Lecture Notes in Computer Science 4227

Commenced Publication in 1973
Founding and Former Series Editors:
Gerhard Goos, Juris Hartmanis, and Jan van Leeuwen

T0189710

Wolfgang Nejdl   Klaus Tochtermann (Eds.)

Innovative Approaches for Learning and Knowledge Sharing

First European Conference
on Technology Enhanced Learning, EC-TEL 2006
Crete, Greece, October 1-4, 2006
Proceedings

 Springer

Volume Editors

Wolfgang Nejdl
L3S Research Center and University of Hannover
Deutscher Pavillon Expo
Plaza 1, 30539 Hannover, Germany
E-mail: nejdl@l3s.de

Klaus Tochtermann
Institute for Knowledge Management
Graz University of Technology
Inffeldgasse 21a, 8010 Graz, Austria
E-mail: ktochter@know-center.at

Library of Congress Control Number: 2006932880

CR Subject Classification (1998): K.3, I.2.6, H.5, J.1

LNCS Sublibrary: SL 2 – Programming and Software Engineering

ISSN   0302-9743
ISBN-10   3-540-45777-1 Springer Berlin Heidelberg New York
ISBN-13   978-3-540-45777-0 Springer Berlin Heidelberg New York

Springer is a part of Springer Science+Business Media

springer.com

© Springer-Verlag Berlin Heidelberg 2006
Printed in Germany

Typesetting: Camera-ready by author, data conversion by Scientific Publishing Services, Chennai, India
Printed on acid-free paper   SPIN: 11876663   06/3142   5 4 3 2 1 0

Preface

With the shift towards a knowledge society, changing working conditions and the continuous evolution of information and communication technologies, peoples' knowledge and skills need continuous development. Technology-enhanced learning is one of the strategic objectives of the EU/IST Work Program, with the goal of "improving the efficiency and cost-effectiveness of learning, for individuals and organizations, independent of time, place and pace." Innovative infrastructures, methods and approaches are needed to reach this goal, and will facilitate transfer and sharing of knowledge between individuals and in organizations. For e-learning, as in e-commerce and e-business, systemic changes wrought by emerging technologies are also changing the relationships between consumption and production—in this case of knowledge—as what many call 'Web 2.0' becomes more interactive and user-generated content becomes more widespread.

EC-TEL 2006, the First European Conference on Technology-Enhanced Learning, provided a unique forum for all research related to technology-enhanced learning in Europe and world-wide, as well as its interactions with knowledge management, business processes and work environments, through specialized workshops and the main conference. Additionally, EC-TEL 2006 provided unique networking possibilities for participating researchers throughout the week and included project meetings and discussions for EU/IST projects funded within the sixth framework program under the action line of "Technology-Enhanced Learning and Access to Cultural Heritage."

EC-TEL 2006 was organized by the Professional Learning Cluster (PRO-LC). PRO-LC has been founded by a cluster of major European research projects in the area of technology-enhanced learning focusing on professional learning: the Network of Excellence in Professional Learning (PROLEARN) and the Integrated Projects PROLIX, APOSDLE, and TENCompetence. Further members are the Specific Targeted Research Projects COOPER and iCamp as well as the projects "Embedding ICT/ Multimedia Standardisation Initiatives into European Vocational Training Development Strategies" (Leonardo da Vinci), EUCAM (Multilingual Communication in European Car Manufacturing), and BASE2 (Broadband Access Satelite Enabled Education).

EC-TEL 2006 received 192 submissions, 146 of those full papers. All submissions went through a rigorous review process, with a final acceptance rate of about 22% for full papers. Based on the reviews, the Program Committee accepted 33 full papers, 16 short papers, as well as 33 posters to be presented in a poster presentation session. In addition, 9 workshops out of 18 proposed and a session on EU/IST funding for technology-enhanced learning research completed the program.

Thanks to this ambitious and competitive selection process, EC-TEL 2006 managed to bring together the leading experts in the field of technology-enhanced learning, addressing the following topics during the conference:

- Collaborative Learning
- Personalized Learning
- Multimedia Content
- Semantic Web, Metadata and Learning
- Workplace Learning
- Learning Repositories and Infrastructures for Learning
- Experience Reports, Assessment, and Case Studies

An event such as EC-TEL 2006 requires much support at different levels: We are grateful to our invited keynote speakers for sharing with our attendees their ideas about the future development of technology-enhanced learning. Many thanks go to all authors who submitted their papers and of course to the Program Committee for their careful reviews. The contributions which were selected by our Program Committee are published in these proceedings.

Peter Dolog worked hard to get the conference proceedings ready in time, and helped with many other tasks necessary for a successful conference, for which we thank him a lot. We also want to thank our staff at L3S in Hannover and the Know-Center in Graz for their high motivation in preparing and organizing EC-TEL 2006. Finally, our special thanks go to all members of our Organizing Committee as well as additional staff from NCSR in Athens and L3S Research Center in Hannover who were responsible for successfully organizing the entire event and in supporting our attendees — and all this without losing patience and gentleness! We are convinced that EC-TEL 2006 was a terrific start for our new conference series and we hope that the conference in Crete provided you with new ideas for your research and with new opportunities for partnerships with other research groups.

July 2006

Wolfgang Nejdl and Klaus Tochtermann
Program Co-chairs
EC-TEL 2006

Organization

EC-TEL 2006 was organized by the Professional Learning Cluster (PRO-LC):
http://www.professional-learning-cluster.org/

Executive Committee

Program Chairs	Wolfgang Nejdl (L3S Research Center and University of Hannover, Germany)
	Klaus Tochtermann (Know-Center and Graz University of Technology, Austria)
Publicity Chair	Erik Duval (KU Leuven and Ariadne Foundation, Belgium)
Workshop Chair	Peter Scott (Knowledge Media Institute, Milton Keynes, UK)
Industry Chairs	Fabrizio Cardinali (Giunti Interactive Labs, Sestri Levante, Italy)
	Luk Vervenne (Synergetics, Antwerpen, Belgium)
	Volker Zimmermann (IMC AG, Saarbrücken, Germany)
Doctoral Consortium Chairs	Katherine Maillet (INT Evry, France)
	Ralf Klamma (RWTH Aachen, Germany)
Organizing Chair	Constantin Makropolous (NCSR Demokritos, Greece)

Organizing Committee

Peter Dolog (L3S Research Center and University of Hannover, Germany)
Sofia Kalokerinou (NCSR Demokritos, Greece)
Vana Kamtsiou (NCSR Demokritos, Greece)
Uwe Thaden (L3S Research Center and University of Hannover, Germany)
Martin Wolpers (L3S Research Center Hannover, Germany and KU Leuven, Belgium)
Helen Zabaka (NCSR Demokritos, Greece)

Program Committee

Heidrun Allert (Austria)	Paul de Bra (The Netherlands)
Kalina Bontcheva (UK)	Paul Brna (UK)

Peter Brusilovsky (USA)
Fabrizio Cardinali (Italy)
Stefano Ceri (Italy)
Pierre Dillenbourg (Switzerland)
Peter Dolog (Germany)
Erik Duval (Belgium)
Dieter Euler (Switzerland)
Monique Grandbastien (France)
Jörg M. Haake (Germany)
Kai Hakkarainen (Finland)
Friedrich Hesse (Germany)
Nicola Henze (Germany)
Wayne Hodgins (USA)
Geert-Jan Houben (Belgium)
Matthias Jarke (Germany)
Ralf Klamma (Germany)
Rob Koper (The Netherlands)

Stefanie Lindstaedt (Austria)
Peter Loos (Germany)
Erica Melis (Germany)
Riichiro Mizoguchi (Japan)
Enrico Motta (UK)
Gustaf Neumann (Austria)
Roy Pea (USA)
Juan Quemada (Spain)
Jeremy Roschelle (USA)
Vittorio Scarano (Italy)
Peter Scott (UK)
Marcus Specht (The Netherlands)
Ralf Steinmetz (Germany)
Julita Vassileva (Canada)
Vincent Wade (Ireland)
Gerhard Weber (Germany)

Additional Reviewers

Jaewook Ahn (USA)
Michael Baker (France)
Monique Baron (France)
Ingo Brunkhorst (Germany)
Mauro Cherubini (Switzerland)
Rosario De Chiara (Italy)
Cyrille Desmoulins (France)
Vania Dimitrova (UK)
Gisela Dsinger (Austria)
Ugo Erra (Italy)
Rosta Farzan (USA)
Christian Glahn (Austria)
George Goguadze (Germany)
Yusuke Hayashi (Japan)
Tsukasa Hirashima (Japan)
Martin Homik (Germany)
Patrick Jermann (Switzerland)
Toshinobu Kasai (Japan)
Akihiro Kashihara (Japan)
Jean-Marc Labat (France)
Tobias Ley (Austria)

Paul Librecht (Germany)
Christoph Lofi (Germany)
Delfina Malandrino (Italy)
Gunnar Martin (Germany)
Nicolas Nova (Switzerland)
Viktoria Pammer (Austria)
Gilbert Paquette (Canada)
Odysseas Papapetrou (Germany)
Dnyanesh Rajpathak (UK)
Christoph Rensing (Germany)
Christoph Richter (Austria)
Mirweise Sangin (Switzerland)
Peter Scheir (Austria)
Wolf Siberski (Germany)
Sergey Sosnovsky (USA)
Markus Strohmaier (Austria/Canada)
Pierre Tchounikine (France)
Roberto Tedesco (Italy)
Armin Ulbrich (Austria)
Carsten Ullrich (Germany)
Claus Zinn (Germany)

Sponsoring Institutions

Platinum Sponsors

Best Paper Award Sponsor

Silver Sponsors

Table of Contents

Short Papers

Posters

From Clicks to Touches: Enabling Face-to-Face Shared Interface

Chia Shen

MERL - Mitsubishi Electric Research Laboratories
201 Broadway, Cambridge, MA, USA
shen@merl.com

Making the interactions with a digital user interface disappears into and becomes a part of the human to human interaction and conversation is a challenge. Conventional metaphor and underlying interface infrastructure for single-user desktop systems have been traditionally geared towards single mouse and keyboard-based WIMP interface design. On the other hand, people usually meet around a table, facing each other. A table setting provides a large interactive visual surface. It encourages collaboration, coordination, as well as simultaneous and parallel problem solving among multiple people. In this talk, I will describe six particular challenges for the design of direct-touch tabletop environments, and present solutions and experiences to these challenges.

The term *display* suggests a device used solely to output visual information, untouched for fear of occluding or dirtying the screen. *Surfaces*, meanwhile, are free of this burden – they are a part of the physical environment, and invite both touching and interaction. What happens, then, when surfaces become displays and when input and visual output spaces are superimposed, creating touchable, interactive surfaces? Such surfaces can be used in any number of ways; one exciting form-factor is as a horizontal, interactive, computationally augmented tabletop. Interactive tables provide three potential benefits for users over traditional displays: First, since a direct touch interactive table serves both as a display and as the user's immediate direct input device, natural hand gestures and intuitive manipulations may be employed to improve the fluidity and reduce the cognitive load of interaction between the user and the digital content. Second, by leveraging the tendency to gather around a table for face-to-face interaction, a horizontal tabletop surface offers affordances and opportunities for building and enhancing co-located collaborative environments. Third, large surfaces such as tabletops offer a spacious work area that may influence working styles and group dynamics. The larger area also provides a larger visual field, which may be utilized as external physical memory in order to extend the working memory capacity of its users, and as an external cognitive medium.

In the past few years, in our pursuit to exploit the advantages and the affordances of direct-touch surfaces, we have designed, implemented and studied a variety of tabletop user interfaces, interaction techniques, and usage scenarios. We have also carried out empirical evaluations, and obtained preliminary findings on how people using a story-sharing table with digital photos, on non-speech audio feedback on multi-user interactive tabletops, and on some of the effects of the size of groups on different aspects of multi-user tabletop collaboration.

W. Nejdl and K. Tochtermann (Eds.): EC-TEL 2006, LNCS 4227, p. 1, 2006.
© Springer-Verlag Berlin Heidelberg 2006

Innovating eLearning and Mobile Learning Technologies for Europe's Future Educational Challenges, Theory and Case Studies

Fabrizio Cardinali

Giunti Interactive Labs, Via Portobello, Baia del Silenzio
16039 Sestri Levante, Italy
f.cardinali@giuntilabs.com
http://www.giuntilabs.com

Abstract. This paper is authored by Fabrizio Cardinali, the CEO of Giunti Interactive Labs (www.giuntilabs.com), provider of Europe's leading SCORM based eLearning and Mobile Learning Content Management Solution, learn eXact™. The paper introduces how new generation Learning Content Management Services and Solutions for rapid and massive content production and personalization can better manage changes needed in the professional and vocational training methods and tools for global corporations entering the new Millennium. Skills based Content Tagging and Mobile, Location Based, Learning Content management are presented as two possible possible trends towards learning personalization to accelerate time to competency in global economies needing to cope with the the demographic and up skilling chellanges launched by New World Economies such as China and India.

Keywords: Personal Learning, Skills & Competency based Education, Location Based, Context Aware, Mobile Learning, Learning Content Management System, LCMS, ePortfolio Management Systems, Skills Management Systems.

1 Introduction

The global labor market is facing clear trends that will dramatically change professional training and development and the way we will use eLearning technologies to better cope with such changes in the next decade. Leading economies, such as the US, Europe and Japan, are clearly shrinking in population whilst emerging economies such as India and China, are recording sky rocketing positions in the global labor market. More than 1 Billion workers from emerging economies have joined the international labor market since 2000. At the same time Ford Motors expects that the number of employees older than 50 will double in Europe by 2008. The demographic drift, a clearly recognized pattern in today's world labor market, hides a slower but even more relevant change: the will of emerging economies to upskill their workforce to gain higher positions in the production chain.

Being well aware of the fact that the world wide production model set up by western multinationals to take advantage of the demographic drift, will be the first to

W. Nejdl and K. Tochtermann (Eds.): EC-TEL 2006, LNCS 4227, pp. 2–7, 2006.

suffer from economic slowdowns, emerging economies want to rapidly upscale their value chain turning their work forces into high level knowledge workers before the conditions change. The Chinese Ministry of R&D has set a goal to reduce dependency of foreign technology to a share of 30 % from more than 50 % today whilst by 2020 Science and Technology Innovation in China is expected to rise to 60 % in Economic Growth. (*China Daily February 2006 on new RD spending boost in China*) With an annual cut of at least 1 % in Europe's growth for the next decade due to median age increase, it is evident that Europe needs to focus on ensuring the leading role as the cutting edge producer of qualitative knowledge workers in this evolving scenario.

This paper introduces new technologies and devices for "Instant Training" and "Personal Learning" solutions to boost personal development plans in Knowledge Economies, to help individuals needing to accelerate their *Time to Competency* and *Time to Knowledge* in this fast forwarding World.

2 Towards Learning Media Based Content Personalization

The development of learning technologies over the last 30 years has been impressive, but only some technologies have better helped to achieve quantum leaps in the possible implementation of new educational strategies and models.

Figure 1 shows that newly emerging Mobile & Broadband Internet technologies are about to boost higher levels of user interactivity and cross community collaboration, favoring a heavy migration from cognitive to constructive models for online learning & knowledge generation. Blogs, Virtual Communities and Mobile devices are starting to demonstrate their effectiveness for online education, giving evidence that where workers and students interact amongst themselves, they construct cumulative knowledge far beyond self learning alone. Interaction amongst students and employees adds a multiplication factor to the cognitive model each one develops when interacting with learning information and contents alone. The learning implication of grouping would therefore alone be enough to justify the expected tenfold increase of mobile access to learning contents and experiences in the educational scenarios to come.

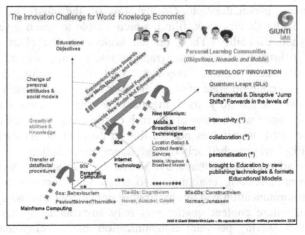

Fig. 1. Towards Personal Learning Communities

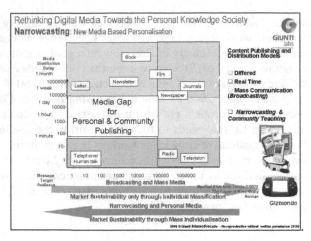

Fig. 2. Towards Narrowcasting (Delivering contents to Ubiquitous, Nomadic and Mobile Personal Learning Communities)

On such evidence many organizations wanting to gain a leading position in the emerging competition towards Global Knowledge Society, are riding the tiger of mobile and ubiquitous access to personalized learning contents based on new innovative media and digital content distribution networks. As a result, today, the economic forces represented by telecom and media industry, are starting again to rally the holy land of digital content for education. Location based, context aware and "always on" access is becoming a must for workers on the move on a continuously evolving labor and professional market; and the nomadic learner is no exception.

Narrowcasting, i.e. delivering filtered information to profiled and clustered communities of interests is emerging as a new marketplace as opposed to the unfiltered and uncontrolled (by users) content delivery paradigm at the basis of the mass media market which has ruled communication over the last 50 and more years.

As the Tomita study performed in late 80s before the advent of Internet well depicts (figure 2), the evolution of media was missing a solution for effective and sustainable content personalization. On the top of the chart we have asynch communication media (letter, book, film.), which enable to reach a variety of users but with no synch capability. Then, on the bottom of the chart, we have the flourishing of synchronous technologies (radio, television and telecom) where "*time to inform*" is the main value... The right side of the chart represents mass communication as a conglomerate of all media to reach mass, the main market which has established over he last 50 years as the main sustainable business models. These three areas are the ones where most of the cash of the Industry flows today, but this happens because until now it was not feasible to do content personalization since "Self Sustainability" was reached only through larger target audience.

Now with the advent of Broadband and Mobile Internet access, *Narrowcasting*, a new way of communication, enabling us to reach very focused communities, is addressing the communication gap left by "traditional" media and more than 50 years of Broadcasting, where content quality was only sustainable by addressing Mass Markets audiences leaving personal communication and development out. Today, publishing just in time educational contents to communities of workers and learners with specific and vertical interests, something quite usual in pre-mass media teaching and communication, becomes again possible. Within Blogs, Podcasts and Mobile networks the Socratic way to teaching to communities re-emerges after years of mass media communication.

3 Towards Skills Based Content Personalization

Given the scenario depicted in the previous paragraph it is not difficult to forecast that in the next years, users, including workers and employees, will want to get increasing nomadic and ubiquitous access to their online contents and communities of interest making Media Content Personalization, or *Narrowcasting,* one of the main teaching paradigms the future Digital Economy, with Mobile & Location Based Knowledge access becoming a converging interest of Publishing, Learning, Media and Telecom players in the very next future. Delivering new Personalized Content Formats to workers on field scenarios, taking into account their devices, position and context of use will anyhow just be one part of the personalization equation. The other big challenge will be to continuously match content delivery to workers pre-existing skills and competences well recorded and interchanged in standard Portfolios and Learner Information Profiles (LIPs).

Ambient Content, i.e. Content designed to favor seamless access to users whilst adapting to their skills and competencies, in the location they are, the digital device they have and the context they are in, will become the main format for content owners willing to position their services in the Knowledge Society. Conceiving new Ambient Content formats able to adapt to the user background and skills, location and context of use, making this media revolution meaningful and satisfactory for the Knowledge Worker of Tomorrow's Learner centric Organizations is the other big challenge in Content Personalization. (see Fig 3 for a positioning of Ambient Content related to other Educational Formats).

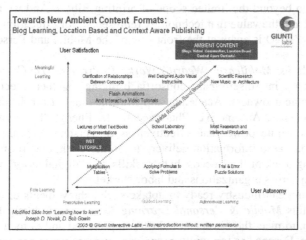

Fig. 3. Towards Ambient Content (Blog Learning,Location Based and Context Aware formats

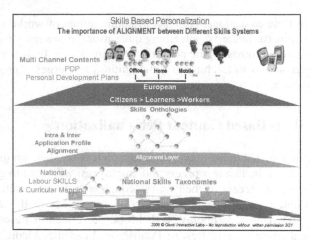

Fig. 4. Skills Based Personalization. The Importance of Alignment between National and International Vocational Systems.

In addition, Skills based Personalization will require an important alignment exercise between different vocational systems at both international and inter-sector level (see Fig.4.) to make acquired skills rapidly recognized and transferable at a pan European level.

4   Mobile and Skills Based Education – Is Europe Ready?

Although Europe has always been at the very front of new learning and media technologies Research and Development programs, in general the European Industry has never been rapid to uptake innovation at start. An unverified anecdote tells that when Gutenberg first disclosed his revolutionary invention to the then European scientific community, he was taken as the inventor of a useless solution presumably not capable to go beyond the limited scope of printing Bibles. And we all know how that story ended and the value that technology represented for Education ...

Today Europe's RD is again at the front row of the Mobile and Personal Learning Revolution.

Projects such as *Mobilearn, WearitAtWork, Prolix and TenCompetence* have managed to set up interdisciplinary consortia bringing together telecom operators, broadcasters, content owners, Academia and Multinationals from leading European sectors (e.g. Avionics, Automotive, Pharmaceuticals, Energy, Telecom & Services) starting to demonstrate power and effectiveness of Personal Learning via context aware & location based information delivery to home, work, classroom and outdoor workers, keeping track of their needs, habits, skills and "digital story" whilst in their nomadic routing across organizations and labor markets.

But is the European Industry ready to uptake such achievements or does the rapid pace at which this *Mobile & Personal Learning Revolution* is likely to take place, risk, once again, to meet the European industry unprepared and unfocused? To avoid a skilling outrun, Europe has to rapidly conceive new learning content production and distribution   models   for   its   learning   contents   being   economically   viable, technologically advanced and pedagogically sounded. To compete in the emerging international markets, higher degrees of content interoperability, localization and personalization must be achieved in Europe, preserving cultural differences yet underpinning alignment of diverse educational systems by means of technology and credits interoperability standards.

Learning Resources must be designed for future proof reusability and internetworking based upon new generation technologies such as XML and Web Services, adopting application profiles and fostering design by Content Objects to support flexible repackaging and re-versioning for different learning paths, contexts, profiles and devices. Good practices in eLearning infrastructures and technologies together with needed pedagogic models, content formats and human resources skills and competencies must be rapidly promoted. Publishing and educational innovation must be combined with new content management technologies, dedicated to learning and mobile deployments; better interchange and interoperability of learning contents across national borders and different vocational systems in Europe must be achieved. Alignment of educational systems and contents become mandatory.

5 Conclusions

Today the demographic drift in World Population brings new challenges to the Labor Market. Together with upskilling strategies starting to emerge from new World economies, this drift can radically change the topology of labor in the next future.

Higher degrees of Knowledge personalization become the main challenge for leading Economies to keep their high stake positioning in such evolving scenario. Personalization that may be achieved by wider uptake of new mobile solutions offering location based and context aware access to Knowledge together with higher adaptiveness to learner's skills, capabilities and backgrounds.

Underestimating the needed urgency for promoting such personalization methodologies and technologies is a great risk to currently leading Economies in the evolving World. A risk no Economy can afford to take in today's high paced trend towards the Knowledge Society.

Considering Human Memory Aspects
for Adaptation and Its Realization in AHA!*

Mária Bieliková and Peter Nagy

Institute of Informatics and Software Engineering
Faculty of Informatics and Information Technologies
Slovak University of Technology
Ilkovičova 3, 842 16 Bratislava, Slovakia
bielik@fiit.stuba.sk

Abstract. Existing adaptive learning systems use various user characteristics for preparing personalized presentation of educational material
for each user (a student). In the process of learning limited capacity of
the human memory plays important role. The student often forgets part
of knowledge acquired during the learning. In this paper we discuss implications of remembering and forgetting for the adaptive learning systems.
We present a proposal of modeling forgetting process in adaptive learning
systems that enables including knowledge repetition into an educational
course. We implemented proposed model within the web-based adaptive system AHA! and demonstrate its viability on domain of learning
English-Slovak vocabulary. This includes also a technique for inserting
concepts for knowledge repeating into a running direct guided course.
Using this technique it is possible to dynamically adapt the sequence of
presented concepts to the actual state of the user model.

1 Introduction

Adaptive learning systems constitute one of the main areas where adaptive web
technologies are used [1]. Their aim is to adapt the presentation of knowledge or
navigation within the educational information space to serve effective learning.
Current adaptive learning systems recognize several aspects of a user – user
characteristics – used during the adaptation, such as user's goals/tasks, level
of knowledge, background, preferences, interests, or user's individual traits [2].
Important aspect considered in adaptive learning systems is undoubtedly a level
of the user's knowledge related to the learned topic (in the IEEE Personal and
Private Information [3] learner profile denoted as the learning performance).

The user's characteristics are represented in a user model. The user model
reflects current state of user knowledge related to the presented information as
it is comprehended by the adaptive learning system. The user's characteristics

---

* This work was partially supported by the Scientific Grant Agency of Slovak Republic,
grant No. VG1/3102/06 and by the Cultural and Educational Grant Agency of the
Slovak Republic, grant No. KEGA 3/2069/04.

W. Nejdl and K. Tochtermann (Eds.): EC-TEL 2006, LNCS 4227, pp. 8–20, 2006.

change (evolve) in the course of learning in accordance with changes of current state of his knowledge (as evaluated by the adaptive learning system). However, most current adaptive learning systems assume that the amount of user knowledge only grows. But increasing knowledge (as a consequence of the remembering) is not the only process. The user can also *lose* (e.g., forget) some of already acquired knowledge. The remembered knowledge is not stored in the human memory forever but in the course of time the knowledge can (and some of them will) drop out from the memory.

Considering remembering and forgetting is important for effective learning process [4]. We presume that a utilization of the human memory aspects while developing an adaptive learning system would also improve the effectiveness of its usage through an improvement of the learning process. Assume for example the following situation: the adaptive book "presumes" that a user possesses adequate knowledge (prerequisites) for understanding a concept just explained. In spite of truly learned concept some time ago, now – after some time passed from this learning session – the user forgot some of the previously acquired knowledge (because of long time without any repeating). The knowledge forgetting causes inconsistencies between the user model as represented in the adaptive learning system (which does not consider the remembering and forgetting in user modeling) and the actual state of the user's knowledge. As a result, we will likely observe incorrect recommendation to the user.

Considering specific characteristics of the human memory can prevent described situation and improve support of learning process by a learning system. In this paper we discuss some issues related to the human memory and implications for adaptive learning systems. We consider the human memory as an aspect of the user's background modeled in the user model. We present a proposal for modeling the forgetting process using current adaptive web-based systems technology together with its implementation for the AHA! system.

The rest of the paper is organized as follows. In the Section 2, we briefly present known facts from psychology about the human memory and the processes of remembering and forgetting. Next, in the Section 3, we give proposal for modeling the forgetting process in adaptive learning systems. Section 4, presents approaches to knowledge repetition. We present a method for dynamic adaptation of the sequence of presented concepts according to findings related to knowledge repetition. Implementation of proposed model within the web-based adaptive system AHA! and demonstration its viability on the domain of learning English-Slovak vocabulary is presented in the Section 5. Finally, we give conclusions and directions for future research.

2 Human Memory and Its Characteristics

The human mind can be viewed as an information processing system. Its architecture is thought to consist of three basic components according the Atkinson-Shiffrin model [5]: sensory memory, working memory and long-term memory. These components roughly correspond to the input (the human mind perceives

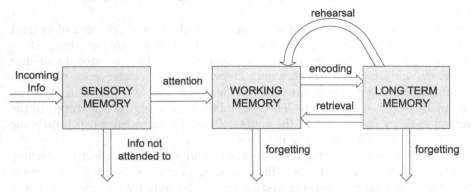

Fig. 1. Human memory model

information from the outside through the senses), processing (information from the sensory memory is processed in the working memory) and storage (processed information is stored in the long-term memory) (see Fig. 1). Naturally, information stored in the long-term memory can be accessed, or activated to help with the processing in the working memory. Accessing information is perceived as the remembering that can be viewed as a usage of the system (ability to find information later again, i.e., to perform information retrieval). Every time we use information from the long term memory this information is repeated. This process is called rehearsal. Described view provides a useful basis for considering the human memory characteristics during the learning [4].

In order to use the human memory aspects for improving the effectiveness of learning through adaptive learning system it is important to know its characteristics. One of the most important characteristics of the human memory is the capacity of the working memory. Its size is well known as the "magical number seven plus or minus two" [6] describing the number of distinct items Miller thought humans could hold in the working memory at any time. In addition, information stored in the working memory can be looked up much faster than in the long-term memory. However, the working memory is characterized also by a relatively brief duration (estimates range from 12 to 30 seconds without a rehearsal), which results in the information loss known as forgetting.

The forgetting is viewed primarily as a consequence of:

- fading (trace decay) over time,
- interference (overlaying new information over the old) or
- lack of retrieval cues.

Function of the volume of remembered information depends on time and has a character of falling an exponential curve. So called the *forgetting curve* was first described by Ebbinghaus in 1885 [7]. To test the retention, Ebbinghaus practiced a list of information items until he was able to repeat the items correctly two times in a row. He then waited varying lengths of time before testing himself again. The forgetting turned out to occur most rapidly soon after the end of practice, but the rate of forgetting slowed as time went on and fewer items could be recalled.

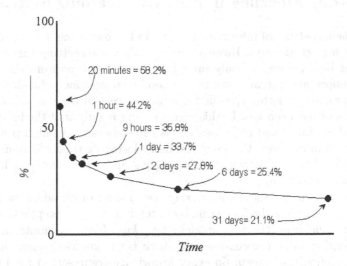

Fig. 2. Forgetting curve

Figure 2 displays typical graph of the forgetting curve. It shows that an individual loses most of the learned information items in first hours (after 9 hours was on average remembered less than 36% information items). After this time is the oblivion less intensive (in average still more than 33% after 24 hours and a bit lesser than 20% after month).

The forgetting can be roughly described with

$$R = e^{-t/S}$$

where R is memory retention, S is relative strength of the human memory and t is time.

Graph on Figure 2 is typical, i.e. related to a human without health problems affecting his memory. Otherwise the curve should be adjusted to the human memory characteristics of such a person. The adjusting process is rather difficult and can be done only experimentally (by an analysis of user behavior). Moreover, the forgetting rate differs little between individuals generally. We believe that this issue is not critical for adaptive learning systems as individual differences can be modeled by setting several levels of the rate at which a user has worked with particular knowledge. Important issue is already considering the forgetting and defining means for estimating the probability that the user have not forgotten an information represented by particular concept.

For the integrity, let us notice that the information items loss can also have biological reasons. It is possible that some biological processes necessary for encoding, storing or searching are disrupted. For example, in a process of embedding knowledge in the memory some structures of brain including hipocamp and amygdala are active. Their mutilation has a negative influence on the process of remembering.

3   Forgetting Modeling in Adaptive Learning Systems

We model the forgetting of information items in the user's memory as an application of the forgetting curve. However, using only the forgetting curve directly is insufficient because we can only infer how much per cent from the original grist of the information items has been remembered in some point of time and we cannot recognize whether specific information item in a given point of time *is remembered* or has been *lost*. In this case we can say only that the information item (learned at time t and not repeated) is remembered with high probability (if according to data about the user's memory-losing at time t is remembered more than K% of learned information items, e.g. more than 90%) or lost with high probability (likewise).

Our proposal is to augment the overlay user model of an adaptive learning system in order to reflect the forgetting by extending every concept's traditional performance value from the user model (e.g., *knowledge* attribute in AHA!) with the retention value (expressing how much is the knowledge remembered). We call it *activity_in_memory*. So every knowledge (represented by a concept in the domain model) has defined for each user a pair of values:

- performance value (from original model) and
- activity in the memory (newly added).

The *activity_in_memory* value is represented by an integer number from a specified range (e. g. $< 0; 100 >$). The greater is the value of *activity_in_memory* there is higher probability that the user's performance value related to the concept corresponds to the value presented within particular concept. Its value must be upon given bound AM, otherwise the knowledge represented in the concept is considered as being *forgotten* by the user. After a successful learning (e.g., concept is visited or a test is passed successfully) the corresponding concept is set as "learned" (performance value is set using standard adaptation rules of the adaptive learning system accordingly) and the *activity_in_memory* attribute is raised. On the other hand, according time passed from the learning of the concept the *activity_in_memory* attribute value decreases according forgetting curve.

In order to reflect the forgetting curve accurately we use the *access_time* attribute for each concept in the user model. This attribute stores the date and time of the last visit of the concept. Worthy results can be achieved also by reflecting the forgetting curve simply by decreasing the *activity_in_memory* attribute value after every new user's session for every concept not being used in the session [8] (i.e., without considering real time passed).

Modeling the forgetting process is performed by the adaptation engine using mentioned attributes defined for each concept for each user in the user model. With every visit to a concept the *activity_in_memory* attribute is raised and the *access_time* attribute is set to the actual date and time. We simulate the forgetting by decreasing the value of the *activity_in_memory* attribute after every user login to the adaptive learning system (at the beginning a session).

For every concept in the user model three steps are performed:

1. Calculation of the time t elapsed from the last access to the concept:

$$t = current\_time - access\_time$$

2. Calculation of the $forgetting\_factor$, which represents an output value of the function expressing the forgetting curve (R):

$$forgetting\_factor = R(t)$$

The $forgetting\_factor$ is a value from the range $< 0; 1 >$ representing probability that the information is remembered after the time t passed from the learning of the information item.

3. Modification the $activity\_in\_memory$ attribute:

$$activity\_in\_memory = activity\_in\_memory * forgetting\_factor$$

The $activity\_in\_memory$ attribute value is calculated for each concept and then it is used for more accurate adaptation that considers possible losing information according time passed. One specific usage is including a repetition in the process of learning.

4   Knowledge Repetition

The speed of forgetting depends on a number of factors such as the difficulty of the learned material (e.g., how meaningful for particular user it is), its representation and physiological factors such as stress. Failing to remember something does not mean the information is gone forever though. Sometimes the information is in the human memory but for various reasons we cannot access it. In this case a repetition can help in regenerating forgotten knowledge. Already Ebbinghaus discovered that distributing learning trials over time is more effective in memorizing than massing practice into a single session; and he noted that continuing to practice material after the learning criterion has been reached enhances retention.

Repeating using the elaborative rehearsal which in contrast to maintenance rehearsal involves deep semantic processing of a to-be-remembered information item[1] is more effective [9]. The maintenance rehearsal involves only simple rote repetition aiming at lengthening periods of time the information item is maintained in the working memory. The elaborative rehearsal can be supported by guidelines.

We have proposed several techniques of repetition for adaptive learning systems using the forgetting model presented in previous section:

---

[1] For example, if an individual is presented with a list of digits for later recall (4968214), grouping the digits together to form a phone number transforms the stimuli from a meaningless string of digits to something that has a meaning.

- repeat when there is an evidence of certain amount of the knowledge considered as forgotten (*periodical repetition*),
- repeat at the beginning of a new lesson the knowledge learned in the previous lesson (*overall introductory repetition*),
- repeat at the beginning of a new lesson the knowledge (assumed) necessary in this lesson (*necessary introductory repetition*),
- repeat at the end of a lesson the knowledge learned in the lesson (*final repetition*).

Selection of particular technique can be supported by adaptive learning system based mostly on evaluation of student's performance. Leaving an option to select the repetition technique for a user is also useful, mainly due to impossibility of precise modeling of particular user.

Often it is not practical or possible to repeat all of the knowledge items marked as forgotten. The adaptive learning system should select a set of knowledge items for the repetition. Certain number of the concepts representing the knowledge items is selected and only these concepts are repeated at the beginning of a new lesson. If there is large number of the lost knowledge the adaptive book offers a repetition-lesson, aimed for the repetition only.

Concepts for repetition are sequenced using the following steps:

1. select the concepts according the type of repetition used[2]:
   - set of concepts from the previous session (overall introductory repetition),
   - set of concepts from current session (final repetition),
   - set of prerequisites for the concepts in the current session (necessary introductory repetition),
2. filter the concepts they have the *activity_in_memory* value lower than the value of given bound AM,
3. sort the filtered concepts respecting the relations between concepts defined in the domain model (e.g., prerequisite relation),
4. generate the sequence of presented concepts.

Sequencing concepts for repetition can be based on several criterions, for example: random sequencing, sequencing based on time of the acquisition an information item (priority is given to the information item acquired longer time ago), sequencing based on a measure of remembering, i.e., the *activity_in_memory* value is used (priority is given to the information item with lower activity in the memory), sequencing based on prerequisite-dependencies (priority is given to the information item which is supposed to be in the need of the user in the next study time).

A repetition can be combined effectively with local guidance adaptation technique to support adaptive navigation. 'Forward' links (realized for example using

---

[2] The set of concepts considered for periodical repetition can vary from all concepts, concepts included in particular part of the knowledge space as the point is to invoke the repetition when the amount of forgotten knowledge exceeds predefined bound.

the "Next" button) determined by standard adaptation mechanisms are dynamically completed by links to the concept with low *activity_in_memory* attribute value.

5 Implementing the Human Memory Considerations in AHA!

In order to evaluate proposed approach for modeling of the forgetting process in adaptive learning systems we decided to use the an open source general-purpose adaptive system AHA! developed and maintained at the Eindhoven University of Technology [10]. We enhanced it in such a way that adaptation according the forgetting curve supplements existing adaptation techniques used in the AHA!.

We looked for an application where we can presume some "minimal amount of knowledge" delivered to the user via the adaptive learning system because the effect of the knowledge forgetting process becomes significant with only relatively large knowledge spaces. Suitable application domain in this sense is the domain of learning foreign language vocabulary. Here we have possibly large amount of concepts (each word is considered as a concept) with possibility of exercising various approaches to knowledge repetition.

5.1 Domain Model

Domain model consists of concepts and their relationships. Our English-Slovak vocabulary course is structured into lessons, one lesson is divided into several parts in such a way that every part includes at most fifteen words. For individual access to the words each word is represented by one concept. That enables us to simulate the forgetting of each word individually. Figure 3 depicts a screen of Graphical Editor tool for AHA! with a part of the domain model.

The AHA! system uses templates for determination which attributes the concept has, and whether it must have a resource associated with it or not [11]. For our course we created a concept template representing one word from the

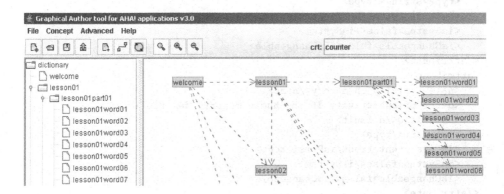

Fig. 3. Concepts of English-Slovak vocabulary domain

vocabulary with the attributes according the model of forgetting presented in the Section 3.

In AHA! the concept attribute type can be only boolean, integer or string. For our needs it is important to work with date and time in the case of the *access_time* attribute. We decided here for the purposes of evaluation of proposed approach to modeling the forgetting to store the *access_time* attribute as a string value. The data conversion is performed at the source code level. The *activity_in_memory* attribute has a type of integer and it acquires in our prototype application values from a range $< 0; 1\,000 >$ for accurate calculations (the range is optional). The bound value AM for determining a level of information item activity in the memory considered as forgotten has a type of integer.

Repetition is best provided using local guidance technique. The user is provided by a sequence of concepts that are advised to be repeated. In order to realize this technique in the AHA! system, we added into the domain model new attribute named *next_concept* of type string. This attribute is used to represent the name of the concept to be presented next in the dynamically created sequence. After the user selects type of repetition the adaptive learning system generates the sequence of concepts for this user. The system filters the concepts intended for repeating. This set of concepts is then included in the generated sequence according to the type of repetition.

Bellow we show part of the word template.

```xml
<?xml version="1.0"?>

<!DOCTYPE template SYSTEM 'template.dtd'>
<template>
<name>word page concept template</name>
<attributes>
  ...
  <attribute>
     <name>access_time</name>
     <description>time of last visiting the concept</description>
     <default>NA</default>
     <type>string</type>
     <isPersistent>true</isPersistent>
     <isSystem>false</isSystem>
     <isChangeable>false</isChangeable>
  </attribute>
  <attribute>
     <name>activity_in_memory</name>
     <description>activity in the human memory</description>
     <default>0</default>
     <type>int</type>
     <isPersistent>true</isPersistent>
     <isSystem>false</isSystem>
     <isChangeable>false</isChangeable>
  </attribute>
  <attribute>
```

```
      <name>next_concept</name>
      <description>name of next concept in generated sequence</description>
      <default></default>
      <type>string</type>
      <isPersistent>true</isPersistent>
      <isSystem>false</isSystem>
      <isChangeable>false</isChangeable>
   </attribute>
</attributes>
  ...
</template>
```

5.2   User Model

AHA! uses an overlay user model, i.e. every concept from the domain model is
defined also in the user model. The value of each attribute for particular user is
stored in the user model. To consider the human memory aspect it is inevitable
to maintain values of the *activity_in_memory* and *access_time* attributes for
each concept from the domain model and each user.

5.3   Adaptation Process

In modeling the forgetting process in an adaptive learning system it is crucial
to define the process of updating values of *activity_in_memory* attribute. On
the beginning of a new session the *activity_in_memory* attribute of all words
(each represented as a concept) in the user model (for the currently logged in
user) are modified. In AHA! the user model of a single user is stored in an XML
formatted file. So the modifications are done in this file. After the user has logged
in the java servlet Get, the system executes the user model update for this user
before the first concept (welcome page) is presented to him. The update process
follows the steps of calculating *activity_in_memory* attribute value presented in
the Section 3.

   We added java servlet GenCourseSequence that generates the sequence of presented words (concepts) according selected type of the repeating. This process
follows the steps presented in the Section 4. The GenCourseSequence servlet
redirects the control to the Get servlet with the name of first word from the generated sequence as parameter. The sequence diagram presenting main communication performed during the process of the user model update and a sequence
of concepts generation is presented in Figure 4.

   AHA! allows a user to navigate through the vocabulary using a tree-view over
the course structure. We used the link annotation adaptation technique of AHA!
to indicate a word considered forgotten. The name of already practiced (i.e.,
visited) word is displayed using violet color. The value of the *visited* attribute
for all words considered forgotten is changed to false during the generating the
sequence of concepts for presentation. Annotations of such words are changed in
the tree-view to blue color.

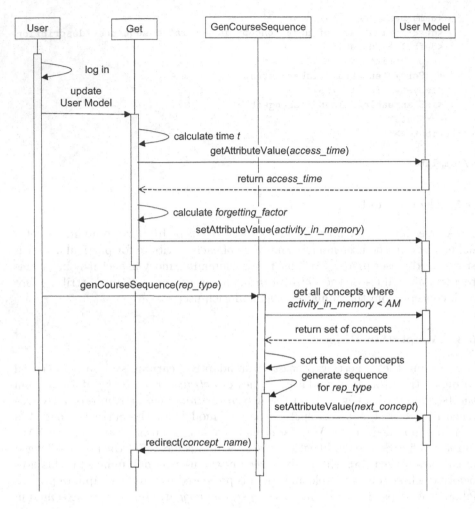

Fig. 4. AHA! servlets operations

During the session after every concept visit (presenting a word to the user) the *activity_in_memory* attribute of this word is increased by a constant value. Also the *access_time* attribute of this word is set to the current date and time.

For presenting a word from the vocabulary we use XHTML files with a form tag to allow processing the data from the page later on. For example, we allow the user to rate his knowledge about the word. This value is then used to evaluate his knowledge level of the English/Slovak word in the vocabulary. The action attribute of the form tag contains a concept name or a string constant value *this.next_concept*. In the first case, the form will be submitted to the listed concept. In the latter case, the destination concept is obtained from the *next_concept* attribute of the currently presented concept. This option is used for the dynamically generating sequence of concepts.

6   Conclusions

The research presented in this paper addresses the possibility of improving effectiveness of learning using adaptive learning system by considering the human memory characteristics. Important aspect is limited capacity of the working memory. We discussed impacts of the human mind nature to the adaptive learning systems. We proposed an approach for modeling the forgetting process together with its usage in adaptation and we realized it in the AHA! system. The base for modeling is the forgetting curve. The forgetting curve can be tuned individually for each user which can result in more effective repeating by utilization of individual differences. At the moment we provide one forgetting curve for all users. Our application of English-Slovak vocabulary teacher proved that in most cases this approach is for such application domain sufficient.

Proposed approach ensures that the repeated knowledge or knowledge more used are being lost more slowly. The knowledge-forgetting model can be supplemented by including hierarchical binds between the knowledge items in a domain. Hierarchical organization of the learned material together with properly defined the prerequisite relation can improve the information access and enables the effective usage of limited capacity of the human working memory. This can be reflected by propagation the *activity_in_memory* attribute value considering the information space structure. We plan to experiment with this issue in our learning course for programming languages [12].

References

1. Brusilovsky, P., Karagiannidis, C., Sampson, D.: Layered evaluation of adaptive learning systems. International Journal of Continuing Engineering Education and Lifelong Learning **14**(4/5) (2004) 402–421
2. Brusilovsky, P.: Adaptive hypermedia. User Modeling and User-Adapted Interaction **11**(1-2) (2001) 87–100
3. IEEE: IEEE P1484.2/D7, 2000-11-28. Draft Standard for Learning Technology. Public and Private Information (PAPI) for Learners, Available at http://ltsc.ieee.org/ (2000)
4. Tuovinen, J.: Optimising student cognitive load in computer education. In Ellis, A.E., ed.: Proc. of the Australasian conference on Computing education, ACM Press (2000) 235–241
5. Atkinson, R., Shiffrin, R.: Human memory: A proposed system and its control processes. In Spence, K., Spence, J., eds.: The psychology of learning and motivation, Academic Press (1968)
6. Miller, G.: The magical number, seven, plus or minus two: sme limits on our capacity for processing information. Psychological Review (63) (1956) 81–97
7. Ebbinghaus, H.: Memory. A Contribution to Experimental Psychology. Reprinted Bristol: Thoemmes Press, 1999 (1885)
8. Ágh, P., Bieliková, M.: Considering human memory aspects to adapting in educational hypermedia. In Aroyo, L., Tasso, C., eds.: Proc. of Workshop on Indifidual Differences, AH 2004: 3rd Int. Conference on Adaptive Hypermedia and Adaptive Web-Based Systems. (2004) 107–114

9. Craik, F., Lockhart, R.: Levels of processing. a framework for memory research. Journal of Verbal Learning and Verbal Behaviour (11) (1972) 671–684
10. De Bra, P., Aerts, A., Berden, B., De Lange, B., Rousseau, B., Santic, T., Smits, D., Stash, N.: AHA! the adaptive hypermedia architecture. In: Proc. of the ACM Conf. on Hypertext and Hypermedia, Nottingham, UK (2003) 81–84
11. De Bra, P., Smits, D., Stash, N.: Creating adaptive applications with aha! Tutorial for AHA! version 3.0. In Aroyo, L., Tasso, C., eds.: AH 2004 Tutorials. (2004) 1–29
12. Bieliková, M., Kuruc, J., Andrejko, A.: Learning programming with adaptive web-based hypermedia system AHA! In Jakab, F., Fedák, V., Sivý, I., Bučko, M., eds.: Proc. of ICETA 2005 - 4th Int. Conf. on Emerging e-learning Technologies and Applications. (2005) 251–256

Creating and Delivering Adaptive Courses with AHA!

Paul De Bra, David Smits, and Natalia Stash

Faculty of Mathematics and Computer Science, Eindhoven University of Technology,
Postbus 513, 5600 MB Eindhoven, The Netherlands
{debra, dsmits, nstash}@win.tue.nl

Abstract. AHA! is an Open Source adaptive hypermedia platform, resulting from 10 years of experience with creating, using and improving on-line adaptive courses and presentations. This paper focuses on some recent additions to AHA! that are especially important for adaptive educational applications, namely *stable presentations*, *adaptive link (icon) annotations* and *adaptive link destinations*. We not only describe the technical aspects of these parts of AHA! but also illustrate their use in educational applications. We describe some fundamental limitations of Web-based adaptive applications, and show how AHA! deals with them in order to provide adaptation to *prerequisite relationships* in the way one would expect.

1 Introduction and Motivation

World Wide Web has changed the world in more than one way. It has radically changed the way in which all kinds of organizations provide information to their employees, customers and the general public. It has also made it possible to have direct interaction between an end-user and provider. But it also changed the *form* in which information is available: linear documents (or hierarchically structured ones) have been replaced by *hypertext*. The navigational freedom that comes with hypertext has stimulated a *browsing* learning style, where the user looking for information or learning material simply picks out the items she is interested in (judging this based either on link anchors or titles or on the opinion of a search engine). This seemingly random user behavior (most suitable for *field-independent* [6] learners) makes it difficult for an author or a course designer to develop content and a link structure that can be fully understood, no matter which path the end-user decides to follow.

Adaptive hypermedia [2,3] comes to the rescue. In "normal" (or static) hypertext it is impossible to offer the right content, the needed definitions and explanations, and at the same time hide or deemphasize already known definitions and unnecessary explanations. When creating the content you have no way of knowing what the end-user has studied before jumping to a certain (web)page. With adaptive hypermedia it is possible to select and present information content based on the user's previous actions (processed and stored in a *user model*) and to select and annotate links in a way that guides the user towards the most relevant information. As we will show in this paper, this added service for the end-user can be created and delivered with little additional effort on the author's side.

W. Nejdl and K. Tochtermann (Eds.): EC-TEL 2006, LNCS 4227, pp. 21–33, 2006.

At the TU/e we started offering a course on the topic of hypermedia in 1994 [8]. This course was offered through the Web, in hypermedia (actually mostly hypertext) form. Initially there were also lectures, but as of 1996 the course was reduced to just its on-line hypermedia form and made available to students of different Dutch and Belgian universities. In order to make it possible to fully utilize the hypertext nature of the course text, with a rich link structure and no hierarchical menu system that would constrain the learner's navigational freedom, we decided to make the course text adaptive. This development has resulted in the Adaptive Hypermedia Architecture AHA!, which is now available in its third major release. (See [9] and http://aha.win.tue.nl/ for details about the AHA! project.) Feedback from authors, researchers and end-users has led us to create a rich feature set, with items that target a large spectrum of possible applications, and with items that are specifically useful for educational applications, including progress reports, inspection (and update) of the knowledge of all the concepts of a course, forms for setting preferences or altering other parts of the user model, and an (externally contributed) authoring and delivery tool for multiple-choice tests. Based on user experience we also designed the main authoring tool for AHA!: the *Graph Author* [10], used to define *concepts*, *concept relationships* and the (one-to-one or one-to-many) connection between concepts and *resources* (like webpages).

Fairly complete information on AHA! can be found on the project website aha.win.tue.nl, including a tutorial. In this paper we only focus on three novel aspects in AHA! that are especially useful for educational applications:

1. *stable presentations*: When an adaptive system continuously adapts the information it presents to the user model (or the user's estimated knowledge state) pages are adapted (and thus changed) each time the user visits them. We have grown accustomed to changing link colors (blue link anchors turning purple when they refer to already visited pages) but not to changing content. We expect a page to present the same information when we revisit it later (although some content is expected to be dynamic, like a weather or traffic report). The *stable presentations* technique in AHA! lets authors decide which pages or objects should always be adapted, or should only be adapted under certain conditions. (And by offering the learner a form to alter a value that influences the condition the end-user can also influence the decision to keep the presentation stable or not.)

2. *adaptive link (icon) annotations*: In several existing adaptive hypermedia systems the "status" of a link (recommended or not, interesting, already visited, etc.) is not or not only indicated through a change in the *color* of the link anchor, but also through some icon, like a small or large checkmark, or a colored ball (in ELM-ART [5], Interbook [4], NetCoach [17], KBS-Hyperbook [12]), etc. The balls or other icons can be placed in front of the link anchor or behind it. Each system has its own rules for deciding which icon to use under which circumstances. In AHA! an author can easily define these rules or conditions, for any arbitrary number of icons. Also, different *views* (or html frames) can use different icons with different conditions for selecting them.

3. *adaptive link destinations*: Link adaptation is not always a simple case of recommended vs. not recommended, but sometimes a matter of *where* to send the user to. A link to a topic may wish to refer a (*field-dependent* [6]) beginner to an introductory page on that topic, and an expert to an advanced page. In AHA! the

binding between the *concept* a link points to and the actual *resource* (or page) that is returned is dynamic. The link destination is selected adaptively, based on the user model.

In each of the following sections we highlight one of these adaptation techniques. We explain how to make use of them in AHA! and illustrate their use in an (educational) example. But first we briefly explain how most Web-based adaptive systems work, and how they deal with the fundamental limitations of using page-based HTTP requests and responses.

2 Architecture and Limitations of Web-Based AHS

AHA! is a typical Java-based web application, using Servlets in combination with a Java-based server like Tomcat. Figure 1 shows the global architecture of such a system, and Figure 2 shows the different files or databases used by the AHA! engine.

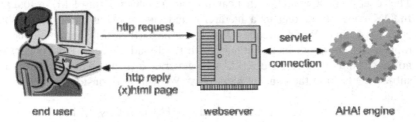

Fig. 1. Global architecture of a Web-based application

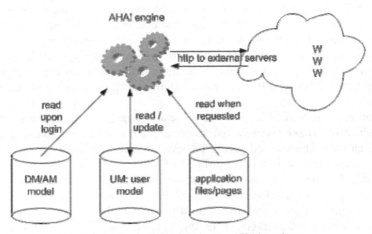

Fig. 2. Data stores used by the AHA! engine

In Figure 2 we see that the AHA! engine uses three types of local information, and potentially also pages that reside on other servers on the Web. The combined domain and adaptation model DM/AM represents a model of the conceptual structure of the application, and the adaptation rules. This information is retrieved when the end-user logs in. As the user is interacting with the application a user model (UM) is used and constantly updated. The interaction involves (mostly) the retrieval of pages and other application files (like images), but it can also involve using forms to update UM or taking multiple-choice tests. DM/AM and UM are used to decide which application file or "page" to retrieve upon a request from the user (and which objects to conditionally include in that page). The request may also result in files being retrieved from other webservers.

As a "pure" Web-Based system, AHA! only reacts to HTTP requests and sends HTTP responses that contain a document (typically in HTML or XHTML, but any XML format is allowed). The interaction between the user and the AHA! application thus happens on a page by page basis. (AHA! allows the use of the novel "Ajax" technologies to allow requests for parts of a page that are updated without refreshing the whole page, but we have not yet considered the UM updates that one might wish to associate with such within-page interaction.) Each time the user issues an HTTP request (typically by clicking on a link) the following procedure is followed:

1. The request contains a URL that can refer to a concept (from DM) or to a page. In DM concepts belong to a hierarchy and can have an associated resource which is a page. When a request refers to a page, the corresponding concept is looked up. The procedure continues with the found concept. If a concept does not have an associated page AHA! will generate a menu-like page that links to sub-concepts from the concept hierarchy. (We will not consider this case in the sequel.)

2. UM is retrieved (if not already cached). AHA! normally caches UM during a session, but it updates the stored version after every request so that other applications can see the changes.

3. The AHA! engine executes rules from AM, starting from the rules associated with the "access" attribute of the requested concept/page. These rules cause updates to some attributes (attribute values) of some (UM) concepts.

4. The updates caused by rules are considered as events that trigger the rules associated with the updated attributes (of the corresponding concepts). Rules thus trigger each other, and this process continues until there are no more triggered rules.

5. A concept may have either just one associated page, or it may have several, one of which is (adaptively) selected, as we explain in section 5 (on adaptive link destinations). The selected page is retrieved (either from local storage or from a remote website) and filtered according to AM and UM, as follows:

    a. The page may contain conditionally included fragments and/or conditionally included objects. Each selected fragment or object is inserted into the parse stream and must thus be a valid piece of (x)html. It may contain other fragments or objects to be conditionally included.

    b. The page may contain "conditional" links (<a> tags) to other concepts or pages. The AHA! engine checks UM to decide how to present the link. Link adaptation typically depends on the suitability of the link destination (concept or page). This suitability determines how the link anchor is annotated (using icons and/or link color changes). The section on link adaptation explains the details.

    c.   Any other content of the page is passed to the browser. Some text fragments may be adaptively presented using a different presentation style, but most content is normally presented without any adaptation.

It is important to note that this procedure implies that UM updates happen before the page is filtered using that UM instance. Using typical adaptation rules (delivered with AHA! by default), the "knowledge value" of a page is updated *before* the page is displayed. This "knowledge value" can thus not be used to conditionally show a *prerequisite explanation* upon the first visit of the page (and not in subsequent visits). The "visited" counter can be used for this purpose. This counter is initialized to 0 so it will have the value 1 when the page is visited for the first time because it is incremented before the page is presented.

There is a good reason why the UM updates happen *before* the page is filtered and presented, not just in AHA! but in all Web-based adaptive systems that use the HTTP request/response paradigm on a page by page basis. This can be illustrated using prerequisite relationships in an educational application. In elementary math you probably have to learn about the "addition" before you learn about the "subtraction". "Addition" is thus a *prerequisite* for "subtraction". Links to "subtraction" will not be shown or recommended until enough knowledge of "addition" is obtained. Now consider that there is a page that provides a lot of information about the "addition" and that contains a link to "subtraction". The author's idea is that the user should read this page and then follow the link to "subtraction". When reading the "addition" page the user will obtain enough knowledge of "addition" to satisfy the prerequisite requirement for "subtraction". So *after* reading this page the link to "subtraction" should become recommended. But the adaptation (including the presentation of the link to "subtraction") is done *before* the reading begins. The UM update on which the adaptation is based must thus be performed before presenting the page.

In the future it may become possible to adapt the page (in a controlled way) while the user is reading, so links may become available and recommended during the reading process. Usability research is needed in order to decide whether adaptation while reading would be a desirable adaptation behavior. For now we only consider the typical architecture in which adaptation must be done *before* the engine sends the page to the browser.

3 Combining Adaptation with Stable Presentations

The hypermedia course (which prompted the start of the AHA! development) contains a page about URLs and their syntax. It briefly refers to the addressing scheme in Xanadu. Learners who visit the URL page before the Xanadu page see the following piece of text:

> In Xanadu (a fully distributed hypertext system, developed by Ted Nelson at Browsn University, from 1965 on) there was only one protocol, ...

Learners who have seen the Xanadu page see a different explanation:

> In Xanadu there was only one protocol, ...

This is a clear and simple form of content adaptation, which Brusilovsky calls the *conditional inclusion of fragments*. There is no discussion that providing such *prerequisite explanations* is a good thing. However, what isn't so clear is whether the learner, who has first seen this fragment, then studies the page on Xanadu and then comes back to the URL page, should be presented the prerequisite explanation *again*, or not. Typical adaptive behavior would remove the explanation on this repeat visit. In this specific example we have not (yet) experienced that learners noticed the ongoing adaptation. But when the changes are more significant it may become desirable to leave a prerequisite explanation (or any content that is conditionally included for some reason) in place even though the adaptation rules dictate that the content is no longer needed.

The on-line adaptive AHA! design paper [11] at http://aha.win.tue.nl/ahadesign/ makes use of the small elementary math example (about addition and subtraction) we described in section 2. The example appears in two places in that paper. It is *explained* on the first of these pages the reader visits, and is *recalled* on the second page:

> In elementary math you probably have to learn about the "addition" before you learn about the "subtraction". "Addition" is said to be a *prerequisite* for "subtraction".

or

> Recall the elementary math example about "addition" and "subtraction".

Whichever page is visited first will conditionally include the explanation. If we call the pages "page1" and "page2" then the rule for including the explanation would be:

```
page1.visited + page2.visited == 1
```

Afterwards (when the example is visited for a second time, or more) the reader no longer needs the explanation, so the example is simply recalled. But it is not desirable to have the explanation disappear completely on all pages, which is what would happen if the above expression would be used for the adaptation all the time. In order to show the explanation again upon a second visit to *that first visited page* (but not show it on the other page) the presentation of the pages must be made *stable*, meaning that adaptation is performed on the first visit, and no more adaptation is performed when the page is presented again (although the "visited" counters are still incremented).

In AHA! *pages* and *objects* can be defined as stable. When a page is stable that stability is automatically inherited by *included objects*. (At the same time small fragments that are conditionally included *inline* are still adapted, as are the link annotations. The Xanadu example in the hypermedia course is realized using *inline* fragments and thus remains "unstable".) In AHA! stability comes in four different gradations:

- *no stability*: this is the default behavior where each UM update immediately influences the adaptation, at all times.
- *always stable*: the first time the concept is accessed UM updates are applied, and the concept is presented based on that UM state; afterwards the presentation is still based on that UM state (even though UM updates are still performed and recorded because other, unstable, pages may depend on these updates).

- *session stability*: the first time a concept is accessed during a session, UM updates are applied, and the concept is presented based on that UM state; afterwards the presentation is based on that UM state for as long as the session lasts. When the user logs out and later resumes the session, adaptation is again applied on the first access.
- *conditional stability*: the stability holds as long as a certain condition (an expression using UM attribute values) is true. When the expression becomes false, adaptation is done based on the new UM state. (The page remains unstable until the expression becomes true again.)

Creating stable presentations is very easy. Figure 3 shows the dialog box used by the Graph Author tool to create a new concept or edit an existing one. Stability is enabled through a simple checkbox. When *conditional stability* is selected the author must provide an expression which "freezes" the page as long as that expression remains true.

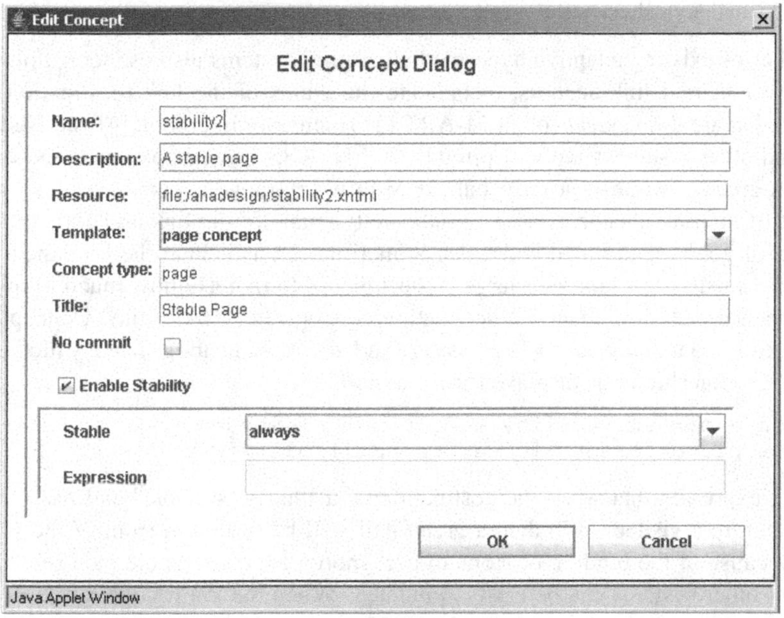

Fig. 3. Edit concept dialog box that allows the selection of stability

4 Adaptive Link Annotation

The (early) Web has been criticized for not having *typed links*. Hyper-G [1], later renamed to Hyperwave, proposed a completely new architecture with links as first-class citizens, but it has not become widely adopted. Using *classes* and *cascading style sheets* (CSS) it is possible to assign a "type" (or "class") to a link anchor, and to associate presentation attributes with that type. This is of course only a small step towards making links become full-fledged objects, but it is a start. AHA! uses link classes to choose a color for the link anchor (text). An arbitrary number of link classes can be defined, but in this paper we refer to the three link classes that have been used most in AHA!-based courses up to now: GOOD (recommended), NEUTRAL (recommended but already visited) and BAD (not recommended). There are two ways to associate these to classes to colors:

1. The author can include a (reference to a) stylesheet in every page, defining the presentation style for each link class. AHA! provides a default stylesheet (aha.css) which defines the standard color scheme with blue, purple and black, for good, neutral and bad links. If the author does not include a stylesheet the AHA! engine will insert one automatically.

2. AHA! offers a special form through which end-users can change the color scheme. (This is only available if the author includes access to that form in the course.) When an end-user changes his color preferences AHA! will automatically insert stylesheet commands in the page, overriding any predefined stylesheet.

A number of existing adaptive hypermedia/learning systems also use icons, placed in front of or behind link anchors, to indicate the status of the link (destination). The systems that are descendents of ELM-ART [5] (including Interbook [4] and NetCoach [17]) and other systems simply inspired by it, like KBS-Hyperbook, make use of such icons. A green ●, white ●, or red ● ball (or yellow or orange in some systems), placed in front of the link anchor, is used to indicate the state of the link and corresponds to the idea of good, neutral and bad links. Sometimes icons behind the link anchors are used, like small ✓, medium ✓ or large ✓ checkmarks to indicate how much knowledge the learner already has about the destination concept. In AHA! a file "ConceptType-Config.xml" contains pairs of expressions and icons, indicating under which condition which icon should be displayed. An example:

```
<icon expr="suitability &amp;&amp; visited==0"
      place="front">icons/GreenBall.gif</icon>
```

This tag expresses that when the destination of a link is "suitable" and has not been visited before ("visited==0") then a green ball will be placed in front of the link anchor. Because of the binding of icons to user model expressions the icon selection of different other systems can be easily simulated. When the knowledge levels of Interbook are translated to values like 0, 30, 60, 90 (so that knowledge increments by 1/10 of a level are also possible, as is done in Interbook when reading non-recommended pages), the checkmarks that follow links to (background or outcome) concepts can be chosen using rules like:

```
<icon expr="knowledge &gt; 29 &amp;&amp; knowledge &lt; 60"
      place="back">icons/SmallCheckM.gif</icon>
```

AHA! supports *forward* as well as *backward reasoning*, meaning that the attributes like "suitability" and "knowledge" may contain either stored values, calculated through rules that are executed when a concept is accessed, or expressions over (other) attributes of (other) concepts, and thus calculated (backwards) from many different user model values.

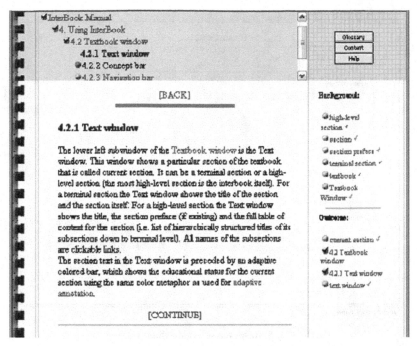

Fig. 4. An AHA! application with adaptive link icon annotations

Figure 4 below shows an AHA! application, generated automatically from the Interbook Manual (which is of course authored for Interbook). This AHA! application shows a clear resemblance to the original Interbook application (including the typical background and the colored balls and checkmarks) but it also uses additional adaptive elements offered by AHA!, including the use of different link colors, not just for links to concepts but also for the "back" and "continue" buttons.

5   Adaptive Link Destinations

In a "normal" Website pages contain link anchors, with link destinations identified using uniform resource locators, or URLs. The connections between pages are thus completely fixed. At the other end of the spectrum we find *open hypermedia* (a rich research field with many publications, among others leading to the FOHM model published in [13]), where the pages do not contain any links, but instead are combined with a link database in order to (possibly adaptively) select the links that are going to be shown to the user. AHA! takes an intermediate approach: the author of pages must include the link anchors, but the link destinations are *concepts*, not *pages* (although that is still possible), and the adaptation engine decides which page to show when a link to a certain concept is followed. So this decision is not made when a page (containing links) is generated, but only when a link on the page is followed.

For most concepts and pages there is a one-to-one mapping between a concept and the corresponding page, and vice versa. However, AHA! allows a concept to be associated with multiple pages, one of which is (adaptively) selected for presentation to

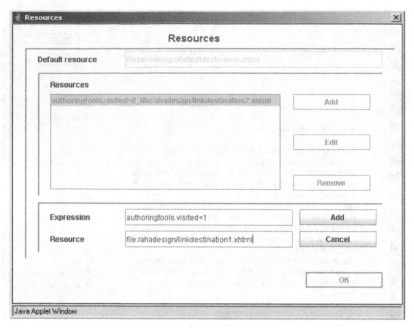

Fig. 5. Resource selection dialog box

the user. Figure 4 shows the dialog box used by the Graph Author tool for creating a list of expressions coupled with resources (pages). The adaptation engine will return the first resource with an expression that evaluates to true.

This dialog box is the same for *conditional link destinations* and for the *conditional inclusion of objects*, and there is also a potential very similar use of these techniques. Research into learning styles [6] has revealed that *field-independent* learners can start a course by diving right into the details of a single topic without first getting acquainted with the whole spectrum of subjects of the course. They can thus follow a *depth-first* navigation path. *Field-dependent* learners on the other hand need more context, and can be helped by offering them a *breadth-first* navigation path. From this we can conclude that at least for field-dependent learners it is a good idea to provide an introductory page on each major topic, before diving into the details. In a course like the hypermedia course that prompted the development of AHA! there are three introductory chapters that can be studied in any order, and there are six "advanced" chapters that should be studied after the first three. A field-dependent learner would like to at least get a glimpse of these advanced chapters before studying any chapter in detail. There are two ways to make this possible:

1. On a page you can conditionally include objects. An <object> tag that refers to a concept is linked to resources in the same way as shown in Figure 5. The resource must be a valid xhtml fragment. (If you wish to conditionally include some media item like an image you have to include it from within the xhtml fragment, e.g. by using an <img> tag.) In order to show an introduction to the field-dependent learner who visits the chapter at the start of the learning process and to show the "normal" page (possibly containing links to

pages with more details) to field-independent learners, or to the field-dependent learner who is ready for it, a skeleton page can be created that includes an object that is conditionally connected to the two resources. However, using conditionally included (page-size) objects to simulate having two different pages is a rather artificial use of this technique.

2. Offering an introductory page and a "normal" page can be done by conditially assigning two pages (or "resources") to the concept that represents the chapter. Through the dialog box of Figure 5 the conditions for presenting each version are defined. Because the selection is now done entirely in the conceptual definition of the application generating adaptive link destination structures is easier than generating skeleton pages and conditional object inclusions. This is especially important for authoring tools that generate AHA! applications from some high-level description format, possibly including learning style adaptation [14]. Tools that perform such translation are the MOT to AHA! convertor [7, 15] and a learning-style authoring tool of [16] (which has since been extended significantly).

6 Discussion and Conclusion

There is no *one size fits all* solution in adaptive (personalized) e-learning. This not only holds for the learners (who have different learning styles) but also for authors. AHA! therefore offers a rich set of possibilities for creating adaptive applications, with different layout, different menu-like structures, different ways to adapt the presentation of links, with or without icons, different ways to adapt the page content, with inline fragments or with external conditionally included objects, and with adaptive link destinations to enable the same link to lead to different pages, all of this depending on the values in the user model.

However, *more* is not always *better* in the area of adaptive hypermedia and personalized e-learning. Too much adaptation may turn an application into an adventure game. In this paper we proposed to use *stable presentations* as an alternative for simply applying less adaptation. Applying adaptation once (and perhaps later again, under controlled circumstances) makes the adaptation invisible to the users because they only see one version of each page. They may only become aware that the application is adaptive when they compare what they see on a page to what other users see on the same page.

Having a rich functionality for creating adaptive behavior, and ways to disable unwanted adaptation, does not guarantee that usable adaptive applications will be produced. The Graph Author tool lets authors create a conceptual structure in a graphical way. An author can for instance simply draw a graph of prerequisite relationships between concepts. And concepts automatically become part of a hierarchy of larger concepts (like chapters) and smaller ones (like pages and fragments). But this conceptual structure must still be *designed* carefully. A drawing tool (with additional features such as cycle detection) for concept relationships of different types is a useful tool but it does not perform the design phase for you.

People have frequently asked us whether creating an adaptive course using AHA! is more work (and if so, how much more) than creating a static Web-based course.

The answer is twofold: yes, it is more work, because one has to consider *prerequisites* and design measures to deal with them. This includes creating the prerequisite relationships in the Graph Author tool so that links are properly annotated (to guide users), and it includes writing *prerequisite explanations* to conditionally include on pages that require prerequisite knowledge that can be sufficiently compensated for by a short explanation (instead of warning the learner not the page at all), or writing introductory pages to replace detailed ones, and have links conditionally refer to the intro or the details. On the other hand, creating a non-adaptive (or static) Web-based course text that can be browsed freely without encountering pages that cannot be understood because of missing foreknowledge is completely impossible. So we argue that it is a matter of putting in some extra effort to create a course of high quality that cannot be obtained without using adaptation. AHA! tries to minimize the required extra effort but cannot completely eliminate it.

Acknowledgements

This work is/was supported by the PROLEARN network of excellence and the NLnet Foundation.

References

1. Andrews, K., Kappe, F., Maurer, M., Serving Information to the Web with Hyper-G. Third International World Wide Web Conference, Computer Networks and ISDN Systems (27) pp. 919-026 (1995).
2. Brusilovsky, P., Methods and Techniques of Adaptive Hypermedia. User Modeling and User-Adapted Interaction, 6, pp. 87-129, 1996.
3. Brusilovsky, P., Adaptive Hypermedia. User Modeling and User-Adapted Interaction, 11, pp. 87-110, 2001.
4. Brusilovsky, P., Eklund, J., Schwarz, E., Web-based education for all: A tool for developing adaptive courseware. Computer Networks and ISDN Systems (Proceedings of the 7th Int. World Wide Web Conference, 30 (1-7), pp. 291-300, (1998).
5. Brusilovsky, P., Schwarz, E., Weber, G., ELM-ART: An intelligent tutorian system on World Wide Web. In Proceedings of ITS'96, Intelligent Tutoring Systems (Springer LNCS Vol 1086), pp. 261-269 (1996).
6. Chen, S., Macredie, R., Cognitive styles and hypermedia navigation: Development of a learning model. Journal of the American Society for Information Science and Technology, 53 (1), pp. 3-15 (2002).
7. Cristea, A.I., Smits, D., De Bra, P., Writing MOT, Reading AHA! - converting between an authoring and a delivery system for adaptive educational hypermedia. A3EH Workshop, AIED'05 (2005).
8. De Bra, P., Hypermedia Structures and Systems. Adaptive course text offered at the TU/e, available at http://wwwis.win.tue.nl/2L690/ (1994, 1996).
9. De Bra, P., Aerts, A., Berden, B., De Lange, B., Rousseau, B., Santic, T., Smits, D., Stash, N., AHA! The Adaptive Hypermedia Architecture. Proceedings of the ACM Hypertext Conference, Nottingham, UK, pp. 81-84 (2003).
10. De Bra, P., Aerts, A., Rousseau, B., Concept Relationship Types for AHA! 2.0. Proceedings of the AACE ELearn'2002 conference, pp. 1386-1389 (2002).

11. De Bra, P., Smits, D., Stash, N., The Design of AHA!. Proceedings of the ACM Hypertext Conference, Odense, Denmark (2006), and on-line adaptive version at http://aha.win.tue.nl/ahadesign/.
12. Henze, N., Nejdl, W., Adaptivity in the KBS Hyperbook System. Second Workshop on Adaptive Systems and User Modeling on the WWW, TU/e CSN 99-97, pp. 67-74, Toronto, Canada, (1999).
13. Millard, D., Moreau, L., Davis, H., Reich, S., FOHM: A Fundamental Open Hypertext Model for Investigating Interoperability between Hypertext Domains. Proceedings of the ACM Conference on Hypertext, pp. 93-102 (2000).
14. Stash, N., Cristea, A., De Bra, P. Explicit Intelligence in Adaptive Hypermedia: Generic Adaptation Languages for Learning Preferences and Styles, HT'05, CIAH Workshop, Salzburg, (2005).
15. Stash, N., Cristea, A.I., De Bra, P., Authoring of Learning Styles in Adaptive Hypermedia: Problems and Solutions, WWW'04 (The 13th International World Wide Web Conference) pp. 114-123 (2004).
16. Stash, N., De Bra, P., Incorporating Cognitive Styles in AHA! (The Adaptive Hypermedia Architecture), Proceedings of the IASTED International Conference Web-Based Education, pp. 378-383 (2004).
17. Weber, G., Kuhl, H.-C., Weibelzahl, S., Developing Adaptive Internet Based Courses with the Authoring System NetCoach, Proceedings of the Third Workshop on Adaptive Hypermedia (AH2001), Springer LNCS Vol. 2266, pp. 226-238 (2001).

Awareness and Collaboration in the iHelp Courses Content Management System

Christopher Brooks, Rupi Panesar, and Jim Greer

Advanced Research in Intelligent Educational Systems (ARIES)
Department of Computer Science
University of Saskatchewan
Saskatoon, Saskatchewan S7N 5C9 Canada
cab938@mail.usask.ca, rup785@mail.usask.ca, greer@cs.usask.ca

Abstract. Traditional learning content management systems have minimal support for awareness among learners, and tend to support only loosely coupled collaboration features. This paper shows how we have integrated user model-based awareness features and collaboration features into our learning content management system for both learners and instructors.

1 Introduction and Motivation

Most popular learning content management systems provide poor collaboration support for learners. These systems, initially aimed at providing simple mechanism for the publishing and consumption of educational content, typically provide only loosely coupled collaboration facilities (e.g. discussion forums, chat systems, etc.). The absence of tighter integration of these facilities with course content impedes the potential of learners to effectively collaborate and learn. In particular, distance education learners are at a severe disadvantage as they are unable to see the subtle societal cues that are prevalent in face-to-face teaching scenarios.

One of our goals is to apply both Social Development Theory [15] and Activity Theory [4] to e-learning environments by encouraging learner collaboration in and around the artefacts of learning. The ability to collaborate, along with the awareness of when and with whom to collaborate, provides a potential to increase learner performance and satisfaction. Further, by extending this awareness to other facilitators of learning (e.g. instructors, tutorial assistants, markers, etc.) we believe that we can provide these facilitators with a means to better scaffold learner interaction.

This paper is structured is follows; the following section will outline the architecture of our web-based learning content management systems, focusing on how learner tracking is employed to create detailed learner models. Section three describes three of our current collaboration tools and indicate how they support learning based on activity theory. Section four provides an overview of some of the features we currently employ to increase awareness of learner activities within the learning environment, and outline a prototype visualization for supporting awareness for instructors over class interactions. Finally, section five will conclude the paper with a look at other research avenues we are investigating with this system.

W. Nejdl and K. Tochtermann (Eds.): EC-TEL 2006, LNCS 4227, pp. 34–44, 2006.

2 iHelp Courses

The iHelp suite of tools[1] was born out of early work in tracking and modeling learners to provide just-in-time expertise location [13]. User models were built up from various observed user interactions (e.g. learners posting questions in a discussion forum), as well as self-declared learning attributes (e.g. learning style, background knowledge, etc.), and intelligent agents were used to match learners with compatible peer helpers on demand.

Since then a number of new directions have been pursued to increase the breadth of this learning environment. The iHelp suite now supports both asynchronous and synchronous discussions, the ability to present packages of standards-based learning objects (e.g. using the IMS Content Packaging format [10]), as well as a shared document annotation tool. One of the focuses of the iHelp environment is to be light weight on the client side yet retain its ability to track what learners are doing. Principle in making this a possibility is the use of asynchronous JavaScript (AJAX) to record user interactions such as when they have viewed a message, posted a message, viewed learning content, or answered the items in a quiz. This information is then stored in the generic tracking model for learner activities and is used to generate derived attributes (e.g. dwell time on a particular learning object).

In addition to this built-in user modeling functionality, iHelp Courses provides a simple API based on the SCORM run time environment [3]. This API allows content packages to store specialized learner characteristics, and helps to support the rapid development of user model-based learning content without modifying the deployed content management system. While this feature is in its infancy, it has been used successfully to create a simple learning-object driven recommender system.

The iHelp Courses system has been deployed and made available to over 1,000 learners in the past two years, and is the primary method of instruction for two fully online courses that teach introductory computer science for non-majors. The asynchronous discussion and synchronous chat systems are available as stand alone tools (named iHelp Discussions and iHelp Chat respectively), and are used by nearly 1,000 students every academic term, resulting in over 5,000 discussion messages being posted and 12,000 chat messages exchanged.

3 Collaboration

One of the principle tenets of activity theory is that the achievement of learning outcomes arises from the interactions between the learner, the artefacts in the environment, the tools to manipulate those artefacts, and the learning community. Mwanza and Engeström indicate that learning is:

> "...driven by genuine developmental needs in human practices and institutions, manifested in disturbances, breakdowns, problems, and episodes of questioning the existing practice." [14].

---

[1] See http://ihelp.usask.ca for more information about these tools.

From this we draw our belief that by providing tools to explicitly link the collaboration of learners with learning artefacts (e.g. content, assignments, interactive simulations) we should be able to positively influence the learning process. This influence could come in many different forms including a decrease of learner attrition rates from online courses, and increase in learner satisfaction in online courses, an increase in learners meeting learning objectives, or an increase in sense of "belonging" in the online community.

Using Activity Theory as an underlying principle in large scale learning systems is not in and of itself novel. Bourguin and Derycke [16] describe a high level architecture for associating CSCL widgets with different learning tasks. Learners can then choose specific tasks to investigate, and get a customized learning environment in which to interact with their peers. We instead take a bottom-up artefact centred view of the problem, and aim to attach collaboration and task features around specific kinds of learning content.

The first approach we have taken is to couple our discussion and chat tools directly with instructional content. This coupling does not occur only at the package level, and instructors are given much latitude in how they would like associations to be made. Further, we aim to make the collaboration as ambient as possible and minimal overhead is needed from the user to initiate collaborations. This is explained in more detail in section 3.1.

The second approach we have taken is to create a groupware application that allows learners to share and collaboratively annotate text (computer program source code in our experiences, though we intend to broaden this to other text artefacts such as student essays). This workspace must be explicitly invoked and accepted by both users, and gives learners the ability to highlight and annotate directly on the shared artefact. This is elaborated in section 3.2.

3.1   Learning Object-Based Collaboration

The iHelp system provides two different discussion interfaces. The first is an asynchronous system, where messages are posted in forums and message threads are hierarchal in nature. Messages can be posted in plain text or a subset of HTML and can contain any number of attachments. The second interface is a synchronous chat system which allows learners to exist in many different channels at once, and operates much like Internet Relay Chat (IRC). Learners can also initiate new private channels for private chats with one another. All learners have the ability to create up to eight pseudonyms for protecting their identity during interaction and, depending on the preferences set by the facilitator, can post to certain discussion forums anonymously.

E-learning standards describe a content package as a collection of hierarchal activities which learners typically traverse using an inorder traversal[2]. Taking a pragmatic approach to defining a learning object, we allow facilitators to create new discussion forums or chat rooms and associate them with any subtree of activities within the content package. As learners traverse the content they are automatically moved into either the chat room or the discussion forum associated with that content.

---

[2] Strictly speaking this traversal can be modified by overlaying a set of sequencing rules to the activity hierarchy and applying a student tracking model. The interested reader is directed to [8] for more information.

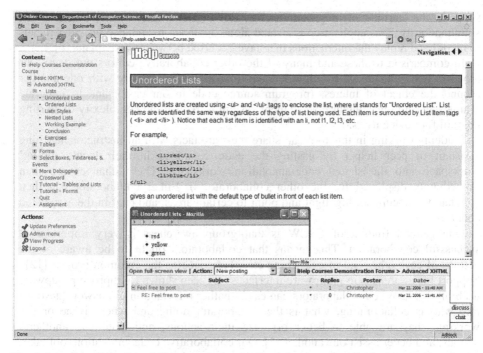

Fig. 1. Learning Object-based Collaboration tools. The left menu shows a single content package with hierarchically arranged activities. Each activity links directly to a file within the content package, which is rendered in the top right frame of the browser. The bottom portion of the right frame holds collaborative tools (with the discussion forum interface shown here), which can be toggled between asynchronous or synchronous discussions using the tabs on the right.

Learners can switch back and forth between chat rooms and discussion forums using a tabbed interface, and new chat rooms automatically open up in the background so current collaborations that might be happening are not lost. Finally, collaboration can be cancelled or terminated by clicking on a "Show/Hide" on the interface and minimizing the chat or discussion forums. Fig. 1 shows an example of this collaborative interface.

3.2 Collaborative Annotation Environment

To help the novices in learning programming concepts in online courses and to enhance the collaboration among them, we have integrated a collaborative annotation tool for text documents within our existing content management system. While this tool is still in the prototype stage, it is quite stable and has been deployed and used in a number of online and blended learning courses over the last eight months.

While not yet commonplace, a number of collaborative editors have been built elsewhere to encourage learners to share text artefacts. CAROUSEL a web based system allows students to share algorithmic representations with their peers. Students can create their algorithmic representation using any utility or software, and can upload those files using the system. These representations are then available for other students to view, evaluate and discuss through discussion forums [9]. GREWP supports the learning of programming by allowing students to edit the same code simultaneously. This application is a stand alone application, and also provides means to record and replay the interactions that have occurred between participants [8].

In comparison to these and many of the other collaborative editors out there, our tool has two main goals: to allow learners to collaborate actively with one another around the object of interest (program source code in our case), and to integrate seamlessly into our content management system to reduce the complexity of starting the tool for novice users.

Students working in this tool can share their artefacts with an instructor, teaching assistant or peer helper by pasting the code contained in their local 'editing' workspace into the shared code-annotation workspace. These changes are then immediately displayed for the other collaborator(s). Either collaborator can then annotate the document, highlight and point to certain areas, and chat in the associated chat tool.

One general finding of CSCW is that group awareness is very important to successful collaboration. This means that collaborators ought to be aware of the actions of each other and of everything else that concerns the common project [12].. Support for awareness in groupware interfaces has been shown to improve groupware usability [6,7]. When collaborators can easily gather information to answer questions like who is collaborating, what is the collaborator doing and where is he or she working, they are able to better organize their actions, anticipate one another's actions, and better assist one another [5]. Our collaborative code annotation tool takes advantage of the iHelp chat window to support informal awareness of presence between participants. This visible list of participants along with the unique color assigned to each collaborator's interactions is explicitly displayed in the interface. Colour makes all users in the group aware of the activities of a particular user. If a user wants to refer to (say) a particular line of code, he/she has to simply select a line of text and the selected line will blink and be highlighted in his/her assigned color, on every other participant's browser screen. The system's representations of other users' activities are implicit. By the mechanism of annotation, users can comment to each other about the text artefact. Replay mode allows collaborators to review each other's activities.

The current implementation of the iHelp collaborative annotation tool enables facilitators and peers to reference and add annotations to the specific lines of code in a software program. Comments attached to a a particular line of code are made immediately visible to the other participating user(s). The annotation mode is a powerful feature as annotations can not only help students to remember, clarify, comprehend, and think about the key points, but they can also facilitate students to engage in discussion [2]. Fig. 2 shows a screenshot of the collaborative annotation tool's interface.

The iHelp collaborative annotation tool is integrated directly within the context sensitive chat system. It can be invoked by clicking on another learners name within the chat room, and indicating that a shared session should begin. Once accepted, a new window opens for each of the users, who then can share a document as they see fit. The ease of starting the application makes it suitable for both computer savvy users and those learners who are new to this kind of environment.

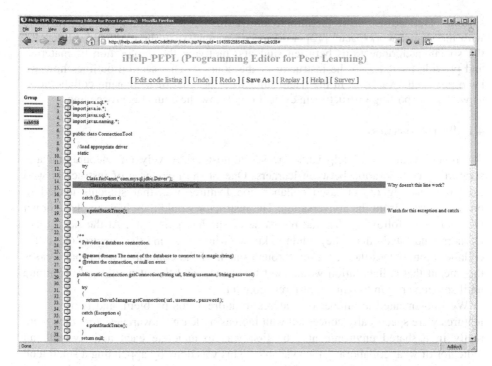

Fig. 2. Collaborative editor interface. The list of participants in this collaborative setting are given on the left, and are colour coded. Each time someone clicks on a line in the interface a bar the same colour as their name flashes to indicate what line has been chosen. Annotations can be added by double clicking on a line, and show up on the right hand side (long annotations are truncated until the mouse hovers over them). The entire session can be replayed using the links at the top of the window.

The prototype is written in JavaScript, DHTML and HTML with a conceptually simple front end. It makes extensive use of asynchronous JavaScript (e.g. AJAX) and DHTML to realize the interactive markup effects and offers capabilities not available in existing systems. The shared-code workspace is basically a framed area, where the code to be shared will be displayed in the browser window of each user in the collaborative group. The shared-code area follows the principle of relaxed WYSIWIS for uniform look. By downloading the most recent version from the shared workspace into their local editing workspace, the students can save the copy of the document locally.

4 Awareness

While mostly absent from content management systems, awareness has been a key field of study for many in the area of Human Computer Interaction. Gutwin et al. break the concept of awareness up into four different types: social awareness, task awareness, concept awareness, and workspace awareness [12]. Of these types, workspace awareness is perhaps most relevant for learning content management systems. Defined as "up-to-the-minute knowledge about other students' interactions with the shared workspace" [12], workspace awareness can be exploited to increase the social interconnections between students, motivate the exploration of material, and provide feedback to the instructor of the course. This section outlines how we have provided awareness in the iHelp suite with the goal of increasing collaboration as well as supporting instructors in evaluation of how the course is proceeding.

4.1 Peer Awareness

Awareness within the iHelp suite focuses almost exclusively on encouraging and supporting collaboration between learners. One of the responses of instructors who used the learning object-based collaboration features was that students tended to browse "away" from the conversation. The instructor would then have to chase down the student by following the chat rooms he or she had gone into. At the same time, learners indicated that they didn't know who was in the environment for collaboration, unless they checked through much of the content first. In many cases this meant that collaboration would start by chance, and that it would only continue until someone began looking at different content.

We implemented a number of features to address this problem, and two of these features were specifically concerned with increasing learner awareness that they were really in a shared environment. The first was to annotate each activity with an indicator of what collaboration is available. This was done by appending a small icon of a person to the end of the title if there were two or three people viewing that piece of content, or appending two such person icons iff there were more than four people viewing that piece of content. In addition, a fractional number was placed after the title of the activity where the numerator indicated the number of asynchronous forum messages on that topic that have been read by the user, and the denominator represented the number of total messages available to read. Figure 3 demonstrates these awareness features.

The second feature was related specifically to the chat channels. To prevent disorientation, new chat rooms open in the background, so current discussions are not disturbed. Awareness of what is happening in background channels is given by changing the title of the channel to indicate the number of messages in that channel that have not yet been read.

4.2 Class Awareness

In addition to ambient awareness within the learning environment, we are working on providing explicit visualizations of learner interaction for instructors (and eventually for learners as well. Most e-learning systems tend to provide only rough statistics on student activity, and scale poorly to large classes. In our initial exploration we have applied sociograms to learner models where the nodes in the sociogram represent individual learners, and the directed edges between nodes indicate some form of interaction (either a reading of or a reply to an asynchronous forum posting). In large classes (e.g. those having more than 100 students), this becomes unwieldy. We further refined this sociciogram by breaking learners into three different groups:

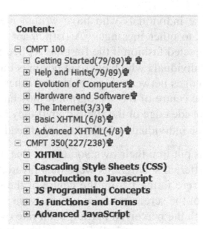

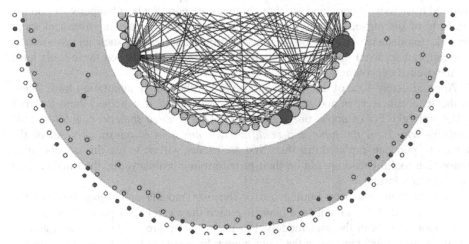

Fig. 3. Peer awareness in the navigation component of iHelp Courses. This figure shows two courses, *CMPT 100* and *CMPT 350*. In the first course the instructor has chosen to add individual discussion modules and chat rooms to each module. The first module, *Getting Started*, contains 89 discussion forum messages, 79 of which have been unread by the current learner. There are currently four or more learners reading content in that module as is indicated by the presence of two small person icons. The setup of the second course is somewhat different – here the instructor has chosen to implement one larger forum and chat room for all modules in the course. As the learners progress through individual modules their collaboration tools will not change.

Fig. 4. Portion of a sociogram for an introductory computer science forum. Dark nodes indicate facilitators, while lighter coloured nodes indicate learners. The inner circle is made up of participants, four of which are very important to the community (as shown by having a larger node size). A casual observation of this network indicates that, while some learners write a fair bit (many interconnected nodes in the middle), there are lots of learners who haven't ever read anything (the outer ring of delinquents), and many lurkers who read very little (as they tend to be closer to the outside of the middle ring instead of the inside of that ring). Note that the ring of delinquents includes a disproportionately high number of facilitators as our currently deployment gives access to this forum to most staff and faculty in the department.

- Participants: Those individuals who have written messages, either on their own or as replies to other messages. A participant is connected to another participant in a directed fashion if the first has replied to the second.
- Lurkers: Those individuals who have read postings but have not written any. Lurkers have no edges between themselves and other nodes, but are situated either closer to the centre of the sociogram if they have read many postings, or closer to the outside edge of the sociogram if they have read few postings.
- Delinquents: Those individuals who have neither read nor written a posting.

Each group of learners was put into their own sociogram that aligned nodes along the exterior of a circle. The different sociograms were then layered on top of one another such that the delinquents were farthest from the centre of the screen, the participants were closest to the centre of the screen, and the lurkers were in between (fig. 4). This corresponded well both with the perceived participation rate of individuals, as well as with the sizes of the different classes of individuals in blended courses. Nodes were further colour coded to represent the different roles of the people involved; red for potential facilitators, and light grey for learners.

5 Conclusions and Future Directions

The iHelp suite aims to be a standards-based research oriented e-learning system where detailed user models can be built. This paper has outlined two specific aspects of this system, collaboration and awareness to support this collaboration. Firmly inspired by activity theory, and the thought that collaboration best happens around the artefacts of discourse, we believe these features have made our environment more suitable for distance and blended learners. Empirically testing such an assertion is difficult, but feedback from instructors and students who have used these tools have been extremely encouraging.

Approximately 40% of the learners who used collaborative annotation tool, filled-in the feedback surveys and responded very positively that it helped them to work collaboratively. For example, one learner quoted "*It enabled students to interact with someone who knew the topic and could answer any kind of questions*". All of the survey respondents reported that their first preference will be to use this collaborative annotation tool for working out on their programming problems and then instant chat or discussion forum.

To date there has been limited use of the user models underlying this system. However, we do have a number of plans to enrich the awareness aspects of the system using more details in the user models. For instance, we are working on a system to motivate student interactions in the environment by allowing them to compare aspects of their activity to that of other learners (including the derived "average" learner, or perhaps an instructor created "ideal learner"). We still believe in grounding this comparison in the artefacts of learning, and are working on ways of changing the course content navigation window to support this kind of user model awareness [1].

Our implementation of class awareness is still in its early stages. We have observed that instructors are both interested in this kind of visualization, as well as willing to change their pedagogical style based on the knowledge they gain of classroom dynamics. We are planning studies to both qualitatively and quantitatively analyse this visualization. In particular, we believe that we can classify the health of class discussions (and individual learners in those discussions) based on graph characteristics of our awareness sociograms. We are also investigating the motivational effects of opening this visualization up to learners and student assistants, where they are able to see clearly how they fit in with the rest of the class.

Acknowledgements. This work has been conducted with support from Science and Engineering Canada (NSERC) and its Learning Object Repositories Research Network (LORNET). Special thanks to Lori Kettel, Robin Dunlop, Ryan Silk, Erik Fredrickson, and Jian Liu for their help in building the technology our research is based upon.

References

1. Brooks, C., Hansen, C., Greer, J. (2006) Social Awareness in the iHelp Courses Learning Content Management System. Workshop on Social Navigation and Community-Based Adaptation Technologies, Fourth International Conference on Adaptive Hypermedia and Adaptive Web-Based Systems (AH2006). In Submission.
2. Chong, N. S. and Sakauchi, M.(2001). Creating and sharing web notes via a standard browser. In Proceedings of the 2001 ACM Symposium on Applied Computing (Las Vegas, Nevada, United States). SAC '01. ACM Press, New York, NY, 99-104.
3. Dodds, P. (ed). (2001) Sharable Content Object Reference Model (SCORM) Version 1.2, The SCORM Run-Time Environment, Advanced Distributed Learning.
4. Engeström, Y., Miettinen, R., and Punamäki, R. (eds.) (1999) Perspectives on Activity Theory. Cambridge, MA: Cambridge University Press.
5. Gutwin C., Stark, G., and Greenburg, S. (1995) Support for Workspace Awareness in Educational Groupware. Pro ACM Conference on Computer Supported Collaborative Learning, pp 147-156, Indiana University, Bloomington, Indiana, USA October 17-20, Distributed LEA Press.
6. Gutwin, C. and Greenberg, S. (1998). Effects of Awareness Support on Groupware Usability. Proc. ACM CHI '98, 511-518.
7. Gutwin, C., Roseman, M., and Greenberg, S. (1996) A Usability Study of Awareness Widgets in a Shared Workspace Groupware System. Proc. ACM CSCW '96, 258-267.
8. Hickey, T. J., Langton, J., & Alterman, R. (2005). Enhancing CS programming lab courses using collaborative editors. Journal of Computing Sciences in Colleges, Volume 20 Issue 3, 157-167.
9. Hübscher-Younger, T. and Narayanan, N. H. 2003. Constructive and collaborative learning of algorithms. In Proceedings of the 34th SIGCSE Technical Symposium on Computer Science Education (Reno, Navada, USA, February 19 - 23, 2003). SIGCSE '03. ACM Press, New York, NY, 6-10.
10. IMS Content Packaging Information Model, Version 1.1.4, IMS Global Learning Consortium Inc., 2004
11. IMS Simple Sequencing Information and Behavior Model, Version 1.2, IMS Global Learning Consortium Inc., 2003.
12. Koch, M. (1994). Design Issues and Model for a Distributed Multi-User Editor. Computer Supported Coop. Work Volume 3, Issue 3-4 , 359-378.
13. McCalla, G., Vassileva, J., Greer, J., and Bull, S. (2000) Active Learner Modelling. In proceedings of the conference on Intelligent Tutoring Systems 2000. Montreal, Canada.

14. Mwanza, D., and Engestroöm, Y. Pedagogical Adeptness in the Design of E-learning Environments: Experience from the Lab@Future Project. E-Learn 2003.
15. Vygotsky, L.S. (1978) Mind in Society. Cambridge, MA: Harvard University Press.
16. Bourguin, G., and Derycke, A. (2001) Integrating the CSCL Activities into Virtual Campuses: Foundations on a new Infrastructure for Distributed Collective Activities. In Proceeding of Euro-CSCL 2001.

Interoperability for Peer-to-Peer Networks: Opening P2P to the Rest of the World

Ingo Brunkhorst and Daniel Olmedilla

L3S Research Center and University of Hanover, Hanover, Germany
{brunkhorst, olmedilla}@l3s.de

Abstract. Due to the information growth, distributed environments are offered as a feasible and scalable solution. Peer-to-Peer (P2P) networks have become one of the most important and used distributed environments inside (and outside) the e-learning community. They bring many advantages such as high flexibility for peers to dynamically join or leave the network, scalability, autonomy and high resilience against peer failures. However, every single one of them typically uses an interface specifically developed for that network, and it requires every peer to implement it in order to join. This is leading to increased development costs for potentially new participants of the network, and usually makes different P2P networks unable to interact with other systems and environments, isolating the network as a whole. In this paper, we report on a solution based on a proxy-based architecture and semantic mappings in order to allow the sharing of content between the set of peers inside a P2P network and other systems outside the network. Furthermore, we present an open-source implementation of the modules described in the paper.

1 Introduction

The World Wide Web has become a well accepted medium for communication among people for private, academic and business affairs. As a consequence, the amount of digital material that is sent along and stored in the network increases rapidly. Obviously, learning is not unaffected by this trend, and the amount of Learning Objects (LO's henceforth) in school, academic and business environments continues to grow rapidly. As a consequence of this evolution, the focus shifts to new questions, like for example "Where shall the LO's be stored?", "Who manages them?" or "Are they easily findable?".

Dynamic sharing of information from end user machines was prohibitively costly in the past due to the lack of storage capacity and network bandwidth available for most desktop computers. As a consequence, networks of computers were mostly reduced to set of interconnected, powerful servers. In this configuration, it is relatively simple to know which servers are available and which information is available where to whom. This is also the typical architecture in business coalitions where several companies share their assets within a network of partners.

W. Nejdl and K. Tochtermann (Eds.): EC-TEL 2006, LNCS 4227, pp. 45–60, 2006.
© Springer-Verlag Berlin Heidelberg 2006

On the other hand, with the boom of web-based file-sharing services (e.g., Napster, Gnutella, Morpheus), peer-to-peer (P2P for brevity) networks have become more relevant. The advantages of the P2P approach include: high flexibility for peers to join or leave the network dynamically, scalability (recently it was shown that for really large networks, a hybrid solution with super-peers scales better [13]), autonomy (as peers do not relinquish control over their resources) and high resilience against peer failures. The main disadvantages are that P2P networks require constant management, as peers join and leave continuously, thereby producing an extra load on the network and slowing down response time during search. The use of specific interfaces for each network usually means, as no standards exist yet, that only peers implementing such interfaces can query for, or provide content in the network.

Obviously, peers must implement specific P2P network interfaces in order to join them, which is typically a different one for each network. This means an extra effort for systems willing to connect, since such systems need to develop a different interface for each network they want to join. This barrier makes P2P networks unable to interact with other systems and environments. However, in many cases such other systems already have a (possibly standardized) interface that could be adapted by re-using connecting components. In this paper, we report on a solution for interoperability in the Edutella P2P network [14] in order to allow the sharing of content from peers within the network with other systems and environments outside the network. Our approach is based on a proxy-based architecture as well as on modules that provide semantic mappings capabilities, thus allowing the communication between a P2P network and any other system. In addition, we provide open-source implementations of the components described in order to encourage re-usability as well as a mapping editor in order to ease the tasks for administrators and developers.

The paper builds on previous work of the authors [17] and is organized as follows: Section 2 starts with an introduction of Edutella, the P2P network we based our work on. The general requirements for interoperability of systems and the assumptions we made for our work are described in Section 3. We continue in Section 4 with a description of our proxy based architecture followed by an introduction of the module with semantic mappings in Section 5. An introduction to an editor developed to help users on the task of specifying such mappings is provided in Section 6. Finally, Section 7 describes related work followed by Section 8 with the conclusions of the paper and a discussion of further work.

2   Edutella

Often, learning object providers do not want to abandon control over their resources to a third party, not even among the members of a coalition. The same concern about abandoning control also often applies to individuals, who may not want to give away their content to any centralized repository. In order to deal with this issue, distributed environments have shown to be a feasible solution for interconnection, integration and access to large amounts of information. P2P networks are one example of the impact the distribution of information might have in the sharing of information. In such networks, peers can offer various services to the user ranging from search and delivery of content, to personalization and security services. In addition, they contribute to the solution of managing the information growth, and allow every learning resource provider to offer its information without loosing control over it.

The Edutella P2P network [14] was developed with these principles as main design requirements. Edutella is a schema-based P2P network for an open world scenario in which LO's are freely offered (at not charge) and everybody is able to join (no agreement with an existing member of the network is required). It has various service facilities implemented, like for example query or publishing/subscription. Schema-based means that peers interchange RDF meta-data (data about data) among each other but not the resources themselves, that is, they interchange information about e.g. title, description, language and authors of a resource. This information can be queried using the QEL query language [15] (based on Datalog). Metadata interchange and search services provide the basic infrastructure needed to retrieve information about resources and services.

3   Requirements and Assumptions

It is important to note that in this paper we only consider the sharing of metadata about LO's. While this metadata is typically available, the learning object itself might not. Therefore, we do not deal with negotiations for the actual use of LO's by users here.

Admittedly, providing transparent access to all available repositories would be easy if all players would use the same metadata profile, query language, storage layer and communication protocol. However, this is not going to happen in the very near future due to the lack of a standard and the proprietary solutions already adopted by most of them.

In the following, we explain what requirements LO's repositories must satisfy in order to achieve interoperability and which are the assumptions within our network.

Common Communication Protocol and Interface. Repositories provide different access methods and interfaces over, among others, Web Services, different Remote Procedure Call methods, HTTP forms or even other appropriate solutions. In order to be able to communicate to each other, it is needed that they agree on a common protocol and a common interface. In this paper, we built on the methods specified in the Simple Query Interface [22] initiative (SQI for brevity), a rapidly maturing standard, using its Web Service binding.

Common Query Language. At the lower levels of data management, metadata is stored in different kinds of repositories, such as relational databases, RDF repositories, file systems, XML stores, etc. On top of this lower level, repositories expose their content through different search and query languages. Some examples are SQL, XQuery, QEL or CQL. In our system we have several wrappers implemented in order to provide access to the most common repositories (relational databases, RDF repositories, RDF files, etc.). Common to all of them is that the wrapper receives a query in QEL and transforms it into the local query language.

Common Metadata Profile. Although IEEE LOM [1] is becoming a standard for e-learning metadata, many repositories are based on specific profiles that may include extensions and specific value spaces. This means that a mapping needs to be provided [12]. This need even increases when content exchanged covers several domains. There are then two possibilities here: either each system maps its schema to a second system schema (in which case we reach semantic interoperability by means of pair of mappings [2,8] or a common global schema is provided and both systems must map into that common schema. Later in the paper, a section on semantic mappings provides a longer explanation and describes a module we developed which allows both approaches.

It is important to notice that although we assume the configuration described above it could be perfectly possible to use a different query language than QEL, a different communication protocol than Web Services and a different interface than SQI though our implementations currently do not support it.

4   Proxying Interoperability

P2P networks are dynamic networks where peers can act as server and client indistinctly and peers might freely join and leave the network over the time. Obviously, peers must implement the specific P2P network protocol in order to connect to it. Consumers and providers try to implement standard interfaces in order to maximize the implementation costs and effort. If they want to access or expose content in a P2P network, this requires the additional extra effort of implementing the specific network interface (one for each different P2P network to be accessed). This barrier makes P2P networks unable to interact with each other or with other systems and environments.

In order to solve this problem, we based our solution in proxies that are used to connect peers in a P2P network with the "outside" world. These proxies bridge two systems with different capabilities by means of implementing the protocol and/or interface supported by each system respectively. This way, a proxy is able to forward requests and responses from one system to another.

Nowadays, systems try to provide their services/resources via standard interfaces like SQI [22] or OKI [25]. In our case, we have implemented proxies able to bridge the proprietary[1] JXTA/Edutella protocol and interface into a the Web Service binding of the Simple Query Interface.

Taking the P2P network as a reference, there are two different desirable scenarios [18]:

---

[1] Here we use the term "proprietary" to emphasize that this protocol is not standard for P2P networks but it does not mean it is not open. In fact, JXTA/Edutella is open-source and anyone can use it easily.

1. **An external consumer/client wants to query content in the P2P network.** For example, let us suppose that we would like to offer the content of a P2P network via Web Services and/or in a web site. The first solution would be to make the (web) server join the P2P network. However, the load of the server would increase considerably and even some problems could arise in case the server wants to provide content from more than one network (it would need to join all of them). A cleaner solution (and the one we follow in this paper) is to forward the query from the server to the P2P network by means of proxies and retrieve the answer with the same mechanism.

2. **An external provider wants to offer content to the P2P network.** We assume that providers that have already implemented a standard interface will not be happy spending more time and money in developing the specific interface(s) of the network(s) they want to join. In contrary, they would like to reuse the one they have which would also ease its administration (as only one interface needs to be maintained).

According to these two scenarios, there are two different types of proxies with different functionality. The former scenario requires the so-called "consumer proxy" and the latter the so-called "provider proxy" (names are assigned according to the role they play). A consumer proxy acts as a mediator between an external client that wants to query the network and the P2P network itself. A provider proxy acts as a mediator in order to provide the content of an external provider into the P2P network.

4.1   Consumer Proxy

As described above in scenario 1, in some cases it is needed to be able to query a P2P network without the need of joining it. A consumer proxy is a peer which is part of the P2P network (and therefore it is able to send queries to and receive the answers from it) and which is also able to receive requests and send responses using a different protocol and interface. This way, an external client is able to query the P2P network through the proxy.

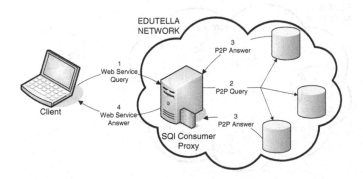

Fig. 1. Consumer Proxy

In our implementation, a consumer proxy mediates between the Edutella/ JXTA and the SQI protocol. As depicted in figure 1, it is responsible for

1. Receiving queries from external clients via SQI
2. Forwarding the query to the Edutella network using the JXTA/Edutella interface
3. Collecting the results sent from peers within the network using the JXTA/ Edutella interface
4. Forwarding those results to the requester system via SQI

This simple mechanism allows any system to query the content of the Edutella P2P network without needing to implement its specific interface. In addition, the proxy can return the results to the client application

Asynchronously. The results are sent to the client as soon as they arrive to the proxy. This is the typical mechanism in distributed environments as not all the results are generated at once but they must be gathered from the different systems in the network.

Synchronously. The results are gathered at the proxy and sent in a single message to the client. Although this is not the intuitive way for a distributed environment it could be desirable in some scenarios (e.g., in mobile devices we do not want our device to receive a new message every time a new result arrives to the proxy but better ask for new results in a proactive manner).

4.2   Provider Proxy

In order to fulfill our scenario 2, a second type of proxy has been developed. This provider proxy is a peer connected to the P2P network which also is able to send requests and receive responses by means of a different protocol and interface. Therefore, it is able to forward queries to external providers and receive their answers providing their content to the network.

As in the the case of consumer proxies, our provider proxy mediates between the Edutella/JXTA and the SQI protocol. As depicted in figure 2, it is responsible for

1. Receiving queries from peers in the network using the JXTA/Edutella interface
2. Forwarding them to the external provider via SQI

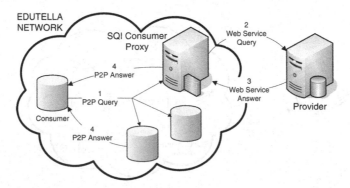

Fig. 2. Provider Proxy

3. Receiving the results from the external provider via SQI
4. Sending them back to the peer that sent the query using the JXTA/Edutella interface

Due to the asynchronous nature of a P2P network, it is possible for the provider proxy to receive the results from the external provider in a synchronous (e.g., in case the external provider is a relational database) or asynchronous (e.g., if the external provider is another distributed environment) way.

5 Semantic Mappings

In previous sections, we have described some of the basics for interoperability, namely common protocol and interfaces (or the use of proxies as presented in previous section) and common query language (or the use of appropriate wrappers). Although these elements ensure that two systems are able to talk to each other they do not guarantee that they will be able to understand each other due to the possible use of different schemas/ontologies.

Nowadays, there is a big effort on standardization of domain ontologies. For example, Dublin Core [4] is intended as standard for cross-domain information resource description and LOM [1] describes attributes required to fully/adequately describe a Learning Object. Unfortunately, still many proprietary schemas are used in each domain (e.g., database schemas within companies). For example, Dublin Core suggests using the attribute "creator" to describe the responsible person of making or writing a resource. While many repositories probably follow this suggestion when annotating their resources, others might use e.g. their own attribute "author" instead. In order to bring interoperability among them, data integration in the form of semantic mappings is needed. In this context, a semantic mapping is a transformation from one data model to another data model according to a set of rules (mappings).

In a distributed network we can distinguish among several integration possibilities:

- If no virtual and unified schema is assumed in the network, systems within the network must provide pairs of mappings between each two systems. Subsequently, the distributed network can be seen as a directed graph in which each arrow represents an available mapping from one node to another. After that, they can be applied transitively in order to infer new mappings which were not explicitly defined. This is specially useful in P2P networks as it is usually not possible to enforce a unique and common schema. Authors in [2,8] study this approach and provide algorithms to estimate the correctness of the inferred mappings.
- If a virtual and unified schema is assumed, there are two approaches for providing integration between the global schema and local schemas at the sources:
  - **Global As View (GAV)** [9]. In this approach, the global schema is expressed in terms of the data sources (an example is depicted in figure 3).

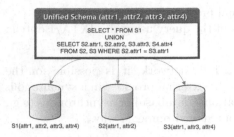

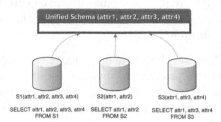

Fig. 3. Global As View Approach   **Fig. 4.** Local As View Approach

- **Local As View (LAV)** [26]. In this approach, each source is defined as
  a view over the global schema. This way, the global schema is specified
  independently from the sources (an example is depicted in figure 4).

A discussion of both GAV and LAV is provided in [11] as well as an introduction to "query rewriting" mechanisms. Query rewriting is the process in which a query expressed in the global schema is reformulated into another query according to a set of mappings [23]. This is the mechanism we have used in the mappings module we describe subsequently.

5.1 Query Rewriting Module

In order to provide semantic interoperability in our network, we have developed a module which transforms a query q_1 into a query q_2 according to the set of mappings specified. This module is intended to work on pairs of mappings without a unified schema, or in GAV or LAV integration approaches.

QEL, the language we use in our network, is based on datalog. In addition to standard datalog constructs, QEL includes some built-in predicates. Taking into account that in our network only metadata (in RDF) is queried and exchanged, the most important one is

$$qel : s(Subject, Predicate, Object)$$

which according to the QEL specification [15] "is true if Subject and Predicate are anonymous or non-anonymous RDF resources, and Object is a non-anonymous or anonymous RDF resource or an RDF Literal and the triple Resource Predicate Object exists in the RDF data". For example, a query like

$$? - qel : s(X, dc : title,' ArtificialIntelligence').$$

will return all the resources which title is "Artificial Intelligence". Other useful built-in predicates are $qel{:}like(X,Y)$ ("used to determine whether an RDF literal or URI contains a string as a substring"), $qel{:}lessThan(X,Y)$ and $qel{:}greaterThan(X,Y)$ which are used to compare two RDF literals.

Given this short introduction to the language, let us present the following simple query that we will use for our examples in the rest of the section:

$@prefix\ qel : < http : //www.edutella.org/qel\# > .$
$@prefix\ dc : < http : //purl.org/dc/elements/1.1/ > .$
$@prefix\ lom : < http : //ltsc.ieee.org/2002/09/lom - rights\# > .$
$? - qel : s(X, dc : title, Title),$
　　$qel : s(X, dc : description, Description),$
　　$qel : s(X, dc : creator, Creator),$
　　$qel : s(X, lom : cost, Cost),$
　　$qel : s(X, dc : subject, Subject).$

This query retrieves all the resources with title, description, creator and subject attributes from Dublin Core and the cost from LOM. The first lines of the query with prefix "@" define the namespaces.

Given such a query, we identified the following requirements:

- The query specifies a property (in the paper we will use property and attribute indistinctly) that does not exist in the source but the source has an equivalent property which could be used instead of. For example, if one data source has its own schema where it uses the property "abstract" instead of the property "description" from the Dublin Core standard.
- The query specifies a property and one value according to a specific taxonomy and the source uses a different taxonomy. For example, if the query searches for resources with "dc:subject" following the ACM classification[3] and the data source does have "dc:subject" but it follows the Dutch Basic Classification [5].
- In general, if one of the attributes is not available at the data source, the whole query fails[2]. However, it might happen that although the source does not have explicitly such an attribute, all its resources would share the same value if it existed. For example, assume a repository where all the resources are offered for free. This repository does not have the property "lom:cost" because it is not needed. However, in case one query contains this attribute, the whole query would fail (even if the constraint in the query is "lom:cost = No" which is actually true though it is not annotated). In such a case, it is desirable to assign a default value to all the resources in the data source without having to explicitly annotate all the resources of the repository.

In order to satisfy these requirements we developed a module that performs two types of mappings and one extra transformation: property mapping, property-value mapping and default value transformation (see table 1 for the whole list of mappings and [16] for technical details).

5.2   Property Mapping

A property mapping specifies how one property in the query must be reformulated. When the mapping module receives a query that contains the triple

---

[2] Here we assume that only conjunctives queries are sent. Edutella and QEL support disjunctive queries but we will omit them here because of simplicity.

Table 1. Types of Mappings

Mapping type	Description
1-to-1 property mapping	$(R, p_1, O) \leftarrow (R, p_2, O)$
1-to-1 property-value-value mapping	$(R, p_1, v_1) \leftarrow (R, p_2, v_2)$
2-to-1 property mapping	$(R, p_1, O), (O, p_2, L) \leftarrow (R, p_3, L)$
2-to-1 property-value mapping	$(R, p_1, O), (O, p_2, v_1) \leftarrow (R, p_3, v_2)$
1-to-2 property mapping	$(R, p_1, L) \leftarrow (R, p_2, O), (O, p_3, L)$
1-to-2 property-value mapping	$(R, p_1, v_1) \leftarrow (R, p_2, O), (O, p_3, v_2)$
2-to-2 property mapping	$(R, p_1, O), (O, p_2, L) \leftarrow (R, p_3, O), (O, p_4, L)$
2-to-2 property-value mapping	$(R, p_1, O), (O, p_2, v_1) \leftarrow (R, p_3, O), (O, p_4, v_2)$
Default value	$(p \leftarrow v)$

$qel : s(X, p_1, Z)$ it rewrites it into $qel : s(X, p_2, Z)$. Using our example query and taken into account the requirement in which the source does not contain the property "dc:description" but "own:abstract" (where "own" stands for their local namespace), it is possible to define the following mapping:

$$(X, dc : description, Z) \leftarrow (X, own : abstract, Z)$$

This mapping is currently a 1-to-1 mapping, that is, there is only one triple at each side of the mapping (separated by the left arrow) but it is also possible to specify 1-to-2, 2-to-1 and 2-to-2 mappings (see table 1). For example, suppose the author in the source is encoded using the property full name from the vcard ontology [20]. In such a case, we need the following mapping

$$(X, dc : creator, Z) \leftarrow (X, dc : creator, Y), (Y, vcard : fn, Z)$$

in order to abstract from the internal representation at the source[3]

5.3   Property-Value Mapping

The mapping described above assumes that one property is completely mapped onto another one. However, mapping can be brought to the granularity of values. A property-value mapping applies only when a query contains not only a specific property but also a specific value for that property and then both of them map into other (possibly the same) property and value. For example, assume that our example query uses the ACM classification in the property "dc:subject" and our source does have the property "dc:subject" but annotated with the Dutch Basic Classification taxonomy. We could use several mappings of the form

$$(X, dc : subject,' Software/Programming\_Languages') \leftarrow$$
$$(X, dc : subject,' Computer\_Science/Programming\_Languages')$$

to specify how the different values from the ACM taxonomy map into the Dutch Basic Classification.

In the same way as the property mapping, it is possible to extend this 1-to-1 to 2-to-1, 1-to-2 and 2-to-2 mappings.

---

[3] Note that we use similar notation as in [26]. Therefore, the right side of the mapping rule is rewritten into the left side.

5.4   Default Value

Property and property-value mappings provide rules which define how source triples are reformulated into equivalent triples corresponding to the destination schema. The "default value" mapping works differently. The properties specified in default values do not exist in the source repository and therefore they must be removed (not just reformulated) in the new query. To our knowledge, default values have not been defined before in literature and therefore, we formalize the process in Appendix A.

Following this approach, when a query is received by our mapping module, if there exists in the query any occurrence of a property specified in the default values, this occurrence is temporarily removed. This way, the query is sent to the local repository without that property (otherwise the query would fail) and a resultset is returned. However, this resultset still does not contain the default values that were requested (the properties previously removed) and therefore they must be added. Therefore, default values are added to each of the rows in the resultset returned by the repository. For example, following with our example query, suppose that our source repository does not have the property "lom:cost" but all the resources in the repository are free of charge. We can then define the following default value

$$(lom : cost \leftarrow' No')$$

This way, any triple in the query referring to the property "lom:cost" would be removed before the query is sent to the repository and added subsequently to the returned resultset together with the default value "No". In contrary, the query may specify that only elements which are not free of charge should be returned. In such a case, since it does not match the default value, the query is not executed and an empty resultset is returned.

6   Generating Mappings Using an Editor

Creating the appropriate mappings for the query rewriting module can be a tedious task, especially when large schemas are involved. Yet another problem is that the rewriting engines are embedded in web services or applications, and therefore have to retrieve the list of mappings from a file or web resource.

In order to help the user to create these files, we have developed an application that can import RDF schemas, displays their properties and allows the user to create mappings by simply clicking on the available elements. Once created, the mappings can be stored on disk in different formats, to be copied into the configuration of the query rewriting engine. Alternatively, the editor can be used to load existing mapping definitions and allow their modification before writing them back to the storage media.

We developed the application as a plugin for the Rich Client Platform [21], using the Jena RDF framework for managing RDF data. The software itself is open source, and is available via CVS from the main Edutella repository[4]

---

[4] http://edutella.jxta.org/

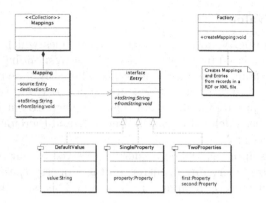

Fig. 5. Classes in the Editor Mapping Data Model

(as the rest of the components described in this paper). The component based approach of the RCP platform makes the editor easy extendable for additional functionality and allows the integration into other RCP tools, like the Eclipse Java Development Platform. The two main parts of the application are the Mapping Data Model and the User Interface.

6.1   Data Model

In the Editor application the mappings are represented as java objects (see figure 5). The Jena RDF API is providing access to the Properties of the involved schemas. The Mappings data Model consists of the classes representing the various forms of possible mappings, as well as an API to create new Mappings (Factory) and to store or load mappings (Parser).

6.2   User Interface

The interface for the user was implemented as an Eclipse plugin, using the Eclipse Rich Client Platform. Therefore, it is easy to integrate the editor into other RCP applications, or to implement additional functionality for the mapping editor, e.g. assistants to support the mappings creation process by doing simple similarity comparisons based on the schema annotation.

After the application startup, a window asks for the location of a RDF schema to use as the source schema (see figure 6). A Schema source can be chosen from a list of common used schemas, or by supplying a URL pointing to the location of the RDF document defining the schema.

Once a schema is selected, the column on the left displays the source schema while the middle column shows the target schema. Figure 7 shows the application where the Dublin Core has been loaded as source schema (left side of the window) and the Friend-of-a-Friend schema [7] as target schema, the right side of mappings (in the middle column). Additionally, default values can be added to the second panel on the left side, below the source schema.

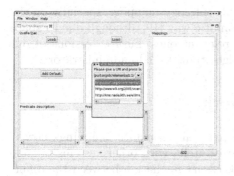

Fig. 6. Choosing a RDF Schema   **Fig. 7.** Creating Mappings

Creating a Mapping is now an easy task. In the lower part of the window are fields for the supported types of mappings. These fields can be filled by selecting elements from the properties listed above them. Then, the mapping is created just pressing on the "Add" button. The new mapping is added to the list of mappings in the right panel. Finally, selecting the appropriate operation from the menu, the created mappings can stored or new schemas loaded.

In order to cover most of the usage scenarios in the early states of development, we first implemented in our editor 1-to-1 and 2-to-1 property mappings and default values. We plan to extend it to the full set of mappings. In addition, techniques for (semi)automatic generation of mappings as described in [19] may be implemented.

7   Related Work

In [18], the authors describe the two scenarios, consumer proxy and provider proxy, and implemented a translation from the JXTA protocols to Web Services and vice versa. In this paper, we enrich our proxies with the possibility of mapping query languages and schemas. In addition, [18] does not use any specific interface but wrap the java objects by means of serialization while in our approach we are using the SQI standard initiative.

[10] presents an interesting approach for interoperability of Learning Repositories. Authors briefly present an "ECL Gateway" which is similar to our idea of proxies. They implemented a translation between ECL and a P2P protocol. In our paper we extend this idea separating the two different scenarios, consuming and providing information, and describing in detail how proxies work and how mappings can be performed. Furthermore, we present our work on default values which, to our knowledge, had not been described yet in any paper. Lionshare [24] includes the possibility to perform federated searches in each of the peers. However, the integration is made at the peer level (users may choose whether to query the network or other federated repositories) thus not providing an interoperability solution at the network level.

There exists a large number of papers on ontology mapping, specially on the creation of such mappings in a (semi)automatic way [19] although due to space limitations we have only cited the most relevant ones. Future versions of our editor may include some of the existing algorithms to help administrators.

8 Conclusions and Further Work

In this paper, we showed by means of proxies and semantic mappings how it is possible to connect a P2P network like Edutella with other systems outside the network. These proxies provide the necessary mediation between the different protocols and interfaces and semantic mappings overcome the problem of schema heterogeneity. Both together allow external systems to query and provide content in the network avoiding the isolation of P2P networks from the rest of the world. We refer the reader to [17] for a detailed description of successfully interconnected systems using our components, like for example ARIADNE and the Media Library (Swedish Educational Radio and Television).

In this paper we have focused the interoperability problem on search. However, although this is of course the most important service, there are still some other issues that must be researched. One of the main topics we plan to research on in the future is distributed ranking algorithms. Currently, a lot of research has been done around web ranking and merging of ranking lists (e.g., on meta-search engines). However, the former assumes that relationships of the form of links exist among resources in different repositories and the latter assumes that there exist overlapping in the content different repositories offer and rank. Unfortunately, this does not apply in a P2P network and the only existing measures are based on trust/reputation of the peers.

In addition, a challenge for the Local As View mappings described in this paper is how they would work in combination with Edutella Retrieval. Edutella Retrieval [6] is a recent addition in Edutella which allows information to be retrieved without requiring it explicitly in the query which would unnecessary eliminate valid matches. Since what is retrieved is not explicitly stated in the query it is difficult to detect which mappings to apply.

References

1. 1484.12.1 IEEE standard for learning object metadata. june 2002. http://ltsc.ieee.org/wg12.
2. Karl Aberer, Philippe Cudré-Mauroux, and Manfred Hauswirth. The chatty web: emergent semantics through gossiping. In *International World Wide Web Conferences*, Budapest, Hungary, may 2003.
3. ACM classification. http://www.acm.org/class/1998/overview.html.
4. Dublin core metadata innitiative (DCMI). http://dublincore.org/.
5. Dutch basic classification codes. http://www.kb.nl/vak/basis/bc98-en.html.
6. ERS: edutella retrieval service. http://edutella.jxta.org/spec/retrieval.html.
7. FOAF the friend of a friend (foaf) project. http://www.foaf-project.org/.

8. A. Halevy, Z. Ives, D. Suciu, and I. Tatarinov. Schema mediation in peer data management systems. In *Proc. of ICDE*, 2003.
9. Alon Y. Halevy. Answering queries using views: A survey. *VLDB Journal: Very Large Data Bases*, 10(4):270–294, 2001.
10. Marek Hatala, Griff Richards, Timmy Eap, and Jordan Willms. The interoperability of learning object repositories and services: Standards, implementations and lessons learned. In *13th World Wide Web Conference (WWW'04)*, New York, USA, May 2004.
11. Maurizio Lenzerini. Data integration: A theoretical perspective. In *ACM SIGACT-SIGMOD-SIGART Symposium on Principles of Database Systems (PODS)*, pages 233–246, Wisconsin, USA, jun 2002.
12. Jehad Najjar, Erik Duval, Stefaan Ternier, and Filip Neven. Towards interoperable learning object repositories: The ariadne experience. In *IADIS International Conference WWW/Internet*, Algarve, Portugal, nov 2003.
13. W. Nejdl, M. Wolpers, W. Siberski, C. Schmitz, M. Schlosser, I. Brunkhorst, and A. Löser. Super-peer-based routing and clustering strategies for rdf-based peer-to-peer networks. In *12th International World Wide Web Conference (WWW'03)*, Budapest, Hungary, may 2003.
14. Wolfgang Nejdl, Boris Wolf, Changtao Qu, Stefan Decker, Michael Sintek, Ambjörn Naeve, Mikael Nilsson, Matthias Palmer, and Tore Risch. Edutella: A P2P networking infrastructure based on RDF. In *11th International World Wide Web Conference (WWW'02)*, Hawaii, USA, jun 2002.
15. M. Nilsson and W. Siberski. RDF query exchange language (QEL) - concepts, semantics and RDF syntax, http://edutella.jxta.org/spec/qel.html, 2003.
16. Daniel   Olmedilla.   Working   with   edutella.   technical   report. http://www.l3s.de/ olmedilla/projects/edutella/edutella.pdf.
17. Daniel Olmedilla and Matthias Palmér. Interoperability for peer-to-peer networks: Opening p2p to the rest of the world. In *WWW Workshop on Interoperability of Web-Based Educational Systems*, volume 143 of *CEUR Workshop Proceedings*, Chiba, Japan, may 2005. Technical University of Aachen (RWTH).
18. C. Qu and W. Nejdl. Interacting edutella/JXTA peer-to-peer network with web services. In *2004 International Symposium on Applications and the Internet (SAINT 2004)*, Tokyo, Japan, jan 2004. IEEE Computer Society Press.
19. Erhard Rahm and Philip A. Bernstein. A survey of approaches to automatic schema matching. *VLDB J.*, 10(4):334–350, 2001.
20. Representing vCard objects in RDF/XML. http://www.w3.org/tr/vcard-rdf.
21. RCP rich client platform. http://www.eclipse.org/rcp/.
22. SQI: simple query interface. http://www.prolearn-project.org/lori/.
23. I. Tatarinov and A. Halevy. Efficient query reformulation in peer-data management systems. In *SIGMOD, 2004.*, 2004.
24. The lionshare project. http://lionshare.its.psu.edu/.
25. The open knowledge initiative (oki). http://www.okiproject.org/.
26. Jeffrey D. Ullman. Information integration using logical views. *Theoretical Computer Science*, 239(2):189–210, 2000.

A   Default Value Formalization

Let T be the set of all triples of the form (R, P, O) such that R, P and O are resource, predicate and object respectively. In addition, let D be the set of default values such that $d = (P, V)$ where P is a property and V a literal.

Then, for all queries Q, define $Q \xrightarrow{D}_1 P$ iff

- $Q = (T_1, \ldots, T_{i-1}, T_i, T_{i+1}, \ldots, T_n)$
- $T_i = (R, p, O)$
- $U = \begin{cases} T_i & \text{if } \exists p, d | T_i = (R, p, O), d \in D, d = (p, V), \\ \emptyset & \text{otherwise.} \end{cases}$
- $P = Q \setminus U$

Finally, we denote with $\xrightarrow{D}$ the reflexive transitive closure of $\xrightarrow{D}_1$ and the unique result of rewriting of the query with default values by $Q_2 = removeDV$ (Q, D).

After this process, the resulting query Q_2 of this process is sent to the repository and a resultset S is received as an answer to the query.

Then, let U be the set of default values applied in the previous process and for all rows R in S, define $R \xrightarrow{U}_1 W$ iff

- $R = (V_1, \ldots, V_n)$
- $V_{n+1} | d = (P, V_{n+1}), d \in U$
- $W = R \cup V_{n+1}$

and finally we denote with $\xrightarrow{U}$ the reflexive transitive closure of $\xrightarrow{U}_1$ and the unique result of this operation as by $S_2 = addDV(S, U)$ where S_2 is the final resultset returned to the query.

Promoting Teachers' Collaborative Re-use of Educational Materials

Emanuela Busetti[1], Giuliana Dettori[2], Paola Forcheri[1], and Maria Grazia Ierardi[1]

[1] Istituto di Matematica Applicata e Tecnologie Informatiche del CNR, Genova – Italy
{emma, forcheri, marygz}@ge.imati.cnr.it
[2] Istituto di Tecnologie Didattiche del CNR, Genova – Italy
dettori@itd.cnr.it

Abstract. In this paper we describe the main lines of a teacher preparation model aiming to promote a culture of sharing and re-use of educational resources. Our methodology is based on the analysis of conceptions of trainee teachers as concerns the production and re-use of educational modules and on the use of a collaborative environment, especially designed to support the construction and development of a community of practice of teachers working on Learning Objects. This approach is meant as a means to support in a collaborative way the construction and diffusion of pedagogical innovation.

1 Introduction

Collaboration through communities of practice is increasingly considered as an effective way for teachers to cope with life-long professional development [14], [5]. We add that such communities could be fruitfully used as a tool to establish a continuity between pre-service and in-service teacher training, favouring the exchange of competence and ideas among teachers with different experience and backgrounds and supporting the development of a culture of sharing and reflection. This could help avoid the individualistic approach to the teaching profession which is currently rather common and hinders the diffusion of innovation. In particular, we argue that communities suitably structured to collaboratively work on Learning Objects (LOs) could results effective in this respect.

Digital LOs were initially conceived as a tool to make distance education efficient, by easing teachers' re-use of self-contained chunks of educational material for course construction. They were subsequently recognized to have the potential to be helpful for education in general [12], since into LOs repositories teachers may find innovative proposals to improve their regular educational practice (such as materials to carry out problem-based activities), as well as simple technological tools (such as java applets for simulating scientific phenomena) whose implementation might be beyond their competence. However, the diffusion of LOs has been slowed down as a consequence of the fact that computers, despite having been introduced into schools from the eighties and being actually used by many teachers, are not yet deeply integrated into school activity: not only does classroom practice often remain unchanged but even many teachers are still dealing with accepting ICT [6], [13]. Moreover, research has

W. Nejdl and K. Tochtermann (Eds.): EC-TEL 2006, LNCS 4227, pp. 61–73, 2006.
© Springer-Verlag Berlin Heidelberg 2006

highlighted a number of difficulties that still hinder teachers' appreciation and actual use of LOs in school, such as the scarce information on the objects' quality and the limited congruence of the metadata standards with the current indications of learning theories [7], [10].

In accordance with other authors [8], we suggest that LOs' diffusion is actually an issue of technological transfer and should be addressed as such. In order to give a contribution in this direction, we propose a methodology for teacher training which integrates personal reflection on LOs with sharing educational material and the related experience of use within communities of practice created on purpose. We implemented this idea by designing and building the prototype of a collaboration environment, and we experimented it in a pre-service teacher training course. We also carried out a study of the conceptions of trainee teachers on the re-use of the educational material in order to give direction to our work and check the feasibility of our approach.

In this paper we describe our methodological framework and outline the output of the experiences carried out with trainee teachers. With his study, we aim to support in a systematic way the collaborative construction of pedagogical innovation, promote a culture of sharing and re-use of educational material and suggest a uniform way to connect pre-service and in-service teacher training.

2 Teacher Training Through Collaboration on LOs

2.1 An approach to Sharing Educational Material

Starting point of our proposal is the observation that, from a pedagogical point of view, re-use of educational material should be focused not only on products but also, and especially, on experiences of use of such products in different contexts [2]. This turns LOs from static materials (as they result in a purely technological view of re-use) into something constantly in evolution, since each experience of use obviously differs from the previous ones, depending on the situation where it takes place, the individuals involved and their pedagogical orientations and personal teaching styles. Reflecting on the variety of experiences carried out with a same material constitutes for the teachers an occasion of learning. Engaging in a re-use activity centred on sharing reflections and comparing experiences can result, for teachers, an effective way of learning and hence become a powerful tool for professional development. Re-use of an educational module in different contexts, moreover, often leads to the re-elaboration of the initial view of the module itself and hence gives rise to a number of variants of it, produced by different teachers to adapt it to different teaching needs and styles. Considering such variants can result useful also to the initial producer, since it leads her/him to take into consideration different perspectives on her/his own work. In this view, re-use constitutes a knowledge transfer process in which both user and producer can equally take part actively, with mutual advantage. Such activity can therefore constitute a good basis for a community of teachers engaged in learning from each others' experience while sharing educational material, and can help building and circulating pedagogical innovation. It can also help creating a deeper sense of community and overcome the problem pointed out by Parr and Ward [11] of

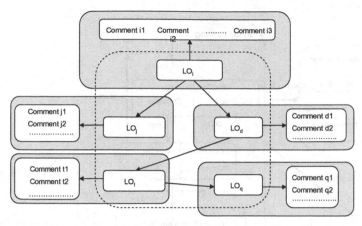

Fig. 1. The conceptual network of educational materials originated by collecting user-produced variants and comments to an original LO

teachers feeling scarcely inclined to share their own productions if they don't perceive the participation in a community of practice as useful and rewarding.

Collecting in a repository variants of a given object produced by different users, and associated reflections, gives rise to a conceptual network of educational material on a given topic, as sketched in Fig. 1. Comments represent the reflections on the experiences of use of different teachers. The presence of variants and comments and connections among them greatly increases the expressive power of the educational material. The creation of a conceptual network of this kind starting from a given learning object is the expression of the collective learning of a community of teachers.

2.2 Preparing Teachers to Share Pedagogical Materials and Experience

It is necessary to prepare teachers to put in practice the above approach, especially since sharing knowledge and experience is not customary in most school systems, and hence a tradition in this sense needs to be established [9]. This entails organizing suitable activities to carry out during pre-service teacher training, apt to promote a culture of sharing and re-use of educational resources. Several components should, in our opinion, be included in this preparation:

- Giving the trainee teachers some basic knowledge about LOs, by explaining their meaning and potential, use of the metadata etc. In order to be effective this activity should be preceded by a study of the conceptions that teachers have on the re-use of educational material, so as to be in condition to explicitly address their doubts and help them building a positive attitude towards sharing experience and pedagogical material in their profession.
- Helping to construct reflective and experiential knowledge by means of an activity on educational modules along the lines mentioned in Sect. 2.1. Reflection on experience should be carried out not only individually, but also collectively, so as to fill a gap that is often present in teacher preparation. Trainee teachers, as a matter of fact, are often not used to collaborative work, due to the limited importance given to this aspect in many school and university systems. This often

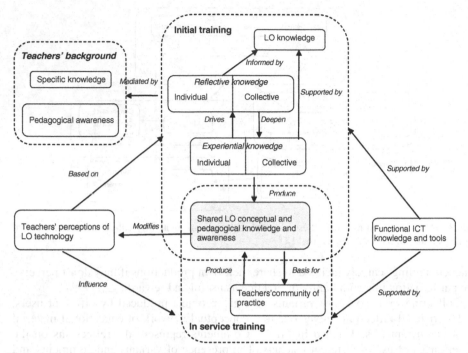

Fig. 2. A model of pre-service and in-service teacher preparation centered on sharing of educational modules

leads in-service teachers to find collaborative contexts difficult, especially with colleagues who have different backgrounds, hence missing good opportunities to improve their professional knowledge and contribute to give their students a more articulated preparation.

- Taking into account teachers' background, which includes both topic-related specific knowledge and pedagogical awareness.
- Making the trainee teachers get acquainted with ICT tools, basic knowledge and terminology which are functional to work easily in technology-based collaborative environments and with technological educational resources.

The aim of this approach to initial teacher preparation is to build a common ground of shared conceptual and pedagogical knowledge on LOs that can form the starting point for learning-oriented, joint, in-service activity and hence constitute a bridge between pre-service and in-service training. It also aims to provide a base of methodological and operative competence apt to favour teachers' collaborative working and learning through communities of practice. The overall structure of this approach to teacher training is sketched in Fig. 2.

2.3　An Environment for Sharing LOs and Experience of Use

In order to implement this approach to teacher training, we designed the collaborative environment LODE (Learning Objects Discussion Environment). We implemented a prototype of it (which is available in Italian and in English) by suitably adapting *ATutor*, an open source, fully inclusive, web-based Learning Content Management System (http://www.atutor.ca/).

LODE's main characteristics, with respect to the collaborative environments currently diffused, is that it is specifically oriented to working with LOs. Hence, not only does it offer the usual variety of communication modalities and file sharing, but also it allows the insertion and cataloguing of new LOs and comments, as well as the definition of connections among them.

Each LO corresponding to an educational module is represented by means of an *ATutor* course. The content of the object is stored by one or more files linked to the LO home page. Each LO has a forum associated, to discuss issues related to its use. Comments can be inserted by any number of people for every LO (including the LO's author); they concern outcomes of experimentations or proposals for pedagogical and operational changes. Moreover, users can define logical connections of different types among objects. At present, four kinds of them are provided: derives from, substitutes, includes and complementary to. This information is part of the metadata set associated to a LO and is represented in LODE environment by the label "links to other LO" (see "legami con altri LO" in the bottom of Fig. 3).

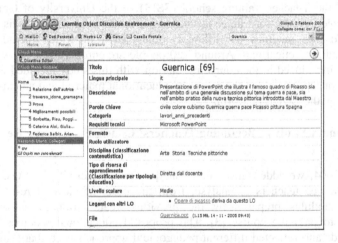

Fig. 3. The home page of a LO in LODE, showing the metadata and the comments available on the left hand side

It is possible to search for material in the environment by any of the metadata on both LOs and comments. It is also possible to browse through the complete list of objects and related comments. A glossary of the terms used in the metadata, a general forum and a help function are also provided.

In order to make the input of LOs simple, metadata have been kept limited to the values strictly necessary to characterize a LO with respect to the educational practice. We paid only limited attention to standards for reuse, both because interoperability issues are outside the scope of our research, and in our view they add a level of unwanted complexity as concerns the applicability of the pedagogical model we propose, as our trainees are new to the LO concept. After considering the most acknowledged metadata standards and specifications developed by international organizations, such as IEEE TTSC LOM, DCMI and related projects such as Gateway to Educational Materials (GEM) and EDNA (Education Network Australia), we selected a set of LO metadata mainly from the LOM scheme, though moving away from it, especially regarding the LOM category "Educational". Rather than thinking of extending this scheme, we preferred to realize a proposal specifically oriented to the school pedagogical context, easily understandable by the trainee teachers and with a limited cost.

Our metadata, then, include: author, language, date, keywords, pedagogical approach, technical requirements, school topics, school level, producer's intention, educational role, connections with other objects. These values are visualized when a LO is opened (see Fig. 3). Comments' metadata include only author, date of creation, key words and LO associated.

3   Towards Implementing Our Teacher Preparation Idea

We tested our teacher preparation approach oriented to knowledge and experience sharing, over the past two years, in a teacher training course on Multimedia in education of the Teacher training school (SSIS) of the University of Genoa, Italy. This is a 3-credit course for trainee teachers of secondary school in all disciplines; it is subdivided into modules on different topics, each of which includes both a theoretical and a practical part. Around 120 people are enrolled in it every year. The activities we introduced in the course in relation with this study included an analysis of trainee's conceptions about the re-use of educational material and an experience of sharing LOs on the LODE platform.

3.1   Preliminary Study of Beginning Teachers' Conceptions on the Re-use of LOs

In the year 2004, we added in the mentioned course an activity on LOs, where we guided the trainee teachers to analyse, from the point of view of re-use, a set of educational modules prepared by the previous years' trainees as one of the assignments to pass the course [3]. The proposed educational modules concerned different fields and reflected different pedagogical approaches, so that trainees could chose among them based on their background and preferences. Aim of this activity was to make the trainees aware of the problems that can be faced in the re-use of other teachers' material, and hence prepare them to pay attention to key elements, both when selecting among their colleagues' materials and when preparing their own materials to be shared with other teachers. Trainees were requested to freely choose a module to analyse in a group of proposed ones, and to deduce its re-use possibilities, technical and pedagogical value, strengths and weaknesses, improvements suggested, etc. They were also asked to mention what features they would select in order to characterize the materials in such a way to make it easy for prospective re-users to chose among them; this request aimed to spot what kind of features trainee teachers would appreciate to find among metadata. We did not give the trainees the summaries and the metadata originally associated with the selected modules, in order not to influence their analysis with the observations and classification reported by the authors but possibly not considered by the trainees who were examining the modules. Then we analysed the trainees' productions, looking for conceptions on the re-use of educational materials. Our aim was to obtain information on several points:

- From what point of view do teachers consider re-usable material?
- Which aspects are considered important in a didactical module? Which important ones are overlooked by the trainees?
- Are trainee teachers able to see a role for a given module in their own teaching?
- What kind of information do teachers consider it important to transfer to their colleagues in view of re-use?
- What relation do teachers see among the selected material and the final users?

A first interesting point, which clearly emerged from this study is that content knowledge was the main (and sometimes only) aspect of the didactical material on which trainee teachers focused. Neither the pedagogical approach nor the technological choices seemed to be considered as being strictly part of the module's overall content and in condition to influence the usability and effectiveness of the analysed material. Trainees mainly assumed to re-use from the given materials the content knowledge (which includes texts, pictures and exercises), adding on their own both the pedagogical approach and the delivery mode. For this reason, they often disregarded any technological mistake or cumbersome pre-requisite. Didactical modules, moreover, were viewed as complete objects, rather than parts of a didactical itinerary.

As prospective re-users, the trainees often did not foresee the range of application possibilities that were prospected by the module's producers.

Some trainees, finally, viewed the didactical modules as chunks of knowledge based on which teachers could work out something useful for their students. Only a few of them expressed the wish to know the guiding ideas underlying the design of the modules and their previous applications, in order to better plan for their re-use.

This study, which was focused only on individual reflections on LOs, allowed us to spot which aspects require special attention when preparing trainee teachers to the use of LOs. It also provided us with useful information to guide the design of the LODE collaborative environment (outlined in Section 2.3) to carry out a training activity on sharing and re-use of LOs. Based on this experience, in the following year we proposed to our trainees a more articulated activity which included both individual and shared reflection, with particular emphasis on the second one.

3.2   A Collaborative Activity on LOs on the LODE Platform

In the year 2005, we introduced in the mentioned teacher training course an activity on sharing educational modules, organized along the methodological lines sketched in Section 2. Before carrying out a practical activity on the LODE platform, the trainees had a class on knowledge management and communication/collaboration systems, one on LOs and repositories, as well as a concise presentation of the LODE environment. Several educational modules developed by the previous years' trainees were uploaded in the environment, to make the work start with some materials at disposal.

The activity with LODE went on for about one month. Trainees were asked to: explore the environment and write a description of their understanding of it; choose a

LO to analyse; write a comment of it; discuss possibly different opinions with the classmates who were analysing the same LO; work out a new LO and upload it in the environment, specifying and justifying pedagogical metadata and connections with other LOs. We evaluated this experience based on the observation of trainees' involvement, the trainee's productions and the answers to an anonymous questionnaire. The results on the three aspects considered were encouraging [4].

The trainees' involvement was rather high. Almost all of them became operative in a short time and used the environment to a wide extent. They often carried out more than the work assigned, and some of them even asked us to leave the environment in use after the end of the course so as to be allowed to work with it again in the future. The reports on the environment confirmed a satisfactory understanding of its structure and aims.

As concerns the trainees' productions, the materials developed resulted to be more clear, articulated and well designed than they had usually been in the previous years. We attribute this improvement to the reflection the trainees had to carry out for writing comments to the materials at disposal, which led them to pay attention to aspects that had been usually overlooked by the trainees of the previous years. The comments produced concerned mainly ideas for school activities to carry out with the commented LOs.

They showed an interest for comparing their work with that of their peers, as well as good self-evaluation abilities. They even tried to evaluate what teacher's competence was necessary for developing and using the considered modules. This led many of them to consider the modules' evaluation as an occasion to become aware of their own competence and a stimulus to get updated if necessary.

The questionnaire, which was returned by 106 people, included 5 groups of closed questions (to be valued on a scale from 1=very poor to 5= excellent), concerning interest for the environment, ease of use and learning, effectiveness of feedback and support received, usefulness of the communication facilities. Some open questions concerned the difficulties experienced and the aspects of the environment most or least appreciated.

The mean value of all answers to the questionnaire resulted 3.74, the standard deviation 0.96, the median 4. If we consider negative answers the values 1 and 2 and positive answers the values 3 (sufficient), 4 (good) and 5 (excellent), the total percentage of negative answers resulted 11.19, while the percentage of positive answers resulted 88.81.

As for the *interest of the environment* for their teaching profession, the respondents expressed a good level of appreciation for both retrieving others' materials and sharing their own (93.96 % of positive answers). Comments and connections among LOs were appreciated more as a way to express their own reflections than for learning those of their peers.

Ease of use and navigation were evaluated from average to high (85.17 % of positive answers). From the open answers, some difficulties emerged, though, as concerns the use of metadata, both for searching LOs based on pedagogical features and for defining the correct ones when creating new LOs. *Ease of learning* to use the environment was evaluated from average to high, with a concentration on average values (88.45 % of positive answers). This matches with the observation that the trainees had started working correctly with LODE in a short time. The *feedback and help* received were considered clear and effective enough (89.64 % of positive answers).

Finally, the questionnaire showed that *communication* with peers was slightly preferred to communication with the teacher; internal mail was appreciated more than forums, which were seen more as a tool to learn from each other than as a place to socialize with peers.

3.3   A Study of Conceptions After Collaboratively Working on Educational Material

In the school year 2005, after the described activity in the LODE environment, we repeated the analysis of conceptions we had carried out with the trainees of the previous year, in order to check if actively working on educational material to be shared and re-used had any positive influence on trainee teachers' conceptions. The task assigned and the guidelines provided to carry it out were the same as the previous years. This activity, however, was carried out after working on the LODE platform, and hence the trainees had gained some familiarity with the concept of learning object. They also had at disposal the metadata and the author's report for each educational module.

This new study of conceptions on educational material confirmed the disorientation as concerns metadata that resulted from the activity in the LODE environment. The trainees tended either to avoid to specify them or to replace them by a wordy description of the educational material's characteristics. In the first case, they seemed to assume that each material would be reused by its author, and this one would have a good enough memory to remind all important features over the years; they also tended to disregard all technical prerequisites necessary to use a material, such as version of the software application used, plug-ins, etc.. In the second case, the trainees seemed to disregard the need to concisely cataloguing the materials and sometimes even considered some fields as ambiguous or meaningless, despite the simplicity of the metadata chosen in our environment. This highlights that metadata, though essential for an effective re-use of educational material, are an intrinsically difficult topic for teachers. Despite the many efforts in this sense made in the past years within the scientific community [1], there is obviously need of some further work on their definition.

Probably due to the activity on LOs carried out before this second study of conceptions, the trainees paid attention not only to the content knowledge of the considered modules, but also to their technological part, showing to understand that this can have an influence on their actual use and educational potential. Hypertexts and multimedia were seen as tools to present in new way topics they knew and to support the exploration of new didactical paths.

Unlike the previous year, they did not appreciate big modules treating thoroughly some topics, but showed a preference for small ones that could better be fitted in their didactical plans.

They attributed great importance to the fact that the modules they were analysing had been made by their peers: not only did they consider the task at their reach, but felt motivated to commit to produce good modules themselves, knowing that they were going to be used by their peers in the following years.

They showed, moreover, great interest in the applicative aspects of the modules. Differently than in the previous year, the trainees managed to figure out and suggest a variety of uses of the considered materials bigger and more diverse than foreseen by the materials' authors. This fact suggests that the activity carried out with digital LOs succeeded in helping the trainees to gain an overall view of teaching more dynamic and open to new and interdisciplinary experiences. This supports our hypothesis that sharing knowledge in a community of teachers, as planned in our model, is a creative activity where also the re-users take part in the production of new knowledge and become motivated to get involved in the process.

3.4 Observations on the Commented and Produced Educational Materials

By analysing the modules' comments and the educational materials produced by our trainees, we noticed some points that highlight the influence of analysing peers' productions on the modules worked out. A relation between some aspects of the commented material and the produced ones was often explicitly admitted by the trainees in their reports. This influence does not consist simply in copying ideas or parts of products, but shows a personal re-elaboration of different module's aspects that suggests a growth of our trainees as producers of educational material. Working in a community focused on re-use and re-elaboration of educational material, trainees seem to improve their critical attitude and this supports the sharing and diffusion of teaching competence.

Let us briefly summarize the main characteristics of the commented and the produced modules.

The materials produced mainly consisted in:
-    multimedia presentations, often including interactive exercises;.
-    constructive activities, where students are guided to explore a topic, and teacher's intervention is rather limited;
-    lessons based on a traditional approach.

From an educational point of view, the produced modules showed different structures:
-    teacher-oriented (to be used by a teacher as support to introduce a topic);
-    problem-oriented (e.g. problems to be solved by the students or paths to be explored);
-    mixed (including both teacher's intervention and students' autonomous work);
-    support for self-instruction.

Students appeared to choose the module to comment based on several different reasons:
-    background and teaching topic;
-    variety of possible uses of the module or support to interdisciplinary activity;
-    interest of the topic with respect to the curriculum, independently of the module's quality;
-    effectiveness of the pedagogical approach in comparison with more traditional ones. We mention as interesting in this respect the request of a trainee who asked to be allowed to comment, instead of a module in the LODE repository, a module she had found in the well known repository Merlot (www.merlot.org), consisting of a set of Java applets for the simulation of chemical reactions. The trainee also

asked to include in LODE a LO consisting in a link to the commented material, catalogued by giving the metadata values that resulted meaningful in our school system, since those used in Merlot reflected a different school context;

We observed different ways to get inspiration from the commented materials for producing their own proposals:

- *General topic*, yet with a different content and a different approach. For instance, a module of archaeological topic, "The Hill of Priamar" (a visit to an archaeological site nearby) inspired two different archaeological modules, "Know your Town" e "The Libarna Archaeological Site". The first of them gets from the original one the idea to deepen the history of one's own town, and includes a link to it; the second one gets from it the idea of a guided tour to an archaeological site.
- *Technical solutions*. For instance, the module "Introduction to networking" inspired "Introduction to micro-processing", based on a similar presentation approach (animation of key elements, arrows to point out main aspects, etc.). Analogously, "Main pictorial techniques" inspired "Painting of flowers in XVII century" with the idea to examine a painting starting from a general view and successively zooming on features.
- *Ideas of possible directions to deepen a topic*. For instance, "The Greek house" suggested the creation of "The Roman house": despite the similar names, however, the content of the two modules has a different focus, due to the different importance given to public and private architecture in the Greek and Roman cultures. What is interesting in these examples is that the second module was conceived as complementary to the first one, so that the two of them allow a teacher to compare not only architectural orientations but also methodology of study of archaeological remains. This added value can result very handy and effective for teachers of humanities.
- *Multiculturalism*. For instance, "Typical aspects of German life", suggested a way to approach the study of a language as a good occasion to analyses and compare different cultures. Getting inspiration from it, "A trip to Berlin" was produced, which features, though, a different content and different target users.
- *Pedagogical approach*. For instance, the module "The symbols of Genoa" (a description of ancient Genoa through its political, economical and religious symbols) owns to "Mirò and the Macroculture of Catalunia" the use of an interactive section (with possibility of zooming and manipulating images) on recognizing the meaning of an image's elements.
- *Multidisciplinarity*. For instance, "Discovering the meaning of labels on food packages" (which includes elements of science and language) inspired "A guide to healthy eating" (which mixes elements of biology and geography).

Also errors and poor solutions proved to be source of inspiration, since several trainees explicitly claimed their will to avoid features they did not appreciate in the commented modules An interesting example is given by a module on philosophy education, a topic where pedagogical studies have so far been limited. A group of trainees observed that the previous years' modules on this topic simply translated a traditional teaching approach into technological presentations, with poor results as concerns both the use of technological tools and the presentation of the content topic.

They worked out, therefore, a more articulated and intriguing presentation which included readings of philosophers' texts and different possible approaches to interpretation.

4 Discussion and Conclusion

The positive response of the trainees in this study highlights the availability and interest of beginning teachers to get involved in the sharing of educational material and collaboratively reflecting on its practical use. The different ways the trainees made use their peers' work to improve their own suggest that critically working with re-usable educational material can result into a creative activity. The good outcomes obtained suggest that our approach to teacher training is feasible and likely effective.

The trainees seemed to learn to evaluate a priori their possibility to re-use a given educational material in different ways, foretelling advantages and drawbacks related to their use. In this sense LODE could even be seen as a tool to learn a methodology for didactic planning.

The study also highlights, though, that some aspects need to be deepened.

The metadata used to cataloguing the material should be revised, trying to find items which result in line with the standards presented in the literature but at the same time take into consideration the meanings usually given to labels by the beginning teachers, in relation with the different school topics. This issue appears to be particularly difficult, since keywords are often used in different ways within different disciplines, let alone within different cultures. If the development of a common language for metadata will not be supported among teachers from different disciplines and environments, however, the diffusion of a culture of sharing and re-use will always result limited.

The effective understanding of the concept of LO gained by the trainees should be further investigated. We think it would be fruitful to provide some examples of excellent materials, explaining the reasons for this excellence. Some activity would also be necessary centred on the articulation of educational paths which include a number of given LOs.

This kind of activity with educational material should be tried out with in-service teachers, to spot issues which are peculiar to them and not shared by trainee teachers. One of this issues concerns how to organize the quality control in a situation where there is no trainer in charge of the activity to select the materials to be included in the repository. The quality control is, on the other hand, essential, to motivate the teacher to make use of a repository. Moreover, it appears necessary to investigate how a community of in-service teachers would self-regulate its own learning activity [15].

Another issue that needs to be addressed is to understand what relation should be established between pre-service and in-service teacher training, at both practical and institutional level, to make these two groups of teachers work together on a same repository, with reciprocal advantage and satisfaction.

If this approach to teacher training will gain diffusion, and many communities of this kind will develop, it will be necessary to adapt its design, so as to create a network of communities, where each teacher could be allowed to potentially be admitted to take part in the activity of any community, yet avoiding the confusion of too crowded groups where the loss of personalization would decrease the possibility of learning from sharing each other's ideas and experience.

Acknowledgements. The work has been partially supported by the Italian Ministry of Education, University and Research, FIRB Research Project 'TIGER-Telepresence Instant Groupware for Higher Education in Robotics' and Project VICE- Virtual Communities for Education

References

1. Anido, L.E., Fernandez, M.J., Caeiro, M., Santos, J.M., Rodriguez, J.S., Llamas, M.: Educational metadata and brokerage for learning resources. Computers & Education 38 (2002) 351-374
2. Busetti, E., Forcheri, P., Ierardi, M.G., Molfino, M. T.: Repositories of Learning Objects as Learning Environments for Teachers. Proceedings of ICALT 2004 IEEE Comp. Soc. Press. (2004) 450-454
3. Busetti, E., Dettori, G., Forcheri, P., Ierardi, M.G.: Preparing Teachers to the use of LOs: an analysis of conceptions. Proceedings of ICALT 2005 IEEE Comp. Soc. Press. (2005) 669-673
4. Busetti, E., Dettori, G., Forcheri, P., Ierardi, M.G.: Teachers' appreciation of a collaborative environment on LOs. Proceedings of ICALT 2006 (2006), to appear.
5. Butler, D.L., Novak Lauscher, H., Jarvis-Selinger, S., Beckingham, B.: Collaboration and self-regulation in teachers' professional development. Teaching and Teacher Education 20 (5), Elsevier (2004) 435- 455.
6. Chen, L.-L.: Pedagogical strategies to increase pre-service teachers' confidence in computer learning, Educational Technology & Society, 7(3) (2004) 50-60
7. Farance F. (2003). "IEEE LOM Standard Not Yet Ready For "Prime Time"", Learning Technology, January 2003, http://lttf.ieee.org/learn_tech/issues/january2003/index.html
8. Friesen, N.: Three Objections to Learning Objects. Online Education Using Learning Objects. In McGreal, R. (ed.) London: Routledge (2004). 59-70.
9. Kezar, A. (2005) Redesigning for Collaboration within Higher Education Institutions: An Exploration into the Developmental Process Research in Higher Education 46 (7), 831-860
10. Jonassen, D.; and Churchill, D.: Is there a learning orientation in learning objects?, Int. Journal of e-learning, 3 (2), (2004) 32-41
11. Parr J.M. & Ward L.: Creating Online Professional learning Communities: A Case of Cart before Horses. In K.-W. Lai (ed.), E-learning Communities – Teaching and learning with the Web, Dunedin, NZ: University of Otago Press (2005) 11-134.
12. Quinn C., and Hobbs S.: Learning Objects and Instruction Components: Formal discussion summary. Educational Technology & Society, 3(2) (2000) http://ifets. ieee.org/periodical/vol_2_2000/discuss_summary_0200.html
13. Robertson J. W. Stepping Out of the Box: Rethinking the Failure of ICT to Transform Schools Journal of Educational Change 4 (4), (2003) 323-344
14. Schlager M. S. and Fusco J.: Teacher professional development, technology, and communities of practice: Are we Putting the Cart before the Horse? In S. Barab, R. Kling, and J. Gray (Eds.) Designing Virtual Communities in the Service of Learning, Cambridge University Press, UK, (2004) 120-153.

A Formal Model of Learning Object Metadata

Kris Cardinaels, Erik Duval, and Henk Olivié

Katholieke Universiteit Leuven, Belgium
Kris.Cardinaels@cs.kuleuven.be, Erik.Duval@cs.kuleuven.be,
Henk.Olivie@cs.kuleuven.be

Abstract. In this paper, we introduce a new, formal model of learning object metadata. The model enables more formal, rigorous reasoning over metadata. An important feature of the model is that it allows for 'fuzzy' metadata, that have an associated confidence value. Another important aspect is that we explicitly address context dependent metadata.

1 The Formal Model of Metadata

In this paper we develop a formal or mathematical model for learning object metadata. Such a model helps to build a formal, rigorous reasoning about metadata in the case of share and reuse. One of the situations in which such a formal model is useful, is, for example, the discussion of automatic indexing of learning objects.

One of the important aspects we introduce in this formal model is the representation of context-awareness in metadata. A context represents a specific situation in which a learning object can be used. These contexts allow us to define more advanced metadata values which enable a better, i.e. more efficient and more effective, retrievability of learning objects. We refer to the automatic metadata generation framework that we implemented (see also [1]) for more information about the use of contexts for metadata generation.

We build our model in different steps, starting with the most simple case in which we only consider the learning objects themselves. Then we extend the model by taking into account contexts in which learning objects are (re)used. In the next step we look at learning objects with a complex structure, such as aggregates.

We conclude the discussion of this model by pointing to an automatic indexing framework we developed that implements this model.

1.1 Learning Objects and Metadata

Learning Objects. The first definitions of our model consider learning objects and metadata. At the beginning we take learning objects in isolation from their contexts in which they are used or reused. As a second simplification we consider learning objects as atomic objects without a specific structure and not part of a larger structure.

W. Nejdl and K. Tochtermann (Eds.): EC-TEL 2006, LNCS 4227, pp. 74–87, 2006.
© Springer-Verlag Berlin Heidelberg 2006

The definition of a learning object is given by the IEEE LOM standard [2]: a learning object is any entity - digital or non-digital - that may be used for learning, education or training.

In our formal model we do not explicitly define learning objects but define a set of learning objects that we use throughout this model.

$$\mathcal{L} = \{l | l \text{ is a learning object}\} \tag{1}$$

The above definition does not include details about learning objects, which indeed corresponds to the given description of learning objects. For the moment, a learning object is an abstract item of which we don't have to know the details.

Metadata. Metadata are data about data. In our research we consider learning object metadata – information about learning objects. In general, two approaches to metadata are used; the first is the record approach (the approach taken by the LOM standard), the second considers metadata items individually (adopted by Dublin Core). To obtain a very general model we follow the second approach; we will, however, also indicate that the record-based model can be derived from the item-based approach.

We refer to metadata facets when we talk about properties. The term facet is appropriate because we, in some way, are dealing with multi-faceted classifications as introduced by Prieto-Díaz in [3]. A facet is defined as a function providing a value for that facet for a given learning object.

$$f_i : \mathcal{L} \rightarrow COD_{f_i} \tag{2}$$

The facet f_i is a function that maps a learning object to a value from COD_{fi}, the codomain of f_i. The codomain of a function is the set of possible values resulting from applying the function. We assume that the set of possible values always includes the value *null* for facets that are not applicable to a certain learning object. We use the value *null* comparable to the use in relational database systems, in which this value may indicate that the value of the facet is unknown, unavailable or unapplicable [4, p.131]. The index i is used to facilitate the distinction between different facets in the further definitions. Throughout this text we refer to the value $f_i(l)$ as f_{il}.

Analogously to learning objects, this definition of facets does not specify anything about the possible values in the codomain. This approach opens the possibility to include all sorts of metadata items, even with a complex structure.

In definition 2 we implicitly made the assumption that every metadata facet can only have one value for a learning object. In many situations this, however, is not the case. Therefore, we immediately redefine a facet to include multiple values also.

$$f_i : \mathcal{L} \rightarrow (COD_{f_i})^n \tag{3}$$

$(COD_{f_i})^n$ is the generalized Cartesian product of the set COD_{f_i}. This definition implies that the value f_{il} can be a tuple $(f1_{il}, f2_{il}, f3_{il}, ...)$ consisting of n values. A simple example of such a facet is the author element; a document can have multiple authors.

1.2   Metadata Records

In the previous definitions we considered metadata as individual items that can be applied to learning objects. This is a flexible and general approach. In practice metadata are often treated within records, such as the IEEE LOM record.

A metadata record is a grouping of metadata facets. A record can be a flat set of facets or it can contain a structure. Our general approach allows us to work with metadata records as well.

A metadata record is defined as:

$$m(l) = \{f_a(l), f_b(l), ..., f_k(l)\} \text{ where}$$
$$l \in \mathcal{L} \tag{4}$$

Remark that the number of facets in a record is not predefined for the general record definition. For each learning object there can be a different number of facets within a record.

Because we did not define the codomain of a facet, a facet could be defined as a complex object which contains other facets. This gives us the possibility to define hierarchies within metadata facets. The definition of these records is the same as that of the general record given above.

The following example shows how LOM metadata can be expressed by this definition.

$$lom(l) = \{general(l), lifecycle(l), metametadata(l),$$
$$technical(l), educational(l), rights(l),$$
$$relation(l), annotation(l), classification(l)\}$$
$$general(l) = (identifier(l), title(l), language(l),$$
$$description(l), keyword(l), coverage(l),$$
$$structure(l), aggregation_level(l))$$
$$\cdots$$

1.3   RDF Metadata

Metadata Facets. The metadata model, based on facets, described above is closely related to the model used in the Resource Description Framework. Formally RDF uses *triples* as the expression mechanism. Each triple consists of subject, a predicate and an object. An RDF expression is called an RDF graph as shown in Fig. 1 [5].

Fig. 1. A Simple RDF Graph

The RDF triplet expresses the relationship 'resource X (Subject) has value Y (Object) for predicate Z (Predicate)'. Every triplet is considered standalone. Technically they can be grouped into descriptions and description sets, but conceptually they aren't available in records. As with our model, RDF properties can be considered functions given the value for that property for the resource [6]:

$$Property : \{Resource\} \rightarrow \{Value\}$$

In our model metadata facets are the properties, the learning objects are resources and the codomain of the facet function contains the possible values of the RDF property:

$$Property \equiv f_i$$
$$\{Resource\} \supset \mathcal{L}$$
$$\{Value\} \supset COD_{f_i}$$

For example:

$$creator("http://www.w3.org/Home/Lassila") = "Ora Lassila"$$

In RDF the value space is defined to be a RDF URI Reference, a literal or a blank node. If the value is a URI Reference, this value can be used as a resource, i.e. statements can be made about that value. In this way, complex structures can be built. An example of such a structured RDF graph is given in Fig. 2.

Comparing our model to RDF, we can conclude that RDF is defined more generally in several aspects:

- Learning objects are only one type of resources in RDF;
- Properties are resources also (defined as a subset of resources). In our model we only consider learning objects as resources and we will not address properties as learning objects or resources;
- Objects ({Value}) are resources also which allows the definition of records as discussed in the next paragraph.

In conclusion, our model for learning object metadata can be considered a simplification of the formal model for RDF focussing on the specific aspects concerned with learning object metadata.

Metadata Records. Metadata in RDF are not defined in records, comparable to our approach. As explained above, an RDF statement can result in a complex graph, which represents a structure, such as defined in a metadata schema. RDF also includes container values for the specification of complex structures.

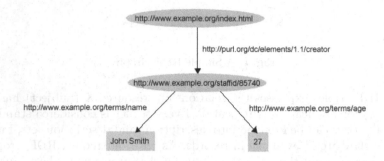

Fig. 2. A More Complex RDF Graph

A grouping of RDF statements is defined within the RDF/XML syntax in which description can be made. A description contains several statements about a certain resource. RDF descriptions are also used in Dublin Core Metadata Initiative Description Model [7]. Within this model a *description set* is defined.

2   Fuzzy Metadata

From a formal point of view the way in which metadata is associated with learning objects isn't a real issue. In this model we aren't interested in the operational aspects of metadata generation, but the possibility to express metadata about learning objects.

For the automatic metadata generation we introduced the aspect of a confidence value for generated metadata (see also [1]). In this section we use this value to define fuzzy metadata.

Fuzzy metadata is related to the fuzzy set theory [8] or fuzzy logic, which is a derivative of the prior. In these theories a *degree of truth* is associated with the elements of the set expression how true the expression is in that set. This degree of truth is also defined with a membership function $\mu \rightarrow [0, 1]$.

We start our discussion on fuzzy metadata applicable for metadata generation in the most simple situation in which we only address the learning objects themselves. Afterwards we extend our mechanisms by also looking at contexts of reuse and taking into account possible complex structured learning objects, such as aggregates.

2.1   Learning Objects, No Context, No Structure

Generally, one cannot tell about a metadata value whether the value is correct or wrong. In many cases the value has a certain degree of correctness. When metadata is associated with the learning object we add this degree of correctness to it. We call this value the *confidence value* of the facet value.

Introducing the confidence value in the definition of a metadata facet results in the following definitions. The simple version of a metadata facet becomes:

$$f_i : \mathcal{L} \rightarrow COD_{f_i} \times [0,1] \tag{5}$$

In the general form in which multiple values can be associated with one facet the confidence value is associated with each individual value.

$$f_i : \mathcal{L} \rightarrow (COD_{f_i} \times [0,1])^n \tag{6}$$

The confidence value can be defined analogously to the membership function of fuzzy logic. This function provides the confidence value of a certain facet value for a learning object.

$$CV_{f_i} : COD_{f_i} \times \mathcal{L} \rightarrow [0,1] \tag{7}$$

Example: Given the values from Table 1 and given a learning object s, the confidence value for the facet language could be the following:

$$CV_{language}("English", s) = 0.95$$

The example states that the confidence value "English" for the facet "language" is 0.95.

The confidence value as we define it should not be confused with an accuracy of an specific algorithm or the probability that a value is correct. From our point of view the accuracy or the probability are possible ways of calculating the confidence value, but these aren't the only possibilities.

Table 1 provides an example of a language classification algorithm and the accuracy of the algorithm according to different languages (see [9] for a discussion on the algorithms). This accuracy value is an excellent example of how the confidence value could be defined for a specific metadata facet.

Table 1. Language Detection Accuracy

Language	Acc (%)	Language	Acc (%)
Afrikaans	97	Italian	95
Croatian	100	Norwegian	95
Czech/Slovak	44	Polish	100
Danish	96	Portuguese	96
Dutch	100	Rumanian	93
English	95	Spanish	95
French	92	Swedish	98
Hungarian	94	Welsh	97

2.2 Multiple Facet Values

Our general definitions of metadata facets allow the possibility that multiple values for one facet are associated with a learning object. For some facets, depending on the application profile, however, this can cause problems because only one value can be retained. This problem arises in the case of multiple metadata generation algorithms returning different values for the same facet.

In some circumstances in the case of conflicting values for a facet, the confidence value can be applied to retain the appropriate values for that facet.

Although a general discussion on this problem quickly results in complex situation, we now try to hint some possible solutions on how confidence values can be used to solve value conflicts.

We define a function MG (which stands for Metadata Generation) that provides the appropriate value for a given facet:

$$MG_{f_i} : \mathcal{L} \times (COD_{f_i} \times [0,1])^n \rightarrow COD_{f_i} \times [0,1] \qquad (8)$$

When every indexer provides only one value for a facet, the simplest solution to retain one value is to keep that value that is returned with the largest confidence value. If multiple values are returned with the highest confidence value an arbitrary decision could be made to retain one of the values.

$$MG_{f_i}(l, f_i^1(l), f_i^2(l), ..., f_i^n(l)) = f_i^j(l) \text{ for that } j \text{ for which}$$
$$CV_{f_i}^j(l) = \max_{\forall k}(CV_{f_i}^k(l)) \qquad (9)$$

Although this simple situation is easy to define, the generalization of the problem of multiple values quickly becomes very difficult to manage. Without going into the details of possible solutions we explain the problem using an example.

Example: In the example we are looking at authors of documents. We use two algorithms to define the author(s) of a given document. Suppose the following situation for a given document:

Algorihm	Value(s)	Confidence Value
1	K. Cardinaels	0.78
	E. Duval	0.74
2	E. Duval	0.76

In the simple solution the result would contain the value "K. Cardinaels" as author because it has the highest confidence value. However, this author does not appear in the result of the second algorithm. This could indicate that the author "E. Duval" could be more appropriate. It is certainly not evidentially clear which solution to apply in this situation.

The situation would still become more problematic when the outcome of the algorithms would be the following:

Algorihm	Value(s)	Confidence Value
1	K. Cardinaels	0.78
	E. Duval	0.56
2	K. Cardinaels	0.43
	E. Duval	0.82

In this result, the two values in the algorithms are more or less contradicting to each other. In this situation a correct solution might be difficult to find.

A possible solution may be found in the rules defined for expert systems by David McAllister [10] for the combination of two positive certainty factors of evidence:

$$CFcombine(CFaCFb) = CFa + CFb(1 - CFa)$$

For example (see [10]):

Consider the predicate: The pilot is suffering from hypoxia.

Given the fact that pilot is flying at an altitude op 4,000m in an unpressured airplane. And, given the fact that the pilot informs us that he is feeling wonderful. We can state that the first factor is a strongly suggestive evidence (certainty factor 0.80) for suffering from hypoxia and the second factor is suggestive evidence (0.6 certainty) for the same.

In combination these two evidences result in a final certainty factor of 0.92 that the pilot suffers from hypoxia.

Although this rule is meant to combine certainty factors of evidence about a single predicate we could use it to make a decision in the situation of multiple facet values. Applying the above rule to the example given earlier would result in the following:

Value	Confidence Value
K. Cardinaels	0.87 = 0.78 + 0.43(1-0.78)
E. Duval	0.92 = 0.56 + 0.82(1-0.56)

In conclusion we can say that the confidence value is a good candidate for solving problems in automatically generated metadata values if only one value may be retained for that certain facet. In simple situations a straight forward solution can be applied, in more complex situations the confidence value can be used to rule out the most appropriate value.

3   Context-Awareness in Metadata

3.1   Contexts

Description. In this section we consider how contexts can be brought into metadata. Making metadata context-dependent allows the users to do more fine-grained searches for learning objects to use in their environment. Context-awareness in metadata also helps to enable more intelligent tutoring systems, based on adaptive hypermedia in which the current learner model is used to select learning objects to be shown (e.g. [11]). This latter is not the focus of this research.

Context-aware systems define a context as follows:

> *Any information that can be used to characterize the situation of an entity. An entity is a person, place, or object that is considered relevant (to the interaction between a user and an application, including the user and application themselves).* [12]

A system is context-aware if

> *it uses context to provide relevant information and/or services to the user (where relevancy depends on the user's task).* [12]

Examples

1. We clarify the use of contexts by writing out the example given in [13] about the Riemann Zeta function.

   An animated fly-through of the graph of the Riemann Zeta function might be considered:
   - Advanced for use in a public mathematics lecture,
   - Moderate for use in a complex analysis course,
   - Beginning as an example of computer animation techniques.

   It makes sense to have different metadata records associated with the same fly-through graph that reflect the intended use of the graph by different communities.

   We define the contexts as follows:
   - PM: public mathematics lecture
   - CA: complex analysis course
   - COMPA: computer animation techniques

   Using these contexts we can for example specify the difficulty

   $$Educational.Difficulty(rz, PM) = \text{'very difficult'}$$
   $$Educational.Difficulty(rz, CA) = \text{'medium'}$$
   $$Educational.Difficulty(rz, COMPA) = \text{'easy'}$$

2. Another example is shown in Fig. 3 in which a picture of La Gioconda is included in a presentation about histograms and in a course about famous painters.

   Probably the time to spend on the same picture by the technicians learning about histograms is a lot less than the time needed to study the painting itself in the context of history.

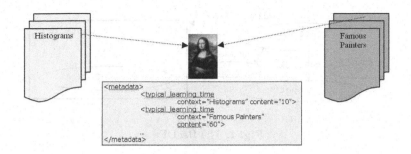

Fig. 3. Context Metadata within an Aggregate Object

In these examples, we modeled a context by specifying its name only. This is a very simplistic approach. Contexts are much more complex and should be modeled adequately for proper use by people or systems. In [14] a *ContextObject* is used to model a context for usage in the OpenURL Framework for context-sensitive services. A ContextObject contains up to six entities to represent its context: the referent, the referring entity, the requester, the request resolver, the referring service and the type of service requested.

Contexts-Independent Facets. We remark that not all metadata facets have to be context-dependent. It is well possible that the metadata set includes facets that have the same value for all possible contexts. Our definitions given in the previous sections also allow this situation. We can apply either the first definition for a facet or the second one depending on the facet we want to use.

> **Example:** The LOM standard defines several elements that can be considered context-independent:
> - Most elements in the **technical** category, such as file size, format or duration.
> - Elements in the life cycle category, about the creation of the object.
>
> In general, the educational facets are most context-dependent. From a educational point of learning objects, this is of no surprise.

3.2 Definitions

Now we redefine metadata and reuse in the case where metadata will be context dependent. This is a major change from the IEEE LOM standard approach or the Dublin Core Metadata Initiative.

At first, we consider a context as an abstract object or black box of which we don't know the inner details. Typically, a context will be a course at an institution, or information about a person incorporating information as described in the previous section.

Comparable to learning objects, we provide the definition of set of contexts:

$$\mathcal{C} = \{c | c \text{ is a context}\} \tag{10}$$

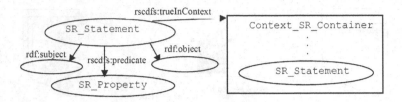

Fig. 4. The RscDF

Given this definition of contexts we can redeclare f_i to take as input the learning object and a context.

$$f_i : \mathcal{L} \times \mathcal{C} \rightarrow (COD_{f_i} \times [0,1])^n \tag{11}$$

This definition of context-sensitive metadata is also used in the RscDF quads ([15] and [16]). An RscDF quad is a Resource State/Condition Description Framework tuple and is represented as (C, S, P, O). C represents the context and (S, P, O) is an RDF tuple (subject, predicate, object). See also Section 1.3 for more about RDF and dynamic metadata. Fig. 4 shows an example of a quad using the property $rscdf : trueInContext$ to include the context in the tuple.

3.3   Context Reification

From the metadata generation point of view a specific category of contexts is of much interest: contexts that can be described as *composite documents* or *content aggregations*. Within a content aggregation, the learning objects are closely related to each other and influence each other's metadata.

In the case of content aggregations, the contexts can be considered learning objects themselves. The granularity metadata element, for example, allows to do this when we are using LOM to describe learning objects. We briefly describe two examples of this situation:

- A learning object is often used within a course defined in a learning environment. This course itself can be considered a learning object to be subject for reuse, for example the next year by the same instructor.
- A slide presentation contains many smaller learning objects, such as pictures, code examples... that can be used individually. In this case, the presentation is a context for all the other learning objects. In [17] this idea is applied for automatically storing the elements of presentation as learning objects in a repository.

In this case we use reification of contexts in our model. Context reification tells that the context itself is a learning object. Then we can use the model to associate metadata to the context. For automatic metadata generation, this metadata can help to create the metadata values of the learning object within the context.

The definition of a metadata facet in this reification becomes:

$$\mathcal{C} \subset \mathcal{L}$$
$$f_i : \mathcal{L} \times \mathcal{L} \to (COD_{f_i} \times [0,1])^n \qquad (12)$$

3.4 Example

Direct Use. Probably the most simple example of reuse is the use of an existing learning object directly within a course. Depending on the learning environment used the course in which the learning object is used is considered a learning object itself or the course is considered a context.

In the first situation the reuse is similar to the creation of an aggregate learning object which we come back to in the next example. An aggregate object is a grouping of related objects into one learning object. A course can be considered such an aggregation.

In the second situation we have again two options to choose from:

1. The course defines a new context for the learning object. In this case the course should be used as a context that defines new metadata for the learning object using the context-aware metadata described above. The course is a new situation in which the learning object is used and the metadata should reflect this.
2. The course already exists as a context for the learning object. This is the simplest case, we only have to indicate the use of the learning object in the course. This could be done using a metadata facet like 'Relation.Kind = 'isreferencedby' of the LOM standard.

4 Automatic Learning Object Indexing

In [1] and [18] an automatic indexing framework is introduced that puts our formal model of metadata in operation for the automatic creation of metadata values. The goal of the framework is to support the learning object developers in the definition of metadata by providing as much as facets values automatically.

The framework uses indexer for different sources of metadata that provide metadata values for one or more facets. Typical types of sources the framework uses are *document content, document context, actual usage* and *document structure*. For each type of metadata source different classes (Indexers) are defined; every Indexer can provide values for multiple metadata facets.

Referring to the model, the classes in the framework implement either the function f_i defined in (6) or the one defined in (11). The prior are subclasses of ObjectBasedIndexer, the latter of ContextBasedIndexer (see also Fig. 5). These classes provide also the confidence value for each value they return.

The class MetadataMerger implements the function MG given in (8) using the simple strategy to resolve conflicts between values we defined in (9): if different indexers provide different values for the same element, the one with the

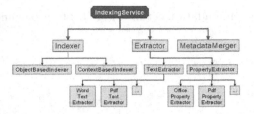

Fig. 5. Overall Structure of the Automatic Indexing Framework

largest confidence value is retained. Currently, no attention is paid in the implementation to solving complex situations as the one mentioned in section 2.2.

This framework provides us with a very flexible and extendible structure for automatic metadata generation, allowing to define new Indexer classes and MetadataMergers if needed. Looking at the tests we performed (see also [1]) the results mainly benefit from the use of context for metadata generation.

5 Conclusions

In this paper we defined a formal model of learning object metadata. The model introduces some new aspects about metadata that become important when doing research about automatic indexing of learning objects.

1. The first aspect we introduced is the use of a *confidence value* to indicate the certainty about a metadata value for a specific learning object.
2. The second is the definition of context-aware metadata. Context-awareness provides the possibility to talk about more advanced uses of metadata in contrast to the very static metadata that is traditionally used.

References

1. Cardinaels, K., Meire, M., Duval, E.: Automating metadata generation: the simple indexing interface. In: Proceedings of the 14th International World Wide Web Conference (WWW2005). (2005) 548–556
2. IEEE: Standard for learning object metadata (2002) Sponsored by the Learning Technology Standards Committee of the IEEE, http://ltsc.ieee.org.
3. Prieto-Díaz, R.: Implementing faceted classification for software reuse. Commun. ACM **34**(5) (1991) 88–97
4. Elmasri, R., Navathe, S.: Fundamentals of Database Systems, Fourth Edition. Pearson, Addison Wesley (2004)
5. W3C: Resource description framework (rdf): Concepts and abstract syntax. http://www.w3.org/TR/2004/REC-rdf-concepts-20040210/ (2004)
6. Melnik, S.: Algebraic specification for rdf models. Technical report, Stanford University (1999)
7. Powell, A., Nilsson, M., Naeve, A., Johnston, P.: DCMI abstract model. Technical report, Dublin Core Metadata Initiative (2004)

8. Zadeh, L.: Fuzzy sets. Information and Control **8** (1995) 338–353
9. Sibun, P., Spitz, A.: Language determination: Natural language processing from scanned document images. In: Proceedings of the Fourth ACL Conference on Applied Natural Language Processing (13–15 October 1994, Stuttgart). (1994)
10. Chassell, R.: Certainty factors. http://www.rattlesnake.com/notions/certainty-factors.html (1997)
11. O'Connor, A., Wade, V., Conlan, O.: Context-informed adaptive hypermedia. In: Proceedings of Workshop on Advanced Context Modelling, Reasoning And Management at UbiComp 2004. (2004)
12. Dey, A.: Providing Architectural Support for Building Context-Aware Applications. PhD thesis, Georgia Institute of Technology (2000)
13. Robson, R.: Metadata matters. Digital Mathematics Library, First DML Planning Meeting, Participant statements, Washington, DC, July 20-30, available http://www.library.cornell.edu/dmlib/robson.pdf (2002)
14. Apps, A., MacIntyre, R.: Using the openurl framework to locate bibliographic resources. In: Proceedings of 2003 Dublin Core Conference: Supporting Communities of Discourse and Practice-Metadata Research & Applications. (2003)
15. MacGregor, R., In-Young Ko: Representing contextualized data using semantic web tools. In: Proceedings of the 1st International Workshop on Practical and Scalable Semantic Systems, ISWC 2003. (2003)
16. Nikitin, S., Terziyan, V., Tsaruk, Y., Zharko, A.: Querying dynamic and context-sensitive metadata in semantic web. In: Proceedings of AIS-ADM 2005. (2005)
17. Cardinaels, K., Duval, E.: Composite learning objects: exposing the components. In: Proceedings of the 3rd Annual ARIADNE Conference, ARIADNE Foundation (2003) 1–7
18. Ochoa, X., Cardinaels, K., Meire, M., Duval, E.: Methodological and technological frameworks for the automatic indexation of learning management systems content into learning object repositories. In: Proceedings of EdMedia 2005. (2005)

Automatic and Manual Annotation Using Flexible Schemas for Adaptation on the Semantic Desktop

Alexandra Cristea[1], Maurice Hendrix[1,2], and Wolfgang Nejdl[2]

[1] Faculty of Mathematics and Computer Science, Eindhoven University of Technology, (TU/e), PBox 513, 5600 MB Eindhoven, The Netherlands
m.hendrix@student.tue.nl, a.i.cristea@tue.nl
[2] L3S Research Center, University of Hannover, 30539 Hannover, Germany
nejdl@l3s.de

Abstract. Adaptive Hypermedia builds upon the annotation and adaptation of content. As manual annotation has proven to be the main bottleneck, all means for supporting it by reusing automatically generated metadata are helpful. In this paper we discuss two issues. The first is the *integration of a generic AH authoring environment MOT into a semantic desktop environment*. In this setup, the semantic desktop environment provides a rich source of automatically generated meta-data, whilst MOT provides a convenient way to enhance this meta-data manually, as needed for an adaptive course environment. Secondly, we also consider the *issue of source schema heterogeneity, especially during the automatic metadata generation process*, as semantic desktop metadata are generated through a lot of different tools and at different times, so that schemas are overlapping and evolving. Explicitly taking into account all versions of these schemas would require a combinatorial explosion of generation rules. This paper investigates a solution to this problem based on malleable schemas, which allow metadata generation rules to flexibly match different versions of schemas, and can thus cope with the heterogeneous and evolving desktop environment.

1 Introduction

Current desktop file structures are surprisingly poor from a semantic point of view. They merely provide fixed folder hierarchies and use simple names to denote entities. The semantic desktop promises much richer structures: resources can be categorized by rich ontologies and semantic links express various kinds of semantic relationships between these resources. For a document, for example, the semantic desktop stores not only a filename, but also information about where this paper was published, when and by whom, which of my colleagues sent it to me, and how often and in what context I accessed it. All these metadata is generated automatically, by the appropriate applications, and stored in an application independent way as RDF metadata, in the user's personal data store. This rich set of metadata clearly makes it easier for the user to retrieve appropriate material for different contexts: for example, when he wants to select appropriate materials for a course lecture. Of course, in this context, we still

W. Nejdl and K. Tochtermann (Eds.): EC-TEL 2006, LNCS 4227, pp. 88–102, 2006.

have to add additional metadata information about course structures and other relevant attributes, like pedagogically relevant attributes, or further contents.

In this paper we first describe course authoring on the semantic desktop. Specifically, we show the interaction and exchange of data between the Beagle++ environment, which is an advanced search and indexing engine for the desktop, generating and utilizing metadata information, and the adaptive hypermedia authoring environment MOT, a sophisticated system for authoring personalized e-courses.

Second, we focus on the problem of schema heterogeneity in this environment. Metadata on the Semantic Desktop are generated by different applications at different times, and have to be described by different and usually evolving schemas. Whilst classical schema integration approaches rely on a set of mappings between these schemas, unifying data through one global schema, these approaches are infeasible in our environment: on the Semantic Desktop, there will always be a good reason for adding additional metadata or metadata attributes, which we did not foresee when starting to collect metadata one, two or more years ago. This paper investigates a possible solution for this problem based on malleable schemas [11], which employs flexible matching against those schemas without the need to continuously modify our metadata generation rules.

The paper is structured as follows. First, in section 2 we present a motivating scenario;. In section 3, the basic metadata schemas are introduced. Section 4 describes the transformation workflow between these schemas. Section 5 introduces impreciseness in the representation, via malleable schemas, as well as discusses some solutions. Finally we draw conclusions in section 6.

2   Scenario

The following motivating scenario for adaptive authoring builds upon both automatically and manually generated metadata.

Dr. Van Bos prepares a new on-line course on Adaptive Hypermedia for undergraduate 4th year TU/e students. The university work distribution allocates a limited amount of time for this, equivalent to the creation of a static, linear course. However,

- o due to the fact that Dr. Van Bos considers it useful to be able to extend the course in the future with more alternative paths guided by *adaptivity*, but also,
- o because he wants to benefit from *automatic help* during the authoring process,

he uses a *concept-based adaptive educational hypermedia authoring environment* with *adaptive authoring support*, MOT [8,15]. This decision costs him slightly more time than the static course creation, as he has to *manually* divide his course into conceptual entities with explicit, independent semantics and semantic labeling.

The advantage is that the *adaptive authoring system* can afterwards *automatically* apply pedagogical strategies. E.g., the system can consider the first, manual version of the course created by Van Bos as the version for *beginner* students, which don't aspire at high grades or deep knowledge. For *advanced* students, wishing to pass the course with high honors, or simply desiring more information for their future professions, the adaptive authoring system can use *semantic personal desktop search* to automatically find on Dr. Van Bos's desktop any stored scientific papers relevant to the current course. These papers can be used as alternative or additional material to the main storyline of the static course. This mechanism builds upon the following assumptions:

o   as Dr. Van Bos is a specialist in the subject taught, his interest is wider than that given by the limitations of the course; he therefore both publishes and reads papers of interest on the subject, which are likely to be stored on his computer;

o   these papers can be considered as useful extra resources for the current course, and can therefore be reused in this context;

o   as this storing process has taken place over several years, Van Bos may not know exactly where each single article relevant to the current course is on his computer;

o   however, Dr. Van Bos has been using Beagle++ Semantic Desktop System [2, 5] to store both papers and all relevant metadata automatically, in RDF format.

This situation can be exploited by the authoring tool; a quick search will find some of Dr. Van Bos's own papers on Adaptive Hypermedia, as well as some by his colleagues on the same topic, e.g., the paper of Brusilovsky, called "Adaptive Educational Hypermedia: From generation to generation" [3], or the paper "Adaptive Authoring of Adaptive Hypermedia" [9]. He may have saved these papers by himself, or might have received them by e-mail, from a colleague working in the same field, or may have used his browser's bookmarks to mark their position on the Web.

In order for these retrieved resources to be relevant to the overall Adaptive Hypermedia course, two conditions have to be fulfilled:

o   the domain concept in the course where each resource is most relevant has to be found (the *right information*)

o   the resource has to be bound to that particular domain concept (in the *right place*).

This means that the first paper can be added in the course at a higher level, somewhere next to the explanation of generic principles of adaptive hypermedia, whereas the second paper should only be placed somewhere in connection with the authoring process in adaptive hypermedia, otherwise its content might be too specific to follow.

How can the system find the right resource and add it in the right place for Van Bos? The search can take place via keywords, labeling both course pieces created by Van Bos, as well as the papers and resources on his desktop (as shown in section 4).

Finally, Van Bos will use several versions of Beagle++ over the years to store his data. He certainly would like the same type of retrieval to work with all the versions of the schemas using during these years.

The following sections will describe in more detail how Dr. Van Bos can enrich his course semi-automatically, without much extra work, as well as keep at all times the overall control and overview.

3   Enriching Metadata

As we have seen in our scenario, both *automatically* generated metadata as well as *manually* added metadata are important. The automatically generated metadata allow description and retrieval of the appropriate articles. The manual annotation step allows addition of additional content, as well as of attributes like pedagogical weights and labels, which are necessary to build the final adaptive course product. The following two sub-sections describe these two kinds of metadata in more detail.

3.1 Input Metadata Schema

Beagle [1] is a desktop search system implemented for Linux that indexes all documents on the user's desktop. *Beagle++* [2, 5] is an extension of Beagle that generates and stores additional metadata describing these documents, other resources, and their relationships. Additional metadata automatically annotate material the user has read, used, written or commented upon. Three obvious sources of desktop behavior information are: *files* on the desktop, *Internet* browsing and downloaded files, and *mail* exchanges and files stored from mail attachments [5, 13]. Figure 1 shows an instance of this ontology depicting files annotated with their publication metadata, file system attributes, web history, and mail context (e.g., files being attached to specific e-mails).

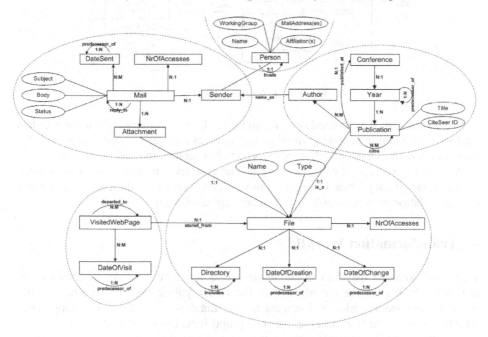

Fig. 1. RDF schema of metadata from Beagle++ [2]

In Figure 1, the upper left ellipse describes emails (with subject, body, sender and status attributes) and their attachments. The upper right ellipse defines publications written by several authors at different conferences (with title, publication year, etc.). The lower left ellipse shows web cache history representation (web pages visited and dates of visits). Finally, the lower right ellipse describes files that are saved on a person's desktop, with their name and specific directory. These files may have been saved via any of the other three processes (from emails, from websites, or from conferences), so an attachment entity and a file entity may refer to the same object.

3.2 Output Metadata Schema

These files and metadata are however not enough to generate a complete course. Specifically, information is needed about the hierarchical structure and order of the material in the context of a lesson, as well as additional pedagogical annotations describing which students the material is best suited for (e.g., *beginner* versus *advanced*). Figure 2 shows this target schema, as defined in MOT [8], an adaptive hypermedia authoring system. The schema describes two models used in the adaptive hypermedia authoring paradigm: the *domain map* (left side of Figure 2) and the *lesson* (right side).

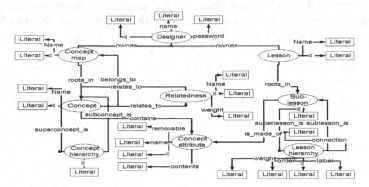

Fig. 2. RDF Schema of MOT [8]

A *domain map* is composed of a hierarchy of domain concepts. Each concept has attributes, containing or linking to e-learning content alternatives describing this concept. In addition to the hierarchy, concepts can also connect to related concepts.

A *lesson* is composed of a hierarchy of sub-lessons. The lesson represents a filtered, pedagogically labeled, weighted and ordered version of the concept attributes (see the relation between sub-lessons and concept attributes).

4 Transformation Workflow

Beagle++ stores all metadata in the Sesame RDF database [18]. All Beagle++ components, which *generate metadata* (e.g., the email, publication, web cache and file metadata generators) add the metadata to this database. All Beagle++ components which *use metadata* (for example, the search and indexing module, the ranking module or the browsing module) retrieve their data from this repository, and, in some cases, write back new data (such as the PageRank value for documents or other resources).

It is easy to accommodate additional modules in this environment by writing appropriate interface components, which read and write from the repository. This is what we have done for *MOT* [8, 15]. In the scenario, we have described semi-automatic addition of articles stored on the user's desktop to a MOT lesson [8]. In MOT, this addition is done to an existing lesson. Based on pedagogic goals, the author can process the data by changing labels and weights and adding other information on the article. After this enrichment, the lesson can be imported back into the

RDF store. We use CAF (Common Adaptation Format [7], a system-independent XML exchange format) to simplify the transformation process from RDF to the MOT MySQL storage format.

4.1 RDF2CAF

In this step, we transform available articles into a CAF sub-lesson. This is a semi-automatic step, where the author selects a lesson in MOT and then the system searches (via keywords and title) for related articles in the Sesame data store. This is done by a Java utility that takes the metadata in the Sesame store and the lesson in CAF format as input and generates an updated lesson as CAF file. As articles are stored locally on the desktop, they have to be than physically transported to the supporting MOT server.

The question is now where in the lesson the new article information is placed? As MOT is mainly a tool for authoring *educational* (adaptive) material, internal information structures are based on strict *hierarchies* (Figure 2). When enriching the domain-model and lesson, we of course want to get the *right information* in the *right place* in this hierarchy. To achieve this, the program first queries the Sesame database, using as search terms title and keywords of each domain concept found in the current lesson:

```
select x from x {p} y where y like "*keyword"
```

This query may result in one file being relevant in many places within the hierarchy. To ensure adding every resource only once, the place 'relevance' is computed:

$$rank\,(a,c) = \frac{card\,(k(c) \bigcap k(a))}{card\,(k(a))}\;;\;\text{where:}$$

rank(a,c) is the rank of article *a* with respect to the current domain concept *c*;

k(c) is the set of keywords belonging to the current domain concept *c*;

k(a) is the set of keywords belonging to the current article *a*;

If a resource is ranked equally for two domain concepts in the hierarchy, we add it to the topmost concept. The number of articles to be added per concept is limited to 3, as adding too many articles to one concept could result in confusing the learner.

4.2 CAF2MOT

The import of CAF files into MOT is implemented as a PHP script and done in two steps. First, the domain map is processed. During this process, an associative array is created, as lookup table. In it, every created concept attribute is stored as follows:

```
[name_of_domain_map\name_of_concept_1\...\
    name_of_concept_N\attribute_name] => attribute_id
```

This allows a faster lookup in the next step than via a direct query on the database. In the second step, the lesson (parts) are generated. While importing, conflicts between lesson or domain map *names* may occur. There are currently 3 ways of handling this:

o The author *ignores* it, allowing one name for multiple MOT domain maps /lessons.
o The author *renames* domain maps /lessons with conflicting names (after the import, from a list of conflicting names).
o The system *merges* (automatically) lessons and domain maps with the same name (handling them as extensions of each other). For domain maps, merging means

that two domain maps with the same name are compared, concept by concept. Domain concepts and attributes that were not present before are added.

In the current implementation, a lesson is exported, then articles are added to the CAF file, and then the CAF file is imported back into MOT with the *merge* option. This is essential, as it allows additions made to lessons between export and import not to be deleted, so other lessons using one of the adapted domain maps are not affected.

4.3 Working in MOT

In MOT, data and metadata imported from Sesame can be manually reordered and edited. Figure 3 shows an extract of editing in the *lesson* environment (the import from Beagle++ generates extra information both for the *domain map* as well as for the *lesson*). The paper called 'Adaptive Educational Hypermedia: From generation to generation' and all its relevant metadata (title, authors, references, conference where presented) have been added automatically during extraction to the 'Adaptive Hypermedia' domain concept, at the highest level in the hierarchy. The paper 'Adaptive Authoring of Adaptive Educational Hypermedia' has been added to the domain concept 'Authoring of Adaptive Hypermedia', in a lower position in the hierarchy, as it is a more specific paper. The author can now manually add pedagogical labels to this new material, e.g., labeling the material 'adv' for advanced learners.

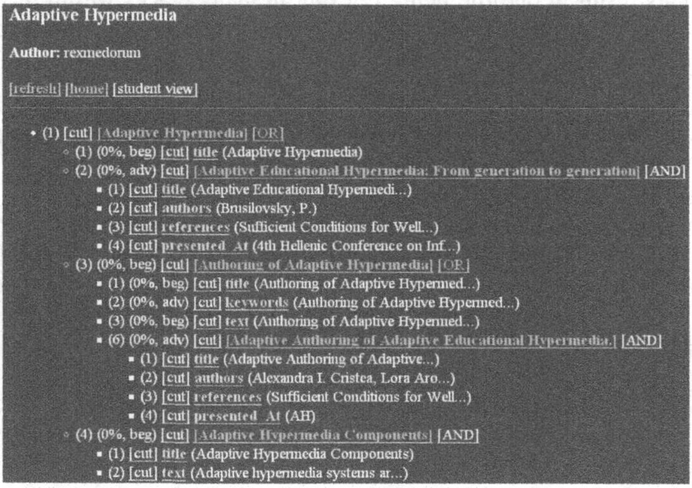

Fig. 3. Adding manual metadata in a MOT lesson

4.4 MOT2RDF

MOT2CAF
Importing MOT into CAF is also implemented as a PHP script. First, the lesson is constructed, based on the lesson hierarchy. During this process, a list of the mappings between lesson objects and domain objects is kept. Next, the corresponding domain map is generated. Every domain map used in the lesson is added to the domain model.

CAF2RDF

For more flexibility, MOT lessons should also be exported as RDF; we are currently implementing this step. These RDF data could be re-used by Beagle++[2]. The RDF metadata schema is described in [9]. Since the CAF file is in XML format, we can use an XSLT style sheet and do an XSLT transformation to convert into an RDF file describing the lesson. The RDF MOT output then looks as shown in Figure 2. If we export the changed information to RDF so that it can again be used by Beagle++, the problem of duplicates arises again. Exact duplicates that overwrite existing information are obviously not a problem. However, information contradicting existing information is less desirable. A solution is to keep track of objects already present, and not export those. However, in this case, changes made to data in MOT [8] would not be reflected. Therefore, if an author manually corrects some error, this would be omitted in the target RDF. On the other hand, an author may make changes only valid in a particular context (e.g., for a given domain map), that do not apply to the resource in general. Therefore, automatic updating, as well as automatic discharging of new information are both undesirable. There are two possible solutions to this problem:

o *manual:* search for existence of resources to be exported and ask the author whether to overwrite the current resources or not.

o *automatic:* save information together with its context as a new information item.

5 Handling Flexible Schemas

The previous sections implicitly assumed fixed schemas. I.e., all schema elements, relationships and attributes are defined and fixed. In reality, however, our Sesame data store contains data based on different schemas, and different versions of these schemas, as metadata and metadata schemas continuously evolve on the Semantic Desktop. Although this does not create great problems in our transformation process (we store all schemas and schema version together with our metadata in RDF/RDFS format), it can lead to problems for metadata generation rules. E.g., rules that specifically refer to certain elements or attributes in a given schema are not viable (cannot be reused) if the schema evolves. The solution we propose in this paper is based on malleable schemas, which allow us to flexibly describe our metadata as well as employ imprecise matching over these schemas, to flexibly refer to the appropriate attributes.

5.1 Extended Malleable Schema

Malleable Schemas (introduced in [11]) are a new concept in the database and web communities. Although the problems with integration of information on the web have been recognized early (various schemas, non-structured data, etc.), solutions proposed often involve either individual *mediating or merging of two or more schemas* [4], or *mapping to a higher level schema* [13, 18] or *ontology* [12]. More advanced solutions deal with *gradually evolving schemas* [23].

Malleable schemas provide a mechanism by which the modeler can capture the imprecise aspects of the domain during the modeling phase in a well principled fashion [11]. This is done based on keyword matching; however, these keywords are elements of the schema, instead of arbitrary keyword fields. Unlike earlier solutions, malleable schemas are an answer to more than one problem when integrating information on the web and especially on the desktop, including:

  o multiple original schemas with varying semantics;
  o evolution of schemas and semantics;
  o need of only partial integration (as opposed to full integration): often, only a part of the existing schema is relevant for a particular application or user; integrating the whole schema can be both an arduous as well as a superfluous exercise.

Malleable schemas help in capturing the important (relevant) aspects of the domain at modeling time, without having to commit to a strict schema. More importantly, the vague parts of the schema can, in principle, evolve later towards more structure, or can just as well remain as they are.

The data model of malleable schemas as described in [11] is an object oriented one, which fits nicely the RDF/RDFS data model [17]. RDF/RDFS represents everything as triples *<subject, predicate, object>*; where subject is represented by *class* elements of the schema (or instances thereof); the predicate represents a *relationship* or an *attribute*, and object can be another class element, an instance thereof, or a value. Relationships have a *domain*, where the domain is a *set of classes*. Attributes have a *range*, specifying *allowed values* for this attribute. Malleable schemas are composed of similar elements as regular schemas. The major differences to conventional schemas are:

  o classes and relationships (properties) do not have to have precise naming; the names can be keywords or phrases, as well as regular expressions; a distinction is made between precisely and imprecisely named elements.
  o structure can vary; a distinction is made between strict structure and variable structure elements. The latter allow us to flexibly refer to classes in paths composed of more than one property.

Malleable schemas thus provide a simplified, unified view on a collection of related and overlapping base schemas. The relationships and overlaps of the base schemas are described by mappings. An example schema is presented in Figure 4.

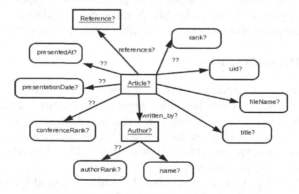

Fig. 4. RDF malleable schema of directory data

This type of malleable schema represents the schema on which queries on several partially known (or evolving) schemas can be based, as discussed in sub-section 5.2. Figure 4 shows the schema on which queries between MOT and the Semantic Desktop data in Beagle++ are made.

Term impreciseness: Flexible class and attribute names
In Figure 4, impreciseness is denoted via *single question marks* '*?*'. For instance, the entity '*Article*' is imprecise (or malleable) and is written as '*Article?*'. In other words, a malleable schema allows impreciseness in the naming of classes. E.g., '*File*' can sometimes appear as '*Article*', sometimes as '*Artikel*'. In the latter, the language has to be identified, whilst in the former, synonyms have to be searched for. Such an uncertainty about class names can appear, as listed above, when the same class has different names in two different schemas, but also, when the target schema that is queried is not known. This malleable feature of schemas is based on the ones proposed in [11]. In the following, the malleability definition in [11] is extended, based on the needs we have found in our transformation and conversion exercise between schemas.

Term impreciseness: Flexible relations or property names
Just as classes can be imprecise, properties of classes can also be only partially known. For instance, we can expect that the malleable class '*Author?*' can have a property '*name*', but it could also be '*firstName*' and '*lastName*', or be expressed in another form. Therefore, we depict this expectation by adding to our schema the malleable property '*name?*'. Again, the *question mark* '*?*'denotes the impreciseness.

Furthermore, composed words can appear, such as in '*presentedAt*' versus '*conference*'. In such a case, synonyms are not enough. First, decomposition into simple words has to be performed, and then, the expression identified.

Flexible paths
Beside the naming differences, schemas can also have different structures. A class can be connected to another class or property via a direct connection, or via an imprecise, indirect connection. In our example (Figure 4), the imprecise attribute '*presentedAt?*' can be directly or indirectly connected to the imprecise object '*Article?*'. This would correspond in Figure 1 to the relationship between the (not displayed) property '*Name*' of the class '*Conference*', to the entity '*Publication*'. '*Name*' in Figure 1 is not a direct attribute of the class '*Publication*'. Therefore, in Figure 4, the property '*presentedAt?*' (equivalent to the above mentioned property '*Name*' in Figure 1), appears as an imprecisely linked property of the class '*Article?*' (equivalent to the above mentioned class '*Publication*' in Figure 1). In Figure 4, such indirect, imprecise connections (of undetermined length) are marked by *double question marks* '*??*'.

The above three types of impreciseness can be resolved in various ways. *Term similarity* [11] ,e.g., can be resolved via Wordnet [24] or by other similarity measures. We can rely on extensive research regarding similarity measures between individual schemas (*instance similarity* [11], *structural similarity*: e.g., editing distance [25], approximate nearest neighbor search [20], unordered tree matching [18], *schema-corpus similarity* [14]).

It is important to note that, for malleable schemas, complete resolution of the impreciseness and schema mapping is not desirable. The resolution is only interesting and important when specific queries are posed against the malleable schema. The elements of the malleable schema which do not appear in the queries do not need to be bound to concrete schema instances or schema alternatives. For malleable schemas, the resolution process of the impreciseness is an *iterative discovery process*.

5.2 Queries and Rules with Malleable Schema Elements

The next issue is how the query process takes place in presence of malleable schemas, and how end-user (e.g., learner) adaptation (personalization) based on malleable schemas can be implemented. As hinted in [11], there are two main query targets: *instances* and *schemas*. Whilst querying based on regular schemas usually targets the instances, for malleable schemas, asking questions about the structure and composition of the schema itself can also be interesting, as it is also, to some degree, unknown.

Instance Querying

Instance querying is the type of querying usually performed: a schema instance is queried about the instances of elements that it contains. For instance, we want to search for articles written by certain authors. We base our instance query system on [11], expanding it, though, as we want to express the impreciseness of *terms* (classes or properties), as well as the impreciseness of *structure* in our queries.

In the following, we exemplify these three types of impreciseness in a query. Let us suppose we want to find an article written by author "Cristea", which was sent to the current user by "Nejdl" via email.

First, in Example 1, we look at how we write this query if we knew the exact structure of the RDFS base schema (as depicted in Figure 1). As we are querying RDF data, the language used a simplified form of SeRQL from Sesame; moreover, this was the implementation language used for our transformation steps described in the first part of the paper.

Example 1 - Standard query:
```
SELECT Title FROM { bplus:Publication} art:title {bplus:Title},
     { bplus:Publication} art:authored_by { bplus:Author},
     { bplus:Publication} rdfs:subClassOf { bplus:File},
     { bplus:Attachment} rdfs:subClassOf { bplus:File},
     {Mail} bplus: Attachment{ bplus:Attachment};
            bplus: email_reply_to { bplus:Sender},
     {Sender} bplus:name {"Nejdl"}
WHERE bplus:Publication = bplus:Attachment
      AND { bplus:Author} like "*#Cristea"
using namespace
 rdfs = <http://www.w3.org/1999/02/22-rdf-syntax-ns#>,
 art = < http://www.win.tue.nl/~acristea/
              schemas/articleSchema.rdf#>
 bplus = <http://www.l3s.de/domain_l3s#>
```

The example returns the desired article(s), if the terminology, as well as the relations used in these query, are correct. We will now gradually relax this query towards a malleable query.

In Example 2, we rephrase this query, based *partially* on the malleable schema in Figure 4. In this case, we are not aware of the precise naming and terminology of the classes of the basis schemas; moreover, we cannot bind the terminology to a given namespace.

Example 2 - Term impreciseness - class impreciseness:

```
SELECT Title? FROM {Article?} title {Title?},
       {Article?} authored_by {Author?},
       {Mail?} Attachment {Article?};
             Sender {Sender?},
       {Sender?} name {"Nejdl"}
WHERE {Author?} like "*#Cristea"
```

As can be seen, Example 2 still assumes some knowledge of the correct terminology of properties, as well as knowledge about the structure, in order to return the desired article(s). Impreciseness is introduced via the imprecise term *'Article?'*, which can be mapped to several classes of the original schema(s): *'Publication'*, *'File'* and *'Attachment'*. As we can see, the impreciseness of terms has the side-effect that queries can be written in a more compact way. Explicit reference to equivalent classes is not necessary in the query.

The following relaxation allows for properties to be also imprecise (Example 3).

Example 3 - Term impreciseness - property impreciseness:

```
SELECT Title? FROM {Article?} title? {Title?},
       {Article?} written_by? {Author?},
       {Mail?} has_attached? {Article?};
             has_sender? {Sender?},
       {Sender?} name {"Nejdl"}
WHERE {Author?} like "*#Cristea"
```

In Example 3, properties such as *'written_by?'* are imprecise. This property will have to be connected during the resolution process with the property *'authored_by'* in Figure 1. This step allows all terms of the query to be vague. This corresponds to the situation where either the actual names of the classes, attributes and properties are forgotten, or they are unknown. The structure of the RDF schema, however, still has to be known.

Finally, we make another relaxation step, as depicted in Example 4a,b. Example 4a is based on the malleable schema in Figure 4, extended with mail information.

Example 4a: Relation impreciseness:

```
SELECT Article? FROM {Article?} written_by? {Author?};
                                ??sent_by? {"Nejdl"},
       {Author?} name? {"Cristea"}
```

The relation *'??sent_by?'* is both imprecise in *terminology* (it should be equivalent to *'email_reply_to'* in Figure 1); this is why it has a question mark on its right side: *'sent_by?'* ; as well as imprecise in *structure* (it actually represents a path between *'Attachment'* and *'Sender'* from Figure 1, i.e., *'Attachment<has_attached-Mail-email_reply_to>Sender'*; this is the reason why it also has two question marks on its left side: *'??sent_by'*).

The query can be relaxed even further, as in Example 4b. This corresponds to a simplified malleable schema, a reduced version of the schema from Figure 4. In Example 4b, the connection between *'Article'* and author name is imprecise as well.

Example 4b - Relation impreciseness:
```
SELECT Article? FROM {Article?} ??written_by? {"Cristea"};
                                 ??sent_by? {"Nejdl"}
```

Notice how in queries 4a,b the query has become more compact, and almost like natural language. This resemblance is due to the fact that the malleable query is similar to the way people ask questions: they only remember partially terminology and relations, and some information about the structure. Moreover, the individual representations remembered by different people differ. Still, individuals are capable of communicating with each other despite these different models (schemas), which provides additional motivation to express uncertainties in the world around us through mechanisms like malleable schemas and malleable queries.

Schema Querying

Schema querying is only necessary when dealing with imprecise schemas [11]. As our malleable schemas are imprecise both in the *naming* of the elements (classes and properties) and in their *structure*, schema queries can serve to identify the actual naming and structure of the base schemas. This is useful in resolving the impreciseness of our malleable schema.

In the following, we exemplify the three types of impreciseness defined above, for a proposed schema query.

In our first example, we want to find the correct term for a *class* or an *attribute*. Here, we want to know how the class *'Article?'* is called in the base schema(s), which is connected via a *'written_by?'*-like property with a class similar to *'Author?'*.

Example 1a - Term impreciseness - class impreciseness:
```
SELECT Name(Article?)
FROM {Article?} written_by? {Author?}
```

For the base schemata in Figure 1, the answer would be *'Publication'*. If we would want to obtain also 'Attachment' and 'File', we would need to relax the triple conditions, as in Example 1b.

Example 1b - Term impreciseness - class impreciseness:
```
SELECT Name(Article?)
FROM {Article?} * {*}
```

In our second example, we want to find the correct term for a *property*. The property name we're looking for is *'written_by?'*, from the same triple as above.

Example 2 - Term impreciseness - property impreciseness:
```
SELECT Name(written_by?)
FROM {Article?} written_by? {Author?}
```

The query result is the property *'authored_by'* from the schema in Figure 1.

In our third and last example, we want to find the *correct path* between two objects (two classes, or a class and an attribute). We exemplify this by looking for the conference rank of a given article (Example 3).

Example 3 - Relation impreciseness:
```
SELECT Path(??conferenceRank?)
FROM {Article?} ??conferenceRank? {ConferenceRank?}
```

The result will retrieve the path between *'Publication'* and *'rank'*, i.e., *'published_at - Conference - has_a'* (from Figure 1).

The two types of queries (*instance* and *schema* query) defined and exemplified above can be performed automatically by search systems, in order to automatically enrich, in our current application, the authored learning material for the adaptive, personalized learning environment of the end-user, the student. The author is expected to use malleable schemas transparently; i.e., he can leave the processing to a query system, and concentrate only in the extra manual annotation and extension of the material.

6 Summary

The semantic desktop is a rich source of metadata about resources as well as relationships between these resources. While many of these metadata can be generated automatically, some additional metadata necessary for adaptive courses still have to be added manually. In this paper we have described how the semantic desktop, building on Semantic Web techniques, can be interfaced with a sophisticated adaptive hypermedia authoring environment. The semantic desktop system provides automatically generated metadata describing publications and other materials relevant for an advanced course. The MOT authoring system adds context and pedagogical information.

Moreover, we have looked at flexible ways to describe metadata in this environment. Conventional schemas are not suited for that purpose, as they cannot cope with changing or evolving schemas, which are very important for the semantic desktop (new tasks make new metadata attributes necessary, additional data sources with additional schemas will be added over time, etc.) The solution we are proposing relies on malleable schemas [11] to flexibly describe our metadata, and on fuzzy querying and matching, based on these schemas, to flexibly retrieve metadata.

In future work we will concentrate on automatic query expansion for malleable schema queries – we have already formulated appropriate expansion rules which we are currently validating and extending -, and on adaptive navigation rules relying on these query expansion mechanisms. Furthermore, we have started to investigate the use of malleable schema-based querying in a search context, and are working on integrating these algorithms into the next Beagle++ version.

References

1. Beagle, http://beaglewiki.org/Main_Page
2. Beagle++, http://www.kbs.uni-hannover.de/beagle++/wiki/pmwiki.php
3. Brusilovsky, P. (2004) Adaptive Educational Hypermedia: From generation to generation. Proceedings of 4th Hellenic Conference on Information and Communication Technologies in Education, Athens, Greece, September 29 - October 3, 2004, pp.19-33.
4. Buneman P., Davidson, S., and Kosky, A. Theoretical Aspects of Schema Merging, Proc. 3rd Int. Conf. Extending Database Technology, Vienna, Austria (March 1992) 152-167.
5. Chirita, P.-A., Costache, S., Nejdl, W., and Paiu, R. Beagle++: Semantically Enhanced Searching and Ranking on the Desktop. Proceedings of the 3rd European Semantic Web Conference, Budva, Montenegro (to appear 11-14 June 2006).
6. Chirita, P.-A., Gavriloaie, R., Ghita, S., Nejdl, W., and Paiu, R. Activity-Based Metadata for Semantic Desktop Search. Proceedings of the 2nd European Semantic Web Conference, Heraklion, Crete, May (2005).

7. Cristea, A.I., Smits, D., and De Bra, P. Writing MOT, Reading AHA! - converting between an authoring and a delivery system for adaptive educational hypermedia -, A3EH Workshop, AIED'05, Amsterdam, The Netherlands (July, 2005)
8. Cristea, A. I. & De Mooij, A. Adaptive Course Authoring: My Online Teacher. Proceedings of ICT'03, Papeete, French Polynesia (2003).
9. Cristea, A., De Mooij, A. LAOS: Layered WWW AHS Authoring Model and its corresponding Algebraic Operators. In Proceedings of WWW'03, Alternate Education track. (Budapest, Hungary 20-24 May 2003). ACM.
10. Cristea, A. I. and Aroyo, L. Adaptive Authoring of Adaptive Educational Hypermedia. AH 2002, Adaptive Hypermedia and Adaptive Web-Based Systems, LNCS 2347, Springer, (2002) 122-132.
11. Dong, X., and Halevy, A., Malleable Schemas, WebDB, Baltimore Maryland (June 16-17, 2005), ACM, webdb2005.uhasselt.be/papers/P-8.pdf.
12. Gardarin, G., and Dang-Ngoc, T-T. Mediating the Semantic Web. 4th journal on extraction and management of knowledge, Clermont Ferrand, Université Blaise Pascal (20-23 Jan. 2004). http://georges.gardarin.free.fr/Articles/MediatingtheSemanticWeb.pdf
13. Ghita, S., Nejdl, W., and Paiu, R., Semantically Rich Recommendations in Social Networks for Sharing, Exchanging and Ranking Semantic Context, International Semantic Web Conference, Galway, Ireland (6 November 2005) 6 – 10.
14. He, B., and Chang, C.-C., Statistical schema integration across the deep web. In Proc. of SIGMOD (2003).
15. MOT homepage, http://wwwis.win.tue.nl/~acristea/mot.html
16. Pottinger, R. A., Processing Queries and Merging Schemas in Support of Data Integration, PhD thesis, University of Washington, US (2004), www.cs.ubc.ca/~rap/publications/thesis.pdf.
17. RDF, http://www.w3.org/RDF/
18. Schlieder, T., Naumann, F., Approximate tree embedding for quering cml data, ACM SIGIR Workshop on CML and Information Retrieval.
19. Sesame, http://www.openrdf.org/
20. Shasha, D., Wang, J., Shan, H., Zhang, K., Atreegrep: Approximate searching in unordered trees, in Proc. of International Conference on Scientific and Statistical DB Management (2002) 89-98.
21. Semantic Desktop, http://www.semanticdesktop.org/
22. Simon, B., Dolog, P., Miklós, Z., Olmedilla, D. and Sintek, M. Conceptualising Smart Spaces for Learning. *Journal of Interactive Media in Education*, 2004 (9). Special Issue on the Educational Semantic Web. ISSN: 1365-893X (2004). http://www-jime.open.ac.uk/2004/9
23. Velegrakis, Y., Miller, R.J., and Popa, L. Mapping Adaptation under Evolving Schemas, with Yannis Velegrakis and Renee J.. VLDB'03, Berlin, Germany, September (2003) 584-595. (full version in VLDB Journal) http://www.almaden.ibm.com/cs/people/lucian/MappingAdaptation_VLDB03.pdf
24. Wordnet. http://www.cogsci.princeton.edu/wn/
25. Zhang, K., Wang, J., Shasha, D., On the editing distance between undirected acyclic graphs and related problems, in Proc. of International Symposium on Combinatorial pattern matching (1998).

eMapps.com: Games and Mobile Technology in Learning

Robert Davies[1], Romana Krizova[2], and Daniel Weiss[3]

[1] MDR Partners, 2b Fitzgerald Road, London, SW14 8HA. +44 208 876 3121
rob.davies@mdrpartners.com
[2] Cross Czech a.s., Spanelska 4, 120 00 Praha 2, Czech Republic, +420 602764247
romana.krizova@crossczech.cz
[3] Ciberespacio SL, Rua Atenas 5 - 15008 A Coruña Spain, +34 609838394
dweiss@chimereguide.org

Abstract. There is a natural alliance between learning and personal mobile technology, making it feasible to equip learners with powerful tools to support learning in many contexts, emphasising the skills and knowledge needed for a rapidly changing society. eMapps.com, under IST EC FP6 in the New Member States, is demonstrating how games and mobile technologies can be combined to provide enriching experiences for children in the school curriculum and beyond, using Advanced Reality Games, played 'live' in the individual territory using Internet, GPRS/3G, SMS and MMS technologies.

Keywords: games, eLearning.

1 Introduction

eMapps.com is a project funded under the European Commission's IST 6th Framework Programme (FP6). Its focus is on demonstrating how games and mobile technologies can be combined to provide new and enriching experiences for children in the school curriculum and beyond. The work will concentrate initially on Europe's New Member States and school children in the age group 9-12. It will support creativity in the classroom and outside and will contribute to practice for developing new teaching.

2 Key Challenges Addressed

The following are among the key challenges which eMapps.com will address:
1. A major potential barrier to integrating games use in learning and the school curriculum, or at any level, is the perceived mismatch between skills and knowledge developed in games, and those recognised explicitly within education systems. The recognition of skill development achievable through games is an important component in breaking down these barriers.
2. Teachers need to be engaged and to recognise and map the relationships between activities in games and the associated learning before they can embed the use of

W. Nejdl and K. Tochtermann (Eds.): EC-TEL 2006, LNCS 4227, pp. 103–110, 2006.

the game within the wider learning context and be enabled to frame tasks, within the game or leading up to or following on from a lesson.

3. Many of the skills valuable for successful game play, and recognised by both teachers and parents, are as yet only implicitly valued within a school context. In future, learning will move increasingly from the classroom and into the learner's environments, both real and virtual.

4. On a cognitive level, play encourages the development of our concepts about the world. By toying with objects and ideas through playful experimentation we develop an understanding of the physical world and our place within it. But as games increase in complexity and freedom, they will be able to accommodate many different playing styles and personal goals, mirroring the inner dynamics of the player's personality.

5. The problem of narrative, of integrating a linear storyline within an interactive game is widely acknowledged as one of the most intractable problems in the field of games design. Although many techniques exist and will attract developers and gamers for a long time to come, none of them solve the hardest problem; creating a truly dynamic narrative, of creating virtual worlds or Mixed Realities (outdoor and indoor) where although the themes and imagery in the world remain consistent, the actions of different players lead to completely different and credible outcomes.

3 Target Audiences

Key target audiences for eMapps.com are:

- Policy makers in school education who will gain assurance of the benefits and confidence in supporting and investing in games-based learning.
- Teachers who will be engaged and encouraged to recognise and map the relationships between activities in games and the associated learning so that they can embed the use of games within the wider learning context and be enabled to frame tasks, within the game or leading up to or following on from a lesson.
- Parents who will gain a better of understanding of the role which games can play in their children's learning and development.
- Children who will be stimulated and whose learning experiences and performance will be improved by exciting adaptations of a technology they already enjoy.

4 Expected Results

The main outcomes of eMapps.com will include:

- A web-based game learning platform for implementation with the target audiences, using games that can be played 'live' in the individual territory on a new generation of mobile devices using Internet GPRS/3G, SMS and MMS technologies.

- A Children's Living Map of Europe which locates the content and games produced during eMapps.com in a format to inspire others and in which any school or locality can participate.
- School teachers/managers or others from each of the eight participating countries will be qualified to implement and disseminate a game training course to other teachers through a series of local events.
- Evaluation of the need, relevance, and practicality of the implemented Game-based learning model will be conducted, and results made public, on the basis of experience in each of the participating countries.
- A Handbook on using games for training in a variety of formats.
- Training courses plus two international conferences on using web-based Games for learning in schools and informal settings, presenting in particular the project methodology and findings in each of the participating countries.
- Exploitation and replication of the results emerging from the project through an extensive dissemination programme including an interactive project website, which will provide access to teachers and other school education staff.

5 Games and Mobile Technology in Learning

The new emphasis in education is on supporting the learner, in collaboration with peers and teachers/managers or other school education staff, through a lifetime of education, both within and outside the classroom.

There is a natural alliance between learning and personal mobile training technology, so that it is becoming feasible to equip learners with powerful tools to support their learning in many contexts over long periods of time, with an emphasis on equipping people with the skills and knowledge for a rapidly changing society.

The approach of eMapps.com is closely related to constructivist concepts of learning which hold that, by reflecting on their own experiences, all learners actively construct their own understanding of the world based on both their previous and current knowledge. Constructivism asserts that the knowledge acquired by students should not be supplied by the teacher as a ready-made product. Children do best by creating for themselves the specific knowledge they need, rather than being instructed in what they must know.

Research shows that people learn best when they are entertained, when they can use creativity to work toward complex goals, when lesson plans incorporate both thinking and emotion, and when the consequences of actions can be observed. The past twenty-five years has produced a substantial body of psychological, educational and development literature highlighting the educational potential of digital games. However, this enthusiasm is tempered by the recognition that the majority of commercial 'edutainment' products have been largely unsuccessful in harnessing this potential to effective educational use.

Key design guidelines for achieving intrinsic integration in digital learning games include:

- Deliver learning material through the parts of the game that are the most fun to play, riding on the back of the 'flow' experience produced by the game, and not interrupting or diminishing its impact.
- Embody the learning material within the structure of the gaming world and the player's interactions with it, providing an external representation of the learning content that is explored through the core mechanics of the game play.
- Rather than pursue learning by listening and/or by reading fact-filled and not-too exciting textbooks, engage students in an immersive world has to perform a set of complex actions to achieve desired learning goals.

The advantage of this approach is that learning through performance requires active discovery, analysis, interpretation, problem solving, memory, and physical activity and results in the sort of extensive cognitive processing that deeply roots learning in a well developed neural network.The educational value of the game-playing experiences comes not from just the game itself, but from the creative coupling of educational media with effective pedagogy to engage students in meaningful practices.

On a cognitive level, play encourages the development of our concepts about the world. By toying with objects and ideas through playful experimentation we develop an understanding of the physical world and our place within it. But as games increase in complexity and freedom, they will be able to accommodate many different playing styles and personal goals, mirroring the inner dynamics of the player's personality.

The problem of narrative, of integrating a linear storyline within an interactive game is widely acknowledged as one of the most intractable problems in the field of games design. Although many techniques exist and will attract developers and gamers for a long time to come, none of them solve the hardest problem; creating a truly dynamic narrative, of creating virtual worlds or 'Mixed Realities' (e.g. outdoor and indoor) where, although the themes and imagery in the world remain consistent, the actions of different players lead to utterly different and credible outcomes.

To solve this problem, we need a way of designing a new learning game where teachers set the theme, the world-space where the game takes place, and the player can then explore and experience whatever permutations of that theme he or she desires. The possibility of different types of interactive narrative that are not bound to specific platforms or stationary mediums, using connected devices, GPS systems or networks (GPRS, UMTS) or multiple users seem limitless. The use of location to trigger events, the presence of other users experience the narrative in the near vicinity, even the ability to bring the narrative into the general culture are all possibilities with emerging technology.

The eMapps.com approach will also require the participants to draw upon a wide range of contextual content and to use new mobile devices in the creation and use of that content, whilst developing and playing game. Playful experiments with objects and ideas help develop our understanding of our place in the physical world.

6 The eMapps.com School Survey

In its early stages, eMapps.com has conducted and analysed a survey of the participating schools in order to establish a baseline on current use of games technology by children, as a starting point for its work. Data was collected from a sample of some 233 children in schools selected to participate in eMapps.com between October and December 2005 in the eight participating New Member States.

Q1. Do you own any of these game platforms?
There is relative uniformity among the schools, across the region, 2.3 platforms per respondent is average for boys, 2.0 for girls. PCs (boys 83%; girls 5%) and mobile phones (boys 60%; girls 77%) are by far the most common platforms among both boys and the girls. Ownership of mobile phones is slightly higher amongst girls. Amongst the 'proprietary' platforms, Sony Playstation (1 and 2) and Game Boy are owned by a significant proportion of respondents, although this amounts to under 20% of respondents in total. Ownership of Xbox or PSP and other platforms is as yet at a very low level.

Q2. Do you play games on any of the platforms listed in Q1?
About 90% of children responding use one or more of the platforms listed for playing games. Just over 60% of the children use PCs for playing games. Many have access to and use PCs to play games, even if they do not actually own them. Mobile phones are used for gaming by 43-44% of the children who own them. Levels of actual use of proprietary games platforms which the children own are high for Sony Playstation but lower for Game Boy.

Q3. What kind of game do you play? Please write down the game's name.
155 identifiable game titles were cited by boys and 148 by girls. The grouping of games by children in the selected schools appears to some extent to be function of peer emulation and/or access to specific titles at school or among schoolmates. The Polish children cited the widest variety of games. The popularity and use of individual game title is more widely dispersed among girls. An average of 2.8 games was cited by each of the boys. This figure was 2.0 for the girls. The suggestion may be that there are fewer attractive games available for girls. There is in general a wide dispersal of game titles cited: a majority of them is cited by only one child. Game titles for PCs and mobile phones are strongly represented. Nevertheless a clear top echelon of the most popular games emerged for the boys and the girls respectively. Action, military strategy and sports games are dominant among those played by the boys. Whilst there are some similarities in the list of top games cited by the girls, mobile phone games are more popular and sports games in particular are less popular. The Sims is by some distance the most popular game title.

Q4. How often and for how long do you play games?
The boys are significantly heavier and more regular players of games than the girls. 53% of boys play games every day as opposed to 27% of girls Differences in access may account for some of the variation between schools in different countries. Only in Lithuania do a majority of the girls play every day. Only in Czech Republic do a minority of the boys play every day.

Q5. Do you have an Internet connection at home?
54% of the boys and 57% of the girls have an Internet connection at home. There is a wide variety of types of Internet connections available at the children's homes. 86% of the boys and 75% of the girls who have a connection have a broadband connection. The proportion of children with an Internet connection at home appears to be significantly lower for the Slovakian schools than in the other countries.

Q6. Do you play games at school as part of the learning process?
More than half of the children regard themselves as playing games at school as part of the learning process. A higher proportion of girls than boys regard themselves as playing games at school as part of the learning process. There is significant variation between countries, possibly depending upon practice and facilities in the selected schools.

7 Alternate Reality Games (ARG)

The eMapps.com approach is based on ARG. Unlike other game genres, ARG have no defined playing field or game space but involve immersive, real world encounters which transcend the limitations of the Internet and reach into the everyday world of the player. They can utilise pre-set scenarios, which represent reality graphically and fragmented narratives which the players are required to reassemble.

By their very nature ARG bring together groups of players together into communities that work cooperatively and collectively in an environment of 'Unrealised Reality' to solve the mysteries of the game. ARG allow interactive authoring whereby the creators are able to observe the players virtually in real time and react to what they are doing and feeling. Equally, players can be motivated by being able to affect what happens in the game. Games are built with multiple levels; players can not move into a higher level until competence is displayed at the current level.

Although ARG originate and take place predominantly online, they employ mobile and other digital devices and allow simultaneous multi-channel communication.

Students are motivated when presented with meaningful and rewarding activities. Games represent a performance-based environment. Learners are gradually challenged with greater levels of difficulty in a progression that allows them to be successful in incremental steps. In this context, games engage users in pursuit of goals, allowing individual students opportunity to assess their own learning and/or compare it to that of others. They can be played with others (e.g. multi-player games) or involve communities of users interested in the same game. Games also allow users to transfer information from an existing context to a novel one.

Three aspects of entertaining digital games help make them intrinsically motivating: challenge, fantasy, and curiosity.

- the player must be able to tangibly affect the outcome of the game
- there must be an overriding goal/challenge as well as sub-goals and challenges to the player with positive and negative outcomes based on their actions
- the game must require mental or physical skill

- the outcome must be uncertain at the outset
- they must require the player to develop strategies in order to win or succeed
- they must offer multiple paths to success
- players must be able to ultimately overcome most obstacles in the game.

The narrative in eMapps.com games is a combination of different factors implementing the narrative implements some of the concepts from games that are played on platforms such as Play Station, Nintendo, Pc, and PSP but at the same time have a strong ARG component.

ARG games are fundamentally cooperative and collective, because of the nature of Internet. By their very nature they bring groups of players together into communities that work collectively to solve the mysteries of the game. They have no defined or implicit rules for playing. There is no simulation of a virtual world through a symbolic interface. The only interfaces in alternate reality games appear to be the same ones regularly used to communicate with the real world. In ARG, rules exist but they are not defined or written out anywhere the player learns these rules through his observation of and interaction with the game. ARG games allow "interactive authoring" so the creators are able to watch the players virtually in real time, as they experience the game, and react to what players are doing and feeling, immediately if necessary.

8 The eMapps.com Platform

The eMapps.com games platform will enable the implementation of ARG. It runs on digital devices such as mobile phones, PDA, Tablet PC over GPRS and UMTS networks and includes game control mechanisms, forum, chat and pre-set map-based local scenarios. The games are played on an open platform through multiple networks and devices. Weblogs, podcasts and videocasts are key components.

'Pins' located in a pre-set scenario (map-based) are linked to information placed in independently edited photo, audio, video and text 'blog' folders, using 'drag and drop'. Any mobile device that supports a browser can be used for uploading the content to any folder. The map also supports external links.

The map is a Graphical Interface that interacts with objects and can be used for mapping existing objects in a given territory, based on UTM Coordinates. The map also has a route editor and comes with a series of tools zoom in and out and move up/down/right/left.

The Graphical Interface is independent of the network or software used for uploading. The map supports unlimited amount of layers ranking from satellite images, aerial images, and maps created ad hoc: these layers are geo-referenced over the original map. The Graphical interface supports any language.

The pin and map information is saved in XML format. An application that works on smart phones, Pocket PC, lap tops that support browser and multiple operating systems (Symbian, Windows, Unix) is being implemented since the platform needs to know who is calling in order to serve the information effectively.

9 Conclusions

eMapps.com will provide a means of designing a new learning game where teachers set the theme, the world-space where the game takes place, and the player can then explore and experience whatever permutations of that theme he or she desires. This approach will also require the participants to draw upon a wide range of contextual content and to use new mobile devices in the creation and use of that content, whilst developing and playing games. The results will have a significant impact in validating new learning paradigms in both school and informal settings and will contribute to strategic thinking about the school and curriculum reform process in the New Member States and more widely across Europe.

References

1. Information and communication technologies in schools: a handbook for teachers or how ICT Can Create New, Open Learning Environments, UNESCO 2005
2. Sefton-Green, J.   NESTA FutureLabs Report 7. Literature Review in Informal Learning with Technology Outside School, 2005.
3. Newhouse, Dr Paul C. A Framework to Articulate the Impact of ICT on Learning in Schools Developed by for the Western Australian Department of Education, December, 2002
4. Godwin-Jones, B.   Messaging, Gaming, Peer-to-Peer Sharing: Language Learning Strategies & Tools for the Millennial Generation. Language Learning & Technology Vol. 9, No. 1, January 2005, pp. 17-22
5. Godwin-Jones,B. Language in Action: From Webquests to Virtual Realities. Virginia Commonwealth University Language Learning & Technology Vol. 8, No. 3, September 2004, pp. 9-14
6. Naismith, N, Lonsdale, P, Vavoula, G, Sharples M. Literature Review in Mobile Technologies and Learning. A Report for NESTA Futurelab, 2005
7. Hawkey, R. Learning with Digital Technologies in Museums, Science Centres and Galleries A Report for NESTA Futurelab, 2005
8. Kirriemuir, J, McFarlane, A. Literature Review in Games and Learning. A Report for NESTA Futurelab, 2005.

Bayesian Student Models Based on Item to Item Knowledge Structures

Michel C. Desmarais and Michel Gagnon

École Polytechnique de Montréal
{michel.desmarais, michel.gagnon}@polymtl.ca

Abstract. Bayesian networks are commonly used in cognitive student modeling and assessment. They typically represent the item-concepts relationships, where items are observable responses to questions or exercises and concepts represent latent traits and skills. Bayesian networks can also represent concepts-concepts and concepts-misconceptions relationships. We explore their use for modeling item-item relationships, in accordance with the theory of *knowledge spaces*. We compare two Bayesian frameworks for that purpose, a standard Bayesian network approach and a more constrained framework that relies on a local independence assumption. Their performance is compared over their respective ability to predict item outcome and through simulations over two data sets. The simulation results show that both approaches can effectively perform accurate predictions, but the constrained approach shows higher predictive power than a Bayesian Network. We discuss the applications of item to item structure for cognitive modeling within different contexts.

1 Introduction

There is considerable interest in the use of Bayesian networks (BN) for student modeling and cognitive assessment (for eg., [14,2,18,19]). In part, this interest stems from the ability of a BN to model the uncertainty that is inherent to cognitive modeling. Moreover, BN lend themselves to automatic learning and offer an attractive alternative to the difficult and error prone effort to parametrize a student model by means of human expertise. Finally, this interest can also be attributed to the fact that the field of BN has progressed at a rapid and sustained pace in the last two decades. It has now matured to a level where commercial and open source software packages and libraries allow their use in a relatively simple manner.

The studies on the use of BN in student models have, to our knowledge, exclusively dealt with modeling relationships from test item responses to concepts and misconceptions, and between concepts and misconceptions themselves. However, items also have an internal structure according to the theory of *knowledge spaces* [6]. Doignon et al. [6] have shown that the structure among items is determined by the order that constrains their learning in time. This order allows the inference of *mastered* (or *non mastered*) items, thereby allowing the assessment of

W. Nejdl and K. Tochtermann (Eds.): EC-TEL 2006, LNCS 4227, pp. 111–124, 2006.

an individual's state of knowledge from partial evidence, akin to the process of evidence propagation in a Bayesian network.

We describe two approaches to building item to item structures and how to use them for cognitive diagnostic. The first approach incorporates a specific method of inducing the structure of item to item structures. It is combined with an inference model based on simple posterior probability model under the assumption of local independence. The second approach is a generic approach of inducing the structure of a BN and performing inference within such structures. First, we describe theoretical underpinning of item to item structures. It is followed by the description of each approach and by a performance comparison to assess their respective ability to predict item outcome.

2 Item to Item Node Structures and the Theory of Knowledge Spaces

Item to item structures depart from the more common way of building student models, which is based on a hierarchy of concepts with items at the bottom of the hierarchy (see, for eg. [13,19,18]). In contrast to hierarchical structures, item to item structures build structures among observable knowledge item themselves [9,6], bypassing concept links. A number of researchers have worked on the problem of building student models within this framework [8,12]. Our own work on Partial Order Knowledge Structures (POKS) [4,5] falls under this line of research as well.

The theory of knowledge spaces asserts that *knowledge items*, i.e. observable elements such as question items, are mastered in a constrained order. Knowledge items define an individual's *knowledge state* as a subset of items that are mastered by that individual. The knowledge space determines which other knowledge state the person can move to. Viewed differently, the knowledge space defines the structure of prerequisites among knowledge items. For example, we learn to solve figure 1's problems in an order that complies with the inverse of the arrow directions. It follows from this structure that if one masters knowledge item (c), it is likely she will also master item (d). Conversely, if she fails item (c), she will likely fail item (a). However, item (c) does not significantly inform us about item (b). This structure defines the following possible knowledge states (subsets of the set $\{a, b, c, d\}$):

$$\{\emptyset, \{d\}, \{c, d\}, \{b, d\}, \{b, c, d\}, \{a, b, c, d\}\}$$

Other knowledge states are deemed impossible (or *unlikely* in a probabilistic framework).

Formally, it can be shown that a directed acyclic graph (DAG), such as the one in figure 1, can represent a knowledge space closed under union and intersection. Closure under union and intersection implies that if we combine two people's knowledge state, it is a valid subset of the knowledge space, and so is the intersection of their two states. We refer to such structures as *partial order knowledge structures*, or POKS. They represent a variant of the general theory

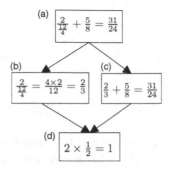

Fig. 1. A simple knowledge space composed of 4 items ($\{a, b, c, d\}$). The partial order constrains possible knowledge states to $\{\emptyset, \{d\}, \{b, d\}, \{c, d\}, \{b, c, d\}, \{d, b, c, a\}\}$. In the Knowledge space Theory, the arrows represent *surmise* relations ($\succ$) that determine the order in which we acquire the knowledge items, represented by the graph nodes.

of knowledge space which assumes closure only under union. The assumption of closure under union and intersection allows a considerable reduction the space of knowledge states. It greatly simplifies the algorithms for inducing a knowledge structure from data and reduces the amount of data cases required.

It can be seen that the theory of knowledge spaces and its POKS derivative make no attempt to structure knowledge in a hierarchy of concepts or any other structure containing latent variables (often called *latent traits*). The knowledge state of an individual is solely defined in terms of observable manifestations of skills such as test question. Of course, that does not preclude the possibility to re-structure knowledge items into higher level concepts and skills. In fact, this precisely is what a teacher does for developing a quiz or an exam, for example.

2.1 Partial Order Knowledge Structures and Bayesian Networks

Although POKS graphs like the one in figure 1 can be conveniently represented graphically by a DAG that resembles to a BN, the semantics of links is different. BN directed links usually represent causal relationships (although they can represent any kind of probabilistic relationship) and the structure explicitly represents conditional independence between variables. A knowledge space link is similar to a logical implication relation, but it represents a prerequisite, or, to use Doignon and Falmagne terminology, a *surmise* relation. For example, if we have a surmise relation $A \succ B$, it implies that the mastery of B will precede the mastery of A, and thus if a student has a success at for A, that student is likely to have a success for B. Moreover, its structure represents a partial ordering of the order in which items are likely to be learned.

That difference in the semantics of links has a number of implications. For one, the closures under *union* and *intersection* of POKS implies that, given a relation $A \rightarrow B$, or in the poks framework $A \succ B$, the absolute frequency of people who master a knowledge item A will necessarily be smaller or equal to the frequency of B. This conclusion does not hold for the case of general BN. For example, assume figure 1's structure is the following (a BN taken from Neapolitan, 2004):

(a) smoking history
(b) bronchitis
(c) lung cancer
(d) fatigue

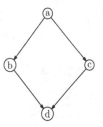

It is clear that *smoking history* (a) can be a much more frequent state than *lung cancer* (c) and *bronchitis* (b). This could not happen in POKS. The frequency of (a) cannot be higher than that of (b) and (c). It is also obvious that, whereas the occurrence *lung cancer* could decrease the probability of *bronchitis* by *discounting* (or *"explaining away"*) that later cause as a plausible explanation for *fatigue*, *discounting* does not play a role in the case of knowledge structures (eg. observing node (c) in Figure 1 would not decrease the probability of (b)).

In short, many interactions found in general BN do not occur in POKS. We conjecture that this reduction in the space of possibilities that characterizes POKS, namely the closure under *union* and *intersection*, can be used to infer knowledge structures with algorithms that rely upon stronger assumptions and more constrained search spaces than for the more general BN models.

In fact, structural induction techniques tailored to the Knowledge structures and the POKS frameworks have been devised by a number of researchers. For example, Kambouri et al. [12] introduced a semi-automated algorithm to construct knowledge structures. They developed an application that combines the use of empirical and an interactive question-answer process with domain experts to successfully construct knowledge structures. Their approach allows the construction of knowledge structures closed under union only, which implies it can represent alternative prerequisites. However, the construction process requires human intervention and cannot be considered as automated learning.

In the current study, we focus on the construction of item to item structures solely from learning approaches. The next section describes a BN learning approach over item to item structures, and a constraint-based structural learning approach to induce POKS.

3   Induction and Inference with Partial Order Knowledge Structures

The topology of an item to item structure can be fairly intertwined and complex. Inducing that structure is a difficult task to perform manually. It entails determining the order of mastery among knowledge items. If the set of knowledge items is large, over a few tens of items for example, our own experience is that this task can be very tedious and error prone.

Thus, finding means of learning the item to item knowledge structures from empirical data is imperative. We study two means of learning item to item structures:

- Bayesian Network structural learning;
- a POKS learning and inference algorithm.

Each approach is discussed below. Experiments to compare their respective performance for predicting item responses outcomes is reported later.

3.1 Bayesian Network Structural Learning for POKS

In spite of the semantic differences between the links of a BN and those of a POKS, the relations of both structures can be thought of as probabilistic implications between nodes. Both can represent evidence that influences the probabilities of neighboring nodes taking on values of true or false, in accordance to a Bayesian framework. It follows that any BN structural learning algorithm is a reasonable candidate for learning item to item structures.

We conducted a study on learning item to item BN structures with the K2 and PC algorithms:

K2 The K2 algorithm [3] is based on a Bayesian method that looks for the most probable structure given the observed distribution. It uses a greedy search algorithm over the space of network topologies.

PC The PC algorithm [17] falls into the *constraint-based structural learning* approach. It uses conditional independence tests with a given level of significance to determine the structure.

These algorithms are regularly used in the BN learning literature. For the K2 algorithm, the general principle is to maximize the probability of a given topology given observed data. Cooper et al. [3] originally used a Bayesian metric, but the well known BIC (Bayesian Information Criterion) is also used. The algorithm performs a local search constrained by a given node ordering pattern to reduce the search space. That order is a topological order which defines a subspace of the permissible DAGs. For our experiments, the initial order is obtained first using the Maximum Weight Spanning Tree (MWST) algorithm by [1] to derive a network topology, and by extracting a topological order from this structure. François et al. [10] have shown that the initial DAG obtained by the MWST is an effective replacement to a random ordering.

We used Ken Murphy's BNT package for learning the BN structures of all the experiments conducted (http://www.cs.ubc.ca/~murphyk/Software/BNT/bnt.html). The results are reported in the section 4.

3.2 POKS Structural Induction

The second approach we study for inducing the relations among items is based on [5,4].

This approach can be considered a constraint-based structural learning approaches since it uses conditional independence tests to determine the structure (see [16]).

The POKS induction algorithm relies on a pairwise analysis of item to item relationships [4]. The analysis attempts to identify the order in which we master knowledge items in accordance to the theory of knowledge spaces [6] but under the stronger assumption that the skill acquisition order can be modeled by a DAG.

The tests to establish a relation $A \succ B$ consists in three conditions for which a statistical test is applied:

$$P(B|A) \geq p_c \tag{1}$$
$$P(\overline{A}|\overline{B}) \geq p_c \tag{2}$$
$$P(B|A) \neq P(B) \tag{3}$$

Conditions (1) and (2) respectively correspond to the ability to predict that B is true given that A is observed true (*mastered*), and the ability that A is false (*non mastered*) given that B is false. The third condition verifies that the conditional probabilities are different from the non conditional probabilities (i.e. there is an interaction between the probability distributions of A and B). These conditions are verified by a Binomial test with parameters:

p_c the minimal conditional probability of equations (1) and (2),
α_i the alpha error tolerance level.

For this study, p_c is set at 0.5. Condition (3) is the independence test verified through a χ^2 statistic with an alpha error $\alpha_i < 0.2$. The high values of alpha errors maximize the number of relations we retain. See [4] and [5] for further details about the parameters.

3.3   Inferences

Once we obtain an item to item structure, an assessment of the probability of success over all items can be computed from partial evidence. In other words, we wish to evaluate the validity of the two frameworks over their item outcome predictive ability. We do not attempt to assess the actual item to item structures themselves because we have no mean to determine their respective true structure. In fact, that issue belongs to the field of cognitive science and was already thoroughly investigated by Doignon and Falmagne (see [6]) and a number of other researchers. Our interest lies in the predictive power of the models which is measured by their ability to perform accurate assessment.

3.4   Inference in BN

For the BN structure, there exist a number of standard and well documented algorithms (see, for eg.,[16]). We use the junction-tree algorithm [11] which performs an exact computation of posterior probabilities within a tree whose vertices's and derived from a triangulated graph, which is itself derived from the DAG in the BN.

3.5   Inference in POKS

For the POKS framework, computation of the nodes' probabilities are essentially based on standard bayesian posteriors under the local independence assumption.
Given a series of relations:

$$E_1 \succ H, E_2 \succ H, \cdots, E_n \succ H$$

where E_i stands for an evidence node (parent) and H stands for a hypothesis node (child), the likelihood ratio of H is computed according to the following equation :

$$O(H \mid E_1, E_2, \ldots, E_n) = O(H) \prod_i^n \frac{P(E_i \mid H)}{P(E_i \mid \overline{H})} \tag{4}$$

In case the evidence is negative for observation i, then the ratio $\frac{P(\overline{E_i} \mid H)}{P(\overline{E_i} \mid \overline{H})}$ is used.
We refer the reader to [5] for more details.

In the current study, we do not use transitive/recursive propagation to perform inference based on partial evidence as was done for previous studies with POKS [5,4]. Instead, we rely on the fact that if we have strong surmise relations $A \succ B \succ C$, then we would also expect to find $A \succ C$ according to the POKS structural learning algorithm. In other words, if we have $A \succ B$ and $B \succ C$, no probability update is performed over C upon the observation of A, unless a link $A \succ C$ is explicitly derived from the data.

The departure from the original POKS framework [4] makes the model simpler. It avoids the definition of a scheme to propagate partial evidence: propagating evidence from A to C in a structure like $A \succ B \succ C$, for example. Given that we expect partial evidence inferences to result in direct, transitive relations, the results are expected to be very similar. This was confirmed in our own experimental results that show that the performance is very close between the two alternatives.

4   Predictive Comparison of the BN and POKS Structural Learning Approaches

The BN and POKS structural learning approaches are compared over their ability to predict item response outcome. We use data from real tests to conduct simulations and measure the performance of each approach for predicting the outcome over the full set of item answers from a subset of observed answers. This validation technique is identical to the ones used by Vomlel [19] and by Desmarais et al. [5].

4.1   Simulation Methodology

The experiment consists in simulating the question answering process with the real subjects. An item is chosen and the outcome of the answer, success or failure, is fed to the inference algorithm. An updated probability of success is computed given this new evidence. All items for which the probability is above 0.5 is considered mastered and all others are considered non-mastered. We then compare the results with the real answers to obtain a measure of how accurate the predictions are. The process is repeated from 0 items administered until all items are "observed". Observed items take their true value, such that after all items are administered, the score always converges to 1.

The choice of the question to ask is determined by an entropy reduction optimization algorithm. The same algorithm is used for the BN and POKS frameworks (for details on this algorithm, see [19,5]). Essentially, the choice of the next question to administer corresponds to the one that reduces the entropy of a set of network nodes. Items with very high or low probability of success are generally excluded because their expected entropy reduction value will be low.

4.2   Data Sets

The data sets are taken from the results of two tests administered to human subjects :

1. **Arithmetic test.** Vomlel [19] gathered data from 149 pupils who completed a 20 question items test of basic fraction arithmetic for grade 6–8 pupils.
2. **UNIX shell command test.** The last data set is composed of 47 test results over a 33 question item test on knowledge of different Unix shell commands. The question range from simple and essential commands (eg. *cd*, *ls*), to more complex data processing utilities (eg. *awk*, *sed*) and system administration tools (eg. *ps*, *chgrp*).

For each data set, a portion of the data is used for training and the remaining ones for testing. Table 1 provides the size of the training and testing sets along with the average success rate of each test.

For each data set, six training and test sets were randomly sampled from both corpus. All performance reports represent the average over all six sampled sets.

4.3   Simulation Parameters

A number of parameters must be set for the different algorithms used.

The BN parameters for both the K2 and PC algorithms were initialized with Dirichlet uniform priors, which correspond to Beta priors in the case of binomial variables.

For the PC algorithm, recall that it relies on a conditional independence test. The significance level chosen for this test in our experiment is 0.2, the same value as the one used for the POKS interaction test (see below).

For the POKS structural learning, two parameters need to be set. They are:

$$p_c = 0.5 \text{ and } \alpha_i = 0.2$$

These values were also used in [4] and they are generally appropriate when the number of nodes is below 50.

Table 1. Data sets

Data set	nb. items	nb. data cases			Average success rate
		Training	Test	Total	
Arithmetic	20	100	49	149	61%
Unix	33	30	17	47	53%

The simulations are run with Ken Murphy's BNT package (http://www.cs. ubc.ca/~murphyk/Software/BNT/bnt.html). Note that it was not possible to test the PC algorithm for the Unix test because it resulted in an error with Matlab©.

4.4 Learned Structures

Over all six randomly sampled sets, the POKS structural learning algorithm created structures that, for the arithmetic data set, contains between 181 and 218 relations, of which 117 to 126 are symmetric, for an average between 9.1 to 10.9 links per node. For the Unix data set, the number of relations varies between 582 and 691, and the number of symmetric relations varies between 348 and 297, and average relations per node that varies between 17.6 to 20.9. The structure of the Unix data set is thus much more populated with an average link per node about twice that of the arithmetic test.

For the BN structural learning results, figure 2 displays the first two structures learned with the K2 algorithm. Recall that the structures of both the K2 and PC algorithms were constrained to 1 parent. It can be seen that the topology differs significantly between the two network shown in this figure. In general, about only half of the relations are common between BN from two samples. However and as mentioned, we do not focus on the actual topologies in this study but solely on the ability of the induced structures to perform accurate inferences.

Processing time for learning differs significantly between the two BN structural learning algorithms.

For the arithmetic data, we obtained these values on a 1Ghz pentium PC running Linux :

PC: ≈ 1080 seconds and K2: ≈ 3 seconds

Learning time for the POKS algorithm is considerably faster than both. It stands around $80ms$. However, these numbers should be interpreted with care as the POKS algorithm is a C program whereas the BN software runs under Matlab. Nevertheless, the POKS algorithm has order $O(ni^2)$ time complexity, where n is the number of cases and i is the number of item nodes, which is far less than the K2 algorithm ($O(ni^4)$ for the current context).

On the performance of the evidence propagation algorithms, the total simulation time for the BN varied between 2120 seconds to 2609 seconds. This is again orders of magnitude greater than for the POKS algorithm which took about 1 second per simulation. Each simulation involves looping over 49 cases and, for each for each of the 20 question item, performing on average 19 inferences

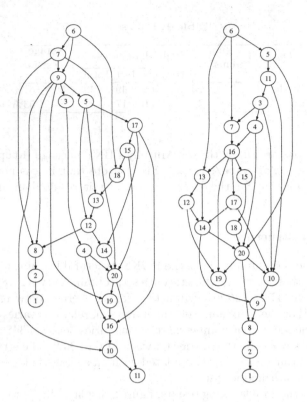

Fig. 2. Two examples of BN structures learned with the K2 algorithm

($n-1$ items). To find the average time of an inference we would thus divide each simulation time by $49 * 20 * 19 = 18,620$.

4.5   Results

The performance results are averaged over all test subjects and random samples. The formula for computing the accuracy of the prediction after each observed item is:

$$\text{Accuracy} = \frac{\sum_i^r \sum_j^m \sum_k^n M_{ijk}}{rmn}$$

where r is the total number items in the test, m is the number of random sample runs of the simulation (6), and n is the number of test subject cases (17 for the Unix test and 49 for the arithmetic test). M_{ijk} represents the item outcome prediction to item i by subject k for the simulation run j. It is 1 if the prediction is correct or if it is an observed item, and 0 otherwise.

Figure 3 reports the simulations results for the item outcome predictive performance. It shows that, for both data sets, the POKS algorithm yields more accurate predictions than the two BN algorithms. Although the difference is only a few percentage points, it is relatively significant. For example, after 20 items,

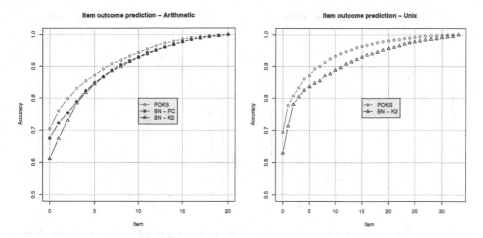

Fig. 3. Item prediction performance for the Arithmetic and Unix tests. Each line represents the average over all 49 test cases and over 6 simulation samples.

the difference between the BN and POKS for the Unix data set is about 95% compared to 98%. Although this represents a 3% difference in absolute values, it should be regarded relative to error reduction. In terms of the remaining error, it represents a 60% relative reduction. Viewed from a different perspective, it means that the accuracy reached by POKS after 20 of the 33 item Unix test is only reached after about 27 items for the BN K2 algorithm. In a context where, for example, we need strong confidence that a specific item is mastered and avoid mistakes, the difference in reliability can be significant.

Looking at the relative error reduction between both tests, we note that the performance difference between algorithms is greater for the Unix than for the arithmetic test. This is potentially due to the fact that this test was meant to discriminate between a wide range of expertise, from basis file manipulation commands to sophisticated data manipulation scripts, whereas the arithmetic test is more focused on closely related skills and notions. The ordering between items that is typical of knowledge structures is more likely to appear for the Unix than the arithmetic test.

We also note that the PC algorithm performs better than the K2 algorithm, apparently due to more accurate priors. However, the difference quickly vanishes after 2 items are observed.

To obtain an estimate of the statistical significance of the performance results, Figure 4 reports the variability of the estimates across subjects. The plot represents the quartiles for the different algorithms. The boxes contain a line indicating the median and span over roughly the upper and lower quartiles around it. The 'whiskers' represent the outer quartiles and outliers are shown by themselves. The arithmetic simulation results of Figure 4 contains two series of boxes for the BN results that respectively correspond to the PC and K2 algorithms, whereas the Unix contains only the K2 algorithm results.

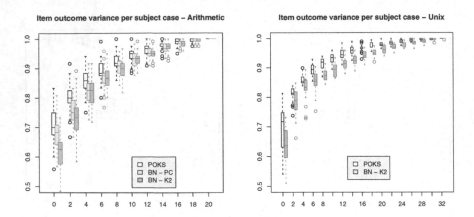

Fig. 4. Box plot of the variance across subjects. Central quartiles are within the box whereas the two extreme quartiles are represented by the "whiskers".

5 Discussion

This study shows that item to item structures can be constructed from data and yield effective predictions of item outcome. Two approaches were investigated, namely standard BN induction techniques and the POKS framework, which stands closer to the Naive Bayes family of models.

Experiments over the two data sets show that the POKS framework yields better predictive results for item outcome prediction than does the general BN framework. Although the strong performance of a Naive Bayes framework is by no means uncommon [7], we conjecture that, for this study, it is consequent with the constrained nature of POKS: knowledge spaces closed under union and intersection. The assumptions made by the POKS framework may be appropriate for the knowledge spaces and, consequently, allow the framework to be applied effectively with small data sets as the ones we experimented with.

Item to item student models are based solely on observable variables. This implies that they can readily be learned through standard and general BN structural learning techniques, or through more specialized techniques such as POKS. The absence of hidden variables makes the learning more robust and more efficient. The POKS approach is particularly efficient for both learning and inference.

These models yield prediction of item responses. As such, they can be used to assess higher level concepts or skills, much in the same manner as we would use test results to assess the mastery of a topic or diagnose learning difficulties. However, they do not model misconceptions, nor build link from specific answers to specific skills or misconceptions as BN can do. Some tutoring systems require such diagnostic in order to provide more relevant remedial material for a student. Nevertheless, their simplicity and the possibility of learning item to item models with relatively small data samples makes them very attractive for many learning systems such as study guides.

Acknowledgments

We are grateful to Jiří Vomlel for providing the data used in this experiment This work has been supported by the National Research Council of Canada.

References

1. C. Chow and C. Liu. Approximating discrete probability distributions with dependence trees. *IEEE Trans. Information Theory*, 14(11):462–467, November 1968.
2. C. Conati, A. Gertner, and K. VanLehn. Using Bayesian networks to manage uncertainty in student modeling. *User Modeling and User-Adapted Interaction*, 12(4):371–417, 2002.
3. Gregory F. Cooper and Edward Herskovits. A Bayesian method for the induction of probabilistic networks from data. *Machine Learning*, 9:309–347, 1992.
4. Michel C. Desmarais, Ameen Maluf, and Jiming Liu. User-expertise modeling with empirically derived probabilistic implication networks. *User Modeling and User-Adapted Interaction*, 5(3-4):283–315, 1996.
5. Michel C. Desmarais and Xiaoming Pu. A bayesian inference adaptive testing framework and its comparison with item response theory. *International Journal of Artificial Intelligence in Education*, 15:291–323, 2005.
6. J.-P. Doignon and J.-C. Falmagne. *Knowledge Spaces*. Springer-Verlag, Berlin, 1999.
7. Pedro Domingos and Michael Pazzani. On the optimality of the simple Bayesian classifier under zero-one loss. *Machine Learning*, 29:103–130, 1997.
8. Cornelia E. Dowling and Cord Hockemeyer. Automata for the assessment of knowledge. *IEEE Transactions on Knowledge and Data Engineering*, 2001.
9. J.-C. Falmagne, M. Koppen, M. Villano, J.-P. Doignon, and L. Johannesen. Introduction to knowledge spaces: How to build test and search them. *Psychological Review*, 97:201–224, 1990.
10. O. François and P. Leray. Etude comparative d'algorithmes d'apprentissage de structure dans les réseaux bayésiens. In *RJCIA03*, pages 167–180, 2003.
11. Finn Verner Jensen. *An introduction to Bayesian Networks*. UCL Press, London, England, 1996.
12. Maria Kambouri, Mathieu Koppen, Michael Villano, and Jean-Claude Falmagne. Knowledge assessment: tapping human expertise by the query routine. *International Journal of Human-Computer Studies*, 40(1):119–151, 1994.
13. Eva Millán, José-Luis Pérez de-la Cruz, and Eva Surez. Adaptive Bayesian networks for multilevel student modelling. In *ITS'00: Proceedings of the 5th International Conference on Intelligent Tutoring Systems*, pages 534–543. Springer-Verlag, 2000.
14. Robert J. Mislevy, Russell G. Almond, Duanli Yan, and Linda S. Steinberg. Bayes nets in educational assessment: Where the numbers come from. In Kathryn B. Laskey and Henri Prade, editors, *Proceedings of the 15th Conference on Uncertainty in Artificial Intelligence (UAI-99)*, pages 437–446, S.F., Cal., July 30–August 1 1999. Morgan Kaufmann Publishers.
15. Kevin P. Murphy. The Bayes net toolbox for MATLAB. Technical report, University of California at Berkeley; Berkeley , CA, October 12 2001.
16. R. E. Neapolitan. *Learning Bayesian Networks*. Prentice Hall, New Jersey, 2004.

17. Peter Spirtes, Clark Glymour, and Richard Scheines. *Causation, Prediction, and Search*. The MIT Press, Cambridge, Massachusetts, 2 edition, 2000.
18. Kurt VanLehn, Zhendong Niu, Stephanie Siler, and Abigail S. Gertner. Student modeling from conventional test data: A Bayesian approach without priors. In *ITS'98: Proceedings of the 4th International Conference on Intelligent Tutoring Systems*, pages 434–443, London, UK, 1998. Springer-Verlag.
19. Jiří Vomlel. Bayesian networks in educational testing. *International Journal of Uncertainty, Fuzziness and Knowledge Based Systems*, 12(Supplementary Issue 1):83–100, 2004.

Towards Community-Driven Development of Educational Materials: The Edukalibre Approach

Jesus M. Gonzalez-Barahona[1], Vania Dimitrova[2], Diego Chaparro[1],
Chris Tebb[2], Teofilo Romera[1], Luis Canas[1], and Julika Matravers[2],
and Styliani Kleanthous[2]

[1] Grupo de Sistemas y Comunicaciones, Universidad Rey Juan Carlos, Mostoles,
Madrid, Spain
[2] School of Computing, University of Leeds, Leeds, UK
{jgb, dchaparro, teo, lcanas}@gsyc.escet.urjc.es,
{vania, chrispy, julika, stellak}@comp.leeds.ac.uk

Abstract. The libre software development model has shown how combining collective intelligence can lead to revolutionary methods that underpin major software advancements. This paper argues that the time is ripe to examine the application of this model to the development of educational materials where not only teachers but also students can become actively involved in the creation of educational content. The paper describes a novel, *truly open* platform, developed within the Edukalibre project [1], to support the creation of collaboratively constructed educational materials. The paper presents the Edukalibre collaborative editing system that provides easy access to core technologies composed of a document repository with version control management and conversion tools to produce several formats for each document. Two different collaborative editing interfaces - COLLAB and ConDOR - have been implemented. Based on evaluation studies with COLLAB and ConDOR, we discuss several pedagogical and technological issues related to the deployment of community-driven development of educational content.

1 Introduction

The libre [2] software development method has tremendously changed the way software is being produced and deployed [1,2] in a number of domains, ranging

---

[1] The Edukalibre project was funded by the European Commission's, Socrates/Minerva program, grant 110330-CP-1-2003-1ES-MINERVA-M. This paper reflects the views of the authors, and the Commission cannot be held responsible for any use which may be made of the information contained therein.

[2] We use the term "libre software" to refer both to "free software" and "open source software". The term "libre" lacks the ambiguity of "free" (which means both "gratis" and "free as in freedom"), and makes reference to the liberty of change that the user of the software gains with it. In short, libre (free, open source) software is defined by the freedom of use, study, modification and distribution that is granted to those receiving a copy of the programs.

W. Nejdl and K. Tochtermann (Eds.): EC-TEL 2006, LNCS 4227, pp. 125–139, 2006.
© Springer-Verlag Berlin Heidelberg 2006

from operating systems (Debian, FreeBSD, Fedora) to desktop environments (GNOME, KDE), web browsers (Mozilla, Firefox), web servers (Apache) or office suites (OpenOffice.org) [3,4,5,6]. It is now widely recognised that the libre software development model, where software is produced by communities of practitioners sharing experiences, methods, and code, has led to revolutionary methods that produced major advancements in software development [7,8].

This paper argues that the time is ripe to deploy the libre, community-driven development model to the creation of educational content. Following the impact on software development, it can be expected that the community-driven development model will lead to innovative educational paradigms and will have a great impact on the way the web is used for teaching and learning. There is a growing interest among the educational community to adopt aspects of the open development model. The first step is being undertaken by the *open learning content* idea which has been taken on board with great enthusiasm in university education[9], and has been implemented in a number of projects, e.g Open Learning Support [10], MIT OpenCourseware [11], Open Learning Initiative [12], Connextions [13], CASCADE[14], WIKI [15].

To fully deploy the community-driven development model both educational practitioners and students should become actively involved in the creation and distribution of open educational content. Until recently, technical challenges made it very difficult to support truly open, dynamic, educational resources constructed collaboratively by large groups of teachers and even students. Nowadays, the libre software community has created a vast amount of technologies to support their practices. However, these technologies have not been explored fully in an educational context. Moreover, many of the existing technologies for collaborative development of software suffer from two problems: (1) they are suitable for software developers but are not intuitive enough to be adopted by teachers and students and (2) they normally tackle small tasks, which is convenient for developers who usually use several tools, but can be inappropriate for use by wide and diverse teacher and learner communities.

New architectures are needed to effectively support the collaborative construction of open educational resources [16]. Moreover, these architectures should themselves be open, enabling customisation and deployment in different settings. An example of such an architecture is proposed in this paper. We describe a novel, *truly open* platform to support the creation of free, collaboratively constructed educational content. The platform was developed within the Edukalibre project [3] which examined the connection between libre software development and the creation of open content for education.

---

[3] The project was funded by the European Commission under the Socrates/Minerva program and ran in the period October 2003 - December 2005. It was coordinated by University Rey Juan Carlos (Spain), and included as partners teams from the University of Leeds (United Kingdom), University of Porto (Portugal), University of Karlsruhe (Germany), University of Lugano (Switzerland), and the Academy of Sciences of the Czech Republic. Project web site: http://www.edukalibre.org.

The paper will first discuss key characteristics of the community-driven development model and its link to the production of educational materials (Section 2). Section 3 will then present the architecture of the Edukalibre system. Two tools that provide a user interface to the system - COLLAB and ConDOR - will be described in Section 4. Section 5 will discuss the deployment of Edukalibre in university teaching. Finally, in the conclusions, we will discuss the contribution of Edukalibre to technology-enhanced learning and will outline future work.

2   Community-Driven Development and Education

The libre software community is one of the best examples of an online community within which there are smaller communities of practice [17] of people solving problems that arise within a particular project and producing solutions that can be used and modified by others [18,19]. The Edukalibre project explores how this community-driven development model can be applied to the education camp to facilitate collaborative development of educational materials. Therefore, we will first outline the key characteristics of the libre software model.

There are several specific issues found across most libre software projects, as discussed in [7,20,3]:

- Frequent and early release of software to enable opportunities to gain external feedback and contributions.
- Decentralised quality maintained by many individuals, including those outside the group of developers.
- Libre software projects, especially when of a certain size, are carried out by a number of geographically distributed developers. They seldom (if ever) see each other face-to-face, and work in a coordinated fashion without formal hierarchies.
- Development is done asynchronously by using software tools for coordination (e.g. mailing lists, bug tracking systems, version control systems, software repositories) and hosting facilities (e.g. SourceForge[4] or Savannah[5]).
- There is a mixture of voluntary and paid work.

In comparison, the deployment of a community-driven, libre development model to education may address the following issues:

Collaboration by educators: Materials will be produced by groups of educators, usually in different institutions, and geographically dispersed. Since the curricula are similar in many cases, it seems reasonable that different teachers have similar needs, and can collaborate in the making of their materials. The collaboration has the implication of sharing the work, coordination, and consensus. Similar situations are found in libre software projects, and it is expected that similar results can be obtained. In the current European context, where collaboration among universities of different countries is encouraged at many levels, this will

---

[4] http://sourceforge.net
[5] http://savannah.gnu.org

increasingly become a common situation, elements of which are demonstrated in several successful European projects, e.g. ARIADNE [6] and EducaNext [7].

Active contribution from students: Materials will also be used, commented, and possibly modified by students. In fact, in many cases, students are already producing their own materials, based on those provided by educators. In the same way that users can contribute to libre software projects highlighting bugs or even proposing useful modifications to the programs (if they have enough knowledge), students (users of the materials) can contribute to the continuous improving of quality. From this point of view, frequent and early release could be as important as it is in the case of libre software.

Intuitive tools: Educators and students will need simple to use, yet powerful, tools to be able to collaborate in the way libre software developers do. For instance, it will be important to mimic the functionality of version control systems and compilation systems, specifically oriented to the production of educational materials. At the same time, authors should be able to use tools in such a way that coordination and work in common is becomes an intuitive process.

Public availability: The public availability of produced materials will enable the collaboration of third parties, such as other professors or students from other institutions who may find the materials useful, and can contribute to their further development.

Agreed licensing terms: Several licensing terms may be explored, some of them allowing for publishers to take the materials and distribute them for profit, in the same way that there are companies distributing GNU/Linux based systems composed only of libre software. The current interest created by some initiatives related to open content (such as Creative Commons[8], the Open Archives Initiative[9], and the the Public Library of Science[10]) is caused by many other projects exploring, particularly in the scientific context, the advantages of this approach.

Of course, this model is difficult to explore without the proper tools and some user groups ready to test and try it, which was the main focus of the Edukalibre project. The following sections will present the Edukalibre system and will discuss case studies in university teaching environments.

3   The Edukalibre Collaborative Editing System

The Edukalibre system is composed of several software components, some of which are widely used in current libre software projects and others have been developed specifically within the project. The architecture of the system is intended to be simple, yet flexible, reusing as many already available components as possible, so that the project can focus on its goals whilst incorporating

---

[6] www.ariadne-eu.org
[7] www.educanext.org/ubp
[8] http://creativecommons.org
[9] http://www.openarchives.org/
[10] http://plos.org

already tested and widespread components, such as the Subversion[11] version control system or the Moodle[12] learning management system. The use of standards compliant technologies and ideology of open access to the different components of the system has been a core design principle. The Edukalibre system has been developed to be as open as possible, using libre software technologies throughout and allowing access to content in as many different ways as is practical.

This paper presents the collaborative editing part of the Edukalibre system. The complete Edukalibre suite of tools includes also a graphical interactive students monitoring tool and a Wiki compiler for mathematical formulas [13]. Collaborative editing with the Edukalibre system enables users to choose from a wide set of tools (from easy-to-use word processors, such as OpenOffice.org[14], to less common XML-based editors), and includes version control facilities and automatic conversion to many end-user formats (ranging from PDF, ready to be printed on paper, to decorated HTML, suitable for previewing when creating a new version or for reading online).

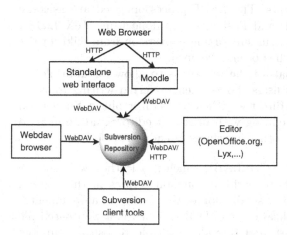

Fig. 1. Components of the collaborative editing subsystem

Figure 1 shows the architecture of the collaborative editing subsystem. The core is a *document repository*, built on top of a *version controlled storage system*, with document conversion and management tools written in **Python**[15] [21]. The main components of the Edukalibre collaborative editing system are:

Version control: Every document created in the system has a main version and a history of older revisions or branches. Each revision can be accessed or modified at any time, and any old revision can be set up as the main version of the document, or assigned as a new branch (for example to adapt higher education teaching materials for a secondary education audience). Currently, the platform uses Subversion as the control version system. Subversion is in some sense an evolution of the more traditional CVS[16], which fixes many of its problems, and adds new features.

---

[11] http://subversion.tigris.org/
[12] http://moodle.org
[13] See www.edukalibre.org for a complete description of all Edukalibre tools
[14] http://openoffice.org
[15] http://python.org
[16] http://www.cvshome.org

Editors and word processors: Our goal is not to create new editors, but to provide ways in which existing editors and word processors can interact in the most flexible way with the system. Authors already have their preferred tools, so our goal is to support as many authoring tools as possible, and offer the same version control and document conversion features to all authors, irrespective of their preferred editing application. The current Edukalibre platform allows a document to be opened, modified and stored using OpenOffice [17] which can edit, in addition to files in its own format, DocBook/XML[18] files (with the help of some code which the project has improved) and Microsoft Word documents. However, any other word processor can be used to modify the documents of the system, if it can manage DocBook/XML or LaTeX[19], the currently supported document formats. Since both are plain-text formats, any text editor can also be used, provided the user knows the syntax of the format. A simple web editor is also provided.

Tools for format conversion: Converting documents from the base formats to other formats more suitable for reading (such as HTML or PDF), is enabled via a suite of conversion tools. Most of the conversions from XML formats are performed using XSLT[20] stylesheets. The XSLT processors used are xsltproc and xalan[21]. Conversions to PDF and Postscript are done using TeX/LaTeX and Ghostscript[22]. A wiki-like system supporting conversion from wiki format to DocBook/XML and vice-versa has been developed.

Web interfaces: One of the goals of the project is to allow for multiple interfaces to the system, and to let users choose their preferred writing tools. In addition to accessing the system directly with a text editor plus a Subversion client (supporting command line editing with unix text editors and familiar to academics mainly in the IT field), other interfaces already provided are:

- A collaborative editing system (COLLAB), which is a Python-written web interface that permits authors to perform common actions in the system, such as listing of documents or visualization of the history of a document.
- A PHP-based groupware application (ConDOR), which is a web based file system view for the repository and provides multiple repository support together with discussion and messaging tools.

Communication protocols: Standard protocols are used to connect the different components. They include the ubiquitous HTTP [22], and WebDAV [23] (an extension to HTTP tailored to the needs of collaborative editing and management of files on remote web servers).

From the perspective of an author collaborating to write some material, the platform provides the two interfaces - COLLAB and ConDOR. Currently, both

---

[17] http://www.openoffice.org/
[18] http://www.docbook.org/
[19] http://www.latex-project.org/
[20] http://www.w3.org/TR/xslt
[21] http://xml.apache.org/xalan-j/
[22] http://www.cs.wisc.edu/~ghost/

interfaces are provided in two forms - as standalone web applications and as integrated components in Moodle. At the time Edukalibre evaluation studies were conducted, see next section, COLLAB was a standalone web interface, while ConDOR was integrated in Moodle. This enabled the evaluation of two types of access and tested the flexibility of the Edukalibre platform.

From the perspective of a developer wishing to incorporate access to an Edukalibre repository into their applications, the platform provides a simple PHP[23] API and Subversion/WebDAV access to the repository for other development platforms.

4   Collaborative Editing Interfaces

In the following subsections, the two collaborative editing interface applications implemented within Edukalibre are described. They show both how the functionality of the system can be integrated with external tools, and how the architecture is modular enough to make room for many different ways of interaction.

4.1   COLLAB: A Python-Driven Web Interface

This is one of the possible interfaces to the system, and allows the users to perform some of the common tasks using just a web browser. A screenshot of the COLLAB interface can be seen in Figure 2. The main page of the interface shows a list of documents in the system, with some information about each of the documents. The interface provides a way to create new documents. An RDF channel with information about the documents recently modified or created is also provided. The information for each document includes:

- Listing of its version history, with the release date and the comments from the release author.
- Listing of links to all end-user formats for every version, so that users can get any format of any version of any document.
- Editing and downloading options for each version, including the possibility to download the base format, modify it and upload the new version using the web interface, or to edit it on-line with a simple web editor.
- Forms to update the document, uploading a new version (written with a standalone editor such as OpenOffice.org).
- Decorated HTML version of the latest version of the document to show a quick preview.

4.2   ConDOR: An Intuitive PHP-Driven Groupware Application

One of the core deliverables of the project was to create a *user friendly* working environment which would allow us to evaluate the effectiveness of web-based Construction of Dynamic Open Resources (ConDOR), see Figure 3.

---

[23] http://php.net

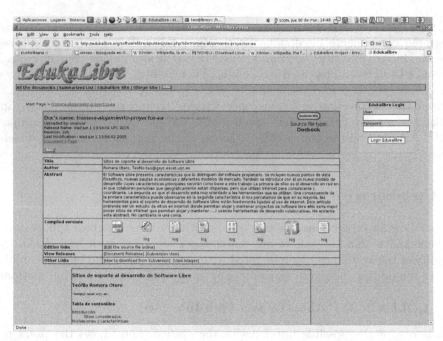

Fig. 2. COLLAB interface: example from evaluation study 3, described in Section 5

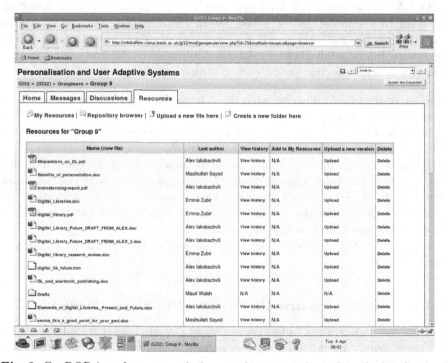

Fig. 3. ConDOR interface: example from evaluation study 2, described in Section 5

ConDOR is a bespoke groupware application which can run standalone, or as a modular component of the libre software learning management environment Moodle. The requirements specification for the groupware was taken from a questionnaire that was filled in by all partners of the project, enquiring into the scenarios in which the platform would be tested. ConDOR provides "explorer style" access to the document repository, allowing intuitive navigation of the file and folder structures, and simple tools for uploading files and creating new folders. To prevent excessive repeated navigation of large folder structures, a "My Resources" section is provided within the ConDOR resource area to allow authors to bookmark documents of special interest within the resource tree. From either the main resources browser or the "My Resources" area, authors can download a document in any supported format (currently XHTML, PDF, docbook and plain text), upload a new version of the document, browse the history of the document and add/remove documents from their "My Resources" list.

The repository allows authors to add any type of file, and put it under version control. Extra features such as format conversion are available for OpenOffice and LaTeX documents. In addition, trial users have been using the repository to manage different kinds of files. A graphic designer using the system used it to manage multiple versions of an Adobe Photoshop document he was working on with another designer, and a systems administrator has used the system to manage various versions of Windows configuration files.

5   Evaluation Studies

The evaluation of the Edukalibre system, given its libre nature, had to deal with several challenges. On the one hand, the highly iterative development process required frequent releases of software (sometimes not fully tested) and demanded quick feedback. On the other hand, user studies in real settings were required to examine the feasibility of the deployment of the libre development model in education. To address these challenges, a flexible, development-led evaluation approach was followed which included two phases - inspection by inspectors and several small scale studies with different Edukalibre tools. The Edukalibre evaluation is presented in detail elsewhere, see [24]. We will refer here only to user studies with COLLAB and ConDOR which highlighted important technological and pedagogical issues of the community-driven development of educational materials. The following user studies were conducted with the Edukalibre collaborative editing tools:

Study 1: Students preparing a group report on an environmental case using ConDOR. The study was conducted at the University of Karlsruhe with 14 students attending an advanced Industrial Engineering seminar [25]. Working in separate groups, the students spent four months researching environmental cases concerning fictitious companies. Each group produced a collaboratively written report based on materials collected by the members. The seminar was run with Moodle and the students used ConDOR for sharing resources and for collaborative writing. The process was monitored by 2 teachers via the Edukalibre student monitoring tool [26]. The students' feedback was collected with a questionnaire at the end of the seminar.

Study 2: Students preparing learning resources on a new topic using ConDOR. The study was conducted at the University of Leeds with 55 students attending a final year undergraduate course on Personalisation and User-adaptive Systems. The students were split into 13 groups. Each group had to research a topic new to them (e.g. personalisation for e-health, digital libraries, or e-learning) and prepare a report which, together with the supporting electronic resources collected, was later used as a learning material by the whole class. The course was run with Moodle and the students used ConDOR for the collaborative writing activities which spanned in one month. At the end, a questionnaire was conducted to collect the students' feedback.

Study 3: Students writing and commenting on papers using COLLAB. The study was conducted at the University Rey Juan Carlos with 24 PhD students who attended a three month course on libre software. The students had to prepare a paper on a topic relevant to the course. They had to help each other by editing and commenting on at least two of the papers being prepared by their peers. The students wrote their papers during the duration of the course and, at the same time, they could read and review papers by their peers. They used COLLAB to download, review and correct papers of their peers and to create and maintain their own papers. At the end of the course, a questionnaire was carried out to find out the users' opinions of the tools. Many of the participants were highly trained programmers, IT technicians or computer engineers, so they offered valuable feedback to the development team and also had less problems to use the tools, since they were familiar with concepts like version control systems and collaborative editing.

Study 4: Teachers preparing a course using COLLAB. The study was conducted at the Academy of Sciences of the Czech Republic. 4 teachers worked together on the preparation of a course on Bayesian Networks suitable for research students. The teachers undertook several iterations of the learning materials. The course included textual descriptions and interactive examples. The teachers gave informal feedback about the usefulness of the tool.

Due to space constraint, we cannot present full details of each study, the reader is directed to the corresponding papers [24,25] and project deliverables [24]. The following section will focus on lessons learned about the deployment of the libre development model to education, based on the combined results from the studies.

6   Using COLLAB and ConDOR for Community-Driven Development of Educational Materials

This section will focus on what the studies with COLLAB and ConDOR told us about the process of community-driven development of educational materials. The results can broadly be divided into pedagogical and technical aspects.

---

[24] Available from the project web site www.edukalibre.org

6.1   Pedagogical Aspects

Team work and collaborative writing. All studies exhibited the three stages of team work: *forming, functioning, finishing* [27]. Since the group members were familiar with each other, we expected that the forming would be quick and there would be a fair degree of trust among group members. However, most student groups had a slow start and the questionnaire results indicated trust problems. For example, 50% of the students in studies 1 and 2 were reluctant for others to be able to see what they write and 64% would not like their writings to be changed by others. In contrast, most participants (83%) in study 3 and all participants in study 4 were willing to share their incomplete writing so they could benefit from reviews, comments and corrections of their peers. Analysis of the discussions with ConDOR in study 2 showed that most groups spent considerable time clarifying the members' expertise and preferences and agreed on what section/subtopic each person was responsible for. The functioning phase showed that most participants actively used the collaborative editing tools. For example, 46% of the students using ConDOR felt that the tool helped them to be more efficient. Most concerns were with regard to the slow access to the document repository, yet 79% were positive that they could share resources with others. In study 2, several conflicts with regard to members' contribution arose and a spilt of three groups was inevitable. Some of the materials produced by the students were not fully coherent and included repetitive or contradicting opinions. The groups who were successful (judged by the quality of their reports) had one or two cognitively central members [27] who would take the leading role in decisions about structure, topics, or resources. In each study, all materials produced were made public to the other participants in the study. While in studies 1 and 2, other groups could only comment on the quality of the produced materials, in studies 3 and 4, everybody could not only comment but also alter what was produced by others. Students in studies 1 and 2 appreciated the feedback from their peers but required some kind of central comment from teachers. This indicates the need of some quality control that is not required in the libre development model (see Section 2) but is important in educational settings.

Building communities of practice. Clearly, there was learning benefit from all studies involving students. Students did not only practise researching a topic and writing materials to be used by others, but also became exposed to a wider set of opinions, engaged in discussions clarifying domain aspects, and became active participants in the course. The evaluation studies showed that the pedagogical impact from engaging students or educational practitioners in collaborative creation of educational materials would be associated with the forming of communities of practice where students and educational practitioners, often from the same or related background, are coming together to share ideas and experience and to tackle common problems and issues [28]. For example, the students in Study 3 spontaneously helped each other with comments, corrections and contributing sections to papers of their peers. Almost all of the students commented that the global quality of the papers they wrote grew because of the help they offered each other. Study 2 also showed elements of learning in communities: initial analysis of the group interactions indicates evidence that by sharing resources and ideas and engaging in a joint task the groups acquired knowledge and the members improved their understanding of the domain.

Integration within the learning environment. The Edukalibre experience showed that engaging students in the collaborative construction of educational materials would be effective only if it is integrated within the overall learning environment. Teachers involved in studies 1, 2, and 3 had to carefully design the collaborative writing exercises linking them to course learning objectives. This link was made clear to the students prior to each study. In studies 1 and 2, which were conducted with undergraduate students, the collaboratively produced reports contributed a small percentage to the students' course assessment. In Study 3, conducted with research students (most at PhD level), all participants were familiar with the libre software development model and its benefits. For them, the study was a valuable experience to examine the feasibility of transferring this model to educational settings.

6.2 Technological Aspects

Flexibility. One of the main design principles of Edukalibre was to provide flexible user access. The collaborative editing tools enabled the conversion between several formats which was appreciated by the participants in studies 3 and 4 who had experience with (study 3) and understanding of (study 4) the benefits of the libre development model. In contrast, the students in studies 1 and 2 did not use the format conversion tools despite being reminded by the teachers several times. Also, the students in these studies did not take the full advantage of the version control functions, whilst this was acknowledged as a very useful feature by the participants in studies 3 and 4. The participants in studies 1 and 2 stressed the need to have an editor integrated within the system, as they found it inconvenient to use an external editor (most of them used Microsoft Word and few used Open Office) which slowed the download/upload/commenting process. An html/docbook editor has been included in the last version of ConDOR released at the end of the project.

Holistic design. The studies clearly pointed out the need for holistic design. It became apparent that resource sharing, communication, and collaborative writing would happen together and should be supported within one environment (as opposed to fragmented tools used in libre software development). This was partly taken into account in the design of ConDOR, but the studies revealed that more features had to be integrated in the interface applications, e.g. appropriate editing tools, links between discussions and documents, and association of roles to participants. Since Edukalibre was designed as a truly open platform, it can easily be extended with new functionality, as discussed above.

7 Conclusions and Further Work

The Edukalibre project makes two important contributions to technology-enhanced learning, namely:

Deployment of the libre development model in education: Edukalibre explores the field of collaborative production of educational materials from a novel point of view: can the common practices of the libre software community be applied to the development of educational content. The project was just an initial step which focused on the development of appropriate tools to support community-driven creation of educational content, and the deployment of these tools in small studies in realistic educational settings. Evaluation studies with COLLAB and ConDOR confirmed that it would be feasible to deploy a more open, community-driven model for the creation of educational resources. Distinctively from other projects that explore sharing, and even collaborative creation of educational resources mainly by teachers, Edukalibre examined opportunities for active engagement of students. Our experience showed that there was a great potential for creative scenarios where students could engage in collaborative writing experiences to create resources that would be used by other students or could help their peers with writing papers.

Deployment of Web 2.0 to the development of technologies for education: The second major contribution of Edukalibre is to demonstrate the application of Web 2.0 to the development of technologies for education. The project followed key tenets of Web 2.0 [29], namely, harnessing collective intelligence, lightweight programming models, sharing and reuse of existing components and tools, build applications that enrich the users' experiences offer creative ways to quickly build effective systems. The project has developed (mainly by reusing already existing components) a web-based system which is built around a Subversion-based repository for document sources, together with access methods to it and automated generation of final formats. The Edukalibre architecture is open and modular in nature, and makes it simple to add new functionality by connecting new subsystems. In some sense, Edukalibre implements a wiki-like syntax, with simple to use interfaces integrated in environments (such as office suites or learning management systems) common to educators. All in all, it lowers the technical barriers for educators to explore the libre software development model applied to educational documents. Also, the whole system is composed of libre software, which makes it easy to try, install and adapt to any environment.

Being an initial step, the project did not examine the full potential of the deployment of the libre development model. Notably, all studies included participants who knew each other and could meet face-to-face. Further studies are required to examine how the Edukalibre system can be tailored and extended to enable the construction of educational resources by large, geographically remote communities. In all scenarios explored so far, we dealt with university settings (which was the focus of Edukalibre). There is notable interest in methods for community-driven creation of content outside the university communities, for example schools [30] and digital libraries [31], and studies in such settings should be conducted. Finally, Edukalibre focused on the creation of educational materials but did not explore how these materials would be reused by different teachers and students. For this, significant extension of the Edukalibre editing tools would be required to generate appropriate meta-data and to export the created resources as learning objects [32]. Finally, some participants pointed that the collaborative editing tools should be customisable, so that the communities could decide what tools would suit them best. Furthermore, offering support tailored to the particular community (e.g. pointing at missing topics, inactive participants, or dominant members) will be beneficial.

Acknowledgements. The authors are grateful to all partners from the Edukalibre consortium for the stimulating discussions that helped clarify the ideas behind the collaborative editing system, and especially to the teams from Lugano, Karlsruhe and Prague who took active part in planning and conducting the evaluation studies. Edukalibre was funded by the European Commission.

References

1. Bezroukov, N.: Open source software development as a special type of academic research. First Monday **4** (1999)
2. Hassan, A.E., Godfrey, M.W., Holt, R.C.: Software engineering research in the bazaar. In: Proceedings of the 2nd Workshop on Open Source Software Engineering at the 24th International Conference on Software Engineering. (2001)
3. German, D.M.: The GNOME project: a case study of open source, global software development. Software Process Improvement and Practice (2003) 201–215
4. Gonzlez-Barahona, J.M., Lpez, L., Robles, G.: Community structure of modules in the apache project. In: Proceedings of the 4th Workshop on Open Source Software Engineering. 26th International Conference on Software Engineering, Edinburgh, Scotland, UK (2004)
5. Reis, C.R., de Mattos Fortes, R.P.: An overview of the software engineering process and tools in the Mozilla project. In: Workshop on Open Source Software Development. (2002)
6. Lameter, C.: Debian gnu/linux: The past, the present and the future. In: Free Software Symposium 2002. (2002)
7. Raymond, E.S.: The cathedral and the bazar. First Monday **4** (1997)
8. Koch, S., ed.: Free/Open Source Software Development. Idea Group, Inc. (2004)
9. Siemens, G.: Open source content in education: Developing, sharing, expanding resources. Pitch: peer reviewed online journal in Instructional and Learning Technology (2003)
10. Utah University Open Learning Support http://ols.usu.edu/.
11. MIT OpenCourseWare http://ocw.mit.edu/index.html.
12. Carnegie Mellon Open Learning Initiative http://www.cmu.edu/oli/.
13. Connextions: Sharing knowledge and building communities http://cnx.rice.edu/.
14. Sapsomboon, B., Andriati, R., Roberts, L., Spring, M.B.: Software to aid collaboration: Focus on collaborative authoring. Technical report, School of Information Sciences, University of Pittsburgh (1997)
15. Wikipedia http://www.wikipedia.org/.
16. Noel, S., Robert, J.M.: Empirical study on collaborative writing: What do co-authors do, use, and like? Computer Supported Cooperative Work: The Journal of Collaborative Computing **13** (2004) 63–89

17. Wenger, E.: Communities of Practice: Learning, Meaning, and Identity. Cambridge University Press (2001)
18. Feller, J.: Thoughts on studying opens source software communities. In Russo, N.L., Fitzgerald, B., Degross, J.I., eds.: Realigning Research and Practice in Information Systems Development: The Social and Organizational Perspective, Boston, Kluwer (2001)
19. Raymond, S.E.: The Cathedral and The Bazaar. O'Reilly (2001)
20. Ghosh, R.A., Robles, G., Glott, R.: Software source code survey (free/libre and open source software: Survey and study). Technical report, International Institute of Infonomics. University of Maastricht, The Netherlands (2002)
21. van Rossum, G., Fred L. Drake, J.: The Python Language Reference Manual. Network Theory Ltd (2003)
22. Fielding, R., Gettys, J., Mogul, J., Frystyk, H., Masinter, L., Leach, P., Berners-Lee, T.: Hypertext transfer protocol – HTTP/1.1, RFC 2616. Technical report, Network Working Group, IETF (1999)
23. Goland, Y., Whitehead, E., Faizi, A., Carter, S., Jensen, D.: HTTP extensions for distributed authoring – WEBDAV, RFC 2518. Technical report, Network Working Group, IETF (1999)
24. Botturi, L., Dimitrova, V., Matravers, J., Tebb, C., Withworth, D., Geldermann, J., Hubert, I.: Development-oriented elearning tool evaluation: the edukalibre approach. In: ED-MEDIA: World Conference on Educational Multimedia, Hypermedia and Telecommunications, Montreal, Canada. (2005)
25. Geldermann, J., Treitz, M., Rentz, O.: Teaching integrated technique assessment based on open-source software. In: EUNITE Conference: European Symposium on Intelligent Technologies, Hybrid Systems and their implementation on Smart Adaptive Systems, Aachen, Germany (2004)
26. Mazza, R.: Gismo: a graphical interactive student monitoring tool for course management systems. In: Technology Enhanced Learning Conference, Milan (2004)
27. Ilgen, D.R., Hollenbeck, J.R., Johnson, M., Jundt, D.: Teams in organizations: From input - process - output models to imoi models. Annual Review of Psychology **56** (2005) 517–543
28. Lewis, D., Allan, B.: Virtual Learning Communities: a Guide to Practitioners. Berkshire, Open University, McGraw Hill (2005)
29. O'Reilly, T.: What is web 2,0: Design patterns and business models of the next generation of software. (2005)
30. Vuorikari, R.: Why europe needs free and open source software and content in schools. INSIGHT (2004)
31. Cushman, R.: Open educational content for public digital libraries. Technical report, The William and Flora Hewlett Foundation (2002)
32. Duval, E.: A learning object manifesto. In: PROLEARN NoE Deliverable D4.2. (2004)

Is There a Way to e-Bologna? Cross-National Collaborative Activities in University Courses

Andreas Harrer[1], Georgios Kahrimanis[2], Sam Zeini[1],
Lars Bollen[1], and Nikolaos Avouris[2]

[1]University of Duisburg-Essen
[2]University of Patras
{harrer, zeini, bollen}@collide.info,
{n.avouris, kahrimanis}@ee.upatras.gr

Abstract. This article describes a study of distance collaborative activities that have been conducted in a cross-national setting between a Greek and a German university. We discuss issues related to organization, technology, and curricula considerations. In addition, we analyze the modes of cooperation that have been chosen in the students' work on creative problem solving tasks and conclude that for complex learning scenarios successful collaboration and peer tutoring in advanced learning support environments is possible, but requires careful preparation and planning. Further we draw conclusions on possible wider implications for such approaches in the emerging common European Area of Higher Education in the frame of the Bologna process.

1 Introduction

Today's work reality involves in a growing degree multi-national activities engaging individuals in remote interaction and collaboration. As a consequence, learning activities, especially at the Higher Education level need to be expanded accordingly in order to prepare students for distant work and cross-cultural communication. This is especially important for the area of computer science, where global projects and multi-national enterprises are a common phenomenon. Thus it is very valuable, both for the students and also for the academic staff, to find opportunities to allow students to experience the challenges, problems, and potential of remotely conducted projects in a multi-national and/or multi-cultural setting. It should be stressed that identification of the conditions for these opportunities and creation of new opportunities for the cooperation of educational establishments across national borders in Europe is one of the main aspects of the Bologna process. The Bologna declaration aims at the creation of a European Area of Higher Education through collaboration among high quality higher education institutions to enforce student mobility, competency development and educational co-operation [1]. In this context, studies which focus on the potential of technology enhanced learning for the integration of the European university systems and the strengthening of reliable computer-supported cooperation between institutions in different European countries are of particular importance. In this article we present the design and implementation of such study that engaged remotely students of the University of Patras in Greece

W. Nejdl and K. Tochtermann (Eds.): EC-TEL 2006, LNCS 4227, pp. 140–154, 2006.

and the University of Duisburg-Essen in Germany. Researchers of the two Universities have been engaged during the last years in study and development of collaboration support technologies. These have been made available to the Academic staff and the students who participated in the study.

In the rest of the paper we present first the organizational and educational framework of the study, followed by a brief description of the technological infrastructure used. Subsequently we discuss the main findings of the study as they emerge from analysis of logs of interaction of cross-national group activities and attempt to draw wider conclusions.

2 Organizational and Curricular Framework

The scenario that was implemented during the study was closely connected to the teaching practice of both parts, i.e. students in the context of real lectures are given short exercises as homework. Usually such exercises are performed individually. In our case they were requested to work in dyads with a partner across the border, using provided collaboration support tools. This scenario left a lot of freedom to the students to approach their task, in terms of when and how to work together or how to divide the work. The use of a more contained lab situation might have been preferable for controlled analysis of some collaboration aspects, but would have produced an artificial environment that would not have been connected well to the students' real world experiences.

In order to proceed with a detailed plan of the activity, we first had to explore the viability of a joint study with respect to curricular opportunities for cooperation and the organizational affordances of it.

To avoid severe grounding problems [2], the students had to have prior knowledge that can be connected with the partner's knowledge, thus it has to overlap or at least to be in each student's zone of proximal development [3][4]. For this end we had to identify courses that were taught at the same time at both partner's sites, in which students could interact and jointly do an assignment. Because of similar profiles of both groups in research and teaching, we managed to identify two opportunities to conduct studies during the last year: The first involved courses in the area of Human-Computer-Interaction for advanced students (5th year in Greece, 3rd year in Germany with quite comparable background knowledge); this opportunity was used for a pre-study to test the setup of technical, organizational, and analytical aspects for a full-fledged study. This first study took place in the summer of 2005 with 9 mixed dyads of Greek and German students. While the joint work was mainly performed cooperatively in asynchronous mode, we obtained valuable insights in the usage of the provided tools and the setup for studies on a larger scale.

The second case involved introductory courses in computer science (the 1st year course for Greek students and an algorithm course for 2nd year German students). In this case we could involve a more substantial number of students for the joint study. Here the background knowledge was well suited for information exchange and grounding, since both populations were more familiar with different aspects of our planned task: the Greek students were quite knowledgeable with diagrammatic representations of algorithms, while the German students were familiar with recursion, iteration, and the transformation between these two concepts. All the courses were conducted in the mixed lecture and lab/exercise format, usually also with online material and communication, which prepares the students nicely for the remote collaboration with the tools that were proposed to be used.

In addition to these curricular considerations such a joint study requires careful preparation of the organizational aspects, too. As the students initially do not know their remote partners, we thought that uncertainty about their role and limited awareness and familiarity with such a task might hinder the whole process. To compensate for this we decided to establish a discussion forum, with a general area for all the participants of the respective study and a specific area for each collaboration dyad. This forum was used for official announcements, the distribution of the task assignment, and questions and answers related to the planned process.

It was thought that there was a need to provide the mixed pairs with ample time to get acquainted with each other. So the time to deliver a solution was at least a full week in both studies. This made the task more realistic with respect to our usual style of assignments that also have one week periods for delivery.

Since the students tend to choose their own pace of work, the replies to their questions need to be provided in a timely manner, an issue that was proven particularly critical in this setting, for avoiding frustration and defection within the groups. In case that problems, especially technical ones, arise, a fast reaction by the support staff is required to enable the students to work on the task and not to fight technical problems. In our experience this is especially important in the phases close to the delivery deadline, because a lot of the collaboration groups tend to start late, even with getting acquainted with the tools. Another issue with the organization of such a study is that the technical environment used, has to be robust, especially with respect to persistent and regular data storage, since a data loss will demotivate students and endanger the whole learning experience considerably.

In the next section we proceed with a brief description of the environments used in the study and their technical characteristics.

3   Technology to Support Co-constructive Distance Scenarios

During our study, the students used a variety of collaborative modeling and communication tools. These tools were either external third party applications (e.g. *ICQ, MSN, Skype*), or available collaboration infrastructure (e.g. *phpBB* based forum) or specific tools that have been developed by the respective Universities to support synchronous collaborative activities (*Synergo* of the University of Patras and *FreeStyler* of the University of Duisburg-Essen). In the following, these tools are described in more detail.

3.1   General Communication Infrastructure: The Patras-Duisburg Web Portal

A forum was established as a source for general information about the studies, as a first meeting point for the dyads and as starting point for the use of other tools, especially for downloads and information about Synergo and Freestyler. The open source phpBB[1] bulletin board was used in this case. This forum consisted of a general discussion space for general questions and comments about the tools and the task, and public and private discussion spaces for each dyad. The forum was also meant as an option to contact the staff as fast as possible in case of organizational or technical problems, since a fast reaction time is crucial in these settings, as discussed above.

3.2 Specific Collaboration Tools

Two tools have been used in the studies to support the students' modeling tasks: *Synergo* and *FreeStyler*. In figure 1 typical screenshots of the two environments are shown. Both tools provide a shared workspace to allow for synchronous collaborative modeling activity, using various visual representations. In addition, both tools provide a chat facility to support direct communication between the partners. Each dyad of students in our study was provided with one of the two tools. One of the objectives of the study was to examine if the use of different tools may impact the collaborative activity and the quality of the produced work.

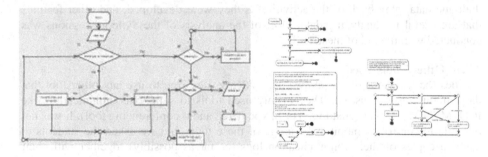

Fig. 1. Synergo and FreeStyler solutions of the given problem

FreeStyler [5] and Synergo [6] bear many similarities. They both enable distance collaborative modeling and discussion scenarios. They are based on a shared workspace architecture, i.e. in a collaborative session, every participant can see all modifications to the workspace done by any participant directly, following the WYSISIS ("what you see is what I see") principle. Both tools are built to support collaborative activities by small groups of students and have been used in Secondary and Higher education settings for teaching various subjects [7].

However since they have been produced independently, they have distinct characteristics in terms of architecture, user interface design and performance:

FreeStyler allows modeling withuse of various visual modeling languages that can be added to the application withthrough a pluginplug-in mechanism. At the moment, there are around 30 pluginsplug-ins available, e.g. for creating Petri Nets, Concept Maps, models in System Dynamics models, Activity Diagrams, State Charts, stochastic experiments etc. In particular, elements of different visual languages can be used in the same workspace at the same time without loosing possibly operational

---

[1] See http://www.phpBB.com for further information.

semantics (e.g. the capability to actually run a System Dynamics simulation). In relation to the task mentioned hereof our study, the suitable plug-in that Freestyler provides is the one for *Activity Diagrams*, the UML diagrams for representing the flow of activities involved in an algorithm,. Activity Diagrams are very similar to *Flow Charts,* a more traditional visual representation of an algorithm.

On the other hand, Synergo provides a smaller number than Freestyler number of fixed libraries for diagram building, which are integrated in the environment by default. Related to the task, Synergo contains a *Flow- Chart* diagram notation library.

What also discriminates the two environments, is that the synchronous dialogue tool that they both provide, is integrated within the shared workspace in the case of Synergo, whereas it appears as an object in the shared workspace in Freestyler.

The shared workspace architecture of Freeestyler is based on the so-called MatchMaker [8], a Java RMI-based synchronization middleware with a central server and a replicated data model. Synergo follows a similar approach; in this case the synchronization component is called Relay Server.

Finally, Synergo provides built-in tools for analyzing log files produced during Synergo activities. It provides automated measurements of logging events, coding of dialogue data, play-back of the activities as they were developed, and other features that are useful for analyzing data. Most of the analysis of the Synergo sessions was conducted with the aid of these tools.

3.2.1 Other Tools Used

Besides the tools mentioned above, the students were free to use any other tool that they might consider useful. They mainly used tools to support communication like ICQ, MSN Messenger (chat tools) or Skype[2] (free audio conferencing tool). It was not possible to control or monitor the usage of these tools, but we asked the students to hand in copies of their communication logs (as far as possibly) together with their solutions, since they had to provide a proof of their collaborative effort.

3.2.2 General Technical Requirements

To conduct this study, several technical requirements have been crucial and needed to be considered beforehand. Some of them are mentioned briefly in this section.

In such diverse multi-national setting, one may face several unexpected problems related for instance to availability of the software in the needed languages, capability of the software to run on the operating systems that are used by the target groups, restrictions on use of the specific software due to security reasons (e.g., some establishments may not allow third party chat tools or have very strict regulations on computer usage regarding security issues.) or other technical difficulties that may arise especially in the case of research prototypes, related to special needs for software installation (e.g. the help of an administrator).

Distant learning setups naturally make use of computer networks. But the setup can be rendered useless if it does not take into account issues like firewalls, NAT (Network Address Translation) schemes or bandwidth limitations that make it impossible to setup a adequate network connection between the participants.

In general, software failures or the loss of data can reduce the students' motivation drastically. Although one cannot expect research prototypes, like the Synergo and

---

[2] See http:www.icq.com, http://messenger.msn.com, and http://www.skype.com.

FreeStyler tools used in our studies, to run with no problems in such complex and diverse learning settings, one needs to decrease the impact of technical problems by e.g. providing robust servers, which are able to restart themselves in the case of a crash and by creating persistent data storage. Both approaches have been realized for this study and they turned out to work well for this kind of scenarios: Although a server crash did happened, the system remained operational without loss of data in either of the two parties and tools used.

In the next section we discuss the context of the study and the findings produced by analysis of the activity logs and the students work.

4   Case Study: Joint Construction of an Algorithm

As a result of the pre-study (see above) we discovered that successful collaboration in advanced learning support environments is possible if properly supported by the setup. For the follow-up study we decided to evolve this hypothesis towards the problem of peer tutoring: with respect to the heterogeneity of the cultural and educational background of the peer students we assume that collaborative modeling and discussion tools can help to overcome the challenges that cross-national learning scenarios impose. Furthermore, by choosing an exploratory design, we aim at finding out and describing *how* such learning processes manifest themselves.

The reported study was conducted during the winter semester of 2005. 16 mixed dyads were engaged in the activity, consisting for the German University of computer science students of third semester in the course "Algorithms and Data Structures" and for the Greek University of computer science students of first semester in the course "Introduction to Computers". Since the lectures were differently conceptualized and had overlapping but not exactly the same contents, we expected a challenge for the peers to find common ground with respect to the task. Thus we expected an initial discussion and peer tutoring phase in various aspects, such as diagrammatic notation and algorithmic knowledge. We also had a similar expectation in the knowledge about the tools and their usage, because the students in Greece were familiar with Synergo, while the German students knew FreeStyler from the lecture.

Half of the dyads were assigned to use FreeStyler while the others to use Synergo as the modeling tool. While, as discussed, both tools provide the possibility for integrating chat in the collaborative workspaces, yet the students were also free to use other chat or communication tools while they were engaged in collaborative activity. Some of them also used e-mail, the forum, and the forum's private messages functionality.

From the 16 teams that were originally formed to participate in the task, 10 managed to complete successfully the assignment. From them 7 were requested to use FreeStyler and 3 Synergo. However, 3 teams that were supposed to use Freestyler, finally decided to use Synergo instead. One reported that they used Synergo because the students were not familiar with Activity Diagrams and preferred to develop their solution in the form of Flow Charts, while the other two faced technical problems with the collaborative use of FreeStyler, and they decided to use Synergo instead. Freestyler had been tested successfully in previous occasions [7], so the technical problems are attributed to the special technical context of this activity, like the special characteristics of the network infrastructure in Greece. So finally the distribution of the collaboration tools was: 6 dyads used Synergo and 4 used Freestyler. An analysis of the log data of synchronous collaborative activity using these tools is included in the following section.

In addition to the two collaboration tools, a forum was provided so that the students would be able to communicate in pairs or publicly with all other participants. Just two out of ten pairs used this forum. One group used the forum in order to negotiate an initial solution to the problem that was provided in pseudo code. The same group also used the forum in order to plan and arrange their sessions. The second group used the forum just to coordinate the initial phase of interaction.

Alternatively, e-mail communication was used by half of the pairs in order to communicate and interchange initial solutions to the problem in the form of pseudo code and arrange their sessions. Surprisingly, half of the students reported that they communicated through other instant messaging applications as well, namely MSN Messenger, ICQ and Skype chatting.

4.1 Methodological Approach

The log files that were collected were analyzed in order to examine patterns of behavior of the different dyads. One particular objective of this analysis was related to the effect of the collaboration tools used. These tools have not been compared formally, so we preferred a mainly qualitative approach enriched by some quantitative measurements. This enables us to interpret the data in the context of the respective tool used and also in a deeper level of detail. A qualitative data analysis software was used in this case. For the quantitative measures we used analysis tools that have been built by the respective research groups. In the case of Synergo the built-in analysis tools [5] produced the indicators for the quantitative measures. The FreeStyler files were analyzed by the Pattern Discovery tool described in [9].

As a part of the analysis of the activity, we conducted a *content analysis* of the dialogues conveyed through different communication tools used. We assigned exchanged messages into categories provided by a content analysis schema that was developed. The purpose of the analysis was to provide an insight on certain aspects of the activity in order to interpret patterns of observed behavior. Content analysis was also useful as a heuristic tool that helped us to focus in parts of the activity that were of most interest. The schema developed is generally constituted of two main sub-schemata: one related to non task interaction and the other to task related interaction.

Table 1. Coding scheme for non task-related categories

CATEGORY		DESCRIPTION OF CASES	EXAMPLE
Coordination		Arranging sessions, planning work, distributing tasks	"Should we meet tomorrow at 12:00?"
Technical	Functionality	Reporting or discussing bugs and inconsistencies noticed in the functionality of the collaborative tools.	"The session was disconnected"
	Usability	Reporting usability problems of the collaborative tools or difficulties of the students to get accustomed with the user interface functionalities	"How can I put text near the connector?"
Social		Social talk, encouraging collaboration	"Good Work ;-)"

The first part of the schema, illustrated in table 1, classifies verbal interactions that do not relate to the task per se. Coordination and planning of the activity, comments on technical aspects or social conversation were included in the schema in order to find what kind of information is conveyed through the tool.

The second part of the schema concerns task-related messages. It refers to instances of *cognitive presence* [10]. The rationale behind that model was inspired by the Interaction Analysis Model proposed by [11].

However, the use of the model differs from Gunawardena's work in some important aspects. Firstly, our study concerns synchronous communication via chatting tools and activity in shared workspace instead of asynchronous communication through forums. Furthermore, the object of knowledge is not the negotiation of meaning of some abstract concepts, but the comprehension of algorithm building using visual notation and the development of algorithm development skills instead. This part of the model is illustrated in detail in table 2.

Table 2. Coding scheme for task-related verbal interaction

CATEGORY	DESCRIPTION OF CASES
Phase 1: Communication of Information	Statements of observation, communication of knowledge about a certain issue, description or realization of a problem, asking questions for clarification, providing examples
Phase 2: Discovering Inconsistencies	Statements of disagreement on a proposed issue or solution to a problem, response to disagreement statements indicating a reform of the initial standpoint or provided solution
Phase 3: Co-construction of knowledge	Reaching consensus, proposing a (partial) solution that integrates new data inspired by contradictions of initial standpoints
Phase 4: Testing jointly constructed solutions / conceptions	Testing the result of the previous phase against certain examples, similar problems, trying to optimize the solution
Phase 5: Further application of new knowledge / meta-cognitive processing	Reflection on the knowledge gained, association to other knowledge, application of new knowledge in similar domains

Concerning the analysis process, what discriminates the model used from Gunawardena's proposal is that not all indications of certain phases are contained in dialogues, as indications of the presence of them can also be found in the shared workspace.

In the model used, it is assumed that knowledge construction evolves from lower to higher cognitive functions as proposed by [3]. Similar distinction can be made in group skills during a collaborative activity [12]. Hence, actions related to higher phases of the model are expected to follow lower phases. However this sequence is not strict, because not all phases have to be manifested in chat dialogues as already discussed. Furthermore, in the tasks analyzed, there were several learning objectives, namely comprehension of flow-chart diagrams, understanding the concept of recursion and the systematic development of algorithm solutions.

During the coding process new categories were detected in the data and introduced to the coding scheme by open coding. Frequently detected codes were discussed between the research partners aiming to find out which new categories would be common to both research approaches in the sense of a generalization process. The category *coordination* for example originally belonged to the global category "non task related". But during the coding we detected that numerous parts of the analyzed discussions were about planning task related issues. So we decided to distinguish between these two different types of coordination activity.

In the case of FreeStyler group the tool atlas.ti[3] was used for coding the conversation data. The conversation data came in this case from messenger chatlogs, forum postings and data extracted from FreeStyler logfiles, since FreeStyler also provides its own chat functionality. A pattern discovery tool was also used during the analysis process. In this case we just counted different types of workspace activities to compare them with the findings in the communication analysis.

The coding of non-task related categories was straightforward. Concerning the task-related categories, emphasis was put on the presence of each category throughout the activity. For example, in a certain phase, several messages indicated appearance of stage 2 of the model. Concerning the message as a unit of analysis, it was not considered important the number of messages that were coded according to it, instead, what seemed to matter was just the fact that e.g. a "discovering inconsistencies" episode occurred in a certain phase of the activity. So, annotated messages did not serve for measuring frequencies of occurrences, rather they were useful for locating most important episodes that would be further analyzed.

Concerning the Synergo group logs, the dialogues were coded using Synergo's analysis tools. Synergo provides a tool for developing a coding schema and annotating events according to it. Summative measures and measures in relation to time intervals are automatically calculated and related graphs are automatically illustrated.

When conducting empirical studies privacy issues are very important to be considered. Therefore, all gathered information was treated anonymously and participation in this study was on voluntary basis.

4.2 Results of the Study

Phases of problem solving activities: The problem solving process was similar in many groups and can be generalized to a phase of grounding, explanation, knowledge construction, coordination, evaluation and modeling. In the following a discussion and examples of each phase are included:

Phase of Grounding. In this phase the peers checked out each other's knowledge by asking each other and trying to develop a common language, e.g. negotiations about definitions. These phases were indicated by the category "communication of information". An interesting example which shows that students also use advanced techniques for grounding is the one in which a Greek student developed a flow chart to explain his understanding of lists:

GR[4]: "the thing is, i'm not really into lists (we only heard about them a month ago) so i'm not sure. if you could please wait, I can scan the flow chart I made for you to see."

---

[3] http://www.atlasti.com/
[4] In dialogue extracts here forth, Greek student shown as GR, German student as DE.

Phase of Explanation: These phases were observed very often while peer tutoring. One of the students who knows a concept tries to teach it to the other student. According to Gunawardena's model this is part of "Communication of Information". A typical example for such a case is where a student teaches recursion to the other:

"DE: as I explained in the other session (Team-2 new2) you see that we need a third parameter
GR :i see"
DE: maybe I should begin and you see what i want to explain to you"

Construction of Knowledge: Theses phases describe the situations in which both students develop common knowledge by the collaborative task. An example for collaborative knowledge construction while modeling the different branches of the function to be developed is:

"GR: now we shall examine what happens if list a is empty
DE: its better than we havent so much recursive calls
GR: no..let's examine what happens if both lists are not empty first
DE: and if u ask not(isEmpty(listA)) then you can do samehting but you never know if listB is not empty.
[Communication break by workspace action] i think its right how you did it know
GR: you think we should change this?
DE: if both are not empty you have to look which value is bigger and stores this in the accu. [Workspace activity] right"

Coordination: As mentioned above we detected some cases of task related planning which comply to the Communication of Information according to the category scheme (Table 2). An example for planning can be shown for the case in which the students decided to take turns while modeling the task:

"GR: nice...your turn to make the if list b empty thing
DE :) [Workspace activity]
GR: nice"

Evaluation: This code is described by the fourth category in the coding scheme (Table 2). These cases were observed frequently in relation to using of pseudo code, for example:

DE: "At the point "stock (first (y)) y<--rest (y)" The operation stock; Doesn't we need two parameters. The first one for the element that we have to add and the next one the list it should be added to?
GR: I think you're right*JOKINGLY*. that needs more thought now..."

Use of auxiliary means during problem solving: Most partners attempted to solve the problem by expressing the solution in an auxiliary form, i.e. in pseudo code or in a programming language (Java) first on their own and then transform it to a flow chart or activity diagram collaborating with their peers. In most cases, both partners had developed or found a solution in pseudo code and presented it to the other at the beginning of the collaboration through Synergo / Freestyler and they interchanged the solutions via mails or forum postings.

In some cases the partners developed or improved their solution on paper while they had real time communication through the tools. Messages like: "I think I have still another idea. I write it down [on paper] at the moment" during a collaborative session indicated such cases. There were also cases that a partner presented the pseudo code solution in the form of a sticky note in the shared workspace, and testing and modifications were done collaboratively.

The number of collaborative sessions that were needed in order to accomplish the task, and the duration of each session varied among the teams.

So the recorded synchronous collaborative activities constituted just a part of the process. Possible learning gains of the activity can not be simply attributed to the collaborative task, but prior (or intermediate) to the collaborative task cognitive elaboration during the phase of solving individually the problem cannot be neglected.

Peer tutoring behavior: One of the main objectives of the study has been to examine if there have been patterns of peer tutoring in the dyads. In most cases, there is an obvious discrepancy in the background knowledge of the partners in the beginning of the task. That is expected since the Greek students have not been taught anything about lists and recursion which is a core concept related to the given problem. On the other hand, concerning the pairs that developed flow-chart diagrams using Synergo, the German partners were not familiar neither with the tool, nor with flow-chart notation. Interestingly, many students seemed to be aware that this difference in prior knowledge could provide benefits for both partners. E.g. the dialogue logs between two collaborators included:

GR ": "so we both know different parts and we will connect them!!"
DE: "sounds good :)"

During the analysis phase we identified peer-tutoring instances and gains of new knowledge. In the following we study further this behavioral pattern, in relation to more specific learning objectives, relating to the use of lists and recursion.

Learning about lists and their usage: The first thing that was necessary for the students to comprehend in order to solve the given problem was lists and their properties. Greek students had limited prior teaching of lists, although they were quite familiar with arrays. On the contrary, teaching of lists was part of the course of the German students. Analysis showed that some students had worked on their own prior to collaborating with their partners, and seemed to have acquired a good knowledge of lists before the sessions started. However, in some cases Greek students initially had misconceptions of the properties of lists. They could assimilate the properties of lists to their previously existing understanding of arrays; they however had not accommodated their knowledge so that it would cover the main distinctive property of lists, i.e. the possibility to access, extract or add only one element at a time. The German partners explained the differences between lists and arrays to the Greeks, and the latter gained the provided knowledge with no significant difficulty. A characteristic example is provided below:

GR: "So now we have to compare a[1] and b[2]. So we add 1 to j and leave i as it was. Check it out."

DE: "But we have only the methods "stock", "first" and "rest" to get the elements of the list. You can't directly take the element 2 or other. You can only take the first element and then you must give out"

DE: "the rest. a = rest(a)"

DE: "You have an idea for handling Arrays, but not for the lists. Do you know what I mean?"

GR: "As far as I have understood, what we do is cut off the biggest element, replace the list that includes it with rest(list) and leave the other list untouched. It is true that I don't know how to deal with lists, I have never faced such problems."

In the first message the Greek partner tries to solve a problem involving lists using the properties and notations of arrays. However, the last message indicates knowledge and comprehension of the list properties. This contradiction becomes more obvious after a while, when the Greek student uses again array notation for representing list elements in the diagram. The depth of Greek students' comprehension of lists does not reach the extent so that she could *apply* this knowledge properly. Applying knowledge corresponds to a higher skill that indicates learning in more depth than just knowing something [13]. The German student responds again:

DE: "You can't take b(i) and a(i), because it isn't a array. You can only put an element at the front of the list. ;-)"

After that, the Greek student corrected immediately the mistake with notations appropriate to lists. Such an extract indicates that collaboration can boost knowledge skills in terms of upgrading from "surface" knowledge to application of knowledge and even reflection. Similar episodes were reported in the activities of most pairs.

Learning about recursion: Learning about recursion in contrast to iteration (in the context of algorithms) by Greek students was the major challenge of the activity, since Greek students were not expected to know what recursion is. We expected to find effective peer-tutoring instances of German students helping Greek students learn what recursion is.

Although almost all German students mastered recursion, the dyads were diverse in terms of initial knowledge about recursion by Greek students and in terms of learning gains. About half of Greek students did not know anything about recursion. Some of them had some related knowledge that they could not associate with the term, and there were a few that had learnt about recursion prior to the collaborative sessions and could apply their knowledge in the development of the diagrams.

In most cases there was an imbalance of knowledge that we expected to be beneficial first for Greek partners, but for German partners as well, because explaining helps learning it in more depth [14]. In about half of the cases there were strong indications of such a success. For example while two partners had developed a first version of the diagram they exchanged the following messages:

1) DE: it is a recursion. and we have to transform it so that it works with loop

2) GR: could we write stock(first(y),merge(x,y))?

3) DE: no that would still be recursion. We can't use merge while we are in merge.

4) DE : shall I send you my code without recursion?

5) GR: but how are we supposed to use the operation stock if we HAVE to add the list name? I mean can we name the new list just "merge" or "list3"?

6) GR : it's the only way of preventing a recursion

7) DE : I think it's ok if we use a new list.

The Greek partner seems to understand what the German stated in message 3 "no that would still be recursion. We can't use merge while we are in merge". Later on not only does he show understanding, but he provides a proposal for the right solution as well: "can we name the new list just "merge" or "list3"?", "it's the only way of preventing a recursion".

However, we noticed other cases that the fact that only the German student knew about recursion prevented true collaboration and learning gains. German students developed solutions almost on their own leaving their Greek partner observing the diagrams and contributing just trivial things. Even questioning about recursion did not necessarily lead to learning. An example is the following dialogue:

GR: "...but could you please explain what a recursive program is and what an iterative program is? Please?"

DE: "Ok, I try it. In German no problem, but in English. :-) Wait a moment, I must think about this. :-)"

GR: "Ok Take your time, it's OK :-)"

DE: "The algorithm in the tasks is a function. The name is "merge". In line 3 and 4 in stock() the algorithm calls itself. That is called "recursiv"."

GR: "Oh, I get it. I know what this is, I just knew only the Greek word for that, not the English...sorry."

Although the Greek student claims to know what recursion is, his practice after this short dialogue proves the opposite. A possible explanation of this problem can be related to the means of assessment of the task which can highly influence the quality and orientation of learning [15]. For the grading of the task, the final solution and the "level of collaboration" were taken into account, but the comprehension of recursion was not demanded in any test that the Greek students had to take in the context of the relevant course. So, they were not highly motivated to gain this knowledge and use it after the end of the collaborative activity.

Technical and usability problems: Some groups were faced with technical problems, so for instance some groups decided to switch tools. These technical problems appeared in different ways. Most of the problems were caused by network latency leaks in combination with usability issues due to the complexity of the tools. For instance, one of the tools (FreeStyler) has many different workspace layers . The tool provides two types of layers, one for handwriting and drawing and the other for building more complex models. The graph layer supports simulation functionality (e.g petri nets) which may cause unexpected waiting in combination with network latency. For example while testing in fast network infrastructure, users "feel" immediately when they are working in the wrong layer or wrong mode and switch natively to the preferred mode. In the observed cases technical problems were attributed to a software limitation that was termed "a bug" by the students:

"GR: the bugs from hell just reappeared, wait a sec, I am going to restart freestyler

DE: for me it works just fine though

GR: okay, (I am) back"

5   Conclusions and Perspectives

In this paper we described organizational and technical affordances for long-distance collaborative activities across national borders. Based on our analyses we conclude that for complex learning scenarios, successful collaboration with advanced learning support environments is possible, yet requires careful preparation and planning of the support structures for the students. An important issue to consider also is the setup of the scenario in a joint pedagogical framework, such that all subjects involved benefit from the learning experience and feel motivated to participate actively, since the withdrawal of a partner cannot be compensated easily in a remote situation; creating personal bonds between the participants up-front is a means to avoid the loss of students. One important lesson learnt is the necessity to embed these learning scenarios into a meaningful and authentic context in the education of the institutions involved, especially in a multi-national or cross-cultural situation.

Both tools used have been proved very relevant for this activity. In addition the students used many communication tools and auxiliary material, often in the form of preliminary versions of the required solution in other representations, like in pseudo code. The fact that both tools used permit logging of student's activity, has been proven very useful for analysis of the actions and understanding the process. Modelling activities in the workspace have shown a wide variety in terms both of the number of actions and the distribution between the partners, as the overall number ranged between approx. 300 and 2500 workspace actions (creation, moving, modification and deletion of objects) and shares of initiative between 5:1 and 5:3 actions. It was found that there was no significant bias in the workspace actions towards either Greek or German students.

An interesting finding has been that from the analysis of the chat logs and the frequent episodes of peer tutoring in both ways we conclude that successful collaboration can even be established while the peers have different background knowledge. The turn taking example demonstrates such collaboration. We observed that – as intended by the design of the learning situation – Greek student gained a solid understanding of recursion and iteration, while German students intensified their skills in handling diagrammatic representations.

We believe that the findings of this study may be useful in setting up similar collaborative activities across boarders, that may lead to enforcement of educational co-operation and competency development, while exposing the students to an environment of multinational work and use of tools for distance collaborative activities, without requiring from them to leave their usual learning practice and environment. Considering this first study a useful experience, we plan to intensify our efforts towards this goal by establishing these joint activities on a regular basis.

Acknowledgment

This work was supported by the IKYDA program (DETAV-CSCA) and the European Research Team CAViCoLA in the Kaleidoscope Network of Excellence (Contract No. 507838).

References

1. Bologna Secretariat website: http://www.dfes.gov.uk./bologna (visited April 2006)
2. Clark, H.H., Schaefer, E.F.: Contributing to discourse. Cognitive Science, 13 (1989) 259-294

3. Vygotski, L.S.: Mind in Society: The Development of Higher Psychological Processes. Harvard University Press, Cambridge, (1978)
4. Murray, T., & Arroyo, I.: Towards measuring and maintaining the zone of proximal development in adaptive instructional systems. In Proc. of ITS, volume 2363 of LNCS, Springer-Verlag (2002) 749–758.
5. Gaßner, K.: Diskussionen als Szenario zur Ko-Konstruktion von Wissen. Dissertation. Faculty of Engineering Sciences, University Duisburg-Essen (2003)ï
6. Avouris N., Margaritis M., and Komis V.: Modelling interaction during small-group synchronous problem-solving activities: The Synergo approach. In Proc. of Workshop on Designing Computational Models of Collaborative Learning Interaction, ITS2004, Maceio, Brasil, (2004)
7. Lingnau, A., Kuhn, M., Harrer, A., Hofmann, D., Fendrich, M., Hoppe, H.U.: Enriching Traditional Classroom Scenarios by Seamless Integration of Interactive Media. In Advanced Learning Technologies: Technology Enhanced Learning, Los Alamitos, CA, IEEE Computer Society (2003)
8. Jansen, M.: MatchMaker - A Framework to Support Collaborative Java Applications, In Proc. of AIED. IOS Press, Amsterdam, (2003) 535-536
9. Harrer, A., Vetter, M., Thür, S., Brauckmann, J.: Discovery of Patterns in Learner Actions. In Proc. of AIED, IOS Press, Amsterdam (2005) 816-818
10. Garrison, D. R., Anderson, T., Archer, W.: Critical Inquiry in a text-based environment: Computer Conferencing in higher education. The Internet and Higher Education 2 (2-3): (2003) 1-19
11. Gunawardena, C N.., Lowe, C. A., Anderson, T.: Analysis of global online debate and the development of an interaction analysis model for examining social construction of knowledge in computer conferencing. J. of Educational Computer Research, 17(4), (1997) 397-431
12. Smith, J. B.: Collective Intelligence in Computer-Based Collaboration. Lawrence Erlbaum Associates, Hillsdale, New Jersey (1994)
13. Bloom, B. S.: Taxonomy of educational objectives, handbook 1: Cognitive domain. New York: Longmans Green (1956)
14. Ploetzner R., Dillenbourg P., Praier M., Traum D.: Learning by explaining to oneself and to others. In Collaborative-learning: Cognitive and Computational Approaches, Oxford: Elsevier (1999) 103-121
15. Knight, P.: Assessment for learning in higher education. London: Kogan Page (1995)

Ontological Support for a Theory-Eclectic Approach to Instructional and Learning Design

Yusuke Hayashi[1], Jacqueline Bourdeau[2], and Riichiro Mizoguchi[1]

[1] ISIR, Osaka University, 8-1 Mihogaoka, Ibaraki, Osaka, 567-0047 Japan
{hayashi, miz}@ei.sanken.osaka-u.ac.jp
[2] LICEF, Télé-université, 100 Sherbrooke W., Montréal, (QC) H2X 3P2 Canada
jacqueline.bourdeau@licef.teluq.uqam.ca

Abstract. Enhancement of learning with technology has been accelerating thanks to the advancement of information technology (IT) and the development of IT standards for learning. The purpose of this study is to build a still more advanced engineering infrastructure of utilization of instructional and learning theories for practitioners in line with such development. This paper discusses a modeling framework for instructional and learning theories based on ontological engineering and the compliance of IMS LD to theoretical knowledge.

1 Introduction

Enhancement of learning with technology has been accelerated thanks to the advancement of information technology (IT) and the development of IT standards in the areas of learning, education, and training. This includes, for example, accumulated knowledge for constructing intelligent educational systems [20] and standardization activity in IEEE LTSC, ARIADNE, ADL, ISO SC36, etc. Thus, increasingly powerful tools for developing advanced educational systems and contents are available. The purpose of this study is to build a still more advanced engineering infrastructure of utilization of instructional and learning theories for practitioners based on such development.

However, the problem of how to build a "good" system using the technologies still remains. Of course, considerable achievement has been made in instructional and learning sciences which would be expected to provide guidelines for building systems. Yet, even though some theories prescribe optimal/desirable methods of learning and instruction, many of the theories are not sufficiently articulated for the use of practitioners. Such theories allow for diverse interpretation and therefore may be difficult to use in practice. Furthermore, age-old question continues to apply: "Is it 'better' to select one theory when designing instruction or to draw ideas from different theories?" Answers to this question depend to a great extent on the purpose of considering instructional theories [17].

One of the reasons such problems come up is that the description of educational theories (learning, instructional and instructional design theories) is made in natural language, using different terminology. As Reigeluth points out, although many theories prescribe the same method for the same situation, these are described in

W. Nejdl and K. Tochtermann (Eds.): EC-TEL 2006, LNCS 4227, pp. 155 – 169, 2006.

different terminology [18]. This leads to a diversity of theories that are all open to interpretation. Even for experts, it is sometimes difficult to appropriately use theories while having a clear understanding of the similarities and differences between them. It is even more difficult to implement knowledge of the theories on computers and make it available to support instructional and learning tasks. We must first establish a common basis for understanding the theories at a conceptual level, along with organized concepts and vocabulary.

As Ertmer discusses, although there are many theories for learning and instruction, every one of them seeks to explain the "Learning" process of human beings [5]. In other words, every theory rests somehow on the common basis of explaining learning and instruction. If we reveal this common basis, we will be able to establish a foundation for comprehensively understanding and using a variety of existing theories.

This being said, the purpose of this study is not to expose a scientifically valid basis for organizing theories nor to reconstruct them on this basis, but rather to find an engineering approximation that allows the building of an engineering infrastructure that enables practitioners to utilize instructional and learning theories. This paper thus proposes a foundation from the view point of ontological engineering, based on the results of previous research in this respect [2][3][14].

Another important issue that this study focuses on is sharing and reuse of the product of instructional and learning design. In this regard, IMS Learning Design (LD) specifications [9] are emerging as a dominant IT standard. IMS LD aims at providing a containment framework of elements that can describe any design of a teaching / learning process in a formal way. In addition, it can be considered as an integrative layer to many existing specifications. This being said, most of the existing LD tools have difficulty to explicitly integrate educational theories, even though the specifications underline their importance. It may be because of the lack of representation of theoretical knowledge as well as the lack of a compliance mechanism between the specifications and the theoretical knowledge. In order to make IMS LD specifications work with educational theories, this study proposes an ontology of educational theories which describes these theories and their links to the LD [16]. It further promotes the discussion of how to organize theoretical knowledge and making theoretical knowledge compliant to IMS LD.

This paper is organized as follows. The next section presents our perspective on learning and instruction. Section 3 proposes a framework for organizing instructional and learning theories. Section 4 discusses an authoring tool based on the framework, after which we conclude.

2 Ontological Approach to Systematization of Educational Theories

2.1 Theories of Learning, Instruction and Instructional Design

According to Reigeluth overview [18], instructional design is a prescriptive science because its primary purpose is to prescribe optimal methods of instruction. However, theories behind instructional design, which are learning and instructional theories, may be discussed in either a descriptive or prescriptive form[1]. In his overview, Reigeluth also summarizes the distinction between descriptive and prescriptive theories. Descriptive ones try to explain learning phenomena by investigating learning actions according to: (1) sets of conditions necessary for making the learning actions successful and (2) expected outcomes. In contrast, prescriptive ones assume sets of conditions and desired outcomes are given and prescribe the best learning actions as the variables of interest. We consider that grasping both aspects of theories is important to understand and design learning and instruction appropriately.

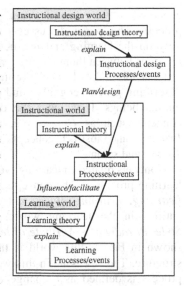

Fig. 1. A nested structure of learning, instruction and instructional design [2]

The relation among theories underlying instructional design is considered as a nested structure as shown in Fig. 1. The bottom of the structure is what we call the learning world. Learning theories explain processes and events in this world[2]. What we call the instructional world is on top of the learning world. Instructional processes influence or facilitate learning one. Instructional theories prescribe effective instructional processes for learning processes leading to desired outcomes. Instructional processes and events are parallel to learning ones. We place what we call instructional design world is on top of the instructional world. Instructional design process is the design process of instructional processes. Instructional design theories prescribe rational processes for designing instructional processes.

One of the major differences among the three kinds of processes is that while the lower two are real world processes, the other is a planning or design process of real world processes/events. However, thinking along the nested structure, we see that all the processes share an essential characteristic: they all rely on the learning process which can be modeled as "state-change of a learner." Therefore, this study has built an ontology with state-change of a learner as the foundation of the conceptual system.

2.2 An Ontology of Learning and Instruction

Roughly speaking, the ontology that this study has been developing is composed of five major concepts: concepts related to the *Common, Learning, Instructional and Instructional design worlds* and *Educational event* in the learning and the instructional worlds. Fig. 2 shows the hierarchy of the upper level concepts. Concepts related to each world are those that describe processes in the respective worlds. The

---

[1] There are also instructional design theories other than learning and instructional theories. These mainly focus on the design *process* and will not be discussed here because we focus on the *product* of design.

[2] Here, learning theories include theories of knowledge, of which there are several paradigms – behaviorism, cognitivism and constructivism – according to the various views about knowledge.

concept of *Educational event* is a description of process. This paper discusses ontology with a focus only on the learning and instructional worlds and the relations between them.

Concepts related to the common world are for describing general cognitive and physical processes of human beings. It includes the definition of concrete concepts such as *Object* (e.g. agent and tool) and *Process*, and abstract concepts such as *Knowledge*, *Theory* and so on.

Concepts related to learning world are for describing learning processes. The concepts include definitions of *Learning*, *Learning object* and *Learning process* as entities in the learning world, *Learning condition*, *Style*, *Paradigm* as *Attribute of learning* and so on. As shown in Fig. 1, this world is the core of the nested structure. The key issue in this world is that a learning process is defined as a change of learner's state. As mentioned before, Ertmer asserts that although behaviorism, cognitivism and constructivism each has many unique features, they describe the same phenomena (learning) [5]. In a similar line of the thought, this study sets up the working hypothesis that the phenomena can be conceptualized by change of learner's state. In other words, while the assumed mechanism of developing knowledge is different for each paradigm, the idea of states in the learning process is common[3]. It is our belief that this hypothesis makes sense as an engineering approximation to build a common ground for understanding and using existing theories.

Concepts related to the instructional world are for describing instructional processes. The concepts include definitions of *Instructional action*, *Instructional strategy*, *Instructional attribute*, etc. The point of the concepts in this world is that instruction is premised on learning. Instruction exists to influence learning, that is to say, to facilitate a change in learner's state. Thus, the meaning of an instructional action is defined by an achieved or intended change of learner's state. However, in this ontology, the relation between a change and an instructional action is defined

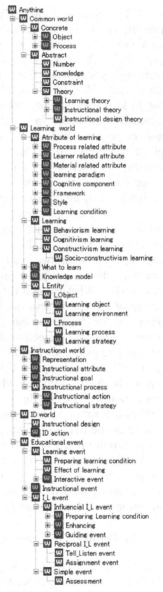

Fig. 2. the upper level concepts (Total number of concepts is 533)

by I_L event, which will be explained at the end of this section, and an instructional action is defined independently of the change of learner's state. This is because a type of instructional action may have different effects depending on the context.

---

[3] Note that we are not saying all the learning theories share the same learning states.

Maintaining independence between instructional actions and changes of learner state is important in order to allow a variety of combinations of instructional actions and the effect.

Educational event is the concept for describing (1) events in each world and (2) relations between them. *Learning event* and *Instructional event* are the concepts describing events in the learning and instructional worlds, respectively. Events of each world are described by concepts of the world and explain the process. A learning event composes an agent as a learner, objects, change of learner's state, and conditions of learning. The relation among them is suggested by learning theories. An instructional event for it part composes an instructional action, its agent, its object and spatial/temporal attributes. The events describe what happens in the respective worlds independently. The important point to note is that the definition of *I_L event* links instructional events to learning events. *I_L event* defines relations between learning and instruction from two points of view. The first is the contribution of instructional events to change of learner's state. The other is the preparation for the following learning event. The role of *instructional event* is to prepare conditions of learning that make learning processes successful. Thus, I_L event also models the contribution to the subsequent learning process. This point will be examined again with examples in 3.1.

2.3   Ontological Modeling Framework of Functional Design Knowledge

The ontology mentioned in the previous section provides basic concepts to describe events of learning and instruction. It has been built with a goal of establishing a basis for describing any learning and instruction. This being said, we need guidelines to determine the composition of the basic concepts. Instructional and learning theories suggest effective composition depending on the situation. This section discusses how to model the prescriptive aspect of instructional and learning theories.

This study adopts an ontological modeling framework of functional design knowledge of artifacts (devices) by Kitamura et al. [11] as a framework to model educational theories. Although the domain is different from educational knowledge, we believe that it is applicable to the systematization of theoretical knowledge for instructional and learning design.

This framework defines a device from two points of view: "behavior" and "function". A "behavior" of a device is defined as the objective independent of designer's intention, that is, the interpretation of its input-output relations considering the device as a black box. A "function" is defined as the teleological interpretation of a behavior given an intended goal.

The key concepts of the framework are *Functional concept* and *Way of function achievement*. The conception comes from the separation of "function" into (a) what to achieve and (b) how to achieve. The

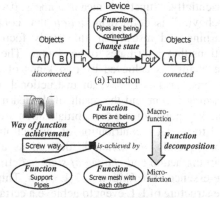

Fig. 3. Functional concept and Way of function achievement

functional concept is a conceptualization of the former (Fig. 3 (a)) and the way of function achievement is one of the latter (Fig. 3 (b)). An important point is the separation between the intended/implemented state-change and the way to achieve the change. This kind of conceptualization makes it possible to provide alternative ways to achieve an intended/implemented state-change because a change is usually achieved in several ways.

Using functional concepts, the functional structure of a device is modeled as a Function decomposition tree and a General function decomposition tree. A function decomposition tree represents the functional structure of a specific device. In contrast, a general function decomposition tree is a composition of some function decomposition trees for similar devices with the same whole-function (the top-function of a function decomposition tree). A (general) function decomposition tree basically shows that a required function (called a macro-function) can be achieved by a sequence of specific sub (micro)-functions. Relations between a macro-function and sub (micro)-functions are described by the ways of function achievement. A general function decomposition tree includes alternative ways of function achievement with an OR relationship. It indicates that there are more than one possible ways to achieve a specific function.

3   Systematization of Learning/Instructional Theories in the Form of Way of Function Achievement

In this section, let us discuss systematization of learning/instructional theories in full detail. This study proposes a framework for systematizing learning/instructional theories/models based on the modeling framework of functional design knowledge described in 2.3.

Before we turn to the discussion of the systematization of learning/instructional theories, it is useful to examine the correspondence of the framework to the domain of learning and instruction. As mentioned before, in a function decomposition tree, the concept of device is defined from two points of view: "behavior" and "function". Essentially, "function" means some sort of *change of state* of the input object and "behavior" is defined as *action* that contributes to the change. In the domain of learning and instruction, this study focuses on the change of learner's state and actions that contributes to the change. The difficulty in modeling these might be that the change is achieved by two kinds of actions: instructional actions and learning actions. That is to say, an instructional action leads a learner to do some sort of learning action and the result of the learning action is the change of learner's state. The key points of our conceptualization are to emphasize the relation among the three and to model a contribution of instructional action on the change of learner's state. Consequently, an *action* is defined as a combination of instructional action and learning action and *change of state* is defined as the change of learner's state. This is the essence of definition of I_L event. This framework therefore enables us to model the structure of I_L event to achieve a certain change of a learner's state.

A structure of I_L event is connected by way of function achievement (referred to as "Way" hereafter), which is defined as a relation between a macro-I_L event and some sub (micro)-I_L events. For example, consider a situation where an instructor wants a learner to understands a piece of knowledge and the necessary condition is that the learner should be aware of prerequisite knowledge. A conceivable process to achieve this is to remind the learner of the prerequisite and then to inform him/her of the thing to learn. The former instructional action brings about the necessary condition, which is to be aware of, and the latter promotes the outcome, which is to understand. A Way is such a decomposition of the required change into the detailed changes and actions to achieve them.

A Way has two interpretations. One is, called bottom-up approach, the sum of changes of learner's state of sub-I_L event promote the changes of learner's state in view of a macro-I_L event. The other is, called top-down approach, that an instructional action of a macro-I_L event is decomposed into detailed/concrete instructional actions of sub-I_L events. The interpretation concentrating on states is descriptive. It describes which outcome is produced by a sequence of changes of learner's state. The interpretation concentrating on action is prescriptive. It prescribes which sequence of instructional actions is required for performing the intended instructional action.

Having examined the correspondence of the framework to the domain of learning and instruction, we return to the issue of the systematization of instructional and learning theories. The prescriptive aspect of Way plays a significant role to model instructional and learning theories. The theories prescribe strategies for designing instructional and learning process according to assumed situations. Therefore, this study proposes to model instructional and learning strategies as Way with not a particular situation but generic situations stated in theories. In this study such a generic Way is called Way-knowledge. Organizing Way-knowledge will contribute to clarification of the conceptual structure of each theory and to setting some flexible design guidelines according to theories.

A hierarchy of I_L event itself may look fairly similar to IMS LD [9]. IMS LD also aims to establish a framework to describe instructional and learning processes at very abstract levels. However, IMS LD is just a framework (at least right now) because the purpose of the specification is to provide a containment framework of elements that can describe any design of a teaching-learning process in a formal way. This means that it allows designers to describe any instructional and learning process without guidelines. Thus, the prescriptive aspect of Way-knowledge proposed in this study will contribute to enhance the expressiveness of IMS LD as guidelines on designing instructional and learning processes [16]. On the other hand, descriptive aspects help check the consistency of learning process influenced by the instructional processes.

3.1 Describing Learning/Instructional Theories as Way-Knowledge

Fig. 4 shows an example of Way-knowledge from learning/instructional theories. This is described using the Hozo ontology editor [12].

The fundamental definition of Way concept is represented Fig. 4 (A). Way is defined as a relational concept [12]. The relational concept is a conceptualization of the relation among concepts. It has slots of participant concepts (*participate-in* relation denoted by "p/i"). Participant concepts in a way class are "whole" or "sub". Constraint of both participants is I_L event.

A learning/instructional strategy derived from a learning/instructional theory is defined as sub-class of the Way class. Fig. 4 (B) is an example of learning/ instructional strategy defined as a Way. The Way describes a motivational strategy that comes from Gagne and Briggs's nine events of instruction [6][4]. It is composed of the first two events extracted out of the events. One is "Gain attention" (Fig. 4 (2)), whose objective is to interest the learner, and the other is "Inform the learner of the objective" (Fig. 4 (3)), whose objective is to orient the learner to learning. We consider both of these extracted events are concerned with learner motivation.

The participant concept assigned to a whole (Fig. 4 (1)) is an I_L event that deals with motivation comprehensively. As mentioned in the previous

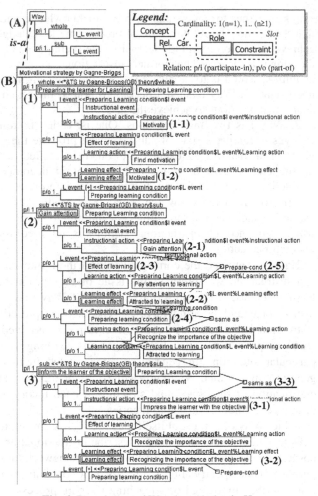

Fig. 4. Description of Way-knowledge in Hozo

section, an I_L event is composed of pair: an instructional event and a learning event. These events are defined independently of each other though when they are paired they form a meaningful I_L event. In our example, the instructional event has an instructional action "Motivate" (Fig. 4 (1-1)). The intention of the action is described not in its definition but in the coupled learning event in the I_L event. Here, the coupled learning event describes the achieved/intended learning condition as "Motivated" (Fig. 4 (1-2)), which means that a learner's motivational state has been modified through the event.

The sub participant concepts include necessary I_L events (Fig. 4 (2), (3)) to achieve the whole I_L event (Fig. 4 (1)). This strategy attempts to achieve the states

---

[4] The strategy shown here is not actually stated in the theory but an interpretation in this study. Gagne and Briggs have identified nine events of instruction as a simple sequence.

in the whole I_L event with the following two states: "Attracted to learning" (Fig. 4 (2-2)) and "Recognizing the importance of the objective" (Fig. 4 (3-2)). That is, the required state in the whole I_L event is achieved if both of the states of sub I_L events are achieved. The sub I_L events also propose instructional actions to achieve the states: "Gain attention" (Fig. 4 (2-1)) and "Impress the learner with the objective" (Fig. 4 (3-1)), respectively.

It can be considered basically that instructional process prepares conditions of learning and succeeding learning processes. An I_L event is described as not only achieved/intended change of learner's state but also preparation of the succeeding learning events. For example, "Gain attention" (Fig. 4 (2)) is modeled with two meanings; one is to change of learner's state to "Attracted to learning" (Fig. 4 (2-2)), which is described as *Effect of learning* (Fig. 4 (2-3)) and the other is the preparation for the following I_L event "Inform the learner of the objective" (Fig. 4 (3)), which is described as *Preparing learning condition* (Fig. 4 (2-4)). The relation of preparation is illustrated in *Prepare-cond* relation between instructional action and learning condition (Fig. 4 (2-5)) and *same as* relation between learning actions (Fig. 4 (3-3)). Conceptualizing instruction with relation of preparation is characteristic of this study.

3.2 Correlating Learning/Instructional Theories by Ways of Function Achievement

It was pointed out above that each theory is respectively organized as a set of Way-knowledge. Such a set can provide guidelines for instructional designers in view of the underlying theory. This section will expand this idea into theory-eclectic guidelines for instructional designers according to multiple theories.

Dependence between instructional theories is best illustrated in the book edited by Reigeluth: "Instructional Theories in Action: Lessons Illustrating Selected Theories and Models" [19]. He asked several authors to design a lesson based on a specific theory, having in common the subject matter, the objectives, and the test items. The objectives included both concept learning and skill development. The lesson is an introduction to the concepts of lens, focus and magnitude in optics. The book offers eight variations of the lesson, each one being an implementation of eight existing and recognized theories.

One of the problems of using theories is best expressed by Reigeluth: *"There are many commonalities among these theories: that is, many theories prescribe the same methods for the same situations (all in different terminology, though!). Most of the differences in methods prescribed by the theories are due to differences in the situations for which they are prescribed."* This clearly shows that it is highly necessary to analyze theories and to discriminate what the terminology essentially refers to. It is further important to differentiate the situations to which each theory pertains. We believe an ontological engineering approach has the potential for solving this problem because it focuses on making "things" clear at a conceptual level. The idea of Way-knowledge and general function decomposition tree based on ontologies is a solution to the problem.

As mentioned in 2.3, a general function decomposition tree includes alternative Ways corresponding to multiple possible Ways to achieve a specific I_L event. In this framework a strategy prescribed in a theory/model is described in terms of

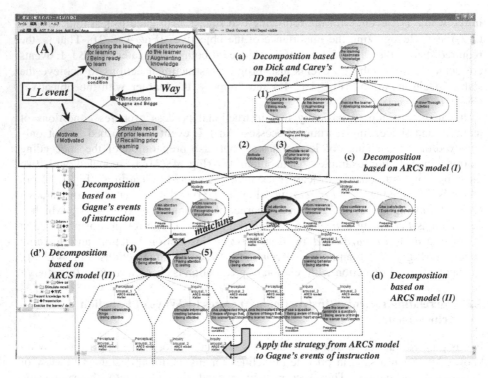

Fig. 5. A part of a general function decomposition tree of learning and instructional design

Way-knowledge. Matching desired outcome and required condition in a Way makes it easy to find points in common among theories/models.

Figure 5 shows a part of a general function decomposition tree of learning and instructional design. An oval node represents an I_L event. Its label expresses combination of instructional action and state-change of learner in the form of "instructional action/state-change of learner". For example, in Fig. 5 (A), "Preparing the learner for learning" is the instructional action and "Being ready to learn" is the state-change of learner[5]. Ideally, this tree provides every possibility of decomposition of I_L events. I_L events in this tree have alternative Ways of function achievement in an OR relationship.

Three theories/models appear in Fig. 5: Dick and Carey's instructional design (ID) model [4], Gagne's nine events of instruction and the ARCS model [10]. The fundamental structure of this tree is based on Gagne's events of instruction. Introducing Dick and Carey's ID model into Gagne's makes the latter more abstract. ARCS model reinforces the I_L event for pre-instruction from the aspect of motivation.

The decomposition of the top I_L event (Fig. 5 (a)) is done by a Way based on Dick and Carey's ID model. In this model Gagne's events are summarized into five

---

[5] A state-change of learner is usually expressed in achieved/desired state of learner because it implies the previous state, that is, a learner has not been in the achieved/desired state.

events. These abstract events are expected to provide pivots for inter-theory relationship at a more abstract level than Gagne's events of instruction.

The first I_L event in the second level, "Preparing the learner for learning/Being ready to learn" (Fig. 5 (1)), can be decomposed into two I_L events: "Motivate/Motivated" (Fig. 5 (2)) and "Stimulate recall of prior learning/Recalling prior learning" (Fig. 5 (3)). The decomposition is based on Gagne's events of instruction but the first two events are put together as an I_L event related to learner's motivation in this tree. Gagne has not himself made it abstract in this way but introducing the abstract event enables learning and instructional designer to have alternatives.

In this tree "Motivate/Motivated" (Fig. 5 (2)) is given two alternative motivational strategies in order to decompose it: based on Gagne's events (Fig. 5 (b)) and based on ARCS model (Fig. 5 (c)). According to ARCS model, learner's state related motivation depends on the following four attributes: Attention, Relevance, Confidence, and Satisfaction. Hence motivational strategy by ARCS model provides four kinds of sub I_L event for each element and detailed strategies to realize the sub I_L events. On the other hand, matching Gagne's motivational strategy with elements in ARCS model, Gagne's theory takes up only Attention and Relevance.

Both Gagne's events and ARCS model have strategies related to learner's attention but these strategies have an important difference. ARCS model is motivational theory so its concern is for getting attention. On the other hand, Gagne's theory is information–processing theory, so its goal is not only for getting attention but also for directing attention to that which is to be learned[10](p. 293). What this statement suggests is that Gagne's strategy for attention is composed of two sub I_L events, which are for "get attention/being Attentive" (Fig. 5 (4)) and "attract to learning/Paying attention to learning" (Fig. 5 (5)). Moreover the I_L event for attention in ARCS model can be same as the former I_L event in Gagne's model. The I_L event for attention in ARCS model can be decomposed into two strategies: "Perceptual arousal" and "Inquiry arousal" (Fig. 5(d)). Consequently, these strategies can be applied to the I_L event based on Gagne's theory (Fig. 5 (4)). The application is shown in Fig. 5 (d').

In this manner, analyzing strategies for desired change of a learner's state not at a terminology level but at an ontological level clarifies intersections of theories and models.

4   Building a Theory-Aware Design Support System for Instructional and Learning Design

This section discusses the application of the ontology of learning and instruction and the framework of function decomposition tree. The usefulness of ontology-based educational systems reported by some studies, for example, [1][7] are for design support and [8] for analysis support. Here, let us focus on design support and discuss the utility of the framework of function decomposition tree with the ontology of learning and instruction.

Existing authoring environments for learning support systems aim at combining authoring tools and knowledge representation [15]. Most of the systems have functionalities to support instructional and learning design based on some sort of fixed theories (or empirical knowledge). Of course, such systems provide designers with guidelines and improve the consistency of design on this basis. However, all of knowledge from the theories in many of the theory-based systems is built in the procedures. The developer, not the system, knows the theory. It causes concealment of relation between the system's functionalities and the theories they are based on.

This study aims to build a theory-aware design support system [14] that understands theories. Such a system has the capability of explaining an author which theory or strategy underlies any suggestion it makes, as opposed to a system in which the theories are implemented as built-in procedures. The following sub-sections present our idea of a design support system called "SMARTIES: SMART Instructional Engineering System", which we have been developing.

4.1 An Overview of a Theory-Aware Design Support System

Fig. 6 shows a block diagram illustrating SMARTIES, which has been under development in this study based on Hozo Core [13]. The scope of support is limited to the design phase of ID process, rather than the analysis and development phases.

SMARTIES helps two types of users; one is design authors, which includes instructional designers, educational practitioners and occasionally learners. The other is knowledge author, which mainly includes researchers and theorists.

A design authors makes a particular instructional and learning process model using the authoring interface. The model manager manages a model design authors made. In addition, the model manager provides the author with guidelines for making a model. Based on the ontology, basic guidelines for modeling instructional and learning process are supplied; concepts and a vocabulary representing them, and the basic structure of concepts. In addition, based on Way-knowledge, instructional and learning strategies from theories are supplied. Besides, generated instructional and learning process model could be finally exported according to IMS LD specification. Briefly put, the structure of a function decomposition tree is reflected in accordance in the activity-structure of IMS LD; instructional actions are compatible with support activities in IMS LD and learning actions are compatible with learning activities in IMS LD.

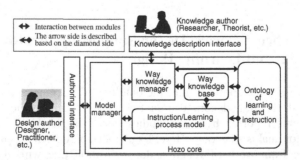

Fig. 6. Block diagram of the design support system: SMARTIES (under development).This diagram focuses only on support for abstract design of learning contents and does not show domain knowledge and learning objects to realize the abstract design.

A knowledge author describes instructional and learning strategies as Way-knowledge with an understanding of theories and put them to the Way-knowledge base. The Way-knowledge manager manages Way-knowledge base and provides knowledge authors with the ontology as basic guidelines as well as the model manager. Describing Way-knowledge makes it possible for design authors to retrieve strategies for inter-theory cooperation and apply multiple theories to a particular instructional and learning process model. The implementation of the retrieval process is being considered using OWL [21] and SWRL [22]. Hozo core can translate ontologies and models into OWL with a set of Hozo features: role concepts, relational concepts and so on. That makes it possible to make ontology and Way-knowledge sharable.

4.2   An Example of Design Support Through Theory-Eclectic Approach

Fig.7 shows a screen shot of SMARTIES. This scene shows how a design author makes an instructional and learning design task using Way-knowledge.

The main window provides an author with an environment to describe a function decomposition tree for an instructional and learning design. Nodes represent I_L events in instructional and learning processes and the decomposition is represented from top to bottom. In this window, an author detemines a function decomposition tree: firstly, an author decides upon the whole-function and then decomposes it step-by-step by choosing applicable ways.

The Way-knowledge window helps an author to choose a Way-knowledge to decompose a function from applicable Way-knowledge candidates. It displays applicable Ways appropriate to the selected function the author wants to decompose. Fig. 7 (a) shows two applicable candidates of

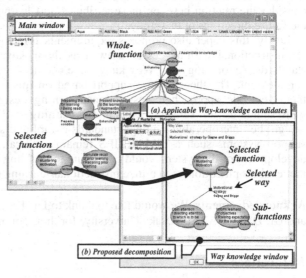

Fig. 7. Screenshot of SMARTIES (under development)

Way-knowledge. When the author chooses one of them, a proposed decomposition is displayed, as shown in Fig. 7 (b). If the author decides to adopt the selected Way, the proposal is applied to the main window. By repetition of the process mentioned above, a design author makes instructional and learning design, moving from abstract levels to concrete ones.

5 Conclusion

We have discussed a modeling framework for instructional and learning theories based on ontological engineering. To summarize, the characteristics of this framework include (1) a theory/paradigm-independent ontology of learning and instruction, (2) a prescriptive model derived from learning/instructional theories, and (3) theory-awareness and compliance with standards for semantic web and e-learning.

Firstly, the independence of an ontology from theories/paradigms allows us to have a common basis for understanding and comparing theories. In this paper, we have discussed the theory-independence of the proposed ontology with the example of Gagne's and Keller's theories in 3.2. The inter-theory relations derived in terms of change of learner's state is one of the key points of the proposed ontology. Although the paradigm-independence has not been discussed, it can be also shown in terms of change of learner's state. From now on, deepening the ontology through organizing many more theories is necessary to examine the effectiveness of modeling in terms of change of learner's state and the paradigm-independence of the proposed ontology.

Secondly, model of theories as Way-knowledge provides us with guidelines for designing instruction/learning at an abstract level. It prescribes which sequence of instructional actions is required to achieve the intended change of learner state. In order to implement such abstract design, it is necessary to link it to learning objects. We have defined attributes of learning and instruction in the proposed ontology. To consider the relation between these attributes and learning object metadata is one of the future directions of this study.

Lastly, this paper also proposes requirements for more advanced support systems for instructional/learning design as well as theory-awareness and compliance with standards. An ontology and Way-knowledge enable systems to understand theories to some extent. The theory-aware support based on this understanding will a facilitate theory-eclectic approach to instructional/learning design. Furthermore, compliance with standards for semantic web and e-learning will make instructional/learning design be interoperable among standards-compliant systems. To develop design support systems such as SMARTIES remains critical. Further research on such a development of the system would contribute to building an engineering infrastructure that enables practitioners to utilize instructional/learning theories.

Acknowledgements. We would like to thank to Dr. Kateryna Synytsya (IRTC, Kiev) and Dr. Daniele Allard (Osaka University) for their comments and suggestions.

References

[1] Aroyo, L., Dicheva, D. and Cristea, A.: "Ontological Support for Web Courseware Authoring", *Proc. ITS2002*, pp. 270-279, 2002.

[2] Bourdeau, J. and Mizoguchi, R.: "Collaborative Ontological Engineering of Instructional Design Knowledge for an ITS", *Proc. of ITS2002*, pp.399-409, 2002.

[3] Bourdeau, J. and Mizoguchi, R.: "Selecting theories in an ontology-based ITS authoring environment", *Proc. of ITS'2004*, pp. 150-161, 2004.

[4] Dick, W., Carey, L., and Carey, J. O.: *The systematic design of instruction*, Fifth edition, Addison-Wesley Educational Publisher Inc., 2001.

[5] Ertmer, P. A., and Newby, T. J.: "Behaviorism, cognitivism, constructivism: Comparing critical features from an instructional design perspective", *Performance Improvement Quarterly*, 6 (4), 50-70, 1993.

[6] Gagne, R. M. and Briggs, L. J.: *Principles of Instructional Design* (2nd Ed.). Holt, Rinehart and Winston, New York, 1979.

[7] Hayashi, Y., Ikeda, M., and Mizoguchi, R.: "A Design Environment to Articulate Design Intention of Learning Contents", *International Journal of Continuing Engineering Education and Life Long Learning*, Vol. 14, No. 3, pp.276-296, 2004.

[8] Inaba, A., Ohkubo, R., Ikeda, M., and Mizoguchi, R.: "An Interaction Analysis Support System for CSCL: An ontological Approach to Support Instructional Design Process", *Proc. of ICCE 2002*, pp. 358-362, 2002.

[9] S Global Learning Consortium, Inc.: IMS Learning Design. Version 1.0 Final Specification, 2003. Retrieved June 30, 2006 from http://www.imsglobal.org/learningdesign/

[10] Keller, J.M. and Kopp, T.W.: "An application of the ARCS model of motivational design", In C. M Reigeluth (Ed.), *Instructional theories in action: Lessons illustrating selected theories and models*, pp. 289-320, 1987.

[11] Kitamura, Y., Kashiwase, M., Fuse, M., Mizoguchi, R.: "Deployment of an Ontological Framework of Functional Design Knowledge", *Advanced Engineering Informatics*, Vol. 18, Issue 2, pp. 115-127, 2004.

[12] Kozaki, K., Kitamura, Y., Ikeda, M., and Mizoguchi, R.: "Development of an Environment for Building Ontologies Which Is Based on a Fundamental Consideration of Relationship and Role", *Proc. of PKAW2000*, pp.205-221, 2000.

[13] Kozaki, K., Kitamura, Y., and Mizoguchi, R.: "Developing Ontology-based Applications using Hozo", *Proc. of CI2005*, pp.273-277, 2005.

[14] Mizoguchi, R. and Bourdeau, J.: "Using Ontological Engineering to Overcome Common AI-ED Problems", *International Journal of Artificial Intelligence in Education*, Vol.11, No.2, pp.107-121, 2000.

[15] Murray, T., Blessing, S., Ainsworth, S.: *Authoring Tools for Advanced Technology Learning Environments: Toward Cost-Effective Adaptive, Interactive and Intelligent Educational Software*, Springer, 2003.

[16] Psyche, V., Bourdeau, J., Nkambou, R., and Mizoguchi, R.: "Making Learning Design Standards Work with an Ontology of Educational Theories", *Proc. of AIED2005*, pp. 539-546, 2005.

[17] Snelbecker, G.E.: "Contrasting and complementary approaches to instructional design", In C. M. Reigeluth (Ed.), *Instructional theories in action: Lessons illustrating selected theories and models*, pp. 321-337, 1987.

[18] Reigeluth, C. M.: "Instructional-design: What is it and why is it?" In Reigeluth, C. M. (Ed.), *Instructional-design theories and models: An overview of their current status*. Hillsdale, New Jersey: Lawrence Erlbaum Associates, Inc., 1983.

[19] Reigeluth, C. M. (Ed.): *Instructional Theories in Action: Lessons Illustrating Selected Theories and Models*, Lawrence Erlbaum Associates, Hillsdale, N.J., 1987.

[20] Wenger, E.: *Artificial Intelligence and Tutoring Systems*, Los Altos, CA: Morgan Kaufmann 1987.

[21] W3C: Web Ontology Language (OWL), 2004.Retrieved June 30, 2006 from http://www.w3.org/2004/OWL/

[22] W3C: SWRL: A Semantic Web Rule Language Combining OWL and RuleML, 2004.Retrieved June 30, 2006 from http://www.w3.org/Submission/SWRL/

Explicit Referencing in Learning Chats: Needs and Acceptance

Torsten Holmer, Andrea Kienle, and Martin Wessner

Fraunhofer Integrated Publication and Information Systems Institute (IPSI)
Dolivostraße 15, 64293 Darmstadt, Germany
{firstname.lastname}@ipsi.fraunhofer.de

Abstract. Chat is used in many learning scenarios and platforms for synchronous communication support. Up to now evaluation of chat communication requires time consuming manual coding and analysis of the chat transcript. In this paper we present a method that combines manual and automatic steps: (1) chat transcripts are manually referenced, i.e. for each chat contribution it is determined to which previous contribution it refers to. (2) the referenced chat transcripts are structurally analysed by calculating different measures. The results of this structure analysis help to evaluate the learning chat and indicate where further (manual) analyses might be helpful. In addition, the ability of chat to support a certain type of learning scenario can be evaluated. We then discuss how chat can be improved by providing functionality for explicit referencing to the participants during the chat. The evaluation of a university seminar in the winter term 2004/2005 that used the tool KOLUMBUS Chat shows that references are used to different extents and not continuously. We analyse the reasons for (not) using explicit references. The results provide hints about the technical and organisational design for learning chats using references.

1 Introduction

Chat is an easy-to-use medium for collaborative learning because of its low requirements for hardware, software and bandwidth. Chat is also accepted by many users, e.g. as instant messaging or web-based chat rooms. Hence, nearly every learning platform offers chat rooms to support communication between the participants. In many learning platforms the chat transcripts (i.e. the list of contributions with author names and timestamps) can be stored and reused. Reuse includes for example providing orientation for late-comers and post-processing the session.

On the other hand chat has disadvantages caused by the specific characteristics of the medium chat. An author of a contribution cannot control the position of his contribution in relation to other contributions because of parallel addition of contributions by different authors. This often leads to incoherent communication and misunderstandings (Garcia & Jacobs 1998).

To evaluate whether a chat can be successfully integrated and utilised in a certain learning scenario or whether other media are more suitable the expected communicative behaviour should be compared to the actual communicative behaviour of the participants (Münzer et al. 2004). Up to now only complex and time-consuming methods exist for the evaluation of communicative behaviour in chats. In this paper

W. Nejdl and K. Tochtermann (Eds.): EC-TEL 2006, LNCS 4227, pp. 170–184, 2006.

we present in its first part a method that combines manual and automatic steps: (1) chat transcripts are manually referenced, i.e. for each chat contribution it is determined to which previous contribution it refers to. (2) the referenced chat transcripts are structurally analysed by calculating different measures.

However, manual referencing has some drawbacks. Errors in the coding can occur because the original intention of a contribution's author has to be determined by a human rater. An approach to avoid this problem is the usage of explicit references that are added by the authors during the chat (Mühlpfordt & Wessner 2005, Kienle 2006). If the authors make proper use of the referencing functionality during the chat the analysis can be accomplished without manual referencing by a human rater. In a study we analysed the usage of explicit references in learning chats. Especially, we focussed on reasons for (not) referencing. The study is presented in the second part of this paper. From the results of the study we derive organisational hints for the design of the learning scenario as well as technical hints for the tool design in order to increase the number of explicit references and thereby minimize the amount of manual referencing by a human rater for the chat analysis.

The remainder of this paper is structured as follows: First, the problem analysis (section 2) and state of the art (section 3) concerning chat evaluation and references in chat tools are presented. Section 4 describes the structure analysis and measures for the evaluation of learning chats. In section 5 the study concerning reasons for (not) referencing in chats is presented. The paper ends with a discussion of findings (section 6), conclusions and an outlook to further research (section 7).

2 Problem Analysis

2.1 The Analysis of Chat Transcripts

When using the medium chat in a learning scenario a certain communicative behaviour is expected of the participants. For a joint discussion of learning content in a learning group the tutor might expect that all users participate in a similar way. For a virtual consultation a sequence of dialogues between the tutor and (single) users can be expected. To evaluate the appropriateness of the medium chat for a specific learning scenario the expected communicative behaviour and the actual communicative behaviour of the participants should be compared. If the actual behaviour differs significantly from the expected behaviour the chosen combination of target group, learning scenario and technology should be reconsidered and eventually changed to ensure learning success.

Direct observation of communicative behaviour of participants in a learning chat requires considerable effort on the side of the tutor. To reduce this effort, evaluation of learning chats should be based on chat transcripts. Especially, the digital chat representation in form of a transcript enables a (semi-)automatic analysis of the communicative behaviour. In the following we assume that the chat transcript contains all references between contributions, i.e. for each contribution it is known to which previous contribution it refers to. If there is no reference, a new communication thread starts. We focus now on a structure oriented view to develop a method that can be used domain-independent. From this point of view three levels can be differentiated:

- **Contribution level**: The contribution level deals with the evaluation of a contribution resp. the order of contributions in a learning chat. The aim is the evaluation of the chat resp. the chat transcript: When do new discussion threads start? How long are the threads? How many parallel threads exist? These analyses should provide hints about the coherence of the communication. We suppose that coherence has positive effects on the readability and reuse of a chat transcript as well as the learning success of the participants.

- **Participant level**: The participant level contains questions on the communicative behaviour of persons. The aim is the assessment of single participants: This includes on the one hand descriptive values such as the (relative) number of contributions and the length of contributions. On the other hand it can be observed to what extent the single user participate in more than one (parallel) threads, whether and how often the user starts or ends discussion threads, and to which amount the user's contributions trigger other contributions.

- **Group level**: The group level focuses on the interaction of participants. The aim is to detect communication structures and to extract information about the group structure. This contains statements about the communication between two participants as well as statements about the group as a whole: For pairs of participants the communicative relation concerning strength and balance should be analysed. These social relations should be aggregated for the group level and compared with typical communication patterns (e.g. star, chain, net, subgroups).

2.2 Explicit References in Chats

Explicit references in chat have three different aims. With references relations between different contributions can be recognized while in chat tools without referencing functionalities these relation can only be interpreted by the reader (1). Additionally, explicit references allow to present the chat not only in the chronological order but also for example in a treeview where contributions are sorted by threads (2). In the case of persistent storage of the chat content this view facilitates reuse, e.g. orientation for late-comers and relearning of the discussion. Last but not least transcripts of chat with explicit references enable an automatic analysis because the step of manual references has not to be applied (3). For (2) (presentation in treeview) and (3) (analysis) a complete reference of the chat is required; if references are missing neither the treeview nor the analysis of the communication structure can be accurate. For (1) (recognizing relations between contributions) references are all the more important the higher the distance between two related contributions is. If two implicitly related contributions are placed adjacent to each other it is from the user's perspective not necessary to have an explicit reference in order to emphasize this relation.

3 Related Work

3.1 Analysis of Chat Transcripts

Related work concerning the analysis of chats resp. chat transcripts can be divided in the two groups, content-related and structure-related approaches. Content-related approaches analyse the content of a contribution (e.g. (Henri 1992)) and its relation to the text as a whole. They require a deeper analysis by a trained, human rater. This requires considerable effort.

Structure-related approaches focus on the evaluation of the relations between contributions. Rafaeli & Sudweeks (1997) analyse the interaction between participants by identifying sequences of reciprocal references between contributions of those participants. On the group level social networks (Wasserman & Faust 1994) are used for the analysis and visualisation of communication patterns. For asynchronous communication (e.g. e-mail, forums) relations between contributions are explicated by using the "reply-to"-functionality. The so developed structure of contributions can be analysed and used for the coordination of e-learning forums (Gerosa et al. 2004).

Furthermore, some approaches propose the combination of both approaches. The Dynamic Topic Analysis (Herring 2003) looks on the structural relation between contributions and topic shifts. This approach turned out to be expensive and error-prone because of the topic related activities.

To conclude it can be stated that existing approaches are either to expensive (content-related approaches) or do not address all levels mentioned in the problem analysis (structure-related approaches).

3.2 Explicit References in Chat Tools

Explicit references to other communicative contributions are already realized in some chat tools, for example in Threaded Chat (Smith et al. 2000). Here a contribution can be related to another contribution as a "reply-to" and all contributions are presented as a tree. This presentation leads to problems, e.g. when new contributions are added to different, potentially distant (out of the current view) branches. To deal with this problem, Academic Talk (McAlister et al. 2004) provides two views in the same window: one presents the contributions in chronological order, the other in logical (tree) order as defined by reply-to relations.

Other tools allow to relate chat conversation and (learning) material. Anchored Conversations (Churchhill et al. 2000) allows chats to be connected to a specific point in a document. This tool does not support references between contributions. Threaded discussions and web pages are linked in Kükäkükä (Suthers & Xu 2002). The GraffiDis tool (Leponiemi 2003) supports relations of chat contributions to texts and graphics and offers a certain persistence: Users enter contributions (which can also consist of graphics and other material) at any places of the chat area. After a time the contributions are faded out to the background colour. With a "history slider" a user can navigate through the chat in chronological order. Relations between contributions are indicated by nearby positions in the chat area. References to contributions are not possible after a certain distance in time as the previous contribution already faded out.

Newer approaches supports references to contributions, references to shared material and a persistent storage of the content. Examples are ConcertChat (Mühlpfordt & Wessner 2005) or KOLUMBUS Chat (Kienle 2006) that was used in the study described later in this paper. Both systems support references between chat contributions as well as the relation of these contributions to (even parts) of material. All chat contributions and the developed material are stored and can be accessed later. If references were used the related chat contributions can be presented in a treeview.

4   The Structure Analysis of Learning Chats

The basis for determining coherence, individual contribution and social relationships in a chat is the chat transcript. A chat transcript is a list of messages sorted by time. The messages usually contain also the name of the author and a time stamp of the sending time. In regular chat transcripts it is not explicit whether a message relates to another message. Thus, this relationship has to be coded manually. In verbal communication the participants assume that a contribution is directly related to the adjacent contribution (Schegloff 2000). So called adjacency pairs are pairs of contributions which relate to each other in a way that the first part requires the second part like in question-answer pairs and greetings. A common observation in chat transcripts are phantom adjacency pairs (Garcia & Jacobs 1998), in which adjacent contributions are not related to each other but seem to because of their adjacent position in the transcript. These events cause irritations for the recipient as he has to search for and identify the related contribution in the transcript.

Identifying the intended relationships between contributions is the starting point for the discourse structure analysis (Holmer 2006). The coding of these relationships is called referencing and means checking for each message if there is a previous message it refers to. If there is no reference to other messages the contribution points to itself and opens a new thread of contributions. Messages which are connected by references are part of a thread. Depending on the structure of the references threads can be chains or more complex tree structures. The analysis of these structures provides insights about the coherence, individual contribution and social networks, which can be used for the evaluation of chat discussions.

4.1   Manual References

If references were not set explicitly by the participants by using referencing functionalities like described above (see sections 2.2 and 3.2) they have to be added manually by trained experts. In order to support the whole process of coding and analysing a software was created which allows the import and referencing of chat transcripts. All messages in a transcript get a number which corresponds to its position in the message list (OID = order ID). The rater's task is to state for each OID a reference ID (=RID) which is the OID of the referenced message. Referencing can be done relatively fast. Depending on the complexity of the transcript (number of participants and parallel threads) it takes approximately a minute per message (Holmer 2006). For video data ten minutes coding activity for one minute of video has been reported, i.e. it takes ten times longer. Table 1 shows an example of a chat transcript taken from (Vronay et al. 1999). In the following sections we demonstrate how this episode can be analysed with the proposed methods.

4.2   Coherence

The linguistic concept of coherence is about how text in verbal or written form belongs together in contrast to unrelated utterances or sentences. Global coherence is the relation of utterances to the topic of the whole text or conversation. Local coherence describes how adjacent utterances refer to each other. In this paper we focus on the aspect of local coherence in chat transcripts.

Table 1. Referenced Chat Transcript

OID	RID	USER	MESSAGE
1	1	Black	Did you see that new Mel Gibson movie - I think it is called 'Payback'?
2	2	Pink	I saw the academy awards last night. Did you watch it?
3	1	Pink	yep.
4	3	Pink	It was very violent, but funny.
5	3	Black	You saw it? You liked it?
6	2	Black	How did it end up - who won?
7	1	Red	I heard it was good.
8	6	Pink	It was OK. At least Titanic didn't win everything.
9	8	Black	I guess you can only be king of the world once.

In order to measure local coherence we calculate the difference between the values for OID (order identification: number of the message) and RID (reference identification: number of the referenced message). This difference is the distance between a message and the message it refers to. The larger this distance the more difficult it is for the reader of a transcript to identify the relationships and to understand the context of the message. The coherence of chat transcripts can be expressed by the values for these differences. In order to show these distances we created a visualisation which shows the reference relationships as semicircles (Figure 1).

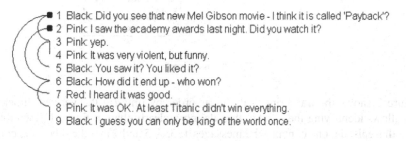

Fig. 1. Visualisation of references as semicircles

Adjacent references are shown as vertical lines while distances more than one are shown as semicircles. The biggest distance is between the message 7 from Red and its reference part, message no. 1 from Black. This figure shows the incoherence of this chat episode. The reader often has to jump more than one line upwards to understand to which message the actual message is responding to.

Another factor which influences the coherence of a chat transcript is the number and amount of topics which are discussed in parallel threads. Overlapping threads make it difficult to follow the line of thought. The presentation of the referenced chat as a graph allows showing this problem.

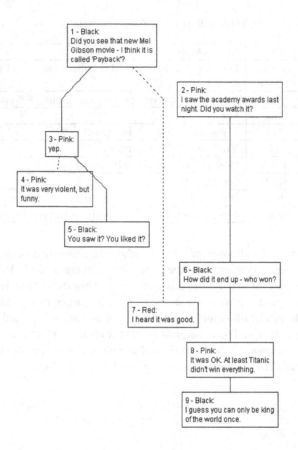

Fig. 2. Chat Graph

Figure 2 shows the transcript in its linear order by time (in the vertical dimension) which allows identifying the parallel threads more clearly than in figure 1. Two threads exist in this episode: one contains the messages 1, 3, 4, 5 and 7 and the other one consists of messages 2, 6, 8 and 9. Both threads are overlapping and interrupting each other.

4.3 Individual Participation

The chat graph (see figure 2) also provides information about the individual behaviour of the participants. In the visualisation there are solid and dotted lines which connect the messages. A solid line shows that there is a pattern of communication which is called "dialog sequence" (Holmer 2006). Dialog sequences are message exchanges in which participants are responding to each other following the the pattern A-B-A. The response of participant B to A and the backward response from A to B show that there is a close interaction between the participants (Rafaeli & Sudweeks 1997). Dialog sequences are important for the evaluation of chat transcripts because they show the intensity of the relationships. The simple counting of sender-receiver transactions is not enough because it does not show in which patterns the messages are exchanged.

Beyond this direct interaction patterns other properties of the messages can provide some insight about the role of the participant in the group. How high is the individual participation rate on the overall communication and in the different threads? How many contributions are triggered by the messages of the participant? It can be differentiated between the whole amount of following messages (impact) and the amount of messages minus own messages (resonance). This distinction is important because if a participant gets no answers to his contributions he has no impact on the discussion. If he is just answering himself in a monologue he will not have high resonance values. The values are calculated by dividing the sum of the following messages by the number of messages of a user.

Table 2. Participation, Impact and Resonance of the participants in the episode

Participant	Messages	Impact	Resonance
Pink	4	1.5	1.0
Black	4	1.5	1.0
Red	1	0.0	0.0

Table 2 shows the result of the analysis for participation, impact and resonance. Pink and Black have the same values while Red has low values in all categories. The results of this small example cannot show the huge amount of differences we found in bigger and more complex transcripts. Interesting patterns are given if a participant has provided just few messages but his impact and resonance values are above the average value. This means that his contributions have raised a lot of discussion and were stimulating the group.

4.4 Social Networks

Groups and their interaction patterns can be represented as social networks (Wasserman & Faust 1994). The participants are represented by nodes, sender-receiver relations are represented as edges. The resulting network can be described and measured by methods of social network analysis. For the analysis of chat sessions it is important, whether the expected communication structures can be found. If an equal distribution of participation and relations is expected then the nodes should be of similar size (size indicates number of messages) and there should be no subgroup structures. Sender receiver relations should be balanced in both directions.

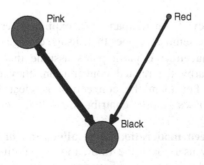

Fig. 3. Social network of the episode

In figure 3 the structure of the interaction is shown as a network. Like in table 2 the users Pink and Black have the highest amount of messages. The new information in this picture is that there is equal communication between Pink and Black, but the relationship of Red is only to Black and only in a one-way fashion. If this episode has to be evaluated the role of Red has to be seen as critical. While Pink and Black seem to interact with each other in a tightly coupled way, Red is not well integrated into the network. This example shows how this kind of social network can be used to compare expected and actual communication patterns and detect critical differences at a glance.

As discussed above, tools exist which allow the users to do the referencing on their own during the chat. This would ease the analysis as ideally no post-processing would be necessary. In the next section we present a study where we analysed the referencing behaviour of students using such a tool.

5 Using Explicit References

A study was carried out in a seminar at the University of Dortmund (Germany), Education Institute, during the winter term 2004/2005. Fourteen students in four subgroups of three to four students participated in this seminar. Each subgroup had to prepare a moderated seminar chat and a talk that had to be given in one of the face-to-face meetings. Both (seminar chat and talk) dealt with a specific topic of e-learning that was on a non-detailed level given by the tutor and provided space for own research questions and solution ideas of the students. For the seminar chats (about 1 hour duration) the KOLUMBUS Chat was used in the moderated modus: each student who wants to add a chat contribution has to request the floor and the moderator grants the floor to one or more persons. KOLUMBUS Chat supports explicit references; users click on a previous message to indicate to which message a new message refers to. For further details concerning the overall study see (Kienle 2006). Here, we focus on the usage of references by the students.

The analysis of the causes for (non-)using explicit references in the seminar considers different levels. A central assumption is that many of the non-referenced contributions are misses. A miss is a contribution that has no explicit reference although its content refers to other contributions. For an appropriate presentation of the discussion structure as well as for its analysis a complete referenced chat transcript is necessary. Based on this we developed research questions concerning the usage of references:

- **Individual constancy:** Do participants use explicit references in a similar way over the course of the seminar or does their usage change over time?
- **Assumption of adjacency:** If participants assume that his/her contribution is probably placed nearby the related contribution, they do not see a need for explicit references. For them the connection is clear because of the spatial adjacency. Are misses those contributions that are nearby the related contribution?
- **Interrelation between moderation resp. allocation of the floor and explicit references:** If many users have the floor, the probability of parallel discussion threads increases and the connection between related contributions becomes more

unclear because of non-adjacent placement. Is there a correlation between the number of persons who have the floor and the usage of explicit references? One assumption is that the usage of explicit references increases with the number of persons who have the floor because the propability of adjacent placement decreases. On the other hand one might assume that the usage decreases because of time pressure.

Results

For the analysis the existing chat transcripts with explicit references were referenced by experienced raters and compared with the original transcripts as shown in table 3. For all chats the post-referenced transcripts have a higher percentage of references. So, a considerable amount of contributions were not explicitly referenced by the participants that had to be referenced according to the opinion of the experts.

Table 3. Comparison of referenced contributions

Moderated chats	Contributions (Sum)	References contributions (existing)	Percentage	References contributions (post-referenced)	Percentage
chat 1	240	95	39,5 %	174	72,5%
chat 2	140	56	40 %	109	77,8%
chat 3	169	87	51,49 %	130	76,9%
chat 4	127	47	37,0 %	79	62,2%
chat 5	146	62	42,4 %	102	69,8%
Sum	**822**	**347**	**42,1 %**	**594**	**71,8%**

Individual constancy

First it can be stated that all persons except of one (participant 8) used the referencing functionality from the beginning of the first chat. This indicates that the participants knew the referencing functionality and its usage. In the following we analyse the

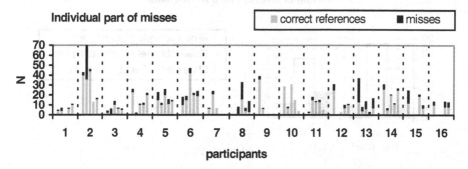

Fig. 4. Individual number of contributions, correct references and misses

development of the misses´ percentage. Figure 4 shows for the 16 participants (14 students and 2 tutors) their participation in the five chats. Here the absolute number of contributions is shown and divided in correctly referenced contributions (white part) and misses (black part).

The analysis of the percentage of misses shows an individual constancy concerning only for some persons: participants 8 and 13 have a continuous high part of misses (50 %), while participants 7, 9 and 10 have never a part higher than 25%. For the other participants high variations can be identified between the chat sessions. It can be concluded that most participants have no individual constancy. For some users the amount of misses decreases over time; here we assume that they adapted to use the referencing functionality.

Assumption of adjacency
Another hypothesis for misses is grounded in the situation of typing a contribution. When writing a contribution one of the following situations has to be the case:

1. Between the appearance of the related contribution and the sending of the referencing contribution no other contributions appear. The participant can act with high probability on the assumption that the related contributions are placed adjacent (side by side).

2. Before the typing of the referencing contribution interrupting contributions are already placed. An adjacent placement is impossible; the participant knows that an explicit reference is necessary (except he wants to start a new thread).

3. After the user started his referencing contribution interrupting contributions appear in the list. In this situation it can happen that the user does not look on the list and recognize that interrupting contributions appeared. He wrongly assumes that his contribution will be placed adjacently.

Figure 5 shows the evidence for the research question mentioned above: in situation 1 (no interrupting contributions) there are more misses than correct referenced messages (25,9% and 12,8%). A quarter of misses are contributions that are placed adjacent in the chat transcript and are no problem for understanding the chat.

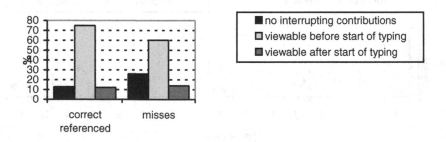

Fig. 5. Part of references and misses before during and after the begin of typing

These findings support the hypothesis that a high percentage of misses might occur under the assumption that the contribution will be placed adjacent to the related contribution. This strategy is marginally thwarted by contributions that appear during typing because in this case the number of misses has to be higher than the number of correct references. But this difference is not significant (13,9% and 12,1%).

Floor and misses
The question if moderation in form of giving the floor has an influence on the number of misses is answered by the correlation between both factors. We calculated for the last ten contributions the average of the number of participants (except moderator) who had the floor and how many misses can be count for the last ten contributions.

Table 4. Correlation between floor and misses (Pearson)

chatsession	chat 1	chat 2	chat 3	chat 4	chat 5	all chats
correlation	-0,94	0,16	0,17*	-0,48	0,04	-0,16**

Results are shown in table 4. Only in chat 3 the value of correlation exceeds the level of significance by 0.05 while for all other chats the value did not reach a significant value. Nevertheless the value of -0,16 for all chats expresses a highly significant interrelation. Thus, giving the floor only has an indirect or contra-inductive effect. The negative coefficient expresses that the number of misses decreases when the number of floor-holders is increased. In the detailed analysis of the data we found two surprising results: when many participants (6 or 7) have the floor, the number of misses decreases while the highest amount of misses occurs when only a small number (2 or 3) have the floor. This means that a high number of misses can not be reduced by limiting the number of typing participants. These findings do not support the assumption that users feel time-pressure in situations with many floor-holders and forget the explicit referencing. In fact the assumption of adjacency is confirmed. When many participants have the floor the probability of adjacent placement decreases and more explicit and correct references occur.

6 Discussion

A structure analysis supports the evaluation of a learning chat and gives important hints for further analyses. The measures of coherence and the different graphical presentations show the relations between contributions, the number of parallel discussion threads and who discusses with whom. The presentation on the individual level helps to evaluate the communicative behaviour of single learners; social networks have the potential to present group structures, the composition of learning groups and its development over time.

The interpretation of these results depends on the underlying learning scenario. An unequal distribution of contributions can indicate a communication that is dominated by a few participants. On the other hand an unequal distribution can also match the expected pattern, for example in the case of virtual consultation-hour. This leads to the more general question of optimum values for the measures. If expectations are clearly formulated (a special communication pattern is expected) it can be controlled whether the chat fulfills the expectations of not. In other cases the structure analysis provides hints on noticeable values and can be seen as a starting point for further (manual) analysis. The question "what is noticeable" has to be answered by the tutor or researcher.

The results of the study on reasons for (non-)referencing showed that only a limited number of persons has an individual constancy for using explicit references in chats. Although some participants adapted to use explicit references it is not sufficient for a complete referenced chat: even in the last seminar chat nearly 30% of the contributions were not correctly referenced.

The strongest support was found for the assumption of adjacency: if the related contribution is placed in a distance (other contributions came in before finishing the contribution) the number of misses decreases. This showed that participants used the referencing functionality to emphasize the relation. A high number of misses can be explained in the way that participants assume (often correct) that their contribution is placed adjacent and therefore do not explicit reference. In these cases the moderator should give hints during the chat session that a complete referenced chat is more helpful for the following reusing of the chat transcript and presentation in a treeview. Without these reminders a normal chat behaviour (typing and sending as fast as possible to reach adjacent placement) arises. A preceding training could emphasize the importance of a complete referenced chat transcript and demonstrate its advantages during and after the chat as well as for the analysis. The analysis of the relation between giving the floor and references further supports the assumption of adjacency: when many people have the floor the probability of adjacent placement decreases and more explicit references occur. Surprisingly, moderation with a limited number of floor-holders doesn't increase the number of explicit references.

Additional to these organisational hints the design of the interface of the chat-tool can influence the number of explicit references resp. the number of misses. In order to increase the number of references the effort for referencing should be very low. In KOLUMBUS Chat explicit references were added by a mouse click on the related contribution. It could be helpful if users can add explicit references also by keyboard actions, e.g. using cursor for selecting the related contribution. This would avoid the need for switching between mouse and keyboard. Another possibility would be to automatically add a reference to the last contribution visible when the typing starts. Thereby the high number of misses with a small distance between related contributions could be avoided.

7   Conclusion and Further Research

Chat is used in many learning scenarios and platforms for synchronous communication support. Its low requirements for hardware, software and bandwidth lead to a high acceptance by many users. To evaluate if a chat can be successfully integrated in a certain learning scenario or if other media are more suitable the expected communicative behaviour and the actual behaviour of the participants should correspond. Up to now only complex and time-consuming methods exist for the evaluation of communicative behaviour in chats. In this contribution a new method for the evaluation of learning chats was described which combines manual and automatic steps. In this method manually referenced chat transcripts are structurally analysed by calculating measures for coherence, individual participation and social networks. The results of this analysis help to evaluate the learning chat and provides hints for further analyses. Thus, the ability of chat to support a certain type of learning scenario can be evaluated.

The functionality of explicit references improves chat tools and eases chat analysis. Explicit references are created by the participants during the chat and make the following manual referencing unnecessary. The evaluation of a university seminar in the winter term 2004/2005 that used the chat-tool KOLUMBUS Chat showed that the references are used to different extents and not continuously. This was a starting point for a further analysis of reasons for (non-)using explicit references. The analysis showed most support for the assumption of adjacency. The evaluation of a relation between moderation and giving the floor also support that assumption. Only for some users an individual constancy can be stated. The results provided hints about the technical (e.g. low effort for referencing) and organisational (e.g. hints by the moderator, usage of typing rights) design for learning chats using references.

Further research concerns on the one hand the method itself. Actually it requires a complete referenced chat transcript for the analysis. This is not given in a chat transcript only with references by the participants as the analysis of the university seminar showed. The method has to be further developed in this direction in order to handle also incompletely referenced transcripts.

On the other hand the design proposals should be tested in experiments in order to improve chat tools with referencing functionalities. The higher the number of correct referenced contributions the more helpful is the chat visualisation and the less time-consuming a complete analysis.

References

1. Churchill, E.F.; Trevor, J.; Bly, S.; Nelson L.; Cubranic, D (2000). Anchored Conversations: Chatting in the Context of a Document. In: Proceedings of the SIGCHI Conference on Human Factors in Computing Systems, 2000, 454-461.
2. Garcia, A.; Jacobs, J. (1998). The Interactional Organization of Computer-mediated Communication in the College Classroom. Qualitative Sociology, Vol. 21 No.3 (1998), 299-317.
3. Gerosa, M. , Pimentel, M., Fuks, H., Lucena, C.: Analyzing Discourse Struc-ture to Coordinate Educational Forums. In Lester, J.C., Vicari, R.M. & Paraguaçu, F. (Eds.), Proceedings of The 7th International Conference on Intelligent Tutoring Systems, LNCS 3220. Springer, New York (2004), 262-272. Available online: http://ritv.les.inf.puc-rio.br/publicacoes/ITS2004.pdf. (Last access 2006/04/10)
4. Henri, F. (1992). Computer conferencing and content analysis. In A. R. Kaye (Eds.). Collaborative learning through computer conferencing: The Najaden papers. Springer, New York, 115 - 136
5. Herring, S. (2003). Dynamic topic analysis of synchronous chat. In: New Research for New Media: Innovative Research Methodologies Symposium Working Papers and Readings. Minneapolis, MN: U. of Minnesota School of Journalism & Mass Communication

6. Holmer, T.: Diskursstrukturanalyse der Chatkommunikation. Dissertation, TU Darmstadt, 2006, in preparation (*Discourse structure analysis, PhD thesis*).
7. Kienle, A.: The integration of asynchronous and synchronous communication support in cooperative systems. Accepted for the 7th International Conference on the Design of Cooperative Systems (COOP), 2006
8. Leponiemi, J.: Visualizing Discussion History. International Journal of Human-Computer Interaction, Vol. 15, No. 1 (2003), 121-134
9. McAlister, S.; Ravenscroft, A.; Scanlon, E.: Combining interaction and context design to support collaborative argumentation using a tool for synchronous CMC. Journal of Computer Assisted Learning, Vol. 20, No 3 (2004), 194-204
10. Mühlpfordt, M., Wessner, M.: Explicit Referencing In Chat Supports Collaborative Learning. Proceedings of the CSCL 2005, Taipei, Taiwan.
11. Münzer, S., Linder, U., Hoffmann, A., & Balzer, E. (2004): Gemeinsam online Lernen: Das Prozessmodell für Konzeption, Durchführung und Qualitätssicherung. (*Joint online learning: the process model for conception, realisation and quality ensurance*) In: Münzer, S. & Linder, U. (Eds.): Gemeinsam Online Lernen: Vom Design bis zur Evaluation kooperativer Online-Übungen. Bielefeld: Bertelsmann, 92-223.
12. Schegloff, E.: Overlapping talk and the organization of turn-taking for conversa-tion. Language in Society, Vol. 29 (2000), 1–63.
13. Smith, M.; Cadiz, J.J.; Burkhalter, B.: Conversation Trees and Threaded Chats. In: Proceedings of the Conference on CSCW. ACM New York (2000) 97-105.
14. Suthers, D.; Xu, J.: Kükäkükä: An Online Environment for Artifact-Centered Discourse. Proc. of the conference WWW 2002, 472-480. Available online: http://www2002.org /CDROM/alternate/252/index.html (Last access 2006/04/10)
15. Rafaeli, S. & Sudweeks, F. (1997). Networked Interactivity. In: Journal of Computer-Mediated Com. Vol. 2 No. 4 (1997). Available online: http://jcmc.indiana.edu/vol2/ issue4/rafaeli.sudweeks.html (Last access 2006/04/10)
16. Vronay, D., Smith, M. & Drucker, S. (1999). Alternative Interfaces for Chat. Proceedings of the ACM Symposium on User Interface Software and Technology. New York: ACM, 19-26
17. Wasserman, S. & Faust,K. (1994). Social Network Analysis. Cambridge Univ. Press, Cambridge.

Integrating Learning Object Repositories Using a Mediator Architecture

Philipp Kärger[1], Carsten Ullrich[2], and Erica Melis[2]

[1] Saarland University, Saarbrücken, Germany
[2] German Research Center for Artificial Intelligence (DFKI), Saarbücken, Germany

Abstract. We propose a mediator architecture that allows a learning system to retrieve learning objects from heterogeneous repositories. A mediating component accepts queries formulated in a uniform query language, translates them into repository specific queries and passes them to each connected repository. For the translation of queries, a novel ontology-based query-rewriting method has been developed. The architecture has been realized in the Web-based, user-adaptive and interactive e-learning environment ACTIVEMATH. Currently, it enables the ACTIVEMATH's course planner to access four heterogeneous learning object repositories.

1 Introduction

In the last years numerous e-learning systems have been developed and more often than not with each system a proprietary repository of learning objects. Consequently many learning object repositories exist (an overview can be found in [1]). Each repository uses a different metadata structure to annotate learning objects and different technologies for storing learning content. This situation makes it almost impractical to retrieve and reuse learning objects from a foreign e-learning system.

Our approach allows an e-learning system to access information in *multiple* repositories and not exclusively in its own. For that purpose we introduce a mediating architecture, which translates queries for a specified set of connected repositories and passes the translated queries to the repositories. The advantage of a mediating architecture is that the querying component does not have to know the specification of the data sources and their query languages [2]. An ontology-based query-rewriting mechanism integrated in our architecture enables the integration of new repositories. The mechanism uses the specified knowledge representation of the repository to be integrated and an ontology mapping to compute the rewriting steps for translating queries sent to the new repository.

The work described in this paper has been realized in ACTIVEMATH, a Web-based, user-adaptive e-learning environment. It comprises a planning component that can create courses adapted to the learner's goals, knowledge, learning behaviour and a specific learning scenario [3]. To select adequate learning objects, initially the course planner queried its proprietary repository MBASE for learning objects with specific characteristics encoded in metadata. The challenge was to integrate more than one repository into ACTIVEMATH's course generation.

W. Nejdl and K. Tochtermann (Eds.): EC-TEL 2006, LNCS 4227, pp. 185–197, 2006.
© Springer-Verlag Berlin Heidelberg 2006

Our mediator architecture solves this problem. It has been integrated into the ACTIVEMATH-environment and enables the course planner to retrieve learning objects additionally from the repository of the DAMIT-system, of the MATHS-THESAURUS, and the LEACTIVEMATH EXERCISEREPOSITORY.

This article is structured as follows. We will first outline the main approach of our work, describing its basic principles and its architecture. Afterwards, in Section 3 we describe the integration of our approach into ACTIVEMATH. Related work is presented in Section 4 and Section 5 provides conclusions and discusses further work.

2   Mediator Approach

The mediator idea relies on the translation of queries based on given ontologies representing the metadata structure of the foreign repositories.

2.1   Queries and Query Language

The mediator provides a single interface for querying several data sources. This interface accepts a query language that specifies metadata of learning objects; therefore, a query sent to the mediator contains a metadata specification of learning objects and returns the Uniform Resource Identifiers (URIs) of the learning objects which meet this specification. A query comprises three parts:

RelationQueries comprise the relational metadata the learning objects to be retrieved has to meet. It is a set of triples (*relation*, `relation`, `LO`) in which the keyword *relation* denotes the type of the query part, `relation` specifies the relation between the learning object `LO` and the learning objects to be retrieved.

PropertyQueries comprise the metadata of properties. It is a set of triples (*property*, `property`, `value`). Each queried learning object satisfies each property-value-pair (`property`, `value`).

ClassQueries comprises all classes the learning objects to be retrieved belong to. It is a set of pairs (*class*, `class`) in which `class` denotes the category the returned learning objects belong to.

A query asking for all learning objects which are easy exercises training the concept *asymptote* looks as follows:

(relation isFor asymptote[1])(class Exercise)(property hasDifficulty easy).

2.2   Ontology Mapping and Query Rewriting

Queries sent to the mediator contain terms taken from the *Ontology of Instructional Objects* (OIO) introduced by Ullrich in [4]. Because existing metadata

---

[1] Usually identifiers of learning objects are URIs. For readability we use simple terms throughout this paper instead.

standards such as IEEE LOM [5] can not represent sufficient information about the sources for a completely automatic search, we use the OIO (see Figure 1) to specify properties of learning objects. This ontology describes different types of learning objects from an instructional point of view. Central to the ontology is the distinction between fundamentals and auxiliaries. The class fundamental subsumes instructional objects that describe the central pieces of knowledge. Auxiliary elements include instructional objects which provide additional information about the concepts.

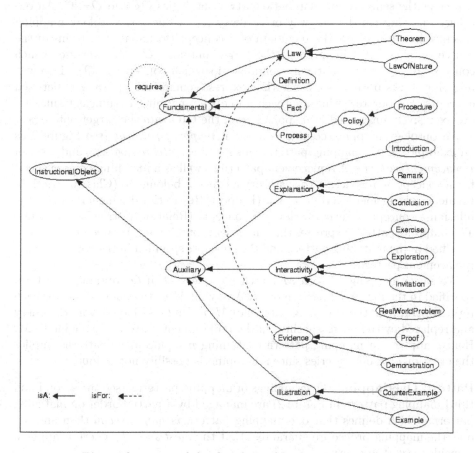

Fig. 1. Overview of the Ontology of Instructional Objects

The terms of the OIO in the queries have to be replaced with the corresponding terms a repository uses to describe its learning objects. Consider a repository using the term *trains* for expressing the relation between an exercise and its topic item and the Boolean property `isDifficult` to express whether a learning object is difficult or not. For that repository the aforementioned query has to be translated into the query

```
(relation exercises asymptote)(property isDifficult true).
```

To guarantee the correct substitution of the terms appearing in the queries one has to define an ontology mapping between the OIO (as the source ontology) and each of the pedagogical ontologies describing the metadata structure of the target repositories. Therefore, to define an accurate mapping definition, one has to make explicit and specify an ontology representing the knowledge structure and metadata semantics of each target repository.

An XML-based ontology mapping language serves to represent the mappings between the OIO and the target ontologies. Generally, an ontology mapping expresses the semantic overlap between two ontologies $\mathcal{O}_S$ and $\mathcal{O}_T$ [6]. An ontology mapping can be one-way or two-way [7]. A one-way ontology mapping specifies how to express the metadata of a concept (formulated in terms of the source ontology $\mathcal{O}_S$) in terms of the target ontology $\mathcal{O}_T$. It expresses which concepts of $\mathcal{O}_S$ are semantically contained in which concepts of $\mathcal{O}_T$. Two-way mapping works both ways, hence they express semantical equivalence between concepts. For our rewriting approach a one-way mapping is sufficient since we are exclusively interested in mappings *from* the OIO *into* the target ontologies.

An ontology mapping comprises a set of *mapping patterns* (see Figure 2 as an example). Each mapping pattern consists of a *matching pattern* and a set of *replacement patterns*. A replacement pattern as well as a matching pattern speci-fies a concept by restricting the category a concept belongs to (ClassRestriction-Element), the property a concept has (PropertyRestriction-Element), and/or the relation a concept connects with other concepts (RelationRestriction-Element). The mapping pattern expresses the semantical containment between the concept specified in the matching pattern and the concepts specified in the corresponding replacement patterns.

We say a mapping pattern M matches a query Q, if Q contains each term specified in the matching pattern of M. Applying M to the query Q means each term appearing in the matching pattern of M *and* in Q is deleted from the query and replaced by the terms specified in the replacement patterns belonging to M. Hence, applying a mapping pattern containing n replacement patterns implies the creation of n new queries since a mapping is possibly not unique.

Pattern Overlapping. Overlappings of mapping patterns (see the second and third mapping pattern in Figure 2) are managed by a partial order on matching patterns which defines that one mapping pattern *is more special* than another one. the mapping procedure guarantees that the *most special* pattern is applied. Consider, e.g., the query

```
(class Example)(relation isFor asymptote)
```

and the ontology mapping shown in Figure 2. Although both mapping patterns match, one has to make explicit that the second mapping pattern is the better choice for the query than the third one is.

Applying an ontology mapping to a query means the following: each most special mapping pattern matching the query is applied. A term for which no matching pattern is found, is left as it is. The rewriting procedure considers this

```
<OIOMapping>

  ...

  <MappingPattern>
    <MatchPattern>
      <ClassRestriction name="Introduction"/>
    </MatchPattern>
    <ReplacementPattern>
      <ClassRestriction name="omtext"/>
      <PropertyRestriction name="type" expected_value="introduction"/>
    </ReplacementPattern>
    <ReplacementPattern>
      <ClassRestriction name="omtext"/>
      <PropertyRestriction name="type" expected_value="motivation"/>
    </ReplacementPattern>
  </MappingPattern>

  <MappingPattern>
    <MatchPattern>
      <ClassRestriction name="Example"/>
      <RelationRestriction name="isFor"/>
    </MatchPattern>
    <ReplacementPattern>
      <RelationRestriction name="example_for"/>
    </ReplacementPattern>
  </MappingPattern>

  <MappingPattern>
    <MatchPattern>
      <RelationRestriction name="isFor"/>
    </MatchPattern>
    <ReplacementPattern>
      <RelationRestriction name="for"/>
    </ReplacementPattern>
  </MappingPattern>

  ...

</OIOMapping>
```

Fig. 2. Extract of a mapping specified in the proposed mapping language

term as used in in both ontologies. This approach allows one to abstain from mapping patterns expressing the pure identity of terms.

Applying the ontology mapping of Figure 2 to the query

```
(class Introduction)(relation isFor asymptote)
```

yields the following two new queries:

1. (class omtext)(relation for asymptote)(property type introduction)
2. (class omtext)(relation for asymptote)(property type motivation).

Query Expansion. The expansion of a query guarantees that the mediator, if asked for category C, returns not only objects belonging to C but objects belonging to subcategories of C, too. For a query Q, the query expansion algorithm returns $\prod_{i=0}^{n} m(C_i)$ queries, where $C_0, ..., C_n$ are the categories specified in Q and $m(C_i)$ counts all recursive subcategories of a category C_i.

2.3   Architecture

Our architecture is a mediation information system architecture as introduced by Wiederhold in [2]. Its main component, called mediator, provides a uniform interface for accessing multiple heterogeneous data resources. Each resource is encapsulated with a wrapper, which can be provided by the data resource or can be a part of the mediator.

To allow an e-learning system to query several data resources we developed a mediator that accepts queries formulated in the query language defined above and returns a set of URIs, where each URI points to a learning object meeting the conditions specified in the query. For each repository a wrapper is integrated comprising the specification of the ontology of the repositories knowledge (as an OWL-ontology-definition) and the mapping between the terms of the Ontology of Instructional Objects and the terms the repository uses (see Figure 3). The mediator utilises the OWL file for query expansion and the mapping specification for query rewriting.

Wrappers. After rewriting, the queries have to be passed to the repositories. To manage the different querying technologies the mediator comprises a set of wrappers. Each wrapper queries the corresponding repository for metadata by creating repository specific commands. These commands are implemented in the following three methods each wrapper offers to the mediator:

queryClass returns the set of categories a given item belongs to.
queryProperty returns the set of property-value pairs a given item has.
queryRelation returns a set of URIs a given item is related to.

Caching. As stated in [8], a repository is not always equipped with a powerful caching mechanism. Hence it is reasonable to integrate a caching mechanism into the mediating component. If a query is sent a second time, the mediator does not query each connected repository again. It returns the cached set of URIs instead, which reduces run-time complexity dramatically. The results of parts of queries are cached, too.

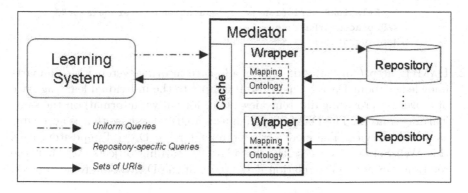

Fig. 3. Mediator Architecture

3   The Course Generator of ACTIVEMATH - A Use Case

The ontology-based mediator has been integrated into the Web-based, user-adaptive learning environment ACTIVEMATH in order to generate adaptive courses from one of four learning object repositories. The ontologies representing the metadata structure of each repository (target ontologies) have been developed, too. For each repository a mapping has been specified which enables the mediator to replace the terms of the Ontology of Instructional Objects with terms of the target ontologies. We introduce the four integrated repositories in the following. To illustrate the different ontology mappings, the mapping of the OIO-relation *requires* is attached to each description.

3.1   Integrated Repositories

1. ACTIVEMATH MBASE (http://www.mathweb.org/mbase) is a knowledge base for mathematical learning objects enriched with metadata. Its representation bases on an extended OMDOC-format [9]. A Java interface is available to access the MBASE's content via XML-RPC. The MBASE-wrapper, comprised by the mediator, uses this interface to query and to retrieve metadata of learning objects. An excerpt of the mapping between the OIO and the ontology the MBASE uses is shown in Figure 2. The relation *requires* is mapped to the relation *domain_prerequisite* and *educational_prerequisite*. That means the relation which is expressed in the OIO with the term *requires* can be expressed in MBASE with the help of the relation *domain_prerequisite* or *educational_prerequisite*. This certain mapping looks as the following:

```
<MappingPattern>
  <MatchPattern>
    <RelationRestriction name="requires"/>
  </MatchPattern>
  <ReplacementPattern>
    <RelationRestriction name="domain_prerequisite"/>
  </ReplacementPattern>
  <ReplacementPattern>
```

```
        <RelationRestriction name="educational_prerequisite"/>
      </ReplacementPattern>
   </MappingPattern>
```

2. DAMIT (http://damit.dfki.de) is an adaptive tutoring system which imparts knowledge about Data Mining [10]. It adapts to the individual learning style of a user by providing different views (e.g. formal vs. informal) on the same learning content. The DAMIT-system uses a DB2 database that is accessible as a Web Service. The mediator's wrapper for the DAMIT-repository calls this Web Service to access the metadata of learning objects. We map the relation *requires* to the relation *depends-on* of the DAMIT system:

```
   <MappingPattern>
     <MatchPattern>
       <RelationRestriction name="requires"/>
     </MatchPattern>
     <ReplacementPattern>
       <RelationRestriction name="depends-on"/>
     </ReplacementPattern>
   </MappingPattern>
```

3. MATHSTHESAURUS (http://thesaurus.maths.org) is an online multilingual Mathematics Thesaurus in nine languages [11]. Its repository uses a MYSQL-database which is not accessible on a central server but can be downloaded from the MATHSTHESAURUS website. To retrieve information from the MATHSTHESAURUS the wrapper of the mediator creates SQL-queries and passes them to a database dump of the MATHSTHESAURUS' content. To express that a mathematical concepts is used to define a another concept, the MATHSTHESAURUS uses the relation *references*:

```
   <MappingPattern>
     <MatchPattern>
       <RelationRestriction name="requires"/>
     </MatchPattern>
     <ReplacementPattern>
       <RelationRestriction name="references"/>
     </ReplacementPattern>
   </MappingPattern>
```

4. LEACTIVEMATH EXERCISEREPOSITORY (http://mathdox.org/repository) is a database of interactive exercises. It has been developed in the context of the LEACTIVEMATH project. This repository uses an EXIST-database. The mediator's wrapper creates XQueries to access the information stored in the EXERCISEREPOSITORY. Since the EXERCISEREPOSITORY uses the same metadata structure as the MBASE, both have the same mapping specification.

Cache size	0	20	500	2000
Number of queries to the mediator	505	505	505	505
Duration, first run	10.1 s	8.2 s	4.9 s	4.9 s
Duration, second run	9.8 s	5.6 s	3 s	0.8 s
Number of queries to MBASE, first run	10,838	1218	1041	947
Number of queries to MBASE, second run	10,838	1103	852	0

Fig. 4. Planning a course with learning objects from MBASE using different cache sizes

3.2   Evaluation of the Mediator's Cache

The course planner of ACTIVEMATH often queries for learning objects with the same or with similar metadata. The mediators cache avoids the repetition of query translation and repository access. The comparison of different cache sizes in Figure 4 illustrates the efficiency of the cache: with deactivated cache (i.e., cache size zero), planning a course for a new user, for learning scenario *Guided Tour*, and the learning goal *Derivative Function* takes over 10 seconds. See the resulting course in Figure 5. The first run was a course generation starting with an empty cache and the second run was the generation of the same course a second time. Increasing the cache to 2000 entries accelerates the planning time for the same setting dramatically.

Using the mediator's cache, the architecture made the course planning more than ten times faster and therefore more usable. The course planner can now generate personalized courses from each of the repositories, and also from several repositories in case the repositories use the same URI for the same concepts.

The mediating architecture proposed in this paper is not only utilized for course planning in the ACTIVEMATH system but was also successfully integrated in DAMIT for dynamic course generation.

4   Related Work

Several approaches for data integration by ontology mapping as well as for federation (i.e., the reuse and exchange) of learning objects exist.

4.1   Federation of Learning Objects

EDUTELLA is a Peer-To-Peer approach for sharing information of the semantic web. One of its first application was the federation of learning objects [12]. EDUTELLA is restricted to RDF-based repositories. Our mediator allows the integration of any repository but is restricted to one consumer which is able to query different repositories. EDUTELLA allows each peer to query which yields distributed mapping and distributed caching and hence is expensive in terms of time and administration. Our architecture has a central rewriting mechanism and a central cache which saves lots of time and makes real-time course generation practicable.

1. Chapter: Definition of a relation
   (a) Definition of a relation
2. Chapter: Definition of a right-unique relation
   (a) Definition of a right-unique relation
3. Chapter: Definition of a left-total relation
   (a) Definition of a left-total relation
4. Chapter: Definition of a function
   (a) Definition of a function
   (b) Examples
   (c) Exercises
5. Chapter: Definition of the difference quotient
   (a) Introduction
   (b) Definition of the difference quotient
   (c) Remarks
   (d) Examples
   (e) Exercises
6. Chapter: Neighbourhood
   (a) Neighbourhood
7. Chapter: Definition of a cluster point
   (a) Definition of a cluster point
   (b) Examples
   (c) Exercises
8. Chapter: Definition of the limit of a function
   (a) Definition of the limit of a function
9. Chapter: Definition of the derivative, resp., differential quotient
   (a) Definition of the derivative, resp., differential quotient
10. Chapter: Definition of the derivative function
    (a) Introduction
    (b) Definition of the derivative function
    (c) Examples
    (d) Exercises

Fig. 5. Generated course for the learning scenario *Guided Tour* and the learning goal *Derivative Function*

The Learning Object Metadata Standard (LOM-Standard) [5] has been developed to achieve interoperable metadata specifications for learning objects. LOM has been extended and modified for many repositories which made our translation architecture necessary. For an educational course generation, LOM is not appropriate because it mixes instructional and technical information about learning objects [4]. For that reason we decided to build the query language upon metadata from the OIO.

4.2   Data Integration by Ontology Mapping

For ontology mapping expressive mapping languages have been developed. In [6] a mapping language as well as a set of pattern templates are proposed. The XML-based mapping language XEOML is introduced in [7]. Both mapping languages are very expressive but are not yet been implemented. Therefore, we decided to develop a query rewriting specific approach which is less powerful but expressive enough for our translation purposes.

In [8] an interface for interoperable learning repositories called SQI (Simple Query Interface) is proposed. It provides various methods for accessing heterogeneous learning object repositories but it does not offer a framework for query rewriting which was needed for our application.

An approach based on the Semantic Web rule language TRIPLE is introduced in [13], where an architecture is described which allows to query for resources in the Semantic Web by specifying their metadata. Since TRIPLE is based on RDF and mainly used for data manipulation which would have made parsing, translating and processing of our simple queries too expensive, we decided to use a simpler query language.

5   Conclusion and Further Work

We propose an ontology-based mediation approach which enables an e-learning system to query several heterogeneous learning object repositories. After analysing and representing the knowledge representation and the metadata structure of a repository it is easy to use the repository as a service by specifying a wrapper which calls the retrieval facilities of the new repository. The mediator is able to rewrite queries for this repository, to retrieve learning objects from it, to cache results, and therewith to offer its service to components of the e-learning system. This technique was successfully implemented and tested for the e-learning environment ACTIVEMATH and four repositories and enhances the course planning af ACTIVEMATH. The mediation architecture proposed here is also used for course generation in the DAMIT system.

Further improvements are planned for the mediator architecture. To ease the creation of ontology mappings an ontology mapping editor would be useful. It can support the user with presenting the ontologies which are to be mapped, with marking not yet mapped expressions, and with advising against insolvable overlapping of patterns. Another planned improvement is to increase the expressiveness of the query language to enable more complex search facilities on repositories (such as text search, provision of disjunctions, etc.).

Our approach focuses on mapping of concepts and not on mapping of instances. To provide an architecture which allows the generation of mixed courses, i.e., courses comprising learning objects from different repositories, we are planning to integrate an instance mapping technology basing on domain ontologies and mappings between them. Note that our architecture does not solve the problem of learning object *presentation*: we are managing heterogeneous metadata standards, heterogeneous knowledge representation and heterogeneous storing technologies. For heterogeneous presentation styles (such as HTML, LATEX, XML, OMDOC, etc.) one has to care about the presentation and not about the retrieval of learning objects.

Acknowledgements

We would like to thank Oleg Rostanin for his help to integrate the DAMiT-repository, Mike Pearson for his advice and provision of an access to the MATHSTHESAURUS, and Mark Spanbroek for his assistance in connecting the LEACTIVEMATH EXERCISEREPOSITORY.

This research was carried out in the context of the LEACTIVEMATH project, funded under the 6th Framework Program of the European Community - (Contract N IST-2003-507826). The authors are solely responsible for its content; it does not represent the opinion of the European Community and the Community is not responsible for any use that might be made of data appearing therein.

References

1. Neven, F., Duval, E.: Reusable learning objects: a survey of LOM-based repositories. In: Proceedings of the 10th ACM International Conference on Multimedia. (2002) 291–294
2. Wiederhold, G.: Mediators in the architeture of future information systems. The IEEE Computer Magazine (1992)
3. Ullrich, C.: Course generation based on HTN Planning. In Jedlitschka, A., Brandherm, B., eds.: Proceedings of 13th Annual Workshop of the SIG Adaptivity and User Modeling in Interactive Systems. (2005) 74–79
4. Ullrich, C.: The learning-resource-type is dead, long live the learning- resource-type! Learning Objects and Learning Designs 1(1) (2005) 7–15
5. IEEE Learning Technology Standards Committee: 1484.12.1-2002 IEEE standard for Learning Object Metadata (2002)
6. de Bruijn, J., Foxvog, D., Zimmermann, K.: Ontology Mediation Patterns Library V1. D4.3.1, SEKT-project (2005)
7. Pazienza, M.T., Stellato, A., Vindigni, M., Zanzotto, F.M.: XeOML: An XML-based extensible Ontology Mapping Language. Workshop on Meaning Coordination and Negotiation, held in conjunction with 3rd International Semantic Web Conference (ISWC-2004) Hiroshima, Japan (2004)
8. Simon, B., Massart, D., van Assche, F., Ternier, S., Duval, E., Brantner, S., Olmedilla, D., Miklos, Z.: A simple query interface for interoperable learning repositories. In Simon, B., Olmedilla, D., Saito, N., eds.: Proceedings of the 1st Workshop on Interoperability of Web-based Educational Systems, Chiba, Japan, CEUR (2005) 11–18
9. Melis, E., Andres, J.B.E., Frischauf, A., Goguadze, G., Libbrecht, P., Pollet, M., Ullrich, C.: Knowledge representation and management in activemath. Annals of Mathematics and Artificial Intelligence Special Issue on Management of Mathematical KnowledgeProceedings of the first Conference on Mathematical Knowledge Management MKM'01 a special issue of the Annals of Mathematics and Artificial Intelligence 38 (2003) 47–64
10. Jantke, K.P., Grieser, G., Lange, S., Memmel, M.: Damit: Data mining lernen und lehren. In Abecker, A., Bickel, S., Brefeld, U., Drost, I., Henze, N., Herden, O., Minor, M., Scheffer, T., Stojanovic, L., Weibelzahl, S., eds.: LWA 2004, Lernen – Wissensentdeckung – Adaptivität, 4.-6.Oktober 2004, Humboldt-Universität Berlin (2004) 171–179

11. Thomas, R.: Millenium mathematics project - bringing mathematics to life. MSOR Connections Vol. 4 (2004)
12. Nejdl, W., Wolf, B., Qu, C., Decker, S., Sintek, M., Naeve, A., Nilsson, M., Palmer, M., Risch, T.: Edutella: A P2P Networking Infrastructure Based on RDF. In: Proceedings of the 11th Iternational World Wide Web Conference (WWW2002). (2002)
13. Miklos, Z., Neumann, G., Zdun, U., Sintek, M.: Querying Semantic Web Resources Using TRIPLE Views. In Kalfoglou, Y., Schorlemmer, M., Sheth, A., Staab, S., Uschold, M., eds.: Semantic Interoperability and Integration. Number 04391 in Dagstuhl Seminar Proceedings, Internationales Begegnungs- und Forschungszentrum (IBFI), Schloss Dagstuhl, Germany (2005) <http://drops.dagstuhl.de/opus/volltexte/2005/47> [date of citation: 2005-01-01].

Guided and Interactive Factory Tours for Schools

Andreas Kaibel, Andreas Auwärter, and Miloš Kravčík

Fraunhofer Institute for Applied Information Technology
Schloss Birlinghoven D-53754 St. Augustin, Germany
andreas.kaibel@fit.fraunhofer.de

Abstract. School education today aims at improving the integration of school and professional life. A popular way to provide first hand experiences to students are guided factory tours. Companies are highly interested in establishing contacts to school classes, but guided tours to factories are subject to constraints on both sides. For schools, they require organizational effort, are not easy to integrate into educational routine, and are limited to the factories within reach. For companies, guided tours for school classes are restricted because of safety issues and because they disturb the working processes. Considering these restrictions, interactive guided factory tours are a valuable opportunity, as they enable school classes to actively take part in guided factory tours via internet. This paper discusses the technical, organizational, and pedagogical requirements of guided and interactive factory tours, presenting an interaction model, a role set, a technical solution, and best practices.

1 Introduction

In most countries educational policies today aim at improving the integration of school and professional life. The German federal government for example created the program *Schule – Wirtschaft/Arbeitsleben* (school – economy/professional life: http://www.swa-programm.de) with the goal to integrate school and economy. The main objective is to give the students inside views into professional life and the economy in general in order to facilitate the transition from school to vocational training and profession. Additionally, in the knowledge society it is of high importance to share not only explicit, but also the tacit knowledge appearing in the corporate settings. But in reality, the integration of school and professional life is achieved in isolated cases only. Partly this is due to the fact that integrating work life experiences into school lessons demands considerable efforts from the side of teachers, e.g. if she wants her class to visit a factory. As a consequence, the contacts between schools and companies are loose or even non-existent; school classes will visit companies twice a year at best.

In this paper we present the concept of *Guided and Interactive Factory Tour* (GIFT) that provides schools with a valuable new opportunity. Its basic idea is to enable school classes to actively take part in guided factory tours via internet. This can easily be integrated into everyday school life and instead of requiring effort from the teachers it may even reduce their workload. Learners, among other benefits, can choose their future careers based on such experiences. For companies GIFT is an interesting opportunity as well. Instead of reaching only schools from the vicinity, they

W. Nejdl and K. Tochtermann (Eds.): EC-TEL 2006, LNCS 4227, pp. 198–212, 2006.

can provide guided tours to schools from everywhere. In this way the learning experience can be shared more effectively and efficiently. The technology behind GIFT is not brand new – mainly videoconferencing and wireless internet. But the constraints and requirements for a widespread use of this approach have not been thoroughly researched so far. This paper describes the needs of schools and companies regarding GIFT, outlines several related efforts, and formulates pedagogical and technical requirements. Furthermore, on the basis of the developments in the Remote Accessible Field Trips project (RAFT) project, an integrated pedagogical and technical solution for GIFT is proposed. Finally some future perspectives are outlined.

2 Need for Guided and Interactive Factory Tours

The integration of learning experiences with working life is a clear goal of present-day *school* education. For instance the conference of the state-ministers for education in Germany [1] declared that "economic education represents an indispensable part of general education and therefore must be embedded in the educational assignment of schools. Economic education should be realized within school lessons, in economy- or profession-related school projects or in cooperation with external partners as e.g. companies." With respect to economic education, guided tours through factories offer an excellent possibility to familiarize the students with working life, professions and economic issues in general. But in everyday school life guided tours through factories are difficult to realize due to organizational issues. The class must leave the school for a whole day accompanied by two teachers, thus disturbing the regular educational process in the school. The transport to the factory must be organized. The factory should be within reach, otherwise the costs for transport are too high and the students will be back too late. Due to these constraints guided tours to factories are only rarely arranged. For these constraints, GIFT offers solutions bringing benefits from the school point of view:

- Schools are not limited to the factories in their neighborhood anymore, instead they can choose companies and factories according to the pedagogical need,
- As GIFT might have a duration of about 90 minutes and the students do not have to leave the school, GIFT can easily be integrated into the everyday school routine,
- GIFT requires only a minimum of organizational effort from the teacher – an accompanying teacher and organization of transport are not necessary and there are no additional regulations to comply with.

Of course, GIFT should not replace real guided factory tours, because seeing, hearing and smelling a factory in reality definitely constitutes a richer experience than taking part via internet. But due to the constraints mentioned above, GIFT can become a valuable and feasible complement.

Most *companies* are highly motivated to establish contacts with schools. Cooperating with schools offers the possibility to get in contact with future customers and workers, to improve the public image of the company and to realize corporate social responsibility [2]. Guided tours through factories are valuable concerning all these goals. Companies can demonstrate the quality of the manufacturing processes to their potential customers. They can display attractive workplaces and professions to possible future workers, who otherwise might not get in touch with this experience. By supporting the educational efforts of schools they can show their social responsibility. But guided factory tours for school classes are subject to several constraints. Managing a high number of guided tours can disturb the production process and may present a safety risk, especially if the visitors are school students who may be difficult to control. Furthermore, only schools within a driving distance of less than two hours will take part in guided factory tours, because in most cases the students have to get back to their school the same day. For both constraints mentioned above, GIFT offers solutions bringing benefits also from the company viewpoint:

- The production process is not disturbed by visiting school classes,
- Companies can offer guided tours to schools everywhere, instead of being restricted to schools in the surrounding area,
- Companies can exemplarily demonstrate their readiness for new developments and their social responsibility.

3   Related Projects

The idea of GIFT originated in the EU-funded *Remote Accessible Field Trip* (RAFT: http://www.raft-project.net) project that was carried out from 2002 to 2005. GIFT adopts the technological development of RAFT as well as parts of the pedagogical and organizational concepts, but obviates the drawbacks. Furthermore, based on the results of the RAFT evaluation, the feasibility of GIFT, as well as its pedagogical value and acceptance in schools are assured. In this section the RAFT concepts, the relevant achievements of the project and the evaluation results are shortly described to give an insight to the fundament GIFT is based on. Furthermore, some other related projects are described shortly.

Learners like to experience the real world and to be actively involved in live events directly or at least via technologies. Field trips enable active learning experience in real world context to improve effectiveness of education. To overcome various obstacles related to their organization (e.g. accessibility and safety issues) the RAFT project aimed at establishing real time collaboration between the field trip site and the classroom. In RAFT learning is considered as a social activity and various learning theories have been taken into account, including collaborative, cooperative, situated, peer assisted, and vicarious learning. Based on them several learning *scenarios* have been developed and a range of *roles* have been identified for pupils [3]. In essence, two basic processes are supported in RAFT: data collection and annotation [4], as well as real time communication between the field and the classroom.

In practice, the field site students take photos, annotate them (with voice annotation), send them to the classroom, answer the requests coming from the classroom, and (technically) support the videoconferences with experts. The classroom students analyze the data coming from the field (photos, audio annotations, and video); they research, ask questions and make further requests to the field site students (via audio or text messaging). Additionally they hold interviews with experts at the field trip site via videoconference. Three main scenarios have been identified to deploy the system: outdoor field trips to landmarks, indoor field trips to areas with restricted access, and guided tours where companies, museums and other institutions can present themselves to remote students and other interested people.

Several RAFT achievements are highly relevant for realizing GIFT [5]:

* *Validated set of requirements:* During the RAFT project requirements for real-time collaboration applications that should be used in schools have been raised and validated during several tens of field trips performed throughout the project. The technical requirements for GIFT are based on this set of validated requirements.
* *Roles and best practices:* Roles and best practices have been derived and validated during the field trips and have been adapted for widespread use in schools.
* *Technical system:* The RAFT system was developed for the use in schools. It fulfills the requirements of widespread use in schools, is robust and easy to use, even for primary school students.
* *Field trip experiences:* The field trips have been performed and evaluated in various educational domains and subjects. Three of these field trips went to factories.

The feasibility and pedagogical value of the highly innovative RAFT approach have been proved by an evaluation study based on more than 30 field trips with more than 400 students [6]. This experience pool is the basis for specification of requirements and recommendations that should be considered by users in order to achieve a widespread use of the RAFT system.

Beside the RAFT project, only a few projects try to realize a concept similar to GIFT. One of them is BliK [7] that enables school classes to have a *videoconference* with partners from several companies that cooperate with this project. Students can talk to trainees and instructors of professions they are interested in. BliK provides teachers with detailed information for planning the videoconference, e.g. concerning roles during the videoconference. But this approach does not use wireless internet connection to offer the classes a guided tour via internet and its widespread use is hampered by the technical platform that is used. BliK rents videoconferencing devices to participating schools. Before participating in the videoconference, the teacher must get the device and ask the technicians in his school to install it. After the videoconference she must return the device. The organizational effort is high and BliK is restricted to areas where its infrastructure is available for renting the equipment.

Some companies offer *virtual guided tours* [8]. In comparison to GIFT their main disadvantage is the missing interactivity. The user can navigate round the factory, but there is no contact partner at the other side. Furthermore, virtual guided tours lack authenticity, because they do not show what is happening right now.

4 Requirements Analysis

While the basic idea and the advantages of GIFT are obvious, it is not trivial to successfully realize these tours. In comparison to movies or broadcasts, the unique selling proposition of GIFT is the possibility to interact with the guide at the factory. If the interaction succeeds, it can lead to an active and satisfying participation in the proceedings of the tour. Thus highest efforts have to be taken to induce and sustain a fruitful and satisfying interaction between the classroom and the factory staff. Furthermore, if factory guided tours want to find a broad audience in schools, their pedagogical requirements, organizational and technical constraints must be considered. Finally, the organizational and technical constraints at the factory site must be taken into account as well.

In the RAFT project, students always were present at the field trip site and were actively cooperating with the classroom from there. Thus from the pedagogical point of view the collaboration of students at different sites was at the core of the RAFT project. But the fact that there are students at the field trip site who actively cooperate with students in the classroom implied some drawbacks that disabled the widespread use of RAFT despite its obvious pedagogical value:

- *High organizational efforts:* For preparing a RAFT fieldtrip, the teacher must check the technical feasibility at the field trip site, mainly assure the internet connection. Furthermore, as there is one group at the field trip site and the other group in the classroom, transport must be organized and the groups at both sides must be accompanied by a teacher. Therefore only technically experienced and dedicated teachers will be ready to run RAFT field trips regularly
- *Accurate preparation:* To realize satisfying collaboration during the field trip, the students must be properly prepared for the roles they will take over during the field trip and the field trip situation must be tested before. This again requires more skills and efforts from the teacher.
- *High price:* RAFT field trips require the use of expensive equipment for the field-trip site, as e.g. tablet PCs and 3G-cellphones. As schools will not afford to buy this equipment, it must be rented somewhere – requiring even more organizational effort and a RAFT infrastructure that is costly to maintain.
- *Questionable quality of transferred data:* Even with training, the students are not professionals and may even disregard requests from the classroom due to their fascination with the field trip site or the technique they work with.

GIFT in comparison is less ambitious. Instead of collaboration of students at different sites, the students participate remotely in proceedings at the factory site. This setting clearly avoids the drawbacks of RAFT:

- *Simple organization:* The teacher needs just to book the GIFT.
- *Minimum student preparation:* To ascertain widespread acceptance, the setup of GIFT will be as simple as possible for school classes.
- *Low costs:* As companies have an interest in a high acceptance of their GIFT, they will not charge excessive fees for schools.
- *High quality of data:* At the factory professional staff is involved.

In general, GIFT attempts to adopt the positive results of the RAFT project, like the validated technical requirements, the technical system as well as the roles and best practices, but avoids the drawbacks.

4.1 General Requirements

Considering GIFT, there are several requirements that are quite general – especially those related to videoconferencing, interaction, and authenticity. GIFT mainly consist of a *videoconference* with two conferencing sites, the guide at the factory and the students in the classroom. The use of videoconferencing in school education has been researched in depth so that guidelines and best practices have been developed [9]. There are comprehensive and easy to read best practice guides for the use of videoconferencing in schools [10]. The research and the best practices assume that the participating partners are ready to invest in acquiring at least some expertise in videoconferencing, concerning both the correct use of technology (e.g. the microphone) and higher level best practices (e.g. aiming at establishing an equal interaction). But in the GIFT scenario this cannot be expected from the classroom side. To achieve widespread acceptance, the barriers for classes to attend GIFT should be as low as possible, both in terms of technology and in terms of preparation. The goal should be to deliver a satisfying experience to the students and the teachers, with only the minimum of previous training. Otherwise only teachers with expertise will embrace GIFT, while the others – especially older and technology-anxious teachers – renounce this offer. Thus the technology and the concepts of virtual guided factory tours must aim at delivering a satisfying interaction in a videoconferencing situation, where there is one highly experienced participant (the guide in the factory who should get explicit training) and a group of inexperienced participants (the students and the teacher). Given the asymmetric situation of the videoconferencing partners in GIFT, there are serious hindrances on the way to a satisfying interaction. As students and teachers are unfamiliar with videoconferencing, they may feel uncomfortable, dissatisfied and thus resile into a passive attitude. Furthermore, due to their experiences with common guided tours, the students may feel uncomfortable to interrupt the tour guide. This undesirable reluctance will even be increased by the unfamiliarity with videoconferencing. Finally, as observed during RAFT field trips, students often have a false impression of their role during interactive guided tours. Given their experiences e.g. with films shown in school lessons, they have to be taken out of their passive and merely receptive role.

The possibility to *interact* with the guide at the factory is the key idea of GIFT. Interaction must be engendered and sustained in an asymmetric videoconferencing situation, where one professional participant (the tour guide) faces a group of inexperienced participants (the students and the teacher). Thus a videoconferencing interaction model should be created, that allows the tour guide to continuously challenge interaction from the classroom and that lowers the interaction barriers for the classroom students. The desirable activities of the classroom students are asking questions and sending requests to the factory staff. These activities must clearly be supported and facilitated by the communication tools and by the setup of the interactive guided tour. Interactive guided tours require an accurate interaction design that ensures the active participation of the students. It is the tour guide who is responsible to take the lead (Fig.1). The students on the other hand will pick up the challenge and thus gain self confidence and experience in videoconferencing situations.

In common guided tours the participants have to some extend the possibility to control and steer their experience of the tour. They can look around for interesting items, they can take a close look at such items, and they can even abandon the guided tour for a few moments to investigate on their own. These possibilities are quite restricted by the web based data transfer. The view the students in the classroom get is determined by video delivered via the camera. Here the "stage direction" must provide possibilities to give the students at least partial control about what they see. GIFT should engender the *authenticity*, the feeling of "being there". In common guided tours it implies that the participants see, hear, smell and feel their environment. Furthermore the environment stimulates emotions in them and they perceive how they move in the environment. Only seeing and hearing are directly supported by the web based communication; the tour guide should try to compensate the others.

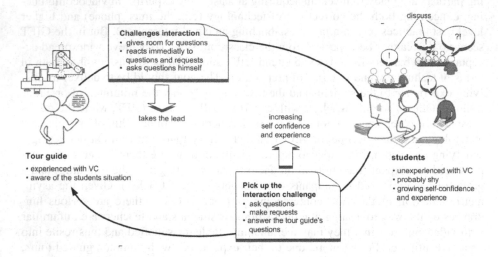

Fig. 1. Asymmetric videoconferencing situation during interactive guided factory tours

4.2 School Requirements

For schools GIFT can constitute a feasible possibility to familiarize the students with the work and the production cycles in factories. To find widespread acceptance, it is necessary to take into account the requirements that schools have both at the pedagogical and technical level. GIFT must be connected to the relevant topics in *curricula*. While the specific possibilities of integration into curricula are dependent of the company and the products they manufacture, a connection to higher-level curriculum topics can in most cases be achieved. This will be demonstrated with two examples for the German secondary school curricula [11]:

* In classes 8 and 9 *occupational orientation* is a topic of paramount importance at all secondary schools. The topic is being discussed in social sciences, German and in the foreign languages. Occupational orientation offers a perfect starting point for a set of GIFT.
* In class 10 *humans and technology* is an interdisciplinary topic that is treated in social sciences, German, foreign languages, biology and art. GIFT can describe the relationship between humans and technology in factories, where the balancing of the relationship between human workers and technology is critical.

Furthermore in natural and social sciences virtual guided factory tours could take over an important role. During the factory tours, the students can see and experience what they have learned in theory before.

From the *organizational* point of view, to achieve widespread acceptance, GIFT should be simple to integrate into everyday school life – this is one of their main advantages in comparison to common factory tours that usually take a whole school day. That means that GIFT should not be longer than 90 minutes (i.c. two school lessons) and classes should be able to participate with a minimum of standard equipment. Furthermore the planning for GIFT should be as simple as possible. Only simple steps should be required:

- The teacher signs up for a tour (via telephone or via e-mail),
- The teacher gets the relevant information (via e-mail),
- The teacher tests the applications a few days before the tour,
- The teacher connects to the guided tour 15 minutes before the tour starts.

Finally, GIFT should be for free or only a nominal fee per student should be charged. Otherwise teachers might run into difficulties justifying the need for the GIFT to the parents who have to pay for it, thus decreasing the number of teachers and students who are ready to participate.

The *technical* requirements for GIFT are derived from the technical requirements for the widespread use of the RAFT system [5]. Low technical barriers are an indispensable requirement for the widespread acceptance of GIFT. Most of the teachers who are interested from a pedagogical point of view (e.g. social science teachers) often do not dispose of high-level ICT competence. And even if they do, a demanding technical preparation of the factory tour would discourage them, given the high workload and the tight schedule teachers in general have. In detail, the system supporting GIFT should comply with the following requirements.

Reliable audio: Audio is the backbone of communication between the factory and the classroom. If the audio communication fails or deteriorates, the collaboration fails, leading to frustration and the feeling of being cut off in the classroom. Therefore reliable audio is even more important than having permanent video. GIFT is often employed in situations that make good audio quality difficult. In the factory there may be high level background noise, in classrooms often a microphone and loudspeakers are used. In common video conferencing systems this would lead to serious disturbances of communication on the field trip side, because the users there would get an echo.

Standard plugins: The need to install software constitutes a high barrier in schools, since most teachers do not have the right to install software on school computers – thus complicating the process of getting started. Installation is even a more serious problem at field trip sites. Here security issues are the main concern. Due to these problems, the application must be browser-based, using only standard plugins.

Avoiding firewall problems: Schools have very different and quite unpredictable firewall configurations. Requiring firewall changes would significantly reduce the number of schools who can participate, because the processes of network administration in schools are often complex and tedious. At the field trip site, the firewall issue is even more important, as companies can hardly be asked to adapt their firewalls for educational purposes.

Avoiding proxy problems: Schools often use proxy servers to handle the data transferred to and from the internet. Proxy servers hide the IP-addresses of clients – but for many videoconferencing solutions IP-addresses are necessary.

Platform independence: In schools, different platforms are used both on the client and the server side.

Acceptable performance: Schools often do not have the financial clout to buy up-to-date hardware and operating systems, therefore mediocre hardware and outdated operating systems have to be considered too.

Scalable bandwidth consumption: Schools often have to share a common DSL internet connection for all classes, thus a broadband connection cannot be guaranteed. Furthermore, the bandwidths at the field trip sites may be unreliable. Fixed bandwidth consumption would either make some field trip sites and some schools inaccessible, or would lead to low video quality, despite of the high bandwidth available.

4.3 Factory Requirements

The tour guide in the factory should be able to move freely while being in contact with the students and transferring video into the classroom. Therefore she needs wireless audio connection and a portable device with a camera connected. Additionally, to create authenticity it must be possible to show the tour guide to the students while she answers questions from the classroom. So two employees are the minimum required staff for running GIFT: the *tour guide* and a *technical assistant* who is responsible for the camera(s) and for the technique in general. But considering the costs of the tour, not more than two employees should be engaged. Given the need to move freely, the tour guide must connect to the internet wirelessly. But even if the factory disposes of a WLAN infrastructure, it often cannot be used for interactive guided tours due to data security restrictions. Therefore the applications should be scalable to either WLAN or 3G internet connection. A major obstacle may be objections by the worker council due to privacy issues of the factory employees. For example, in Germany, photographing or filming employees during their work requires the written consent of the worker. This is difficult to achieve in factories with hundreds of workers.

Due to image awareness most companies will not be ready to deliver mediocre *video quality* to the outside world. Furthermore for many procedures in factories, especially for the most interesting ones, detailed views are necessary to really get an impression, e.g. for robots in a car assembly line. Therefore high video quality is an important issue.

5 Solution

The aim of GIFT is to develop and adapt a suitable technical solution based on sound organizational and pedagogical concepts. Technical, pedagogical, and organizational developments are obviously interconnected with each other. The technical implementation has to take into account the pedagogical and organizational requests, while the corresponding developments must consider the technical constraints of GIFT.

The current research and development at Fraunhofer FIT focus on a prototype for GIFT that will be implemented at the Volkswagen factory and is being developed according to the requirements of the Volkswagen visitor center in Wolfsburg. This prototype based approach opens up the possibility of development in realistic settings. As the settings at the Volkswagen factory and the requirements of the visitor center are not unique, the results can be transferred to factories in other sectors of industry too. The Volkswagen factory in Wolfsburg is quite large, thus guided tours span several kilometers. Visitors can take a tour train for about 40 persons and they are not allowed to leave it during the sojourn in the factory. Beside the tour trains for common visitors there are also individual tours offered to VIPs. Up to seven persons can use a tour car (VW Touran Cabrio) driven by the tour guide. During a 90 minute tour, about seven points of interest are visited and at some of those the tour guide and the visitors get off the car to take a closer look. The driving time between the points of interest is up to five minutes and is filled with more general information by the tour guide. Obviously the VIP tours are the model that GIFT should be based on.

5.1 Technical Solution

The technical solution for GIFT at the Volkswagen factory represents a further development of the RAFT system that was created to realize remote accessible field trips for schools. As the RAFT system was developed for widespread use in schools, it fulfills all the technical requirements of schools described above. The RAFT applications offer solutions for the accessibility and audio quality demands of schools and for the network access requirements in factories. The technical solution of the RAFT system has been described in detail in [5].

Simple accessibility: To meet the accessibility requirements of schools, the GIFT system uses the Flash Communication Server as a communication backbone. On the client side, only a browser with a Flash-plugin is needed. This ensures interoperability and platform independence. Since schools often do not have the latest Flash plugins installed on their computers, the development is based on Flash 6.0, the oldest Flash version providing the needed communication features. Audio- and video-streaming is done with port-80-tunneling. This avoids firewall problems with all but the most restrictive firewalls and the RAFT system is always accessible as long as streaming is not blocked completely. Because the Flash Communication Server does not need to know the IPs of the participating clients, problems with proxy servers are minimized. These settings ensure that at almost all schools the GIFT system is accessible without any special installation and without additional reconfiguration of firewalls, even in cases where outdated operating systems as e.g. Windows 98 are used. The drawback of using Flash is that the GIFT system currently can not be used on Pocket PCs, because their hardware or Flash-plugins do not provide sufficient performance to handle Flash-video streaming. So at the factory, tablet PCs or notebooks must be used, which are comparably bulky. These limitations will change with hardware of higher performance and better flash plugins for pocket PCs that will soon become available.

Reliable audio: During the RAFT project several technical problems have been identified that obstruct or even disable audio communication between the factory and the classroom. One of them is deterioration of audio quality due to low bandwidth. The Flash plugin does not give audio priority over video. So with low bandwidth both video and audio qualities go down. As observed during the field trips, the deterioration of audio quality leads to severe disruptions of the communication, because then sentences arrive in fragments that are no longer understandable. Therefore to ensure acceptable audio quality, the GIFT system is scalable and adaptable to changing bandwidths; four levels of bandwidth consumption are implemented. If audio deteriorates, then users can switch to a lower bandwidth setting, assuring that audio quality is preserved. If the bandwidth is changed by one client, it automatically adapts for all clients, ensuring that no client pushes video streams with too high bandwidth consumption.

Echo problems have to be avoided too. In the classroom typically loudspeakers and microphones are used for audio communication. This might lead to serious acoustic feedback problems for the tour guide at the factory. To avoid this, the GIFT system works with "speaking on demand". Only one user can speak, while others have the option to interrupt him. Of course speaking on demand has an impact on the free flow of communication, but given the possible disruptions as experienced during the RAFT project, speaking on demand is still preferable. The communication flow must be assured by other technical measures and by organizational and pedagogical concepts. Generally speaking, this communication protocol can become very efficient when users get used to it. Additionally, it might be supported by another communication channel – text chat.

Network solution: In the factory GIFT can be used either with WLAN or 3G internet connection. Thus it is up to the specific factory to make a choice considering WLAN infrastructure, data security issues and 3G coverage. To give an example, internet access can be delivered by 3G-WLAN-Routers, which are provided by cellphone companies. They offer the necessary flexibility and establish a high speed access to the internet. Fig. 2 shows a different network solution, using 3G cell phones for data transfer.

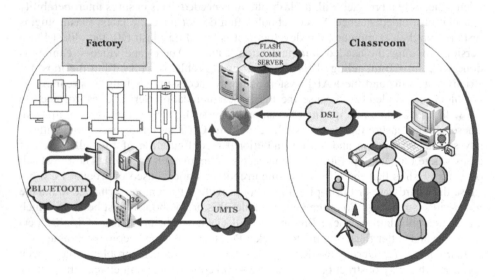

Fig. 2. 3G-based network connection for interactive guided factory tours

5.2 Setup in Factory

The goal in the factory is to create an application that enables interaction and authenticity without hurting the technical constraints and without overstraining the capacities of the staff involved. Both the technical development and the best practices depend on the roles of the staff. Therefore the setup in the factory will be derived from their roles. As stated before, two roles at the factory will be involved in GIFT, the tour guide and the technical assistant. The *tour guide* is responsible for the communication with the classroom. It is his duty to stimulate the interest and interaction with the classroom students. Furthermore she has to drive the tour car, at least in the envisaged prototype in the Volkswagen factory. While the tour guide can focus on the (audio-) communication with the classroom, the *technical assistant* has a wide range of tasks to solve. He must ensure the functionality of the equipment and the net-connection. Furthermore, he has to adjust the audio (volume, background noises vs. the voice of the tour guide) and the video (sharpness, general view vs. focusing on details or the tour guide) settings. In doing so he must try to provide the classroom students with a clear view of the proceedings in the factory, support the interaction (e.g. by immediately reacting to requests for detailed views) and create authenticity, e.g. by showing the location of the tour guide in the environment of the factory. All together the technical assistant could easily be overwhelmed by the tasks he has to solve. Therefore the technical and organizational setup should facilitate the tasks of the technical assistant as much as possible. The GIFT system will encompass the following audio and video recording facilities:

- *Audio:* A microphone for the explanations of the tour guide, a second microphone for the surround sound, that is highly important for creating authenticity. The activity of the microphones can be switched by the technical assistant. Both the tour guide and the technical assistant receive audio from the classroom via headset. To maintain the mobility of the staff, the headsets are connected via Bluetooth to the computer in the tour car.
- *Video:* A fixed camera for the front view and a turnable camera to show the view to the sides. Both these cameras are attached to the tour car, providing a steady view and simplifying the technical assistant's task. Furthermore a third camera is attached to a tablet PC allowing the technical assistant to leave the tour car, to walk to places of interest and show them in detail.

As described before, engendering and sustaining *interaction* and creating the feeling of *authenticity* is paramount to GIFT. To achieve both goals, a suitable tour setting has been developed. To give the classroom students the feeling of really participating in a guided tour, their "eye", the camera, is seated behind the driver. This creates authenticity by simulating the guided tour situation: The students "sit" in the car, seeing the car and the driver/tour guide while the car moves forward. Furthermore this setting offers clear advantages in regard to interaction.

While driving and explaining what the classroom students can see, the tour guide is always present to the classroom students. They see her explaining and can even have eye contact with her via the review mirror. From the interaction point of view this situation conveys the message to the classroom students that they may ask questions, but that looking at the surrounding factory and listening to the explanations of the tour guide are the principal expected activities.

The situation completely changes when the tour guide stops the vehicle and turns round to camera. It immediately becomes clear to the students that now they must definitely leave their passive situation and interact with the tour guide. The tour guide can enhance this situation change be requesting questions from the classroom or by asking some questions herself.

These two interaction situations should also be created when the tour guide and the technical assistant leave the car to show something, e.g. a machine in detail. First the machine is displayed, while the tour guide explains, then the tour guide is shown in front of the machine, requesting activity from the side of the students just by changing the situation. Thus during the whole tour explanation phases and interaction phases alternate and can clearly be distinguished by the classroom students, giving them orientation and self-confidence in the unfamiliar videoconferencing situation.

Interaction should also be supported in explaining situations. The students may have urgent questions, but due to the situation they will feel awkward to put them forward, because this means disrupting the tour guide. To enable interaction here, technical support is deployed – the students can push a "question"-button. The tour guide is adverted by an audio signal – she can finish her sentence and then request the students to ask their questions.

In large factories there may be several driving periods from one point of interest to another. Due to the low speed these driving periods may last up to five minutes. Instead of trying to fill all the driving periods by providing explanations, they may partially be used to support interaction in a different way – the tour guide explains to the classroom that she now has to drive for several minutes and that she will switch off the sound in between. She advises the classroom students to use the time to discuss internally and to formulate questions that she will answer as soon as she comes back.

5.3 Setup in School

To enable widespread use, the setup in schools must be as simple as possible and should not require unusual organizational efforts and technical know-how. The *hardware requirements* are very basic:

- PC with broadband internet connection,
- video projector,
- headset (or microphone),
- loudspeakers,
- webcam is recommended.

The technical system should be tested several days before the factory tour. To facilitate the preparation, roles and best practices should be reduced to the minimum that is necessary to establish a satisfying interaction between the classroom and the factory staff. From the experiences of the RAFT project the following essential *roles* have been derived:

- *Interviewer* leads the interview with the tour guide, makes requests, and asks questions. Of course, other students may directly ask interposed questions, but the interviewer is mainly responsible for the communication. The interviewer should dispose of high communicative competences.
- *Technical assistant* cares about the technical quality of the transmission, e.g. adjusting the volume or the webcam. If there is a question from the classroom he notifies the tour guide via audio signal.
- *Requests gatherer* collects questions from all students and transfers them to the interviewer in a sequential order. Thus she relieves the interviewer from the organizational effort of deciding which question to ask first.

More detailed role sets have been put forward [12, 13, 5]. These role sets lead to the involvement of more students in the classroom and thus to richer interaction. They may be offered to school classes, but their use is not imperative. As described before, mainly the tour guide in the company is responsible for engendering and sustaining satisfying interaction.

But nevertheless, some basic *best practices* should be followed by the interviewer. She should try to ask short and precise questions and she should inform the tour guide in case the class needs some time for internal discussion, as the tour guide may not be aware of this and may want to continue. Furthermore, she should command the courage to interrupt the tour guide, if the tour guide does not react to the "question" signal sent by the technical assistant. During the guided tour the teacher may take over the role of the requests gatherer or retreat to the role of a spectator. Therefore GIFT realizes the rare situation that the deployment of advanced technologies makes life easier for teachers instead of complicating their tasks.

6 Conclusion and Outlook

GIFT are a highly innovative concept for giving students inside views in professional life and the economy. They represent a solution to the needs and constraints of both companies and schools. Based on the experiences and the technology of the Remote Accessible Field Trips (RAFT), a validated set of requirements, a technical system, an interaction model, roles and best practices were developed. They enable school classes to take part in GIFT without effort and the tour guide in the factory can deliver an authentic and interactive guided tour experience. Given the experiences and the evaluation results of the RAFT project, the feasibility of GIFT and their pedagogical value are sure. As GIFT are easier to realize for schools and as their reach is not limited to factories in the vicinity, they can be a valuable complement to traditional guided factory tours in practice.

Due to the fact that there are no students at the factory site, GIFT is definitely more feasible and more widely applicable than RAFT. But having no students at the factory site may entail disadvantages from the pedagogical point of view: In RAFT field trips, having students at two sites cooperating induced a high level of responsibility and self determination concerning the learning process. The students were involved in the field trip planning and were responsible for the organization and communication at the runtime of the field trip. Thus having successfully achieved a RAFT field trip filled them with pride and self confidence. Furthermore, by establishing and maintaining efficient remote communication via video conference, in RAFT the students were able to greatly improve their communicative and organizational skills. Finally, seeing their peers at the field trip site provided the classroom students with a high level of authenticity. After the field trip the students were then able to exchange their experiences at the different sites, leading to further reflection of the field trip topics and the communicative experiences. By contrast in GIFT, the responsibility and self determination of the students is reduced, because in GIFT the tour guide at the factory takes the lead and is responsible for the tour proceedings. Having a professional tour guide in the factory, the communicative skills of the students are less challenged and less important for the success of the tour. That is the pedagogical price for the feasibility, the effortless organization and the broad reach of GIFT. It is not yet clear, whether the less demanding setup of GIFT leads to lower acceptance rates among students. This will be evaluated during the prototype testing.

A prototype of the GIFT system is planned to be tested this autumn at the Volkswagen factory in Wolfsburg. The tests will be evaluated in regard to technical and organizational feasibility as well as student and teacher acceptance. If the tests are successful, Volkswagen visitor services will implement the system. In the near future improvements in 3G connection, in internet connection of schools, and in wearable computers will further enhance the feasibility and technical quality of GIFT. Then also other institutions (e.g. museums, historic sites) may adopt the GIFT concepts and technology.

References

1. Wirtschaftliche Bildung an allgemeinbildenden Schulen – Bericht der Kultusministerkonferenz vom 19.10.2001. http://www.kmk.org/doc/publ/wirt-bildung.pdf (2001)
2. Fritz, W., Wagner, U.: Soziale Verantwortung als Leitidee der Unternehmensführung und Gegenstand der akademischen Ausbildung, Management mit Vision und Verantwortung. In Wiedmann, K.P., Fritz, W., Abel, B. (eds.): Eine Herausforderung an Wissenschaft und Praxis. http://www.univie.ac.at/marketing/Publikationen/Fritz_Wagner_formated.pdf (2004)
3. Rentoul, R. M. S., Hine, N. A., Specht, M., Kravcik, M.: Beyond Virtual Field Trips: Collaboration and m-Learning. In Hall, R. (ed.): Proceedings of NAWeb 2003 Conference, http://naweb.unb.ca/proceedings/2003/PaperRentouletal.html (2003)
4. Kravcik, M., Kaibel, A., Specht, M., Terrenghi, L.: Mobile Collector for Field Trips. In Educational Technology & Society, 7 (2), http://ifets.ieee.org/periodical/7_2/5.pdf (2004) 25-33
5. Kaibel, A., Braeuer, D., Kaul, J., Auwärter, A., Kravcik, M.: Perfoming Remote Accessible Field Trips in Schools. In Proc. IMCL Conference (2006)
6. Bergin, D.A., Anderson, A.H., Molnar, T., Baumgartner, R., Mitchell, S., Korper, S., Curley, A., Rottmann, J.: Providing remote accessible field trips (RAFT): an evaluation study. Computers in Human Behavior (in press), http://dx.doi.org/10.1016/j.chb.2004.10.034
7. BliK – Berufe live ins Klassenzimmer (Jobs live into the classroom), http://www.blik-bayern.de/projekt_start.htm (2005)
8. BASF Virtuelle Werkführung (BASF virtual guided factory tour) http://www.rheinneckarweb.de/basf/erleben/werkfuehrung/ (2006)
9. Woods, T.J.: Instructor and student perceptions of a videoconference course. Lethbridge, Alberta , 04/2005. http://www.uleth.ca/edu/grad/pdf/thesis_woods.pdf (2005)
10. Videoconferencing: A Digital handbook for teachers and students. http://www.d261.k12.id.us/VCing/index.htm (2006)
11. Bildungspläne, Lehrpläne und Richtlinien der Bundesländer (School curricula of German states) http://www.bildungsserver.de/zeigen.html?seite=400 (2006)
12. Hine, N., Rentoul, R., Specht, M.: Collaboration and roles in remote field trips. In: Attewell, J., Savill-Smith, C. (eds.): Learning with Mobile Devices Research and Development (2004) 69-72
13. BliK – Rollen- und Aufgabenverteilung (BliK – distribution of roles and tasks), http://www.blik-bayern.de/projekt_ablauf_3.htm (2005)

Adult Learners and ICT:
An Intervention Study in the UK*

Maria Kambouri, Harvey Mellar, and Kit Logan

Institute of Education, University of London, 20 Bedford Way, London
{M.Kambouri, H.Mellar, K.Logan}@ioe.ac.uk

Abstract. The study's aim was to develop effective ICT based teaching strategies through a series of trials using theoretically grounded ICT task designs targeted at specific adult literacy, numeracy and ESOL learning objectives. Both the development of literacy skills through the use of ICT and the acquisition and development of ICT skills were examined. Working with a group of nine practitioners who agreed to participate both as teachers and as action researchers, we developed nine teaching interventions based on schemes of work that embedded ICT literacy within adult Literacy, Language and Numeracy classes as well as introducing new pedagogical techniques. Seven of these projects were taken into an intervention phase were the approaches and strategies employed were evaluated. Involvement of tutors was a key element of this process, both in deciding on the development of the ICT interventions and in the research process through reflection on their developing practice using ICT. Participants were, interviewed, observed, and the learners were assessed at the start and end of their 8 week course for attainment in reading and listening skills in English, as well as background, attitude and attainment in ICT literacy through bespoke questionnaires and assessment materials matched to the Skills for Life ICT curriculum. Findings support hypotheses that use of ICT boosts adult learners' confidence in learning as well as rapidly gain ICT skills and double the value of study time by acquiring two sets of skills.

1 ICT to Support Skills for Life: The UK Case

One important aspect of the strategy proposed by the Moser report [1] was the use of ICT to support delivery of basic skills, "At the heart of improved quality in delivery and materials must be increased use of Information and Communication Technologies (ICT) to improve basic skills". Specific claims were:
- ICT is a powerful tool to raise levels of literacy and numeracy.
- Computers and multimedia software provide attractive ways of learning.
- The Web enables access to the best materials and the most exciting learning opportunities.
- ICT offers a new start for adults returning to learning.

And:

---

* This project was part of a group of Effective Practice Projects supported by ESF and NRDC (the National Research and Development Centre for adult literacy and numeracy).

W. Nejdl and K. Tochtermann (Eds.): EC-TEL 2006, LNCS 4227, pp. 213–226, 2006.

-     Learners who use ICT for basic skills double the value of their study time acquiring two sets of skills at the same time.

By 2003, ICT was itself coming to be seen as a "Skill for Life", in the White Paper, *21st Century Skills: Realising Our Potential* [2], ICT skills are for the first time included within the Skills for Life programme:

> *"Until now, basic skills have referred to literacy and numeracy. In today's society, we believe it is as important that everybody can also use Information and Communications Technology (ICT), particularly in the workplace. So we shall offer basic ICT skills as a third area of adult basic skills alongside literacy and numeracy within our Skills for Life programme."*

This has been a time of great change in adult education in UK and the use of ICT in Skills for Life. During the period that the present study was being carried out, the standards for adult ICT user skills were developed [3], a pilot project looking at the implementation of these standards was carried out [4] leading to the development of a draft for the ICT Skill for Life Curriculum [5] and the ICT Skills for Life Pathfinders project which is currently under way in England. These measures and strategic developments are part of a series of changes the present UK government has implemented as technology is recognized to play a major part in the solutions to each of three major challenges which globalization is setting modern governments - economic productivity, social justice and public service reform.

2   ICT, Teaching and Learning

The issue of how to teach ICT skills in adult education has not been explicitly addressed. Tutors who adopt a wide range of strategies for developing learners' literacy and numeracy skills sometimes adopt a purely didactic form of teaching when approaching ICT skills, or alternatively adopt a time intensive strategy of individual tuition. There is little research in this area of how best to use ICT to teach basic skills and this study has sought to fill this gap.

We have based our thinking about the role of ICT in teaching and learning on the framework developed by Ivanic and Tseng [6], summarized in Fig. 1. We incorporated within this framework some of the insights derived from the literature on ICT and learning. (An overview of approaches to learning and ICT can be found in Mayes and de Freitas [7]).

Ivanic and Tseng classify the use of ICT under 'use of resources' in the context of teaching/learning events. However, in this study we are focusing on the learning and teaching of ICT skills themselves as well as the learning of language supported by ICT, so each aspect of the framework (which originates in linguistics) has implications for our study. We would argue that ICT is actually implicated in most, if not all, of the factors identified by Ivanic and Tseng, and so has a much more significant role in learning and teaching than is implied by describing it merely as an educational resource. Below we will indicate some of the ways that we believe ICT further adds to the density of each of the factors they have identified. Evidence from our case studies (see appendix 1 for a summary and a full account shortly in www.nrdc.org.uk) provides additional illustration for these interactions. Within the following discussion we will highlight those areas that specifically informed the design of our interventions, and which may be of specific concern for ICT in adult learning.

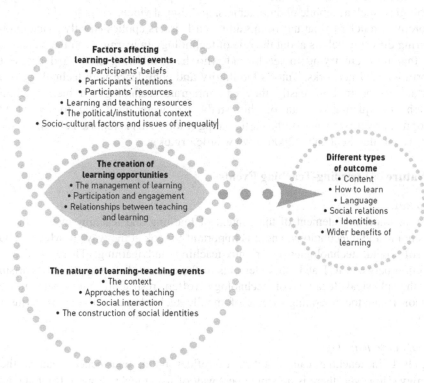

Fig. 1. The relationships between teaching and learning: a conceptual framework (Ivanic and Tseng 2005, p 9)

Factors Affecting Learning-Teaching Events

Participants' beliefs, intentions and resources
Learners come with beliefs about the role of technology in learning which impacts upon the way that they use technology. Earlier work on media more generally has shown that the impact of media on learning and on motivation for learning is itself related to learners' beliefs and expectations about their reactions to the media and not just the media themselves [8].

Learners also have different intentions relating to what they want to get from the courses in terms of the balance of ICT skills and literacy skills, rarely (in these courses at least) is ICT seen purely instrumentally, as simply the means to another learning objective. Access to ICT resources (ownership of technology and access to the internet), personal resources in terms of ICT experience and attitudes to technology, as well as supporting social networks of ICT knowledgeable family and friends all play important roles in learners' take up and use of technology.

The ability of ICT to motivate adult learners, both to come into learning and to stick with learning has often been discussed, however, 'traditional' digital technologies, such as the desktop computer, may well be losing their appeal, and this project was keen to explore the motivational impact of the use of a variety of technologies, such as mobile phones, tablets, and digital video.

Moreover, much of what has been said about learners applies equally to the tutors, who bring differing beliefs about the role of technology in learning and the balance of skills that they are trying to teach, and who have differing skills and access to supporting social networks. Tutor's familiarity and confidence with technology is an important factor in how easily they can integrate technology in their teaching. Through the qualitative data of this study we were also able to record the development over two years of the participating tutors. This is reported elsewhere (see NRDC report due September 2006 at www.nrdc.org.uk).

The Nature of Learning-Teaching Events

The context

ICT is an important element of the context of learning and teaching events, though ICT is not a single technology, and it is important to look at the ways in which a wide range of digital technologies enter into teaching and learning. There is also an interaction between ICT and other elements of the context, for example issues arising from the physical location of technology (often restricting movement in the classroom) and the liberating effects of mobile technologies (at least in terms of space).

Approaches to teaching

Using ICT in teaching caused tutors to reflect upon, and hence change, their pedagogy. However, there is no single best way of using technology in teaching, and a wide range of approaches needs to be adopted. In attempting to put some structure on the discussion of this range of approaches Conole et al [9] suggest three axes along which to describe uses of technology in education: 'Information – Experience', 'Reflection – Non-reflection' (discussed later under the heading 'How to learn'), and 'Individual – Social' (discussed later under the heading 'Social interaction').

The dimension 'Information – Experience' highlights the use of ICT for repetitive practice (also referred to as 'drill and practice') at the one extreme, and at the other learning involving the construction of concepts through the construction of artefacts (see for example Papert and Harel [10]). In our projects tutors rarely used ICT for repetitive practice (though this was sometimes done, particularly in the use of Web sites for practice of literacy skills), but commonly took the construction of an artefact as the central part of their activity. Another way in which ICT was used, was to allow the learners to experience a variety of roles (for example as news interviewer) thus aiming at both literacy and language skills through the medium's affordances (video camera/tape recorder).

Much discussion of learning in recent years has centred on Lave and Wenger's concept of 'communities of practice' [11], and some work in adult and community learning has put the idea of learning communities centre stage (see Cook and Smith [12]). We have evidence of one case study only where the tutor was already working with this idea before his involvement with the project and incorporated this thinking within his scheme of work [13].

Social interaction and construction of social identities
Because of the nature of adult education, all tutors were interested in the benefits of social interaction between learners in the classroom and its effect on learning. Some tutors used technology to promote social interaction and learners' reports show appreciation of an 'improved ambience' in class. Earlier research in use of ICT in schools has shown the difficulties with children in developing successful collaborative activities around ICT [14-16], and more recent work by Mercer [17] looked at modes of talking in learning contexts (including the use of ICT). They all suggest that careful preparation is necessary for 'group chemistry' to work.

The Creation of Learning Opportunities

The management of learning
One of the vital elements for us in thinking about the management of the learning was the role that ICT was seen as having in this learning. Ginsburg [18] identified four rationales for the use of ICT in adult literacy; "Technology as curriculum", "Technology as complement to instruction", "Technology as instructional tool", and "Technology as delivery mechanism". Tutors reflected on their particular approaches and strategies by being explicit about why they were using ICT. They were also encouraged to move away from the view of the 'tutor as expert', often attributed to them by learners, to a more realistic view of the tutor as facilitator for learning, and supporting the development of learner autonomy [19]. This clarity about the role of ICT in the learning process, we believe, plays an important role in encouraging learner autonomy which is a crucial for adults who need to take charge of their own learning outside the formal learning contexts.

Different Types of Outcomes

Content
We were always concerned with two kinds of content, ESOL, literacy and numeracy on the one hand and ICT skills on the other. To build the ICT literacy test we used the definitions of ICT skills adopted by the recent ICT Skill for Life Curriculum [3]. Although restrictive these definitions incorporated a concept of 'purposeful use' which is very intuitive in this field. A number of other definitions have guided us to a wider definition as well as concept of informal development of ICT skills. Two approaches which we found particularly useful were those of Carvin [20] and The International ICT Literacy Panel [21]. Carvin [20] distinguishes a number of elements of relevant new literacies, including:

i.   Technological Literacy: the ability to utilize common ICT tools, including hardware, software, and Internet tools like search engines.
ii. Information Literacy: the skills to ascertain the veracity, reliability, bias, timeliness, and context of information.
iii. Adaptive Literacy: the willingness to learn new tools and to apply previous ICT learning to new situations.

How to learn
ICT has often been seen as allowing learners to reflect upon their own learning processes [22], and some of our tutors saw this as an important aspect of their work.

Use of Language of ICT
The use of the language of ICT within the literacy/language classroom can be seen as a distraction from more useful language. The use of this language clearly presented a challenge for literacy and ESOL tutors and they developed different ways for dealing with this challenge. Some incorporated it in the vocabulary lists to be mastered as technological terms and others left the learners discover the terms and their meaning for when they were needed.

It is clear that digital technologies are changing the nature of literacies; in particular there is a changing relationship between graphic and textual elements. Whilst this changing nature of literacies was not reflected in the literacy and ESOL tests used here it was nevertheless an important element of changing practice that we observed.

Wider benefits of learning
For many learners developing ICT skills is crucial in their everyday lives, whether it opens up work opportunities, enables them to help their children with homework or communicate with distant relatives by email.

3 Aims and Methods

This study's aim was to develop effective ICT based teaching strategies through a series of trials using theoretically grounded ICT task designs targeted at specific adult literacy, numeracy and ESOL learning objectives. We examined both the development of literacy skills through the use of ICT, and the development of ICT skills.

Our main questions were firstly to identify effective ways of using ICT to support the learning of other Skills for Life, and secondly to identify effective ways of learning ICT skills themselves. In doing this we would be testing whether the principles we had derived from our previous work [23] and from a consideration of the literature were useful in building effective ways of using ICT.

Side by side with these main questions we sought to gather data on a number of other specific issues:

i.   The motivational impact of ICT on learners
ii. How ICT was impacting on the wider learning context
iii. Effective support for the development of tutors in the use of ICT in Skills for Life.

An interventionist approach was used inspired to some degree by the design-based research perspective [24], developing approaches to using ICT, and also developing the skills of the tutors in using ICT for teaching. These approaches incorporated elements of learning theories discussed in workshops with the tutors, who were encouraged to express their teaching interventions using technologies in terms of existing paradigms. For example, a constructionist approach (theoretically derived from constructivism, but incorporating the idea of construction within the educational process) was considered. This approach involved multimedia authoring (including digital video) for teaching literacy, and computer-based problem-solving (including simulation and modelling approaches) in the teaching of numeracy.

In Phase 1 (2003-4) we worked with a group of nine tutors to develop a number of teaching interventions based on the recommendations arising from our earlier work, a research review and practitioner perspectives. We met with the tutors on a monthly basis, and between these meetings two development officers visited the tutors and worked with them in developing their practice. Each week the tutors completed an on-line reflective diary, and each term they drew up an intervention plan. The projects developed included a range of technologies and techniques: WebQuests, e-Portfolios, Tablets, m-learning, Digital Video, Mindmaps, National Test, Cyberlab and Family numeracy.

A brief summary of each of these case studies can be found in Appendix 1.

In Phase 2 (October 2004 – March 2005) we ran a series of trials to evaluate these approaches in the areas of literacy and ESOL (we were unable to continue the numeracy trials for practical reasons).

Based on the development work of the previous phase, seven scenarios of ICT use (also referred to as 'schemes of work' by tutors) covering a range of technologies, software and pedagogical approaches such as use of video, web searches, collaborative work etc) were identified to take forward for evaluation. Each project was led by the tutor who developed the approach and usually included another tutor (a 'buddy') who also implemented the same scheme with the tutor's help.

At the start of this phase the learners were given a series of tests – on ICT skills, knowledge and confidence (CICT), ESOL listening skills and in half of the cases a reading comprehension test (NFER,GO). The teaching sessions lasted approximately 40 hours and spread over two terms. Each classroom was observed on three or more occasions (focusing on the teacher) in addition to which a sample of individual learners was observed carrying out tasks at each observation. The observational data involved recording the activities in class following a set of codes developed in a previous phase. Analysis of these activities was both quantitative (counting the occurrence of certain codes) and qualitative (describing the meaning of the activities in relation to the learner data to understand the pedagogic processes involved).Learners were tested again at the end of the teaching sessions. 180 students undertook the tests; pre-and post test data were available on the ICT knowledge and skills assessment (ICTKSA) for 81 students, on the ICT Confidence assessment (CICT) for 91, on the GO reading test for 60, and on the ESOL listening test for 67, with complete data (i.e. ESOL and/or GO, ICTKSA and CICT, and Profile) for 61 learners (Table 1). Fluctuations in numbers were a result of students in some classes either improving and being moved up a class or dropping out.

4 Summary of Results

In the evaluation learners improved in almost all cases first in ICT skills and in literacy or language (ESOL) skills though, as expected, different groups showed different balances between improvements in the two sets of skills. Table 1 shows the gains in ICT knowledge and skills (ICTKSA), in confidence with ICT (CICT), reading (GO), and in the listening (ESOL) tests. The learning gains for classes were in most cases statistically significant and the effect sizes large. The effect size was calculated as the difference between the pre and post-test means divided by the pooled standard deviation. This lends strong support to the claim in the Moser Report [1] that *"Learners who use ICT for basic skills double the value of their study time acquiring two sets of skills at the same time."*

Table 1. Comparison of the mean improvements and effect sizes found between the different schemes of work on the four assessments used for the 61 learners where all data was available

	ICTLA		CICT		GO		ESOL	
	Mean Change	Effect Size	Mean Change	Effect Size	Mean Change	Effect Size	Mean Change	Effect Size
Webquests	12.14	2.68	1.76	0.58			3.00	1.08
e-Portfolio	1.76	0.33	0.27	0.18	10.26	0.66	0.87	0.72
Tablets	4.65	0.72	1.92	0.75			0.07	0.05
m-Learning	5.16	0.84	0.70	0.21	9.64	0.76	0.74	0.24
Digital Video	3.33	0.87	1.74	1.24	16.00	1.49	-0.20	-0.33
Mindmaps	17.57	4.56	3.85	2.06	10.00	0.54		
National test	12.25	1.02	2.00	4.83	3.50	0.14		

Factors Affecting Learning-Teaching Events

ICT confidence
Initial levels of ICT confidence were found to have an impact on learners' persistence, particularly in classes with young learners, where those with lower levels of ICT confidence were likely to attend less frequently, and were more likely to eventually drop out (Table 2). The reverse was however noted for one particular class (National Test) of learners. This class was comprised of more mature students and a conjecture is that age may be a factor affecting the relationship between confidence and attendance (the lower the confidence initially the higher the attendance for older students). However, there is limited data to support this hypothesis and the negative correlation is based on a small number of students (8).

Learning and teaching resources
The use of ICT was found to be motivating for most learners across a range of technology use, though a few learners saw the technology as a distraction from their language work. Use of mobile technologies (Tablets, PDAs, mobile phones) was found to be particularly motivating, and enabled greater flexibility in teaching.

Table 2. Correlations between percentage of lessons attended by a learner and their initial levels of ICT confidence (CICT). Where * correlations significant at p = 0.05 or better.

	Pearson Correlation (r)	Significance (p)	Sample available (n)
Webquests	0.135	0.711	10
e-Portfolio	**0.504**	0.002*	34
Tablets	- 0.050	0.792	30
m-Learning	**0.515**	0.010*	24
Digital Video	--	--	0
Mindmaps	0.205	0.571	10
National Test	**- 0.773**	0.025*	8

Age
The learners' age was a significant factor in predicting learning gains. There was a negative correlation in gaining ESOL skills (older learners made least progress), and for men (but not for women). Positive correlations were found for ICT skills and for confidence (older learners made most progress). It may be that younger males at the start of the courses overestimated their abilities and by the end they had a more realistic view of their skills.

The Nature of Learning-Teaching Events

Use of technology
Increased ICT skills and confidence were positively correlated with the amount of time learners spent using the technology within the classroom. More specifically learner use of the internet, PowerPoint and word processing were found to be positively correlated with gains in ICT skills, though only the use of word-processing was also correlated with increase in confidence (partly due to insufficient sample). These changes point to an increase in learner overall confidence and autonomy.

Collaboration
Particular emphasis was put on the introduction of collaboration, and observations indicated that tutors were often successful in managing a classroom with groups/pairs of learners collaborating.

Those classes where individual learners spent more time working on their own showed better gains in ICT skills than those classes which spent more time working in small groups. However there were no corresponding gains in confidence levels related to time spent working individually.

Examination of the qualitative data showed that there were issues about the way group work was organised. When collaborative work was forced by the need to share technology it was not as successful as when tutors developed tasks that required peer interaction. One person sometimes dominated the use of the technology, and this may have undermined the usefulness of collaborative work for developing ICT skills. Observations do however point to collaborative working being useful for increasing confidence in using ICT as well as persistence with the course.

Artefacts
Most of the courses involved learners in the construction of an artefact – often jointly. Evidence from classroom observations indicates that this was often a useful focus, generating motivation, collaboration and purposeful action. Observations also pointed out the value for using ICT in this way which allowed differentiation within the classroom.

The Creation of Learning Opportunities

The management of learning
There were no correlations found between any of the teaching practices and change in performance in literacy and ESOL, but a number of interesting correlations were found for ICT skills and literacy. (It is likely that the ICT tests were closer to measuring what the learners were learning and were therefore more sensitive, and so these results may be indicative of what might be happening to a lesser degree in the literacy/ESOL area as well.)

We encouraged teaching strategies that aimed to increase the autonomy of learners so that they were able to engage in self-directed learning.

There was a positive correlation between the amount of time spent by tutors '**Managing activities**' (tutors engaged in helping individuals or small groups while the class works on an activity) and gains made in both ICT skills and confidence.

The most effective teaching strategy was '**Extending**', where the tutor built on/added to material previously introduced by them, or added to a comment by a learner. There was a strong correlation between this type of teaching activity and changes in ICT skills and confidence scores.

One strategy was found to be negatively correlated with changes in ICT skills and confidence, and that was '**Explaining**' (a one-way dialogue from the tutor to the students on 'how' to complete a task). This is possibly due to not allowing sufficient time for learners to understand the task.

Tutors' use of PowerPoint also correlated negatively with change in ICT skills. These results suggest that tutors' one-way presentation was not effective in developing ICT skills or confidence.

5   Different Types of Outcomes

It was interesting to observe how ICT changed the nature of knowledge to be learned, so tutors talked more about managing information and less about learning it, they talked about browsing and scanning and less about reading as comprehension.

Tutors were aware of the wider range of ICT skills that need to be developed, in particular being able to evaluate resources, willingness to learn new skills and the transfer of skills from one context to another.

6   So What Is Effective Practice?

The specific components of our approach to changing classroom dynamics for the use of ICT in adult literacy and ESOL classes were shown to be effective in supporting the development of ICT skills and confidence. Tutors were most successful when they managed the following strategies:

i.   Have clear reasons as well as a plan for using the technology.
ii. Encourage learner autonomy (through managing activities, extending activities, discussion and reducing tutor presentation time), and consequently release teacher time to observe and get to know their learners better and so carefully adapt their teaching to learners' needs. This often meant understanding how to encourage self-directed learning through boosting their confidence.
iii. Use of technology to construct (often shared) artefacts.
iv. Use of a wide range of technologies, and in particular mobile technologies to support greater flexibility in learning in any place at any time.
v.   Collaborative learning was shown to be effective in terms of gaining confidence and speaking skills, but this was not always so; further work is needed to understand and develop more effective approaches to the use of collaboration with adult learners.

This study would not have been possible without the close collaboration and active participation, in terms of development as well as practice, of the strong team of teachers (tutors in adult education) who not only were open to change through constant updating of their ICT skills and reflecting on their pedagogic skills, but also took risks with experimentation.

References

1. DfEE, A fresh start: improving literacy and numeracy (The report of the working group chaired by Sir Claus Moser). (1999), DfEE: London. Available from: http://www.lifelonglearning.co.uk/mosergroup/index.htm, [Accessed: 9 March 2006].
2. DfES, 21st Century Skills: Realising Our Potential. (2003). Available from: http://www.dfes.gov.uk/skillsstrategy/_pdfs/whitePaper_PDFID4.pdf, [Accessed: 9 March 2006].
3. Qualifications and Curriculum Authority, Standards for adults ICT skills. (2005), Available from: http://www.qca.org.uk/2791.html, [Accessed: 28 Jul, 2005].
4. NIACE, ICT Skill for Life - Action Research Project, Report to DfES, October 2005. (2005). Available from: http://www.niace.org.uk/Research/ICT/ICT-SfL-Action-Research-Project.pdf, [Accessed: 9 March 2006].
5. Qualifications and Curriculum Authority, Skill for Life ICT Curriculum (draft). QCA. (2006), Available from: http://www.qca.org.uk/downloads/qca-05-1887-ict-skill-for-life-curriculum-draft.pdf, [Accessed: 6 March 2006].
6. Ivanic, R. and M.-i.L. Tseng, Understanding the relationships between learning and teaching: an analysis of the contribution of applied linguistics. (2005), Available from: NRDC, Institute of Education: London. ISBN: 1-905188-00-5.
7. Mayes, T. and S. de Freitas, Review of e-learning theories, frameworks and models. (2004), Available from: http://www.jisc.ac.uk/uploaded_documents/Stage%202%20Learning%20Models%20(Version%201).PDF, [Accessed: 9 March 2006].
8. Salomon, G., Television is 'easy' and print is 'hard': The differential investment of mental effort in learning as a function of perceptions and attributions. Journal of Educational Psychology, (1984). 76: p. 647-658.

9. Conole, G., Dyke, M.,...Oliver and Seale, J., Mapping pedagogy and tools for effective learning design. Computers and Education, (2004). 43: p. 17-33.
10. Papert, S. and I. Harel, Constructionism. (1991): Ablex Publishing Corporation.
11. Wenger, E., Communities of practice: Learning, meaning and identity. (1998): Cambridge University Press.
12. Cook, J. and M. Smith, Beyond formal learning: informal community e-learning. Computers and Education, (2004). 43(1-2): p. 35-47.
13. Harris, S.R. and N. Shelswell, Beyond Communities of Practice in Adult Basic Education, in Beyond Communities of Practice: Language, Power and Social Context, D. Barton and K. Tusting, Editors. (2005), Cambridge University Press: Cambridge.
14. Crook, C., Computers and the collaborative experience of learning. (1994), London: Routledge.
15. Hoyles, C., L. Healy, et al., Groups work with computers: An overview of findings. Journal of Computer Assisted Instruction, (1994). 10: p. 202-215.
16. Hoyles, C., L. Healy, et al., Interdependence and Autonomy: Aspects of Group Work with Computers. Learning and Instruction, (1992). 2: p. 239-257.
17. Mercer, N., Words and Minds. (2000), London: Routledge.
18. Ginsburg, L., Integrating Technology into Adult Learning, in Technology, basic skills, and adult education: getting ready and moving forward, C.E. Hopey, Editor. (1998), ERIC Clearninghouse on Adult, Career and vocational Education, Ohio State University: Ohio.
19. Letertre, E., Multimedia pedagogical resource and learner autonomy. (2003), Available from: http://www-deis.cit.ie/biteCONFERENCE/Papers/BiTE_FR.pdf, [Accessed: 9 March 2006].
20. Carvin, A., 'More than Just Access',. (2000), Available from: http://www.educause.edu/apps/er/erm00/erm006.asp?bhcp.
21. International ICT Literacy Panel, Digital Transformation: A Framework for ICT Literacy. (2002), Educational Testing Service (ETS): Princeton, NJ. Available from: http://www.ets.org/resesarch/ictliteracy.
22. Wegerif, R., Literature Review in Thinking Skills, Technology and Learning. (2002), NESTA Futurelab. p. 1-44.
23. Mellar, H., et al., ICT and adult literacy, numeracy and ESOL. (2004), NRDC, Institute of Education: London. p. 1-100. Available from: http://www.nrdc.org.uk/uploads/documents/doc_258.pdf, [Accessed: 9 March 2006].
24. The Design-Based Research Collective, Design-Based research: an emerging paradigm for educational research. Educational Research, (2003). 32(1): p. 5-8.

Appendix 1

Developing the Interventions
We worked together with the tutors in developing approaches to the effective use of ICT, starting from the tutors' work in the classroom, incorporating the recommendations from the earlier Stage 1 study and reflecting on the resulting designs in terms of the research literature on teaching and learning in adult skills for life and on ICT and learning. Each approach was trialled and refined over three iterations. Below we briefly describe each of these approaches; full descriptions of these will be available in the form of Case Studies on the NRDC web-site at www.nrdc.org.uk. The first seven of these approaches were taken forward into the second phase for trialling and testing. Unfortunately the eighth and ninth studies

(which were the two numeracy studies) could not be taken forward because it was not possible for the tutors involved to continue to commit to these studies as a result of other commitments.

Web Quests

This course used Web Quests with entry level ESOL learners – a Web Quest was developed based around local sites giving an element of familiarity which helped to overcome the difficulties caused by the low level of language skills. A variety of strategies of arranging pairs in order to encourage collaborative learning and to improve confidence in speaking were trialled. The personal tutors and the ICT tutors worked very closely together to keep the language focus and the ICT focus matched.

e-Portfolios

This course used OPEUS e-Portfolios, a web-based technology that allows users to design websites in which they can store and display their work thus creating electronic books or portfolios. This allowed quick display of learners' work (learners can design a web page and email someone with a link to their website) and allowed email feedback This was intended to both develop both learners' language skills (writing and communication) and ICT skills (web design, word processing, email, etc).

The learners were Entry 2 literacy group of 16 ESOL learners aged 16-20 at an FE College, who attended on a full-time basis. About half of the lessons for this class were held in rooms with computers, and the learners also had access to computers outside class hours in the Learning Centre.

Tablets

Tablets were used in an FE College setting with two groups of about 25 ESOL students in one 2.5 hour weekly session. This course aimed at creating language learning opportunities through the use of mobile technologies (incorporating ICT in classes where this would otherwise not be possible) and also laid emphasis on collaborative working in groups with the learners sharing use of the Tablets. The learners were also actively involved with the local community through participation in a neighbourhood project.

m-learning

ESOL and literacy learners used camera phones and handheld computers with mobile phone functionality and built-in cameras to send text, images and sounds as multimedia messages or emails to a website to create a mobile photolog/weblog, or moblog. The intervention was presented as a project during which learners became photo-journalists and prepared a photo record of college open day.

Digital Video

This course was titled 'ESOL and Computing', its aim was to develop both ICT and language skills, and it was run in an FE College. It was an optional course for second language learners, most learners were in an ESOL E3 course and they came to this course to get an introduction to ICT skills. Video Nation - a collection of amateur short streamed videos on the BBC web site - was used as a source of examples and material to work on. The learners then used a digital video camera to create films, and they were encouraged to take turns and assume different roles in filming the college's new building.

MindMaps

In this course the tutor used mind mapping software in an adult Basic Skills Literacy classroom in order to help improve the planning of written work through organising thoughts and structuring work into separate paragraphs. These maps could be saved directly into Word in order to be used as a basis for writing. This was a class of mostly retired learners who ranged in terms of literacy levels and who had a common interest in acquiring ICT skills.

National Test

This course took place in the evenings in a Community Centre which hosted a UK Online Centre accommodating up to seven learners The aim was to encourage residents who lived on the estate to join a basic ICT class with embedded basic literacy skills. Tutors used Skills for Life resources and the BBC Skillswise website alongside other paper based and web based material and to prepare learners for the National Test in Literacy..

CyberLab

Cyberlab was a course for a literacy and numeracy embedded into topics including science, technology, history and culture in a framework of ICT-enabled activities. The intervention included a mixture of constructional, instructional and exploratory teaching and learning approaches. This has included the use of Logo and robots when investigating algorithms, and when investigating fractals, learners used digital cameras to take pictures of real life examples.

Family numeracy

This course used website resources to allow parents to assess and practise numeracy skills. The workshop was tailored around the needs identified by the assessments. A tablet computer was used to enable parents to model how they would undertake calculations. Different strategies that parents could use with their children were discussed and practised using freely available online children's games and school's software.

Community Aware Content Adaptation for Mobile Technology Enhanced Learning

Ralf Klamma, Marc Spaniol, and Yiwei Cao

Lehrstuhl Informatik V, RWTH Aachen University, Germany
{klamma, spaniol, cao}@i5.informatik.rwth-aachen.de

Abstract. Mobile technology enhanced learning pertains to the delivery of multimedia learning resource onto mobile end devices such as cell phones and PDAs. It also aims at supporting personalized adaptive learning in a community context. This paper presents a novel approach to supporting both aspects. The community aware content adaptation employs the MPEG-7 and MPEG-21 multimedia metadata standards to present the best possible information to mobile end devices. Meanwhile, interest patterns are derived from a community aware context analysis. We designed and developed a technology enhanced learning platform supporting architecture professionals' study at city excursions and other mobile tasks.

1 Introduction

In the past few years, technology enhanced learning has experienced a boom. With the development of wireless communication, the number of mobile multipurpose devices is constantly increasing (surpasses several times the number of humans on the planet). Compared to the previous devices, the handheld mobile devices nowadays generally have larger storage and display screens. The wireless transfer speed is also enhanced greatly. The terms m-learning or MobiLearning appeared around 2000 with the increase of cell phone users, defining learning technologies using wireless transmission [28]. It was seen as an important technical means of enhanced learning in the 21st century, instead of e-learning started around 1995 [16]. Equipped with mobile devices, professional learners can conduct learning activities flexibly and ubiquitously, i.e. at anytime, anywhere. Mobile technology enhanced learning is yet still not so powerful as technology enhanced learning on desktop computers [19].

In the aspect of information provision, the development of new digital information technologies introduces novel approaches to learning. You can get answers by a finger clicking to surf the internet instead of checking the answers from a book shelf of encyclopedia at home. The number of Wikipedia articles in many languages shows the rapid even exponential increase of information provision. Currently over 1 million English articles were written for Wikipedia and the number has doubled within the past year.

In parallel, the desire of consumers to access information at any time and anywhere has given the birth of ubiquitous/pervasive computing. The mobility

W. Nejdl and K. Tochtermann (Eds.): EC-TEL 2006, LNCS 4227, pp. 227–241, 2006.

of ubiquitous computing can be depicted as how to deliver the right information to the right place and at the right time to the right user. In the context of mobile technology enhanced learning, we observe the following questions. (1) Who are the target learner communities? (2) What kind of learning material needs high mobility to transfer? (3) How can the right information be related to a certain location, to the temporal context, and to the community context? (4) How can the right learning resources be delivered to mobile devices?

With these questions addressed, we did an indepth survey of the state-of-the-art e-learning and m-learning systems. One of the target communities to be involved is architecture professionals. We have analyzed their community requirements and provided a solution to mobile learning for architecture professionals with a context aware content adaptation mobile learning environment. We use the term mobile technology enhanced platform to make clear, that it is only a starting point for a comprehensive solution for mobile learning. Yet, the systematic use of metadata standards make it much easier to combine the work already done with other metadata standard based solutions. Especially the use of MPEG-7 [18] and MPEG-21 [5], allows effective metadata crosswalking with other XML based standards in technology enhanced learning by means of simple mapping rules realized e.g. in XPath.

The rest of the paper is organized as follows. In Section 2 we propose the concept of a mobile technology enhanced learning platform with community aware content adaptation. In Section 3 the MPEG-7 and MPEG-21 metadata standards as a comprehensive framework for the creation of multimedia adaptations are discussed. Then the learning communities of our platform by means of community awareness concepts and context patterns are introduced in Section 4. After that we present the implementation of the mobile technology enhanced learning platform with community aware content adaptation. The system evaluation was performed in a mobile learning scenario within the community of architecture students. The paper closes with the conclusions and gives an outlook on future research.

2 Mobile Technology Enhanced Learning for Architecture Professionals

The research work of current technology enhanced learning as well as mobile technology enhanced learning platforms focuses on either content-centric learning or user-centric learning. The former supports learning resource creation, adaptation, management and delivery [33,29]. The latter supports learning activities through interaction between teachers and learners. The MIT media laboratory presents several applications of mobile technology enhanced learning in classrooms, such as opinion metrics to rank lecture contents in real-time, and reality mining & conversation analysis to record and analyze students' conversations [28]. Compared to the proposition of [12] that "mobile computing is more sophisticated than using a computer while moving", m-learning is neither merely delivery learning resources to mobile end devices, nor a simple clicking ranking buttons to interact with lecturers.

PROLEARN (http://www.prolearn-project.org), the EU IST Network of Excellence in Professional learning, focuses on technology enhanced professional learning. Our approach is heavily influenced by the results from the work package about personalized, adaptive learning. We add two specific results here. First, we incorporate multimedia content adaptation to the capabilities of the used mobile devices by means of MPEG-7 and MPEG-21. Second, we include a community context into the adaptation process, arguing that addressing stereotypical users is less restricting and that it avoids undesired cognitive and social lock-in situations.

30 mobile learning initiatives are demonstrated and surveyed systematically in [16]. The success of mobile technologies depends greatly on social and cultural aspects [4,7]. Thus, an important application area of mobile technologies is to deliver contextualized information. Here, *context* includes the location, the time, the personal preferences, and the current task [11]. Another important type of context is the community context, which includes the community preferences and community tasks.

Furthermore, in the cases that mobile technologies are necessary to be applied, another problem arises. Although there are huge numbers of multimedia learning resources available on the web, users have many problems trying to access these contents with the constraints of their mobile end devices. In the first step, users have to select content needed in their current situation. In the second step, the selected content has to be adapted. It is highly complex for users to obtain the right information anytime and anywhere, when the contexts of mobile end devices change continuously. In order to solve those problems smart solutions are needed to help the learners in the *content selection process* and simultaneously *adapting the multimedia content* to the capability of the used mobile devices.

Current *adaptive recommender systems* are a step forward in this direction. Here, user preferences are a decisive factor in the content selection process. User preferences are externalized metadata about content gathered by explicit user feedback (e.g. "Do you like it?") or implicit ones (e.g. time elapsed watching the content). Most approaches therefore concentrate on "simply" taking user preferences into account [3,8,22,24,6,30,15]. However, terminal characteristics and network conditions are considered only to a very limited scale. A more advanced approach is the combination of user preferences and terminal/network capabilities for presentation, as in [27]. Recently the *community context* has been considered in the adaptation process [20]. There are still little research work in this field. As a result, users are not aware of the communities formed around their habitat and might not gain additional information from them. This lack of community awareness leads to several deficits for the user.

In summary, there are three problems, when users try to access multimedia learning resources via mobile devices. First, it might cause *less accurate addressing*, especially with the increase in the number of multimedia contents. Since mobile devices have limitations to list available items or even to preview contents, the selection process becomes very tricky for the user. Second, with an increasing amount of multimedia contents, the diversity of these items increases, too. It is almost impossible for the user to take an ad hoc decision which might be most informative under current learning circumstances. Thus, the risk increases. The user's preferences may either not cover the whole set of items properly or be *too restrictive*, so that other contents might be skipped due to the narrow classifications. A community oriented classification can broaden the classification again, a well-known effect in social recommender systems. Third, users miss the chance of having *identification* as a member of a community. Identity is an important concept for putting information into action.

In order to overcome the previously described deficits, our approach combines adaptive multimedia content with community awareness. By doing so, the professionals not only gain access to contents based on their individual preferences but also benefit from the experiences achieved in the professional learning communities they belong to. Thus, we bring *content adaptation* and *recommender systems* together under one roof. Conceptually, this approach improves the Universal Media Access (UMA) [21] based on multimedia metadata description standards by integrating the aspect of community awareness into the mobile technology enhanced learning platform.

Mobile technology enhanced learning has been targeted to diverse user communities. The case of computer science education on a global scale is surveyed in [10]. In our context, the target groups are communities of professionals with special interest, on which physical location has a great impact. For example, architecture or art professionals usually get used to computer-aided design software or graphic design. The penetration of information technologies is less than other disciplines, since craft and technologies are two independent domains. However, usability is an important evaluation parameter for e-learning systems [32]. Architecture professionals do need such a platform to support their architecture excursions as well as non-aimed learning during travels. Thus, architecture professionals are chosen as the main target community in the research work.

In addition, architecture learning resources are of high interest in mobile technology enhanced learning. The reasons are as follows: The learning resources are greatly associated with existing physical instances like buildings and urban spaces at a location. Some of the greatest architects have never studied architecture at universities and have learned by perception. Moreover, learning resources are distributed to a great extent and the formats are various. Multimedia contents play an important role among architecture learning resources, e.g. videos of architecture as well as of interviews with architects, audio slides and pictures of building facade and internal design, a large number of plans and drawings, and various 3D models. Another factor is that community awareness has a great impact on architecture learning. Besides the delivery of learning resources from repositories, architecture professionals are quite interested in resources from the community. The experiences from other professionals such as architects, very famous architects, engineers, architecture lecturers and students are highly requested.

However, how are the architecture learning resources organized and delivered currently? Much architecture learning stuff is written or organized in a virtual database schemes with attributes like architects, building title, building years, location, description, and images. So the online stuff is also deployed in table sheet with those attributes and multimedia like 3D models as well as images. One of the largest online architecture databases, the ArchINFORM (`www.archinform.net`), is not accessible anymore, without giving any information about the access rights. This database was created by architecture students at Karlsruhe University in Germany and had been published online since 1996. Another important university-developed architecture database is from University of California, Berkeley. In the frame of the Museum Informatics Project, an architecture visual resources library SPIRO (Slide and Photograph Image Retrieval Online) has been launched (`www.mip.berkeley.edu/spiro/`). Students' design work is also archived in it. In addition, some offline architecture databases are specialized in *architectural history*. The stuff is well collected by universities and research institutions. However, those databases are accessible only with a strict license within a chair or institute. They only deliver architectural materials to the authorized researchers rather than support collaborative research and learning among architectural communities. Certainly, some online architecture databases might be accessible with a strict user management. ArchINFORM might be such a case after being published publicly for good 10 years. Another still public online database, the Great Building Online, hosted by Artifice, Inc. has extended its architectural stuff since 1997 (`www.greatbuildings.com`).

Nevertheless, the aforementioned open comprehensive architecture databases are not adaptive to different contexts or to different end devices with wired or wireless connections. They deliver the same content to user communities who look up information with different purposes. There are diverse use scenarios for architecture professionals. For instance, the architecture databases can be used to get general design ideas, to draw inspiration for a design work at hand, to get up-to-date information and multimedia about a building nearby when an architect is en route, or to get to know how to draw a sketch at a museum visit through learning from other professional sketches. Those diverse demands can be met effectively in mobile technology enhanced learning with context-aware and community-aware content adaptation. We aim at a personalization and adaptation of information to meet the user's needs and interest. One of the goals is to integrate the variety of perspectives on personalized and adaptive learning. We focus on personalization issues in collaborative learning more intensively than on personalization in individual learning situations. One of the important factors is the content adaptation which is discussed in the next section.

3   Content Adaptation with MPEG-7 and MPEG-21

Taking the various techniques applicable for media adaptation into consideration, our system focuses on the media's target context. In particular, we have implemented an approach that covers the professionals' infrastructure in terms of the device capabilities, as well as the preferences of the learner and the community he belongs to. In order to guarantee a high quality of the multimedia contents provided by our system, we concentrate on static adaptation. This means, in contrast to dynamic adaptation, that the content variations will be created and tested beforehand. In addition, this helps to reduce response times since the multimedia contents need not to be transcoded when being requested. In terms of media formatting we mostly stick to media adaptation instead of cross-media adaptations, since the media formats we use are compliant to the most end devices. However, we also provide cross-media adaptations with respect to picture previews. Finally, the presentation supported in our system regarded from an abstract level is physical, but not semantic. That means, we support the adaptation of multimedia content presentations with respect to the aspects mentioned before, but do not modify the meaning. Figure 1 contains an overview on media adaptation techniques and highlights the techniques supported by our system. As it can be seen, our system is capable of supporting these aspects on a broad-scale with a focus on community awareness.

With regard to various multimedia metadata, MPEG-7 provides a large set of pre-defined elements to describe multimedia contents. In particular, these elements are composed of two different types: Description Schemes (DS) and Descriptors (D). Depending on the fields of applications, a specific description scheme can be defined by freely combinable descriptors (i.e. tags). Each descriptor itself refers to a specific feature or attribute of multimedia content [18,21]. In addition, the Description Definition Language (DDL) of MPEG-7 makes this standard more powerful than other metadata standards, since it allows the creation of new descriptors and description schemes within the standard. Hence, it makes the vocabulary of MPEG-7 to be extensible by employing the XML-Schema.

The MPEG-7 standard consists of eight parts. However, the first five constitute the core MPEG-7 technology, whereas the others are supplementary to the standard. For the purpose of multimedia adaptations for mobile, only the part 5 dealing with "Multimedia Description Schemes" (MDS) will be deployed [13]. The MDS contains several high-level description schemes which are particularly suitable for description and management of versatile multimedia contents.

Despite MPEG-7's capabilities to describe and administrate multimedia contents, it lacks dedicated features to capture information for user modeling, end devices descriptions and copyright management. These issues are approached by the MPEG-21 framework [5]. Here, the so-called digital item defines a structured digital object (an interaction unit) which is represented in a standard format, identified uniquely in the environment. In addition, a digital item also encapsulates the metadata associated with the object. A digital item can be anything such as a video, an image along with its metadata, an HTML page composed of several media files, photos etc. Thus, a digital item is a combination of resources, associated metadata and the structuring information. In this aspect, any digital object within the MPEG-21 infrastructure, such as textual information or any other related digital content, are digital items.

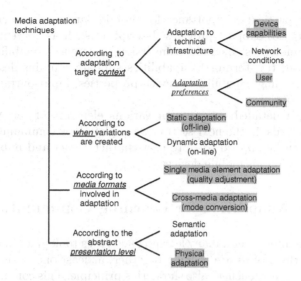

Fig. 1. Community aware media adaptation

In general, MPEG-21 consists of twelve parts [9,18]. These parts are independent of each other. So the excerpts of the standard might also be applied. Alone for the purpose of managing multimedia contents in mobile end devices we confine the system to the MPEG-21 Digital Item Adaptation (DIA) and MPEG-21 Digital Item Declaration Language (DIDL). The MPEG-21 DIDL contains six top level descriptors (tags) as follows, of which the first four are particularly important for mobile data management.

- *Container* is a data structure to group other containers or items. In addition, it may contain a descriptor.
- *Item* is used to group other items or components.
- *Component* is used to fasten the resource and its descriptor (metadata).
- *Resource* is a physical object, e.g. a video file. Location of the object, e.g. URI, can be specified as a resource.
- *Condition* puts a condition on the enclosed element by means of (multiple) predicates.
- *Choice* restricts the selection on the enclosed elements, e.g. user may only choose one of the resources within this tag.

In our context, a digital item is defined as a video file along with its content description in (MPEG-7), and all of its available variations (as items) and their media properties (again in MPEG-7). Thus, the digital item consists of MPEG-21 descriptors that embed MPEG-7 multimedia metadata descriptions. Usage Environment Description Tools, the first major category of MPEG-21 DIA, are intended to describe the usage environment. In this aspect, it is the key element to achieve interoperable transparent access to rich multimedia content [5]. The MPEG-21 DIA itself is again subdivided into four more subparts which contain sophisticated descriptors for mobile data management. Two of these DIA subparts are of particular importance for mobile data management. First, the User Characteristics subpart provides descriptors such as content preferences, presentation preferences, modality conversion preferences, mobility character- istics etc. Second, the Terminal Capabilities subpart contains descriptors that cover coding-decoding capabilities, device properties, input-output capabilities and interaction options.

After giving a detailed overview on various elements of the MPEG-7 and MPEG-21 standards, in the next section we explain how community aware con- text patterns can be applied to store user characteristics and improve learning content presentation for mobile devices.

4   Content Adaptation for Learning Communities

Even before the internet era, many learning activities took place in communities. The saying "if three of us are walking together, at least one of the other two is good enough to be my teacher" also shows this principle. This community context is stressed in the concept of "community of practices", which has dimensions of mutual engagement of communities and a shared repertoire of knowledge [31]. As knowledge management and learning management become more and more exchangeable, learning activities can be carried out and supported in community of practices.

In addition, personalization has become one of the major success factors in current information services as well as in learning [27,1]. In this aspect, our approach aims particularly to adapt global learning media (video, image, multilingual-text, etc.), taking the learning community background of each indi- vidual into consideration. Thus, apart from individual preferences, community- specific knowledge will be used in the adaptation process initiatively. We try to integrate community information as another item of context into existing ones, such as device capabilities or user preferences. This forms the user's context which is probably the most important concept in adaptation, since the whole adaptation is based on it. In a mobile scenario we can specify the mostly used context in learning resources adaptation as device capabilities, usage environ- ment (system software, application software), network capabilities (which can also be considered in usage environment), and user skills and preferences (a complex working model of context can be found in [25]).

The previously described aspects are of different nature. On the one hand, some of these criteria might be extracted automatically as much as possible. On the other hand, others might be integrated manually in the most accurate way. Up to now, most of the current systems take only network capabilities (such as effective bandwidth, bottleneck bandwidth, latency, etc.) automatically into consideration. However, we also consider software properties, since information about the encoder in use might influence the adaptation process significantly. Information that has to be inserted manually (at least initially) into our system is the learner preferences. Nevertheless, we collect these data systematically, e.g. by means of an interest profile. Moreover, the information will be put into the learning community (preferences) context where not only a single learner will be considered separately but also the learning community will be included. For that reason, our approach aims at detecting communities from the learner preferences and the system data which merge to community context patterns. The developed community context patterns help learners to search and retrieve learning resources effectively.

4.1   Community Clustering Strategies

In order to detect community patterns we apply clustering techniques. In this aspect, there are two main points to be considered. First, a distance or similarity metric which guides the grouping process needs to be specified [23]. Second, a clustering algorithm has to be chosen and potentially adapted to suit as well as possible the needs for community detection. In our case, the distance among professionals (i.e. dissimilarity among user preferences) is the most suitable metric to measure similarity among them. Here, the *Euclidean distance* is by far the most popular one and seems to be a suitable metric to be used [14]. We consider the user preferences as a vector that contains discrete positive integers ranging form "1" (i.e. ignorable) to "5" (i.e. very important). In this case, the Euclidean distance can be easily used to measure the distance between these vectors. Concerning the clustering algorithm, an approach should be chosen to allow updating clusters with any new learner entering the system. Therefore, an *incremental clustering algorithm* is selected.

However, again there are two options in building the clusters: top-down or bottom-up. The top-down approach is based on predefined stereotypes for each possible cluster. On the basis of similarity (respectively distance) computations are done between the user profiles and the pre-defined stereotypes assignments of users to community clusters. As a result, each user is assigned to one cluster at any time (hard-clustering) whose distance to the user is below a threshold. In the bottom-up approach, users are classified directly based on similarity measures on their corresponding profiles. Here, the distances between user profiles are calculated in order to create clusters by determining whether any two users correlate to each other, i.e. whether they belong to the same community. Figure 2 gives a graphical overview on both previously approaches. For further reading, an intensive review on clustering methods can be found in [14].

Apart from the aforementioned benefits of updating community clusters by incremental clustering, this algorithm also causes less computation complexity and thus faster updates. A bottom-up approach requires $m*(m-1)$ computations of distance vectors (delta values) at any point when the community clusters require to be updated. Thus, it leads to a complexity of $O(m^2)$. In the case of deploying a top-down approach and assuming there are n community stereotypes and m users, $m * n$ distance vectors (delta values) need to be calculated and compared ($m * n$ comparisons) with a pre-defined threshold. This leads to an overall complexity of $O(m)$ assuming that the number of users is much greater than the number of community stereotypes ($m >> n$). Consequently, a top-down community clustering approach has been implemented in our system.

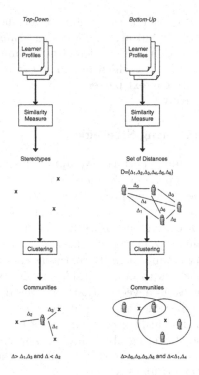

Fig. 2. Comparison between top-down and bottom-up clustering

4.2   Community Context Pattern Maintenance

With an increasing numbers of learners making use of our platform, the maintenance of community context patterns becomes critical. The reason is that new learners joining the system or changing the individual user profiles also influence the overall view of the community, which these learners are assigned to. As a consequence, updating of user profiles might lead to shifts in community assignments of the respective learners. Additionally, the community stereotype needs to be updated, when every time a learner joins or leaves a community. Finally, it might turn out that two or more community stereotypes should be merged due to correlation while new ones appear.

Considering the previously described aspects we have selected a top-down, incremental clustering algorithm again. In our system we've implemented a modified version of the Doubling Algorithm [26]. Our system calculates for each new learner the distances between the learner's vector and the clusters' centroids (in our case the mean community stereotypes). Then, based on the community clustering criteria of our algorithm, either a new community cluster is formed or the learner joins in an existing one. Additionally, if a new cluster is formed, it is checked whether the number of clusters has exceeded a predefined value. In general, this value prevents a too fragmented clustering. Thus it is possible to

Table 1. Structure chart of the community clustering in our system

Community Clustering		
Step-1: Check current number of clusters	Case a: If less than 2	Create a new community and add the user to this community
	Case b: If more than or equal to 2 and less than k_1	If the minimum distance from the user to any community is less than MIN_DISTANCE_LIMIT, then add the user to that community
		Otherwise, same as case a
	Case c: If more than k_1	If the minimum distance from the user to any community is less than 2*MINIMUM_DISTANCE, add the user to that community
		Otherwise, same as case a
Step-2: Set new MINIMUM_DISTANCE value: the minimum distance from any two communities in the set		
Step-3: Check if number of communities has exceeded k_2	If yes, merge communities	
	If no, <none>	

make sure that individuals are not considered as separate communities, but are more likely to be integrated into a "real" community together with others.

The main difference between our implementation and the standard algorithm concerns the k-means clustering technique. Different to the original algorithm we use two k values. The first k-value (k_1) is used as the threshold to let the system form a set of clusters like in the original algorithm, in order to have a stable and reliable *MINIMUM_DISTANCE* value (i.e. the distance between the two nearest clusters in the current set), which is the key to the maintenance of the clusters. The main difference now is that after having exceeded the k_1 value, there is initially no force to merge clusters. In our approach, the previously computed *MINIMUM_DISTANCE* on the basis of the k_1-threshold acts as "community awareness" by trying to associate new users with a community *instead of* making them alone in an isolated "community". Here, the *MIN_DISTANCE_LIMIT* is applied to avoid the separation of closely related communities in the initialization phase. The second k value k_2 (maximum number of communities allowed) acts exactly the same as the k-value in the original algorithm: In case k_2 is exceeded, some communities will be merged. Actually, there is no deterministic rule to fix k_2. However, experience shows that $k_2 = 2 * k_1$ is a balanced presetting. Table 1 contains a structure chart of our community clustering process.

5   Platform Implementation and Evaluation

The modern architecture is equally international. However, culture has a deep impact on architecture. Europe has been considered as a live museum for architecture study and attracted architecture professionals worldwide since more than a century ago. A use scenario of our system has been performed in Aachen (Germany) in the past months. As Aachen is a "small" university city with a

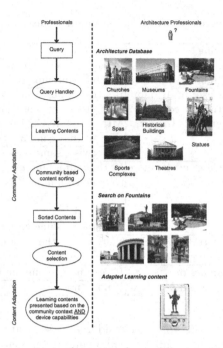

Fig. 3. Community aware content adaptation for architecture professionals in Aachen

historic core, most of the city center is covered by WLAN. For that reason, it was possible to perform the case study by users equipped with WLAN compliant PDAs. Moreover, Aachen, as the home town of one of four modern architecture founders, Mies, has quite a lot of learning resources for architecture professionals.

The stereotypes of the architecture professional communities include students working on sketch, painting, and on-site survey exercises, graduates working for interships in architects' offices, and young archtects working on different projects. In details, our platform was deployed in a learning scenario helping architecture students to find the spots they are interested in. Therefore, we created 35 videos (10sec-1,5min), with which we produced about 80 variations containing of more than 50 videos (MPEG-1, AVI) and about 30 pictures (JPEG, BMP) of historical buildings, modern architectures, museums, urban spaces and statues. These variations have been prepared to suit several types of content quality ranging from high quality videos (original content) to images (preview).

In our mobile learning environment the Java client was installed on the WLAN compliant PDAs of our test users (architecture students in Aachen). In the beginning, the students were first asked to fill out three questionnaires about user preferences, device capabilities and settings. In the user preference section, we asked the students to manually fill the personal interests and their importance for the professionals in this scenario. Device capabilities and settings were extracted mostly automatic with a subsequent manual refinement option. The so collected information was stored in a central repository, in order to create context patterns for a latter community aware content adaptation. Then, the students were able to use the system by querying content which they were interested in (e.g. buildings or statues) via the mobile client. As a result, a two-stage server side computation was performed. The first step is a community adaptation process, where the list of contents is sorted for preview, based on the user's query and current community context. That means the listing is based on the community which a professional has been attributed to in the aforementioned community clustering process. In particular, the sorting depends on the best average rating given to an item by other members of the community. The second step is content adaptation process, where the selected item of the learner is transmitted to the mobile device. Here, the best suiting variation based on the user's device settings is presented on the mobile client. Finally, the user is asked to give feedback about the content consumed. Thus his positive, neutral or negative experiences are brought into the system for further enquiries by members of his community. Figure 3 illustrates the previously described procedure and highlights the key features of our mobile technology enhanced learning.

6   Conclusions and Outlook

In this paper, we introduced a mobile technology enhanced learning platform for architecture professionals and presented an approach to content adaptation in mobile end devices based on community aware context patterns. In addition, we have given an overview on multimedia metadata technologies and standards. As we have pointed out, the combination of MPEG-7 and MPEG-21 offers a comprehensive framework for multimedia management on mobile end devices. However, it does not provide any dedicated features for the brokering of learning objects as in e-learning specific metadata standards such as LOM or SCORM [2]. Within the PROLEARN network of excellence such a integration can be realized by joining this work with those of the partners. The prototype has shown that these technologies help to gain maturity of mobile technology enhanced learning applications in the rapidly developing market of mobile multi-purpose devices. Even more, the mobile technology enhanced learning platform is advantageous for users to consider both their own preferences and their community context. By doing so, it is possible to gain a better overview on the content relevant for them, even with the limitations of a small mobile device.

Current research pursues several issues. First, we want to embed localization technologies into our mobile clients, e.g. GPS. By doing so, we hope to combine these information with the existing community context into a more powerful information system, combining community and place. In this aspect, we have already undertaken first studies in geospatial content management and retrieval in a desktop computer application [17]. The second issue that we currently research on is to implement a mobile community hosting environment. Unlike classical community hosting, we want to allow learners to identify and use community services based on their actual spatial position and available community members in their proximity. Third, the establishment of a metadata repository for online architecture databases will be useful to deliver more architecture information onto mobile devices. Thus, web 2.0 related technologies like RSS might be employed. The last issue is to detect other learners within the community for collaboration on future learning activities.

Acknowledgements. This work was supported by German National Science Foundation (DFG) within the collaborative research centers SFB/FK 427 "Media and Cultural Communication", the SFB 476 "IMPROVE", and by the 6th Framework IST programme of the EC through the Network of Excellence in Professional Learning (PROLEARN) IST-2003-507310. We'd like to thank our colleagues for the many discussions. In particular, we thank Oguzhan Özmen and our student worker Evanela Lapi for the implementation.

References

1. G. Adomavicius and A. Tuzhilin. Personalization technologies: A process-oriented perspective. *Commun. ACM*, 48(10):83–90, 2005.
2. L.E. Anido, M.J. Fernandez, M. Caeiro, J.M. Santos, J.S. Rodriguez and M. Llamas Educational metadata and brokerage for learning resources. *Comput. Educ.*, 38, 4:351-374, 2002.
3. T. W. Bickmore and B. Schilit. Digestor - device-independent access to the world wide web. In *Proc. of the 6th Intl. WWW Conf.*, pages 1075–1082, Santa Clara, CA, USA, 4 1997.
4. J. Blom, J. Chipchase, and J. Lehikoinen. Contextual and cultural challenges for user mobility research. *Commun. ACM*, 48(7):37–41, 2005.
5. J. Bormans and K. Hill. MPEG-21 Overview v.5. http://www.chiariglione.org/mpeg/standards/mpeg-21/mpeg-21.htm, 2002.
6. L. Böszörmenyi, H. Kosch, H. Hellwagner, M. Libsie, and S. Podlipnig. Metadata driven adaptation in the ADMITS project. *Signal Processing Image Communication*, 18(8):749–766, 9 2003.
7. K. Brown. *How does the Java logging API stack up against log4j?*. http://builder.com.com/5100-22-1046694.html, July 2002.
8. P. Brusilovsky and W. Nejdl. *Adaptive hypermedia and adaptive web*. CRC Press, 2004.
9. I. Burnett, R. Van de Walle, K. Hill, J. Bormans, and F. Pereira. MPEG-21: goals and achievements. *IEEE Multimedia*, 10(4):60–70, 2003.
10. U. Fuller, J. Amillo, C. Laxer, W. M. McCracken, and J. Mertz. Facilitating student learning through study abroad and international projects. *SIGCSE Bull.*, 37(4):139–151, 2005.
11. T. Gross and M. Specht. Aspekte und Komponenten der Kontextmodellierung. *i-com*, pages 12 – 16, 3 2002.
12. P. Hagen, T. Robertson, M. Kan, and K. Sadler. Emerging research methods for under-standing mobile technology use. In *Proceedings of OZCHI 2005, Canberra, Australia*, November 23-25, 2005.
13. ISO. Information technology – multimedia content description interface – part 5: Multimedia description schemes. Technical Report ISO/IEC 15938-5:2003, Intl. Organisation for Standardisation / Intl. Electrotechnical Commission, 5 2003.
14. A. Jain, M. N. Murty, and P. Flynn. Data clustering: a review. *ACM Computing Surveys*, 31(3):264 – 323, 1999.
15. D. Jannach and K. Leopold. Knowledge-based multimedia adaptation for ubiquitous multimedia consumption. *Journal of Network and Computer Applications, Special issue on "Intelligence-based adaptation for ubiquitous multimedia communications"*, 2006.

16. D. Keegan. The future of learning: From elearning to mlearning. Technical report, Fern Univ., Hagen (Germany). Inst. for Research into Distance Education, Postfach 940, D-58084 Hagen, Germany, 2002.

17. R. Klamma, M. Spaniol, M. Jarke, Y. Cao, M. Jansen, and G. Toubekis. ACIS: Intergenerational community learning supported by a hypermedia sites and monuments database. In P. Goodyear, D. G. Sampson, D. J.-T. Yang, Kinshuk, T. Okamoto, R. Hartley, and N.-S. Chen, editors, *Proc. of the 5th International Conference on Advanced Learning Technologies (ICALT 2005), July 5-8, Kaohsiung, Taiwan*, pages 108–112, Los Alamitos, CA, 2005. IEEE Computer Society.

18. H. Kosch. *Distributed Multimedia Database Technologies Supported by MPEG-7 and MPEG-21*. CRC Press, Boca Raton et al., 2003.

19. M. Kravcik, A. Kaibel, M. Specht, and L. Terrenghi. Mobile collector for field trips. *Educational Technology & Society*, 7(2):25–33, 2004.

20. T. Lutkenhouse, M. L. Nelson, and J. Bollen. Distributed, real-time computation of community preferences. In *HYPERTEXT '05: Proc. of the 16th ACM Conference on Hypertext and Hypermedia*, pages 88–97, New York, NY, USA, 2005. ACM Press.

21. J. M. Martinez, C. Gonzalez, O. Fernandez, C. Garcia, and J. de Ramon. Towards universal access to content using MPEG-7. In *Proceedings of the 10th ACM International Conference on Multimedia*, pages 199–202. ACM Press, 2002.

22. R. Mohan, J. R. Smith, and C.-S. Li. Adapting multimedia internet content for universal access. *IEEE Transactions on Multimedia*, 1(1):104–114, March 1999.

23. M. O'Connor and J. Herlocker. Clustering items for collaborative filtering. Technical report, Univ. of Minnesota, Dept. of Computer Science, USA, 2000.

24. L. L. Sampath, A. Helal, and J. Smith. UMA-based wireless and mobile video delivery architecture. In *Proceedings of the SPIE Voice, Video and Data Communications Symposium*, November 2000.

25. A. Schmidt, M. Beigl, and H. Gellersen. There is more to context than location. *Computers & Graphics*, 23(6):893 – 902, 1999.

26. G. Somlo and A. Howe. Incremental Clustering for Profile Maintenance in Information Gathering Web Agents. In J. Müller, E. Andre, S. Sen, and C. Frasson, editors, *Proc. of the 5th Intl. Conf. on Autonomous Agents*, pages 262–269, 2001.

27. O. Steiger, T. Ebrahimi, and D. Sanjuan. Mpeg-based personalized content delivery. In *IEEE Int. Conf. on Image Processing, ICIP2003, Barcelona, Spain, September 14-17, 2003*. IEEE, 2003.

28. M. Sung, J. Gips, N. Eagle, A. Madan, R. Caneel, R. DeVaul, J. Bonsen, and S. Pentland. Mit.edu: M-learning applications for classroom settings. Technical Report Technical Note 576, MIT Media Laboratory, 3 2004.

29. J. Tane, C. Schmitz, and G. Stumme. Semantic resource management for the web: an e-learning application. In *WWW Alt. '04: Proc. of the 13th Intl. World Wide Web Conf. - Alternate track*, pages 1–10, New York, NY, USA, 2004. ACM Press.

30. S. Ujjin and P. J. Bentley. Building a lifestyle recommender system. In *WWW10: Proceedings of the 10th Intl. World Wide Web Conf.*, 2001.

31. E. Wenger. *Communities of Practice: Learning, Meaning, and Identity*. Cambridge University Press, Cambridge, UK, 1998.

32. P. Zaharias. Usability and e-learning: the road towards integration. *eLearn*, 2004(6):4, 2004.

33. G. Zhao and Z. Yang. Learning resource adaptation and delivery framework for mobile learning. In *Proceedings of 35th ASEE/IEEE Frontiers in Education Conference, Indianapolis, USA, October 19-22, 2005*. IEEE, 2005.

Pattern-Based Cross Media Social Network Analysis for Technology Enhanced Learning in Europe

Ralf Klamma, Marc Spaniol, Yiwei Cao, and Matthias Jarke

Lehrstuhl Informatik V, RWTH Aachen University, Germany
{klamma, spaniol, cao, jarke}@i5.informatik.rwth-aachen.de

Abstract. It is extremely challenging to get an overview of the state-of-the-art in technology enhanced learning in Europe. Rapid technological and pedagogical innovations, constantly changing markets, a vivid number of small and medium enterprises, complex policy processes, ongoing political and societal debates on the pros and cons of technology enhanced leaning, combined with many languages and different cultures, make it almost impossible for people to be informed. We want to introduce the media base and the measure tools for pattern-based cross media social network analysis, created by the PROLEARN network of excellence in professional learning. The main goal of this endeavour is the reduction of complexity for actors in digital social networks by applying ideas from social software and already successful methods for complexity reduction, such as information visualization, social network analysis and pattern languages.

1 Technology Enhanced Learning in Europe

Networking is one of the buzzwords for the information and knowledge society in the 21st century. Our spheres of life are networked, especially with digital media having impact on all forms of human action. According to the Lisbon Strategy, Technology Enhanced Learning is one of the major goals of the European Community, which should also be reached by access to ICT, networks and resources. Due to the different languages in Europe, the market of the enhanced learning has a larger diversity than the USA. The development levels of technology enhanced learning vary from country to country. Above all, the United Kingdom, the Netherlands and Sweden play the leading roles in enhanced learning in Europe [31]. The reasons are software industry and the high internet penetration rates. The United Kingdom dominates the software sector with 29.6% of the market share (EUR 43.8 billions). Statistics show that internet usage by individuals in Sweden (82%), Denmark (76%) and Finland (70%) reached the highest levels in Europe in the first quarter of 2004 [48].

Through this continuing process new network phenomena occurs, such as distributed learning repositories [12], virtual learning communities and digital networks, such as the European School Net (www.eun.org/portal/index.htm) and the PROLEARN Virtual Competence Center (www.prolearn-online.com),

W. Nejdl and K. Tochtermann (Eds.): EC-TEL 2006, LNCS 4227, pp. 242–256, 2006.
© Springer-Verlag Berlin Heidelberg 2006

offering services for education in general or to businesses. As there are many pedagogical innovations in technology enhanced learning and a growing number of technical infrastructures, the demand for technology enhanced learning services is growing, too. Due to the extending research on economic feasibility, commercial relevance, usability, sociability, and educational benefits, the overall situation of the European technology enhanced learning market is getting more complex. Information in these networks, is far beyond the human capabilities of analysis and understanding, due to the sheer mass of contents, the number of companies, as well as the different languages, cultures, and markets.

This paper introduces one of the endeavours of the PROLEARN Network of Excellence in Professional Learning (www.prolearn-project.org) [52]. In the scope of the work package "Social Software", we aims to create a European media base, containing digital information about technology enhanced learning for different target audiences, i.e. actors in digital media networks, including scientists, business people, policy makers, and normal citizens who are interested in ongoing discourses in technology enhanced learning. We store information from mailing lists, newsletters, blogs, rss feeds, web sites, podcasts, etc. The PROLEARN media base is far from being complete. Like any kind of social software, the media base depends on the participation of the people using the software. Being started with an excellence network of hundreds of partners is good for having a critical mass of content. However, the barriers of participation have to be very low [6,46]. Therefore, the tools should be used easily and offer added value services. We also aim to provide actors self-monitoring tools to help them better understand the impact not only of their own activities, but also of the other actors' activities in the digital media network. By now, we do not know definitely what result the idea of a European media base for technology enhanced learning will lead to. What we know by now is that we need to reduce complexity. So the toolset PROLEARN Measure offers a series of computer-based tools for analysis of the media in the PROLEARN media base.

Computers are deployed to facilitate our understanding of complex network phenomena. A network is a set of autonomous entities, connected in a specific way. Natural or artificial networks share a set of entity-, sub-network or network-specific features which could be observable empirically sometimes. These features can be expressed by empirical measures or probabilistic models. With the common mathematical basis, it is possible to exchange knowledge about networks between different theoretical or observation contexts. In contrast to explanations, gained in isolated scientific disciplines such as sociology, genetics or economics, this leads to a dramatic increase in the appreciation of network phenomena.

In the following we introduce three approaches to complexity reduction: information visualization, (social) network analysis, and pattern languages. All three approaches are interwoven. The subtle interplay which happens sometimes between visualization and network analysis as well as pattern presentation respectively has to be taken into account, too [29].

Information visualization [3] is certainly a promising way to reduce complexity, but we have to go beyond visualization, since the amount of information is challenging even for advanced information visualization strategies [44]. A survey we have conducted in 2002 shows that a particular requirement of non technique-experienced users were especially interested in a sophisticated cross media analysis with hidden computational complexity. The visualization of networks with generally available algorithms creates (sometimes even undesirable) evidences for abstract numerical correlations. Those network representations are one more digital medium in the trace of media usage. Re-contextualizing them in scientific and societal discourses facilitates knowledge creation, since societal processes and structures are mediated over digital media. The importance of digital media for our life is constantly growing while trust in digital media is an issue. On the one hand, digital media offer actors in networks new possibilities to act. On the other hand, these actors themselves are more often a target of undesired actions of others. This relation of agency and patienthood [43] is most critical in our appropriation of information technology at large, e.g. in vocational training situations people are very unsure about the future. Challenges are to balance structural analysis and content-related analysis of media. Both content-based and structural analysis can be tackled by media-extended social network analysis.

This second way to reduce information complexity is to apply social network analysis (SNA) [10]. Within structural traditions in sociology, SNA is applied to handle large complex relational data sets, covering information about social relations. Working on this idea, we want to present cross media extensions arguing that actors act through the media which they produce and consume. The basis for cross media social network analysis is the Actor-Network Theory (ANT) [30]. It provides an approach which does not distinguish between people and objects. For that reason, it is an appropriate method for modelling digital social networks.

The third approach to reducing complexity are pattern languages. A pattern includes the description of an observable and known behaviour related to the media base. We later call this a disturbance. From the tradition we take elements like the context where the pattern is applied, forces which come into play, the recommended solution and the rationale behind it [1]. Patterns are most useful if they are seen in relations with each other [42], since the human mind is always searching for regularities and similarities [41]. Patterns were already successfully applied in other areas to reduce complexity, such as architecture [1], economics [11], and computer science [18]. A pattern language could be crucial for forecasting the possible development of digital media. Since the formalization and applicabiliy of patterns are most urging for the media base in the moment, we discuss differences and similarities with other pattern language approaches in a later phase of the project.

The rest of the paper is organized as follows. In the next section we will introduce the cross media social network analysis theory. Then, we will present the PROLEARN media base. On top of the media base there are a series of exploratory and interactive tools, PROLEARN Measure. After that pattern-based methods to combine structural and content specific analysis on large data sets are presented. The paper concludes with an outlook.

2   Cross Media Social Network Analysis

Cross media Social Network Analysis creates evidences on acting and being a target of actions in media networks. These evidences are starting points for learning processes within the networks to develop competences of acting in a networked world or at a global stage. We are aware that all tools presented here can be used to observe the online behaviour of people. Therefore, it is most important that the media base and the tools presented here are not in the hands of a few but are given to the network members for self-monitoring. For the sake of clarity, we introduce the theories which influence our cross media social network analyis theories in short.

- The structural properties of dynamic, evolving and real-world networks are part of **(social) network analysis** [36].
- **Media operations** have been studied mainly in the humanities [21] while a unifying view on media agents and patients is possible with **Actor-network theory** [30]. The **structural dependencies** between actors can be expressed best with the i*-Framework [53].
- **Learning processes** based on reification of intuition, shared practice and beliefs are studied in the context of **Knowledge Management** and **Organisational learning** [38,51].

Every network supports certain types of media. They influence how the communication links between the members are created. The members as edges and the communication links as vertices define a graph $G = (V, E)$. Properties which have their roots in the network analysis can be defined for the network and the members. The most important network properties are the small world [50] property and the scale free network [2] property. In those networks that are both small world and scale free, there exist special members, so-called *hubs* which control media opeations being a well-connected node. We model this within the i*-framework [53]. Apart from the network, there are three special types of actors that compose a social network. The *member* stands for an existing person or a sub-community. The *medium* enables the members to do certain activities, among which the most important ones are establishing communication links and exchanging information. The *artefacts* are objects created by the members, using some medium. The communication links among the members can be traced using the artefacts. The basic social unit, which forms a digital social network is the member. Members have properties which are derived from SNA, describe their positions, and are used to estimate the importance of the members in the network modeled than in the i*-framework.

Some important types of centrality are: the *Degree* centrality, a property which measures in the most straight forward way the member's social capital in the network; the *Closeness* centrality CC_m, taking into account the closeness of the member m to every other member [4,10,15]; the *Betweenness* centrality, estimating the possibility of a member to influence the communication of others [4,10,15]. Efficiency is used to detect structural holes in the neighbourhood of a member v. Structural hole is a relationship between two non redundant

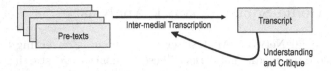

Fig. 1. Transcription creates interpretations of media in media

neighbours of a member [7]. The more structural holes exist for a member, the greater his social capital is [19]. The efficiency is a function of the time and the energy which a member invests into the relations with each neighbour.

Referencing ANT, we apply SNA on networks built by media, artefacts and individuals. All media are social entities. A media-specific theory helps us understand digital media support for cross media SNA. It is based on the following media operations [14,21]. New concepts are developed through making selections from an initially unstructured set of media-based 'pre-texts' and converting them by a process called *intra-* or *inter-medial transcription* into a so-called transcript, a media object describing the new concept.

- It condenses and structures the set of pre-texts by designating some of them as evidences, counter-examples, or points of critique, while de-emphasizing others. *Transcription* is a media-dependent operation to make media collections more readable (cf. Figure 1).
- Thus, it enables a new reading of the pre-texts where the kind of readership is determined by the media, through which the transcript is prepared and communicated. Well-designed transcripts can significantly increase the community of practice for a certain piece of knowledge, or may intentionally focus on specific 'insiders'. *Localization* means an operation to transfer global media into local practices.
- The term of *(Re-)Addressing* describes an operation that stabilizes and optimizes the accessibility in global communication.

Thus, transcription not only changes the status of passive understanding by others, but also enables further cooperative knowledge creation by stimulating debates about the selected pre-texts and about the transcription itself. More details can be found in [22,23]. We will now synthesize these media-specific operations with learning processes by human actors. The result is a media centric re-formulation of the previously introduced media operations on knowledge creation and social learning processes adopted from Nonaka and Takeuchi [38] and Wenger [51]. The knowledge creation theory, especially the SECI model, by Nonaka [38] has been widely acknowledged in management theory and practice. Also in the fields of CSCL and professional learning, the most prominent knowledge management theories are those of Bereiter, Engeström and Nonaka [39]. We are building our media base on the assumption that digital social networks, informal sub-networks or communities of practice, want to share knowledge about business, markets, their professions etc. Knowledge sharing in this setting is primarily a social process [9,47,20]. The SECI model makes a basic distinction between *tacit* and *explicit* knowledge [40,38,35,26,27]. The processes include the related media specific operations: *transcription, localization,* and *addressing.* In the *internalization & socialization* we focus on actions performed by actors. Starting with an individual who has internalized some media-specific knowledge, there are two ways to communicate with others. On the one hand, there is an option to present this information to others by *localized* actor-actor interaction, which allows the content's socialization within the community of practice and is equivalent to the development of a shared history vice versa. On the other hand, individuals may also perform an *actor transcription* of their knowledge by generating new medial artefacts (*externalization*). This operation brings to the processing of media from the digital social networks. The externalized artefacts of a member are now further processed by formal information system. This is done by a *transcription* of the medial artefacts (*combination*). The final *addressing* closing the circle is the context depending presentation of the medial artefacts or a cross media concatenation. From then on, the process might be repeated infinitely, oscillating between tacit and explicit knowledge on the epistemological axis and between actors and the digital social network on the ontological axis.

Moreover, we want to address two other issues: (a) the prerequisites for any knowledge transformation and (b) a phase model for knowledge creation. This phase model of learning (sharing tacit knowledge, creating concepts, justifying concepts, building an archetype, cross-leveling of knowledge) makes it clear that learning is an action-oriented process. The aim of knowledge creation is to build something (the archetype). Thus, the PROLEARN media base needs to define a mission, a vision which brings the members together. The overall goal of the PROLEARN Network of Excellence, the PROLEARN outreach instruments, the PROLEARN Academy and the PROLEARN Virtual Competence Center is essential for the creation of a mission. With the cross-leveling of knowledge, the process starts again. As important as the process model are the prerequisites of learning, which are intention, autonomy, fluctuation, creative chaos, redundancy and requisite variety. All these ideas might amount to a nightmare for western style organizations. However, Nonaka and Takeuchi are arguing that these prerequisites are inevitable. Furthermore, the concept of 'ba' [37] and the concept of CoP [51] are quite similar.

3   A Technology Enhanced Learning Media Base for Europe

The first question addressed is why to build up a media base. Briefly, this enables us to perform a model-based analysis of different kinds of processes in existing digital social networks to describe and relate concepts of communication, coordination, and knowledge organization, compare and extract use of these concepts in different contexts, identify patterns of communication and knowledge organization, and study common and distinct features of digital media usage. An important feature is to offer members a functionality to collaboratively administrate and retrieve medial artefacts. Of course, there are many projects dealing with thematic classification of artefacts for a latter retrieval. For instance, there are several social software tools indexing and classifying bookmarks, references, images, and

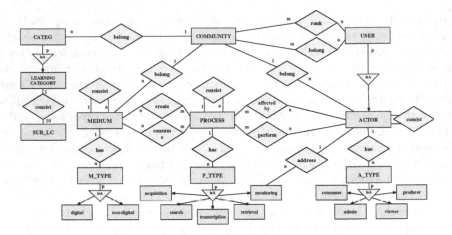

Fig. 2. ER Diagram of the Community centered PROLEARN Media Base

videos in general. We analyze the correlation between digital social networks and the media they use. For that purpose, we support the members by tools to classify, comment and review the projects they monitor. In this aspect, projects in the cultural sciences cover discussion groups, newsletters, web-sites, feeds, and blogs.

The second question addressed is how to build up such a media base. We decided to build the core of the media base on top of an operational community memory system, called GRAECULUS [27]. The strategy was preferred, because the system already interrelates patterns of knowledge organization and patterns of communication and coordination. As cited in [6], we are members of hundreds of different overlapping communities all the time. To interrelate the knowledge organisation processes with the community processes, we construct an Entity-Relationship model that emphasizes the coherence between the community process models and the knowledge organization processes. The ER model depicted in Figure2 is based on an extended entity-relationship approach. Each box represents an entity of the model, with the attributes omitted here. Relationships are linked by diamonds with links to the entities, while isA-relationships are presented as triangles. The most important concepts of the ER model are summarized in the next paragraph.

A *Community* is the central concept of the PROLEARN media base, as it is a sub-network of a whole network and indicates trustful relations between the individual members. In every kind of social software, there are means to facilitate such sub-structures. Without them, social software would not be usable any more because of the high communication complexity and trust issues. Community activities contain important knowledge, which is stored on media belonging to the community. Actors also belong to Communities and perform processes (modeled by process models expressed in a language chosen by the actors). The *Process* concept describes community and knowledge processes of actors. All Processes can be refined by consist-relationships. Each process belongs to a process type taxonomy (*P_TYPE*) which is defined collaboratively by each community. We define a standard taxonomy [42,49] with five different process types: a) acquisition processes which are used to acquire new media, b) search processes for media, c) transcription processes for media, d) retrieval processes for media, and e) monitoring processes for media. An *Actor* characterizes humans or groups of humans (consist-relationship) performing a process. Each actor belongs to an actor type taxonomy which is defined collaboratively by each community. From past experiences with knowledge management projects [34], we have already defined a standard taxonomy consisting of four different actor categories: a) Actors who produce media, b) Actors who consume media, c) Actors who view media, and d) Actors who administrate or manage media within a community. The *Medium* concept describes artefacts created or consumed by the processes, according to the transcription theory. For later use in cross media social network analysis and in the pattern language, we can differentiate between media and artefacts. But this is not shown here. Each *Medium* belongs to a media type (M_TYPE), describing a taxonomy of media types which is also defined collaboratively by each community. ANT states that actors not only perform processes, but also are affected by processes (patienthood). A *User* is a special actor that uses the PROLEARN media base. Therefore, the User has a certain rank within the community. Each Community has a classification. The classification can be done by 'tagging' of the community members or can be defined in other categorization hierarchies. Here, we put a learning classification developed by the PROLEARN network of excellence to characterize their work in work packages. Other classifications which can also be used in parallel are geographical distributions of the media and language distribution etc.

Retrieval and Exploration Tools
Retrieval of data is realized on top of the content management system Plone, which is built on the application server ZOPE. For each medium in the media base, we have created web-based access structures, e.g. for reading mails, newsletters, blog entries, rss feeds and so on. All web sites in the media base are mirrored completely on local file systems, so we can access them even if the original web site is not available temporarily or gone forever. For accessing the huge amount of information, we have predefined - apart from a simple free text search function - several queries that enable even a not experienced user to discover dependencies among various media offers in order to explore its content by the structure defined in the ER diagram. First, users might *pass through* the media structure and its components. Here, various characteristics of the projects are displayed, which have been automatically extracted upon its creation and can be modified manually later on. Another way is to deploy information visualization strategies.

Figure 3 shows a treemap visualization of the PROLEARN Measure mailing lists. The mailing lists are categorized according to their languages and according to some categorization schemes on learning. The latter is derived by adopting some of the PROLEARN work packages as the categories. The treemap is computed by using the squarified treemap algorithm [5]. The size of the rectangles on the lowest level reflects the number of mails that have been sent within the corresponding mailing lists. For each mailing list, some statistics, such as the

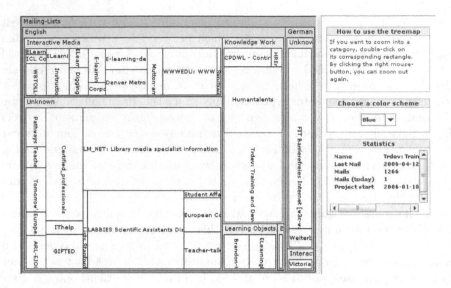

Fig. 3. Treemap Visualization of the PROLEARN mailing lists

overall number of mails, can be displayed. In order to provide a close look at the mailing lists, it is possible to zoom in the treemap. Further development aims at visualizing the mails themselves as well, i.e. going to one level deeper.

In Figure 4 a simple tool for the cross media social network analysis of the PROLEARN Measure mailing lists is shown. The user can select different networks, explore them and perform an interactive cluster analysis. In the following, this process is depicted in a more detailed way: at first, the user has to select the mailing list he wants to explore and a time frame for this exploration (see form "Data" in Figure 4). Then the user has to decide on the nature of the data that he wants to visualize as a network.

In this context, four different kinds of information (and arbitrary combinations of them) can be displayed: 1) If the option "Mails Member ->Member" is chosen, this results in a network reflecting the communication structure between the members of the selected mailing list. More precisely, if the member A has replied to a mail by the member B, the network contains an edge from A to B. 2) With the option "Mails Member ->Mailing List" turned on, each member to whom A has written a mail in the selected mailing list, results in an edge from A to a node representing this list. The last two options concern the reference structure of the mailing list. 3) If some web site W has been referenced in one of the mails by the member A, the resulting network contains an edge from A to W (third option). 4) Basically the same as 3), only that all mails of the mailing list (also those that have been sent by the mailing list itself) are considered. In this case, for each mail in which the web site W is referenced, the network contains an edge from the node representing the mailing list to W. If the user selects several options at the same time, the corresponding networks are merged.

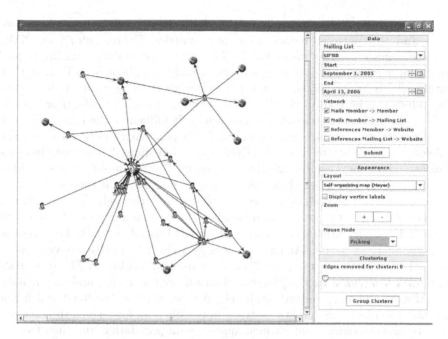

Fig. 4. Cross media Social Network Analysis for PROLEARN Measure

After having submitted the "Data" input, the final network is displayed. The selected mailing list is represented by a mail icon, an individual by an actor icon and a website by a globe icon. This network can be further explored through the functionalities of zoom-in and zoom-out, moving it within the network window, moving single nodes or groups of nodes and choosing different layout algorithms. Four different layouts are available: self-organizing map by Meyer [33], Fruchterman-Reingold [17], Circle, and Kamada-Kawai [25]. As mentioned, apart from simply exploring the network, it is possible to cluster it interactively. The clustering is based on the Edge Betweenness Centrality (EBC) [16]. With a slider, the user can choose the number of edges N he wants to be removed from the network. This results in the removal of the N edges with the smallest EBC. The different colours of the nodes then indicate the latter's cluster membership. When clicking the button "Group Clusters", all nodes that belong to the same cluster are grouped together.

4 Pattern-Based Repositories for Technology Enhanced Learning Media

Our PALADIN (PAttern LAnguage for DIsturbances in digital social Networks) approach is an application, developed to research into a set of digital social networks with patterns on the basis of the ANT model and a pattern language. We call behaviour observed in digital social networks behaviours, because it is the start of a learning process triggered by the difference between the actual behaviour and the desired behaviour. PALADIN offers a web interface to define, browse and store patterns, actors and actor properties. The repository is an XML database management system. PALADIN includes a general network implementation that focuses on the structural properties of the members. In PALADIN a digital social network is a set of actors along with their relations. It has properties which can be used in the definition of the patterns. A medium or a set of media is the basis of the digital social networks. It influences the networks, their structures and the way to communicate [45]. Dependencies between actors are modeled with the i*-framework [53]. Every type of medium defines how the communication links between the members are built. The media are emails, mailing lists, blogs, transaction-based web sites, wikis, URL, and chat rooms.

The communication between members is realized through the exchange of artefacts. An artefact is created by a member in a certain medium. The artefacts represent the information circulating in the digital social network. The types of artefacts, analyzed in PALADIN, are messages, threads, bursts, conversations, blog entries, comments, web pages, transactions, and feedbacks. The properties which are mostly used for the pattern definition are the author and the creation date. Most of them are defined intuitively. An exception is the burst which is a conceptual artefact, based on the activity in the network for a given time period. It can be used to detect topics which appear, gain popularity, and then fade.

According to the activity of the members and their patterns of communication, we defined several patterns based on the analyis of literature [8,13,32,49] like questioners, answering persons, trolls, conversationalists, and spammers. A questioner is a member, who seeks help and information. A answering person provides answers to the raised questions without going into discussions. A conversationalist is a member who actively participates in discussions. A troll aims at drawing attention and starting useless discussions. A spammer sends messages irrelevant for the community, which are mainly advertisements or binary files.

The pattern language includes a pattern structure definition, the Formal Expression Language for Patterns (FELP), and algorithms for the application of the patterns in digital social networks. A pattern has a name, a disturbance, a description, forces, force relations, a solution, a rationale and pattern relations. The name of the pattern is short but descriptive. The disturbance is a condition, which indicates the existence of the pattern in a social network. It is defined by a FELP expression. It consists of variables and rules for constructing formal expressions. When a pattern is defined, the variables of an expression are bound to variables from the network model. The description explains the problem to which the pattern provides a solution and the settings when the pattern occurs. The force is the basic component of the pattern. It represents an actor relevant to the disturbance. The forces in a pattern are automatically extracted at the moment, when the user binds the variable from the disturbance expression. The force relation corresponds to a relation between actors, included in the pattern as forces. The solution contains the actions which are proposed to be carried out in the situation, to which the pattern refers. The rationale is used for reasoning about the forces and the disturbance. It may include examples, past success stories or failures. The pattern relations show whether the pattern, being currently defined, has anything in common with other patterns. The pattern relations are important for the structure of the pattern language. An example may illustrate our approach. A **troll** is a person which only answer in threads started by himself. This behaviour may be recognized as disturbance by other actor in a network. It depends on the existence of *thread* artefacts in the medium. In order to identify the trolls of a given medium we have to create a pattern expression which is then an instance of an existing pattern **troll**. The expression looks like

$$(\exists[troll|(\exists[thread|(thread.author = troll)\wedge$$
$$(count[message|(message.author = troll)\wedge$$
$$(message.posted = thread)])> minPosts])\wedge$$
$$(\neg\exists[thread_1, message_1|(thread_1.author_1 \neq troll)\wedge$$
$$(message_1.author = troll \wedge message_1.posted = thread_1)])])$$

A sample set of patterns has been defined and tested on the social networks built upon the available database sources. The patterns reflect the existence of trolls, spammers, conversationalists, questioners, answering persons, bursts and structural holes in the digital social networks. The storage of the patterns as XML documents enables their automatic application. More details are in [28].

5   Conclusions and Outlook

In this paper we have presented first realization ideas for the ongoing work on the PROLEARN media base and the PROLEARN Measure tools for technology enhanced learning in Europe. The main goal of this endeavour carried out in the PROLEARN Network of Excellence in Professional Learning and Training is to give actors an overview of current discourse of technology enhanced learning relevant to Europe. The main idea is to reduce complexity in order to give the control of the actions back to actors in digital social networks. Not only the impact of their own actions (media agents), but also that of the other actors' actions of (media patients), should be made visible by three strategies to reduce complexity. The first strategy is information visualization with simple principles, such as 'Overview first, details later'. We have presented retrieval and exploration tools which can be easily applied within the context of the PROLEARN media base. A second strategy is the combination of existing social network analysis tools with cross media and knowledge management theories to produce new cross media analysis tools dealing with both the content and the structure of information. A third strategy is the development of a pattern language. With a predefined pattern, describing problems and solutions within complexity reduction on a natural language level which can be understood by non technical actors easily. We can give monitoring tools to a broad target audience to make possibly new interactions among them. Our hope is that new learning processes in communities, supported by the PROLEARN media base, take place. Furthermore, this will be a never-ending circle of knowledge creation.

These are the first experiments we undertake with social software in the context of professional learning. The PROLEARN media base and the PROLEARN

Measure tools are integrated in the PROLEARN Academy portal www.prolearn-academy.org to reach a broad audience inside and outside the network. We have ongoing discussions among the network members to add media to the media base and to join forces with fellow projects, such as the EU STREPS ICamp (www.icamp-project.org) [24] and the other projects from the Professional Learning Cluster (www.professional-learning-cluster.org). We do not know how the media base will develop in future. As stated in [6], some of the best communities are not built - they emerged.

Acknowledgements. This work was supported by German National Science Foundation (DFG) within the collaborative research centers SFB/FK 427 "Media and Cultural Communication", the SFB 476 "IMPROVE", and by the 6th Framework IST programme of the EC through the Network of Excellence in Professional Learning (PROLEARN) IST-2003-507310. We'd like to thank the reviewers for the comments and our colleagues for the support. In particular, we thank Dimitar Denev and our student worker Heike Haegert for the implementation.

References

1. C. Alexander. *A Pattern Language: Towns, Buildings, Construction (Center for Environmental Structure Series).* Oxford University Press Inc, USA, 1978.
2. A.-L. Barabási. The physics of the web. *Physics World*, 14:33–38, 7 2001.
3. B. B. Bederson and B. Schneider, editors. *The craft of information visualization.* Morgan Kaufmann, 2003.
4. U. Brandes and T. Erlebach, editors. *Network Analysis - Methodological Foundations, LNCS 3418.* Springer, Berlin Heidelberg New York, 2005.
5. D. Bruls, C. Huizing, and J. van Wijk. Squarified treemaps. In W. de Leeuw and R. van Liere, editors, *Data Visualization 2000, Proceedings of the joint Eurographics and IEEE TCVG Symposium on Visualization*, pages 33–42, Vienna, 2000. Springer.
6. L. Bryant. Smarter, simpler, social. Technical report, Headshift.com, 2003.
7. R. S. Burt. *Structural Holes: The Social Structure of Competition.* Havard Business Press, Cambridge, MA, 1992.
8. K. S. Cheung, F. S. Lee, R. K. Ip, and C. Wagner. The development of successful on-line communities. *International Journal of the Computer, the Internet and Management*, 13(1):77–89, 4 2005.
9. R. Daft and R. Lengel. Organizational informations requirements, media richness and structural design. *Management Science*, 32(5):554–571, 1986.
10. A. Degenne and M. Forse. *Introducing Social Networks.* Sage Publications, 2003.
11. V. Dhar. Data mining in finance: Using counterfactuals to generate knowledge form organizational information systems. *Inf. Systems*, 23(7):423–437, 1998.
12. P. Dolog, N. Henze, W. Nejdl, and M. Sintek. Personalization in distributed e-learning environments. In *WWW Alt. '04: Proceedings of the 13th international World Wide Web conference on Alternate track papers & posters*, pages 170–179, New York, NY, USA, 2004. ACM Press.
13. D. Fisher, M. Smith, and H. T. Welser. You are who you talk to: Detecting roles in usenet newsgroups. In *Proceedings of the 39th Hawaii International Conference on System Sciences*, 2006.

14. J. Fohrmann and E. Schüttpelz. *Die Kommunikation der Medien.* Niemeyer, Tübingen, 2004 (in German).
15. L. Freeman. Centrality in social networks. conceptual clarification. *Social Networks,* 1:215–239, 1979.
16. L. C. Freeman, S. P. Borgatti, and D. R. White. Centrality in valued graphs: A measure of betweenness based on network flow. *Social Networks,* 13:141–154, 1991.
17. T. M. J. Fruchterman and E. M. Reingold. Graph drawing by force-directed placement. *Software - Practice and Experience,* 21(11):1129–1164, 1991.
18. E. Gamma, R. Helm, R. Johnson, and V. John. *Design Patterns: Elements of Reusable Object-Oriented Software.* Professional Computing. Addison-Wesley, Reading, 1994.
19. M. S. Granovetter. The strength of weak ties. *American Journal of Sociology,* 78:1360–1380, 1973.
20. E. Hollender, R. Klamma, D. Börner-Klein, and M. Jarke. A comprehensive study environment for a talmudic tractate. *DS-NELL,* 2001.
21. L. Jäger and G. Stanitzek, editors. *Transkribieren - Medien/Lektüre.* Wilhelm Fink Verlag, Munich, 2002 (in German).
22. M. Jarke, X. T. Bui, and J. M. Carroll. Scenario management: An interdisciplinary approach. *Requirements Engineering,* (3):155–173, 1998.
23. M. Jarke and R. Klamma. Metadata and Cooperative Knowledge Management. In A. Banks Pidduck et al., editors, *CAISE 2002, LNCS 2348,* pages 4–20, Springer, Berlin, 2002.
24. B. Jerman-Blazic, T. Klobucar, T. Arh, B. Kieslinger, F. Wild, and E. L.-C. Law. An approach in provision of interoperability of elearning systems in enlarged EU - the case of ICamp project. *aict-iciw,* 0:6, 2006.
25. T. Kamada and S. Kawai. An algorithm for drawing general undirected graphs. *Information Processing Letters,* 31:7–15, 1989.
26. R. Klamma and M. Jarke. Driving the organizational learning cycle: The case of computer-aided failure management. In W. R. J. Baets, editor, *Proceedings of the 6th European Conference on Information Systems (ECIS'98), Aix-En-Provence, France,* vol. 1, pages 378–392, Euro-Arab Management School, Granada, 6 1998.
27. R. Klamma and S. Schlaphof. Rapid knowledge deployment in an organizational-memory-based workflow environment. In H. R. Hansen, M. Bichler, and H. Mahrer, editors, *Proceedings of the 8th European Conference on Information Systems (ECIS 2000), Vienna, Austria,* pages 364–371, 2000.
28. R. Klamma, M. Spaniol, and D. Denev. PALADIN: A Pattern Based Approach to Knowledge Discovery in Digital Social Networks. *Proc. of I-Know 2006, Special Track on knowledge visualization and knowledge discovery,* 2006.
29. L. Krempel. *Visualisierung komplexer Strukturen: Grundlagen der Darstellung multidimensionaler Netzwerke.* Campus Verlag, New York, 2005 (in German).
30. B. Latour. On recalling ant. In J. Law and J. Hassard, editors, *Actor-Network Theory and After,* pages 15–25. Oxford, 1999.
31. elearning - Kapital für die Zukunft. http://www.ecin.de/state-of-the-art/ elearning, 2001 (in German) (June 30, 2006).
32. T. Madanmohan and S. Navelkar. Roles and knowledge management in online technology communities: an ethnography study. *International Journal of Web Based Communities,* 1:71–89, 2004.
33. B. Meyer. Self-organizing graphs- a neural network perspective of graph layout. LNCS 1547, pages 246–262. Springer Verlag, 1998.
34. P. Mika. Flink: Semantic web technology for the extraction and analysis of social networks. *Journal of Web Semantics,* 2005.

35. J. Mylopoulos, A. Borgida, M. Jarke, and M. Koubarakis. Telos - a language for representing knowledge about information systems. *ACM Transactions on Information Systems*, 8(4):352–362, 1990.
36. M. Newmann, A.-L. Barabási and D. Watts, editors. *The structure and dynamics of networks*. Princeton University Press, Princeton and Oxford, 2006.
37. I. Nonaka and N. Konno. The concept of 'ba': Building foundation for knowledge creation. *California Management Review*, (40):3, 1998.
38. I. Nonaka and H. Takeuchi. *The Knowledge-Creating Company*. Oxford University Press, Oxford, 1995.
39. S. Paavola, L. Lipponen, and K. Hakkarainen. Epistemological foundations for cscl: A comparison of three models of innovative knowledge communities. In G. Stahl, editor, *Computer Support for Collaborative Learning: Foundations for a CSCL community. Proceedings of the Computer-supported Collaborative Learning 2002 Conference*, pages 24–32. Erlbaum, 2002.
40. M. Polanyi. *The tacit dimension*. Anchor Books, New York, 1966.
41. E. Rosch. Principles of categorization. In *Cognition and Categorization*, pages 312–322. Lawrence-Erlbaum Ass., 1978.
42. N. A. Salingaros. The structure of pattern languages. *Architectural Research Quarterly*, 4:149–161, 2000.
43. E. Schüttpelz. Die Spur der Störung. In G. Fehrmann, E. Linz, and C. Epping Jäger, editors, *Spuren Lektüren, Praktiken des Sekundären*, pages 121–132. Wilhelm Fink Verlag, München, 2005 (in German).
44. J. Scott. *Social Network Analysis - A Handbook*. Sage Publications, London et al., 2nd edition edition, 2000.
45. C. Seeling, Spaniol, M., B. A., and K. R. Discourse visualization strategies for a comprehensive medial analysis of cultural science communities. In K. Tochtermann and H. Maurer, editors, *Proceedings of I-KNOW '04, Graz, Austria*, J.UCS, pages 337 – 344. Springer, 2004.
46. C. Shirky. Social software: A new generation of tools. *Esther Dyson's Monthly Report*, 10, 2003.
47. E. W. Stein and V. Zwass. Actualizing organizational memory with information technology. *Information Systems Research*, 6(2):85 – 117, 1995.
48. Compendium of projects until 2003: A world of learning at your fingertips — pilot projects under the elearning initiative. `http://europa.eu.int/comm/education/programmes/elearning/projects_en.html`,4 2004 (June 30, 2006).
49. T. C. Turner, M. A. Smith, D. Fisher, and H. T. Welser. Picturing usenet: Mapping computer-mediated collective action. *Journal of Computer-Mediated Communication*, 10:7, 2005.
50. D. J. Watts and S. H. Strogatz. Collective dynamics of small-world networks. *Nature*, 393:440–442, 1998.
51. E. Wenger. *Communities of Practice: Learning, Meaning, and Identity*. Cambridge University Press, Cambridge, UK, 1998.
52. M. Wolpers and G. Grohmann. PROLEARN: technology-enhanced learning and knowledge distribution for the corporate world. *International Journal of Knowledge and Learning*, 1(1/2):44–61, 2005.
53. E. S. K. Yu and J. Mylopoulos Towards Modelling Strategic Actor Relationships for Information Systems Development – With Examples from Business Process Reengineering *Proc. 4th WITS, Vancouver, Canada*, pages 21-28, 1994.

User Effect in Evaluating Personalized Information Retrieval Systems

Effie Lai-Chong Law[1], Tomaž Klobučar[2], and Matic Pipan[2]

[1] Institut TIK, ETH Zürich, Gloriastrasse 35, CH-8092 Zürich, Switzerland
[2] Institut Jožef Stefan, Jamova 39, 1000 Ljubljana, Slovenia
law@tik.ee.ethz.ch, {tomaz, matic}@e5.ijs.si

Abstract. Evaluation of personalized information retrieval (IR) systems is challenged by the user effect, which is manifested in terms of users' inconsistency in relevance judgment, ranking and relevance criteria usage. Two empirical studies on evaluating a personalized search engine were performed. Two types of relative measures computed with different mathematical formulae were compared. The ranking similarity and the randomness of relevance criteria usage were estimated. Results show some undesirable personalization effects. Implications for the future development and research of adaptive IR systems are discussed.

1 Introduction

Digital library (DL) is broadly defined as "information systems (IS) and services that provide electronic documents – text files, digital sound, digital video - available in dynamic and archival repositories" ([10], p.1023). DL, as a kind of information retrieval (IR) system, is an integral part of e-Learning as it enables users to store, retrieve and reuse learning resources. The extent to which DL supports users to fulfill their learning needs is determined by the efficacy of IR. Personalization is seen as a promising means to increase the effectiveness, efficiency and satisfaction (i.e. usability) of IR, because a user's profile (i.e. goals, interests, habits, preferences) decides a tailor-made or customized solution for the user's information problem. Conceptually personalization is easy to understand but practically it is difficult to implement. Creating and maintaining accurate user profiles is a bottleneck of personalization, because users' needs and interests are highly situational and their knowledge and experience are evolving. Of particular concern is that the number of empirical studies evaluating personalized IR systems is limited. It can be attributed partly to the fact that there exist only a handful of such systems and partly to the changing concept of 'relevance' that becomes ever increasingly dependent on user-based values; this dependency is particularly prominent in personalization. A robust evaluation framework for personalized IR systems is yet to be developed. We have assumed this challenge.

In the literature of IR, a palette of evaluation metrics (e.g. *recall*, *precision*, *relative relevance*), theoretical assumptions (e.g. the problem-solving paradigm; situated cognition) and mathematical models (e.g. the Jaccard formula, the cosine function)

W. Nejdl and K. Tochtermann (Eds.): EC-TEL 2006, LNCS 4227, pp. 257–271, 2006.

have been documented. Nevertheless, their inherent limitations are addressed by the IR researchers and practitioners. For instance, *recall* is limited by how to define the set of *all* relevant information objects (**IOs**), and it is impossible to get the accurate value of 'all'. The limitation is attributed to the very fact that human interpretation is involved. Whether an IO is considered relevant is determined by the user's perceptual, cognitive and affective states; these psychological constructs change moment-to-moment [23], leading to the inconsistency problem observed within as well as between users. We coin this as **user effect in relevance and ranking**, which is defined as: *The varied propensity of individual users as defined by their stable and dynamic characteristics to judge and rank relevance of information entities consistently, given the particularities of the context of an evaluation test.* Clearly, user effect has substantial impacts on the reliability and validity of evaluation results of IR systems, e.g. algorithmic versus situational rankings [4].

2 Literature Review

User-based evaluation of personalized IR systems is challenging because of the user effect in terms of the inconsistency in ranking and in relevance criteria usage. The paradigmatic shift in Information Science (IS) is characterized by user-centred (in place of the earlier system-based) design and evaluation. End-users are seen as ultimate assessors of the quality of the information and of the systems as well as services that provide information [1]. The notion of relevance judgment has instigated a vast number of conceptual and empirical studies since the 1950s [e.g. 3, 8, 20, 21]. Here we highlight previous research that has crucial impact on our work (cf. see [19] for a comprehensive review on relevance research).

Relevance judgments are influenced by a number of factors related to user psychological states (e.g. goals and needs), intrinsic information quality (e.g. topical appropriateness and recency) and contextual constraints (e.g. task requirement). Many models are built on distinct assumptions about users' cognition, knowledge, perception and affect (cf. an overview in [1]). These models can well exemplify the complexity of factors underlying relevance judgment. Users employ a set of criteria to determine whether information at hand can help resolve their information problems or meet their information needs. How these criteria are related to each other is the research question that has led to a diversity of relevance models [e.g. 5, 8, 24, 25]. Notwithstanding recent efforts to scientifically classify relevance criteria, there is still no consensus on the categorization and labeling of the classes of criteria [25]. A valid and reliable criteria classification scheme can presumably help IR system designers focus on metadata that are critical for users to make relevance judgment.

Borlund and Ingwersen [4] introduced the relative relevance (**RR**) measure as an attempt to bridge the gap between the objective system-driven topical relevance assessments versus the subjective user-centered situational ones. The RR measure computes the degree of agreement between two results of relevance assessments R_1 and R_2, which may be objective or subjective. Specifically, *algorithmic relevance* as the system's output is interpreted and assessed by users in accordance with their dynamic perceptions of a real or simulated work task situation, resulting in *situational relevance*. The same output can be judged by an assessor in terms of the *nearness* between the IO retrieved and the topic represented by the search query, resulting in *intellectual topicality relevance*. Non-binary values (i.e. 1- relevant, 0.5 – partially relevant, 0 – irrelevant) are permissible.

In their earlier work, Borlund and Ingwersen [4] claimed that the Jaccard association coefficient (Formula 1) was preferred to the cosine measure (Formula 2) because pairs of sets not vectors were dealt with. However, in her more recent work [3], Borlund revoked this previous claim and remarked that the cosine measure is more robust because the Jaccard measure is not capable of handling fractional counts.

$$\text{Jaccard Association } (R_1, R_2) = \frac{\Sigma\,(R_1R_2)}{\Sigma R_1 + \Sigma R_2 - \Sigma(R_1R_2)} \qquad \textbf{[Formula 1]}$$

$$\text{Cosine Association } (R_1, R_2) = \frac{\Sigma\,(R_1R_2)}{(\Sigma R_1{}^2)^{1/2} * (\Sigma R_2{}^2)^{1/2}} \qquad \textbf{[Formula 2]}$$

$$\text{Euclidean distance } (R_1, R_2) = \left[\sum_{i=1}^{n} (R_{1i} - R_{2i})^2\right]^{1/2} \qquad \textbf{[Formula 3]}$$

Table 1. Cosine association coefficients for hypothetical data

Information Object (IO)	R_1	R_2	R_3
IO 1	1.0	1.0	0.5
IO 2	0.8	0.8	0.4
IO 3	0.6	0.6	0.3
IO 4	0.4	0.4	0.2
IO 5	0.2	0.2	0.1
Sum	3.0	3.0	1.5
Precision = Sum/ Number of IOs	0.6	0.6	0.3
RR:			
Cosine(R_1, R_2)	1		
Cosine(R_1, R_3)	1		

Nonetheless, Borlund [3] fails to mention one obvious drawback of the cosine measure. As shown in Table 1, the cosine coefficient of 1 can be obtained when the values for each of the IOs in R_1 and R_2 are completely identical or when the value of each of the IOs in R_3 is of the same fraction of its counterpart in R_1, in this case is ½. If R_1, R_2 and R_3 are based on the same scale (min: 0.0; max: 1.0; interval: 0.1), then the cosine measures cannot reflect accurately the real differences. Furthermore, Euclidean Distance (ED: Formula 3) is a method commonly used in various domains to estimate the similarity of the retrieved IOs. The magnitude of the distance reflects the degree of similarity between the two sets of relevance assessments [cf. 18]. As applied to the hypothetical data in Table 1, ED (R_1, R_2) = 0, ED (R_1, R_3) = 0.8.

3 Research Questions

The current study has the objective of developing evaluation metrics for IR systems. Furthermore, based on the foregoing arguments, we formulate four research questions and attempt to answer them with the empirical data collected:

RQ1: How serious was the user effect in terms of inconsistency in applying different relevance criteria to system-generated search results and in ranking them?
RQ2: To what extent did different relative relevance (RR) measures estimated by the three mathematical models (Jaccard, Cosine and Euclidean) converge?
RQ3: To what extent was the users' level of satisfaction with the search results correlated with the effectiveness of the search?
RQ4: What was the general pattern of relevance criteria usage?

4 Evaluation of Personalized IR Systems

Subsequently, we present two evaluation studies – Study 1 and Study 2 – on a personalized search engine (PSE), which is integrated into two e-learning platforms. Study 1 focused on assessing relative relevance (RR) measures whereas Study 2 focused on identifying user relevance criteria.

4.1 Systems Overviews

The PSE evaluated was developed by the ELENA project (http://www.elena-project.org) and the EducaNext project (http://www.educanext.org/ubp). The PSE enables users to find a variety of learning resources (LRs) in a federated network of repositories, and aims to improve search results by taking user profiles into account and by implementing the ranking algorithm in the network search client based on *Lucene[1]* (for details see [6]). As LRs are unique within each repository and they do not link to LRs in other repositories, ranking of search results is far more challenging than in other cases, for instance, a centralized LR repository or a meta-search engine in the Web. The eclipsed feature in Fig. 1 shows the "Personalized Search Results" check box and the three personalization scales: User Interests, User Goals and User Learning History. Users have control over the personalization features, turning it on and off contingent on their situational needs. Previous research [14] suggests that users be given control over when the automated assistance during the search process should be invoked.

Note that in the current version of the ELENA-PSE prototype, the personalization based on User Learning History is not yet implemented. In EducaNext-PSE prototype there is only one personalization scale (User Interest) instead of three. Otherwise, the user interface of the search engine in both platforms is essentially the same. The main rationale of using the two platforms (Study 2) is that their respective target groups are different (corporate learners for ELENA and academic learners for EducaNext). With the shift of the platform and the associated new task requirements (see below), users are supposed to be more aware of the contextual change and thus their interests/goals appropriate to the situation can better be elicited.

---

[1] *Lucene* (http://lucene.apache.org/) is a free text-indexing and searching API written in Java. It is a technology suitable for nearly any application that requires full-text search.

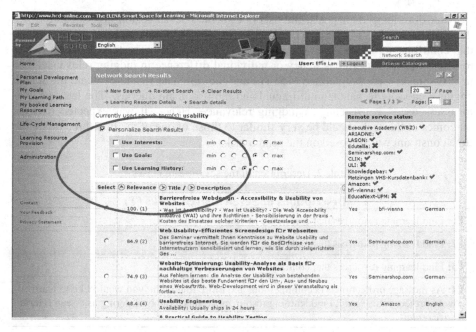

Fig. 1. The user interface of the ELENA-PSE

4.2 Study 1

4.2.1 Participants

The evaluation tests consisted of two rounds. In **Round 1** a total of 22 test persons from Slovenia, Austria, Germany, Spain, and Switzerland were involved. They were faculty members of academic institutions with rich experience in search engines. In **Round 2** two information professionals (or assessors) were involved. They were senior researchers in computer science and HCI, respectively, and possessed expertise and experiences in e-learning.

4.2.2 Method

4.2.2.1 Round 1 Tests

Tasks and instruments

The evaluation tests were performed in summer 2005. The users were given a simulated work task situation, which served as the trigger of the user's information need and as the platform for relevance judgment [3]. They were first asked to imagine working in a company in a particular position, and to think of the learning goals they might have in this situation. The users were then required to enter into their learner profiles three goals. Each goal was captioned with a title and elaborated with free-text description (see the example cited below):

> *Information systems access control – To investigate and learn about the most recent technologies and frameworks for access control to information systems, such as security policies, authentication mechanisms (e.g. biometrics), authorization mechanisms or privacy-enhancing technologies*

After describing their goals, the users performed seven search tasks (Table 2). In the first three tasks (T1, T2, T3) the users were asked to find learning resources (LRs) that contribute to the three pre-specified goals, respectively. The fourth task (T4) was to assess between-user consistency or individual difference in judging relevance. The next two tasks were pre-defined (T5, T6) and the rationale was to evaluate the search engine's capacity to handle multilingual and multi-domain queries. The last task was to assess users' consistency in judging relevance. Hence, it was expected that the outcomes of this task should be very similar to those of one of the first three tasks. No time constraint was imposed on the search tasks.

Table 2. Description of the seven search tasks

Descriptions of Seven Search Tasks (T)
T1: Find learning resources that contribute to your first goal.
T2: Find learning resources that contribute to your second goal.
T3: Find learning resources that contribute to your third goal.
T4: As message protection is becoming more and more important, you would like to learn how to protect your e-mail. Find learning resources on this topic by entering as a search term *secure e-mail*.
T5: Select a foreign language you would like to learn. Find free learning material or seminars that help you to learn the language.
T6: Find seminars on Java programming in your local language.
T7: Find a learning resource that contributes to your MOST important goal of the three you have identified.

Relevance Judgment

By default the personalization feature of the search engine is deactivated. User can activate it by checking the appropriate box (Figure 1). For each of the search tasks, the users were asked to complete a template (see the excerpt in Figure 2). In total, the 22 users performed 99 *complete* search tasks. Partially completed tasks were not analyzed.

4.2.2.2   Round 2 Tests. The two assessors performed search tasks based on the users' goal-driven queries (with and without personalization) that were implemented in Round 1. Then they assessed the outcomes in accordance with two types of relevance. For the list of returned LRs *without* personalization, the assessors judged the first 15 by determining how an LR corresponds to the topical area required by the perceived information need, resulting in *intellectual topicality* [4]. For the list of returned LRs with personalization, the assessors judged first 15 by determining how useful the viewed LR was by addressing the relationship among the LR, the goal and task underlying the user's information need and the user's current cognitive state observed, resulting in *situational relevance*.

****

1. Write down what you are trying to find (i.e. Search Term):
   Answer: LEARN EXCEL
3. What is the total number of the returned results?
   Answer: 117
4. How many of the returned results are relevant for you, i.e. they are what you were looking for?
   Answer: 5

No personalization

5. How many of the top 10 ranked results are relevant for you?
   Answer: 1
6. Write down the five most relevant results for you from the overall results list and their ranking numbers (not relevance). Please write the most relevant result the first, then the second most relevant, and so on.

Your rank	Engine-Rank	Learning resource title
1.		
2.		
3.		
4.		
5.		

Personalise Search Results → Use Goals

9. How many of the top 10 ranked results are now relevant for you?
   Answer: 1
10. Please write down how the ranking of the most relevant results has changed after personalization

Your Rank	Previous Engine-rank (before personalization; see item 4)	Current Engine-rank (after personalization)
1.		
2.		
3.		
4.		
5.		

****

Fig. 2. An excerpt of a template for a search task

4.3 Study 2

4.3.1 Participants

Eleven users from two academic institutions in the UK and Slovenia were involved. Five were postgraduates and six were faculty members. Seven of them had academic background in computer science, two in economics, one in medicine and one in law. All of them had medium to rich experience in working with Web-based search engines. One was English native speaker and the others were fluent in English.

4.3.2 Method

The evaluation tests were conducted at the two institutions in early 2006. The users were required to perform two search tasks with the ELENA-PSE and another two with the EducaNext-PSE. The order of the systems tested was counterbalanced. In the context of the ELENA-PSE, the same procedure for eliciting **user goals** in Study 1 (see 4.2.2.1) was performed. In the context of the EducaNext-PSE, the users were asked to imagine delivering a new course and pursuing a research topic; these activities were actually part of their real-life work. Then they were required to enter into their personal profile one **lecturing interest** and one **research interest**; each should be classified into an academic discipline (selected from a drop-down menu) and described in free text format. An example of research interest is:

> `Description:` Security and privacy aspects of the next generation networks, in particular pervasive and ubiquitous systems, and technology-enhanced learning
> `Classification:` Computer Science

The users were required to carry out four search tasks to find learning resources (LRs) that contribute to each of their self-defined goals and interests. No time constraint was imposed on the search tasks.

A list of items with each of them consisting of a title and a snippet (up to three lines of text) was returned as search results. Each item was hyperlinked to a website where more information of the LR were presented (cf. Amazon-format such as title, description, author, publisher, year of publication, number of pages, price, table of content, editorial/customer review). We coin this information object as **metadata-surrogate**. The users had no access to complete LRs catalogued in the two platforms, partly because of the intellectual property right issue and partly because of the technical constraint.

Similar to Study 1, the users were required to make relevance judgments on the search results produced when the personalization feature was on or off. In addition, when examining metadata-surrogates for relevance, the users were required to think aloud and to highlight onscreen keywords that influenced their relevance judgment with a mouse (cf. [9]). All onscreen activities and think-aloud protocols were captured with Camtasia® or Hypercam®. In addition, the users were asked to fill in a template similar to that of Study 1 (Figure 2).

5   Results

5.1   Study 1

5.1.1   Findings of Round 1 Tests
Personalization Effect
The descriptive statistics of the search tasks were shown in Table 3. Ranking without personalization placed on average 4.99 relevant LRs among top 10 ranked. The most important LR for a user was top ranked 25 times (i.e. 25% of the total search tasks), on the second place 7 times, and on the third place 8 times (40% of the time among top 3). We calculated the differences between no personalization and with personalization in terms of (i) the *number* of relevant LRs among 10 top ranked (i.e. *NoP-10* vs. *GOAL-10*); (ii) the *rankings* of the 5 most relevant LRs, namely *Rank-NoP* and *Rank-P,* of which the averages result in *NoP-R* and *GOAL-R*, respectively. Paired sample t-tests and Kendall's correlation tests were performed on (i) and (ii), respectively. Both results were statistically significant: (i) $t = 2.77$, $p = 0.007$, $N = 99$; (ii) $\tau = .71$, $\alpha = .0$, $N = 462$.

Table 3. Descriptive statistics of the search tasks results

Variable	Mean (SD)	Explanation
Tot-IOs	33.3 (26.9)	Average number of information objects (IOs) returned in total
Rev-IOs	8.9 (6.5)	Average number of relevant IOs out of the total
NoP-10	5.0 (2.4)	Average number of relevant IOs among top 10 ranked (without personalization)
GOAL-10	4.6 (2.3)	Average number of relevant IOs among top 10 ranked (with personalization on goals)
NoP-R	8.9 (9.7)	Average rank of the 5 most relevant IOs for a user (without personalization)
GOAL-R	9.5 (11.6)	Average rank of the 5 most relevant IOs for a user (with personalization on goals)

In the literature of IR, an association measure based on Kendall's correlation coefficient (τ) is commonly employed to estimate the change in system rankings (e.g. [7]). The similarity of two rankings is defined as the Kendall's τ between them (range: 0.0 to 1.0). Previous work has considered all rankings with correlations greater than 0.9 as equivalent and rankings with correlations less than 0.8 as containing noticeable differences in general [26]. *Rank-NoP* (without personalization) and *Rank-P* (with personalization) are expected to be different, with the latter having the more relevant items higher on the ranking list, because of the 'push' driven by the personalization effect. If the two ranks are similar (i.e. $\tau >= 0.8$) then there is no personalization effect because no change occurs. Conversely, if the two ranks are dissimilar (i.e. $\tau < 0.8$), then it may imply that there is some personalization effect. The question is whether it leads to better or worse ranking results.

These findings clearly indicate that the ranking algorithms for the PSE were not successful and require revisions, because both the number of relevant LRs among 10 top ranked (i.e. the higher the better) and the average rank of the 5 most relevant LRs (i.e. the lower the better) were more desirable when the personalization was switched *off* than when it was switched *on* (Table 3). Out of the 462 monitored rankings, 205 were ties, 100 negative ranks (i.e. better) and 157 positive ranks (i.e. worse).

Within-User and Between-User Consistency
In Round 1 tests, Task 7 (T7) and Task 4 (T4) were meant to evaluate within-user consistency and between-user consistency (see Table 2), respectively. Nonetheless, only six users followed the instruction of performing Task 7 in the way that they entered exactly the same query that was used in one of the first three goal-related tasks (i.e. T1, T2 or T3). For instance, one user entered 'digital signature acceptance' for Task 1 but 'digital signature competence' for T7. As the system's outputs could be very different, it is necessary to discard such data. For one user, we computed the ranking similarity in terms of Kendall's tau_b (τ) between T2 and T7 when the personalization was on and off; the average τ over the two conditions is 0.2, which is very low, implying no similarity at all. For the other five users, we applied the same analysis method; the average association coefficients over the two conditions were: 0.6, 0.3, 0.7, 0.5 and 1.0 (i.e. this user had identical rankings).

For each user, the duration of each of the seven search tasks was recorded. From these data we computed the average time lapse between the two repetitive tasks (i.e.

T1/T2/T3 and T7), which was equal to 89 minutes (range: 33 min to 169 min). There was no significant correlation between the magnitude of τ and the length of time lapse. It seems to suggest that memory did not play an important role in determining within-user consistency. In summary, these findings show that the users were generally inconsistent in ranking the search results. It can somewhat confirm the assumption that human information need is highly dynamic and unstable.

Next, we look into the problem of between-user consistency. All the users were required to perform the same search task T4. Some users failed to comply with the instruction and their data had to be discarded. Consequently, we examined the data of the ten users. Table 4 shows individual users' first five ranked LRs; the numbers in rows were the system-generated ranks for the corresponding LRs. These findings show that the users could interpret the same system's output very differently.

Table 4. Between-user rankings on the same search task

Rank	J1	J2	J3	W1	W3	J7	J8	J9	J10	J11
1st	12	21	12	5	5	1	1	1	8	8
2nd	25	47	15	11	11	4	4	8	20	20
3rd	21	15	11	12	12	8	7	2	1	4
4th	50	25	16	15	13	7	8	4	2	15
5th	39	12	13	1	17	15	10	20	5	1

Correlation Between Satisfaction and Effectiveness
After each search task, the user was asked to rate on a 7-point Likert Scale (1 = lowest, 7 = highest) her level of satisfaction with the search results (i.e. SUCCESS) and with the amount of time it took to locate what was being looked for (i.e. TIME). While no significant correlation was found between SUCCESS and *precision* (i.e. = Rev-IOs/Tot-IOs in Table 3), there was significant correlation between TIME and the *precision* ($r = 0.3$, $p = .002$, $N=99$). Nevertheless, the level of satisfaction with the search results was determined not only by the number of relevant LRs, but also by how they were ranked in the system's output. Hence, for each search task we computed the average change in ranking before and after personalization and correlated it with SUCCESS, no significant difference was found, indicating that the user satisfaction was not solely determined by the effectiveness of the personalized ranking.

5.1.2 Findings of Round 2 Tests
Relative Relevance (RR) Measures
In Round 2, two assessors performed relevance assessments on altogether 38 goal-related search tasks. For each task, the assessors looked at the top 15 top ranked LRs, and for each of these LRs they judged whether it was relevant (1.0), partially relevant (0.5) or not relevant at all (0.0). Two sets of outcomes were obtained: when no personalization was used (i.e. intellectual topicality; the column "Topic" in Table 5) and when the knowledge about the goals was considered (i.e. situational relevance; the column "Situate" in Table 5). Besides, for each of the two cases, the system's algorithmic relevance were generated (the columns Algo(on) and Algo(off) in Table 5) when personalization was switched off and on, respectively. We computed Relative Relevance (RR) for four combinations of different types of relevance, including:

- Intellectual Topicality (subjective) vs. Algorithmic Relevance (objective) {personalization = off}
- Intellectual Topicality (subjective) vs. Situational Relevance (subjective)
- Situational Relevance (subjective) vs. Algorithmic Relevance (objective) {personalization = on}
- Algorithmic Relevance (objective) {personalization = on} vs. Algorithmic Relevance (subjective) {personalization = off}

Table 5. Computation of RR with three methods

	R_1 R_2	Topic Algo(off)	Topic Situate	Situate Algo (on)	Algo(off) Algo(on)
Jaccard measure		0.38	0.49	0.33	0.46
Cosine measure		0.7	0.73	0.64	0.92
Euclidean distance		8.08	7.84	7.67	3.27

Specifically, we employed the three methods described in the foregoing section, namely the Jaccard measure, the Cosine measure and the Euclidean Distance. Interestingly, the results (Table 5) show that the three methods could lead to inconsistent conclusions. According to the Jaccard measure, the best match was between the two subjective relevance assessments (RR = 0.49). However, for the Cosine measure the best match was between the two objective ones (RR = 0.92), and it was supported by the Euclidean Distance (= 3.27; the lower the magnitude the more similar the two values). Indeed, it is reasonable to assume that the two system outputs (i.e. two types of Algorithmic Relevance) should have the highest degree of overlapping, given that no dynamic information need or fuzzy human interpretation was involved. Nonetheless, for the second best match, the three methods suggest three different combinations.

5.2 Study 2

As mentioned earlier, Study 2 focused on the usage of relevance criteria. The empirical findings on the personalization effect, which were somewhat consistent with those of Study 1, are not reported here due to the space constraint. The content analysis of the users' think-aloud protocols and highlighted text onscreen yielded data on their usage of relevance criteria. Altogether eighteen unique criteria were identified, based on the literature of relevance research [1, 9, 15] as well as on inductive analysis during the coding process. As we aim to present the findings on the distribution and application of relevance criteria, the definition of individual criterion is not presented here due to the space limit.

391 instances of 18 criteria used for assessing altogether 182 metadata-surrogates. Our results were somewhat consistent with those of previous relevance research:

- Topical appropriateness (i.e. specificity) was the most often used criterion being supplemented by an array of extra-topical criteria with a large range of frequency:
- The distribution of relevance criteria approximated a decaying exponential model, with the predominance of a few widely used criteria being followed by a long tail of occasionally used ones. Specifically, twelve of the 18 criteria (Figure 3) identified for meta-surrogates represented less than 5% of the respective total number of criteria.

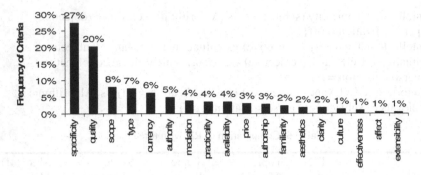

Fig. 3. Distribution of relevance criteria for assessing meta-surrogates

To see how consistent individual users applied their selected criteria, we employed the concept of information entropy (H), which describes how much randomness (or uncertainty) there is in a signal or random event. Since frequency for some criteria is not very high (e.g. 'affect''), while other are very common (e.g. 'specificity'), the selection of criteria is not really as random as it might be. On the other hand, since we cannot predict which criteria the user will apply: it is, to some degree, 'random'. Entropy is a measure of this randomness, as suggested by Shannon [22]. Accordingly, entropy (H) is defined in terms of a discrete random event x, with possible states (or outcomes) $1..n$ as:

$$H(x) = \sum_{i=1}^{n} p(i) \log_2 (1/p(i))$$

(x is a random event where a user applies a specific relevance criterion to j search tasks, where $j = 1..4$; $n = \{0, 1\}$ and $p(i)$ is the probability that the criterion is applied (n = 1) or not applied (n = 0))

The resulting entropy H was divided by the total number of relevance criteria applied by the user to standardize the attribute, which has the range from 0.0 to 1.0. The lower the s(tandardized) H the higher the consistency the user applied the selected criteria is. The average sH was 0.54 (SD = 0.21), indicating that generally the users were somewhat neutral with respect to the consistency of criteria application.

6 Discussion

Subsequently, we discuss the four research questions (Section 3) with reference to the empirical results obtained:

RQ1: User Effect: Ranking and Relevance Criteria Relevance
The empirical results of this study further corroborate the observation about the user effect. The users were inconsistent in judging the relevance of information objects and in ranking them, even when the same search query was entered and the same overall results list was produced. Specifically, the criteria the users employed for making relevance judgment varied from a metadata-surrogate to another, even when the same set of metadata attributes was available. Put simply, the user searching and seeking behaviour is essentially unpredictable, although many attempts to model and formalize this kind of behaviour have been undertaken in the literature of IR (cf. the

papers of recent SIGIR conferences). Considering the fuzziness of psychological constructs like goals, interests and needs, the provocative question whether personalization is doomed to fail can be raised. Nonetheless, in the recent years the notion of individual differences has been attracting more research attention and effort in the field of human computer interaction (HCI) and IS. It is intriguing to explore the related theoretical models (e.g. [16]) to deepen the understanding of the user effect.

RQ2: Estimation of Relative Relevance with Different Mathematical Models
It was interesting to observe that the three methods could lead to inconsistent conclusions about the relationships between different types of relative relevance (RR). A number of previous IR research attempted to compare so-called *distance coefficients*, which vary in inverse proportion with the degree of similarity, with *association coefficients*, which vary in direct proportion with the degree of similarity [11, 18]. However, the results appear inconsistent and inconclusive, i.e. there seems no clear-cut answer to the question which measure best fits which application context. In fact, the Jaccard formula has been used in IS and HCI (e.g. any-two agreement [13]). Not until recently has its robustness been challenged. However, as shown above, the resilience of the cosine measure can be challenged as well. Perhaps it entails an alternative measure. However, we should bear in mind that an array of tools may not be better than a single powerful one.

RQ3: User Satisfaction and Search Efficacy
In the current study, we are not able to derive from the empirical data which factor plays a stronger role in determining the level of satisfaction: the number of relevant IOs retrieved or the way how these IOs were ranked. In fact, the user satisfaction was evaluated *after* all the seven tasks were performed. It thus further complicated the picture. It is speculated that users themselves may not be able to isolate these factors. Emotional responses are based on intricate interactions between cognitive and affective attributes. *Satisfaction* is a composite term, amalgamating a cluster of "felt experience" [17], and is measured in a coarse-grained manner. The current research efforts on User Experience (UX) attempt to reduce the composite *satisfaction* into elemental attributes – fun, pride, pleasure, surprise, intimacy, joy, to name just a few – and thrive to understand, define and quantify such attributes. Evaluating UX is an emerging area. As remarked by the UX pioneers, what has been done in the last few years is just the beginning [12]. A number of theoretical, methodological and empirical issues germane to UX need to be researched. More important, outcomes of such research can inform the practice in design and evaluation.

RQ4: Pattern of Relevance Criteria Usage?
There is limited or even no study that reports the distribution of relevance criteria on an individual basis. Nor is there any study that investigates how consistent users apply their criteria to different IOs. Our results show that the users seemed to apply the criteria in a rather random manner. This proposition is somewhat supported by our results on computing the consistency of criteria usage, which is expressed in terms of information entropy – a critical concept in the information theory that we borrow and adapt for developing this new metric. The standardized entropy sH of 0.54 indicates that the level or randomness of the relevance criteria use is medium. Put differently, while the users possess some strategies for the criteria use in relevance judgment, there are no deterministic rule governing the actual application. These findings are consistent with the notion that the relevance judgments are highly dynamic and situational.

7 Limitation and Future Work

Several constraints - technical, political, conceptual and methodological – have limited the scope of our empirical findings:

- The PSE under evaluation is a prototype under development; there is much room to improve the ranking algorithm (e.g. the category filter [6]) and to make the associated changes in the user interface. Specifically, users should be enabled to sort, delete, insert or select personal goals and interests with ease at anytime they want to activate the personalization feature (cf. with the current interface one can apply personalization only to all or none of pre-defined goals/interests), thereby having their specific, situational information need addressed more appropriately.

- The use of metadata-surrogates does not allow us to study so-called stage-dependent criteria use [e.g. 2, 5, 25], i.e. whether users apply different criteria to judge the relevance of a metadata-surrogate and its corresponding full text document. While the technical constraint on the access to a complete information entity can be overcome in the future, the copyright issue is trickier to deal with.

- The focus of our analyses was on individual criteria rather than on categories or clusters of criteria. The pattern of change in criteria use can better be illustrated by instances rather than types of criteria. While a classification of criteria may help distinguish between essential and subordinate and between subjective and objective criteria, it may mask the distinction between individual criteria. Besides, IR system designers can focus attention on improving metadata if they are well informed which specific relevance criteria are of great importance and frequent use. There is a need to sustain the work to map relevance criteria across information search process stages, variations in IO representations, tasks and application contexts [25].

- The number of users employed for both studies was relatively small. In addition, the ecological validity of laboratory-based studies is generally not particularly high. More interesting data would be garnered if more users with larger heterogeneity (e.g. academic disciplines) could be engaged in a longer period of time for evaluating a general-purpose tool.

The current study and the list of quoted previous work clearly point to the fact that user-based relevance evaluation is a complex topic. The relevance of this topic to the technology-enhanced learning community is substantial; the most significant criterion is *practicality*, thereby informing the design and evaluation of personalized IR systems.

References

[1] Barry, C.L., & Schamber, L. (1998). Users' criteria for relevance evaluation: A cross-situational comparison. *IP&M, 34(2/3)*, 219-236.
[2] Bateman, J. (1998). Changes in relevance criteria: A longitudinal study. *Proceedings of the 61ˢᵗ Annual meeting of the American Society for Information Science*, 35, 23-32.
[3] Borlund, P. (2003). The concept of relevance in IR. *JASIST, 54(10)*, 913-925.
[4] Borlund, P. & Ingwersen, P. (1998). Measruse of relative relevance and ranked half-life: performance indicators for interactive IR. In *Proceedings of SIGIR'98* (pp. 324-331).

[5] Boyce, B. (1982). Beyond topicality: A two stage view of relevance and retrieval process. *IP&M, 18,* 105-109.

[6] Brantner, S. (Ed.) D4.4 Smart learning space description: the ELENA project (http://www.elena-project.org/en/index.asp?p=3-4).

[7] Buckley, C., & Voorhees, E.M. (2004). Retrieval evaluation with incomplete information. *SIGIR'04,* Sheffield, UK.

[8] Cosjin, E., & Ingwersen, P. (2000). Dimensions of relevance. *IP&M, 36,* 533-550.

[9] Crystal, A., & Greenberg, J. (in press). Relevance criteria identified by health information users during Web searches. *JASIST.*

[10] Elliot, M., & Kling, R. (1997). Organizational usability of digital libraries. *JASIST,* 48(11), 1023-1035.

[11] Ellis, D., Furner-Hines, J., & Willett P. (1994). On the measurement of inter-linker consistency and retrieval effectiveness in hypertext databases. In *Proc 17th SIGIR Conference,* Dublin (Ireland), pp.51-60.

[12] Hassenzahl, M., & Tractinsky, N. (2006). User experience – a research agenda. *Behaviour and Information Technology, 25*(2), 91-97.

[13] Hertzum, M., Jacobsen, N. E. (2001). The evaluator effect: A chilling fact about usability evaluation methods. *Int'l. J. Human Computer Interaction, 13*(4): 421-443 (2001).

[14] Jansen, B.J. (2005). Seeking and implementing automated assistance during the search process. *IP&M, 41,* 909-928.

[15] Maglaughlin, K.L. & Sonnenwald, D.H. (2002). User perspectives on relevance critera: A comparison among relevant, partially relevant, and not-relevant judgments. *JASIST, 53*(5), 327-342.

[16] Magoulas, G.D., & Chen, S. Y. Chen (Eds) (2004). Proceedings of the Workshop in Individual Difference in Adaptive Hypermedia (http://www.dcs.bbk.ac.uk /~gmagoulas/ AH2004_Workshop/Individual_Differences_WorkProc.pdf).

[17] McCarthy, J., & Wright, P. C. (2004). Technology as Experience. MIT Press.

[18] Michel, C. (2003). Poset representation and similarity comparisons of systems in IR. In SIGIR Workshop on <Mathematical/Formal Methods in IR> (MF/IR 2003) – July 2003 – Toronto, Canada.

[19] Mizzaro, S. (1997). Relevance: the whole history. *JASIST, 48,* 810-832.

[20] Park, T.K. (1994) Toward a theory of user-based relevance. *JASIST, 45,* 135-141.

[21] Saracevic, T. (1996). Relevance reconsidered '96. In P. Ingwersen & N. Ole Pors (Eds.), *CoLIS2* (pp. 201-218). Copenhagen, Denmark.

[22] Sloane, N. J. A., & Wyner, A.D. (1993) (Ed.), *Claude Elwood Shannon: Collected Papers,* New York: IEEE Press.

[23] Suchman, L. (1987). *Plans and situated actions.* Cambridge: Cambridge University Press.

[24] Swanson, D.R. (1986). Subjective versus objective relevance in bibliographic retrieval systems. *Library Quarterly, 56,* 389-398.

[25] Tang, R., & Solomon, P. (2001). Use of relevance criteria across stages of document evaluation. *JASIST, 52*(8), 676-685.

[26] Voorhees, E.M. (2001). Evaluation by highly relevant documents. In *Proceedings of the 24th Annual International ACM SIGIR Conference on Research and Development in Information Retrieval (pp.* 74–82).

Data and Application Integration in Learning Content Management Systems: A Web Services Approach

Ivan Madjarov and Omar Boucelma

Laboratoire des Sciences de l'Information et des Systèmes
(LSIS) - UMR CNRS 6168,
Aix-Marseille Universités
Domaine Universitaire de Saint-Jérôme
Avenue Escadrille Normandie-Niemen
F-13397 Marseille Cedex 20
ivan.madjarov@iut-gtr.univ-mrs.fr
omar.boucelma@lsis.org

Abstract. This paper describes a service-oriented approach for the integration of third-party external applications and resources into an existing open source e-Learning environment. We detail the architecture for creating customized learning environments composed of existing open source applications and systems. As a result, a Web services-oriented framework for e-Learning systems is proposed, providing a flexible integration model in which all the learning components and applications are loosely connected. Web services provide a suitable deployment environment to realize dynamic and interoperable e-Learning systems by facilitating application-to-application interaction.

Keywords: Web Services, Learning Object, Interoperability, XML.

1 Introduction

Many of existing e-Learning systems are based on plain monolithic, component client-server or peer-to-peer models and therefore suffer from drawbacks like poor scalability or complicated interchange of content [30]. Although there exist standards like LOM [10], SCORM [1], and IMS [14] the interchange of educational content between servers or peers is still a problem for which satisfactory solutions still need to be provided. Some solutions do concentrate on the architectural design, like the pattern approach [25], or framework systems (Cisco, WebCT, IBM), which allow the use of plug-in components. However, difficulties still remain, since the interconnections between heterogeneous systems are not made easy. Such solutions are not flexible and do not allow interoperability because they are based on monolithic or component client-server architecture (e.g., Blackboard or WebCT). Most content providers have large monolithic systems where e-Learning standards adaptation will not significantly change the underlying teacher-learner model. Emergence of Web services is an attempt to provide interoperability. Web services are a set of open standards that facilitate application-to-application interaction [37].

W. Nejdl and K. Tochtermann (Eds.): EC-TEL 2006, LNCS 4227, pp. 272–286, 2006.

Traditional Web-based e-Learning applications generally interact with a server in submitting forms, exercise results or questions/answers, most of these data being completed by a learner. In response to each request, the e-Learning server responds by sending back a new web page, slowing down application execution. The new AJAX technique (*Asynchronous JavaScript and XML*) [21] is a term that refers to the use of a group of Web-based and Web services-based technologies together. AJAX applications can send requests to the Web server-engine to retrieve only the data that is needed, usually using SOAP or some other XML-based Web service dialect.

We believe that a future e-Learning system should consist of a set of independent but cooperating non-monolithic services-based applications that integrate pedagogical data between common *Learning Content Management Systems* (LCMS).

In this paper we propose a service-oriented architecture (SOA) in which the pedagogical content is encapsulated inside a Web service in order to increase interoperability and reusability for learning data and applications [31]. The role of SOA we suggest is to integrate existing free and open source LCMS, in which different external components are implemented as Web services. For course authors, course administrators and learners, e-Learning systems can be individually assembled by using distributed components to provide the functionality they really need. In addition, we propose a new Web service-based client in an e-Learning system in using AJAX technique.

The remainder of this paper is as follows. Section 2 presents the state of the art in e-Learning, Web services, and e-Learning systems architecture and standards; work related to AJAX is also described. Section 3 presents our approach for a SOA-based LCMS. Finally, concluding remarks are given in section 4.

2   Background

In this section we briefly introduce the background relevant to our work, that is: (1) the integration of LCMS and (2) the third-party external resources and applications in using Web services. Some XML-based semantic-oriented tools, usually not directly supplied by a LCMS, are described as well.

2.1   E-Learning

E-Learning is defined as: "the convergence of the Internet and learning, or Internet-enabled learning; the use of network technologies to create, foster, deliver, and facilitate learning, anytime and anywhere" [22].

In a typical e-Learning environment, there are several groups of people involved: authors and learners; administrators and trainers. The core of an e-Learning system typically consists of a LMS (*Learning Management System*) or LCMS. An LMS provides functionalities like the management of learners and their profiles, their progress tracking, collaboration facilitation, or event scheduling. An LCMS is aimed at managing a learning content which is usually stored in a database [8], [16]. In addition, an LCMS eases content reusability, provides workflow support during content development, or delivers content via predefined interfaces and presentation layers.

Choosing an e-Learning system is not an easy task. One known approach is to adopt a proprietary system (e.g., WebCT, Blackboard, or Docent) irrespective of specific users needs. Another one is to customize an existing *open source e-Learning environment* (e.g., Moodle, Atutor, or Dokeos) by modifying its source code. While this solution affords maximum flexibility, it may be also very costly. In this paper we propose a SOA for creating customized e-Learning environments comprised of existing *open source* applications and systems.

The development of Learning Objects (LOs) [10], which are reusable units of study, exercise, or practice, influenced the way how e-Learning content is handled in the core of e-Learning systems. LOs can be authored independently of the delivery media by using an authoring system, they are stored inside or outside a LCMS, and they may be distributed on demand over the Web. LOs represents building blocks for a solution that solves interoperability and reusability problems, since LOs are based on existing standards (SCORM, IMS, LOM), and intended for use in many different e-Learning systems. The second possible solution consists in a collection of Web services that can be used to handle e-Learning content: courses, functionalities and other services. From our perspective, Web services represent a suitable technology for LOs implementation. Our system consists, among others, of an *Open Semantic Editor Suite* (OSES) that is a set of XML-based tools (editor and plug-ins) for creating, editing, and storing learning content in a native XML database (NXDB). XML is used for encoding textual and non-textual information such as vector graphics, mathematical expressions, synchronized multimedia documents, complex forms, quizzes, etc [16], [18]. Integration of OSES with a LCMS is made possible through the Web services technology.

2.2 Web Services

Web services are independent software components that use the Internet as a communication and deployment infrastructure. They provide a high level abstraction view of applications, together with a standardized stack of protocols and languages, as depicted in Fig. 1. In a typical Web service invocation, a client may use a UDDI registry (*Universal Description Discovery and Integration*) to find a server that hosts a service then it requests from the server a document, encoded in WSDL (*Web Services Description Language*), which describes the operations supported by a service. For the communication, SOAP (*Simple Object Access Protocol*) can be used, which build

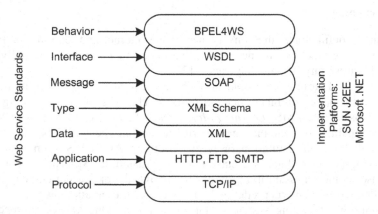

Fig. 1. Web Service Standards Stack (*adapted from [27]*)

upon HTTP (*Hypertext Transfer Protocol*) to transport the data. More complex Web services can be composed out of existing services in using, for example, BPEL4WS (*Business Process Execution Language for Web Services*) [6], [3].

To develop Learning Object Web services (LOWS), a content provider has to implement an interface that supports Web services. There are several different possibilities to provide LOs as Web services [31], [37]. In our work, we choose a technique detailed as follows: the content is stored in a NXDB or in an XML file, it is extracted and enriched by a presentation specification; a SOAP message is constructed and sent back to the authoring OSES suite, finally another service is in charge of publishing parsed data in the LCMS.

2.3 Combining Web Services with AJAX Technology

As mentioned above, usual e-Learning Web-based applications essentially submit forms, exercise results or questions answer, completed by a learner. The e-Learning Web-based server responds by sending back a new web page, at each request time. AJAX is a web application development technique that uses a mix of modern web technologies to provide a more interactive user interface. These technologies are JavaScript, HTML, CSS (*Cascading Style Sheets*), DOM (*Document Object Model*), XML, XSLT, and *XMLHttpRequest* [33]. AJAX applications can send requests to the Web server-engine to retrieve only the data that is needed, usually in using SOAP messages or some other XML-based Web services dialect.

LOs, which consist of exercises and quizzes, have a major importance in e-Learning platforms as they make it possible to keep students challenged when taking a course. The exercise concept is therefore an essential ingredient in the assimilation of knowledge. Existing e-Learning systems provide different means of exercise construction in the form of QTI type questionnaires [15]. Most of e-Learning systems also include tools that help in assessing the effectiveness of student learning. Students can be invited to answer questions, solve a problem or write a computer program. These kinds of exercises lacks for interactivity and immediate feed-back to the student: an immediate comment, an immediate suggestion or an evaluation of its answer are not offered. In our conception, the exercise is an exclusive LO that ensures interactivity and an immediate answer. This becomes possible by applying AJAX technique on the e-Learning client-side, where the learner interacts with a Web browser.

The core idea behind AJAX is to make the communication with the server asynchronous, so that data is transferred to a background process. AJAX-enabled applications rely on a new asynchronous communication method between the client and the server. This method is implemented as a JavaScript engine, loaded on the client side during the initial page loading. This engine serves as a mediator that sends only relevant data to the server and subsequently processes server response to update the relevant page elements. In contrast, the traditional synchronous (*post back*) communication would require a full page reload every time data has to be transferred to or from the server [2]. Fig. 2 below illustrates the AJAX-Web application model:

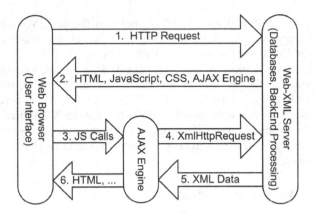

Fig. 2. AJAX Web Application Model

1. The user requests a specific URL.
2. The complete page is sent by the server to the client.
3. All subsequent requests are initiated as function calls to the AJAX engine.
4. The AJAX engine makes a request to the server [33].
5. The server processes the request and sends a response in XML format to the client. It contains only the data of the page elements that need to be changed. In most cases this data represents just a fraction of the total page markup.
6. The AJAX engine processes the server response, updates the relevant page content or performs another operation with the new data received from the server.

AJAX technique offers the possibility to invoke SOAP Web Services from within a Web browser. In the e-Learning client context this means a dynamic management of course page sequence, exercise sequence or question sequence.

The implementation of a pedagogical strategy relies on facilities for delivering and presenting course LOs from both traditional and adaptive ordering viewpoints. Traditional sequencing is most straightforward as the system delivers LOs according to the order defined by the course author. Adaptive sequencing manages LOs distribution according to students' answers to exercises or quizzes. In this case, this sequencing results from the nature of student actions and/or answers rather than being set on a pre-established order selected by a course author. In the adaptive approach, sequencing of course pages, exercises, or questions is never static and is always driven by student capabilities [24]. A Web service is responsible for the guided generation and the update of the content sequence invoked via AJAX.

2.4 E-Learning Systems: Architecture and Standards

The purpose of e-Learning interoperability standards is to provide standardized data structures and communications protocols for e-Learning objects. When these standards are incorporated into vendor products, users of e-Learning can purchase content and system components from multiple vendors, based on some quality criteria and appropriateness, and also the confidence that interoperability is ensured [12]. Learning standards can be organized into five categories as follows [23]:

- *Metadata*: learning content must be labeled to support the indexing, storage, search, and retrieval of LOs by multiple tools across multiple repositories. Data used for this purpose are referred to as Learning Object Metadata (LOM) [10].
- *Content Packaging*: content packaging specifications (SCORM) [1] and standards (IMS) [4] allow courses to be transported from one system to another.
- *Learner Profile*: learner profile information can include personal data, learning plans, learning history, accessibility requirements, certifications and degrees, assessments of knowledge and the status of participation in current learning.
- *Learner Registration*: learner registration information allows learning delivery and administration components to know what offerings should be made available to a learner [4].
- *Content Communication*: when content is launched, there is a need to communicate learner data and previous learner activities [1].

An e-Learning architecture consists of three components: access tools, learning applications and the underlying network infrastructure [7].

- *Access tools* ensure the availability of learning resources. They provide a variety of audiences with convenient access to courses, briefing sessions, white papers, multimedia and online tests.
- *Learning applications* fall into four broad categories: business operations, content management, delivery management and LMS.

Fig. 3 below illustrates how various elements of the system might work together. It describes a simple functional model for an e-Learning application environment. This model provides a visual representation of the components that make up an e-Learning environment and the objects that must be passed among these components. SCORM defines a highly generalized model of a LMS as a suite of *Services* that manage the delivery and tracking of learning content to a learner. But it does not specify the LMS functionality. The functional model proposed in [16] is strongly influenced by the SCORM model where two different platforms are defined: LCMS and LMS.

LMS and LCMS really have two very different functions [8]. The primary objective of a LMS is to manage learners, in keeping track of their progresses and performances across all types of training activities. At the opposite, a LCMS manages the content and it is a multi-user environment where end-users and developers can create, store, reuse, manage and deliver LOs from a central database. The use of standardized learning metadata structures plus standardized learning content import and export formats also allows LOs to be created and shared by multiple tools and e-Learning software. To ensure interoperability across systems, LCMS is designed in compliance with standard specifications for content metadata, content packaging, and content communication [23]. E-Learning platforms, based on LMS or LCMS, and their functionalities resemble one another to a large extent. Recent standardization efforts [10], [1], [14] in e-Learning concentrate on LOs reuse, but not on the reuse of application functionalities [31], [17].

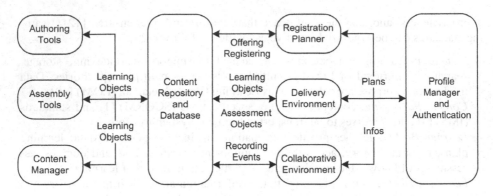

Fig. 3. E-Learning Functional Model (*adopted from [11]*)

In our work we consider that the functionalities of a LMS can be included in a LCMS to acquire a broader interoperability and the reuse of mandatory components and functionalities. Then, we complement the system with some Web service-based functionality to cover most of the functions that an e-Learning environment should provide. These functions are built on the hypothesis that a typical LCMS is a collection of activities or processes that interact with authors and learners. We subdivide the main functionalities of a LCMS into a number of stand-alone applications. For this reason we include additional functionality in an open source LCMS, which is implemented as a set of Web services.

Some solutions, such as described in [31], suggest a complete decomposition (unbundling) of a LMS or LCMS into a number of stand-alone components, which can then be implemented as services. To fulfill specific application requirements, a composition of chosen services is made on demand in some enterprise-based integration software. This unbundling process is not an easy task; besides it may impose extra requirements at the implementation and deployment levels. In adopting free and open source components, we believe that we provide a flexible method that allows a high level of abstraction at the design level, and many choices at the implementation one. Our approach, leverages of many existing open source LMS or LCMS, some of them being already adopted by universities or companies. Besides, including new or complementary functionalities is always based on free and open source java-based software components and interfaces. Their integration with a selected LCMS is performed via XML-based free solutions. As a result, this integration is made possible for any Web-based e-Learning system.

3   Service Oriented Architecture for LCMS

In this section we discuses our proposal for learning content and applications integration. We also describe our Web services-based e-Learning platform, still under development. Work described in this section is part of a research project, supported by the French AUF or *Agence Universitaire de la Francophonie* (www.auf.org).

3.1 Learning Content and Applications Integration

A central piece of the system we are currently building is our XESOP open source software [18], [19]. XESOP provides a flexible XML-based suite of tools for author customization, editing, storage and publication of LOs compliant with existing e-Learning standards (e.g., SCORM, IMS, and LOM).

Depending on course specificity, e.g., a math course, an author can represent diagrams, mathematical formulas or data in tables. It is well recognized that material consisting of figures or tables is worth a long discourse and is of a great pedagogical value [29]. For these reasons we developed a MathML editor for mathematical expressions, a SVG editor for vector graphics creation, a schema for table generation, a SMIL editor for multimedia presentations, and a QTI editor for student's progression evaluation. In this case, XML is used for encoding non-textual information [26] such as vector graphics, mathematical expressions, synchronized multimedia documents, complex forms, etc. For encoding textual information and content assembly, an XML semantic editor is used and a tree structure of a generic learning document is generated, while a validation grammar of XML Schema type is used [16].

Formatted texts, diagrams, formulas, tables and images are the basic structure of most learning materials. In our authoring suite, binary data of multimedia content is embedded directly into the XML course data itself. As a result, the course collection can be managed easily since all materials relating to the course are stored in a single XML collection. During the editing process, if the user inserts an image or any binary data into the edited content, the semantic editor will encode it using Base64 encoding method (RFC2045, RFC3548). The encoded binary is surrounded by XML tags marking its filename, content type and encoding method. For example, `<image filename="name" type="gif|jpg|png" code="Base64">` ... `</image>` tags can be used for inserting an image into the course content. Currently three image formats are supported: JPG, GIF, and PNG.

Once created, a course can be saved as an XML document and shared by making local copies, or in using HTTP protocols in the Internet environment. That does not imply the creation of a course warehouse, ready to be shared by several LMS/LCMS systems. According to the evolution of the course, authors or teachers may need to modify its contents. Therefore, the correct operation of a collaborative authoring system imposes the storage of learning collections, possibly in an appropriate database, for a better re-use and diffusion of these documents. The choice of an appropriate database is essential: we have chosen eXist [13], a native XML database which allows the storage of XML documents in their native format. Our choice, in opposition to that of a relational database, is explained by the nature of learning documents which are in general of narrative types, i.e., document-centric and not data-centric. Although relational database products today provide built-in XML document and query support, native XML databases are arguably the best choice for metadata storage. As far as query language is concerned, IMS recommends XQuery [35].

To achieve maximum flexibility, XML is used for internal representation of the learning material. A large number of media-rich contents can be stored using the abundant set of available XML schemas. Also in providing proper XSLT [36] transformation files, the XML content can be presented in many forms, such as HTML for web-based learning or PDF for printing and off-line learning and than published in a LCMS via Web services.

An exercise service is provided by a RDE (*Remote Development Environment*). In our vision, an exercise is an exclusive LO that ensures interactivity and an immediate answer. The real time execution of the exercise is associated with a Web service-based framework. The meaning of this approach resides in the student autonomy towards an operating system while bringing an effective solution to the phases of set up, compiler configuration and licenses management [18].

To implement this *semantic-oriented authoring suite*, a cooperative open Web services-based environment is proposed.

3.2 Web Services Implementation

Web Services [6] are self-contained, self-describing, and present a modular XML message-centric approach, that allow building loosely coupled, highly distributed e-Learning systems [37]. Web Services are a good technology for ensuring the interoperability of e-Learning systems for three main reasons [23]:

1. The information exchanged between e-Learning systems like LOM [10] and IMS content packaging [14] all have standard XML [32] binding.
2. Web Services architecture [3] is a language independent platform. It can promote interoperability and extensibility among various applications, platforms, frameworks and workflows.
3. Web Services provide a unified programming model [9] for the development and usage of Internet Services. As a result, the choice of network technology can be made entirely transparent to the developer and consumer of the service.

A Web service application interaction is quite simple as defined by W3C [34]. A requester entity might connect and use a Web service as follows: the requester and provider entities become known to each other; the requester and provider entities agree on the service description and semantics that will manage the interaction between them; the requester and provider entities exchange messages. Some of these steps may be automated, others may be performed manually. The Web services may be implemented on LCMS and then includes: authoring, content managing and publishing, remote exercising, service discovering, etc.

In our system, all LOs, contents and applications are built as services with XML front-end and described with standardized metadata [10], [1], and [14] so the service requesters are able to discover and match these services with their needs. Once they are built as services, they are described by a WSDL document to let requesters know how to invoke them. WSDL file and XML metadata are wrapped in a SOAP message that will be sent to the WSDL-SOAP server (like UDDI server). Through this UDDI, Learning Service Requester (LSR) are able to find Learning Objects Services (LOS), Learning Contents Services (LCS) or Learning Service Applications (LSA) by sending a SOAP request over HTTP and then facilitates the loose connection between two applications.

As shown in Fig. 4, the learning-centric data and the management-centric data are clearly separated. LOs are developed and stored in a native XML database (NXDB), while information relevant to learner personal data, learner profiles, course maps, LOs sequencing, information presentation and general user data is stored in a relational database (RDB). The database interfaces interact with Web services via SOAP messages.

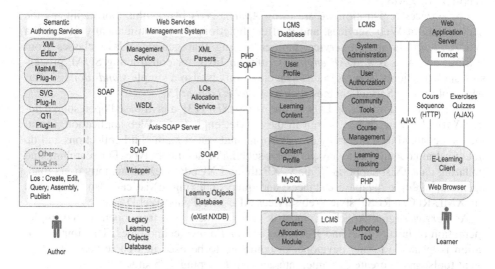

Fig. 4. Service-Oriented System Architecture

The left side of Fig. 4, highlights OSES, our *Open Semantic Editor Suite*, while the right side illustrates *Web-based and open source LCMS*.

The interconnection of these two parts is carried out by Web services. Thus external applications can be integrated with a LMS/LCMS while being based on the dynamicity and the flexibility of Web services. For a service-oriented integration with typically Web-based LCMS, Web services are the right technology to use. The communication of different learning applications using SOAP has already been suggested in [28]. The IMS Global Learning Consortium [14] recently underlined the interoperability of SOAP-based services.

Scenarios. The left side of Fig. 4 highlights also the author's interactions with *OSES services*. Thus he can store created *LOs* in the *NXDB* or publish a course in a suitable format (XML, XHTML, and PDF), using *WSMS services*, in the LCMS *Learning Content Database* (RDB). WSMS can help him to reach pedagogical content, via suitable wrappers, in an external *Legacy Learning Objects Database* (LLOD). The data integration process is made within *OSES services*.

The right side of the same figure illustrates user's interactions with *LCMS* via an *e-Learning client*. The learner can be registered and follow an already on-line published course in the *Learning Content Database*. To seek complementary elements the student can address himself to the LOs native database or given LOs from an external LLOD via WSMS. Based on the potential for Web services in data integration the wrapped result set is send in a suitable format to the learner browser.

Implementation Details. For a proof of concept, we are using Dokeos[1], a LCMS based on PHP and MySQL as a storage back-end. An implementation of the LCMS interface via Web Services offers a high degree of flexibility and ease of use, in particular as SOAP libraries for PHP already exist, which leads to an easily extensible Web-based LCMS.

For services registration we are using *Apache Axis* [4], as this tool facilitates the deployment of Web Services, and it offers functionality to automatically generate a WSDL description of a service, emitter tooling that generates Java classes from WSDL, etc. Axis is a *SOAP engine* (written in Java, for constructing SOAP processors such as clients, servers, gateways, etc). Axis is also a simple *stand-alone server*, which plugs into Servlet engines such as *Apache Tomcat* [5].

For storing and managing LOs we are using *eXist* [13], a java-based open source *native XML database*. It can be run in the Servlet engine of a Web application. Documents are stored as a hierarchy of collections that can contain child collections and do not constrain documents to any particular schema or document type. For searching and updating data eXist supports XQuery, XPath, and XUpdate. eXist supports users management, multiple database instances, and query indexing. eXist can also be invoked via XML-RPC, a REST-style Web services API, SOAP, and WebDAV.

As *Servlet engine* Apache Tomcat is used. Tomcat is a free, open-source implementation of Java Servlet and JSP (*Java Server Pages*) technologies. This implementation is available to any developer or company to be used in web servers, development tools, and to create dynamic, interactive e-Learning web sites.

3.3 Use Case Scenario

In this section, we describe some sequence diagrams related to a use case initiated by a course author. In Fig. 5, the author populates an XML content. Once the content is submitted, it is sent to Tomcat *Servlet engine*. The Axis SOAP client API is used to create and send a SOAP RPC request message that specifies that the *submit* method of the XML content should be invoked with the *Content* object as the parameter. When this message is received by the Axis SOAP runtime the request is forwarded to the *database repository service*. After the request is processed the response is sent back to the Axis SOAP runtime. The return value is then encapsulated in a SOAP message and sent back to the *Servlet engine*. Than a response message is generated and sent back to the *author suite*.

As stated in the previous section, it is possible to invoke Web services in the *AJAX model* by using SOAP for message exchange. Here, we describe and illustrate the generic framework for integrating AJAX into browser-based Web Service applications. There are two main components in the integration architecture: the Web-based e-Learning client and Web Services-based e-Learning system. For a Web-based e-Learning client this model offers a dynamic management of page, exercise or question sequences. The *client browser* sends a request to the *Servlet engine*, which in turn makes a request to the *Axis SOAP server*, where the Web service resides. The response from the *Web service* is then transformed by the *Servlet engine*, and presented to the client browser.

---

[1] www.dokeos.com

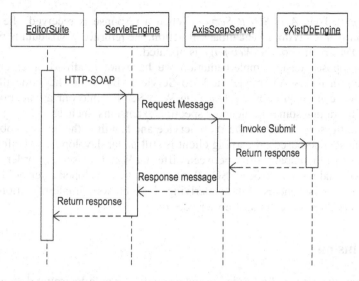

Fig. 5. Web services system interactions initiate by the course author

In Fig. 6, a Javascript code running within the *Web browser* creates an instance of the *XMLHttpRequest* and a function that serves as an asynchronous *callback*. The object is then used to perform an HTTP request to the *Servlet engine*. Than a Web

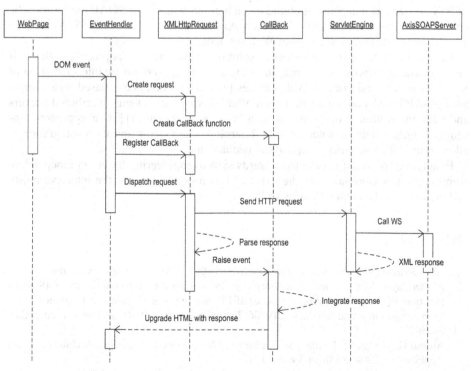

Fig. 6. XMLHttpRequest Object Functions (*adapted from [20]*)

service is called via *Axis SOAP Server*. When a response is received, the callback function is invoked. Within the callback function, the returned XML data is processed and the DOM structure of the *Web page* is updated.

In our proposed design implementation we have not modified or extended any technologies in the AJAX model or Web Services. By using the same theoretical standards, we can integrate any e-Learning Web Service into our application framework just by doing some application specific extensions such as creating requests according to the service API of the Web Service and handling the returned objects.

Our Web service-based e-Learning client is still under development. Unfortunately there exist some incompatibilities between different Web browsers. In order to invoke Web services and reliably process SOAP messages, we developed a script library that abstracts the inconsistencies of the underlying XML browser implementations, allowing us to work directly with the Web services data.

4 Conclusion

In this paper, we proposed a service-oriented model for an e-Learning data and application integration system. We adopted Web services technology in order to provide a flexible integration model in which all the learning components and applications are well defined and loosely connected.

As a result, we suggested a SOA platform, where the reuse of both learning materials and application functionalities is supplied. Components and functionalities of the LCMS are seen as independent entities which communicate via SOAP messages. The generic integration architecture, based on AJAX technique for a LCMS Web-based client, can be adapted to any kind of Web services.

Recall that existing interoperability solutions advocate two approaches: the first one is oriented towards the integration of the e-Learning systems by intermediation of SOAP interfaces and external Web services [30]; the second one is based on a distributed SOAP-based communication with Web services on several distributed servers and their integration is orchestrated by a Workflow system [31]. Our approach concentrates on the independence of the e-Learning components and their integration is allowed by a Web services composition mechanism.

Finally, our proposal is oriented towards system engineering based on independent components to ensure not only the reuse of Learning Objects but the interoperability and the reuse of the applications as well.

References

1. ADL Sharable Content Object Reference Model (SCORM) 2004, http://www.adlnet.org/.
2. Ahmet Sayar, Marlon Pierce, Geoffrey Fox, Integrating AJAX Approach into GIS Visualization Web Services, Proceedings of IEEE International Conference on Internet and Web Applications and Services ICIW'06, February 23-25, 2006 Guadeloupe, French Caribbean.
3. Alonso G., F. Casati, H. Kuno, V. Machiraju, Web Services – Concepts, Architectures and Applications. 2004. Springer-Verlag. Berlin.
4. Apache Axis, Web services-Axis, Available at: http://ws.apache.org/axis/index.html.

5. Apache Software Foundation, Apache Tomcat, Available at: http://tomcat.apache.org/.
6. Booth, D., Haas, H., et al. (eds.), Web Services Architecture, W3C Working Draft 11 February 2004. Available at: http://www.w3.org/TR/2004/NOTE-ws-arch-20040211/.
7. Calvo, Rafael A., E-Learning Infrastructure, Available at: http://www.weg.ee.usyd.edu.au/courses/ebus5002/ slides/6.1-elearning.pdf.
8. Chapman B. and B. Hall, Learning Content Management Systems, Comparative Analysis of Systems Used to Construct, Organize and Re-Use Learning Objects, September 2001.
9. Chauvet J. M., Services Web avec SOAP, WSDL, UDDI, ebXML..., Eyrolles, 2002.
10. IEEE LOM, Draft Standard for Learning Object Metadata, IEEE 1484.12.1-2002.
11. E-learning Application Infrastructure, White paper of Sun Microsystems, 2002.
12. E-learning Interoperability Standards, White paper of Sun Microsystems.
13. eXist, Native XML Database, Available at: http://www.exist-db.org.
14. IMS, "IMS Content Packaging Best Practice Guide", IMS Global Learning Consortium, Inc., Version 1.1.3, June 2003.
15. IMS Question & Test Interoperability Specification, Available at: http://www.imsglobal.org/question/.
16. Ivan Madjarov, Abdelkader Betari, Un éditeur XML sémantique pour objets pédagogiques stockés dans une base de données XML native, In : Les Nouvelles Technologies de la Répartition NOTERE 2004, Saidia, Maroc, p. 218-233, Juin 2004.
17. Ivan Madjarov, Des services Web pour le e-Learning, in: Revue électronique sur la recherche en TIC (eTI-2005), n° 1, ISSN 1114-8802, 28 Octobre 2005. Available at: http://www.revue-eti.net/document.php?id=354.
18. Ivan Madjarov, Abdelkader Betari, Zohra Bakkoury. Web Service Based Remote Development Environment for an e-Learning System. ICHSL5/CAPS5, Vol. Human System Learning Who is in control, Europia, Paris, pp 79-95, November 2005.
19. Ivan Madjarov, Bogdan Shishedjiev, A Collaborative and Adaptive Authoring Environment for an e-Learning System, Proceedings of Second International Scientific Conference of Computer Science, October 2005, Chalkidiki, Greece.
20. James Snell, Call SOAP Web Services with Ajax, IBM, 2005.
21. Jesse James Garret, Ajax: A New Approach to Web Applications. Available at: http://www. adaptivepath.com/publications/essays/archives/000385.php.
22. Line Zine, Learning in the new economy, Available at: http://www.linezine.com/elearning.htm.
23. Liu, Xiaofei, An Implementation Architecture of An E-Learning System, Available at: http://www. site.uottawa.ca/~elsaddik/abedweb/publications/architecture.pdf.
24. Madjarov Ivan, Boucelma Omar, Betari Abdelkader. An Agent- and Service-Oriented e-Learning Platform. In: Wenyin Liu, Yuanchun Shi, Qing Li (Eds.): LNCS, Vol. 3143: Advances in Web-Based Learning - ICWL 2004: Third International Conference, Beijing, China, August 8-11, 2004, pages 27-34. Springer-Verlag Berlin Heidelberg, 2004.
25. Michael Derntl, Patterns for Person-Centred e-Learning, Ph.D. Thesis, Universität Wien, 2005, Available at: http://elearn.pri.univie.ac.at/derntl/diss/diss-derntl.pdf.
26. Quint V., Vatton I. Techniques for Authoring Complex XML Documents, ACM symposium on Document engineering, Milwaukee, Wisconsin, USA, p 115 – 123, 2004.
27. Richard Hull, Jianwen Su, Tools for Design of Composite Web Services, SIGMOD 2004 June 13-18, 2004, Paris, France, ACM 1-58113-859-8.
28. S. Wilson, Gluing learning applications together with SOAP, Bangor, U.K.: Center for Educational Technology Interoperability Standards, 2001.
29. Vercoustre A. M., McLean A. Reusing Educational Material for Teaching and Learning: Current Approaches and Directions. CSIRO, Australia, 2003.

30. Victor Pankratius, Olivier Sandel, Wolffried Stucky, Retrieving Content with Agents in Web Service E-Learning Systems, In: AI, IFIP WG12.5 - First IFIP Conference on Artificial Intelligence Applications and Innovations (AIAI). Toulouse, France, August 2004.
31. Vossen G., and P. Westerkamp, "E-Learning as a Web Service", In: 7th International Conference on Database Engineering and Applications (IDEAS), IEEE Computer Society Press, Hong Kong, China, 2003, 242–249.
32. W3C-XML, Extensible Markup Language, Available at: http://www.w3.org/XML/.
33. W3C, The XMLHttpRequest Object, W3C Working Draft 05 April 2006, Available at: http://www.w3.org/TR/ 2006/WD-XMLHttpRequest-20060405/.
34. W3C, Web Services Architecture, W3C Working Group Note, 11 February 2004.
35. W3C-XQuery, XQuery 1.0: An XML Query Language W3C Working Draft 04 April 2005. Available at: http://www.w3.org/TR/2005/WD-xquery-20050404/.
36. W3C-XSLT, XSL Transformations (XSLT) Version 2.0 W3C Working Draft 4 April 2005. Available at: http://www.w3.org/TR/2005/WD-xslt20-20050404/.
37. Zhengfang Xu, Zheng Yin, Abdulmotaleb El Saddik, A Web Services Oriented Framework for Dynamic E-Learning Systems, CCGEI 2003, Montreal, May 2003.

Using Virtual Learners' Behaviours to Help the Development of Educational Business Games

Nicolas Manin, Sébastien George, and Patrick Prévot

ICTT Research Laboratory, INSA de Lyon
21 avenue Jean Capelle, 69621 Villeurbanne Cedex, France
Nicolas.Manin@laposte.net
{Sebastien.George, Patrick.Prevot}@insa-lyon.fr

Abstract. Educational business games can be of a great help for initial and continuous learning, in the engineering field among others. These games have as major asset the possibility for learners to intervene or act as they wish. Nevertheless, there are numerous possible paths in such games. Designing the appropriate game structure and defining the optimum parameters so as to achieve the pedagogical objectives of business games are not straightforward. Presently, only users feedback allows the adjustments required and the appropriate structure modification needs to be identified. Waiting for feedback may take months and leave users a negative appreciation of the product. In this project, our aim is to conceive a "Simulator of Learners' Behaviour" to ensure the pedagogical quality of educational games. In order to provide realistic players' behaviours, mathematical and economical methods are used.

1 Introduction

During the designing of a computer environment for educational purposes, it is impossible to consider all the possibilities of learners' behaviours. Educational games are so complex that adjusting and finalising them are particularly difficult. It is thus interesting to possess a system that simulates learners' behaviour so as to statistically evaluate the performance of a game without having to wait for an extensive user feedback that could take several months. The objective of this research work is to design a generic simulator of learners' behaviour that can be instantiated for different business games.

In this paper, we shall firstly present educational business game principles and the context of our work. We shall then define virtual learners and a method to simulate real learners' behaviour by using metadata and mathematical methods. At last, we suggest a model named SIMCA which can be adapted to several games, and describe its framework and its functioning.

2 Educational Business Games

Educational business games are pedagogical applications that teach people several aspects of the functioning of a company, of a business or industry. During the past

W. Nejdl and K. Tochtermann (Eds.): EC-TEL 2006, LNCS 4227, pp. 287–301, 2006.

fifteen years, the ICTT laboratory of the *INSA de Lyon* has gathered a lot of experience in the designing of business games [1], [2], [3]. Most of these environments have been developed as group projects by 4th year students (master level) of the Industrial Engineering department under the supervision of research lecturers of the laboratory. These business games have then been used for training in this department and others at INSA. The ICTT laboratory can thus directly gather a large quantity of feedback.

The use of educational business games make up a relevant training method for engineering students. The objective of these games is to establish a virtual environment in which we can artificially recreate on a smaller scale (time, space and actions) the conditions that allow learners to find themselves in a context similar to the situations they will face in their professional life. Business games cover a wide range of subjects (finance, commerce, industrial maintenance, collaborative problem solving...). As a variant of role-playing games, business games confront learner groups, usually associated to different companies, to each other. Endowed with specific powers or skills (tools, competences, protections...), players must take up the challenge and attain goals such as decreasing the stock level, increasing productivity, winning market shares, etc.

2.1 Educational Business Games Models

As researchers, one of our objectives is to situate the development of business games in an organized and structured approach. The goal is to define a common root that make it possible to speed up the development of specific games and at the same time benefit from a common infrastructure that allows designers to create, refine and extend these games without having to start from scratch each time. Our approach is generic and aims at the identification of invariants in order to define a design technology which creates a genuine workshop for configuration and as development help for this type of pedagogical products. The identification of invariants has led us to elaborate the following models: the conceptual, the dynamic, the pedagogical and the computer models.

The Conceptual Model. It is based on three fundamental elements in the game structuring:
- the attractor (i.e. "educational bait"): a challenge that must be taken up by the learner,
- the case: real-life contextual situation (defining the rules, environment ...),
- cognitive places: knowledge, concepts, know-how, behaviour, competences... which are objects of the training. The learner is not necessarily conscious of these places but he is compelled to pass these places to take up the challenge proposed to him;

The Dynamic Model. It consists in cutting up the scenario into phases:
- discovery phase,
- analysis and diagnosis phase,
- strategy construction phase,
- decision-making and implementation phase,
- assessment and evaluation phase;

The Pedagogical Model. It integrates the animator role as from the original design of the game:
- briefing sessions, to start the game or phases,
- debriefing and sharing sessions for analysis,
- multimedia sessions that alternate the conceptual and action sections;

The Computer Model. It is based on a multi-agent approach for the following reasons:
- In multi-agent systems, as in games, acts are the structuring elements of the system,
- The cooperative aspects of educational business games dictate a distributed vision,
- Business games must be able to adapt themselves to modifications to the structure or environment brought about by the author.

2.2 Research Issues on Business Game Designing

During the designing of an educational business game, it is impossible to predict all the possibilities in learners' behaviour (navigation, activity choice, answers given to questions, course or route taken...). The richness of this type of educational games makes their realisation difficult (in terms of parameters, game structure, need for interaction...). The only way of creating such a game is to make actual learners test the game and then correct it according to feedback. From experience, we know that this process takes about two years to achieve a finalised version of the game (from a pedagogical point of view). This long testing time causes the lost of product credibility. This happens particularly if the learners having the "appropriate behaviour" (in terms of learning objectives) are not the ones who are rewarded...

Our research objective is thus to suggest models and tools for testing the games prior to their use. To sum up, we aim at designing a simulator of learners' behaviour to test the game's parameters. This simulator can be considered as a test bed sufficiently universal to test thoroughly the game progress with virtual learners (with random actions and events) so as to statistically evaluate how far the pedagogical objectives have been achieved. This solution will be used in conjunction with the user-centered and participatory design approaches. So the final solution will be a sort of hybrid approach that involves both virtual players and working with real users.

The closest work on which we can base ourselves are about virtual players [4], [5] and companions [6], [7], [8]. As in these works, we must define players'/learners' behaviour and a mechanism to retrieve information about what happens all through the game session so that the simulator can act consequently. However, the needs of our learners' behaviour simulator are quite different. In particular, we do not want to create a simulator dedicated to a specific game but to design a simulator for a class of business games.

2.3 Study of Two Business Games

To come up with a model for the simulator, two educational business games have been studied and analysed. The "maintenance game" (in the field of industrial maintenance) and the game called "Garde à Vue" (French for "police custody" – concerning the law field) have been chosen. These two games, both event-based, are nevertheless different enough in their objectives and the knowledge to acquire. This study has contributed to our researches on desired features, the constants and some of the parameters necessary to design a learners' behaviour simulator for educational business games.

These two games are board games with well-defined steps or "squares" and events (with various consequences) that take place at each step. At any moment, in order to play, one must be able to know his or her location (which step he/she is at), his or her game score or the amount of money he or she has, or the available objects or accessories. Hence, the simulator must be aware of the values of variables that indicate the status of the game and that of the player/learner. As for interaction, there are situations where choices are possible (multiple-choice questions, purchases, sales, etc.). These choices of course have an impact on the rest of the game. To be able to make theses choices, the simulator must include a game strategy. That is, he must know the player's objectives and the types of player behaviour to obtain these objectives. For example, in the two games considered, there are means of avoiding risks and decreasing losses or sanctions. There are also actions that have long-term or short-term effects. In the two games, there are both random stages/steps and default ones. In these cases, the simulator passively undergoes what happens to it and is not given any choice. The values of variables and the rest of the game change subsequently.

3   Defining Virtual Learners

The objective is to define virtual learners able to take decisions in business games like human learners. In this part, we will present how to simulate their behaviour, with the combination of two methods: one based on the strategic sense of the game actions, and the other based on the game events and their influence on the objectives.

3.1   Strategies-Based Behaviour

We have defined a method to simulate learners' behaviour using game strategies and player profiles. We explain these strategies and profiles below before discussing how behaviours are simulated.

Game Strategies. Strategies are used to annotate actions of the games with behaviour criteria. We have been able to identify the following strategies partly by observing the use of educational business games by actual learners. Some can coexist (but at different intensities or proportions) while others are totally opposed one to another.

- favoured *term* (long, medium or short),
- type of *interaction* with the other players (competition, collaboration...),
- need for *adventure* (explore – active , discover – passive...),
- *risk taking* (maximum, average or minimum),
- *enthusiasm* (maximum, average, minimum – "endure" the game),
- *time* spent on the game/*duration* of the game (playing for the longest time or trying to end the game before the other players),
- *desire to win* (winning at all cost or doing everything to lose).

Player Profiles. In business games, some players seem to use similar strategies in the way of solving problems: some are careful while others take more risks; some are more helpful than others, etc. Such behaviours are characteristic of some well-known profiles:

- the *aggressive* player can do anything in order to win the game;
- the *ambitious/calculating* player. Everything he does is motivated by victory;
- the *curious/inquisitive* player wants to learn and to explore the game levels;
- the *careless/thoughtless* player is one who has the necessary knowledge but who does not pay much attention to what he does;
- the *go-ahead/audacious* player does not have a strategy and does not care about risks;
- the *kamikaze* player does all he can to sabotage his chances of winning;
- the *neutral/average/standard* player does not take lots of risks but is not excessively cautious;
- the *nonchalant* player is not really a type of user but is rather a type of behaviour that we want to simulate. It can be that of a person who is not much involved in the game and who will make random choices or that of a program module that needs to test a game's reactions;
- the *hurried* player wants to have the maximum gains as quickly as possible;
- the *cautious* player is the one who takes the minimum risks.

Simulating Behaviour. Each virtual learner has a player's profile, and each game action is annotated with strategic marks. During the game, when a virtual player must choose between different actions, strategic marks of each solution are compared with the strategic preferences of his profile. Then, he can choose the action which is the most similar to his profile. For instance, a cautious-defined virtual player will choose safety actions, while an aggressive-defined opponent will choose instead hazardous actions. This is a method of behaviour simulation that can lead to varied, realistic behaviours. However, it implies that each action of the game has a strategic sense.

The quality of the simulated behaviours depends on the quality of the actions marks. Defining them is a difficult task, because the strategic value of an action can be differently interpreted by people. Therefore, these marks are also the expression of their creator's own judgment, thus the decision of virtual players could not be entirely objective. Another problem is that the strategic value of an action cannot be judged alone, but the whole context and its consequences must be considered. For example, an action is dangerous when it can lead to bad situations. If there is no bad situation, then the same action should no more be considered dangerous. Details on the simulation of behaviours can be found in the article George *et al.* [9].

3.2   Events-Based Behaviour

It appears that this strategic-based behaviour is centered on the learner's psychology. Virtual players take decision following their psychological preferences, in a reactive process that isn't directly linked with the winning conditions. Do aggressive-defined

Table 1. This table matches game strategies and player profiles. The parameters on the horizontal axis represent the strategies and the standard profiles are on the vertical axis. The sections marked with a cross specify the strategies corresponding to each learner or player type.

Player profiles	Player strategies																				
	Term			Interaction			Need for adventure			Risk-taking			Enthusiasm			Time/Duration			Desire to win		
	long	middle	short	competition	collaboration	independent	maximum	average	minimum	maximum	average	minimum	maximum	average	minimum	maximum	average	minimum	maximum	indifferent	none
Aggressive			X	X						X	X		X				X		X		
Ambitious	X			X			X						X	X			X		X		
Curious	X				X		X			X			X				X			X	
Careless			X		X					X	X		X				X			X	
Go-ahead			X	X						X	X		X						X	X	
Kamikaze			X			X				X	X			X		X					X
Neutral		X		X				X			X			X			X			X	
Nonchalant			X			X				X	X			X		X				X	
Hurried			X			X				X	X		X						X	X	
Cautious	X				X		X					X		X			X			X	

virtual players must have a suicidal behaviour in their actions, while sometimes the danger is so evident for human learners? Since the virtual learners are also players, they have to pay attention to game objectives.

Freud used to distinguish instinct and reason in the human psychology. For philosopher Bergson, in 1907, instinct and the intelligence represent two solutions of the same problem. We have thought about reproducing this duality in the decision making, providing virtual players instinctive (strategies-based) and rational (events-based) decision units.

Some Theoretical Concepts of Decision. To define a player's behaviour centered on the game events, we have looked at mathematical and economical works, such the Game Theory of John von Neumann and Oskar Morgenstern [10] or the Prospect Theory of Daniel Kanheman and Amos Tversky [11]. We will present here some concepts used in these famous theories that should serve to simulate the virtual player's decision-making process.

Utility Function. In most games, in order to win, the players have to maximize the values of specific resources (e.g. score, money), and/or to minimize other values (e.g. time). While attempting to achieve game objectives, players are attracted by positive events that tend to maximize or minimize their resources. So the evaluation of the variation of a resource in a game event can be expressed in term of attraction or repulsion, like the strategic preferences: this is the utility function. We will use specific utility functions to simulate players' choice between several solutions.

Expected Value. If X is a discrete random variable which can take x_1, x_2... values with p_1, p_2... associated probabilities, the formula of the expected value of X is:

$$E(X) = \sum_i p_i (x_i) . \tag{1}$$

Using this mathematical formula as a utility formula is a very simple method to have objective and evaluated comparisons of game solutions. For example, if a virtual player's objective is to maximize the gain, he calculates the expected value of gain of each solution, and then chooses the solution with the highest value.

However, using the expected value as the utility function is not a sufficient solution. The simulated behaviours are different from that observed on real players – what about the popularity of national lotteries in spite of negative expected gain values? Worst, they can lead to paradoxes, such as the Saint Petersburg's paradox.

The Diminishing Marginal Utility. The mathematician Daniel Bernoulli solved the Saint Petersburg's paradox by introducing psychology parameters. In this theory, the attraction for a gain is not only linked to its value, but also to its utility for the receiver according to his/her initial resources (i.e. the marginal utility). For example, 10 € have more utility for a player who has 10 € than for a player who has 1000 €. In the first case, the 10 € gain represents a 100% gain, and in the second one, only a 1% gain. The more resource someone has, the less s/he feels utility to have more: this is the diminishing marginal utility.

Risk Aversion. When someone plays a double-or-quits game, this player must choose between an assured gain and a lottery with the same expected value of gain. Experience shows that, in the majority of cases, he keeps the guaranteed gain: this is risk-aversion.

Introducing risk aversion to virtual player's profile will be a medium of giving them more realistic behaviour. To simulate the risk aversion, economics use convex functions such as the logarithmic function; however, since it is defined only for positive numbers, we can use another function, like the square root. So we modify the expected value formula to obtain the following utility formula:

$$U(X) = \sum_i p_i \sqrt{(x_i)} . \tag{2}$$

The utility of a 100 € gain X_1 is $U(X_1) = \sqrt{(100)} \approx 10$, whereas the utility of the gain X_2 of the corresponding double-or-quits lottery $L = \{(½; 200); (½; 0)\}$ is $U(X_2) = ½ \sqrt{(200)} + ½ \sqrt{(0)} \approx 7.071$. So the certain gain is more attractive for a risk-averse person.

Loss Aversion. It is a psychological concept which explains that loss-averse people are more sensible to a loss than to a gain, even if they have the same value. Like the risk aversion, adding loss aversion in the mechanism of decision-making is an opportunity to make virtual players' behaviour more realistic. To simulate it in the virtual players' decision, we use the following utility formula that inserts a multiplier coefficient to all losses' values:

$$U(X) = \sum_i p_i (y_i) + \sum_j q_j (\lambda z_j) . \tag{3}$$

The y_i are the positive values (gain) and p_i their probabilities, and the z_j are negative values (loss) and q_j their probabilities. λ is the loss aversion coefficient: $\lambda > 1$ for a loss aversion, $\lambda = 1$ for a loss neutrality, and $0 < \lambda < 1$ for a loss attraction.

Simulating Behaviour. All of these concepts could be used to simulate human players' behaviours. We combine each one of them in an ultimate utility function that will be used to calculate attraction/repulsion of game events. In this function, y_i are the positive values (gain) and p_i their probabilities, the z_j are negative values (loss) and q_j their probabilities, and λ is the loss aversion coefficient.

$$U(X) = \sum_i p_i \sqrt{(y_i)} + \sum_j q_j \sqrt{(\lambda\, z_j))}\,. \tag{4}$$

3.3 Coordinating Decisions

Virtual players, with both instinctive and rational decision units, dispose of two distinct solutions for the same problem. Decisions can be compatible, but they can also be opposite. Thus, players need an arbitration process to choose only one solution.

To avoid this problem, each decision unit won't provide only the most attractive solution, but the list of all solutions and their probabilities of choice, depending on their attraction or repulsion for the player. Then, an arbitration unit combines the two probabilities of each solution in a unique probability. An advantage of this probabilistic method is to define varied behaviours.

4   The SIMCA Model

We have defined a method to simulate virtual learners' behaviours for business games. Now, in this part, we describe the global functioning of the simulator. The designed model is named SIMCA ("*SIMulateur du Comportement d'Apprenants*" which means "simulator of learners' behaviour").

4.1 Global Functioning of a Simulation

The simulator is composed of an inference engine that contains functioning rules and parameters that describe behaviour characteristics of virtual players. Business games on which we experiment the simulator have a game engine separated from the graphical interface. In this way, the simulator does not use Human Computer Interface of business games but intercepts the messages coming from the game engine and sends some commands and actions directly. The global functioning of the SIMCA model is depicted in figure 1.

To use the simulator on a particular business game, the game administrator has to list all the important data of the game that will be used by the virtual learners (variables representing choices, game states, scores and players progress). This list is then given (1) to the simulator administrator who associates the parameters of the simulator with the game variables (2).

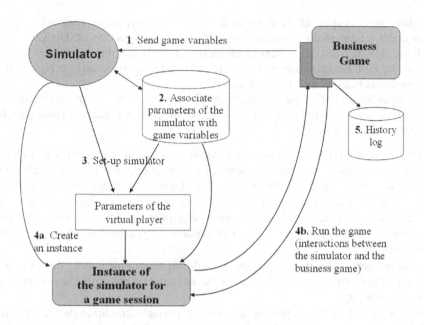

Fig. 1. The SIMCA Model

Before launching the simulator, the administrator chooses the parameters of the virtual player for a game session (3). He can choose among a set of existing players' profiles, those defined in the table 1, or specify a particular player profile by configuring the different strategies (interaction, need for adventure, risk-taking, etc...). He also defines the player's objectives policy.

Finally, an instance of the simulator is created from the game information and for a virtual player profile (4a). A game session could then be run. Some messages are then exchanged (4b) between the game (choices, events ...) and the simulator (decisions, actions ...). During the session, the simulator engine will interact with the virtual players when they will have to take decisions in order to reach the set goals and to follow their strategies.

Exchanged events are recorded in a history log (5) that aims to help the game designer to identify necessary modifications before the use of the game in real situation with learners. It should be noticed that the actual model does not take the interaction between learners into account.

4.2 Virtual Learners in the SIMCA Model

Virtual players are an essential component of the SIMCA model. We have previously defined their theoretical decision-making process. In this part, we describe how to integrate them and their decision process within the SIMCA architecture.

Metadata and Graphs of Actions. In the Game Theory, game trees are graphs in which nodes represent the situations, and edges the different moves. Decision takers use them, starting from the present situation (root), to choose the actions that can lead them to the best future situation. We want to use similar structures to represent the game metadata used by the virtual players.

We define graphs of actions as structures that contain both the strategy-related and event-related marks. Nodes and edges can be of different nature. There are four different kinds of nodes:

− *Decision nodes* (D-nodes) represent a decision situation, and signify a choice for the player. Their out edges represent all different possible actions. Each one is annotated with strategic marks related to the players' list of strategies (cf. part 3.1).
− *Events nodes* (E-nodes) contain a list of events in relation to objectives, in term of gain or loss (e.g. score: -50, time: +10). According to his objectives, the paths leading to some E-nodes will attract or repulse the player. They have no or only one out edge.
− *Random nodes* (R-nodes) represent a randomly-determined fork, for example a lottery. Their out edges correspond to the universe of possibilities, and each one has a probability.
− *Tests nodes* (T-nodes) represent a game or player's condition-determined fork. Their out edges correspond to the different possibilities of satisfaction of the condition, and each one has a list of conditions.

These graphs have an entrance node, always a decision node, since it represents the initial decision situation. The exits of graph are the events-nodes, as they are the final consequences of the chosen actions, but not all of them are exits.

One advantage of using graphs of actions is that virtual players take decisions with the metadata they contain. So a simulation can be run without the finished game, just with the data files of its graphs. That can be useful to test the game parameters before or during the implementation. Another advantage is that the game structure can be easily changed, just by replacing a graph file by another.

Virtual Learners' Decision. The decision-making process is the key of the simulation because it reflects the quality of the simulated behaviour. Each virtual learner has:

− a strategic profile: aggressive, ambitious, curious, careless…, or cautious.
− a list of objectives, in the form of a list of weighted resources/objectives, indicating their priority. Virtual players seek to maximize resources with positive weight (e.g. score), according to their value, and to minimize resources with negative weight (e.g. time). They are neutral to resources with null weight; this can be interesting to test only specific objectives of the game.

The virtual player evaluates the solutions of a problem starting from the D-node root of the corresponding graph of actions. Attraction( ) is the function that calculates the attraction of an action, node or event. The repulsion corresponds to a negative value of attraction. We say that the attraction of an action (a D-node's out edge) is equal to the attraction of the successor node. There is now two distinct evaluations of the solution, leading to two distinct decision attractions.

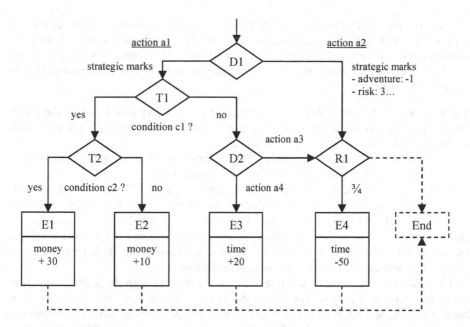

Fig. 2. An example of graph of actions. The virtual player who uses this graph is in a decision situation represented by the D1 decision node, where he can choose between the "a1" and the "a2" action. The first action leads to the T1 node and the other one will lead to the A1 node. D2 is another decision node, with "c" and "d" possible actions. T1 and T2 are test nodes representing respectively conditions "c1" and "c2". R1 is a random node; ¾ is an example of probability leading to E4 node. E1, E2, E3 and E4 are events nodes, with examples of events.

Instinctive Attractions. To express instinctive attractions, the virtual players use a simple comparison algorithm of the strategic marks. The marks of the starting D-node's out edges (i.e. possible actions) are all compared with the player's strategic preferences. If the strategy of the mark matches with the player profile, then the attraction will be positive; otherwise, it will be negative. All marks are compared one by one, and the sum of the attraction gives a global attraction value.

Rational Attractions. To express rational attractions, virtual players use a path graph algorithm. The attraction of an event is calculated using a utility function as previously defined. If the graph contains cycles, i.e. a situation leading to a previous one, then the algorithm could run in an infinite time. So it is important to define a limited number of covered nodes. We define the following recursive algorithm:

- attraction (E-node) = $\sum_i$ utility(event$_i$) + attraction (succ), where event$_i$ are the E-node's events.
- attraction (R-node) = $\sum_i$ probability(succ$_i$) * attraction (succ$_i$), where succ$_i$ are the R-node's successors.
- attraction (T-node) = attraction (succ$_i$), where succ$_i$ is the T-node's successor who completes all conditions of the node's out edge.
- attraction (D-node) = max(attraction (succ$_i$)), where succ$_i$ are the D-node's successors.

For example, from the node D1 in figure 2, the two possible solutions are the actions "a1" and "a2". If the conditions "c1" and "c2" are both completed, then the attraction of "a1" is : attraction (T1) = attraction (T2) = attraction (E1) = utility (money, +30); and the attraction of "a2" is : attraction (A1) = ¾ attraction (E4) = ¾ utility (time, -50).

The Choice of a Solution. After 1) the strategic marks comparison and 2) the graph exploring, each algorithm gives to virtual players an evaluation of each solution, such as this example list (independent of the fig. 2):

Solution "A": attraction = 0; solution "B": attraction = 15; solution "C": attraction = -5; solution "D": attraction = 25; solution "E": attraction = 10

What does the attraction mean in this example? The B, D and E solution, with positive attractions values are attractable for the players; the A solution, with null value is neutral; the C solution, with negative value, is repulsive. In this case, the choice of the solution will concern the first three ones. If there are no positive values, virtual players will choose between the neutral solutions. And if there are no null values, they will choose between the repulsive solutions.

The easiest way to select a solution is to choose the one with the highest attraction value, because it is the "best" (or at least the worst) one. But there are opportunities to build a more varied behaviour. For example, we can add a probability to each solution depending on its attraction value. So in the precedent example, the "D", "B" and "E" solutions would have respectively 50%, 30% and 20% chance of being chosen, according to their attraction of 25, 15 and 10. The other solutions would have a 0% chance.

When the virtual player selects a solution, the simulator informs the game of the chosen action, the information is saved in the game log file, and the game session continues.

4.3 Implementation and Uses

We have developed a prototype of simulator using java language, and XML data files, one for each graph of actions of the game. They are represented in XML, because it is an easy way to describe the graph structure. The game administrator uses an editor to create the graphs easily. The simulator administrator has then to reference the files, so that the simulator engine can find the graph corresponding to each decision situation. For example, he associates a graph to a board case of the game.

There is also one data file that contains all player profiles. The simulator administrator uses it to initialize the virtual players before the start of the game session.

Creating Graphs of Actions. Below is an example of an XML file that represents a graph of actions. The XML syntax is adapted to our process algorithm.

```xml
<?xml version="1.0" encoding="ISO-8859-1"?>
<graph>
  <Dnode name="D1">
    <outEdge name="Action1">
      <strategy name="risk">2</strategy>
      <!-- other strategic marks -->
      <succ type="Tnode ">T1</succ>
```

```
        </outEdge>
        <!-- other out edges -->
      </Dnode>

      <Rnode name="R1">
        <outEdge>
          <proba num="2" den="3"/>
          <succ type="Enode">E1</succ>
        </outEdge>
        <!-- other edges -->
      </Rnode>

      <Enode name="E1">
        <event name="money">-15</event>
        <!-- other events -->
        <outEdge>
          <succ type="END">END</succ>
        </outEdge>
      </Enode>

    <Tnode name="T1">
        <outEdge>
          <test type="=">
            <object>time</object>
            <value>100</value>
          </test>
          <!-- other tests -->
          <succ type="Rnode">R1</succ>
        </outEdge>
        < !-- other out edges -->
      </Tnode>

  <!-- other nodes -->

  </graph>
```

List of Player's Profiles. Example of the XML file that contains the list of player's profiles.

```
<?xml version="1.0" encoding="ISO-8859-1"?>
<profiles>
  <profile>
    <name>Aggressive</name>
    <strategies>
      <strategy id="risk">3</strategy>
      <!-- other strategies -->
    </strategies>
  </profile>
  <!-- other profiles -->
</profiles>
```

5 Conclusion

The development of business games is delicate and limits very often their use. We have proposed in this article the base of a simulation model of learners' behaviour aiming at favouring the testing of business games in compressed time. This model, named SIMCA, is based on the definition of players' profile types and game metadata (graphs of actions), which ensures tests as comprehensive as possible. Technologies used allow an easy set-up of the simulator despite the existing differences in the development of business games. The SIMCA model leads to the implementation of a prototype that will be tested soon on two business games.

There are many futures directions of this work. First, in an incremental development approach, the actual model could be improved so as to refine interactions between learners. In the same direction, we aim at simulating more realistic behaviours by adding for example the change of strategies during a game session. Furthermore, the simulator runs currently in compressed time, which allows fast virtual testing. A real time mode could be added in order to simulate virtual players that can be able to play with or against human players.

Finally, this work is part of a global study on an integrated environment for the design of business games. Beyond the testing environment, future work will concern a complete software suite for the development and configuration of educational business games.

References

1. Akkouche I., & Prévôt P.: Cooperative distance learning-sessions management: A transportation model application to Role Distribution. IEPM'97: International Conference on Industrial Engineering and Production Management, Lyon, France (1997) 166-174
2. David B., Gibaud O., Roland J.-P., Tarpin-Bernard F., & Vial C.: Cooperative learning Systems: Extension of the micro-world concept. Telecommunications for Education and Training, Prague (1997) 48-54
3. Babari M., Mahi A., & Prévôt P. : Approche générique pour la conception et l'ingénierie de jeux d'entreprise multimédias coopératifs - Cas du jeu de la maintenance multimédia. Colloque international TICE 2000, Troyes, France (2000) 377-384
4. Bouzouane A., Dionne C., Stiharu-Alexe I., & Gagné D. : Jeu de rôle virtuel à base d'agents intelligents. 6ème journées Francophones d'Intelligence Artificielle et Systèmes Multi-Agents (JFIADSMA 98), Pont-à-Mousson, France (1998) Hermès, 147-161
5. Roge O., & Labat J.M.: Integration of Virtual Players into a Pedagogical Simulator. Computer Aided Learning In Engineering Education (CALIE 2004), Grenoble, France (2004) 227-232
6. Gazzaniga G., Morrone G., Ovcin E., & Scarafiotti A.: The "virtual" companion: a "real" help for educational hypermedia. International Conference on Educational Use of Technologies (ICEUT 2000), Beijing, China (2000) 363-366
7. Zapata-Rivera J.D., & Greer J.: Exploring Various Guidance Mechanisms to Support Interaction with Inspectable Learner Models. Sixth International Conference on Intelligent Tutoring Systems (ITS 2002), Biarritz, France, (2002) 442-452.

8. Burleson W.: Affective Learning Companions. Doctoral consortium in conjunction with the 7th International Conference on Intelligent Tutoring Systems (ITS 2004), Maceio, Brasil (2004)

9. George, S., Titon, D., Prévôt, P. : Simulateur de comportements d'apprenants dans le cadre de jeux d'entreprise. Conference Environnement Informatique pour l'Apprentissage Humain, Montpellier, France (2005) 389-394

10. Von Neumann, J., & Morgenstern, O.: Theory of Games and Economic Behavior. Princeton University Press (1944)

11. Kahneman, D., & Tversky, A.: Prospect Theory: An Analysis of Decision under Risk. Econometrica, 47 (1979) 263-291

A Mechanism to Support Context-Based Adaptation in M-Learning

Estefanía Martín, Rosa M. Carro, and Pilar Rodríguez

Escuela Politécnica Superior, Universidad Autónoma de Madrid
28049 Madrid, Spain
{Estefania.Martin, Rosa.Carro, Pilar.Rodriguez}@uam.es

Abstract. In this paper we present a mechanism that supports the generation and management of adaptive mobile learning systems. Such systems are accessed by students and teachers for the accomplishment of diverse individual or collaborative learning activities. The main aim is for the systems to suggest the most suitable activities to be tackled by a given user in a specific context (location, idle time, devices). The basis of this mechanism, as well as an example of the context-based adaptation carried out for three different users in a specific scenario, are presented.

1 Motivation

Mobile and wireless technologies constitute innovative infrastructures that support the access to the Web at any time from any place through diverse devices. The widespread use of different devices daily, such as tablet PCs, PDAs, mobile phones or laptops, among others, suggest the convenience of supporting an adaptive access to Web-based applications through these types of devices. Apart from that, it is a fact that nowadays information is updated frequently because of research. Therefore, professionals must learn continuously. The Web is a great mean to spread updated information quickly and it is widely used to support e-learning. Besides, time has become a really valuable good. People use to spend a lot of time working and, in many cities, a great deal of time travelling from one place to another. Therefore, it is pretty common to find persons making use of personal devices at public transportation to take benefit from idle time. These facts motivate researchers and developers to provide web-based applications to support not only information access, but also mobile learning. Mobile-learning (m-learning) has been defined as e-learning through mobile and handheld devices using wireless transmission [1].

The fact that different learners may have distinct needs, interests, preferences, personal features or learning styles [2] has been considered with adaptation purposes in e-learning systems [3]. With the aim of guiding each individual during the learning process, adaptation techniques have been used to customize the information space, the organization of information in this hyperspace, the navigational possibilities and the contents to be presented to each user in the corresponding web pages.

Some applications have also been developed with the aim of supporting information access from different types of devices. In this respect, adaptation techniques have

W. Nejdl and K. Tochtermann (Eds.): EC-TEL 2006, LNCS 4227, pp. 302–315, 2006.
© Springer-Verlag Berlin Heidelberg 2006

been normally used for the customization of the multimedia contents to be showed through different devices [4].

In the context of m-learning through the Web, not only the devices but also the situations can be completely different each time a learner connects to the corresponding web-based system. New features must be taken into account, such as the student's location, idle time and available devices, which we have called the user's context and have been considered as the key issues to be modelled in mobile learning. The suitability or availability of certain learning activities may vary depending on the users' features and their particular context. Even the same activity can be appropriate for a user in a certain context while being inadequate for other user in the same context, because of his/her particular learning style, for example. This fact motivated us to use adaptation techniques to support the generation and management of mobile learning environments so that, given a specific user accessing to a Web-based system in a particular context, the system is able to suggest him/her the most suitable learning activities to be accomplished in that specific situation.

The rest of the paper is organised as follows: section 2 presents the basis of the mechanism that supports the adaptation; section 3 contains an example of the context-based adaptation carried out in an m-learning environment for three different users in a specific scenario; section 4 describes related work; and, finally, section 5 is devoted to conclusions and future work.

2   The Adaptation Mechanism

The main aim of the mechanism presented in this paper is to support adaptation in m-learning systems in order to satisfy the needs of different users when connecting and interacting with these systems, either individually or collaboratively. This mechanism supports the creation of adaptive collaborative m-learning environments in which the activities to be proposed to a user at a certain time can depend on: i) the user's particular features, learning styles, preferences or previous actions, ii) his/her partners' personal features, learning styles, preferences or previous actions, iii) the specific context of the user at that time, including his/her location, idle time and devices to support the interactions, and iv) the specific context of his/her partners at that time, among others.

This mechanism is fed on the specification of the information about the users to be taken into account during the adaptation process, as well as on the description of the activities that can be performed in the m-learning environment plus the rules describing the adaptation capabilities. Each of these sources of information is explained in detail next. The general schema of the system that implements this mechanism is shown in figure 1.

2.1   Users and Groups

As it has been stated before, it is necessary to store the information about each user that will be considered with adaptation purposes. It is possible to consider any user feature whose possible values can be represented by means of a set of either discrete values or continuous intervals. In that way, users can be classified with respect to

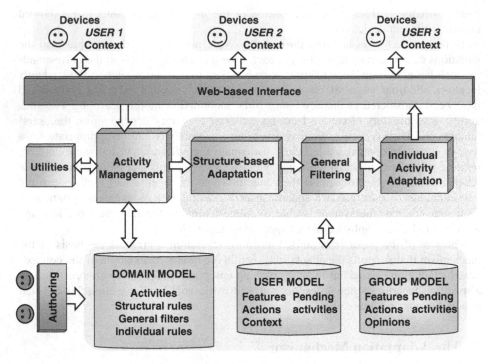

Fig. 1. General schema

each feature according to the corresponding value. These characteristics are stored in the user model and are taken into account in order to select the most suitable activities to be presented to each specific user in a certain context. The user model can contain information such as:

– Static user features: This information is stable throughout the time. Some examples of these features include personal data information (such as name, address, email, and telephone number), personal characteristics (language, background, abilities, etc.), preferences (learning style, type of information desired), role of the user (teacher, student), and so on.
– Actions: In order to supply a proper adaptation, it is necessary to store information about the actions done by the user, such as the activities started but not finished (pending), the activities already finished, the results obtained during the accomplishment of these activities, etc.
– Context: Users can interact within the m-learning environment in different contexts. The context of a user includes information related to his/her location, the available devices at that moment and the idle time.
– Agenda: The users' agendas are also stored in the system so that they can be used for checking the expected availability of each user at a certain time.

The designer of the m-learning environment is the responsible of the description of these features, although models by default can be used. As the users can perform activities both individually and collaboratively, it is also necessary to store information about groups, which is stored in the group model. This model contains information about the members that compose each group, such as the activities in which they collaborate (either in progress, finished or pending), the results of each activity (when corresponding), each user's role and their opinions about previous activities.

2.2 Activities and Adaptation

Concerning the activities that can be performed by the users, the following types of activities are supported so far:

- Individual learning activities, such as reading/interacting with an example, studying a theoretical explanation or solving an exercise (test/free-text answer).
- Collaborative learning activities, such as discussing, solving an exercise collaboratively or doing practical work.
- Other activities that involve more than one user and that can be generated on the fly, such as sending a file, sending a message or asking for a tutoring request.

With respect to the adaptation capabilities of the system, they are specified in three different ways, by means of:

- Structural rules, establishing the convenience of presenting specific activities to the students, as well as the curricula sequencing and the dependences among them, which can be different for distinct types of students.
- General filters that determine whether certain types of activities should be proposed to all or some students depending on their specific situation and on their personal features.
- Conditions associated to specific activities with special requirements. These requirements can be established in different ways depending on the students which the activity is intended for (student's model).

All this information is stored in the domain model. The adaptation mechanism is implemented in three steps: structure-based adaptation, context-based general adaptation and individual adaptation (see figure 1). Each of them is in charge of processing the corresponding filters/rules in order to select, from a set of activities, the most appropriate ones for a user at a specific each context. This selection is done according to the information about the user, stored in the user model. In the case of collaborative activities, the information stored in the group model is beard in mind too. The output of this process is a list with the available activities for the user.

Structure-based Adaptation. The goal of this type of adaptation is to support the selection of the activities to be proposed to a student at a certain time, depending on the relationships between activities, their requirements and the navigational guidance offered for each set of activities, which can be different for each type of student. For example, it could be considered convenient for non-experimented students to be directly guided through a set of activities, while it could be though much more appropriate for experimented students to navigate freely and get firstly involved in the activities they prefer. Or, to give another example, it could be necessary to include basic extra activities for novice students to learn in deep a certain subject (i.e., practising with simulations or doing individual exercises) before engaging in collaborative activities with other students.

With this purpose, structural rules, which are stored in the domain model, are used. These rules, which have been previously used for the description of adaptive web-based courses [5], show the way in which each activity is split in several sub-activities, and contain information about the curricula adaptation. They are formed by:

- Optional activation conditions related to information about the users. These conditions determine the rule activation for the corresponding type of users. If no condition is given, the rule will always be triggered.
- A composed activity.
- Activities that form the composed activity.
- Sequencing mode, which indicates the navigational guidance offered to the users with respect to the activities that form the composed activity (direct guidance, free navigation or alternative paths).

Structure-based adaptation consists of processing structural rules in order to get a first set of available activities for a certain user at a specific context. It compares the activation conditions for the rules (if any) with the information available about the user. If either a rule has no conditions or the existing conditions are satisfied, the corresponding activities are added to the list of available activities according to the indications of the sequencing mode.

Content-based General Adaptation. This type of adaptation supports the inclusion/exclusion of activities in/from the list of recommended activities, depending on the suitability of the type of activity for the particular context of the user. For example, if a user is in the classroom with his/her PDA switched on, it makes no sense to suggest him/her to engage in a collaborative synchronous task, since he should be participating in the class and paying attention to the teacher and students comments. However, it could make sense for the teacher to ask the students to answer a question through their PDAs during a lecture, so that their answers were immediately sent to the system, and the system were able to check them and present the corresponding statistics at that time. This last possibility would also be useful for students that can not attend a lecture, who would not necessarily miss that lecture, since they can connect to the system from outside the classroom and answer to the questions posed.

Apart from that, it could be desirable to propose different types of activities to dissimilar users in the same situation, depending on their personal needs and features, such as their learning style. For example, it can be considered desirable to propose review or individual short activities to students with an active learning style while travelling in public transportation for about twenty minutes, while it could be considered unsuitable to propose those activities to reflective students in the same situation.

With the aim of supporting this type of adaptation, general context-based rules can be included. They are constituted by:

- Conditions related to information about the user, such as location, idle time, available devices, learning style, etc.
- Types of activities suitable/unsuitable for a certain type of user according to his/her situation, specified in the conditions of the rule.

Context-based adaptation consists of triggering the corresponding rules for each user and of updating the list of the most suitable activities for this user. Therefore, the output here is the list of available activities generated during structure-based adaptation updated accordingly.

Individual Adaptation. It could the case that specific conditions should be satisfied for some particular activities. These conditions may be related to any user feature or situation. For example, if it is required for an activity to be done in the laboratory, the corresponding condition must be associated to this activity.

The means of supporting this adaptation is quite simple and consists of creating individual adaptation rules for the corresponding activities. These rules are formed by:

- Activity identifier.
- Conditions for the activity execution, related to any feature stored in the user or group models. In the case of collaborative activities, information about the minimum number of users needed to form a group to work on the activity can also be specified.

Therefore, the last step of the adaptation process consists of checking whether the activities in the list of available activities have individual activation conditions and, if so, whether they are satisfied. The list of available activities is updated accordingly and the final output is the definitive list of the most suitable activities to be proposed to a specific user in a particular context. This list is presented to the user, who decides the activity to perform. When a user either finishes an activity or disconnects from the system or his/her context changes, the information about the activities is stored / updated in the user model to be used subsequently.

As it can be noticed, this mechanism facilitates the adaptation of learning activities in a mobile environment according to the user features, preferences and context. Furthermore, it supports different adaptation decisions for different users interacting with the same system and even in the same context, since the user personal features, learning styles and so on are also considered within the adaptation rules. Finally, with respect to this mechanism, it should be remarked that there is no need of including rules in every step.

3 Example of the Context-Based Adaptation Process

With the aim of illustrating the adaptation process explained in the previous section, an example related with the 'Informatics' subject of the Computer Engineering studies is presented. Firstly, the way of describing the m-learning environment (activities, adaptation capabilities, user and group features considered) is presented. Afterwards, the functioning of the mechanism in a specific scenario is explained.

3.1 Description of the M-Learning Environment

In this example, students can accomplish several types of activities related to Boole's Algebra, such as: studying theoretical explanations, learning procedures, observing examples, interacting with simulations (applets), accomplishing collaborative activities, answering open-ended questions individually, answering test questions individually either at any time or during a class, asking for a tutoring, downloading course materials or sending/reading messages to/from other users.

Next, the information about the users is considered during the adaptation process, which the set of activities that compound the system is and how the adaptation desired are specified.

User and Group Models. In this example, characteristics related to the user's personal features, actions and context will be stored in the user and group models. In particular, concerning the information related to the user's features, the starting point of the users (whether they are taking the course for the first time or they did before but failed), their previous knowledge about the subject (novice or advanced) and one dimension of their learning style (active/reflective) is stored. With respect to information about the context, the place in which the users are (home, classroom, lab or unknown) and their idle time (value between 0 and infinite) are considered. Regarding the student's actions, all of them are stored automatically. This information (see table 1) is stored in the user and group models to be used with adaptation purposes. Note that it is not necessary to create the user and group models from scratch, since features used previously are made available each time a new model is created.

Table 1. Some characteristics forming the user model

Id	Characteristic	Possible Values
1	starting_point	zero/background
2	knowledge	novice/advanced
3	learning_style	active/reflective
4	place	home/classroom/lab/unknown
5	available_time	$(0,\infty)$

Activities and Adaptation. The next step concerns the specification of the activities to be accomplished. The activities supported in this example are:

- Boole's Algebra (*BooleA*).
- Theory about Boole's Algebra (*BA_Theo*).
- Interactive simulations using applets to support the learning of logical operations, logical gates and logical circuits (*BA_Sim*).
- Individual exercises to check the understanding of the theory (*BA_Exer*). These exercises are intended for students taking the course for the first time.
- A collaborative activity to design a logical circuit synchronously (*BA_Collab*).

- Review of already studied subjects (*Review*).
- Test questions posed during a lecture (*Test_Theory*).
- Test questions posed in the lab (*Test_Practice*).
- Course materials sent by the teachers for the students to download them and use them during the lecture (*Material*).
- Tutoring meetings (*Tutoring*).
- Messages to/from other users (*Message_S, Message_R*).

Concerning the relationships between activities and the guidance supported, structural rules have been defined (see table 2). The students taking the course for the first time, when accessing to the activity *BooleA*, must accomplish the following activities: theory, simulations, exercises and collaborative activity (table 2, rule 1). They will be directly guided through this set of activities, as indicated by the sequencing mode. Through the individual exercises, the students are forced to practise before engaging in a collaborative activity with other students. However, it is not necessary for the students to take the course again to do those exercises. Furthermore, they are allowed to accomplish the other three activities (theory, simulations and collaboration) in the order they prefer (table 2, rule 2). According to the knowledge of each student, the *BA_Sim* activity is structured in two different ways: novice students must experiment with logical operations and logical gates, doing the corresponding sub-activities in any order (table 2, rule 3). However, advanced students can access to simulations about logical gates and circuits, and it is not necessary for them to accomplish both activities (table 2, rule 4). Note that novice students are presented with basic simulations about logical operations while advanced students will be able to interact with circuit simulations. Both novice students and advanced students can interact with simulations about logical gates. The *BA_Sim* activity consists of simulations about AND, OR, NAND, NOR and XOR gates (*BA_AndGate, BA_OrGate, BA_NandGate, BA_NorGate, BA_XorGate* activities) for all the students. That is why the corresponding rule has no activation condition (table 2, rule 5).

As it can be noticed, in this example structural rules have been used to support the variation of the activities presented to each type of student according to their starting point and knowledge, as well as to offer distinct guidance support to each of them.

Concerning general filters, in this example it is considered that reviews, individual exercises or simulations are activities suitable of being accomplished by active users with more than 15 minutes available, connecting to the system from an unknown place (different from the university or home) (table 3, rule 1). In the case of reflective users, only if they have more than 40 minutes available they will be proposed with theory, reviews or simulations, but no individual exercises (table 3, rule 2).

Table 2. Structural rules for an example about 'Informatics'

Id	Activation condition	Seq.	Activity	Activity Composition
1	starting_point = zero	direct	BooleA	BA_Theo, BA_Sim, BA_Exer, BA_Collab
2	starting_point = background	free	BooleA	BA_Theo, BA_Sim, BA_Collab
3	knowledge = novice	free	BA_Sim	BA_Operations, BA_Gates
4	knowledge = advanced	alternative	BA_Sim	BA_Gates, BA_Circuits
5	-	direct	BA_Gates	BA_AndGate, BA_OrGate, BA_NandGate, BA_NorGate, BA_XorGate

Table 3. Context-based general rules for the example

Id	User-related Conditions	Conditions	Type
1	lstyle_ap =active	place = unknown, time > 15	review OR ind_exercise OR simulation
2	lstyle_ap =reflective	place = unknown, time > 40	theory OR review OR simulation

Table 4. Individual conditions for specific activities

Id	Context-related conditions	Activity
1	place = lab	Test_Practice

Finally, activities may have individual conditions associated. In this example, a test related to the practical work done by the students (*Test_practice*) is posed by the teacher at the beginning of the laboratory class to check whether students understood the concepts involved in the previous practical work. This activity must be performed in the laboratory. Therefore, this condition for that specific activity is specified in the way shown in table 4.

3.2 Scenario of Use

The evolution of the adaptation mechanism in a scenario of use with three students interacting with the m-learning environment described above, in different contexts, is presented next.

Users' features. In this scenario, three users are considered: Irene, Marius and Alice. All of them are engaged in the course 'Informatics'. Alice and Irene are students in the first course, and this subject is completely new for them. Therefore, they have no background on the subject and are novice students. On the contrary, Mario studies the subject for the second time, although he is still novice with respect to the course contents. Concerning learning styles and regarding the dimension used in this example (active/reflective), Alice is a pretty active student, while Mario and Irene were classified as reflective ones.

Context and evolution of the mechanism. Irene has an ankle sprain today, so she will not be able to go to the university. Marius and Alice are travelling to the university by train. The trip lasts 20 minutes. As soon as Alice enters the train and sits down, she switches on her laptop and connects to the system to see what she can do during the trip. She already connected to the system once before and, as it was the first time she studied Boole's Algebra, the first structural rule's activation condition was satisfied and rule 1 (table 2) was triggered. At that time, she studied *BA_Theory* and left the system. Therefore, the next activity to be performed, according to the rule (direct guidance), is *BA_Sim*. As Alice is a novice student, she will have access to simulations related to operations and gates (activities *BA_Operations* and *BA_Gates* from table 2, rule 1). Then, the context-based general filters indicate that, as Alice is an active person and has more than 15 minutes available, reviews, individual exercises or simulations are recommended for her (table 3, rule 1). Therefore, the *Review*

activity is added to the list of activities for Alice. Notice that, as no atomic activity related to individual exercises is defined, nothing else is added to the list. Finally, as no
specific activation conditions are established for the activities *BA_Sim* and *Review*, both
of them are suggested to Alice so that she can choose which one to do during the trip.

Concerning Marius, he switches on his PDA and connects to the system. Since he
has not started accomplishing any activity yet, and it is the second time he takes the
course, the structural rule 2 (table 2) is activated. This rule indicates that he can
choose among all the sub-activities (free guidance): *BA_Theory*, *BA_Sim* and
BA_Collab. Concerning the collaborative synchronous activity *BA_Collab*, since his
partners are not connected at that time (what is checked automatically by the corresponding external module), it can not be tackled. Since he is a reflective student but
has no more than 40 minutes available, neither rule 1 nor rule 2 (table 3) are activated.
Therefore, no general filter is applied. Consequently, the activities *BA_Theory* and
BA_Sim are available for Marius. He starts reading the theory (*BA_Theory*). He does
not understand most of the explanations, and he asks for a tutoring meeting with the
teacher of 'Informatics'. This action generates a new activity that is stored in the database as an atomic activity (*Tutoring*). The corresponding module compares the
teacher and student agendas and looks for possible common free time. Whenever it
finds it, the activity is added to the list of available activities for both of them (with
the date and time associated). Then Marius switches his PDA off and tries to get off
with Alice, who is pretty concentrated with the simulations.

When Marius and Alice arrive at the school, Marius connects to the system through
his PDA again. The system informs him that the teacher is in his office at that time
and confirms that the assessment meeting can take place at this moment. Thus, Marius
runs to the teacher's office. Meanwhile, Alice goes to the lab to check her emails. She
connects to the system through a PC and receives a message from Irene saying that
she will not be able to travel to the university (*Message_R* activity, which was pending for Alice, is finished when Alice reads the message).

Now it is time for the lecture of "Informatics". The teacher sends the electronic
slides to be used during this lecture to the system and goes to the classroom. Marius
and Alice go there too. That sending generates a new activity in the system, corresponding to the reception of the slides (*Material*). It has a deadline associated (next
class). As soon as Marius and Alice switch their laptops on, the system checks for the
most suitable set of activities to be performed, and finds out that *Material* is pending.
Therefore, the slides are made available to the students. Irene receives the slides too,
since she is connected through her PC to follow the class from home.

During the lecture, the teacher decides to do a quick test related to the concepts explained (*Test_Theory*). This activity can be performed by all of them, since no requirements are specified. Therefore, Irene is also informed that she has an available
activity to be performed, although she is at home.

After the lecture, Marius and Alice go to lab to start a new programming practice.
When they arrive at the lab, the teacher proposes them an activity to be done at that
precise time in that lab (*Test_Practice*). He wants to check whether each student did
really participate in the elaboration of the previous practice. Because of the condition
established for this activity (table 4, rule 1), Marius and Alice can do it, but Irene can
not. However, Irene starts accomplishing other activities according to the corresponding rules.

4 Related Work

M-learning has evolved quite quickly during the last years, mainly due to the increasing use of mobile and wireless devices and also to the continuous need of training, as it has been discussed in the motivation. Conferences and workshops devoted to this specific subject have been organised [6] [7] [8].

In mobile systems, the context is treated as a key element to be considered. Different definitions of context have been given. One of the most referenced definitions is presented in [9]: *"context is any information could be used to characterize the situation of an entity"*. An entity is a person, a place or an object that could be important to the interaction between a specific user and an application, including the user and the applications themselves. A classification of the characteristics to take into account for modelling the context is presented in [10]. In our case, the context of a user at a certain time has been defined as the conjunction of his/her physical location, his/her idle time and the devices available at that moment.

Concerning adaptation techniques, adaptive hypermedia has been used to adapt the delivered information and the services offered to the users and groups according to their context. In their majority, they deal with the adaptation of multimedia and web-based information content to the characteristics of mobile devices [4]. Some of the first examples of adaptation for content delivery are location-based services and museum information systems, in which the multimedia material is presented according to the user's situation and the device used [11]. In some cases, not only the contents, but also the navigational paths to be followed are adapted to the user [12].

In any adaptive system it is necessary to represent the user model so that it can be used during the adaptation. In learning systems, user models usually include factors such as the student's preferences, interests, goals, knowledge or learning styles. Apart from those, in web-based learning environments there exists a lot of information about people's behaviour that can be at least partly used in mobile environments [13]. Some of the most significant characteristics to be used with adaptation purposes in mobile learning environments are presented in [14]. A mechanism that takes into account some aspect about user's context for adaptation is presented in [15]. This mechanism models student's learning styles and adapts the course contents to individual learning style, based on the Felder-Silverman learning style theory and the device used by the student. In our work, it is possible to consider any user feature whose possible values can be represented by means of a set of either discrete values or continuous intervals. In the examples we have created so far, the users' personal features (learning style, knowledge, background and preferences), actions (activities started, finished, results) and context (idle time, location, available devices) is used.

Some recent adaptive m-learning systems are presented in [12], [16], [17] and [18]. A context-based filtering process is proposed in [16]. It is based on the current user's physical context (location, device and application), user's organizational context (group, role, member, calendar, activity, shared object and process) and general profiles. General profiles are the descriptions of a potential context that might characterize the user's real situation. Filtering rules should apply accordingly. The filtering process identifies the general profile to be applied and selects the awareness information. This context-based filtering process is devoted specifically to collaborative activities and the characteristics to be taken into account in the user's context (both physical and organizational) are pre-established.

JAPELAS is a context-aware language learning support system for Japanese polite expressions learning. This system provides learners with the appropriate polite expressions according to their situation (i.e. meeting room, office) and their personal information. It is focused on supporting only the learning of the Japanese language [17].

Two different mobile adaptive learning systems are presented in [18]. In the first one, adaptation is based on the learner knowledge, the time available for studying and location-related features related to concentration level. The second one provides easy access to commonly used files, applications and tasks, according to use location. The features taken into account for adaptation process are limited to the student's knowledge, the time available for studying and the locations characteristics. Both of them are centred in the concept of location.

Finally, IWT, an e-learning platform that supports simple and intelligent courses, is presented in [12]. For each student, an intelligent course generates the best learning path starting from the student model, mainly based on the acquired knowledge and his/her learning preferences. Furthermore, users can collaborate and communicate among them through messages, forums, chat, content sharing and videoconferencing, even if they are using different devices. This e-learning platform is only focused on courses, not in collaborative environment where people collaborate with other purposes.

As it has been mentioned above, our main goal is to provide means to support the development of adaptive m-learning systems able to suggest the most suitable learning activities to be tackled by each specific user in a particular context. Our approach is general enough to support an adaptation based not only on the context, but also on any user feature that could be considered as relevant, such as learning styles. It provides three different levels of adaptation and it can be used in different application areas. A reflection about these features of the described mechanism is presented in the next section. Details of the architecture of an m-learning system based on this mechanism can be found at [19].

5 Conclusions

The main goal of this work concerns the development of a mechanism to support the generation and management of adaptive mobile learning systems. Students and teachers can use these systems for the accomplishment of a variety of learning activities in different contexts (at different times, from diverse physical locations and through different devices). The main aim is for the system to be able to suggest the most suitable learning activities to be tackled by each specific user in every particular context.

Three different modules compose the adaptation mechanism presented, which is being currently implemented. Each module supports a different adaptation capability. Therefore, it is possible to provide adaptation based on: i) the relationships among activities and the navigational guidance through them, ii) the suitability of certain types of activities in defined contexts, and iii) specific requirements for particular activities. This fact makes it feasible either to endow systems with the three types of adaptation altogether (by means of the corresponding rules) or to ignore any of them.

Furthermore, adaptation at different levels of granularity can be provided. It is possible to specify general rules affecting to all the activities of the system, rules in which only groups of activities are involved or rules to establish special requirements for individual activities.

With respect to the diversity of users, it has been taken into account that the same activity can be appropriate for some users in a certain context while being inadequate for other users, even if they are in the same context. The users' particular needs, preferences or learning styles, among others, can influence this aspect. Therefore, the rule-based mechanism has been created to support the consideration of these differences too, so that the i) the relationships between activities and the navigational guidance offered, ii) the suitability of learning activities depending on their type and on the context the user is in, and iii) the restrictions imposed in specific activities, may be established in different ways depending on the users' contextual and non-contextual information.

The mechanism presented is general enough to be used in different application areas, since: i) adaptation rules are expressed in terms of activities, sub-activities (when corresponding), types of activities and conditions related to features stored in the user model, and ii) groups can be devoted to learning together, working, or doing any other collaborative activity. One can establish the types of activities to be included in the system, define or reuse the user model, and then specify the relationships among activities and the adaptation capabilities by means of the corresponding rules.

The adaptation capabilities and the flexibility of the mechanism presented constitute the main benefits of the presented mechanism in the area of m-learning. The use of this mechanism in further m-learning environments will give rise to more conclusions about the effectiveness of the mechanism presented as well as about potential new needs.

Acknowledgements

This work has been supported by the Spanish Ministry of Science and Education, project number TIN2004-03140.

References

1. Ktoridou, D. and Eteokleous, N.: Adaptive m-learning: technological and pedagogical aspects to be considered in Cyprus tertiary education. In: Recent Research Developments in Learning Technologies. Formatex, Badajoz, Spain (2005) 676-683
2. Alfonseca, E., Carro, R.M., Martín, E., Ortigosa, A. and Paredes, P.: The Impact of Learning Styles on Student Grouping for Collaborative Learning: A Case Study. User Modeling and User Adapted Interaction. Special issue on User Modeling to Support Groups, Communities and Collaboration. In press.
3. Brusilovsky, P.: Adaptive hypermedia. In: Kobsa, A. (eds.): User Modeling and User Adapted Interaction, Vol. 11, 1/2 (2001) 87-110
4. Conlan, O., Brady, A. and Wade, V.: The Multi-model, Metadata-driven Approach to Content and Layout Adaptation. W3C Workshop on Metadata for Content Adaptation, Dublin, Ireland, 12-13 October (2004).

5. Carro, R.M., Ortigosa, A., Schlichter, J.: A Rule-based Formalism for Describing Collaborative Adaptive Courses. In: Palade, V., Howlett, R.J. and Jai, L.C. (eds.): Knowledge-Based Intelligent Information and Engineering Systems. Lecture Notes in Artificial Intelligence 2774. Springer-Verlag (2003) 252–259.
6. World conference on mLearning, mLearn: http://www.eee.bham.ac.uk/mlearn/, http://www.lsda.org.uk/events/mlearn2003/ , http://www.mobilearn.org/mlearn2004/, http://www.mlearn.org.za/, http://www.mlearn2006.org/
7. IEEE International Workshops on Wireless and Mobile Technologies in Education, http://lttf.ieee.org/wmte2002/, http://lttf.ieee.org/wmte2003/ http://lttf.ieee.org/wmte2005/
8. IADIS International Conference Mobile Learning: http://www.iadis.org/ml2005, http://www.adis.org/ml2006
9. Dey, A.: Providing Architectural Support for Building Context-Aware Applications. Ph. D. Thesis, Department of Computer Science, Georgia Institute of Technology, Atlanta. (2000)
10. Yau, S.S. and Karim, F.: An Adaptive Middleware for Context-Sensitive Communications for Real-Time Applications in Ubiquitous Computing Environment. In: Real Time Systems, 26. Kluwer Academic Publishers (2004) 29-61
11. Zimmermann, A., Specht, M. and Lorenz, A.: Personalization and Context Management. User Modeling and User-Adapted Interaction, 15, Springer (2005), 275-302
12. Capuano, N., Gaeta, M., Miranda, S. and Pappacena, L.: A system for adaptive platform-independent mobile learning. Proceedings of Mlearn 2004, Roma, Italy, (2004), 53-56.
13. Benyon, D.R. and Murray , D.M.: Applying user modelling to human-computer interaction design. AI Review, 6 (1993) 43-69. www.dcs.napier.ac.uk/~dbenyon/AIReview.pdf
14. Jäppinen, A., Nummela, J., Vainio, T. and Ahonen, M.: Adaptive Mobile Learning Systems - The Essential Questions from the Design Perspective. Proceedings of Mlearn 2004, Roma, Italy, (2004), 109-112
15. Kinshuk and Lin T.: Application of Learning Styles Adaptivity in Mobile Learning Environments. Third Pan Commonwealth Forum on Open Learning, Dunedin, New Zealand, (2004).
16. Kirsch-Pinheiro, M., Villanova-Oliver, M., Gensel, J. and Martin, H.: Context-Aware Filtering for Collaborative Web Systems: Adapting the Awareness Information to the Users Context. In: 20th ACM Symposium on Applied Computing (SAC 2005). ACM Press, Santa Fe, Nuevo Mexico, USA, (2005) 1668-1673
17. Ogata, H. and Yano, Y.: Context-aware support for computer-supported ubiquitous learning. In: Proceedings of IEEE International Workshop on Wireless and Mobile Technologies in Education. IEEE Computer Society, Taiwan (2004) 27-34
18. Bull, S., Yanchun Cui Robig, H. and Sharples, M.: Adapting to Different Needs in Different Locations: Handheld Computers in University Education. In: Wireless and Mobile Technologies in Education (2005) 48-52
19. Martín, E., Andueza, N., Carro, R.M.: Architecture of a System for Context-based Adaptation in M-Learning. In: Kinshuk, Kope, R., Kommers, P., Kirschner, P., Sampson, D.G. and Didderen, P. (eds.): Proceedings of the 6th IEEE International Conference on Advanced Learning Technologies (ICALT 2006). IEEE Computer Society (2006) 252-254

Production and Deployment of Educational Videogames as Assessable Learning Objects

Iván Martínez-Ortiz[1], Pablo Moreno-Ger[2], Jose Luis Sierra[2],
and Baltasar Fernández-Manjón[2]

[1] Centro de Estudios Superiores Felipe II, Aranjuez, Madrid, Spain
imartinez@cesfelipesegundo.com
[2] Department of Computer Systems and Programming, Universidad
Complutense de Madrid, Fac. de Informática, 28040, Madrid, Spain
{pablom, jlsierra, balta}@fdi.ucm.es

Abstract. The generalization of game-based Learning Objects as serious learning material requires their integration into pre-existing e-learning infrastructure (systems and courses) and the inclusion of gameplay-aware assessment procedures. In this paper, we propose an approach to the production and development of educational graphic adventure videogames that can be deployed as normal Learning Objects in a Learning Management System. The deployment is carried out using a game engine that includes a built-in assessment mechanism that can trace and report the activities of the learner while playing the game.

Keywords: game-based learning; adventure educational videogames; edutainment; assessment; learning management systems; learning objects; IEEE ECMAScript content to runtime service communication; IEEE Data Model for Content; <e-Game>.

1 Introduction

The e-learning arena is faced with a number of challenges such as the quality of the learning achievements or improving students' motivation to prevent mid-course dropouts. These problems have been addressed in different ways. For instance, a distinctive characteristic of multimedia-based approaches [21, 26] is to catch the attention of the learner by using a lot of eye-candy in the content, while collaborative learning [2, 22] attempts to motivate the learner by generating peer-pressure, group-belonging and close feedback. An alternative approach is to take advantage of videogames as a highly motivating and entertaining activity that can be used to deliver the content.

We will focus our attention on educational games and how they can be integrated in an e-learning system. A serious learning process cannot consist merely of playing, without any kind of supervision or assessment of the activities within the game and the learning outcomes. Another issue with game-based learning is whether it can (or should) be integrated in pre-existent learning processes without altering already established learning procedures.

The most typical e-learning scenario in which we may try to introduce educational videogames is in a Learning Management System (LMS), a web application that

W. Nejdl and K. Tochtermann (Eds.): EC-TEL 2006, LNCS 4227, pp. 316–330, 2006.

delivers content and assesses the activity of the learner inside the system. Most LMSs try to comply with a number of specifications and standards regarding content formats or course structure to facilitate the interoperability of content between different LMSs. This interoperability/reusability process is founded on the Learning Object (LO) Model [18].

This work describes <e-Game>, an environment in which educational videogames are integrated in a complex LMS and treated as LOs. This tries to resolve the two key issues presented: assessment within an educational videogame and LMS integration. In order to further integrate the videogames into the learning process, an engine is used to execute the videogames that can profile the activity of the learner during gameplay and generate reports that are notified to the LMS. In addition, the LMS can send data to the videogame so that the game experience can be adapted.

The paper is structured as follows: Section 2 surveys the applicability of computer and videogames to educational processes. Section 3 presents the development model for educational graphic adventure games induced by <e-Game>, while section 4 presents the <e-Game> built-in assessment mechanism that enhances its educational value. Section 5 deals with the deployment of educational games into LMSs using <e-Game> and, finally, section 6 outlines some conclusions and future lines of work. All these sections have figures related to the experimental development of a short adventure game in the field of workplace safety regulations.

2 Computer and Video Games in Education

Applying games in general (not only videogames) to education is not a new idea. Playing is an inherent trait of human beings which is closely tied to the learning process [23]. The basic claim for supporting the introduction of games into learning processes is that games, unlike more traditional educational situations, are fun to play. Playful activities in a classroom (like role-playing events of history in class) [17] can be a very appealing and effective way of learning, although it is not cost-effective and it is very unlikely that a system involving such a high ratio of instructors/learners may ever be implemented. However, technologies bring up new possibilities for gaming environments with computer and video games, hereafter referred as videogames or simply games.

2.1 Can Videogames Educate?

Videogames allow the immersion of the student in richly recreated environments with a relatively low cost per student. Also, videogames support many educational approaches such as collaborating and/or competing within the game or, alternatively, simulating artificial peers in order to achieve similar results to collective playing in a cost-effective way. In any case, the experiences from in-game activities can then be shared with real peers and monitored by instructors to compensate for the lack of direct human intervention. In addition, the entire process can be fun and appealing to the learner. This description derives from four traits observed in and around modern videogames [9] as follows:

- *Videogames are fun.* And not only for small kids or young male teenagers. As of 2005, the average age of a videogame player is 30 and 43% of players are female [7].This suggests that *entertaining* educational videogames would be appealing for a broad audience and applicable not only for primary/secondary school learners, but also in corporate and long-life learning.

- *Videogames are immersive.* A videogame immerses the player in an environment by using a number of approaches. The most direct one is to allow the player to navigate the environment from a first-person perspective. A second approach is to project the identity of the player onto an avatar. Another alternative is to give the player the power to affect the environment without any visible agent, by clicking on the environment or using a graphic interface (videogames presenting this kind of interaction are often called god-like games, although they may just be simulating the functioning of a corporation or a railroad system). Regardless of the interaction model, videogames transfer the identity of the player to the recreated world and immerse him/her in whatever reality the designer of the game wanted. In [10] the psychological details of this immersion and transfer of identity are elaborated. Educational videogames can thus provide a constructivist and embodied learning process.

- *Videogames stimulate cooperation/competition.* Games are fun and immersive due to their short and efficient feedback loop [22]. Although this feedback loop is manifested in a variety of forms, humans are naturally inclined to interaction with other humans. Thus, the environments in videogames are often populated by characters that provide interaction. Although typical games have the player playing the central role in the story, multiplayer videogames involve several players at the same time and make them collaborate or compete in the achievement of goals. In either case, in most videogames the player interacts directly with other human or human-like entities. When applied to education, videogames can serve as a medium for collaborative learning even without requiring the involvement of actual peers. Alternatively, competitive factors can be employed to motivate learners to perform better.

- *Videogames promote the creation of communities of practice.* Playing a videogame, even a single-player game, is not an isolated activity. Videogames transcend their medium and generate communities around them, proving to be a brilliant example of Communities of Practice [30]. New players soon learn details about the games, strategies, play styles, etc. These communities are essential vaults for learning about a game, and it all happens on a peer-to-peer basis. There are no instructors and no learners, yet some vast vaults of knowledge and learning are formed without external influence. Expert users spend time answering newbie questions and enthusiasts write extensive guides (sometimes above the 300 page count) while only seeking peer recognition. The bottom-line is: Gamers enjoy talking about games after playing them. In the educational field, this suggests potential for discussion and argumentation of the concepts delivered by educational games, ideally directed by an expert instructor (an example of this approach can be found in [31]).

2.2 Integration of Videogames in an E-Learning Process

Regardless of the potential advantages of educational games, it is neither possible nor reasonable to revamp all existing e-learning programs and dispose of the entire existing web-based infrastructure (i.e. LMSs) and content. Educational games should be able to co-exist in the present web-oriented situation. Acknowledging the current trends in web-based education, educational games should be able to fit in an environment in which standards compliancy and the Learning Objects Model are dominant features.

Videogames as Learning Objects

Integrating a huge videogame that can be used to learn an entire domain will usually be difficult. However, if the domain is divided into small pieces of content, it is possible to create and integrate small videogames that focus on a single well-determined concept. This is precisely the concept used in the LO model, where the content is divided into small discrete pieces that can be assembled to form a course.

Many modern LMSs support this model, and their courses are divided into LOs. These LOs are typically made of web documents, but powerful LMSs barely restrict the content format as long as they can be delivered within a web browser. Therefore, this is the perfect situation for the inclusion of small educational videogames in a pre-existing course. The educational videogame can simply substitute one of the learning objects included in the course, as long as it covers the same materials and behaves externally the same way (the last part is not difficult, as most learning objects are passive content).

Videogames as assessable content

The instructors of any e-learning program will usually want to assess the activity of the learner in order to make sure that he/she achieves the results desired. This assessment can be a direct examination of the knowledge of the learner (which typically verifies the results through tests) or an examination of the learning *process* itself (which verifies the activities of the learner, the effort, the learning path, etc.).

Assessing the learning process itself in a web environment consisting of passive web documents is simple and rigid: It is possible to obtain data such as the order in which the themes were displayed and the time that the learner spent reading that content. This kind of measure by itself is not accurate because it does not reflect the real interaction. A sophisticated system may take note of the hour in which a learner accessed a document and when the learner triggered a new event, but this data may be inaccurate since it does not reflect whether the learner actually did anything while the content was being displayed. There is a lot of research related to obtaining assessment information by applying data-mining techniques to get the best out of these measures [13, 14], but with passive web documents, it is not technologically possible to go much further with regard to assessing the learning process.

However, educational videogames offer new opportunities, without rejecting their nature as LOs, because games are more interactive than standard web content. Since the actual learning will occur through a series of player decisions and interactions, it would be very interesting to assess the detailed activities of the player/learner within the game. Questions like "what decisions did the learner make?", "in which order?" or "what was the result of the action?" are a key point in the assessment of learner activity inside the videogame.

3 Creating Educational Games: The <e-Game> Project

The <e-Game> Project [19,20] proposes a new model for the development of educational games. Game development demands skilled technicians like designers, programmers or artists. Educational videogames also require the participation of expert tutors that provide the instructional design and decide how to deliver the content within the game. In order to facilitate the collaboration between technicians and tutors, the <e-Game> project applies a well-proven technique: The Documental Approach to Software Development [27, 28].

3.1 A New Development Approach

The <e-Game> project applies the advantages of document-driven developments and XML technologies [4] to facilitate the development of educational games. The key idea behind <e-Game> is to allow instructors to develop educational videogames by following a simplified procedure, without requiring the heavy involvement of experts in ICTs.

However, it is not necessary to permit the creation of *any* kind of game. We are interested in Adventure Games, which have been identified as a valuable genre for learning [3, 32]. Besides, studies like [16] indicate the main traits of adventure games and identify a clear bias for content instead of just plain action. In addition, most adventure games have a very similar structure and functionality, which is very valuable to our objective of simplifying the development process.

Our aim is that an author should be able to specify an adventure (we call them eGames) with only basic knowledge on how to use a computer, a text editor and a few notions of XML and the <e-Game> syntax. The next subsections describe this development process.

3.2 Designing and Marking an <e-Game> Adventure

The <e-Game> development process, described in greater detail in [19], starts with the elaboration of a document with the script/storyboard of the game. After writing the storyboard (or at the same time) the author adds descriptive markup to that document that indicates the conceptual meaning of each part of the script [5, 12]. The <e-Game> engine will receive this document along with a set of art assets (graphics, animations, sounds, etc.) and will directly produce the final executable game.

The storyboard writing process starts by defining the different game scenes and indicating their content (i.e. like in a theater play). Scenes have exits that lead to other scenes and the complete set of scenes defines the environment for the game. However, scenarios in an adventure videogame are static: background artwork and exits leading to other scenarios. Although it is possible to include learning content in the scenarios (embedded in the artwork, for instance), that is not their purpose. The storyboard should instead populate the scenarios with objects and characters.

Once the basic structure of the game is laid out in the form of a network of scenes, the next step is to define the objects and characters that populate the game in detail. From a learning perspective, these objects and characters are the interface that delivers most of the learning content, not the content itself. The actual content is delivered by the potential interactions between the learner and those objects and characters.

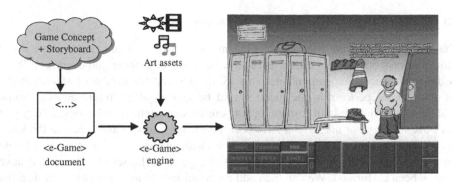

Fig. 1. Outline of the <e-Game> development process model. The storyboard is marked up with the <e-Game> XML syntax and fed to the engine together with the art assets.

```
<scene id="DressingRoom">
  <resources><!-- Art assets --></resources>
  <exits>
    <exit>
      <target idTarget="Corridor"><position x="0" y="300" />
    </exit>
  </exits>
  <elements>
      <item-ref idref="Boots"><position x="40" y="300" /></item-ref>
      <char-ref idRef="Foreman"><position x="485" y="410" /></char-ref>
  </elements>
</scene>
```

Fig. 2. Definition of a scene. There is a section for external assets, a section for exits (leading to other scenes), and a section with references to the elements that populate the scene (objects and characters). Objects and characters are detailed separately.

```
<item id="Boots">
  <resources> <!-- Art assets --> </resources>
  <description>
    <brief>A pair of sturdy boots</brief>
    <detailed>These are special safety boots for construction. The regulations
    demand that they be worn at all times.</detailed>
  </description>
  <actions>
    <use-with>
      <target idRef="Locker" />
      <effect>
        <speak-player>I think I shouldn't leave them here until I go home</speak-player>
      </effect>
    </use-with>
    (...)
  </actions>
</item>
```

Fig. 3. Definition of an item. There are two descriptions, a section for external assets, and a set of actions that can be performed on this element. Every action contains a description of its outcome.

The definition of an object must mention what happens when an object is examined roughly (a brief description), examined in detail (a more detailed description), combined with another object or given to another character. On the other hand, interactions with characters also include offering objects and, most important of all, conversations. The different interactions and conversations that the user performs are the main element for delivering content.

3.3 Adding Narrative Flow and Customization

The previous section has presented the means to describe a simple game, where every door is always open, every character always says the same thing and every exit leads to the same place. We can enhance this by introducing the notion of *state*. All the actions that we perform in the game should be able to affect future actions. Some objects may be hidden until something happens or some exits may be locked (e.g. you can't use the elevator unless you have been instructed to do so and received the key). The <e-Game> syntax allows each interaction (with an object or character) to activate a condition. The state at any given point in the game is the set of actions that have already been performed. We can then add preconditions to anything we want as a list of conditions that indicate which actions must have been performed.

```
<exit>
  <target idTarget="Rooftop" />
  <condition>
    <active flagRef="SAFETY_EQUIPMENT_READY" />
  </condition>
</exit>
```

(A)

```
<conversation id="CheckEquipment">
  <speak-char>Are you wearing all the safety equipment?</speak-char>
  <speak-player>Yes, sir</speak-player>
  <speak-char>In that case, go to the rooftop and help David</speak-char>
  <end-conversation>
    <activate flag="SAFETY_EQUIPMENT_READY" />
  </end-conversation>
</conversation>
```

(B)

Fig. 4. A conditioned exit (A) and a conversation that triggers it open (B). After the conversation ends, the flag "SAFETY_EQUIPMENT_READY" is activated.

```
<conversation id="FirstGreeting">
  <speak-char>Ah, you must be the worker. What's your name?</speak-char>
  <speak-player>Yes, sir. My name is <param name="username"/> </speak-player>
  <speak-char>Welcome on board, <param name="username"/> </speak-char>
  (...)
</conversation>
```

Fig. 5. Text customization. The <param name="username" /> markup will be substituted by a value written in the configuration file when the game is executed.

Finally, most of the content of these games is text, and it may be desirable to customize some pieces of text in order to enhance the gaming experience. The <e-Game> syntax supports this kind of personalization with the inclusion of a special markup indicating that a piece of the text should be read from a configuration file.

This customization mechanism can be used for trivial modification like including the name of the user in conversations. However, the system can be pushed further: if all the texts are derived to a configuration file, we are actually implementing an internationalized game.

4 Assessment in <e-Game>

<e-Game>, as described thus far, is a tool for the documental development of adventure videogames in general. However, <e-Game> is actually oriented to the development of *educational* adventure videogames. For this purpose, <e-Game> has a built-in assessment mechanism. When an author defines an eGame, learning designers can include in the documents information about which tasks are relevant for the learning process. When the videogame is executed, the activation of the relevant tasks is logged and a report can be elaborated for the instructor.

```
<assessment id="WEAR_HARDHAT" type="achievement" importance="high">
    <condition>
      <active flagRef="WEARING_HARDHAT"/>
    </condition>
    <effect>
      <assessment-concept>The user equipped the hardhat</assessment-concept>
      <assessment-text>
        The user grabbed the hardhat before entering the construction site
      </assessment-text>
    </effect>
</assessment>
```

Fig. 6. Assessment action conditioned to the activation of a flag that indicates that the user is equipped with the safety hardhat

4.1 The Assessment Syntax

As depicted in Fig. 4, the state of the game is characterized for the set of flags that are active. <e-Game> allows learning designers to determine which game states are relevant to the assessment process. For this purpose, they include *assessment actions* using assessment elements. As depicted in Fig. 6, these assessment actions are associated to conditions in the game state.

An assessment action includes information using different attributes and nested elements that will subsequently be used in the production of reports:

- The type attribute: When a report is generated, the assessment elements can be grouped by their type. Initially, <e-Game> suggests the values achievement (important events are triggered), behaviour (things that the user does within the game and reflect his/her playstyle), stuck (points of the game that suggest the user got stuck at a certain moment) and impossible (points that should never be reached, mostly for testing purposes). However, the different possible values can be decided by the author for each specific game.
- The importance attribute: Reports can be generated with different levels of detail. Thus, the author can decide on the relative importance of each action and assign it a value. Later, the instructor will be able to generate reports with different levels of detail in which elements of lower importance are not included. Again, it is possible to customize the names and order of the possible values, although <e-Game> suggests using verbose, low, average and high, with the first one only being used for testing purposes.
- The assessment-concept element: It is a description of the action being assessed. Different assessment may have the same concept associated.

- The `assessment-text` element: A text describing how the learner triggered the assessment action.

Of course it is not necessary to fill in all these fields and attributes. Indeed, all assessment actions are assumed to be of type `achievement` and of `average` importance. Also notice that assessments can be included in a separate document. Therefore, the same game can support different assessments tailored to different learning scenarios.

4.2   Assessment Logs and Reports

When the eGame is executed, the <e-Game> engine will keep track of all the assessment actions and log their activation. During the play session or after its completion it is possible to access the assessment log that allows the instructor to understand the behaviour of the student within the videogame. This log is marked up using descriptive markup in order to facilitate its subsequent processing and presentation. For each action triggered, there will be a timestamp and the reference to such an action.

```
<assessment-log>
    <assessment idTarget="WEAR_HARDHAT" timestamp="00:09:30"/>
    <assessment idTarget="FOREMAN_IS_DECEIVED" timestamp="00:21:30"/>
    (...)
</assessment-log>
```

Fig. 7. An assessment log generated by <e-Game>. Assessments actions have an associated timestamp. The XML markup permits the generation of formatted reports on demand.

The logs, together with the assessment actions, can be used to generate enriched HTML reports for the instructors (Fig. 8). To view a report, the instructor can select a level of detail and all actions with a lesser importance will not be displayed. This way, if the instructor selects "average" as the detail level, actions marked as having "average" or "high" importance will be displayed while "verbose" and "low" importance actions will be filtered out.

ASSESSMENT OF ACTIVITIES

Achievements
00:04:23 - Flag ID: DISCOVER_HARDHAT
Event: The user found the hardhat inside the Locker
Description: --

00:09:30 - Flag ID: WEARING_ HARDHAT
Event: The user equipped the hardhat
Description: The user grabbed the hardhat before entering the construction site

Behaviour
00:21:30 - Flag ID: DECEIVE_FOREMAN
Event: The user tried to deceive the foreman
Description: The user lied about the height of the scaffold

Fig. 8. An assessment report where assessments are classified by their types

The open structure of these reports allows the author to use them for a variety of purposes. On one hand, when the author is concerned about the path followed by the learner, the reports can be used to trace the activities of the learner in detail with thorough descriptions. On the other hand, if the objective is to give a single mark based on the last objective achieved (for eGames with multiple possible endings), it is possible to mark only those final actions and put a numeric mark in the text of the assessment element. In the latter case, the report will only contain the name of the final state of the game, the score associated and the time it took the learner to complete the game.

5   Integration of <e-Game> Educational Games in a LMS

As described in the previous sections, the main goal of the <e-Game> Project is to allow authors to create small games that can replace some pieces of static learning content such as an HTML or a PDF file. eGames, like Learning Objects, tend to be small and cover a specific set of learning objectives. Once an eGame has been fed to the <e-Game> engine, it can be executed as a stand-alone program. However, it can also be deployed in a web-based LMS.

5.1   Delivering Games in a Web-Based LMS

As the <e-Game> engine uses Java as supporting technology, the eGames produced can actually be packaged as Java Applets that can be easily embedded into a HTML page. Thus, an eGame can be deployed into practically any LMS that supports web pages with embedded objects as content. In fact, any LMS compliant with the "de-facto" standard IMS Content Packaging [15] can easily have the game deployed as an IMS Resource, with the (applet version of the) <e-Game> engine, the <e-Game> document and the art assets as support files, and a container HTML file as the main file.

This integration, although very straightforward and compliant with almost all the existing LMSs, only offers the motivational advantages of game-based content but does not offer any assessment advantages over alternative simple formats such as a PDF file or a standard applet. The next subsection offers some insights on how an eGame can have a more sophisticated integration with a LMS.

5.2   Communication of the Assessment Reports to the LMS

Games developed with <e-Game> can let a LMS know about the activities of the learner within the game. Depending on the standards supported by the LMS and its implementation, the integration of an eGame within the LMS can be more or less sophisticated:

Blackbox Integration: As described above, this is the most straightforward methodology and almost any LMS that supports web-pages can integrate an eGame. From the LMS point of view, games-based resources are treated as black boxes, with no knowledge of what happens within the game. In this scenario, the best that the LMS

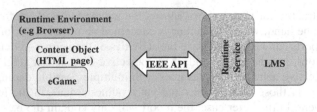

Fig. 9. Use of the IEEE ECMAScript API for communicating assessments logs to the LMS

can do is to obtain the same set of external measures that can be obtained from a simple content file (number of accesses, duration of the visit, etc.).

Standardized communication, not <e-Game>-aware: When the LMS supports it, the IEEE ECMAScript API for Content to Runtime Service Communication [24] can be used for communicating assessment data to the LMS. This Runtime Service is designed as a bridge between the environment (typically a web browser) where the learning content runs and the LMS itself. This communication mechanism can be used with different kinds of LOs, such as, for example, SCORM SCO (Shareable Content Objects) [1]. In general terms, this standard provides a communication protocol between a Content Object and the LMS, but does not specify what kind of information is actually interchanged between the content (in this case, an eGame) and the LMS. To tackle this issue, a recent IEEE Standard, the IEEE DMC (Data Model for Content) to LMS Communication [25], provides a general Data Model for communication exchange.

```
(a)  (assessment-identifier,
         Timestamp:type:importance:assessment-concept:assessment-text)

(b)  (WEAR_HARDHAT, 000930:achievement:high:
                     The user equipped the hardhat:
                     The user grabbed the hardhat before
                     entering the construction site)
```

Fig. 10. Attribute-value pairs transmitted to the LMS. (a) General syntax. (b) Sample entry according to the example in figure 6.

A LMS with even basic support of the IEEE ECMAScript API will be able to receive basic information from the eGames deployed, as depicted in Fig. 9. For this purpose, the applet version of the <e-Game> engine processes the assessment log and uses the ECMAScript API[1] to push basic information to the LMS in the form of simple attribute-value pairs, as in Fig. 10.

In this way, assessment information is passed to the LMS, which is responsible for storing it. Of course, if the LMS is not <e-Game>-aware, it is very unlikely that the system will be able to do much with all the information received other than simply displaying it without type or level filtering as described in Section 4.2.

---

[1] Bidirectional communication between Java Applets and ECMAScript is feasible when using for instance the API supported by the Java™ Plug-in.

The LMS is expected to have a mechanism that puts together all the information gathered from a specific resource (in this case, all the attribute-value pairs for a specific game). A simple and comfortable use of this approach is to have the learning designer assign a final score to a specific action.

Standardized communication, <e-Game>-aware: The simple data described above is highly compatible, but it does not exploit the full potential of <e-Game> assessment mechanisms. Even if the engine pushes all the relevant information towards the LMS, the LMS will not necessarily know what to do with that information. However, instead of using a generic inspection tool, it is possible to create a specific application profile aware of the information provided by the engine and get the most out of the <e-Game> assessment system. A prototype of such a tool has been tested in the <e-Aula> LMS [29].

When this tool is present, it lets instructors generate reports for the activity of each learner during each play session. The tool queries the instructor about the types of assessment elements that should be included and the level of detail desired, always according to the default nomenclature and semantics presented in Section 4.1. The tool gathers the information from the LMS storage layer and generates enriched HTML reports that are displayed to the instructor.

In the runtime initialization, the engine can discover if there exists a communication mechanism with the Runtime Service, and if there does, the engine verifies what features are supported. In particular, the engine will check whether the <e-Game> Data Model is supported. If there is no support for any kind of communication, the logs are never generated. Otherwise, if there is support for basic (standard-compliant) communication, or the LMS is <e-Game>-aware, the engine will push all the relevant information contained in the log document using the standard IEEE ECMAScript API.

6 Conclusions and Future Work

The <e-Game> Project, as presented in this work, offers a valid alternative for the gradual inclusion of small games into pre-existing online courses and LMSs. Its documental approach to the development and maintenance of educational adventure games allows authors without an extensive programming background to develop these adventure games.

The games developed by those authors can be executed by using an engine equipped with a built-in mechanism that supports the assessment of the activities performed within the game. For this purpose, <e-Game> includes a flexible syntax that allows the assessment of different aspects of these activities. In addition, the games can be integrated into almost any modern LMS although the depth of the integration will depend on each specific LMS. Nonetheless, <e-Game> supports the three different levels of integration described in this work.

This flexibility and the viability of the development approach have undergone some preliminary testing which suggests a great potential. A group of volunteer authors participated in the development of short adventure games covering different aspects of workplace safety regulations. The authors were provided with a number of art assets and basic storyboards and managed to mark up those documents and generate the corresponding eGames with hardly any assistance. It must be noted however that all the authors had previous experience with XML applications, which is actually the main concern regarding the applicability of the development model: developing an eGame is an XML-intensive task and many authors without any experience may find the process excessively complicated. On the other hand, the process still has a great advantage over a traditional game development and many authors in the e-learning arena are familiar with XML technologies as long as these support most standardization processes in the field.

Regarding the integration of eGames into different LMSs, the trivial Blackbox integration model described in Section 5.2 was tested in publicly available LMSs such as Moodle [6] and Sakai [8] as well in the commercial WebCT [11] deployed at the Complutense University of Madrid. As for more sophisticated integration mechanisms, the <e-Game>-aware inspection tool developed for the <e-Aula> experimental LMS has demonstrated the viability of the approach.

It is interesting to note that the aforementioned IEEE ECMAScript API and Data-Model Communication standards also support communication in the other direction: The content can query the LMS for specific pieces of information with different purposes. Next steps in <e-Game> are to support this type of communication with different objectives:

- The basic approach is to customize the game with data pulled from the LMS. As described in Section 3.3, the <e-Game> syntax allows the configuration of eGames from external data read by the engine from a configuration file. This data may be stored within the LMS instead and be pulled in real time with this mechanism.
- An <e-Game>-aware LMS could store data corresponding to preconditions of a specific eGame. The potential of such a mechanism is almost unlimited: Since preconditions are the basic utility for game flow, it would be possible to configure the entire eGame from the LMS itself. It would be possible to adapt the game to different learner profiles (since the preconditions can open and close game branches), to save the game in the LMS itself (since preconditions are the current state of the game) and even to allow the result of previous LOs and learning paths to affect the behaviour of the eGame.

Acknowledgements

The Projects TIN2004-08367-C02-02 and TIN2005 08788 C04-01 and the Regional Government of Madrid (4155/2005) have partially supported this work.

References

1. ADL. Advanced Distributed Learning Sharable Content Object Reference Model (ADL-SCORM). 2006; Available from: http://www.adlnet.org/ 20th January, 2006.
2. Alavi, M., Computer-Mediated Collaborative Learning: An Empirical Evaluation. Management Information Systems Quarterly. Vol. 18(2). (1994) 150-174.

3. Amory, A., Naicker, K., Vincent, J., and Adams, C., The Use of Computer Games as an Educational Tool: Identification of Appropriate Game Types and Game Elements. British Journal of Educational Technology. Vol. 30(4). (1999) 311-321.
4. Birbeck, M. et al, Professional XML 2nd Edition. Wrox Press.(2001).
5. Coombs, J.H., Renear, A.H., and DeRose, S.J., Markup Systems and the Future of Scholarly Text Processing. Communications of the ACM. Vol. 30(11). (1987) 933-947.
6. Dougiamas, M. and Taylor, P. Moodle: Using Learning Communities to Create an Open Source Course Management System, in World Conference on Educational Multimedia, Hypermedia and Telecommunications 2003. Honolulu, Hawaii, USA: AACE (2003).
7. ESA, E.S.A. Essential Facts about the Computer and Videogame Industry. 2005; Available from: http://www.theesa.com/files/2005EssentialFacts.pdf 20th February, 2006.
8. Farmer, J. and Dolphin, I. Sakai: eLearning and More, in 11th European Univeristy Information Systems (EUNIS 2005). Manchester, UK (2005).
9. Garris, R., Ahlers, R., and Driskell, J.E., Games, Motivation and Learning: A Research and Practice Model. Simulation & Gaming. Vol. 33(4). (2002) 441-467.
10. Gee, J.P., What video games have to teach us about learning and literacy. New York; Basingstoke: Palgrave Macmillan.(2003) 225 p.
11. Goldberg, M.W. and Salari, S. An Update on WebCT (World-Wide-Web Course Tools) - a Tool for the Creation of Sophisticated Web-Based Learning Environments, in NAUWeb '97 - Current Practices in Web-Based Course Development. Flagstaff, United States (1997).
12. Goldfarb, C.F., A Generalized Approach to Document Markup. ACM SIGPLAN Notices. Vol. 16(6). (1981) 68-73.
13. Heathcote, E. and Dawson, S. Data Mining for Evaluation, Benchmarking and Reflective Practice in a LMS, in E-Learn 2005: World conference on E-learning in corporate, government, healthcare & higher education. Vancouver, Canada (2005).
14. Huang, H.M. and Wu, C.H., Applying Data Mining in E-learning Environment. Learning Technology Newsletter. Vol. 6(2). (2004) 31-32.
15. .IMS. IMS Content Packaging Specification v1.1.4. 2004; Available from: http://www.imsproject.org/content/packaging/ March 17th, 2005.
16. Ju, E. and Wagner, C., Personal computer adventure games: Their structure, principles and applicability for training. The Database for Advances in Information Systems. Vol. 28(2). (1997) 78-92.
17. Keller, C.W., Role Playing and Simulation in History Classes. The History Teacher. Vol. 8(4). (1975) 573-581.
18. Koper, R., Combining re-usable learning resources and services to pedagogical purposeful units of learning, in Reusing Online Resources: A Sustainable Approach to eLearning, A. Littlejohn, Editor., Kogan Page: London. p. 46-59 (2003).
19. Martinez-Ortiz, I., Moreno-Ger, P., Sierra, J.L., and Fernández-Manjón, B. Production and Maintenance of Content Intensive Videogames: A Document-Oriented Approach, in International Conference on Information Technology: New Generations (ITNG 2006). Las Vegas, NV, USA: IEEE Society Press (2006).
20. Moreno-Ger, P., Martinez-Ortiz, I., and Fernández-Manjón, B. The <e-Game> project: Facilitating the Development of Educational Adventure Games, in Cognition and Exploratory Learning in the Digital age (CELDA 2005). Porto, Portugal: IADIS (2005).
21. Oz, E. and White, L.D., Multimedia for better training. Journal of Systems Management. Vol. 44(5). (1993) 34-38.

22. Pivec, M. and Dziabenko, O., Game-Based Learning in Univeristies and Lifelong Learning: "Unigame: Social Skills and Knowledge Training" Game Concept. Journal of Universal Computer Science. Vol. 10(1). (2004) 4-12.
23. Prensky, M., Digital Game Based Learning. New York: McGraw-Hill.(2001).
24. Richards, T., IEEE Standard for Learning Technology - ECMAScript API for Content to Runtime Services Communication. (2004).
25. Richards, T., IEEE Standard for Learning Technology - Data Model for Content to Learning Management System Communication. (2003).
26. Schank, R.C., Learning via multimedia computers. Communications of the ACM. Vol. 36(5). (1993) 54-56.
27. Sierra, J.L., Fernández-Manjón, B., Fernández-Valmayor, A., and Navarro, A., Document Oriented Development of Content-Intensive Applications. International Journal of Software Engineering and Knowledge Engineering. Vol. 15(6). (2005) 975-993.
28. Sierra, J.L., Fernández-Valmayor, A., Fernández-Manjón, B., and Navarro, A., ADDS: A Document-Oriented Approach for Application Development. Journal of Universal Computer Science. Vol. 10(9). (2004) 1302-1324.
29. Sierra, J.L., Moreno-Ger, P., Martinez-Ortiz, I., Lopez-Moratalla, J., and Fernández-Manjón, B., Building learning management systems using IMS standards: Architecture of a manifest driven approach. Lecture Notes in Computer Science. Vol. 3583. (2005) 144-156.
30. Squire, K., Video games in education. International Journal of Intelligent Simulations and Gaming. Vol. 2(1). (2003) 49-62.
31. Squire, K. and Barab, S. Replaying History: Engaging Urban Underserved Students in Learning World History through Computer Simulation Games, in 6th International Conference of the Learning Sciences. Santa Monica, United States: Lawrence Erlbaum Assoc. (2004).
32. Young, M. An ecological description of videogames in education, in Annual Conference on Education and Information Systems: Technologies and Applications. (2004).

Two Technology-Enhanced Courses Aimed at Developing Interpersonal Attitudes and Soft Skills in Project Management

Renate Motschnig-Pitrik

Research Lab for Educational Technologies
Faculty of Computer Science, University of Vienna
renate.motschnig@univie.ac.at

Abstract. Recent strategies in the European Union encourage educational styles which promote the development of attitudes and skills as a basis for knowledge construction. The question is whether technology-enhanced settings have the potential to support such educational styles. The Person-Centered Approach, developed by the American psychologist Carl Rogers and adapted in several innovative educational settings holds great promise in promoting experiential, whole person learning. In this paper we illustrate technology-enhanced, person-centered education by describing two course settings and scenarios in which we emphasize, respectively, constructive, interpersonal attitudes and soft skills in the context of project management. As a result of each of the two courses students stated that they had learned significantly on the level of attitudes and soft skills. They considered exchange and discussion with colleagues and active participation during the course as the top factors from which they benefited. Furthermore, the majority of students felt that it was easier for them to work in teams and to establish social relationships in the two courses presented in this article than in traditional courses.

1 Introduction

"We know [...] that the initiation of such learning rests not upon the teaching skills of the leader, not upon scholarly knowledge of the field, not upon curricular planning, not upon use of audiovisual aids, not upon the programmed learning used, not upon lectures and presentations, not upon an abundance of books, though *each of these might at one time or another be utilized as an important resource*. [Emphasis added] No, the facilitation of significant learning rests upon certain attitudinal qualities that exist in the personal relationship between the facilitator and the learner."

(C. Rogers on significant learning [18])

Authors from constructivist, learner-centered [10], and person-centered traditions have argued that learning is most effective if it includes not only the intellect but also feelings, meanings, ideas, skills, attitudes, etc. More recently, this requirement of taking the whole person into consideration while educating has explicitly been voiced in the course of the Bologna process that aims at modernizing education in the European Union and making it more accessible to a broad range of learners. In

W. Nejdl and K. Tochtermann (Eds.): EC-TEL 2006, LNCS 4227, pp. 331–346, 2006.

particular, in the context of determining core competencies in our society, The European Association for the Education of Adults [8] notes that: *"There is a need for new curriculum. Traditionally the curriculum consisted of three elements: knowledge, skills, attitudes, which tends to value knowledge above skills, and skills above attitudes. Experience of life suggests different priorities: positive attitudes are key to a rewarding life and job, skills are also more important than knowledge. These priorities should be asserted in the development of new curriculum, which would raise the value of social capital, civil society and the role of non-formal learning."* But how can these principles and strategies be put into practice? A key question is whether academic, blended learning courses are proper settings to support these needs and if so, what are the most important factors that enable whole person learning. A closely related question is how development at the skills and attitudes level can be assessed.

Recent research indicates that technology-enhanced learning settings, i.e. settings that mix face-to-face and online learning, offer the required flexibility [7, 15] in which resourceful persons can foster experiential, whole person learning that addresses the learner at the level of intellect, social skills, and attitudes/dispositions [13]. In this paper we aim to share the goals, scenarios, and settings, reactions, and results of two academic courses that follow the same didactical approach. Both are intended to complement the strongly intellect-focused education with addressing learners at all three levels of learning: attitudes, skills, and intellect, however with different emphasis according to particular learning targets. In other words, we ask the question what we can do to allow students to become better communicators, negotiators, and constructive teammates in cooperative tasks aside of acquiring knowledge in some subject area?

We hope that the following snapshots of practice and research on technology-enhanced, person-centered education in the context of two academic courses on communication and on soft skills in project management provide vivid examples how important the whole person's concept is for education. Both courses have been conducted at the University of Vienna as part of the masters program in computer science and business informatics. They have undergone some evolution in their designs since they were first held three years ago. By sharing our experience with our readers we hope to facilitate further development that builds on these experiences and extends as well as transcends their and our current context. If this paper turns out to be an inspiration for professionals and students to find new ways of bringing meaningful learning, creativity, fun, personal resources, and wisdom into the classroom, the purpose of this paper will be fulfilled.

The paper focuses on the didactical approach in the context of the particular processes, i.e. the nature and sequence of activities and the aspect of blending face-to-face and online elements within the course design. Furthermore, the paper reflects on some methodological questions regarding research design. We suggest applying a mix of qualitative and quantitative methods in order to deal with research questions such as: What are the factors that students perceive as most influential in their learning? What is the role of online support? Can the course contribute to building positive social relationships and facilitating teamwork? While the overall participatory action research framework has been specified and illustrated in [6, 11], in this place we share some results of the qualitative and quantitative studies in the sense of a proof of concept.

The paper is structured as follows. The next section provides a concise introduction into the didactical and technological baselines underlying our approach towards applying technology in order to enhance learning. Section three presents the course on project management soft skills (PM-SS), while section four is devoted to illustrating a course on communication and New Media that focuses on the development of interpersonal attitudes such as congruence, acceptance, and empathic understanding. In Section five we discuss the results of the course evaluations and students' reactions and include personal experiences that other educators may find useful. The final Section summarizes the paper and identifies questions for further research.

2 Underlying Didactical Approach

Our approach to technology-enhanced learning builds upon humanistic educational principles as realized in the Person-Centered Approach (PCA) by Carl Rogers [16, 18]. Person-Centered learning is a personally significant kind of learning that integrates new elements, knowledge, or insights to the current repertoire of the learner's own resources such that he or she moves to an advanced constellation of meaning and resourcefulness [2]. It can be characterized by active participation of students, a climate of trust provided by the facilitator, building upon authentic problems, and raising the awareness of meaningful ways of inquiry [18]. We view the open, self-responsible, and yet relationship-focused tendencies inherent in the PCA as smoothly complementing the open spaces and free contacts enabled by current web-based environments.

Research in the Student-Centered Approach proved [1, 4, 16] that students achieve superior results along with personal growth in terms of higher self-confidence, creativity, openness to experience, self-respect, and respect towards others and their environment, etc., if they learn in an atmosphere or climate in which the facilitator (instructor, teacher, etc.) holds three core attitudinal conditions and if they perceive them, at least to some degree [16]. The core conditions are realness or congruence of the facilitator, acceptance or respect towards the student, and empathic understanding of the students and their feelings. Consequently, personal resourcefulness of the facilitator and his or her relationship with students has significant influence on the students' learning. This, along with the insight that facilitators equally learn in the facilitation experience, causes us to prefer the term "person-centered" rather than "student-centered". Person Centered Learning is a shared responsibility where human beings (teacher and student) meet to inspire each other and to bring the best out of them imparting knowledge, skills, attitudes, and experiences in a creative, promoting environment.

The way in which these core conditions can be expressed in blended learning situations in general is discussed in more detail in [12, 14]. The current paper shares two course designs that provide space for the core conditions to be expressed. To fill the space, however, instructors personally need to be sufficiently open to experience, real and transparent in their communication, yet respectful and acceptant, and endeavoring to understand students' inner worlds: their meanings, feelings, potentials as well constraints.

3 Course on Project Management Soft Skills

Industry and educational strategies call for the development of skills and attitudes aside of knowledge. Our challenge has been to approach the needs voiced above and to examine, as objectively as we could, the direction we decided to choose.

The course on project management soft skills (PM-SS) is aimed at addressing students at all three levels of competence or learning: knowledge, skills, and attitudes with an emphasis on experientially developing soft skills. In more detail, goals pertaining to each of the three levels were specified as follows:

- **Goals on the level of knowledge and intellect:** Theory of interpersonal communication, conflict management, group processes, negotiations, presentation, moderation, rhetoric
- **Goals on the skills and capabilities level:** Perceive the potentials and limitations of exercises aimed at improving communication; Improve teamwork; Moderate meetings; Gain active listening skills; Experience the interactive presentation, moderation, and discussion of a theme; Increase one's problem solving capability and creative approach to tasks; Gather and reflect experience in the application of computer-mediated communication
- **Goals on the attitudes, awareness level:** View learning as a personal project and take co-responsibility for it; Gain self-experience in expressing own intentions; Live the group process and develop as a team; Gain openness to experience; Experience the meaning of active listening and develop one's own attitude towards it; Perceive the creative influence and self-organization through the open design of a topical unit; Perceive a constructive working climate and offer it to the group.

The course scenario (depicted in Figure 1) blends face-to-face and web-supported learning such that the strengths of both settings, mediate and immediate, can be exploited and the learning process can proceed closer to the intentions and needs of individuals. In order to provide room for active interaction in class, fundamental material, links, and a list with references to further literature are supplied by the instructor over the learning platform at the time of course initialization. Also, key data on the course such as time, location, goals, brief description, etc. are provided such that students have initial information before enrolling in the course. The initial meeting is used to discuss the innovative course style, requirements, and learning methods, as well as to introduce the learning platform and to finalize the list of participants. Then students are asked to fill out an online questionnaire aimed at capturing their initial motivation, attitudes towards learning, ways they tend to profit from academic courses, etc. Furthermore, students are asked to assign themselves to small teams of about three to four students for cooperative work.

The face-to-face thread of the course consists of ten moderated workshops, 4 hours each, where individual topics within the gross framework of "soft skills in project management" are elaborated following a strongly interactive style. The first three workshops are moderated by the instructor who practically introduces students to elements of the moderation technique. This is done by conducting team discussions on selected aspects of the course, collecting expectations on a flip chart, using moderation cards to reflect on attitudes of good listeners, drawing mind-maps, having students prepare a flipchart on frequent barriers in communication, etc. Accompanying descriptions of these techniques and more theoretical background on

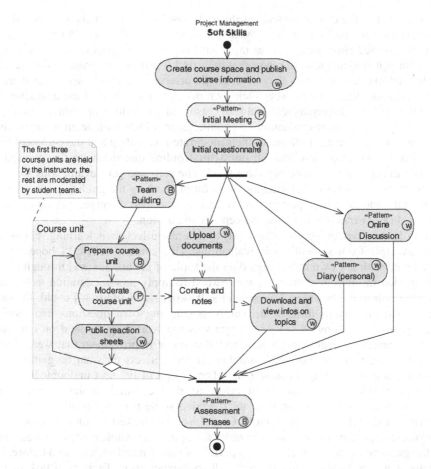

Fig. 1. Course scenario for project management soft skills (PM-SS) specified using UML [19] and including web-based (W), blended (B) and face to face (P) elements [5]

their application is provided via the learning platform and can be inspected on demand. The material was initially compiled by the instructor and has been complemented by numerous sources in the course of a master's thesis. The remaining seven workshops are prepared by teams of students on topics we agree upon during the initial sessions. Preparation of a workshop includes the provision of e-content regarding the selected topic. Preparation also encompasses consultation with the instructor with regard to the moderation sequence and elements. After each workshop, students submit online reaction sheets that can be read by all participants and are aimed at providing multi-perspective feedback to the team that moderated the workshop. At any time, students have access to the basic material provided on the platform. Concurrently, they are expected to briefly document their learning activities in a personal diary that shall support them in writing their self-evaluation in the end of the course. Furthermore, a discussion forum is available for communication with the instructor, web master, and fellow students on all course relevant issues.

At the end of the course students evaluate themselves online. This is accomplished by responding to questions such as: What did I contribute? What could I take with me from the course? How intensive was my contribution with respect to my team mates? etc. Although students tend to report that they find it difficult to evaluate themselves, in the vast majority of cases they evaluate themselves accurately such that there is only a minimal difference between their own perception and that of the instructor. So far, all cases of discrepancies could be resolved in follow up conversation. In addition, an online peer-evaluation in conducted in which each team anonymously evaluates all other teams in terms of their moderated workshop and the e-content they provided. Furthermore, students fill out a final online questionnaire that is used to evaluate the course on a more objective level. The self- and peer-evaluations are used by the instructor in his or her grading, thus complementing the grading process by an individual- and a group perspective reflecting the participative, person-centered didactic strategy inherent in course conception and design.

In order to give an idea in which ways students reflect their learning, below we share excerpts from student's self-evaluations: One student writes: "I hope I have contributed with my own inputs regarding the topic of negotiation and through active participation in all course units. I have learned to apply new moderation techniques and have acquired a balanced overview of soft skills ... In addition I could, for sure, gain maximum benefit through frequently posing my own questions and thereby framing the discussions. A key experience was the workshop we held on our own: Despite intensive preparation I have realized ways of improvement that were shown up by the feedback we received." Another student reflects on what he gained from preparing and moderating a course unit. "The design of the unit undoubtedly was a challenging task. I took me much effort to decide which topics to select for presentation and which just to refer to. I needed some time for reading, getting an overview, and making my own picture. Once I had overlooked the theme I considered everything important and necessary in order to capture the whole context. It was a real challenge to moderate the theme over a period of time I never experienced before, but equally it was a highly interesting and valuable experience. Tackling a task of this dimension shows how one manages to integrate oneself into a team and goes about solving problems in that team. In my view, our team did grow together quite intensively in the preparation phase. ... I think the constructive criticism of the group was more than justified in order to learn from it."

4 Course on Person-Centered Communication and New Media

When considering the major causes of project failure, experts agree that people issues clearly dominate technology issues. For example, in the Bull survey [3], the item "bad communications between relevant parties" heads the list of reasons for project failure.

Keeping these insights in mind and relating them to the EU strategic statement on key competences (mentioned in the introduction), we felt the need to design a technology-enhanced learning course that explicitly integrates all three levels of learning in the context of person-centered communication and new media (PCC). Unlike the course on soft skills, the course on PCC was designed to emphasize the level of interpersonal attitudes. This should allow students to gain some self experience such as to base their communication on a better understanding on their own inner world and, as a consequence, on the inner worlds of their communication partners. Let us introduce the PCC course by stating its course goals that we tend to extend by students' expectations as elaborated in initial course units.

- **Level of knowledge:** Knowledge about: Interpersonal attitudes, active listening, developmental tendency in the Person-Centered Approach, encounter groups, process stages, community building in real and virtual communities.

- **Level of skills:** Improvement of skills regarding: Ad hoc communication and online communication, speaking in a group, active listening, short ad-hoc presentations, teamwork, reflection and feedback.

- **Level of personality and attitudes or dispositions:** Development towards: Inner flexibility, transparent communication as a result from increased congruence, improved online communication, higher acceptance and better understanding of self and others, dealing with problems in everyday life more constructively.

As specified in course scenario given in Figure 2, the course information and lecture notes were published in an interactive course space, realized by means of CEWebS [9]. During a brief initial meeting students are selected to participate in the course following pre-specified criteria. The students are asked to fill out an online questionnaire and to read the initial part of the lecture notes along with an article on active listening. This is to ensure that the first workshop can be spent with getting to know one another and elaborating and discussing issues rather than lecturing. After the first workshop, students are asked to form teams of about three persons and to choose one out of about 10 small projects proposals listed on the platform to be elaborated by the team in self-organized fashion. Also, students should form pairs and select, co-read, summarize and discuss an article included in the course's lecture notes. Summary and discussion were to be published in the course space.

The four half-day workshops were spent with elaboration of topics in teams and subsequent presentations, small and large group discussions, brief presentations of the students' concept of working on their team projects, an exercise in active listening and its reflection, role play, discussions of students' reactions sheets, and watching a video on Carl Rogers, the founder of the Person-Centered Approach and Person-Centered Encounter Groups [17]. In the fourth workshop students were acquainted with the free and open style of encounter groups and their inherent potential for personal development. The subsequent Person-Centered Encounter Groups are scheduled to last 1.5 days each and provide wide space for experiencing one's own and the group's communication behavior. Each encounter group and workshop is followed by writing personal reaction sheets that are uploaded on the platform and can be read by all participants to allow for continuous development of the course. After the deadline for uploading the team projects, students are asked to evaluate themselves and each student is supposed to read and comment upon the project work of two teams that can freely be chosen. The final workshop is devoted to reflecting the students' personal experience in the course process as well as to collectively reflect on the Person-Centered Encounter Group process. In the end, students are asked to fill out the final online questionnaire including questions on teamwork, interpersonal relationships, course elements, learning on each of the levels, etc.

Since academic courses require grading, we looked for a grading procedure that would allow us to include as many facets of learning as possible into the final grade. Currently, the latter takes into account students' self evaluation, the evaluations of the students' project work by peers and the facilitator, and the facilitator's assessment of each student's participation in face-to-face and online activities.

To get an impression on the course setting and atmosphere let us inspect some students' reaction. A student noted: "I liked the first workshop and appreciate a course in which students get the chance to openly talk to one another, discuss, and share their views. Sitting in a circle was a well planned setting that has facilitated face-to-face communication. I consider it very appropriate to work in teams and subsequently present the ideas. This allows us to learn how to present our views effectively. The feedback after each presentation helps to see the strengths and weaknesses and to work on overcoming the weaknesses later."

Another student commented on a later workshop: "I consider talking about the reaction sheets in the beginning of the workshops as very meaningful. This way we can discuss and put into practice comments and suggestions, such as the idea to use name cards which, in my view, considerably contribute to creating a relaxed atmosphere. The moderation cards regarding the themes 'What is important for me as a speaker/listener' enabled one to identify issues of common concern as well as versatile issues that one has not considered on one's own."

Summarizing, the workshops were targeted at building knowledge about communication by means of elaborating material and served to practice concrete communication situations and thereby to heighten the sensitivity of students regarding relationship issues and feelings. The consequences of online media on reducing many essential assets of communication, possible workarounds and their potentials and limitation were thoroughly addressed, such that students could continue observing the different modes while meeting online and/or face-to-face to work on their projects.

The consequent Person-Centered encounter groups [2, 17] were foreseen to develop, in the first place, the level of feelings, attitudes, and dispositions. The lack of structure in such groups required participants to co-construct meaning by relying solely on their personal resources. In encounter groups, my primary task as a facilitator is to provide an open, respectful and understanding atmosphere in which participants and the whole group can move forward in a constructive process to build community and at the same time develop as individuals. The open sharing among, say, all participants, contributed to deep personal learning. Personally, I hypothesize that the openness expressed in the reaction sheets significantly contributed to building a safe and trustful climate in the group that allowed for deep learning at all levels.

Participants who talked less during group session often wrote insightful reactions and thereby became "known" to the group. This, in my view, built trust in the group and accelerated the group process, such that the group moved quickly to the constructive phases, in which the expression of positive feelings, respect, and change towards more openness and transparency dominated. The following excerpts from students' reactions after the first and second group meeting is intended to serve as an illustration of the encounter group process. Note also the more personal style in writing when compared with the reaction sheets after the initial workshops.

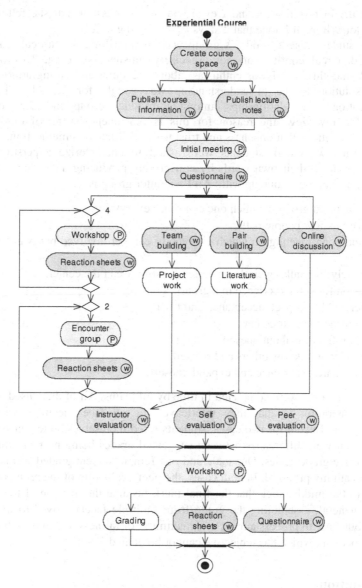

Fig. 2. Course scenario of Person-Centered Communication specified using UML [19] and including web-based (W), blended (B) and face to face (P) elements [5]

After the initial 1.5 day encounter a female student wrote: "I really liked the first encounter group. I did not expect that there will be no schedule at all, but that worked really well. I was surprised by the way in which themes appeared. ... Also, it was cool how the exchanges became more personal and meaningful and I could 'see' the increase trust among us. What I really appreciated was that persons, who tended to remain silent, finally contributed a lot more. Jean (name was changed here) really impressed me in this respect and I even had the impression that she felt well and profited a lot. All in all I hope that it stays as interesting as it is."

A male student noted: "Today's group was very thrilling, in particular, since we experienced a real conflict, or more precisely, misunderstanding. The discussion developed smoothly and I was enthusiast about the quiet and caring atmosphere in which a solution to the misunderstanding was sought for. ... Also, I felt the communication and relationships among individual group members improved gradually. In my view, the reason for this is our open sharing of our personal experiences. I believe that openness and trust truly facilitate communication. ..."

In the final workshop, students were asked to characterize a person-centered encounter group in their own words by collectively producing a flipchart. Here is a transcript on what they came up with: An Encounter group is:

- a non-structured group in which one can share everything
- and learn to know people better
- a free and open meeting, in which everybody can get involved but is not forced to do so
- a completely free talking circle, in which persons are at the center
- an occasion for self experience in a group
- characterized by respect, acceptance and trust
- location for growing together
- a form of reflecting about oneself
- a place to learn to know others and oneself
- a place to share experience and expand oneself.

The project works were completed in time by all teams. All of them used a blended way of cooperation in that they interleaved face-to-face meetings with online communication. Except for two cases, students rated themselves quite consistent with my evaluation with differences between suggested grades being no more than half a grade on a five grade scales. One male and one female student graded themselves 1.5 grades beneath my proposal. In both cases, the peer evaluation of the project work lay precisely in the middle such that the final mark became the average of the differing views. In general, assembling the grade from multiple facets proved to be a work-intensive but smooth process aiming at a maximum of fairness as can be achieved in a grading process in which the subjective cannot be denied.

5 Evaluation

In order to find out from which aspects of the respective course students benefited most and how this is related to traditional courses, we included 25 profitable aspects in the online questionnaire. In the beginning of the course we asked students to indicate to what degree they benefited from each of them in a "general" course in their studies, while in the end we wanted them to rate their benefit in the course on PM-SS and PCC, respectively. The complete results are depicted in Figure 3. On scales from 1 meaning "not at all" to 5 standing for "very much" the top three features in PM-SS and their average values were:

- Practical exercises during the lab hours (4.71)
- Active participation during the course (4.67)
- Exchange and discussion with colleagues (4.62)

All these items (and some others) were statistically significant at the p < 0.05 level using the Mann-Whitney-U test. In PCC, students indicated to have benefited most from "considering situations from different points of view" (4.87). As in PM-SS, "active participation during the course" (4.73) came second and "exchange and discussion with colleagues (4.71) was ranked in third place, both being significantly different (p < 0.05; Mann-Whitney-U test for 2-sided testing) from a typical course.

Figure 3 illustrates that there are only minimal differences regarding the item "materials and literature references" between a "traditional course" and PM-SS and PCC. Interestingly, however, students consistently rated items relying on active participation and interaction higher that learning from material resources. Figure 3 further indicates that the courses on PM-SS and PCC substantially differ from the "traditional course" in those aspects of learning in which interpersonal relationships are essential, while they are rather similar to each other regarding items such as active participation and sharing. The ratings in these items clearly surpass those given for a traditional course.

Interestingly, the feature "Support by a web based platform" came in place 9 and 13, respectively, with an average value of 4.14 and 4.13. This illustrates that although support by new media clearly is considered helpful, students do not view it as one of the primary features for their learning in the context of the courses on PM-SS and PCC.

To get a further perspective on how important students perceive online course elements when compared with structured workshops and unstructured encounter groups, we asked them to rate these three course elements in terms of the perceived importance in PCC. Approximately the same amount of course time was scheduled to these three course segments. As expected from the students' feedback in face-to-face meetings and online reaction sheets, the encounter groups were perceived as the most important in both course instances of PCC that we investigated. Interestingly, as depicted in Figure 4, they were perceived as slightly more important in the course instance PCC group 2 (scenario given in Figure 2) that allocated about 9 hours more to workshops than to encounter groups. This indicates that, despite the highest potential attributed to the encounter groups by students, structured workshops are essential for preparing students for the experience and allowing them to collaboratively reflect on it in a final face-to-face workshop. Although online contributions came in third place only, the difference between them and the other elements appears quite low. From this we conjecture that they can be seen as a highly suitable element to complement the more intensive face-to-face elements.

Regarding learning/development on the levels of knowledge/intellect, skills, and personality, we were interested, whether students' perceptions matched the course goals. Therefore, in the final online questionnaire, we included the question: "Please indicate, how much you benefited on the individual levels of learning." On a scale where 1 indicated very little and 5 meant very much, the level of skills received the highest rating in both courses, followed by the personality level and the level of knowledge/intellect. The result can be seen as a confirmation of the course goals in PM-SS so far, as emphasis has been given to development at the level of soft skills.

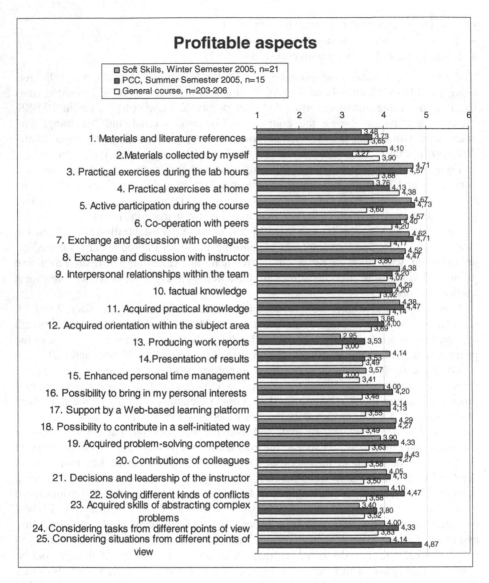

Fig. 3. Aspects from which students benefit in a "traditional course" as compared with PM-SS and PCC. Scales from 1…"not at all" to 5…"very much".

Interestingly, in PCC learning at the level of personal attitudes having been in the focus, was perceived as lower than learning of skills. This was the case despite the fact that "considering situations from different points of view" – typically a feature reflecting the attitude of openness – headed the list of profitable items on the same questionnaire. Also, the majority of items in the self evaluation of participants in PCC could be classified as pertaining to the attitude level. This shows that multiple perspectives are required to interpret data as well as that the distinction between the

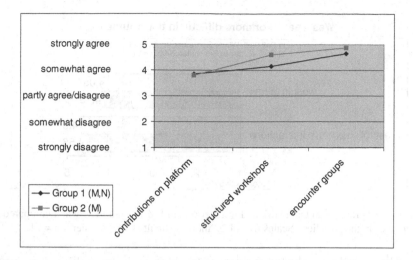

Fig. 4. Perceived importance of course elements in two groups (n1 = 15, n2 = 14) of the course on PCC. The Figure illustrates to which degree students agreed when asked: The contributions on the platform, the encounter groups, the structured workshops, respectively, were important.

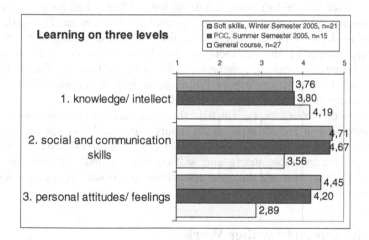

Fig. 5. Learning at three levels in a conventional course and the course on PM-SS and PCC

social skills and attitudes level may be fluent and fuzzy. Last but not least Figure 5 can be seen to confirm the superiority of whole person learning. Intuitively speaking, the collective contribution of the three levels for each of the courses PM-SS and PCC is higher than that for a traditional course. Note that students perceived the facilitator as congruent, respectful and understanding according to the rating of these person-centered attitudes, namely 4.66, 4.75, and 4.60, respectively in PM-CC on scales where 1 meant "does not apply" and 5 stood for "applies fully." There were no statistically significant differences between the ratings of the same instructor in different courses held during the same academic year.

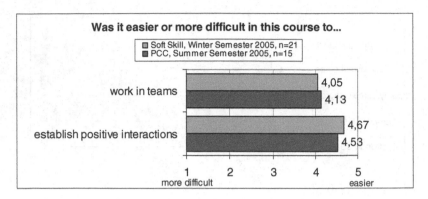

Fig. 6. Students ratings on teamwork and interactions in PM-SS and PCC when compared with other courses in their studies. Scales from 1…"more difficult" to 5…"easier"; n = 21.

In order to find out, whether students found it easier or more difficult to work in teams and to establish positive interpersonal relationships in PM-SS and PCC, two further questions were included in the final questionnaire. As shown in Figure 6, most students felt that in the course on PM-SS and PCC it was somewhat easier to work in teams and easier to establish positive interactions. When asked for the reasons, one student responded: "Because of the intensive contacts between us. The work in small teams, the moderation of the course, but also the sitting arrangement in a circle significantly supported the interactions and building of positive relationships. Regarding teamwork a student comments: "I knew my colleagues already from other courses, hence I knew what to expect. At the same time, the course offered sufficient inputs and space to coordinate team work well."

From the second reaction we conclude that care must be taken in interpreting the results, since several factors aside of the course style and atmosphere may be co-responsible for the students' perceptions on teamwork and relationships. Nevertheless, the reaction sheets and self-evaluations indicate that the positive atmosphere in the course and the open discussions contributed to highly constructive cooperation and interaction.

6 Conclusions and Further Work

Whereas the lead in effective learning still stays with persons, their capabilities, and social- and interpersonal values, thoughtfully designed scenarios, customized web services, and easily accessible content have the potential to significantly support persons in their striving to support learning by new technology. Clearly, this requires not only highly usable tools but also personal skills and a high degree of transparency, openness, acceptance, flexibility, and understanding from the facilitators. During a flexible course process, usable learning technology supports the higher degree personalized and active learning.

When balancing the power differential in class, one realizes that students and professors become something different. Rather than playing roles, they become whole persons with thoughts, meanings, feelings, behaviors which come fully into effect. In this style of person-centered methodology the professors become facilitators where learning can happen fully, as has been shown in the evaluation section of the courses on project management soft skills and person-centered communication. Perhaps more vividly than figures can show, a student from PCC notes: "In the end I would like to thank all of you for contributing to the success of this course. Each unit was a special experience for me and I appreciate having been able to be a member of this group und share these experiences with all of you." Another student writes: "I am sure that everybody profited from this course, at least, I did. ... What I experienced in this course is something that I will never forget." Personally, the author is convinced that the educator's or better facilitator's attitudes, skills and experiences in project- or group situations can serve as an essential input for students' experiential learning. To develop and smoothly complement these processes by flexible, highly usable web-based tools appears to be a challenging task for institutions that propagate technology-*enhanced* learning.

Our exploration of two teaching/learning settings has confirmed that no single research paradigm suffices to provide answers to the questions that typically arise when investigating socio-technical systems such as technology-enhanced courses. In our experience, participatory Action Research, complemented by qualitative and quantitative methods, has proved helpful for investigating learning scenarios.

Further work will proceed with method triangulation in teaching/learning processes and their modeling in reusable scenarios and patterns [5]. One issue of particular interest is to accompany person-centered encounter groups with online elements in order to confirm or modify initial findings on accelerating group and team building processes. Furthermore, we intend to transfer the concepts and tools to profit and non-profit organizations and other institutions for higher- and adult education. Readers interested to join our efforts are invited to contact us at http://www.cs.univie.ac.at .

Acknowledgement

The author sincerely thanks her colleague Kathrin Figl for her contributions and support regarding the course evaluation and Michael Derntl, Jürgen Mangler and Klaus Spiegl for several discussions and learning platform support.

References

[1] Aspy, D. N.: Toward a Technology for Humanizing Education. Research Press Company, Champaign, Illinois (1972).
[2] Barrett-Lennard, G. T.: Carl Rogers' Helping System - Journey and Substance. Sage Publications, London (1998).
[3] Bull: Bull survey on project failure statistics, available at http://www.it-cortex.com/ Stat_Failure_Cause.htm (1998).
[4] Cornelius-White, J. H. D., Hoey, A., Cornelius-White, C., Motschnig-Pitrik, R., and Figl, K.: Person-Centered Education: A Meta-Analysis of Care in Progress. Journal of Border Educational Research 3 (2004) 81-87.

[5] Derntl, M.: Patterns for Person-Centered e-Learning. PhD Thesis, University of Vienna, Vienna, Austria (2005).

[6] Derntl, M. and Motschnig-Pitrik, R.: A Pattern Approach to Person-Centered e-Learning based on Theory-Guided Action Research. Proc. 4th International Conference on Networked Learning (NLC), Lancaster, UK, (2004).

[7] Derntl, M. and Motschnig-Pitrik, R.: The Role of Structure, Patterns, and People in Blended Learning. The Internet and Higher Education 8 (2005) 111-130.

[8] European Association for the Education of Adults: Strategic Statement on Key Competencies, available at http://www.eaea.org/doc/Strategic_document_2004.doc (2004).

[9] Mangler, J. and Derntl, M.: CEWebS - Cooperative Environment Web Services. Proc. 4th International Conference on Knowledge Management (I-KNOW '04), Graz, Austria, (2004).

[10] McCombs, B. L. and Whisler, J. S.: The learner-centered classroom and school: strategies for increasing student motivation and achievement. John Wiley & Sons, San Francisco (1997).

[11] Motschnig-Pitrik, R.: An Action Research-Based Framework for Assessing Blended Learning Scenarios. Proc. ED-MEDIA 2004: World Conference on Educational Multimedia, Hypermedia & Telecommunications, Lugano, Switzerland, (2004).

[12] Motschnig-Pitrik, R.: Person Centered e-Learning in a major academic course: What are the results and what can we learn from them? Proc. 4th International Conference on Networked Learning (NLC), Lancaster, UK, (2004).

[13] Motschnig-Pitrik, R. and Holzinger, A.: Student-Centered Teaching Meets New Media: Concept and Case Study. Journal of Educational Technology & Society 5 (2002) 160-172.

[14] Motschnig-Pitrik, R. and Mallich, K.: Effects of Person-Centered Attitudes on Professional and Social Competence in a Blended Learning Paradigm. Journal of Educational Technology & Society 7 (2004) 176-192.

[15] Reichelmayr, T.: Enhancing the Student Team Experience with Blended Learning Techniques. Proc. 35th ASEE/IEEE Frontiers in Education Conference, Indianapolis, IM, (2005).

[16] Rogers, C. R.: On Becoming a Person - A Psychotherapists View of Psychotherapy. Constable, London (1961).

[17] Rogers, C. R.: Carl Rogers on Encounter Groups. Harper Row, New York (1970).

[18] Rogers, C. R.: Freedom to Learn for the 80's. Charles E. Merrill Publishing Company, Columbus, Ohio (1983).

[19] Rumbaugh, J., Jacobson, I., and Booch, G.: The Unified Modeling Language Reference Manual. Addison Wesley, Reading, MA (1999).

Developing Collaborative Virtual Learning Community for the Korean Community Health Practitioners

Woojin Paik[1], Eunjung Ryu[2], Jaewook Choi[3], Hyeongsu Kim[4], and Eunmi Ham[2,*]

[1] Dept. of Computer Science, Konkuk University,
322 Danwol-Dong, Chungju-Si, Chungcheongbuk-Do, 380-701, Korea
wjpaik@kku.ac.kr
[2] Dept. of Nursing Science, Konkuk University,
322 Danwol-Dong, Chungju-Si, Chungcheongbuk-Do, 380-701, Korea
{go2ryu, hem2003}@kku.ac.kr
[3] Dept. of Preventive Medicine, Korea University,
Anam-dong Seongbuk-Gu, Seoul, 136-701 Korea
shine@korea.ac.kr
[4] Dept. of Preventive Medicine, Konkuk University,
322 Danwol-Dong, Chungju-Si, Chungcheongbuk-Do, 380-701, Korea
mubul@kku.ac.kr

Abstract. Community Health Post workers are mainly registered nurses. They provide first-level primary health care to the numerous underserved rural communities in Korea. The primary goal of our project is to provide technological foundation for the community health practitioners to form a virtual community that collaboratively solves problems and learns to improve their patient caring and treatment skills. The main enabling technology is a collaboratively maintained knowledge management system, which assists the community health practitioners to make appropriate diagnoses and also to determine the corresponding expected outcomes and interventions to perform given the patient's symptoms. The knowledge management system includes a knowledge base, which is converted from the standardized nursing process guidelines. In addition, the knowledge management system is also used as a case retrieval system so that the community health practitioners can compare the current case in progress with the similar prior cases. We have developed a prototype system and finished a preliminary evaluation of the system.

1 Motivation and Background

Korean government established Community Health Posts to provide various health care services to rural population in 1980. Currently, there are 1,866 community health practitioners working at 1,889 community health posts. Each community health post is working with about 1,000 residents and thus there are about 2 million responsible people, which is about 5% of the total Korean population [1].

Various missions of the community health practitioners are: 1) delivering first-level primary health care including health assessment, hypertensive disease management,

---

* Corresponding author.

W. Nejdl and K. Tochtermann (Eds.): EC-TEL 2006, LNCS 4227, pp. 347–356, 2006.

glycosuria management, ophthalmology related health management, infectious disease management, and tuberculosis management; 2) consulting with and educating rural community residents about the general health related issues; 3) dealing with maternal and child health related issues and family planning; and 4) various other chores including medication receipts and disbursements, insurance related form filing, activity reporting to the overseeing regional government, and monetary transaction managing.

With respect to how the community health practitioners spent their time while on the duty, 64% of the community health practitioners' time was spent on client care activities and 36% on management. Half of the time spent on client care was taken up by preventive activities, 16% by health assessment activities, and 33% by treatment [2].

Most of the community health practitioners either have 3-year associate's degree or 4-eyar bachelors' degree in nursing science. Ones, who want to become a community health practitioner, have to get 24 weeks of supplementary training about the community health post operation before they can actually apply for a position at a particular public health post. There is government mandated yearly maintenance training, which can lasts six days or less, for the community health practitioners to attend [3]. However, the initial supplementary training is one time education for the life of a community health practitioner. Furthermore, the topics covered in the yearly maintenance trainings are limited due to the time and space constraints. The large lecture type trainings are usually conducted for a few hundred practitioners at one time. Thus, it is impossible for the community health practitioners to get individualized attentions to their particular problems or the cases. More importantly, there is no formalized way for the community health practitioners to inquire about the immediate health care related problems they face while they work except for sending the patients to a hospital located sometimes one hundred kilometers or more away from the particular community health post. Informally, the community health practitioners have been discussing their cases and receiving advices from other nearby community health practitioners mainly via phone or email communications with certain degree of satisfaction. But, this sort of communication does not usually leave any records for the later use. To enhance this informal and small scale collaboration practice, we are working on an ongoing project to develop a knowledge management system, which can be used to store the experiential knowledge and also to share accumulated knowledge amongst a larger group of community health practitioners.

Currently, Korean Ministry of Health and Welfare is working on the Phase 2 of the Community Health Post Information Technology Modernization Project. By introducing the government mandated standardized information management system, the government is trying to accomplish the following: 1) increase the efficiency of the community health posts' work flow; 2) reduce the operating cost of the community health posts; and 3) automatically generate and collect the statistical information about the services provided and population served by the community health posts to guide the future policy introduction. While this government project is mainly focusing on the administrative aspect of the public health care management, our project is focusing on the performance of the community health practitioners. Our goal is to improve the patient care and treatment skills of the community health practitioners by helping them to work together and also to form a co-evolving virtual community even they are geographically dispersed.

Although most of the community health practitioners are originally trained as nurses, they are working at the locations where the medical doctors are not usually nearby. Thus, they are given limited authority to perform simple and routine medical treatments, which do not require complicated reasoning or extensive training. The community health practitioners can also prescribe or dispense medications to cure common symptoms such as flu. However, the practitioners are fully qualified to follow the standard nursing process to provide nursing care. The nursing process consists of assessment, diagnosis, planning, implementation, and evaluation of the patients' health problems. For example, nursing diagnoses address human responses to actual and potential health problems or life processes such as activity intolerance, ineffective health maintenance, and ineffective airway clearance. The nursing diagnoses change as the client's situation or perspective alters or resolves. In comparison, medical diagnoses are illness or conditions such as diabetes, heart failure, hepatitis, cancer, and pneumonia that reflect alteration of the structure or function of organs or systems. The medical diagnosis usually does not change [4].

We allow the medical treatment related knowledge to be stored and shared by the practitioners by using the collaborative learning knowledge base. However, we determined that the nursing process related knowledge to be the main target subject for the community health practitioners to learn through the use of our system.

2 Collaborative Learning for Knowledge Building

The process of knowledge building in collaborative learning is characterized by six cognitive activities [5]. They are: 1) mutual exploration of issues; 2) mutual examination of arguments; 3) agreements and disagreements; 4) mutual questioning of positions; 5) dynamic interaction; and 6) weaving of ideas.

2.1 Collaborative Learning Example

Our system facilitates all six activities and also allows them to occur in a Peer to Peer (P2P) information sharing environment. Our system supports the 'mutual exploration of issues' by enabling the community health practitioners to collaboratively review and clarify the patient information. Our system also allows the practitioners to 'examine the arguments mutually', 'agree and disagree', and 'question positions mutually' by providing the functionalities to question or comment in response to the evaluations or the analyses of the patient information posted by other practitioners. These exploration, examination, agreement, disagreement, and questioning form the 'dynamic interactions' amongst the practitioners thanks to the built-in synchronous and asynchronous communication functionalities of the system. Finally, our system provides the capability to 'weave ideas' during the collaborative generation of nursing diagnoses, outcomes, and interventions.

The following Korean example was a narrative about a 47-year old divorced male patient written by a community health science internship student, who participated our preliminary evaluation of the system. The student concluded the narrative with a defense mechanism assessment, which is a type of a psychiatric nursing diagnosis.

This narrative was posted on the threaded discussion board by the student to get the reactions about her assessment from other system users.

<Question> 왜 술을 많이 마셨는지에 대해 물어보았을 때 </Question> <Answer> 환자는 자신이 술에 손을 대게 된 계기와 폭주를 하게 된 계기가 모두 이혼한 아내 탓이라고 말하며 </Answer> <Observed> 침울한 표정을 지었다. </Observed> <Definition> 이는 자신의 불쾌한 감정, 사고 및 태도를 다른 사람의 탓으로 돌리는 </Definition> <Assessment> 투사의 방어기제로 보여진다. </Assessment>

The English translation of the first clause marked as 'Question' is 'when asked about why the patient had been drinking excessively'. The translation of the second clause marked as 'Answer by Patient' is 'the patient described that he started to drink and had been drinking a lot because of his divorced wife'. The translation of the third clause marked as 'Observed' is 'his face looked somber'. The fourth 'Definition' clause is translated as 'the preceding description indicates that the patient blames other person for his unpleasant feeling, thoughts, and attitudes'. The final clause marked as 'Assessment' can be translated as 'the symptoms indicate the projection as the defense mechanism of the patient'. In response to this post, two students agreed with the original assessment by posting approval replies. This is an example of 'agreements and disagreements ', which is the third cognitive activity described by Harasim [5].

2.2 Knowledge Management System

The main enabling technology to sustain a virtual learning community is a collaboratively maintained knowledge management system, which assists the community health practitioners to make appropriate diagnoses and also to determine the corresponding expected outcomes and interventions to perform given the patient's symptoms. The knowledge management system includes a knowledge base, which is converted from the standardized nursing process guidelines. In addition, the knowledge management system is also used as a case retrieval system so that the community health practitioners can compare the current case in progress with the similar prior cases. The community health practitioners can review and learn from the records of the interventions applied, patient reactions occurred, and the outcomes achieved.

Probably, the most difficult stage of the patient care is the selection of the most appropriate nursing diagnosis given the physical and mental state and symptoms of a patient. The main component of the knowledge base is a set of 142 nursing diagnoses, which are organized as ontology of a three-layer hierarchy. Each diagnosis is associated with the definition and one or more defining characteristics. The practitioners learn to navigate the hierarchy and differentiate diagnoses by reviewing the existing cases and also by observing what other do.

The nursing outcomes are also organized as ontology of a multi-level hierarchy. In addition, each diagnosis is linked to one or more potentially suitable nursing outcomes. Therefore, the practitioners select the most appropriate nursing outcomes based on the nursing diagnosis, the state, and the symptoms of the patients.

Similarly, the nursing interventions are organized as ontology of a multi-level hierarchy in the knowledge base. Each diagnosis and outcome is linked to one or more potentially suitable nursing interventions. This leads to the selection of the most appropriate nursing interventions based on the nursing diagnosis, nursing outcome, the state, and the symptoms of the patients. Yet again, the practitioners learn to select the correct outcomes and interventions by reviewing the existing cases and also by observing what others do namely exploring the outcomes and interventions ontology.

Typical case reports include the background information about the patients such as the general biographical information, the medical history, various health related information, physical and mental state assessment results, nursing diagnoses, suggested interventions, and expected outcomes. Often certain information such as the medication records is entered in a tabular form. However, much of the information is conveyed as narratives of the practitioners and the direct quotes from the patients. Patient data are regarded as either subjective or objective data. Subjective data are what the client reported, believed, or felt. Objective data are what can be observed such as vital signs, behaviors, or diagnostic studies [4]. The practitioners record patient's condition in the form of facts that they observed, monologue by the patient, patient's answers to the practitioners' questions, and the patient's condition conveyed by others such as family members. Then, the practitioners often summarize the factual information. The practitioners form their evaluation of the patient's condition based on the summarized factual information.

2.3 Peer to Peer (P2P) Information Sharing

Another important supporting technology for the collaborating and learning community is the P2P information sharing technology that connects the case knowledge bases and the geographically dispersed community health practitioners. Since each case knowledge base is developed and maintained independently by each community health practitioner, the use of the P2P information sharing technology allows one practitioners to refer to all knowledge bases, which are developed by other fellow practitioners. To solve problems that require immediate attention or to discuss matters online, the P2P information sharing technology enables computer-mediated multimedia communication such as real-time audio and video chats amongst the practitioners. The community health practitioners can take care of their difficult ongoing treatment cases collaboratively by jointly reviewing the patient assessment data in the forms of photo images, sound recordings, and written records. In summary, our system is designed to promote the evidence and standard based treatment of the patients as well as the team-based approach in the patient caring by the community health practitioners by forming a virtual learning and collaborating community with the knowledge management and emerging P2P information sharing technology.

3   Implementation and Preliminary Evaluation

We are working on a 2-year project to develop a virtual learning community for the community health practitioners. We are continuously collecting information about 1) the difficulties that the practitioners face in terms of providing quality health care, 2) how the practitioners currently learn new patient care and treatment skills, and 3) how they collaborate with each other to develop a virtual community model describing

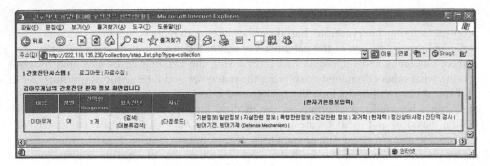

Fig. 1. Treatment Case Report Initial Entry Screen

how the public health care professionals can remotely collaborate with each other to learn new knowledge and share their experiences.

Although the software requirement generation phase has not been completed, we developed a prototype knowledge management system based on the P2P information sharing technology by following an incremental software development methodology. We wanted to allow the community health practitioners, who are early adopters, to tryout our system to provide us with early feedback. While not all the functionalities are fully implemented, the prototype system allows the practitioners to 1) enter treatment case reports based on the standardized nursing process guidelines; 2) retrieve ranked list of previously entered case reports, which are similar to the current case in progress; 3) collaboratively or individually select the most appropriate nursing diagnoses as well as the corresponding nursing outcomes and nursing interventions given the symptoms discovered from the patient assessment stage of the nursing process; 4) collaborate with other remotely located practitioners to come up with the best possible nursing diagnoses, outcomes, and interventions by sharing pictures images and written/verbal recordings about the patients though real-time voice and video chats; and 5) post questions and publish ideas about the patient care for other public health care professionals to review.

Figure 1 shows the screen where the community health practitioners enter the patient information as a part of the case report. This is the main window, which is shown in the beginning of each data entry session. It includes the very basic patient information such as name and sex as well as the number of nursing diagnoses selected. It also shows various section headings for the case report. The headings are: 'basic and general information', 'suicide information', 'violence related information', 'health related information', 'past health history', 'present health status', 'mental health assessments', 'diagnostic test results', and psychiatric health information including defense mechanisms'. These headings are hyperlinked buttons leading to the respective data entry windows. For example, a pop-up window shown as Figure 2 appears if the button labeled as '현재력', which can be translated as 'present health status', is selected. The Figure 2 shows the entry for 'main symptom', which is the first part of the 'present health status' section.

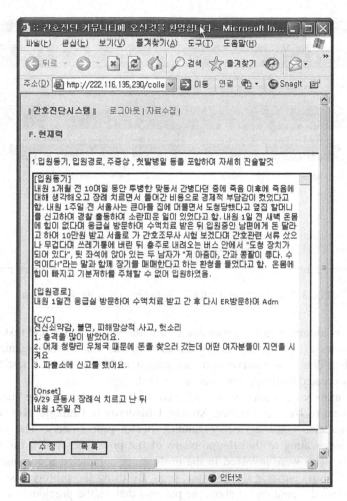

Fig. 2. Present Health Status Information Entry Screen

The Figure 3 shows the window listing one of three nursing diagnoses selected for this patient. The diagnosis is 'constipation'. The community health practitioner chose 'bowel elimination' as the expected outcome. She selected a number of interventions to be administered. The embedded knowledge base includes all possible diagnoses, outcomes, and interventions. The practitioner makes tentative selections from the possible options by navigating the knowledge base. At this point, the practitioner has two choices. One option is to post her diagnosis and the link to her case report on the active threaded discussion board. This usually happens when the responsible practitioners is not confident with her choice and thus soliciting others to review and comment. Another option is not to take any particular action with respect to her choice. In this case, the responsible practitioners are usually confident about her reasoning.

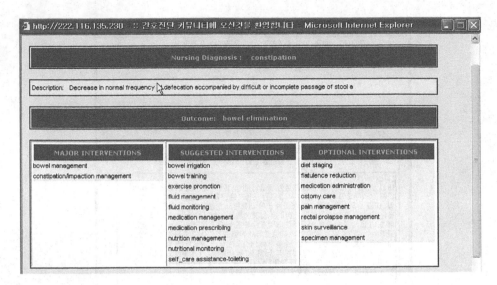

Fig. 3. Nursing Diagnosis/Outcome/Intervention Review Screen

The online communication screen consists of the video, voice, and text communication windows as well as the active threaded discussion boards organized by the themes such as diagnosis, intervention, medication, and home visits. These themes are dynamically created by the practitioners as needed.

The preliminary evaluation was conducted with six senior nursing students from the Department of Nursing Science, Konkuk University in Chungju, Korea in March 2006. All students acted as the community health practitioners. The goal of the evaluation was mainly to find the problems of the prototype system functionalities. The students, who were involved in the evaluation, completed a community health science internship course in the previous year. By using the prototype system, each student re-created a case report about the patients that he/she previously worked with in the internship course. During the re-creation, the students were not allowed to meet in person but encouraged to virtually collaborate with each other.

We used a formative evaluation methodology. It is usually conducted with a small number of people to test run various aspects of a program or product. According to Scriven [6], formative evaluation is conducted often more than once with the intent to improve. It is referred as having someone look over your shoulder during the development phase to help you catch things that you miss, but a fresh set of eye might not.

Based on this preliminary evaluation, we have mainly identified a number of usability problems, which can confuse and also mislead the users to enter wrong information to search for potentially relevant cases to their problems at hand. Based on this preliminary evaluation result, we are revising the system for the later full scale usability and the effectiveness evaluation with the actual community health practitioners in the field to assess the usefulness of the system in building continuously evolving learning community for the community health practitioners.

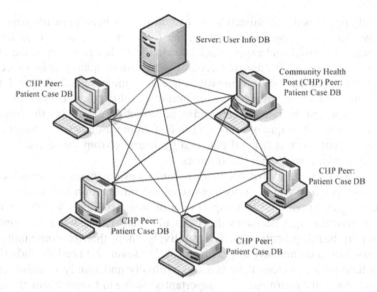

Fig. 4. Peer scheme of the Collaborative Learning Knowledge Management System

The P2P information sharing technology based collaborative learning knowledge management system is developed in Java using JXTA, which is a set of open protocols initially developed by Sun Microsystems that allow any connected device on the network to communicate and collaborate in a P2P manner [7]. Specifically, JAL, which abstracts the functionality necessary for the P2P systems, was used for the system development [8]. Figure 4 shows the structure of our system, which is a hybrid architecture between client-server model and peer-to-peer model. The server provides user registration and authentication services to ensure only the valid community health practitioners can use the system. This security measure exists to provide privacy protection against the misuses of the patient information. Each peer, which corresponds to a community health post, is a desktop PC with a PC camera, a microphone, and a headset. The nursing process related knowledge base and information about the patients, who gets health care service from the respective community health post, are stored in a database implemented with MySQL database management system. The overall architecture of the system is similar to the one used to share radiological images and diagnoses [9].

4 Summary and Future Work

Although we are clearly in the early stage of developing a prototype Collaborative Learning Knowledge Management System for the community health practitioners, we find prototype implementation and preliminary evaluation of the system to be quite promising. Thus, we are eager to share our experiences in developing a system to build a virtual learning community with other researchers. We are in the process of upgrading the prototype system based on the preliminary evaluation. However, we plan to conduct a formal evaluation of the system with the actual community health practitioners.

Once fully developed and utilized by many community health practitioners, we expect our system to contribute in generating the following outcomes: 1) faster health care information transfer and experiential knowledge exchange amongst the community health practitioners, 2) improved capability to deliver quality health care to the people in the rural area, 3) overall improved health of the people in the rural area, 4) increased job satisfaction amongst the community health practitioners and thus decreased job displacement rate, 5) knowledge preservation even after the community health practitioners either quit or retire, and 6) faster time for a new community health practitioner to start work at her full potential by learning from the stored knowledge and virtually working with other practitioners.

However, we understand that our work is limited as our main research focus was on the system usability and the effective use of the information technology. We neglected to study an important social aspect of community building, which will eventually help us to make right decisions that can truly improve the work performance of the community health practitioners. We intuitively know that the community health practitioners form a community of practice [10]. However, we need to study them by observing how they carry out their tasks individually and jointly to understand the type of community they formed. Most importantly, we need to study how the learning actually takes place amongst the community health practitioners to facilitate them with the proposed technological advances.

References

1. Lee, C.Y., Yu, T.U.: Service Analysis of Community Health Nurse Practitioner using Information Systems. In: Journal of Korea Community Health Nursing Academic Society, Vol. 17. No. 1. (2003) 26-34
2. Kim, E.S.: Research on the Community Health Practitioner Activity Analysis and Education Curriculum Development. In: International Development Research Centre Research Report (1988)
3. Republic of Korea. The Special Measures Law Enforcement Rule for Health and Medical Care for the Farming and Fishing Villages: Ministry of Health and Public Welfare Decree No. 264 (2003)
4. Doenges, M. and Moorehead, M.F., Application of Nursing Process and Nursing Diagnosis: An Interactive Text for Diagnostic Reasoning 4th Edition, F.A. Davis Co., Philadelphia, Pennsylvania. (2003)
5. Harasim, L., Collaborating in Cyberspace: Using computer conference as a group learning environments. Interactive Learning Environments, 3(2). 119-130. (1993)
6. Scriven, M., Beyond Formative and Summative Evaluation. In: McLaughlin, M.W. and Phillips, ED.C. eds., Evaluation and Education: A Quarter Century. Chicago: University of Chicago Press (1991)
7. Project jxta. http://www.jxta.org
8. Jxta abstraction layer. http://ezel.jxta.org/jal.html
9. Blanquer, I, Hernandez, V., Mas, F.: A P2P Platform for Sharing Radiological Images and Diagnoses: In: Proceedings of Distributed Databases and processing in Medical Image Computing Workshop, Rennes, France (2004)
10. Wenger, E.: Communities of Practice: Learning, Meaning, and Identity. Cambridge University Press, Cambridge, UK. (1998)

Simulation as Efficient Support
to Learning Business Dynamics

Alexander Karapidis[1], Lucia Pannese[2], Dimitra Pappa[3],
Mauro Santalmasi[2], and Wolfgang Volz[4]

[1] Fraunhofer Institute for Industrial Engineering (IAO),
Nobelstrasse 12, 70569 Stuttgart, Germany
Alexander.Karapidis@iao.fraunhofer.de
[2] imaginary s.rl. c/o Acceleratore d'Impresa del Politecnico di Milano,
via Garofalo, 39, 20133 Milano, Italy
info@i-maginary.it
[3] Division of Applied Technologies, National Centre for Scientific Research
(NCSR) "Demokritos", 15310 Agia Paraskevi, Greece
dimitra@dat.demokritos.gr
[4] Klett Lernen und Wissen GmbH, Educational Concepts,
Rotebühlstr. 77, 70178 Stuttgart, Germany
w.volz@klett.de

Abstract. The aim of this paper is to provide insight in the important role simulation technologies can play in the context of effective business process-oriented learning. The gap between business processes and HR carrying out concrete tasks could be bridged by integrating knowledge management and learning needs with respect to business processes. First, the importance between business processes, learning and simulations is illustrated. Second, simulations and their impact for company efficiency is outlined. Third, the benefits of the PROLIX e-simulation are described according to specific requirements out of a business process perspective. A company case study is also presented. The conclusion is that decision support for management under specific performance conditions and the learning environment itself are key elements that contemporary e-simulations bring together for the benefit of work performance and effectiveness as well as efficiency of companies.

1 Business Process-Oriented Learning with e-Simulations

Nothing is constant but change, especially in a turbulent, complex and globalized world. To survive, an organisation should develop the capacity to learn continuously (Watkins & Marsick, 1993). Change and complexity also mean that people in organisations must constantly learn and adapt.

Enterprises are faced with a number of vital business issues to improve operational efficiency in terms of product time-to-market, cost retention, quality improvement, regulatory compliance etc. New approaches are needed for companies to effectively plan, structure and manage their activities so as to gain or maintain their competitive advantage. Creating strategic advantage and improving organisational competitiveness requires changes in business organisation (a shift towards performance driven

W. Nejdl and K. Tochtermann (Eds.): EC-TEL 2006, LNCS 4227, pp. 357–365, 2006.

processes) and continuous investment in human capital growth, as the success of modern corporations increasingly depends on its intellectual assets.

Out of this perspective, learning emerges as a key enabler for organisations to support and enhance performance. This process entails linking individual training needs to the key business priorities by building links between business and learning processes. Since business processes define organisational roles and associate functions, each with its own specific requirements in terms of competencies, learning processes can be defined based on the lacking competencies of individual employees assigned to specific organisational roles: whenever there is a gap between the competencies profile of an individual assigned to a specific role and the competencies profile of the role (i.e. the competencies required for this particular role), the most suitable training plan must be designed and the most suitable learning resources must be mobilised, in order to fill it.

In response to the need of organisations and enterprises to improve their response to business change and reduce the time needed to fill competency gaps (Time2Competency) that result from business needs (e.g. business process changes, reorganisations), the European project **PROLIX** ("Process-oriented Learning and Information exchange"[12]) aims to couple business processes with learning processes in corporate environments, so as to facilitate business process oriented learning. This will support:

1. **Continuous tactical improvement (small scale):** This concerns tactical operations (short term decisions and small scale changes) aimed at the continuous improvement of organisational operations (day to day business, incremental performance improvements based on existing resources).

2. **Goal oriented change (large scale):** This relates to large scale changes in corporate strategy and/or goals (e.g. wide range business process re-engineering activities, implementation of a new strategic plan).

For example, aligning organisational change and learning will enable organisations to:

- adapt to changes in business processes (business process reengineering)
- effectively introduce new employees to a project and /or role
- overcome performance problems caused by heterogeneous company culture among different company's departments, branches or within project teams (e.g. due to mergers and acquisitions)
- adapt to changes in organisational and/or management structure
- optimize the alignment between business process and competency management

The optimisation of business processes by means of learning entails the combination of business process intelligence tools with knowledge management and learning services provision applications. In this context e-Simulations are expected to play an important role, for both business process optimisation and learning delivery. The aim of this paper is to investigate the double role of simulation technologies in the framework of business process-oriented learning. In this light the application of e-simulations in the framework of the PROLIX project in the publishing sector (Klett AG) will be discussed.

2 The Power of an e-Simulation

2.1 Management Perspective

Business process simulation (BPS) is a tool used to assist in the management of change in a variety of manufacturing and service settings. BPS can "assist decision making by providing a tool that allows the current behaviour of a system to be analysed and understood. It is also able to help predict the performance of that system under a number of scenarios determined by the decision maker"(Greasley, 2003).

From this perspective, simulation technologies can have a double role. They can either be a **vehicle for learning along processes** or a **decision support instrument** to help decide how to improve processes and the overall effectiveness of staff. Also, simulation techniques can be used to **validate decisions associated with the learning solution.**

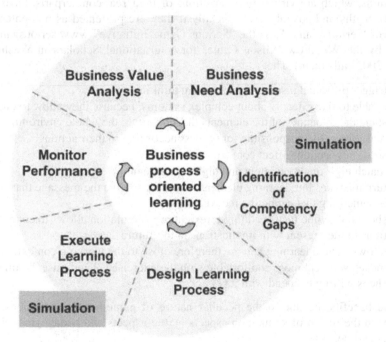

Simulation has been available as an **operations management** technique in industry for approximately 50 years (compare Kelten & Sadowski 1998). BPS can facilitate the successful implementation of redesigned processes, within the context of business-process-reengineering activities. When faced with the need to adapt to business change, simulation can provide the answer to a critical from an operational point of view question, namely:

"Under which conditions can we have the correct resources to meet the performance requirements of a specific business process, in terms of execution time, cost, quality etc?"

Viewed as a **learning instrument**, simulations have the potential to add enormous value to corporate training environments. Simulation exercises are fun and engaging and allow learners to internalize knowledge by applying new skills in a risk-free environment. This can dramatically increase motivation and retention rates—and provide a high return on training investments.

The main benefit of a simulation is that it allows users to be as close as possible to reality; therefore if learning happens through simulation, new acquired competences can immediately be applied to ongoing business, raising the return on investments. Also, if the simulation system is based on machine learning technologies, it has the capability to learn together with the user, resulting in an auto-adaptable tool. This means that the real and the virtual environment of the user change at the same time, making simulation even more efficient and learner-oriented.

2.2 User's Perspective

Simulations, which are virtual representations of their real counterparts, have a long list of strengths and advantages, especially if they are presented as non-entertaining games (or "serious games", as the "Serious Game Initiative" www.seriousgames.org funded by the Woodrow Wilson Center for International Scholars in Washington, D.C. in 2002 calls them). They:

- trigger profound insights for long-term thinking
- enable to think deeply about complex systems, because they allow to understand the dynamics of the elements that constitute the whole environment [1]
- make users feel responsible for success according to their actions
- show how actions affect context
- match high-quality content and high engagement [4]
- turn mistakes into learning elements avoiding to give the message that an error is something that cannot be recovered [3]
- shorten the time factor: adding foresight to a simulation allows to connect actions in the present with implications in the future
- allow situated learning and are therefore close to the working context
- make users feel more comfortable with the exercise [2] and raise the time he or she is willing to spend with it [1]

These benefits are due to the peculiar nature of game-based simulations, which profit from the match of simulation aspects, game aspects and pedagogical elements at the same time. [1]

Some studies carried out in the educational sector [2] as well as their follow-up carried out in the business environment substantially show a high degree of enjoyment in this new means of learning:

Simulation tools are generally perceived as pleasant, about usability surveys in general show that they are considered easy to use and in particular that they are considered effective tools for:

- change
- reflection
- assumption of new behaviours
- transferability of the information treated in daily situations

The simulators are considered as non-invasive tools. In fact, the subjects declare to feel free during the deployment of the assignment and in the choice of the answers. As far as the degree of involvement is concerned, users seem

- to be prepared to repeat the experience
- to have succeeded in identifying themselves in the situation
- that they would prefer this particular training means if they were free to choose
- to have succeeded in maintaining a high degree of interest and attention towards the treated topic

The simulations are not considered as being boring and they are perceived as less tiresome than frontal lessons in a classroom.

2.3 Application of Simulations in Business

Despite their potential online simulations are still under-used by corporate training departments. While many HR-managers in companies support the idea in principle, most have not integrated simulations into their corporate training offerings, Furthermore, the use of simulation as a decision-support tool for the optimisation of corporate training is still in its early steps.

One of the limitations of simulations until now, which possibly explains why they are not yet largely used in business, is that either these tools simulate processes but they do not have anything to do with training, or they represent very nice and effective training tools, that unfortunately are not linked to business processes.

The authors try to close this gap with a new type of simulation that can be a decision support system, simulating complex business processes and a training tool at the same time.

3 Competency-Based Simulation – The PROLIX Example

e-Simulations are part of the toolset of the PROLIX system [12] that will couple business processes with learning processes in corporate environments, in order to achieve optimal performance and reduce the time needed to fill competency gaps. Their role in the context of the PROLIX system is illustrated in figure 1.

The quest for organisational excellence calls for innovations and a continuous improvement of organisational operations. Business processes are generally identified in terms of beginning and end points, interfaces, and organisation units involved, particularly the customer unit. Davenport & Short (1990) define business process as "a set of logically related tasks performed to achieve a defined business outcome." A process is "a structured, measured set of activities designed to produce a specified output for a particular customer or market. It implies a strong emphasis on how work is done within an organisation" (Davenport 1993). In their view processes have two important characteristics: (i) They have customers (internal or external), (ii) They cross organisational boundaries, i.e., they occur across or between organisational subunits.

Nowadays, amidst constantly changing organisational operations, training is one of the most frequently applied solutions for dealing with business change. In this context learning and business process management need to be more strongly connected and coordinated in order to exploit learning as a key enabler for change.

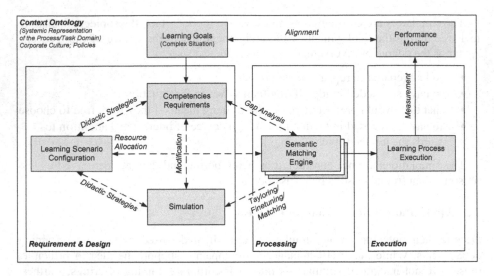

Fig. 1. PROLIX Process-oriented Learning Architecture

Based on this understanding, the aims for simulation-enabled learning developed in the PROLIX project are:

the reflection of workplace conditions, the involvement of realistic and authentic activities, the support of holistic judgement and undergoing quality assurance to guarantee the effectiveness of the simulation.

The **effectiveness** of the simulation is meant on one hand in terms of "interactivity" and of "performed actions" [11], because it is always much easier to remember and to understand the consequences of what one did than of what one heard or read; on the other hand it is to be understood in terms of "closeness" to the business situation. (The effectiveness of the simulation in terms of "simulation results" will be cross-checked by another module of the PROLIX architecture).

In fact, in the PROLIX project, the competency oriented process simulator will be a highly interactive web-based tool based on the concept of experiential learning that will be customizable for each customer's processes and sets of competencies, thus resulting always extremely close to business reality.

So, based on these pre-assumptions the competency-based simulator consists of a resource-based approach (person power and competencies necessary to cope with the requirements of a process step) interlinked with business process performance relevant criteria, namely time, cost and quality. This means, based on an evaluation matrix for each process step, the status of specific performance conditions can be seen and re-adjusted in a way, that it fits most optimal for overall business objectives (e.g. like very high quality criteria for the products/ services etc.).

The outcome can be described as a real-time learning simulation based on different blueprints of the defined business process and requirements raised by organisational issues brought up out of "real" work-situations to run these processes. So the PROLIX simulation tool that tries to bring together learning and process management aspects has three main characteristics:

- **User support tool based on a single business process as a good practice.** The result of the simulation is used as learning content in an instructional way. The employee on the shop floor can use the information as factum.

- **Business process configuration tool / simulation of possible scenarios by the business process engineer.** This simulation considers the "surroundings" of the process, in order to be able to identify its impact of different variables on the related processes. The aim is to try to reduce the risk of redundancies and of delays in the information transfer across different processes, trying to optimize the "whole" business environment.

- **User learning tool / "Edugaming" for staff training (shop floor level).** The idea is to simulate the different logical links of the tasks which build up the process in order to let the user understand how the process works and what the consequences of wrong logical links could be. The employee should understand what the relevance of his work is and what kind of impact a failure in his work task could have for the complete business process.

4   Application Example for the Competency-Based Simulator: The Educational Publishing Sector at Klett AG, Germany

The German publishing house Klett AG is one of the pilot users of the PROLIX system for business-process oriented learning,

The editorial environment
The core competence of an educational publishing house is to publish – develop, produce and market – teaching and learning materials for institutional education. Therefore, in the PROLIX project and especially in the competency-based simulator, a main process of education publishing should be modelled for the benefit of closing the gap between business process needs and an optimal condition to cope with all process steps. The traditional business process in the field of educational publishing consists of six main phases:

1. Product sketch
2. Product planning
3. Realisation
4. Production
5. Archiving
6. Sales / Distribution.

According to the outlined major process steps and its underlying sub-processes, different issues emerged that are critical for success to cope with a modified process:

Issues in developing business processes more adequately
Nonetheless, the need for structural changes in the business processes may emerge, even in this environment, which appears to be stable from an organisational point of view. A couple of such cases have been identified:

- Achieving greater efficiency in the planning and realisation phase, e.g. decreasing the time to market
- Introduction of a new editing environment, e.g. introducing a content management system
- Changing the business process at the conceptual level, e.g. addressing a new customer group
- Tailoring business processes according to specific customer's needs e.g. high-level quality for specific target groups

In shorter product/service life-cycles, a well-prepared and defined process with low barriers between human-machine-interaction and employees with adequate competencies are the key factors to resist in turbulent markets.

So, gaps between competency profiles needed to carry out a business process and work process related lacks due to changes in business processes should be discovered in order to decide whether to spend resources for re-organising or re-training employees or to run a process on a sub-optimal level.

What happened in the competency-based simulator scenario "educational publishing"

In this framework, the educational publishing scenario simulation based on different blueprints of the defined business process and requirements raised by organisational issues brought up starting from "real" work-situations can play a significant role in making business process changes smoother. In concrete, Klett's issues are to find options to e.g. reduce costs, raise quality, save resources, use competencies adequately in the described business processes. Especially the competency levels needed to fulfil a process step and the person power with adequate competences for each process step are critical for success from the Klett perspective. So, the need for an "ex-ante" simulation of real business processes could help especially decision-makers and responsible managers deciding about a business process according to their specific needs. Based on a pre-defined setting of the educational publishing process steps the process chain manager can start simulating this setting by adjusting performance indicators for the whole educational publishing business chain and/or for some of its sub-process steps. As a (round-based) result, the process chain manager receives information about the condition of the business process that varies for each process step. So, non-ideal conditions can easily be re-adjusted until they fit to the pre-assumptions or desired conditions. As a result, e.g. the product realisation phase could be qualitatively enlarged by a competence increase of the involved employees. This means, competency gaps that are specific for a process step can be identified. Furthermore, the simulation can support the decision e.g. to spend money for a process-step-focussed training.

The main benefits for Klett are:

- To increase the awareness for business processes and their costs
- to identify business process gaps in advance,
- to estimate costs and quality levels in a better way for specific business process conditions,
- to use an appropriate condition for a quick-start learning scenario for employees and

- to reveal capacity and competency bottlenecks in the planning phase for a business process

5 Conclusions

Simulation is a tool that is used to predict performance and to understand the impact of change. This ability of simulation, not only to provide answers to different "what if" questions, but also to transport users into a virtual environment where they can experience alternative pictures/views? of the future, makes it ideal for supporting both decision making and experiential learning. It represents a particularly animated and participatory form of learning, where users learn by virtually "living" in a reconstruction of the real-life environment, where they will soon have to apply their new knowledge. In the latter case, simulation techniques are used to validate decisions associated with the learning solution.

Currently there are numerous process simulation tools available on the market. But there is a shortage in simulation tools integrated in a process- and competency driven framework for interlinking business process intelligence tools with knowledge management and learning environments. The simulation of real working situations, easy adaptable to different companies' scenarios, is still an issue for many simulations dealing with work processes. Especially, solutions for modelling simulation settings in the area of HR, e.g. competencies of staff and their behaviour in real work-contexts, arc weak. The conduction/bringing together of learning goals and business processes, including didactical strategies, competencies and the modelling of specific learning processes configurations is still unsolved for simulations.

References

[1] Aldrich, C.: Learning by Doing, Wyley, 2005
[2] Pannese, L.; Cassola, M.; Grassi, M.: Interaction with Simulation Tools: Analysis of Use Cases, I-KNOW Conference, 2005
[3] Kelten, W.D.; Sadowski, R.P.; Sadowski, D.A.: Simulation with Arena, Boston: McGraw-Hill, 1998
[4] Kindley, R.: The Power of Simulation-based e-Learning (SIMBEL), The eLearning Developers' Journal, 17 September 2002.
[5] Prensky, M.: Digital Game-Based Learning, McGraw-Hill, 2000
[6] Quinn, C. N.: Engaging Learning, Wiley, 2005.
[7] Pannese, L.; Nitti, V.; Santalmasi, M.: Simulation-based solutions for performance enhancement in companies from different industrial sectors, Stuttgart, "Professional Training Facts" conference, 2005.
[8] Watkins, K.E., and Marsick, V.J. Sculpting the learning organisation: Lessons in the art and science of systemic change. San Francisco: Jossey-Bass, 1993
[9] Greasley A. "Using business-process simulation within a business-process reengineering approach" Business Process Management Journal Vol. 9 No. 4, 2003 pp. 408-420
[10] Gopinath C., Sawyer John E., (1999) "Exploring the learning from an enterprise simulation", Journal of Management Development, Vol. 18 No. 5, 1999, pp. 477-489.
[11] Van Eck R., "Digital Game-Based Learning", Educause, March/April 2006, pp. 17-30.
[12] PROLIX ("Process-oriented Learning and Information exchange") Integrated Project, IST FP6-2005-027905, www.prolixproject.org

MD2 Method: The Didactic Materials Creation from a Model Based Perspective

Carmen L. Padrón, Paloma Díaz, and Ignacio Aedo

DEI Laboratory Computer Science Department.
Universidad Carlos III de Madrid
Avenida de la Universidad, 30, CP 28911, Leganés, Madrid, Spain
{clpadron, pdp}@inf.uc3m.es, aedo@ia.inf.uc3m.es

Abstract. The creation of didactic materials is a complex task that needs an effective support for all practitioners involved in such process. This is the goal of the MD2 method presented in this paper. We propose the MD2 model to describe didactic materials requirements like its contents, pedagogical, technical and quality features. The rationale is to use some of those descriptors to provide mapping from high level technical descriptions of learning technology standards to simpler and closer descriptions to practitioners about material requirements. Those model mappings are used as foundation of MD2 creation method, and we show how they can guide the selection and composition phases of creation. By other side, another set of MD2 descriptors are used in the evaluation phase to control the usability and quality of the obtained material. A log of the whole process including the values of all model elements and the material's design rationales will be stored as extended semantic annotation. Thus, important properties of the created material like its interoperability, accessibility and reusability will be ensured.

Keywords: Authoring Tools, Metadata, Learning Objects, Modeling, Development Methods.

1 Introduction

E-Learning provides, among other advantages, the means to integrate teaching and learning into every facet of each person's life, promoting the life-long education and increasing the globalisation of education [8]. Thanks to e-Learning there are accessible a wide range of new opportunities for instructional reusability and personalised learning needed for long-life education. But those opportunities can not be efficiently deployed if there are not available authoring tools to create didactic materials able to support those features.

The didactic materials creation is not a simple task; it can be seen as four-phase process. The first phase is related to the analysis of material requirements. The second one is the selection of resources, which is concerned with finding the most appropriated resources according to knowledge, pedagogical and technical requirements to compose the material. The third phase is the composition that is related to the integration of those resources in the final material. And the fourth phase is the evaluation, where the fulfilments of creation requirements in the obtained material features are checked. Each phase has own singularities and there different

W. Nejdl and K. Tochtermann (Eds.): EC-TEL 2006, LNCS 4227, pp. 366–382, 2006.

issues arising on their execution, like what is the best procedure to select the most appropriated resources, which guidelines must be followed to integrate resources in the material or when obtained material successfully satisfies particular pedagogical, technical and knowledge requirements. The use of creation methods can give us answers to those questions, since they provide development frameworks to systematically and rationally aid the creation of didactic materials.

In addition, from early stages of creation it is also required to take into consideration a set of general views to ensure material features such as: its quality and pedagogical value, its reusability, its usability and conformance with current learning technology standards and specifications [21]. But usually some of the practitioners involved in the creation process, teachers and educators, are not very familiar with each one of those perspectives. That is another reason why is needed the support of creation method with mechanisms that model material general features like its content, pedagogical, technical and quality requirements. Quality authoring environments based on such development methods will help reducing the workload of creation considering all those aspects and will properly guide practitioners during the whole process of didactic material creation.

The need of authoring tools has not been ignored in recently years and there is available an important number of those tools. Among them are worthy to mention: RELOAD [24], CopperAuthor [4], Aloha [2] and OLAT QTI Editor [19]. They have in common the successful technical implementation of learning technology standards and specifications such as IMS LD [10], IMS LOM [12], IMS QTI [13] and ADL SCORM [26]. That is a first step in order to ensure important features of the obtained materials like interoperability, accessibility, reusability and personalization. But unfortunately those aims can not be completed reached if the use of those tools does not provide means to ensure that created materials have appropriated semantic annotations. Although some of those tools implement the integration of Instructional Design in the standards [29], they lack of development methods support to guide practitioners during the creation process. Usually, the use of those tools represent an increment in the workload for some of their intended users due to the technical knowledge level about e-Learning specifications required to understand and effectively use those tools is very high for many of those intended users.

In this paper we explore an approach to solve some of those issues. We propose a model to generally describe didactic materials requirements like its contents, pedagogical, technical and quality features. The rationale is to use some of those descriptors to provide mapping from high level technical descriptions of learning technology standards to simpler and closer descriptions to practitioners about material requirements. Those model mappings are used as foundation of a creation method, since they allow guiding selection and composition phases of creation. By other side, during the evaluation phase, another set of requirement descriptors or model elements are used to check if obtained material features satisfy stated requirements and to control material usability, pedagogical value and quality. A log of the entire process including the values of all model elements and the material design rationales will be stored as extended semantic annotations. By this way, important properties of the created material like its interoperability, accessibility, reusability and personalization will be ensured. In section 2 we present a characterization of the didactic material creation process as four-phase process: the analysis of material requirements, the selection of material resources and the composition of material using those resources, and the evaluation of obtained material. We also analyze why this process must be supported by a creation method. Section 3 is devoted to explain the MD2 model, the basis of MD2 method for development of didactic materials. Later in section 4 we present MD2 method and a working example. And finally in section 5 some conclusions and future works are outlined.

2 Characterization of the Didactic Materials Creation

Didactic materials are any kind of digital (or not digital) element that assists actors of the teaching/learning process to achieve their objectives during the entire process [21]. Didactic materials are herein considered as the conjunction of contents and a pedagogical strategy, defined by an instructional design and, used to guide learning and teaching processes.

There is a set of perspectives or requirements needed to take into consideration during the creation of didactic materials. Those perspectives ensure the attainment of desirable didactic material features for the deployment of any educational process. Some of those features can be summarized in the following: reusability, quality and pedagogical value, usability and conformance with current learning technology specifications and standards. Next we briefly explain each of them.

Reusability: The reusability character of didactic materials is based on their capability to be used in different learning situations or in diverse knowledge domains [23]. There is a group of determining factors enabling the didactic material reusability. Those factors are: granularization (relation between its size and its pedagogical value)[29], conformance with current learning technology specifications and standards, appropriate dealing with intellectual property rights [18], a material design based on separation of contents from presentation and, contents from instructional design [23]. And also the presence of some embedded or associated semantic information in the material [21].

Thus, during the didactic material creation those factors must be controlled in order to achieve the desired reusability.

Quality: The quality of a didactic material can be defined, according to Tagushi [28], as "the degree in which the characteristics of the material can cover the felt o pre-felt needs of users during a period of time". Those users are practitioners involved in the creation process like teachers, pedagogical advisors, instructional designers, software developers and designers, and also final users such as learners or trainees.

The quality of didactic materials must be analysed from two points of view: the material as a product itself, and its development process. From the point of view of the product, to facilitate the measurement of user satisfaction, formal specifications of the user needs, the required attributes of the didactic material and some analytical tools must be provided. Hence, the creation process must contain an evaluation phase in order to check the quality of obtained material.

From the point of view of the process, it is needed an analysis of the protocols, that guide how didactic materials are built, and how these can improve efficiency and reduce costs of the creation process.

Usability: The usability of a didactic material is a feature that synthesizes its quality from the Human Computer Interaction perspective. The usability of didactic material can be defined according to ISO 9241-11[14] as the material ability to effectively, efficiently and satisfactorily support its target audience (learners and academic staff) in development of their tasks and achievement of learning objectives and outcomes in a specified context of use.

To obtain usable didactic materials is necessary to consider two aspects: its technical usability and its pedagogical value [7]. The technical usability aims to ensure an efficient and error-free interaction with the material. Meanwhile the pedagogical value is related to material's capability to effectively support the learning process. A usable didactic material aims to minimize the cognitive load resulting from interaction with the material in order to free more resources for the effective support of the learning process. Consequently, usability evaluations will be essential during the development of didactic materials, since they provide to creators with certain confidence about material quality and capability to effectively support the educational process and the attainment of learning objectives.

Pedagogical value: In the case of didactic materials, the pedagogical value is a kind of instrumental value [25] concerned with the effective achievement of a set of learning objectives and competences. So, the pedagogical value of material must be ensured during its creation process providing to developers with means to assess the material utility based on the perceptions of what is required and what results can be obtained.

Standards and specification conformance: The perspectives hereinbefore described should also take into account current learning technology standards and specifications. They provide common means to make materials interoperable among heterogeneous systems (e.g. IMS CPIM [9]; SCORM [26]); accessible with suitable dealing with intellectual property rights (e.g. IMS LRMDI [12]); capable for management and personalization (e.g. IMS LIP [11]) and, flexible enough to perform composition and integration into new materials (e.g. IMSLD [10], IMS QTI [13]).

The didactic materials creation or development process, we intend to support, can be seen as four-phase process. The first phase is the analysis of material requirements, which must take into account perspectives previously described according to the specific creation situation. The second phase is the selection of resources, which is concerned with finding the most appropriated resources according to the knowledge, pedagogical and technical requirements for material creation. The third phase is the composition, related to the aggregation and integration of those resources in the final structure of the material. And the fourth phase is the evaluation of the created material.

There are different ways to proceed for the selection phase. The election of the most appropriated or lower cost procedure depends on the accessibility rules and availability of those resources that meet particular knowledge domain and pedagogical requirements of the material. For instance, a selection approach could be the creation from scratch of needed resources when there are not available proper resources or when the cost for paying the access and use of those resources is higher than the cost of creating them from scratch. Other option can be the retrieval of "ready to use" resources from repositories, if those resources are available and accessible, and they exactly match with creators requirements. But if they do not exactly match to those needs, other option can be the versioning of those resources. Sometimes the best procedure for the selection phase is not one of those options but a combination of them. At this point is important to count with aids to guide developers (novice or not) to choose which is the best procedure to follow during the selection phase. Such aids must contain expertise knowledge from other similar creation situations and their solutions.

By other side, during the composition phase all resources are aggregated and integrated into a material structure defined according to pedagogical requirements of the type of material needed to create and, the most adequate e-Learning standard or specification used to meet technical material requirements of delivery and presentation. Thus, guidelines and mechanisms for material's composition are needed to effectively help the integration and aggregation of resources into such material structure.

Once material is composed and after its preview, its features must be controlled in order to check if they properly satisfy all creation requirements during the phase of evaluation. Then material quality, usability and pedagogical value must be inspected. In those cases whether they do not achieve acceptable levels, material must be redesigned, some times making modifications in its contents, its structure or in presentation parameters. That is why metrics and rules to effectively control material features and mechanisms for material's redesign are needed.

The creation of didactic materials is a complex process, is the first conclusion we can extract from this analysis. There are many requirements needed to be considered, which in many cases are unknown for some of the professionals involved in the creation process. Also, each of creation phases has own particularities which require of special aids, rules and mechanisms to assist and guide practitioners involved in the creation. Hence the creation process demands of method support, which provides development frameworks to ensure effective, systematic and rational solutions for the creation. And also high-quality authoring environments based on such development methods are needed in order to effectively help and guide developers facing the complexity of the creation process.

3   The MD2 Model

Our approach to support didactic material creators in the material development process is based on the MD2 model. We had named it MD2 after the Spanish acronym for Development Method of Didactic Materials (and their automation) [21].

We believe that creation of didactic materials can be effectively supported if we count with means to describe material main features: contents and pedagogical strategy and, a method as guide for the different creation phases: selection, composition and evaluation. The MD2 model generally describes didactic material's features like its contents, pedagogical, technical and quality requirements. The rationale behind the model is to use those descriptors to provide mappings form high level technical descriptions of learning technology standards and specifications to simpler and closer descriptions to practitioners about material requirements. MD2 model is the foundation of a MD2 creation method, presented in Section 4. The mapping from some MD2 model elements allows guiding the selection and composition phases of the didactic material's creation process. Meanwhile another set of MD2 model elements are used in the evaluation phase to control the usability, pedagogical value and quality of created material. They are used to guide checking related with the fulfilment of requirements. Also, all values of MD2 model elements will be automatically stored as extended semantic annotations of the created material, allowing it future localization and it retrieval for reutilization purposes.

The model tries to attain such aims through the use of a four-view description of didactic material. These views are composed by a set of distinguishable and measurable elements belonging to the areas which gather the perspectives needed to take into consideration during the development process. Those generic areas are the main disciplines involved in the educational process: a knowledge domain, the pedagogical one and the technological area as support of the process [15]. Next, we explain the relation between MD2 views and those generic areas using the information of their elements generally represented in the Figure 1.

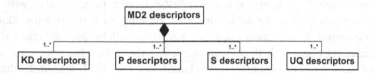

Fig. 1. MD2 model descriptors

Knowledge domain (KD) view: Its elements represent main features from the knowledge domain of the subject or discipline enclosed in the material contents. We use as reference knowledge structure similar to those used in Dublin Core [6], the Library of Congress Cataloging System (LCC) [17] and the Body of Knowledge of ACM Computing Curricula [1]. The subject contents structure for didactic material we use for MD2 model can be seen in Figure 2. Such structure is mainly based in the Body of Knowledge of ACM Computing Curricula, which uses a three-level hierarchical organization: knowledge area, knowledge units and set of topics. The highest level of the hierarchy is the knowledge area (KA), which represents a particular disciplinary sub-field. Each knowledge area is broken down into smaller divisions called knowledge units (KU), which represent individual thematic modules within an area. And the lowest is a set of topics (s(T)), which further subdivides each knowledge unit. Each topic has also associated a group of learning outcomes addressing skills to be promoted and a time estimation to achieve those outcomes.

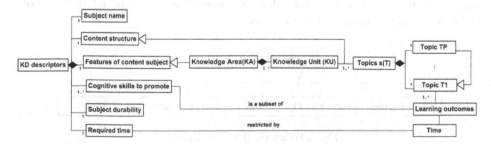

Fig. 2. Knowledge domain KD view elements

This type of structure allows more exact descriptions about knowledge and pedagogical requirements needed for the selection phase of creation. It is also used in the composition phase to establish appropriated content structure mapping and content integration with the presentation and execution patterns provided by e-learning publishing and delivering standards like IMS LD, IMS QTI or SCORM. For instance, a didactic material about Programming Fundamentals course [1] can cover topics like Fundamental data structures and Programming constructs, subjects belonging to s(T) of the Fundamental Programming Constructs- KU from Programming Fundamentals- KA. Some of this course learning goals or cognitive skills are relate to "Use and apply current technical concepts and practices in the core information technologies".

If the standard of the delivery and presentation used is IMS LD, during the phase of the composition, the course will be structured using an IMS LD based pattern like a unit of learning of two acts, one for each topic. According to the pedagogical strategy each act will include learning activities related to one topic. It also will include assessment activities about the achievement of learning goals or cognitive skills. The list of those cognitive skill associated to each topic will be used to select the most adequate questions to check if students achieved those learning outcomes. If those assessment activities presentations are based on the QTI standard, then each assessment activity will be composed and presented as QTI assessment composed by a set of QTI items (questions) in proper formats (type of questions) to check such learning outcomes.

Pedagogic (P) view: Its elements describe the material pedagogical requirements such as features and guidelines to follow during the educational process (pedagogical strategy). They are presented in Figure 3. The material type element describes the possible types of material which have adequate granularity to ensure reusability: assessments, activities or learning objects. Each one of them has associated certain pedagogical strategy. The Cognitive skills needed element contains a list of those learning objectives needed to achieve in a certain learning situation. Such list is controlled by the element Cognitive skills to promoted from the KD view.

The Estimated effort to effectively execute material is an element that describes the time needed to successfully achieve learning outcomes. It is limited by the KD Time required for coverage. And, the Difficulty element describe how hard is to work with the material for the target audience. This descriptor has a direct mapping to Difficulty from Educational category of LOM [12] and its values represent levels of difficulty, which are also used to control the values of some features of material' presentation and delivery, described by S view elements.

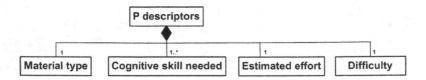

Fig. 3. Pedagogic (P) view elements

Support (S) view: It contains technical support requirements for the educational process. S view elements are presented In Figure 4 and they are used during the composition phase to ensure that created material is reusable, interoperable among heterogeneous systems, accessible, capable for management and personalization. The Learner interaction type element must be selected from a list of restricted and fuzzy values [High, Medium, Low], and it is checked to accomplish rules restricting the type of interaction according to the Delivery or publishing medium element. The rest of S view elements are defined according to relations provided by elements from KD and P views. And they provide information about what kind of material structure for the implementation of certain pedagogical strategy is needed and how contents can be connected or plugged to such structure. Their values are obtained as the result of the mapping from the creator requirements descriptions to the learning technology specifications descriptors.

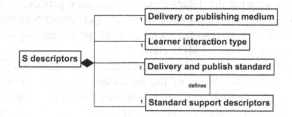

Fig. 4. Support (S) view elements

Usability and quality (UQ) view: This view is close related to other three views (KD, S, P) and its elements are presented in Figure 5. The elements of UQ view define a set of properties used during evaluation phase to provide developers with certain confidence about the quality and pedagogical value of created material. We use as reference the findings of research done by Chao-Min et al in [5]. They empirically showed that measurement of usability, quality and value of e-Learning system must be done independently but their results have a summative and positive effect on the user satisfaction and confidence about the system. Thus, a set of UQ view elements (Q) are used to check if created material can effectively support educational tasks and the achievement of defined learning objectives. Their values belong to fuzzy sets corresponding to linguistic terms [Low, Medium, High] or [Good, Average, Poor]. They are used in fuzzy computations of Pedagogical value. And the obtained value is compared to a predefined Quality threshold to check if the material has an adequate Pedagogical value. In similar way, the other set of UQ view elements (U) are used to calculate Observed Usability element. Its value is compared to Usability threshold to control if the material has acceptable usability. Such comparisons will provide to developers with confidence information about the material quality and effectiveness. If the material does not reach acceptable levels of quality and usability, all information gathered during the evaluation is used for the material redesign to modify the involved features until the material will reach appropriated quality and usability levels.

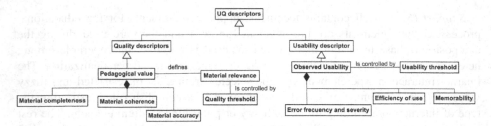

Fig. 5. Usability and quality (UQ) view elements

4   The Creation Process Supported by MD2 Method

The MD2 method is based on the MD2 model hereinbefore presented. This method will guide developers during the didactic material creation process. It is composed by a set of 13 steps based on simple questions to developers about material requirements. It will be verified that their answers have an appropriate correspondence with the valid values of some of the model MD2 elements.

The method steps follow a logical order, first are going questions (1) related to the KD view since they are foundation of the educational process. In second place are questions (2-5) about P view elements; they will determine the material's pedagogical requirements. Next, the questions (6-12) are related to S view will define the technical support needs. Developer or creator answers to those questions are input data for inference mechanisms based on MD2 model, which helps finding or creating the most appropriated resources during the selection phase. The inference mechanisms also uses another set of those answers to obtain mappings from the stated requirements to the proper information model elements of the selected delivery and publishing standard, thus the material's presentation structure can be defined and can be fulfilled through the composition phase of creation. Final method step (13) is concerned with the evaluation of created material. Developer is asked about material features described by some of QU view elements. His answers are used to calculate QU elements: Relevance of created material and Observed usability. Then, their values are compared to Quality and Usability thresholds to check if the material has adequate levels of Quality, Pedagogical value and Usability. Such comparison will provide developers with confidence information about the quality and effectiveness of the created material. MD2 method also defines that all those data exchanged with creators during the whole creation process will be stored as an extended set of material semantic annotations in a Repository. Such kind of annotations contains material descriptions and its design rationales. The availability of such information will allow easier and proper retrieving resources from Repositories for material composition in such creation situations when other practitioners need to create didactic materials with similar requirements.

Let us introduce a simple example to explain how MD2 method will guide step by step the creation process. This example is related to the example we presented in Section 3 to describe the KD view elements. In this case, a professor needs an assessment activity based on tests to check if learners have achieved certain learning outcomes related to Fundamental Data Structures, especially about the AVL Trees

Data Structure. He will use an authoring tool which implements the MD2 method and there is also available a repository of questions.

In Figure 6 is represented the creation process supported by MD2 method. There are represented the authoring tool modules which implements main MD2 method functionalities: Filters definition, items recovering or creation's modules for the selection phase, material's composition module and evaluation module. And also each functionality results are represented.

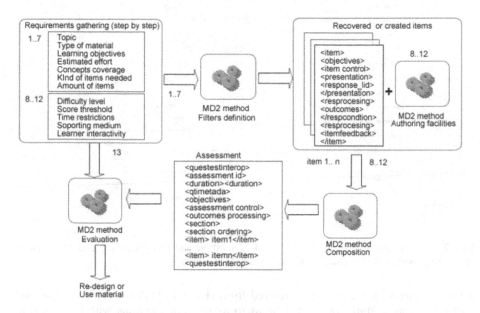

Fig. 6. Creation process based on MD2 method

Method steps from 1 up to 7 will provide information to MD2 inference mechanism to define the values of some MD2 model elements. They are used to create filters (i.e. queries to the Repository) to select and retrieve the most suitable questions (items) for the professor needs, as is shown in the Figure 6. The nature of those queries is progressive and iterative, i.e. information from Step 1 will define the first filter about the subject of material to query the Repository. If there are not available items after the first query to local Repository, another search will start using web services like Item bank services from SPAID web services [27]. The rest of filters defined from steps 2 until 7 will refine the results of the set of questions retrieved from the first filter. Thus, at the end of 12th step will be a set of the most probable or suitable questions for the composition of the assessment. If no adequate items are found, then Inference mechanisms based on the MD2 model, will check which query (belonging to n step, n>1) did not produce results. It will transfer the results obtained from its previous filter (n-1 step) to the MD2 authoring facilities in order to create adequate items. All data gathered from the n-1 until 12 will be used by authoring module to create such items. The authoring module will select patterns for items presentation based on the chosen delivery and presentation standard according to the data collected from steps 2, 6 and 11. It will prompt the professor to complete

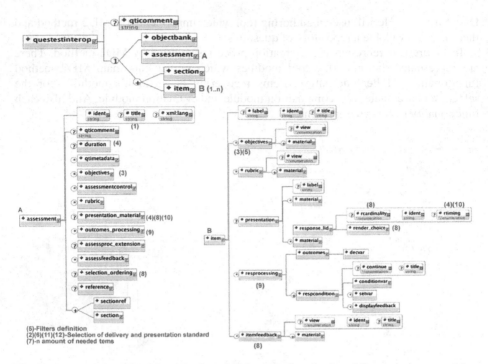

Fig. 7. A material composition based on MD2 method and using delivery and presentation structure provided by the XML binding of IMS QTI standard

such structure with the contents retrieved from step n-1. This authoring module also will control all features of created items to avoid contradictions with requirements stated from Steps 8 until 12.

Once selection phase is completed the MD2 composition module, using an integration and delivery engine based on the chosen standard (i.e. for this example, an engine based on IMS QTI), is in charge of the integration of items into the final material's composition. The Figure 7 represents how MD2 method steps are used to define elements value of material's structure during the composition phase. The MD2 composition module will use information gathered from steps 8 to 12, to define values for the S view elements. It uses such data to define material's presentation structure and to integrate the set of retrieved (or created) items into that structure therefore is made up a candidate of assessment. Then the professor can visualize and run a candidate of the assessment. Once he finished its preview, he is asked to assess if the obtained material satisfies his initial requirements during the evaluation phase. For this purpose Quality and Usability thresholds are defined. They are used to delimit the acceptable minimum values for material's pedagogical value and usability.

Next we explain how the professor will be guided step by step during a creation process based the MD2 method:

1.   *Selection of material content's discipline or subject.* The professor will be asked about the name of the subject or discipline to be enclosed in the material's contents. It will be checked if such subject or discipline belongs to a valid Knowledge

domain. In the example, professor answer is AVL Trees Data Structure. This answer is used to gather information from a Knowledge Ontology about learning AVL Trees and the main features of the Structure of Body of Knowledge enclosing that topic, which belong to the same s(T) presented in Section 3. Once this information is recovered, the professor will be required to confirm if these are corresponding features of the required subject. If that is confirmed, the elements of the KD view will stored those data.

2.   *Type of material definition.* The professor must answer what kind of material he needs from a list of possible types (i.e. activities, LO-learning object, and assessment). He selects assessment. This answer will be stored and used to define some S view elements like Delivery or publishing standard and the Standard support descriptors element which contains references to the information model elements of that standard.

3.   *Selection of required learning objectives.* The professor is requested to select which competences are needed to attain from a list of cognitive skills (or competences) to be promoted by the AVL Trees Data Structure retrieved in Step 1. This list contains for each competence, data about Competency Types [3], [22], Competence Names and related concepts. Such structure represents a semantic reference that allows better descriptions and easier comparison to find and retrieve adequate resources. In the case of our example, some of the data from this list are: (1) Knowledge- Know- AVL tree data structures representation, operations and use; (2) Comprehension- Describe-AVL tree data structures memory allocation and its use of memory. The professor selects both of them and those values will be stored as the P view element List of cognitive skills or competences to achieve using the material.

4.   *Definition of the estimated effort to execute material and to effectively achieve the learning objectives.* The professor is asked to select time estimation from a list of legal values. The maximum value of such list of Time is restricted by the KD element Time required for coverage (2hrs) that has been retrieved in the Step 1. He selects 45 minutes.

5.   *Definition of concepts coverage.* The professor is queried to select from two possible options: All concepts or some concepts. The professor selects concepts (2) from the list of concept names retrieved in the Step 3. Those selected concepts will be used to define filters that refine the list of retrieved questions from the Repository.

6.   *Definition of the kind of items needed for the material.* The professor is asked to select what kind of items he needs for the material from a list with all possible item types. Those types are restricted by his answer to Step 2. He had selected Assessment in Step 2, so he is just allowed to select from a list of types of Questions (i.e. True False, Fill in, multiple valid answers, etc). He selects all those types and this selection is also used to define new filters to refine results from previous queries to the Repository.

7.   *Definition of amount of items needed for the material.* The professor is required to provide a number of items he considers necessary to compose the material. His answer is 15 and is used to select the number of most relevant resources for composing the material. In the example, this information is used to retrieve the 15th most suitable items from a Repository. If there are not found appropriated items

in the repository for his needs, then the professor will be provided with authoring facilities to create such number of items as we explained before in this Section.

8.   *Selection of desired level of difficulty for the material.* The professor must select an option from the list of possible fuzzy values [High, Medium, and Low]. His answer is Medium. This answer is used to obtain suitable values for the S view elements related to the Delivery or publishing Information Model for the composition of material. In this case it will define assessment presentation parameters like number of possible correct answers, random order of questions and answers presentation, types of feedback to learner after he complete each answer.

9.   *Definition of score threshold.* The professor must define if some score threshold is needed to consider that learning goals are achieved. He must select an option from a list of two valid values (Yes, No). If he selects Yes, then he is prompted to provide a range of values for the score threshold and he gives a range between 2 and 5 points. Those values are also be used in the material composition to obtain suitable value for S view elements related to the Delivery or publishing Information Model. For this example, his answer is used to setup a minimum value for processing learning outcomes per questions of the assessment, that means learners who obtain less than 2 points per answer have no achieve the desired level for learning objectives checked in such question.

10.   *Definition of Time restrictions for the material.* The professor must define if the material needs time restrictions, he will be asked to select an option from a list of two valid values (Yes, No). If his answer is Yes, then he is prompted to provide a range of values to restrict the assessment execution time. That answer is also controlled by a maximum value corresponding to his answer to the Step 4. In the example, he answered Yes, and he set 2 minutes per questions. Thus, 2 min * 15 questions = 30 minutes is lower than the estimated effort of 45 minutes provided in Step 4. That value (2 minutes) is also used in the material composition to obtain suitable values for S view elements related to the Delivery or publishing Information Model. In this case, it will define the maximum time available to allow learners to complete each question before the next question is presented.

11.   *Selection of supporting medium.* The professor must select the desired supporting medium for the material from a list of possible media (Printed, hypertext, hypermedia-web, pervasive computing element). He selects hypermedia-web, that answer is used by the Inference mechanism to define the S view element Delivery or publishing standard for the material's composition phase. Since he needs an assessment (answer to Step2) and the hypermedia-web is adequate supporting medium for kind of items selected in Step 6, the MD2 based inference mechanisms propose that appropriated Delivery and presentation standard for this case can be IMS QTI.-

12.   *Definition of the learner interactivity level.* The professor is asked to define what kind of learner interactivity with the material is needed to effectively achieve the stated learning outcomes. He is prompted to select of one type from the list of fuzzy values [High, Medium and Low]. The inference mechanisms control the adequacy of his selection with respect to his answer to Step 11. For instance, if he would select Printed material in Step 11, it would not have sense a selection of High learner interactivity with material, since there is a MD2 model axiom which defines that interaction between learners and printed material is considered as passive or low. Thus, professor is allowed to select between Medium and High interactivity according

to another MD2 model axiom that states that hypermedia-web supporting medium facilitates achievement of learning outcomes by means of Medium or High levels of learner interactions. In the example, he selects Medium and that answer is used by the inference mechanisms to confirm the proposal from Step 11 about the IMS QTI as presentation and delivery standard. Because items and tests conformant to that standard allow rendering and executing the type of questions (answer to Step 6) which support such levels of learner interactivity.

13. *Evaluation of the created material.* Once the composition module presents a candidate of assessment to the professor and he has visualized and interacted with it. The professor will be asked to evaluate some properties of the obtained material like Material completeness, Material coherence (related to contents), and Accuracy of the material contents. He must assign values belonging to a set of fuzzy values corresponding to linguistic terms [Good, Average, Poor] Coherency (Completeness or Accuracy). These values are used by the MD2 evaluation module to check material Quality and Pedagogical value by means of fuzzy aggregation operations. In the example, he assigned values like Good Coherency, Good Completeness and Average Accuracy. Thus, the material has a suitable Pedagogical value.

The material usability is also checked by MD2 evaluation module considering the professor evaluations for Error frequency and severity, Efficiency of use and Memorability elements of the QU view. Their valid values belong to fuzzy sets corresponding to linguistic terms [Low, Medium, High] Frequency of errors; [Good, Average, Poor] Efficiency and [High, medium, very low] Memorability. He selected Low frequency, Average efficiency and High Memorability. These values are used by the MD2 evaluation module to compute fuzzy aggregation for the Observed usability.

In the example, the obtained values for Pedagogical value and Usability are higher than defined Quality and Usability thresholds, so, the professor can be confident about the usability, quality and pedagogical value of the created material. In cases whether the Pedagogical (or Usability) value would be lower than Quality (or Usability) threshold, the material must be re-designed. In such cases, the professor will be provided with information about what parameter didn't reach an acceptable value and the authoring facilities will help him adjusting the features of obtained material to his requirements. Some possible adjusting actions can be asking to the MD2 filter definition module to select and retrieve new items to compose the material or to create from scratch items for the material.

All information exchanged between the MD2 modules and professor during the whole creation process is also stored as an extended set of material semantic annotations in the Repository. Those annotations contain material descriptions and its design rationales. Thus, material's reutilization can be ensured since it has associated such semantic information and its design is based on separation of contents from presentation, and from the instructional design. Also the availability of such semantic information can help reducing creation efforts in cases that this professor (or other user of the MD2 based authoring tool) will need didactic materials with similar requirements to the obtained didactic material.

Once the professor obtain the assessment in form of QTI test, he can use the MD2 method based authoring tool to include it as a resource of an activity belonging to an IMS LD compliant course about AVL Trees Data Structure. In that case, he will be asked if he needs to include the obtained test into another kind of material. He gives an affirmative answer and selects as Type of material, activity, from the list of available material types. In this case, the selection phase is considered as completed and MD2 inference mechanisms pass to composition phase. Those inference mechanisms will retrieve semantic information from the previous creation process of the QTI test in order to select a presentation pattern for the activity. Then another integration and delivery engine for the activity composition is selected. In that case, an IMS LD based engine will be responsible for the definition of learner and staff roles and the integration of QTI test as resource of that activity environment. At that point professor will be able to visualize the obtained activity and to asses its quality and usability properties following the procedure previously explained for evaluation phase.

5 Conclusions and Future Works

In this paper we had presented the MD2 model, which describes general requirements for the didactic material creation. The MD2 model descriptors of contents, pedagogical, technical requirements are used to provide mappings to high level technical descriptions of learning technology. Such mappings are the foundation of MD2 method and we explain how they are used to guide practitioners during selection and composition phases of creation. The interoperability of created material is ensured thanks to those mappings as well. Meanwhile the quality descriptors of MD2 model are used to check if the features of obtained material satisfy usability and quality requirements. Thus, creators or developers will have some confidence about the achievement of those properties at the end of evaluation phase. MD2 method also defines that all those data exchanged with creators during the whole creation process will be stored as an extended set of material semantic annotations in a Repository. Such kind of annotations contains material descriptions and its design rationales. We are working on the definition of IMS LOM extension to include information about design rationales. The availability of such semantic information will ensure material's accessibility, reusability and its personalization capability.

The MD2 model and method are the foundation of MD2tool, a generative authoring tool for didactic material creation. The main idea is that users will specify material's features at a high level of abstraction and the MD2tool will be capable to infer and fill the information for lower level of design, allowing to assemble material's components in delivery time or runtime and to generate accurate semantic annotations. The tool will also control the quality and usability of material based on the coherence and completeness of contents and their capability to effectively support the achievement of stated learning objectives.

At the time of this writing we are involved in the refinement of the fuzzy aggregation mechanisms for the evaluation phase based on MD2 method. We are also working in the definition of presentation and delivery patterns based on XML bindings of the IMS Learning Design to represent different pedagogical strategies for other material types. We are also considering the content modeling experiences from ML3 [20] for the creation of learning objects and their integration into such presentation and delivery patterns for the composition phase. And we start the design and development of the MD2tool, especially care is paid to key facts like information and graphical tool design centered in practitioners involved in the creation. By that way the MD2tool usability will be ensured. Other future lines of work are related to evaluation of the effectiveness of the creation process guided by MD2 method.

Acknowledgements. This work is part of the MD2 project (TIC2003-03654), funded by the Ministry of Science and Technology, Spain.

References

[1]   Computing Curricula 2005- Chapter 5. Overview of the CS Body of Knowledge: Programming Fundamentals. Retrieved from http://www.acm.org/education/curric_vols/ IT_October_2005.pdf

[2]   Aloha project website Retrieved December 16, 2005 from http://aloha2.netera.ca/

[3]   Bloom Benjamin. Taxonomy of Educational Objectives: the classification of educational goals. 1975. New York. D. McKay.

[4]   CopperAuthor project website. Retrieved February 3, 2006 from http://www. copperauthor.org/

[5]   Chao-Min C., Meng-Hsiang, H.,Szu-Yuan, S., Tung-Ching, L., Pei-Chen, S. Usability, quality, value and e-leaning continuance decisions. In Computers & Education journal 45 (2005), pp.399-416. Retrieved November 2005 http://www.sciencedirect.com/

[6]   Dublin Core Metadata Initiative (DCMI) Retrieved from http://dublincore.org/ documents/dcmi-terms/

[7]   Erica Melis et al. Lessons for (Pedagogic) Usability Design of eLearning Systems. In Proceedings of the World Conference on E-Learning in Corporate, Government, Healthcare, and Higher Education (eLearn-2003), 2003. http://www.ags.uni-sb.de/ ~melis/Pub/elearn03Usability.pdf

[8]   Hummel, H., Manderveld, J., Tattersall, C. and Koper, R. Educational modelling language and learning design: new opportunities for instructional reusability and personalised learning, *Int. J. Learning Technology*, Vol. 1, No. 1, pp.111–126, 2004.

[9]   IMS-CPIM. IMS Content Packaging Information Model. Version 1.1.2 final specification, 2001. Retrieved from http://www.imsproject.org/content/packaging/cpv1p1p2/ imscp_infov1p1p2.html

[10] IMS-LD. IMS Learning Design. Version 1.0 - final specification. Retrieved April, 2005 from http://www.imsglobal.org/learningdesign/index.html

[11] IMS-LIPS. Learner Information Package Specification. Version 1.1-final specification, 2001. Retrieved from http://www.imsglobal.org/profiles/lipinfo01.html

[12] IMS Meta-data Best Practice Guide for IEEE 1484.12.1-2002 Standard for Learning Object Metadata Version 1. Retrieved April, 2005 from http://www.imsglobal.org/ metadata/mdv1p3pd/imsmd_bestv1p3pd.html

[13] IMS Question and Test Interoperability: Information Model. Retrieved April, 2005 from http://www.imsglobal.org/question/index.html

[14] ISO 9241-11. Ergonomics requirements for office with visual display terminals (VDTs) – Part 11: Guidance on usability. Geneva: International Organization for Standardization (ISO). 1998.

[15] Jochems, W., van Merrienboer, J., Koper, R. (Eds) Integrated e-Learning: implications for pedagogy, technology and organization. Routledge Farmer, London, 2004.

[16] Koper, R. From change to renewal: Educational technology foundations of electronic learning Environments (2000) Retrieved December, 2005 from DSpace OUNL site http://hdl.handle.net/1820/38

[17] The Library of Congress Cataloging (LCC). Available at http://www.loc.gov/catdir/
[18] LitleJohn, A. Issues in reusing online resources in Reusing Online Resources: A sustainable approach to e-learning. Editor LitleJonh A. Kogan Page London/ Kogan Page US, 2003.
[19] OLAT web-based Open Source Learning Management System (LMS) project website. Retrieved February 3, 2006 from http://www.olat.org/public/index.html
[20] ML3 Multidimensional Learning Objects and Modular Lectures Markup Language website available at http://www.ml-3.org/
[21] Padrón, C., Dodero, J.M., Aedo, I. and Díaz, P. The collaborative development of didactic materials. *Computer Science and Information Systems Journal* Volume 02, Issue 02 (December), 2005
[22] Paquette, G., Rosca, I. (2004) An Ontology –based referencing of Actor, Operations and Resources in eLearning Systems. SW-EL/2004 Workshop. Einhoven, The Netherlands, August 2004.
[23] Polsani, P. "Use and abuse of reusable learning objects." *Journal of Digital Information*, Volume 3, Issue 4. (2003). Retrieved January, 2006 from http://jodi.ecs.soton.ac.uk/ Articles/v03/i04/Polsani/
[24] RELOAD Reusable E-Learning Object Authoring and Delivery project Retrieved January 5, 2006 from http://www.reload.ac.uk/
[25] Rokeach, M. J. The nature of human values. New York: The Free Press. 1973.
[26] SCORM. Sharable Content Object Reference Model (SCORM). 2004. Retrieved form http://www.adlnet.org/scorm/history/2004/documents.cfm
[27] SPAID web services site http://www.learningservices.strath.ac.uk/spaid/spaid.html.
[28] Tagushi. Methods: A hands-on approach to quality engineering. Addison -Wisley, 1998
[29] Wiley, D. A. "Connecting Learning Objects to Instructional Design Theory: A Definition, a Metaphor, and a Taxonomy", in D. A. Wiley (ed.), The Instructional Use of Learning Objects, Agency for Instructional Technology and Association for Educational Communications and Technology, pp. 3-23, 2002.

DynMap+: A Concept Mapping Approach to Visualize Group Student Models

U. Rueda, M. Larrañaga, A. Arruarte, and J.A. Elorriaga

University of the Basque Country (UPV/EHU)
649 P.K., E-20080 Donostia
{urko_rm, mikel.larranaga, a.arruarte, jon.elorriaga}@ehu.es

Abstract. Computer supported learning systems such as Intelligent Tutoring Systems, web-based learning systems, etc. gather data from students' interaction. Teachers and students may find useful a medium to inspect information of students and student groups in an intuitive way. This paper presents DynMap+, an approach to generate and visualize Group Student Models generated from data gathered by a computer supported learning system. DynMap+ represents student models graphically by means of Concept Maps. Some graphical resources are used to highlight important data. The use of those resources allows DynMap+ to provide users (e.g. teachers) with a viewpoint that helps him/her to make decisions in order to improve the students learning process. The generated group student models record not only the last state of knowledge of the students but also their evolution during the learning sessions. As the knowledge of the students change over time, the updating of those models is also considered.

1 Introduction

Inside the computer based teaching-learning area the inspection and visualization of students´ knowledge has been widely explored. The necessity of having a Student Model for representing such information is commonly agreed [1]. Moreover, it has become apparent the benefit of having Open Student Models to facilitate the inspection and, in some cases, the modification of these models [2]. There are diverse reasons that different authors argue for making the Student Model available [3]. For example, the teacher could detect what parts of the domain are difficult to achieve and so, consider the inclusion of some additional material (e.g. more examples, tutorials, etc.) in order to improve the understanding of such contents.

A Concept Map is a useful resource for opening Student Models to final users (e.g. teachers or students). Since Novak [4] placed Concept Maps in the educational agenda, they have been broadly used as a medium to represent and interchange knowledge [5]. A Concept Map is a graphical way of representing and organizing knowledge. It is comprised of nodes and links, arranged in some order to reflect the domain being represented. Nodes symbolize concepts, and links represent relationship between concepts; both concepts and links are labeled and may be categorized. The use of Concept Maps can help to improve the understanding of the information contained in Student Models.

W. Nejdl and K. Tochtermann (Eds.): EC-TEL 2006, LNCS 4227, pp. 383 – 397, 2006.

The knowledge of a student during the learning sessions changes continuously. Although most of the Student Models are able to manage the last state of knowledge of students, only few of them take into account the evolution of the model [6]. A medium where the evolution of knowledge can be analyzed is of great interest as the user can have an image of the way student's performance has evolved.

It is also important to remark that, in some situations, students get better results while learning with peers rather than working individually [7]. To adjust activities to group characteristics it is necessary to face new research questions such as Group Models [8]. Inside the research community some works defend the need of having Group Models to support the learning processes of students that work as a group [7]. Furthermore, Jameson *et al.* [9] propose an explicit Group Model or a dynamic combination of Individual Models as needed. From their point of view, an explicit Group Model can serve as a focal point for discussion.

Along this paper, the authors present an approach for Group Student Models. Using Concept Maps, the Group Student Models are opened. In this way, a better way of visualizing the raw data contained in such models is provided. Raw data can come from different sources such as learning data generated in a web-based learning system. Moreover, the models provide the students' knowledge evolution during the learning sessions. Thus, the changes in the knowledge of students can be displayed dynamically. Therefore, learning systems designers, teachers and students can benefit from a medium that shows useful learning information, helping them to make decisions to improve learning.

The rest of the paper is organized as follows. First, DynMap is introduced, a tool to graphically visualise Individual Student Models by means of Concept Maps. Then, the approach to Group Student Models using the DynMap+ tool, which is based on DynMap, is presented. Finally, some conclusions and future research are pointed out.

2 DynMap

Although a lot of effort has been made in the construction of Student Models to support the learning processes in computer based systems, not so much has been done to externalise such models to the final users (e.g. teachers and students) [10]. Inside the human-computer interaction community the development of software that is easy to use and understand is an important aim. Focusing on this objective DynMap has been developed [11], a system that facilitates the inspection of Student Models. More precisely, it is designed to externalise Student Knowledge Models (SKMs) to the final user. A SKM is a model of domain-related information and represents the student's state and level of knowledge of course material [12].

DynMap provides a visual representation of Student Models using Concept Maps and it is based on CM-ED, a general purpose Concept Mapping tool [13]. DynMap uses the data gathered by a computer supported learning system and represent it as a dynamic concept map. The knowledge of students is represented following an overlay approach [14]. Thus, the knowledge the student has is viewed as a subset of the whole learning domain.

As the knowledge of students' changes over the learning sessions, the Student Models should support this dynamic behaviour. DynMap is able not only to maintain the last state of knowledge of students, but also the knowledge evolution during the learning sessions. Using the facilities provided by the Concept Map Editor (CM-ED) to record the operations performed over a Concept Map (operations logs), DynMap stores the evolution of Student Models (evolution logs) and allows the user to view, using video-like buttons, how the knowledge of students changes during the learning sessions. Thus, the system is able to show the performance evolution over the learning sessions. In this way, DynMap users, for example teachers, can inspect the performance of students and, depending on it, plan appropriate didactic actions to improve learning. Such Dynamic Student Models are stored in two parts. One part corresponds to the last knowledge state of the student. The other part is related to the evolution of the knowledge since the first learning session. Both parts are stored in xml documents, so the corresponding schemas to define the structure and data contents of the xml documents have been established.

DynMap shows student data gathered by a computer supported learning systems, such as Intelligent Tutoring Systems, web-based learning systems. Each system has its own representation for the student data. Therefore a general purpose intermediate schema for the incoming student data has been defined. Thus, before DynMap can generate the models, the data has to be translated from the internal representation of the Computer Supported Learning System (CSLS) to the intermediate representation. The translator is a piece of code that has to be implemented for the CSLS, which converts students' learning data to xml format following a schema. The schema defines the structure and contents of the xml data and it is composed of two parts: *domain data definition* and *students learning data definition*. The *domain data* part defines the following elements: topics contained in the domain, didactic resources (learning objects) to learn the topics and skills that can be achieved performing learning activities with the didactic resources. The domain specific data part also includes some other particular information such as: evaluation parameters for the learning activities (e.g. required mark to successfully pass the learning activity), whether a didactic resource is shared or not by a group of students[1], etc. The *students learning data* part defines the format that the incoming data about students learning must follow. In this data part, the realization of learning activities with specific didactic resources is collected. The incoming data is formatted as follows: student identification, domain topic, didactic activity used to learn the topic, date when the didactic activity was carried out, skills that achieved if successfully performed and mark obtained in the learning activity when assessable. As not all this information could be available in the computer supported learning systems, the schema defines some data as optional and DynMap uses just the available data.

Once the students learning data is stored in xml format, a Base Concept Map (BCM) is generated using CM-ED. The BCM represents the domain and includes the topics represented in the *domain specific* part of the xml document. This BCM is the domain model from which the overlay Student Models are generated. The structure of the Concept Map is hierarchical and includes, in the higher part of the tree, the topics of the domain. The learning activities worked by students are represented with the

---

[1] This information will support the generation process of Group Students Models in DynMap+, which is detailed later.

nodes at the bottom of the tree linked to the corresponding topics represented in the Concept Map.

A medium where a Student Model is open for inspection should meet some criteria: understandability, effective inspection and reducing the cognitive load [15]. Focusing on these criteria and having validated the graphical approach selected for showing different circumstances in the student's knowledge about the domain contents [11], a set of graphical resources are used in the nodes of the DynMap Student Models:

- **Thickness**: the thickness of the border represents the student's level of knowledge about the concept. In order to determine the thickness the number of learning activities and their marks are taken into account. The thicker the border is, the more knowledge the student has about the concept.
- **Continuous/Dashed Line**: a dashed border represents that the concept is not completely achieved, e.g. the performance of the student when working with the learning activities related to the concept has gone beyond a threshold, otherwise the line will be continuous.
- **Flag**: this graphic resource is used to show when the concept has attached learning activities (for example, lectures , labs , assignments). Thus, the Concept Map shows the type of learning activities used in each part of the domain.
- **Form**: type of concept represented by a node (e.g. modules of the domain, units in each module, learning activities, etc.). The types of concepts are defined in a template using CM-ED before making the BCM of the domain.
- **Shadowed line**: shows whether the node is contracted (shadowed) or not. A contracted node contains a subset of the Concept Map related to the node.
- **Green Rectangle**: used to highlight new nodes in the Student Model (student's knowledge changes).

In order to meet Dimitrova's criteria [15] presented above DynMap includes the following resources: contraction mechanism, views and filters. DynMap uses a contraction mechanism to reduce the cognitive load of the SKMs. It involves collapsing parts of the Concept Map in a node and marking it with a shadowed line. CM-ED has the possibility to define views and filters over the Concept Maps and DynMap takes advantage of them to provide the user with different points of view of the data contained in the models. On the one hand, the filters DynMap defines allow the filtering of data depending on the learning activities performed by students. On the other hand, the view changes the way data is displayed in the Concept Maps, facilitating in this way an effective inspection of the student's knowledge. A direct benefit of these mechanisms, supported by DynMap, is the scalability of this approach. The major disadvantage of using Concept Maps in qualitative work seems to be their complexity. The maps can be difficult for participants unfamiliar with the format to read and the linkages may be harder to see as the maps get more and more complex [16]. With the visualization facilities provided by DynMap, the models represented as Concept Maps can be visualized in a simplified way avoiding the scalability problems of big Concept Maps.

Fig. 1 displays, making use of the graphical resources mentioned, the usage of DynMap in a real situation. It shows a Student Model in the context of a Computer

Security course at the University of the Basque Country [11]. The Concept Map of the model is organized hierarchically from top to bottom and includes the most general concepts at the top and the most specific data at the bottom. In the figure the top node represents the complete domain, the second level in the hierarchy represents the modules in which the domain is organized and the third level represents the basic topics in each module. These three top levels correspond to the BCM, and the last level in the hierarchy represents the student learning data in the domain. For example, the topic *System access control* shows three learning activities (two lectures and one lab) performed by the student.

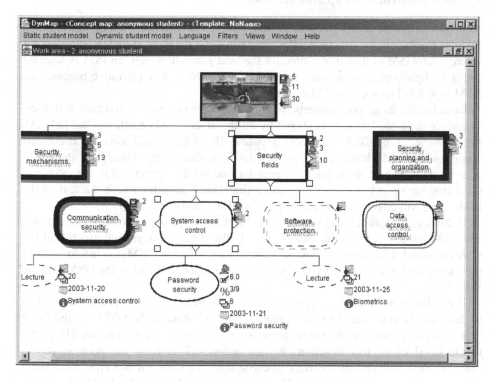

Fig. 1. Student Model in DynMap for a Computer Security course domain

3 DynMap+

Nowadays, it is common practice to learn inside a group (e.g. lectures in a school, group assignments, etc.). Research has been performed to improve the learning performance of a group [9] [17] [18]. The necessity of having a Group Student Model (GSM) that stores the learning characteristics of a group has been analysed [7]. If these models are open they can be used to inspect the learning performance of the group and so, make the appropriate changes in the teaching processes in order to enhance the knowledge of each individual member.

With this aim, DynMap has been enhanced to support GSMs. Such enhancement is implemented in DynMap+ tool where GSMs share structure with the Individual Students Models (ISMs) generated in DynMap. However, some extra information inherent to a GSM is added to the model as will be discussed below. The similarity between GSMs and ISMs makes it possible to reuse the functionality provided by DynMap. In the following subsections several aspects with regard to DynMap+ are analyzed: generation of GSMs, representation of GSMs, updating considerations of GSMs and GSMs visualization issues.

3.1   Generation of a Group Student Model

As proposed in [19] and [20], the GSM in DynMap+ is obtained from the ISMs of the students that belong to the group. The generation of a GSM is an incremental process where a new ISM is joined at a time. In the first generation step, an ISM is selected and it is slightly adapted to meet the GSM format. Next, in an iterative process, the GSM is updated taking one ISM each time.

Learning in a group, students perform both group and individual activities. Therefore some student data is shared by all the students while other is not [21] [8]. For example, in the Computer Security course above mentioned there are individual (assignments) and shared (lectures and labs) student data. Therefore, the GSM generation procedure has to take into account that the data contained in the ISMs can be shared (group activities) or not shared (individual activities) with the rest of the ISMs. This will affect the integration process of the ISMs into the GSM.

If the data is shared, the update procedure of the GSM depends on whether or not the GSM already reflects the shared data. If the data is not yet represented in the GSM, it is added to the model, but if it already exists in the GSM, the information of the shared data is updated making some statistical operations using the GSM and the ISM data.

If the data is not shared the update procedure is more complex. The main problem to deal with is to decide the way of representing this data in the GSM. As the GSM represents data related to the whole group activity, the non-shared data must be added to the GSM taking this characteristic into account. This issue has been solved as follows. First, the non-shared data is classified depending on the type of didactic resources (learning objects) used. Next, this data is added to the GSM taking into account the type of didactic resource in two steps. The first step involves the generation of statistic information from the non-shared data of all students related to each didactic resource type. This information includes: number of didactic resources used, average mark obtained with the didactic resources, etc. The GSM represents group information of non-shared data through this statistical data. The second step involves the linkage of such global data with the specific non-shared data of each ISM. In order to improve usability when inspecting the GSM, the specific non-shared data of each ISMs is added to the GSM. How the shared and non-shared data is integrated in the GSM is detailed in section 3.2 (representation of a GSM).

Using the dynamic support facilities for Student Models provided by DynMap, DynMap+ is able to maintain not only the last state of the GSM, but also the progress over the learning sessions. As stated in [8] a Group Model should keep information with regard to the student performance in each learning activity. Following this statement, DynMap+ maintains in the GSM a reference to the ISMs that is based on. The dynamic version of a GSM is obtained from the ISMs' evolution logs and implies the generation of an evolution log for the GSM. This log, represented in xml format, collects each individual operation included in the evolution logs of the ISMs ordered by time. In order to meet the format of the GSM, the evolution log generated for the GSM includes some operations not contained in the evolution logs of the ISMs. However, the evolution logs of an ISM and a GSM share structure and thus, the functionality of DynMap for displaying dynamically a Student Model can be used in DynMap+ for showing the evolution of a Group Student Model.

3.2 Representation of a Group Student Model

Using the graphical visualization facilities provided by DynMap the GSMs are also represented as Concept Maps. In addition to the graphical resources used in DynMap for the representation of different aspects of the Student Models, DynMap+ uses one more: the attenuation of the colour of the nodes. This new graphical resource is used to represent the number of students that contribute in the corresponding node of the GSM. If the colour is full (not attenuated) it means that all the students have contributed in the corresponding node. In the case of an attenuated colour (a gradient of it), the more attenuated it is the smaller the amount of students that have contributed in the corresponding node. The main advantage of the attenuation graphical resource is that a clear view of the distribution of students work can be obtained at a glance. It is easy to identify what parts of the domain are the most worked by the group and what other parts are not. This information could be used, for example, for planning future teaching covering less worked domain topics.

Fig. 2 shows a screenshot of a GSM using the mentioned graphical resources. The GSM is based on the Individual Student Models generated in the Computer Security course at the University of the Basque Country [11] (see **Fig. 1**). In figure 2 it is perceptible that few students of the group have performed "*Legato*" and "*Backup devices*" learning activities, which are lab sessions. However, looking at the attenuation graphical resource, it can be noticed that "*Backup devices*" has been performed by more students of the group than "*Legato*". In contrast, the learning activiy *Lecture* titled "*Failure tolerance*" has been performed by most of the students of the group. This could suggest for example, that students could have acquired some knowledge in "*Failure tolerance*" as the mayority of them have attended the lecture. But as few of the students have taken part in the practical lab sessions of the topic "*Back-ups*" it can be supossed that the group have not achieved the required skills for the topic. Also, looking at the topics of the module "*Security mechanisms*", the topic "*Back-ups*" is less attenuated than the corresponding topics of the same level. This suggests the work distribution (using learning activities) that the students of the group have performed over the topics of the module. Another circumstance visible in the figure is the distribution of "*assignment* type" learning activity in the modules "*Security mechanisms*" and "*Security fields*". The distribution of work is balanced between both modules: 58 *assignments* for the former and 56 for the latter.

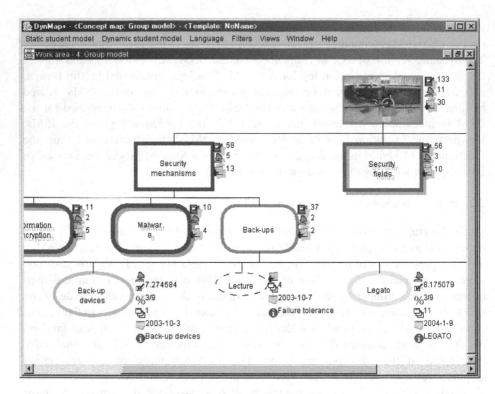

Fig. 2. Group Student Model

As mentioned in previous section (Sect. 3.1), the data that each ISM contains can be shared or not by the rest of the ISMs. For the case of shared data, DynMap+ has no changes, with respect to DynMap, on the graphical visualization of the GSM (with the exception of the attenuation graphical resource). The reason of having no changes is that the GSM represents group information when the data is shared by all the ISMs. However, for non-shared data some changes must be included in DynMap+ because that data is individual to each student and do not represent group information. As presented in section 3.1, DynMap+ supports the inclusion of statistical data in the GSM. Also, such statistical information is linked with specific non-shared data of each ISM. The statistical data is represented as a node in the GSM and the related ISM-specific information is linked to that node.

Fig. 3 shows a fragment of a Group Student Model that contains both shared and non-shared data. The selected node of the Concept Map (bottom part of the figure) corresponds to statistical information of non-shared data related to some students of the group. The information displayed inside this node is similar to the one displayed in the intermediate nodes (nodes of the Base Concept Map of the domain) of the GSM. However in an intermediate node (*i.e.* topics of the domain) the statistical data is shown in the right side of the node. For example, the topic of the figure "*Information encryption*" has four flags attached which represents, from top to down, the average mark obtained by the group in that topic (7.8 over 10), the percentage of assessable learning activities performed satisfactorily compared with the threshold that is required for the topic (9 out of 9) and the number of learning activities performed (2 labs and 11 assignments). On the other hand, the statistical data of non-shared data is displayed inside a node. For example, the node selected in the figure displays inside it the following statistical information: 7.4 (out of 10) average mark obtained, 66% (6/9) of domain achieved and 11 assignments performed. The specific non-shared data of each student related to the topic can be reached through this node. The mechanism to access the specific data is the same as used in other parts of the model, and implies expanding the collapsed node.

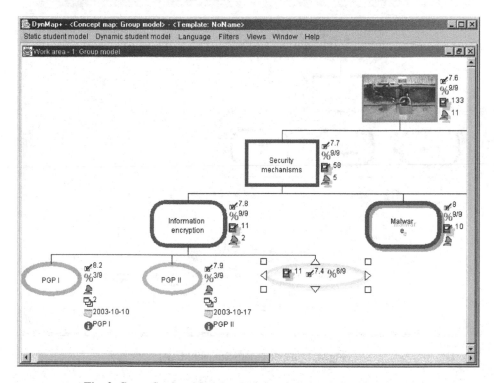

Fig. 3. Group Student Model containing shared and non-shared data

For the dynamic visualisation of GSMs, DynMap+ extends the functionality available in DynMap that supports the display of the evolution of a Student Model over time. In Fig. 4 an example of a dynamic Group Student Model is presented. The dynamic GSM is similar to the dynamic ISMs of DynMap, with the exception of non-shared data. For example, the selected node in the Concept Map corresponds to the last non-shared learning activities performed by the group in the topic *Malware*. Concretely, it collects three learning activities: *Express assignments*. The "green rectangle" graphical resource provided by the dynamic part of DynMap highlights the last learning activities performed in the current state of the dynamic GSM: one lab (*Backdoors*) and three assignments (*Express assignments*). The evolution of the GSM can be viewed at different time units and implies moving in the time sequence of learning events. This means that the user can choose the time unit of the jumps in the evolution. In addition, the GSM can be viewed dynamically taking into account a specific student of the group. Thus, the steps when playing the evolution correspond only to the activities performed by that student. Therefore, the performance of the student in the group is displayed according to the events of one student, *i.e.* the state of the group knowledge is shown when the knowledge of the student changes.

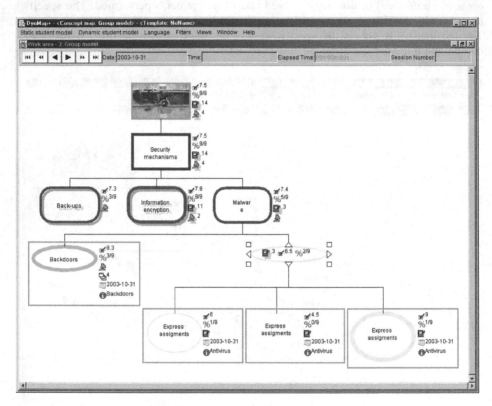

Fig. 4. Dynamic Group Student Model

3.3 Update of a Group Student Model

During the learning sessions of students their ISMs are updated over time. As the GSMs generated in DynMap+ are based on those ISMs, the updating procedure of the GSM is an important issue. [12] analyses methods of updating Student Models. However, in DynMap+, as the GSM is linked with the ISMs (see Section 3.1) such methods are not necessary because the GSM can be updated dynamically each time the GSM is accessed for inspection. This is similar to the GSM update procedure selected in [17], which takes place at every start-up of the program.

Another update issue of GSMs that should be taken into account is the change in the composition of the group. There can be different reasons why a group loses or gains members: student timetable incompatibilities, teachers´ decisions to improve the performance of a group, etc. Therefore, the GSM must be also updated when students come into a group or leaves it. In DynMap+ these changes are supported updating the references from the GSM to the ISMs that is based on (see Section 3.1). If a student leaves the group, the corresponding reference to its ISM is removed from the GSM. In the same way, if a student enters the group, the corresponding reference to the ISM is added to the GSM. The modification of the group composition is stored in order to maintain the evolution of group members and also, to obtain the proper GSM at a specific date. GSM is also updated adding or removing from it the data related to the ISMs of the students that join or leave the group. Moreover, for the dynamic version of the GSM, its evolution log is updated to reflect the group member formation.

3.4 Visualization of a Group Student Model

As DynMap does DynMap+ uses three mechanisms to reduce the cognitive load [15] of the SKMs: contraction mechanism, filters and views. Parts of the Concept Map can be contracted and represented in a node and marking it with a shadowed line. These mechanisms guarantee the scalability of this approach. The ability to effectively filter information is necessary when presenting large amounts of data [22]. Following this idea, DynMap+ uses views and filters functionality implemented in DynMap to simplify the visualization of information contained in the GSMs. The inclusion of such resources allows the user to view the data from different points of view and to focus on a particular aspect of the model. Having a simplified vision of the data, a greater perception of special circumstances in the GSM is achieved. For example, a filter that shows data related to one type of didactic resource facilitates the visualization of the distribution of the use of that kind of didactic resource over the domain. This could be used for analysing the learning performance achieved with a particular set of didactic resources and so, the teacher would have valuable information to consider the inclusion and degree of usage of such type of didactic resources in future teaching sessions. In Fig. 5 an example of a filtered version of a Group Student Model is shown. The applied filter is based on a particular type of didactic resource (*lab sessions*) used by students in the Computer Security course. The filter only displays the nodes of the Concept Map related to that didactic resource and hides the information related to other types of didactic resources. Also, the information displayed in the view of the Group Student Model is adapted to the applied filter. This means that the knowledge achieved by the group of students in each of the topics of the domain is based taking into account only the type of didactic resource corresponding to the filter being used. A direct benefit of this filtering approach is the visualization of students knowledge at different levels of detail. In the example, a teacher could check how the performance of the group is in the whole domain considering the *lab sessions* learning activity. Furthermore, as the instructor (e.g. the teacher of the subject) can filter the GSM for each type of didactic resource, s/he could detect what types of didactic resources are obtaining the worst performance in students' learning. This can be easily seen at a glance looking at the different graphical resources used in DynMap+ for remarking special circumstances. For example, nodes in the model with dashed lines would denote parts of the subject that have not been achieved with the correspondent type of didactic resource.

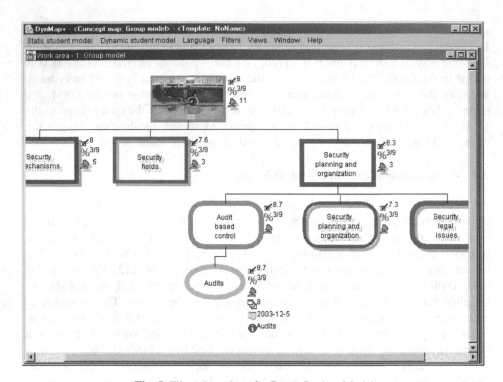

Fig. 5. Filtered version of a Group Student Model

In addition, GSMs offer more possibilities of filtering data than the ones defined in DynMap for an ISM. A GSM could show data depending on several perspectives related to the criteria used to show data in the GSM; e.g. show data in the GSM only if all students of the group have contributed in that data. These criteria take into account the following set of variables: the level of achievement or degree of knowledge about the domain contents, the number of didactic resources used and the subset of the domain that is being worked. As the GSMs that result from this type of filtering are not equal nor a subset of the original GSMs, the filtering process is not a simple process and it is advisable to perform it at generation time. In the generation of a GSM, DynMap+ offers to the user a list of optional filters. At the end, DynMap+ maintains a global GSM as described previously and a set of GSMs for each type of filter selected. Finally, at runtime, the user can apply one of the filtering approaches already generated or, if needed, generate the ones that have not been generated. However, it is desirable to perform all the GSM generations at generation time due to performance issues, as the generation processes are more time consuming than just applying a view or filter over a GSM.

Furthermore, a GSM can also be filtered with respect to the members of the group. As a result of those filters, Subgroup Student Models are obtained. The procedure to obtain those filters is similar to the update procedure when there are changes in the composition of the group (see Section 3.3). Another advantage of this filtering is the visualization of influence of a single student (or subgroup of students) in the group. For example, if a student is removed from a GSM, the influence of this student in the knowledge achieved in the group is shown graphically. Also, with regard to the dynamic version of a GSM, the influence of a student (or subgroup of students) can be viewed over the learning sessions of the group. The way to inspect the changes between a GSM and a filtered version of a GSM is to open both versions using the Multiple Document Interface provided by DynMap. In this way, any important influence of a student or subgroup of students in the group can be noticed.

4 Conclusions

In this paper, DynMap+, a tool for supporting Group Student Models has been presented. The tool represents not only the last state of a model but also its evolution during the learning sessions. The models that follow the overlay approach are graphically visualized by means of Concept Maps. Moreover, some graphical resources are used to highlight important data. In order to keep information with regard to students' performance in each learning activity, the Group Student Models maintain a reference to the Individual Student Models that are based on. Along the paper, several aspects have been discussed about generation, representation, updating and visualization of Group Student Models.

Students learning data can be gathered from different sources such as Intelligent Tutoring Systems, web-based learning systems, etc. DynMap+ is designed to show graphically the student data generated by those computer based learning systems. First the systems' internal student data must be transformed to an intermediate representation supported by DynMap+. The raw students data can be graphically visualized using the tool in a Concept Map. DynMap+ provides a medium to analyze the knowledge achieved during the learning sessions of a group of students (or just an individual or a subgroup). With this tool, useful information is opened for inspection, allowing teachers to make teaching decisions (e.g. new teaching planning) in order to improve the students learning. Therefore, the tool can be classified inside the Decision Support Systems as it externalizes the state of knowledge of individuals and groups of students for decision making purposes.

A direct application of the tool is the formation of group of students. By suggesting appropriate group arrangements, many problems might be solved even before they arise [18]. Furthermore, it is interesting to know how a member of a group influences the learning outcomes of a group [21]. DynMap+ can be used for this purpose providing a vision of how the learning performance of a group and of a student changes when moving students to different groups. This would also help in group formation decisions when seeking a specific performance of learning in a group.

As future research, an evaluation of the different aspects of DynMap+ presented in this paper will be performed. DynMap has been already evaluated in a real use context [11] and DynMap+ has been tested based on the Individual Student Models generated in this study. Therefore, the evaluation of DynMap+ will be performed in the same context: a Computer Security course at the University of the Basque Country [11]. As DynMap+ provides many facilities to visualize the knowledge of students of a group, the evaluation will have to be performed incrementally at different levels of complexity: group, group with differential loads/paritipation, etc. Also, DynMap+ will be extended to detect student's knowledge performance similarities and complementarities. Thus, using for example the Complementarity criterion [19], which states that a student can be helpful to another student if the first one knows a topic and the second has difficulties in that topic, the formation of appropriate subgroups or reorganization of existing groups would be easier to decide.

Acknowledgments

Work funded by the Univ. of the Basque Country (UPV00141.226-T-15948/2004), the CICYT (TIC2002-03141) and the Gipuzkoa Council in an EU program.

References

1. Workshop on Open, Interactive, and other Overt Approaches to Learner Modelling. AIED'1999, Le Mans, France, July, 1999.(http://aied.inf.ed.ac.uk/members99/resources/modelling/modelling.html).
2. Hartley, D. and Mitrovic, A.: Supporting Learning by Opening the Student Model. In Cerri, S. Gouardères and Paraguaçu (eds.) Proceedings of International Conference on Intelligent Tutoring Systems (2002) 453-462.
3. Kay, J.: Learner Control. User Modelling and User-Adapted Interaction, Vol. 11 (2001) 111-127.
4. Novak, J.D.: A theory of education. Cornell University, Ithaca, NY (1977).
5. Bruillard, E. & Baron, G.L. (2000). Computer-based concept mapping: a review of a cognitive tool for students. In Proceedings of ICEUT2000, 16th IFIP World Computer Congress (eds. D. Benzie & Passey, D.), pp. 332-338. PHEI.
6. Eva Millán, José Luis Pérez-de-la-Cruz, Felipe García, Dynamic versus Static Student Models Based on Bayesian Networks: An Empirical Study, Lecture Notes in Computer Science, Volume 2774, Oct 2003, Pages 1337 – 1344.
7. *Tongchai N., Brna P. (2005)*. Enhancing Metacognitive Skills through the use of a Group Model based on the Zone of Proximal Development. Workshop on Learner Modelling for Reflection, to Support Learner Control, Metacognition and Improved Communication of the 12th International Conference on Artificial Intelligence in Education (2005).
8. Miao, Y. and Hoppe, U. (2005). Adapting Process-Oriented Learning Design to Group Characteristics. Proceedings of Artificial Intelligence in Education, Looi, C., McCalla, G., Bredeweg, B., Breuker, J. (eds.) IOS Press, 475-482 (2005).
9. Jameson, A., Baldes, S., and Kleinbauer, T. Generative Models of Group Members as Support for Group Collaboration. Workshop on User and Group Models for Web-Based Adaptive Collaborative Environments Proceedings of the International Conference on User Modeling, 1--14, 2003.
10. Workshop on Student Modeling for Language Tutors. AIED'2005, Amsterdam, Netherlands, 2005 (http://www.research.ibm.com/people/a/alpert/AIED05/).
11. Rueda, U., Larrañaga, M., Kerejeta, M., Elorriaga, J.A., Arruarte, A. (2005). Visualizing Student Data in a Real Teaching Context by Means of Concept Maps. International Conference on Knowledge Management I-Know 2005.
12. Brusilovsky, P. (1994). The construction and application of student models in intelligent tutoring systems. Journal of Computer and System Sciences International, 32(1), 70-89.

13. Rueda, U., Larrañaga, M., Arruarte, A., Elorriaga, J.A. (2004). Applications of a Concept Mapping Tool. In: Cañas, A.J., Novak, J.D., González, F. (eds): Proceedings of the First International Conference on Concept Mapping (2004) 545-553.

14. Golstein, I.P.: The Genetic Graph: a representation for the evolution of procedural knowledge. In: Sleeman, D. and Brown, J.S. (eds.): Intelligent Tutoring Systems, Academic Press (1982) 51-77.

15. Dimitrova, V. (2002). Dimitrova, V., Brna, P. and Self, J.: The Design and Implementation of a Graphical Communication Medium for Interactive Learner Modelling. In Cerri, S. Gouardères and Paraguaçu (eds.) Proceedings of ITS'2002 (2002) 432-441.

16. Daley, B.J. Using concept maps in qualitative research. In Cañas, A., Novak D. and Gonzales, F.M. (eds.) *Concept Maps: theory, Methodology, Technology: Proceedings of the First International Conference on Concept mapping*, Pamplona, Spain, Volume 1, 2004, pp. 191-197

17. Kinshuk, Hong H., Albi N., Patel A., Jesshope C. (2001). Client-Server Architecture based integrated system for education at a distance. In Ruokamo H., Nykänen O., Pohjolainen S. & Hietala P. (Eds.) Intelligent Computer and Communications Technology - Learning in On-Line Communities, Proceedings of the Tenth International PEG Conference (June 23-26, 2001, Tampere, Finland), Tampere, Finland: Digital Media Institute, Tampere University of Technology, 57-61 (ISBN 952-15-0627-X).

18. Muehlenbrock, M. (2005). Formation of Learning Groups by using Learner Profiles and Context Information. Proceedings of Artificial Intelligence in Education, Looi, C., McCalla, G., Bredeweg, B., Breuker, J. (eds.) IOS Press, 507-514 (2005).

19. Hoppe, U. (1995). The use of multiple student modelling to parametrize group learning. Greer, J. (Ed.), Proceedings of World Conference on Artificial Intelligence in Education, pp. 234-241.

20. Mühlenbrock, M., Tewissen, F., Hoppe, H.U. (1998). A framework system for intelligent support in open distributed learning environments. *International Journal of Artificial Intelligence in Education*, Vol. 9, 256-274.

21. Fischer, F. & Mandl, H. (2001). Fostering shared knowledge with active graphical representation in different collaboration scenarios (Researchreport Nr. 135). München: Ludwig-Maximilians-Universität, Lehrstuhl für Empirische Pädagogik und Pädagogische Psychologie.

22. Pettersson, D. (2000). Aspect filtering as a tool to support conceptual exploration and presentation. Technical Report TRITA-NA-E0079, KTH Stockholm, December 2000.

Knowledge Management in Schools—From Electronic Schoolbag to Social Software

Harald Selke

Heinz Nixdorf Institute, University of Paderborn
Fürstenallee 11, 33102 Paderborn, Germany
hase@upb.de
http://www.hni.upb.de

Abstract. This contribution examines how teaching and learning in schools can be enhanced by employing computer technology. For that purpose, a web based system was developed in an evolutionary and participatory design process to serve as a platform for knowledge management in schools and then developed further into a system that can be characterized as social software for schools. The development was carried out in three stages. A powerful content management proved too complex and thus too difficult to learn for most users and resulted in poor usage. After reducing the functionality and re-implementing the user interface, the system was successfully introduced in schools. An evaluation of this "electronic schoolbag" showed that while the system was very well received, additional features were demanded. The third stage of the development thus added support in particular for use of the system in class, so that cooperation, communication, and coordination are now supported by an integration of several components of social software.

1 Introduction

Within the initiative *Bildungswege in der InformationsGesellschaft (BIG)* – ways of education in the information society, documented in [1] – a solution was required for making the material developed for school use available to teachers. For this purpose, the content management system *Hyperwave Information Server* [7] was employed. This system had already been used successfully by us in other projects. One reason for using such a system instead of a simple web server was that teachers were not only to access published material but work with this material actively – be it individually or together with other teachers of their own school or from other schools with whom they cooperated in teacher training courses or in work groups on specific topics. To that end, teachers needed to select and arrange material as needed and also add own documents; another requirement was the possibility to modify the documents in order to use them in a specific context. Since not all of the material was supposed to be accessible to the public and, when used in class, documents were to be released to particular groups of learners, access rights granting read or write access needed to be assigned to specific users or user groups. The solution provided for this purpose is described very briefly in the second section of this contribution.

W. Nejdl and K. Tochtermann (Eds.): EC-TEL 2006, LNCS 4227, pp. 398–410, 2006.
© Springer-Verlag Berlin Heidelberg 2006

Very soon it turned out that use of the platform, while providing all functions needed, was difficult to learn for most of the users. Also, most of the functions the platform offered were not needed. Thus, it was necessary to replace the web interface which was the main means for applying the server's functions by a new one that was tailored to the needs of every-day teaching and working in schools. For that purpose, the functionality offered to the users was reduced to the minimum needed, thus reducing the effort needed for learning how to use the platform and also the inhibitions in using the server. Instead of creating a system that implements a large number of useful functions the goal was rather to make possible a knowledge management on an elementary level and making the system very easy to use. This system which in its core functionality may be characterised as an "electronic schoolbag" is described in the third section.

As of March 2006, three servers with more than 5000 users from some 500 schools were in operation. The usage in the respective schools is highly varying. While at some schools virtually all teachers have a user account (yet using the server to a very different degree), at others only single teachers are registered. Also several registered users do not use the server at all. Thus, these numbers have to be interpreted with care. The reasons for using the server to different degrees are manifold, the technology itself being only one factor, others lying in the necessities of every-day work life. In the fourth section, an independent evaluation is described that has been conducted in a separate project "School Wide Web" by the Bertelsmann Foundation. Within that project, teachers from three schools were trained in using the server and concepts for a methodic deployment of knowledge management in schools were developed.

For reasons irrelevant to this contribution, the Hyperwave server forming the basis of the system during the project phases described so far, was replaced in a third stage by the open source system open-sTeam which is based on the concept of virtual knowledge spaces [5]. At the same time, several new functions were implemented; these new features had been requested by teachers either within the evaluation mentioned or through other feedback channels. Most of these functions which may be assigned to the domain of "social software" [8] resulted from the use of the platform in class. All of these functions are available to every user and every group in their own work area and can be used whenever needed without having to contact an administrator. The fifth section describes this system.

The evolutionary development process was coordinated by a technical advisory board that determined the requirements by questioning the users, gathering feedback provided in training seminars and also from the evaluation described in section four. Concerning the latest development stage, first experiences and feedback are available but have not yet been determined systematically.

2 The First Step: Hyperwave's Original Interface

The Hyperwave Information Server is in its origins a server based hypermedia system that has been developed into a content management system. In the process of extending the system, a multitude of functions were added. The user interface shipped with the server allows the access to virtually all of these functions. While this interface may be customised on several levels, this possibility was not utilised within the BIG

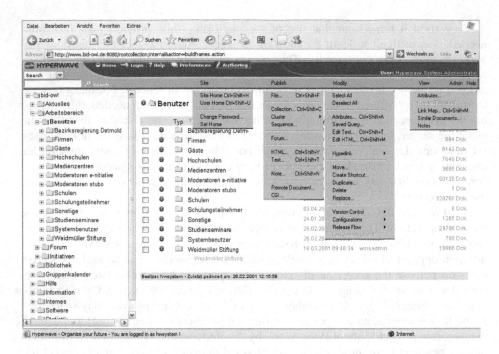

Fig. 1. All menus (without submenus) of the Hyperwave Information Server's standard user interface. When using the system, only one of the menus is visible at any time, of course.

project. Thus, users were required to work with the user interface as shipped. This interface was also used in other school projects, where no budget for customising the user interface was assigned.

In this contribution, the functions provided will not be described in detail. What is important in this context is a result from the "Network Media Schools", a best-practice network of experts in use of computers in schools ([9], p. 12). Although this network consisted solely of teachers experienced in using computers in school, it turned out that even after trainings that were restricted to the basic functionality a considerable amount of uncertainty in using the software was felt. In the schools this uncertainty was of even more importance because teachers were not using the server on a daily basis. Also, the teachers that had participated in the trainings often felt not to have the ability to introduce the system to learners or other teachers who had not yet worked much with web based tools. While the user interface resembled the Windows Explorer to a certain degree, using it was not intuitive. The main reasons identified in [2] (p. 316) are the many different functions which can not be reduced to the necessary basic functions like, e.g., uploading documents and linking them. As a result, many teachers and learners were reluctant to use the system. Within the Network Media Schools it was thus decided to use Quickplace, a reduced variant of the Lotus Notes system. In the final report, it is emphasised that this platform is a sensible reduction of a complex system ([2], p. 317).

3 The Electronic Schoolbag

The server employed can be customised in a number of ways. Simple modifications are possible by removing individual menu items, thus not offering this particular function to the users. Hyperwave's concept of document classes [6] allows to define new object types that possess object specific and thus possibly reduced functionality. However, the user interface is not simplified but rather extended by the introduction of document classes. A reduction of Hyperwave's dialogs is very time-consuming because of the complexity of the web based front-end. Thus, it was decided to develop a completely new front-end which can be achieved using server-side JavaScript and the Hyperwave-specific macro language PLACE. While it would also have been possible to implement the new front-end in PHP on a separate web server, this possibility was not considered.

The development was coordinated by a technical advisory board consisting of up to seven members: teachers from different school types, a representative of the Weidmüller Foundation which conducts cooperation projects of schools with companies, the representative of the regional government (Bezirksregierung Detmold) who is responsible for media education, a representative of Gütersloh's regional media centre and the author of this contribution – being responsible for the technical realization. Through their own experience and that of their colleagues on the one hand and feedback in trainings on the other hand, this board was useful in determining the concrete requirements and shortcomings in using the system formerly employed. This was done by talking frequently to users rather than in a formalised process. Prototypical implementations were then firstly tested by the technical board and then by a small group of test users before they were released.

According to the main goal to lower the inhibition threshold for working with the system, the resulting application was a kind of minimalist solution. Among the basic functions offered were the creation of folders, up- and download of documents of arbitrary type, the creation of texts directly on the server and the filing of references to web addresses as social bookmarks. It was also deemed essential that users were able to delete, move, and copy documents, assign access rights to define which persons were allowed to read or modify the objects created. The ability to search for keywords or within the full text of documents was also considered vital.

The dialogs for accomplishing these tasks were drastically simplified in comparison to the dialogs of the Hyperwave server. In the dialog for creating objects, e.g., only those fields were displayed that were definitely indispensable. Further attributes were only available via a "properties" dialog. While users were introduced to these attributes in the trainings, they were only very briefly explained in more detail. Users who had been working with the Hyperwave server and its original user interface before as well as users who had been working with other web based systems sometimes asked for additional functionality in addition to these basic functions. This was made possible by providing access to the standard interface via a separate port.

Every user has their own work area where initially only they have read and write access. However, they may allow other individual users and groups of users to access or modify this personal work area as well as any other object (folder, document, etc.)

created by them. Every group of users also own a work area where all members of the group have read and write access. Here also objects with different access rights may be stored, in particular objects may also be publicly accessible.

The considerations in the development process are best illustrated by looking at the dialog for setting access rights. Hyperwave's default dialog requires the user to enter the name (or a partial name) of a user or user group into a search field. The user sought-after can then be selected and read or write access rights may be assigned. In the case of the use in schools as targeted here, users usually cooperate in steady contexts, i.e. individual users or groups usually cooperate over a long term like, e.g., during teacher trainings, in school classes or in study groups. As a consequence, we decided to implement a procedure in two steps: The dialog for setting the access rights displays only those groups the user is member of. In order to assign an access right to another user or a group one is not member of, this user or group must first be added to this dialog via a separate "Favourites" dialog. These favourites are also displayed in the access rights dialog so that the user can assign read or write access to any of them. While this procedure is cumbersome for a "one-time cooperation", it is much simpler in the "steady cooperation" case of this use context.

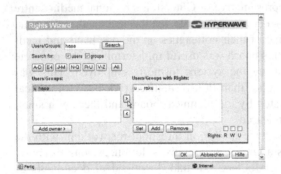

Fig. 2. A comparison of the dialogs for setting access rights. The original Hyperwave dialog is shown on the left, the newly developed one on the right.

A similar procedure was followed for other functions: First the requirements within the particular context of use were determined before designing the user interface elements specifically for this purpose. In virtually all parts this led to a reduction of available possibilities and, thus, complexity for the user.

The functionality realised at this stage can be characterised as an "electronic schoolbag". It allows users to file and transport documents that hereby are available wherever they are needed – provided that an internet access is accessible. However, the system also offers elementary support for cooperative work already. These mechanisms, e.g. the filing of references to web addresses in a group's work area (social bookmarks), may be attributed to the domain of "social software". Another example for a "social" function is the shared text editing made possible by a special type of folder. In these folders, individual learners (or groups of learners) may be assigned a part of the text that only they may modify while everybody can see what others have written so far. In that way, a class may work on a single document with defined responsibilities, thus allowing a teacher to grade the work afterwards.

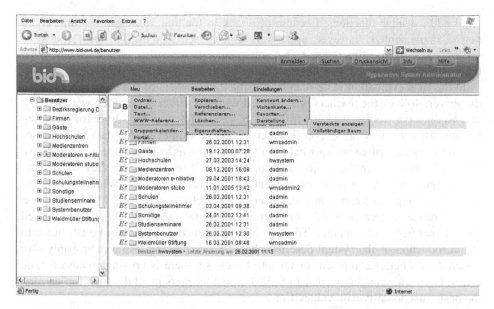

Fig. 3. All menus of the server "Bildung im Dialog" (Education in Dialog) as implemented in the last Hyperwave-based version. Calendars and Portals were missing in earlier versions. When using the system, only one of the menus is visible at any time, of course. Also, this user interface was only available in German language.

4 User Feedback

In the project "School Wide Web – Intranets in Schools" conducted by Heinz Nixdorf Foundation and Bertelsmann Foundation [3] the system as described in the previous section was systematically introduced in three schools. The decision for using this system was made by the project's steering group consisting of four to six teachers from each of the participating schools, some of whom were familiar with the system described in the second section.

In a number of meetings, the steering group developed a catalogue of requirements ([3], p. 57ff.). Most of these requirements were already met by the system described in the previous section, in particular the functions for managing documents, assigning access rights and searching. Other essential criteria were a simple handling and that every teacher and learner should be able to learn how to upload, edit, and remove documents within one or two short training sessions ([3], p. 59). Most of the requirements for user administration were realised rapidly by developing scripts for an import of authentication and directory data from an LDAP server where those data were already administrated.

The system had shortcomings with regard to the functions characterised in the project as groupware. However, these functions were regarded as less important during the project's initial phases. The steering group's catalogue listed discussion forums, a chat function, email lists, and appointment calendars for individual users and user groups. In the course of the project, the server was thus amplified to provide the requiredd calendar functions. Because of a lack in funding, discussion forums could not be implemented; however, users were able to access these via the Hyperwave server's standard user interface. A chat and email lists were also not implemented, the latter being utilisable via the LDAP server.

In the final evaluation more than half of the 220 teachers of the three schools used the server. 40% of the teachers who worked with the server stated they were using it at least once per week (all results from [3], p. 42ff). 67% used the server for preparing lessons, 48% for developing course material, and 40% in class. No data on the absolute numbers how often and to what extent the server was used in these activities have been published. When the project started, 42% of all teachers said, they were using the Internet at regular intervals or frequently for preparing lessons. While 19% stated, they were using the Internet at regular intervals in class, none used it frequently. At the end of the project those values rose to 58% and 38% respectively; 10% now used the Internet frequently in class. To a certain degree this increase may be attributed to the introduction of the system described here. The usage in class was probably also fostered by a better equipment in school classes; so, there is no single cause for the effect. On a scale ranging from 1 to 6, 58% of the teachers rated the time for learning the basic functionality with values 1 or 2.

The most frequently used functions were those for retrieving and making documents available. Only 35% were using the possibility to search for documents frequently or regularly (all results from [3], p. 61). This low value is probably due to the fact that users worked most of the time with documents within an environment created by themselves (like, e.g. within their school class). For this reason, users were familiar enough with the structures in these areas that they were able to directly navigate through the folder structures instead of using the search functions. The web references were used by some 20% of the users frequently or regularly; in most cases they were used by teachers to make external web resources available to their pupils in the class folder.

The appointment calendars that had been integrated in the meantime were only used by 10% of the teachers frequently or regularly, the reason being probably technical problems that had not been foreseen in the development. Also rarely used were the discussion forums (15% used them frequently or regularly); this is probably due to the fact that they could only be used via the standard user interface of Hyperwave and thus were not really integrated into the system. Talks with teachers of the three schools showed that the forums had only been used at one of them.

In addition to this evaluation, feedback from the users was gathered continuously during the complete development process. The demand for an integration of forums was uttered there as well. Another deficit that had been observed early was a missing feature that allowed users to present results from their work in an easy-to-use way. For that purpose, we developed a simple editorial system that allowed for such a presentation without requiring the users to have any knowledge of HTML. School classes were thus able to publish project results cooperatively and keep that presentation up-to-date. In the evaluation of the project "School Wide Web" already 30% of the teachers using the server stated that they used this editorial system – dubbed "portals" – frequently or regularly.

5   Social Software for Schools

By now, the third stage of the development has been realized. The underlying Hyperwave server was replaced by the open source system open-sTeam which is based on the concept of virtual knowledge spaces [5]. The user interface described in the third section has been retained unchanged to the largest possible extent for two reasons: It was well proven and any larger modification would have resulted in a considerable need of training for teachers and learners. However, several problems were eliminated. In particular, functions that had turned out to be complicated to use were simplified. Assigning access rights was also simplified further because the new underlying platform brought with it a rights concept that was more suitable in the given usage context.

A major challenge, however, was the increasing functionality of the system. On the one hand more experienced users – who had also been participating in the project "School Wide Web" or been working with other attractive platforms like the lo-net server (http://www.lo-net.de/) – demanded additional functions. On the other hand, the main goal was maintained that as many teachers and learners as possible should be able to work with the system without the need of time-consuming trainings.

The already existing social software components (social bookmarks, shared editing of texts, appointment calendars and portals) were revised thoroughly. In intensive talks with users feedback was acquired on the existing functions and requests for modifications and extensions were collected. Among the new functions demanded were much more flexible portals that now can also be used in a blog-like fashion, integrated forums, a wiki-style extension of the text editing features, and additional communication features some of which are integrated into the system while others provide quick access to external applications.

5.1   Cooperative Editing of Text

While text could easily be created in the old version of the system, formatting of text required users to employ HTML tags. To edit text thus users needed to modify the HTML source code or use a tool that allowed WYSIWYG editing of HTML documents. This meant in the first case that at least a basic knowledge of HTML was necessary or in the latter that an appropriate tool was at hand. In the latter case, the document to be edited also had to be downloaded, then edited, and uploaded back to the server.

In the new version, the HTML syntax for formatting text is still supported. However, BBCodes, a syntax used frequently in web based bulletin boards, can additionally be employed. As another alternative, wiki syntax can used, though for the time being in a version reduced in scope and flexibility. Both alternatives are currently being tested by the users; depending on their feedback, either or both will be offered in the long term. The goal here is to find a reasonable compromise between flexibility in layout on the one hand and ease-of-use in editing on the other.

The shared creation of text as described in section 2 is another feature still supported. However, in some aspects the handling – e.g., sorting the individual text fragments – were not optimally supported. This has been optimised in the new version. By supporting wiki syntax, texts now can easily be linked together. In fact, every text document can now be used as a wiki document so that every folder effectively is a wiki. In that way, a school class can maintain their own wiki without much effort. They may assign access rights so that, e.g., only the teacher and the pupils of that class have read and write access. If they wish, however, they can also make their wiki accessible to the public. Links across different wikis are also possible.

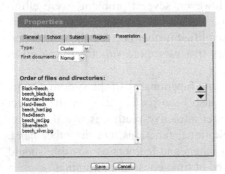 

Fig. 4. The dialogs for sorting the parts of a text with included images that is being written cooperatively (left) and for assigning access rights (right), shown here for a wiki

5.2 Portals and Blogs

The original concept of the portals was very easy to use but also very static. In general, they consisted of four components: a headline; a column where links to other websites, optionally annotated, could be published in a structured way; a column with messages, each of which was made up by a title, a subtitle a message text, and optionally a link to another web page and an image; and finally, a column where important dates could be announced. After an evaluation showed that this last component was rarely used, a facility was implemented to hide this component when it contained no entries.

In the new version, the portals were made more flexible in two ways. Firstly, arbitrary grid layouts can now be created so that learners can produce a kind of online news paper, e.g. Currently, the user can only choose from a few fixed layouts as no satisfactory way has been found so far to offer the full flexible functionality in a way that is readily understood by unexperienced users.

Secondly, the individual segments of the layout can in principal hold arbitrary components. While only few are available for the time being, new ones are under development or being planned. In addition to the components mentioned above (annotated link lists, messages, and date announcements), RSS feeds can be embedded by simply specifying the respective address (and optionally which additional data from the feed are to be displayed). Further components can easily be developed by anyone who has basic knowledge of PHP and the API of the open-sTeam server. It will be tested if pupils of a school's computer science course are capable of accomplishing such a development. Components now can also be linked into different portals so that, e.g., a date component can be displayed in the portal of every class in a school while it is updated and maintained centrally.

Portals can also be used in a blog-like fashion with reduced functionality by using the message component for that purpose. Annotations for blog entries are technically feasible; however they are not planned currently. Since the portals are fully integrated with the access management of the server, a blog can be created cooperatively and its visibility can be restricted to any group of users.

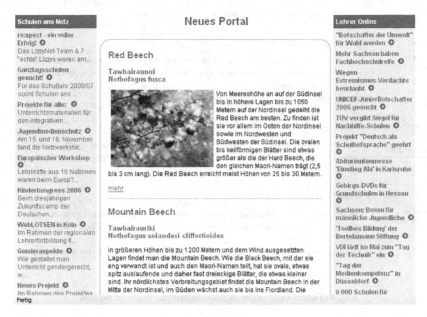

Fig. 5. A portal page with two RSS feeds on the left and right and a message component in the middle column

5.3 Forums

Forums were already available in the old version of the system; yet, they were not integrated into the user interface but could only be used with the Hyperwave server's original user interface. Because of the high demand for easy usable forums, these were now to be integrated. Based on the experiences made and after discussing different alternatives with selected users, we decided not to implement complex forums with hierarchical structures and threaded discussions although these would have been supported by the open-sTeam server. Instead, they were implemented as bulletin boards in a similar way that is often employed in forums on the world wide web. Such bulletin boards are simple sequences of topics with every topic consisting of a sequence of articles. Thus, users can start a discussion on a new topic or contribute an article to an existing topic. Articles can only be added to a topic and are always appended at the end of the sequence; they can not be appended to another article. Experiences made when applying forums in learning platforms in university teaching have shown that the structure in threaded forums often does not reflect the logical structure as many users post their contributions in a wrong part of the thread ([4], p. 13). Since users of our application are often even less familiar with complex discussion forums, we decided to implement forums in the more easily usable form as bulletin boards.

› Thema: Grundfunktionen	
dschubert	**Grundfunktionen**
erstellt am 18.05.2005 14:08	Hier sollen Anregungen zu den Grundfunktionen gesammelt werden.
dschubert	**Texte zwischenspeichern** ○
gesendet am 18.05.2005 14:10	Unter Neu -> Text können wir nun Texte mit leichten Formatierungen versehen. Will ich aber Fehler korrigieren oder längere Mitschriften zwischenspeichern, fehlt mir eine Funktion, um gespeicherte Texte weiter editieren zu können. *Der Inhalt wurde vom Benutzer dschubert am 30.5.2005 13:22 geändert.*
dschubert	**WWW-Referenzen** ○
gesendet am 30.05.2005 13:26	Ist es eigentlich nicht möglich, die Adressen, die ich unter dem IE als Favoriten ablege, durch einen einfachen FTP-Upload mit Hilfe eines Skript als WWW-Referenz auch in bidsteam zur Verfügung zu haben?
adettke	**Inhalte ordnen** ○
gesendet am 31.05.2005 22:31	Ich möchte gern die Möglichkeit haben, die Inhalte eines Ordners gezielt ordnen zu können, so wie das früher mit der Sortierfunktion (die mit den negativen Zahlen!) möglich war. Vielleicht sogar ganz bequem mit Auf- und Abpfeilen? Jedenfalls gefällt mir die jetzige Ordnung nach Erstellungsdatum (woran ich **nichts** ändern kann) überhaupt nicht.

Fig. 6. Forums are implemented as simple bulletin boards

Users may edit their own articles and even delete all text within them after they have been posted. However, the contribution itself, i.e. its subject along with a note that the content of the article has been modified or deleted, is always preserved. The administrator of a forum is the only person to completely delete a topic or an article. Forums are also completely integrated with the access management of the server; thus, the creator of a forum can specify who may read the contributions and who may participate actively, i.e. post their own contributions. Thereby, a school class can realise an internal forum only visible to the pupils of that class.

5.4 Appointment Calendars

Appointment calendars had also been available in the old version of the system. However, they offered rather limited functionality allowing users to specify a date and place, a short description and a link to further information for every appointment. Additionally, any appointment could be assigned a colour in which it was to be displayed, thus basically assigning an appointment to a category. When a user or a group of users were invited to an appointment, every invited user received an invitation in their personal calendar. The users were then individually able to accept or reject that invitation while all invited users could check the current status of the appointment, i.e. they could check who had accepted or rejected that particular appointment.

The basic conception of the appointment calendars was retained; yet, its integration was improved in two respects. Firstly – and very basically for the time being – , desktop integration was introduced. Any appointment can now be exported in a standardised format (iCalendar) and thereby imported into desktop calendar applications. Depending on user feedback, further functionality like, e.g., the export of a number of appointments with a single action or an import of appointments will be included.

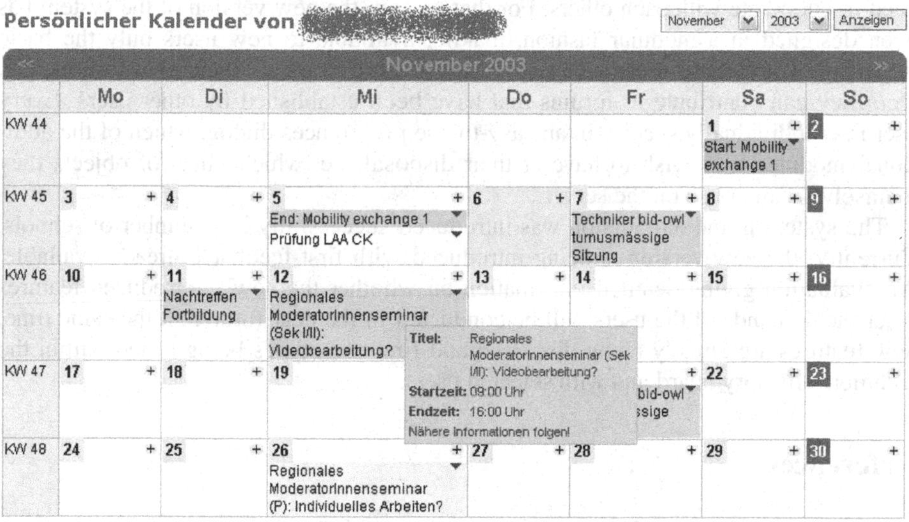

Fig. 7. Appointment calendars for individual users and groups of users support coordination

Secondly, the integration with the server's document management facilities has been improved. Thereby, it is now possible to attach arbitrary documents to an appointment like, e.g., an agenda or – after a meeting has been held – the minutes of that meeting. Also any other files that are of importance to an appointment can thus be coupled with the appointment, being easily accessible to all participants and, by default, only to them. We will have to explore in which way these new features will be used or if users prefer to file documents connected to an appointment in the way they did until now, i.e. within a folder structure and link to these documents from the appointment.

6 Conclusion

Starting from a system rather restricted in its features, a new platform was developed that now offers considerable functionalities and that will keep growing with new requirements as they are put forward from our users in schools. In this contribution, we have described how that process has been organized, how feedback was acquired, and which results this process has produced. The system has thus been developed in an on-going evolutionary process, where existing functionality is altered and new features are introduced in small steps and evaluated in order to determine how to improve the platform. We have concentrated here on the web front-end and on the aspects of social software in particular rather than the document management functionalities or the communication features provided by additional clients like a chat or a whiteboard which are also available to the users.

With increasing functionality, the gap grows between experienced and demanding users on one side and easily irritated novices on the other. Still, these users with very different knowledge and abilities will have to use the same system since they have the need to cooperate with each others. For that reason, the new version of the system has been designed in a modular fashion, making available to new users only the basic functions. Thus, these users will at first not be able to create their own forums, e.g. Yet, they can contribute to forums that have been established by other users. Every user may individually specify in an easy-to-use preferences dialog, which of the additional modules they wish to have at their disposal, i.e. which kinds of objects they themselves can create on the server.

The system in the old version was introduced successfully in a number of schools. Currently, the new version is being introduced with first feedback already available. An evaluation giving detailed information on whether the newly introduced features meet the demands of the users will be conducted in the near future. At the same time, new features are already being discussed and first prototypes being tested within the technical advisory board and with selected users.

References

1. Bentlage, U., Hamm, I.: Lehrerausbildung und neue Medien. Verlag Bertelsmann Stiftung, Gütersloh (2001)
2. Dankwart, M.: Aufbau von Intranets in Schulen – Erfahrungen, Anregungen und Empfehlungen. In: Vorndran, O., Schnoor, D. (eds.): Schulen für die Wissensgesellschaft. Ergebnisse des Netzwerkes Medienschulen. Verlag Bertelsmann Stiftung, Gütersloh (2003) 313–323
3. Dankwart, M.: School Wide Web. Kommunikations- und Kooperationsplattformen in der schulischen Praxis. Gütersloh: Verlag Bertelsmann Stiftung, Gütersloh (2005)
4. Fritsch, H.: Host contacted, waiting for reply. Zentrales Institut für Fernstudienforschung, Hagen (1997)
5. Hampel, T., Keil-Slawik, R.: sTeam: Structuring Information in a Team – Distributed Knowledge Management in Cooperative Learning Environments. ACM Journal of Educational Resources in Computing 2 (2002) 1–27
6. Hyperwave: Hyperwave User Manual. Hyperwave AG, München (1999)
7. Maurer, H.: Hyper-G now Hyperwave: The Next Generation Web Solution. Addison-Wesley, Reading (Ma.) (1996)
8. Tepper, M.: The rise of social software. netWorker. Vol. 7, Nr. 3 (2003) 18–23
9. Vorndran, O.: Netzwerk für die Schulentwicklung: Reflexionen am Beispiel des Netzwerks Medienschulen. In: Vorndran, O., Schnoor, D. (eds.): Schulen für die Wissensgesellschaft. Ergebnisse des Netzwerkes Medienschulen. Verlag Bertelsmann Stiftung, Gütersloh (2003) 11–29

Satellite-Enabled Interactive Education: Scenarios and Systems Architectures

Tacha Serif[1], Lampros Stergioulas[1], Gheorghita Ghinea[1], Michalis Moatsos[2],
Constantinos Makropoulos[2], Sofia Tsekeridou[3], and Thanassis Tiropanis[3]

[1] School of Information Systems, Computing and Mathematics
Brunel University,
Uxbridge, Middlesex,
UB8 3PH, UK
{Tacha.Serif, Lampros.Stergioulas,
Gheorge.Ghinea}@brunel.ac.uk
[2] National Center of Scientific Research "Demokritos"
153 10 - Agia Paraskevi, Athens, Greece
{mmoatsos, cmakr}@dat.demokritos.gr
[3] Athens Information Technology (AIT)
P.O.Box 68
19.5 km Markopoulo Ave.
GR- 19002 Peania, Athens, Greece
{sots, ttir}@ait.edu.gr

Abstract. There are specific sectors of the economy that can benefit from satellite-based tele-education. Areas, such as maritime and agriculture, share common needs for both broadband connectivity at remote geographical areas that cannot otherwise be covered, and for innovative content for tele-education purposes. Furthermore, each area has special requirements with regard to the type of content to be delivered. In this paper we propose a set of architectural designs and case scenarios that will realise such interactive end-to-end education systems based on satellite communications. Services requirements in this setting are also identified and discussed.

1 Introduction

This paper explores how innovative and efficient tele-education solutions can be offered over satellite to communities that would otherwise be excluded from the ongoing revolution in the area of tele-education and eLearning. That is not just because with satellite technology broadband accessibility will be offered to previously isolated communities, but because using innovative content and efficient tele-education platforms, such communities will be able to actively participate in an exchange of knowledge that is crucial for building a knowledge economy.

It is increasingly recognised that professional communities, which are distributed in remote places, will benefit significantly by using tele-education applications over satellite. In this study, we will consider the agricultural communities (farmers etc.) and the maritime communities (crew etc.) as two important exemplar groups for employing satellite based education systems. Farmers at remote areas, who often produce

W. Nejdl and K. Tochtermann (Eds.): EC-TEL 2006, LNCS 4227, pp. 411–423, 2006.

specialised products of designated origin, require continuous targeted training to increase or very often guarantee the quantity and quality of their production. Maritime workers also have continuous needs for tele-education and have been handicapped for many years by the lack of reliable and efficient network infrastructure that would help them reach this target. The structure of this paper is as follows: Section 2 presents an overview of distance learning systems; Section 3 identifies the user requirements of the two target communities; Section 4 describes three satellite network architectures that can be used for electronic learning purposes; Section 5 considers the main possible scenarios and their objectives. Section 6 details the services required for the implementation of satellite-based education systems. Finally, Section 7 draws the conclusions from this study.

2   Networked Learning Environments for Distance Education

Urdan and Weggen [1] define e-Learning as "the delivery of content via all electronic media, including the Internet, intranets, extranets, satellite broadcast, audio/video tape, interactive TV, and CD-ROM" In that way, e-Learning encompasses all currently available instruments, including digital or electronic tools, to facilitate learning and impart the contents of a course. Urdan and Weggen [1] also define e-Learning as a subset of distance learning, as depicted in the Fig. 1.

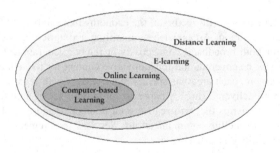

Fig. 1. Subsets of distance learning [1]

e-Learning is a term that nowadays covers almost any type of learning process based on information and communication technologies. E-learning is not just a course converted to be stored in a personal computer, but it rather represents a new mix of resources, interactivity and achievements; new structures for learning, a combination of teaching services using technological tools that adds value, anytime and anywhere [2]; [3]; [4].

As depicted in Fig. 2, e-learning is a composition of three main areas: Contents, Technologies and Services [5].

The Contents are the didactic units or reusable modules of the e-Learning process. The Technologies are the technological tools (platforms) that support the educational systems, including communication networks, protocols, and Learning Management Systems among others. The Services refer to the tracking and support offered to the students; e.g. Tutorials, periodic reports, assessments, course management, student motivation, course quality, etc.

CONTENT

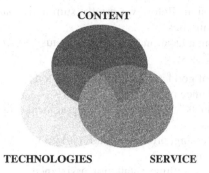

TECHNOLOGIES   SERVICE

Fig. 2. E-Learning components [5]

e-Learning systems are defined as the platforms or systems offering features that support educative services through electronic media. These systems can be Learning Management Systems (LMS), Learning Content Management System (LCMS), Knowledge Pools, or Brokerage Systems.

A Learning Management System is an application running in a web server that is used to perform learning activities. It is also called a Platform or Virtual Campus. It is a place where students, tutors, teachers and coordinators connect through the Internet to download contents, examine the topics of each course, send e-mail to the teachers, chat with students, discuss in a forum, assist to a tutorial, etc.

A Learning Content Management System is a system that is independent or integrated into a LMS. It manages the learning contents. Once the contents are into the system, they can be assigned to each course, combined, downloaded, etc.

The Knowledge Pools are distributed repositories of metadata compatible with the Learning Object Metadata (LOM) standard which assure an efficient publication, search and restore of educative contents. An interesting characteristic of these servers is that they can be federated.

The Brokerage Systems store the description of the educative resources available locally or at remote locations.

3   e-Learning System Requirements of User Groups

This study focuses on the educational needs of agrarian and maritime communities that are in general remote communities with considerable networking and bandwidth constraints. It is often the case that access to e-learning services is not possible to remote villages or on a ship, since either no network is available or any existing bandwidth which might be available to these communities does not allow for fully-featured and rich multimedia-enabled services offering. Nevertheless, education and information updating is of vital importance to such communities to preserve their competitiveness and extend their activities or ease up their workload. Thus, a number of e-learning service requirements stem from the needs of such communities. Both require easy access to services, utilising common means and routines in the best possible way (natural interaction with new technology). However, with respect to educational content, the requirements differ according to the targeted community and the nature of their profession. Below we briefly summarize such requirements for each type of targeted communities.

The needs regarding educational content and thus services supporting such content are summarized as follows;

- Application of good agricultural practice codes.
- Cross compliance policies
- Quality products and products of geographical origin.
- New products
- Product processing, promotion and marketing
- Management issues
- Young farmers settling/installation assistance
- Special policies on rural women activities
- EU Policy changes in agriculture and the agrofood industry

Some of the above subjects constitute horizontal issues that concern all users. Others constitute vertical matters that concern a specific audience. In all cases, content preparation will have to be adjusted to the local needs and the products or sectors each area specializes in.

The content of a satellite-based tele-education service is designated primarily by the needs of the maritime vessel crew who aim to maintain their excellence and receive credit in their job. In order to provide an outline of such appropriate educational content, the major categories of educational needs and detailed specialised topics of education for the maritime community have been identified as follows:

Security-related education requirements:

- Methodology of ship security assessment. On scene survey. The threats that the vessel facing during the trip and methods to reduce the risk of this threats.
- Methods of ship security surveys and inspections. How to search the vessel or specific place for explosive devices after threat phone call.
- Instruction techniques for security training and education including security measures and procedures.
- Knowledge of current security threats and patterns.
- Recognition on a non–discriminatory basis of characteristics and behavioural patterns of persons who are likely to threaten security
- Methods of physical searches and non-intrusive inspections.
- Negotiations with terrorists.
- First Aid. General information. Care of casualty, physical examination–symptoms and signs

Safety-related education requirements:

- Firemen Training. Familiarization with fire fighting equipments, fire suits, breathing apparatus.
- Fire Fighting. Human Risk during fire fighting. Command and control the Incident.
- Different types of fire.
- Passenger mustering and crowd management. Method of safe evacuation and mustering during emergency situation. (ex. fire).

- Fighting Sea Pollution. Guideline Procedures to reduce the sea pollution after collision or grounding or bunkering, materials and chemicals that you can use.

General Training-related education requirements:

- Computers & software. Training and familiarization with word, excel, outlook and power point programs
- Shipboard Management.
- Marine risk assessment. To identify the source of risk that face but also to know how to deal with them effectively. Implementing risk management strategies in the increasingly sophisticated ad competitive environment.
- Marine accident prevention and analysis. Accident prevention and Human Factor.
- Training methods

4 Satellite-Network Architecture for Distance Learning

We consider three distinct satellite network architectures for education applications. The rationale in supporting multiple satellite communication environments stems from: (1) the variability of expected user requirements (some users have inflexible legacy communication systems, while others can be open for very innovative deployments), and (2) the existence of a number of satellite platforms with a wide range of capabilities and cost.

The main architectures for satellite education can be identified as follows:

4.1 VSAT Architecture

Land-to-Land VSAT Architecture
This architecture includes a number of VSAT enabled sites and further interconnection using WiFi and/or WiMax wireless infrastructure for delivering the service to more users (Fig. 3). Different usage scenarios can involve point-to-point, point-to-multipoint interactive communication, live lectures and video on demand capabilities, as well as interconnection between the network sites in order to ensure the necessary collaboration between the learning groups, which is an essential eLearning element.

In the VSAT architecture, each VSAT station has its own distinct purpose. A central VSAT is needed for the broadcast of the live lectures using a fully equipped studio and the provision of the educational offline material from the eLearning platform. This VSAT station acts as a central node in the process of educational content consumption. Another VSAT antenna provides the eLearning service to users attending the course live at the tele-education hall or through a WiFi connection from other premises. The third VSAT antenna is used to facilitate the testing of VSAT and Wi-Max in combination with the WiFi networking. The VSAT network will have mesh topology and thus will provide the possibility of collaboration among sites.

Land-to-Vessel VSAT Architecture
It includes one or more ship(s) connected with a VSAT station at the central node with a fully equipped studio (Fig. 4). Live lectures and video on demand capabilities using IPv4 are to be integrated in the scenario.

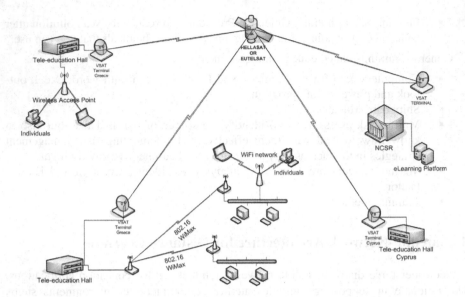

Fig. 3. VSAT networks

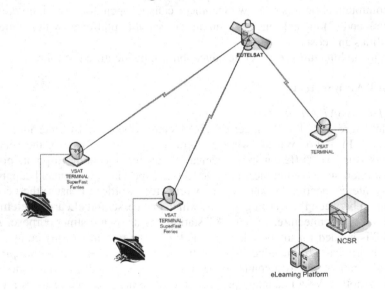

Fig. 4. Maritime network structure

4.2 DVB-S/S2 Architecture

This architecture involves DVB-S or DVB-S2 enabled sites for tele-training. It can support tele-training scenarios, such as point-to-point and point-to-multipoint interactive communication and collaboration, as well as live lectures and video on demand capabilities using IPv4 and IPv6 protocols (Fig. 5).

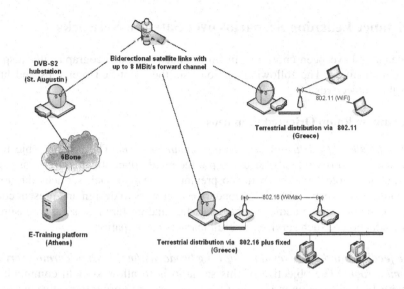

Fig. 5. DVB-S/S2 network structure

4.3 DVB-RCS Architecture

This architecture involves DVB-RCS enabled sites connected with the central DVB-RCS platform (Fig. 6). Similarly to the previous architecture, this architecture can support live lectures and video on demand capabilities using IPv4.

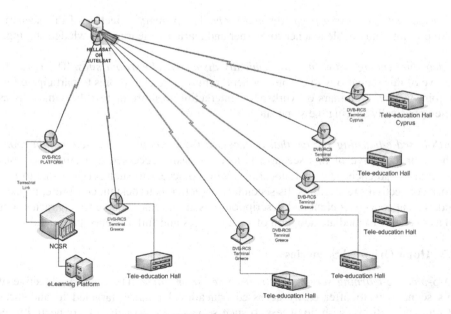

Fig. 6. DVB-RCS network structure

5 Distance Learning Scenarios over Satellite Networks

Ten scenarios have been chosen to fulfill the needs of our geographically dispersed target communities. The following section lists the identified scenarios and briefly details their objectives.

5.1 Common Room Oriented Scenarios

Broadcast/multicast e-learning service to a common room. The primary objective of this scenario is to offer easily accessed pre-recorded educational courses targeted to audiences at remote locations, with no previous access to such services due to network connectivity restrictions. Its secondary objective is to design and present courses content based on remote audience characteristics and preferences so as to ensure immediate adoption of such services and full learners participation.

Offline feedback and Q&A session following broadcast/multicast e-learning service to a common room. The objective of this scenario is to allow smooth communication and interaction with the tutor after an e-learning session in order to resolve questions.

Virtual Classrooms with Remote Tutor; fully interactive; pre-scheduled for all participating sites or on-demand for specific sites (tutor is based on a central site). The main objective of this scenario to allow the creation, support and maintenance of a virtual classroom that provides similar tools and capabilities as in a real classroom without the physical presence of the interacting learners and teachers/tutors in the same space domain but only in the same time domain.

Webcast that is accessed from common room. The primary objective of this scenario is to promote and enable teacher-to-learner and learner-to-learner knowledge sharing.

Videoconferencing between geographically dispersed classroom sites. The core objective of this scenario is to enable learners from remote classrooms to participate live in joint lectures, seminars or workshops, interacting in more or less the same way as when physically sharing the same site.

LMS-based e-learning service that is accessed from a common tele-education room. The main objective of this scenario is to offer easily accessed educational courses targeted to audiences at remote locations, with no access to such services due to network connectivity restrictions. Its secondary objective is to design, configure, manage and present courses content and descriptions based on remote audience characteristics so as to ensure immediate adoption of such services and full audience participation

5.2 Home Oriented Scenarios

LMS-based e-learning service that is accessed from home. The primary objective of this scenario is to offer easily accessed educational courses targeted to audiences at remote locations, with no access to such services due to network connectivity restrictions. The secondary objective for this scenario is to design and present courses content based on remote audience characteristics so as to ensure immediate adoption of such services and full audience participation.

Access to Virtual classroom from home. The first objective of this scenario is to allow the creation, support and maintenance of a virtual classroom that provides similar tools and capabilities as in a real classroom without the physical presence of the interacting learners and teachers/tutors in the same space domain but only in the same time domain. The second objective is to provide the flexibility to the users to join the virtual classroom from home, and the final objective is build a Virtual Classroom environment that can facilitate standalone users to communicate whenever they want with others co-workers or users from their homes in order to be informed for their work sector or to be trained / educated.

Webcast that is accessed from home. The main objective of this scenario is to enable and promote teacher-to-learner and learner-to-learner knowledge sharing from home.

Videoconferencing from home. The objective of this scenario is to enable learners from their homes to participate live in joint lectures, seminars or workshops.

6 Satellite-Enabled Education Services

Starting from the user requirements and the scenarios presented in the previous sections, a number of services can be identified. The process of identification of these services is informed by the previously derived scenario specifications.

6.1 Virtual Classroom Service

A virtual classroom is defined as a computer accessible, on-line learning environment intended to fulfil many of the learning facilitation roles of a physical classroom. It provides a distributed learning environment at any time, any place and at any pace.

By using Virtual Classrooms, one can hold face-to-face conversations and collaborate with co-workers around the world. The features supported by these tools are concentrated on the following topics:

- Video and Audio Conferencing
- Chat
- File Transfer
- Program Sharing
- Whiteboard
- Remote Desktop Sharing

These features can be used in a point-to-point connection through the predefined networks topologies to create multi-user connections from different sites to collaborate in a conference or presentation.

The types of content that can be delivered in a virtual classroom environment can be categorized into the following functionalities:

- Lecture Material (Course notes provided by the tutor)
- Embedded Tools (Simulations, spread sheets, calculators, etc.)
- Real time Video and Audio
- Note Taking and Annotation
- Major Exams
- Quizzes (Embedded in the coursework)
- Homework (Written material, worked problems)
- Reading Assignments (Instructor guide to readings and actual readings)
- Collaborative Projects (Teams and team projects)
- Chat and Discussion
- Messages and Email
- Feedback, Questions, and Course Evaluation

6.2 Learning Content Management System (LCMS) Service

Among the services that have been identified as relevant to the scope and objectives of the satellite-enabled education is the deployment of a Learning Content Management Service. An LCMS supports the authoring, publication and management of learning content, including multimedia content adaptation aspects, from the viewpoint of the system administrator and author but at the same time it will provide for personalised access to combined Learning Objects (LOs) in a Learning Path that suits best the learners of the participating communities.

An LCMS typically accommodates LOs with the following types of content:

- Video (both high quality and low quality video)
- Audio (high quality)
- Presentations (combining different formats)
- Images
- Documents
- Assignments (for both individual learners or groups of learners)
- Tests (deployed for access via Web browsers)

The above formats seem to be able to cover requirements for content to be delivered to the computers of individual learners or for content to be delivered to a classroom with many learners present over a variety of access networks and available bandwidth.

It is envisaged that the LCMS will be combined with content adaptation systems to support further personalised and quality assured access to learning solutions by the learners. Content adaptation will consist of both pre-configuring high quality content to a variety of formats, generating associated metadata descriptions to describe each content variation (pre-adaptation stage), as well as research on scalable content formats and MPEG-21 profiles generation, as well as the design of resource and metadata adaptation engines, to account for dynamic content adaptation throughout the transmission and reception path.

6.3 Tele-conferencing Service

This is a core service enables live sessions connecting many geographically dispersed sites, either ad-hoc or prearranged manner. The functionality offered by a tele-conferencing service is similar to that of the Virtual Classroom, however it is more focused on live interaction and more flexible with regard to time scheduling and site participation, but with limitations in terms of delivering materials. Tele-conferencing can be defined as bi-directional communication between two or more groups, or between three or more individuals, who are in dispersed sites.

Depending on the interaction capabilities offered, there are a number of teleconferencing modalities ranging from plain audio to fully multimedia-enabled. For example, small, quick and short tele-meetings can be held "over the phone" via an audio conference. The following description considers a full service, which is both audio- and video-enabled. It does not include teleconferencing intended for delivering content/LOs in an integrated environment of multiple sites or in a Virtual Classroom, as this is covered in the definition of other Services.

The remote groups (learning communities) or the individual learners from their homes get together to participate in the educational activities (e.g. attend seminars/workshops or meetings/conversations, and collaborate with colleagues/ fellow learners at other sites). Transmission of live video to and from the set-top box or PC is performed bi-directionally over a satellite network, and possibly also via wireless LAN/MAN connection. The teleconference is launched at each site by logging in to a multipoint web service at the desired time. The sessions can be either arranged "ad-hoc" or prescheduled.

Such a service attains the following features:

- Real time Video and Audio (multimedia networking)
- Session Scheduling tool
- Collaboration tools (Teams and team projects)
- Chat and Discussion
- File Transfer
- Program/Application Sharing
- Whiteboard
- Shared Notepad
- Remote Desktop Sharing
- Document camera

Commercial Off-the-shelf teleconferencing solutions for implementation

A number of platforms and tools can be used depending on the specific user needs:

- The Isabel conferencing tool [6] can support any possible case of delivery, providing high speed connections with many users from different geographically disparate sites.
- In the case of just one point-to-point connection with very basic functionality, a simpler tool such as Microsoft's NetMeeting [7] can also be used.
- For audio conferencing, less demanding applications based on Voice-over-IP platforms would be sufficient.

6.4 Webinar/Webcast Service

This service consists of a unidirectional, live or pre recorded, transmission of content from one site to the rest of remote sites. The date and details of each session should be announced previously in order for the receiving site to tune in properly.

The main actors that interact in the educational process could be teachers and learners, or just learners among them. There are no restrictions on the communities that could be able to use this service; In principle any community (including agrarian and maritime) can benefit from it.

While the content can be pre recorded at the transmitting site, this service does not involve on-demand download. In that way the receiving site can not distinguish if the content being played is live or pre recorded. The only difference in this case is at the transmitting site.

The content could be received at a common room or at the learner's home. Both scenarios are pretty similar. The main difference is the need for a more sophisticated common room setup. It is expected to use common-of-the-shelves player software at the receiving site.

6.5 Other Services

Another potential service that accommodates the needs of already defined e-learning scenarios is the "Broadcast/multicast e-learning service". In such a service, pre-recorded educational content is either broadcasted over satellite core and access networks (DVB-S2, VSAT) or multicasted over broadband satellite and wireless IP-based access networks (DVB-RCS, Wi-Fi, Wi-Max) respectively to remote groups of learners gathered in a tele-education hall, equipped with receiving satellite antennas and hubs or wireless access points, set-top boxes or PCs, video projectors, VCRs, TV sets, microphones and speakers. The session is initiated either at pre-scheduled times or by the course coordinator and involves initially passive viewing of the educational course and later on communication and interaction possibilities for Q&A sessions. Such a service involves use of an LMS/LCMS to store educational pre-recorded content, configured in a variety of formats to accommodate differentiated networking bandwidths. Associated annotations/descriptions along with course information and scheduling are stored along with the content into the LMS/LCMS. Access to this service is feasible either through a purely satellite network and client terminals (VSAT, DVB-RCS), or through a core satellite network interlinked with broadband wireless access networks (DVB-S2/VSAT + WiFi/WiMax). Broadcasting or multi-casting is implemented based on IP protocols for streaming over Internet such as IPv4 and IPv6. Return channel communication for the Q&A session takes advantage of the bidirectional capabilities of DVB-RCS and VSAT satellite networks, while in the case of unidirectional DVB-S2 satellite networks, the possibility to use SCPC for back-channel communication is considered. User means of communication and interaction with the tutors/coordinator are through emails, chats, forums, audio conferences, etc.

Several other types of services may be applicable in case that targeted community requirements are not met by the currently defined ones, or system and infrastructural requirements are faced with technology limitations and feasibility risks.

7 Conclusions

This paper has discussed the need for satellite-based tele-education in the context of providing tele-training services to professional communities, which are distributed in remote areas. The satellite-based service requirements have been identified for two important communities (agricultural and maritime). Three network architectures have been described that fulfill the system requirements. A number of usage scenarios have been identified and critically examined in terms of their applicability and potential benefits to the two communities. Finally, a raft of services has been proposed to implement the envisaged scenarios based on designed satellite architectures. It is the authors' strong belief that the development and wider adoption of such satellite-based services will extend the benefits of ICT-enabled education to an even larger proportion of the workforce worldwide. It is also expected that that emergence of such learner-oriented systems for distance education via satellite communication will lead to sustainable solutions to the problem of delivering education to geographically dispersed learner communities in the developing countries, most of which suffer from a lack of any network infrastructure.

Acknowledgments

The authors are grateful to Mathias Kretschmer, Andreas Voigt, Gabriel Huecas Fernandez-Toribio, Carlos Barcenilla, Vouyioukas Demosthenes and Dimitra Pappa for their valuable comments and for fruitful discussion. The presented work is supported by the Aeronautics and Space programme of European Commission, as part of the BASE2 project (Contract no.: 516159)

References

[1] Urdan. T., Weggen, C.: Corporate E-Learning: Exploring a New Frontier: http:// www. spectrainteractive.com/pdfs/CorporateELearingHamrecht.pdf (Accessed on 3 April 2006)
[2] Hambrech, W.R.: Corporate e-Learning: "Exploring a new Frontier" http://www. learnchamp.com/upload/e-Learning _Exploring_New_Frontier.pdf (Accessed on 3 April 2006)
[3] Koskinen, T., Stergioulas, L.K., and Denoual, Y.: European Roadmap for Professional e-Training, Barcelona (2004).
[4] Stergioulas, L.K., Kamtsiou, V. and Koskinen, T.: A roadmapping framework for technology-enhanced professional training In: Proceedings of the 8th IFIP World Conference on Computers in Education (WCCE '05), Cape Town, South Africa, 4-7 July 2005.
[5] Santos, M.; Tendencias en la formación con medios digitales: el e-Learning. http://www.unav.es/digilab/ric/textos/e_learning.html (Accessed 3 April 2006)
[6] Isabel: Isabel Technical Documentation. Available on http://www.agora-2000.com/ products/isabel/documentation.html (Accessed on 12 April 2006)
[7] Netmeeting: Microsoft Netmeeting Features, Available at http://www.microsoft.com/ windows/NetMeeting/Features/default.ASP (Accessed on 12 April 2006)

Motivational Effects
Within Scientific Experimentation Scenarios

Astrid Wichmann, Markus Kuhn, Kay Hoeksema, and Ulrich Hoppe

Collide Group, Institute for computer science and interactive systems,
University of Duisburg-Essen, Forsthausweg 2, 47057 Duisburg, Germany
{Wichmann, Kuhn, Hoeksema, Hoppe}@collide.info

Abstract. This paper reports on scientific experimentation activities conducted in the EU project COLDEX. Learning scenarios have been developed that allow students to carry out scientific experiments in various fields of science such as astronomy, probability etc. The activities were supported by a collaborative experimentation environment called "CoolModes". The environment will be described in detail regarding its support for experiments from different areas of science. The focus of this study was evaluating the learning scenarios. Students' motivation was assessed right after participating in the scenarios. Attitudes regarding computers and science in general were investigated to gain additional background variables.

1 Introduction

Pedagogical perspectives on how to get students interested in science learning have been studied to a large extent [1], [2]. According to Chinn and Malhotra [3] authentic learning settings in science are one way to motivate students effectively to engage in scientific thinking. Authentic approaches in science include exploring problems with unknown outcome and providing students with tools that scientists use. Especially when it comes to complex problems, students need a structure that on the one hand allows them to investigate a scientific problem on their own but on the other hand guides them within their inquiry process to avoid frustration. In authentic inquiry, this structure includes formulating hypotheses, manipulating variables to run appropriate experiments etc. These activities are unique in the field of science but applicable across subjects. Supported appropriately they can allow students to face challenging scientific tasks.

When Jonassen [4] referred to mindtools he described techniques using software tools such as system-dynamics or mind-mapping programs, which are useful for supporting cognitive activities in various areas. For example the "Mindtool" Stella [5] can be used for visualizing concrete systems such as traffic in a city, but also for representing theoretical constructs in the field of psychology. Respectively, Hoppe et al. [6] focus on the development of "Collaborative Mindtools" to provide scientific tools such as modelling, within one environment called "CoolModes". CoolModes contains different kinds of visual languages to support knowledge representation collaboratively by sharing workspaces. These workspaces allow combining different visual languages which support activities in various fields of science such as astronomy, stochastics etc.

W. Nejdl and K. Tochtermann (Eds.): EC-TEL 2006, LNCS 4227, pp. 424–436, 2006.

This study was conducted in the context of a European funded project called COLDEX (IST-2001-32327). COLDEX stands for "Collaborative Learning and Distributed Experimentation" [7].

2 Pedagogical Aims

A pedagogical framework [8] including learner requirements guided the development of scenarios in the COLDEX project. The requirements focus on aspects to engage students in science learning by stimulating interest in complex phenomena in rich scientific environments. These requirements include:

- *Authentic activities.* Presenting authentic tasks that conceptualise rather then abstract information and provide real-world, case-based contexts, rather than pre-determined instructional sequences. Learning activities should be anchored in real uses, to avoid that knowledge remains inert.
- *Knowledge Construction.* Learners should be constructing artefacts and sharing them with their classmates.
- *Collaboration.* The environment should support collaborative construction of knowledge through social negotiation.
- *Reflection.* Reflective practice through modelling activities
- *Situating the context.* To enable context and content dependent knowledge construction.
- *Multi-modal representation. To* provide multiple representations of reality, representing the natural complexity of the real world.

The Cool Modes Environment supports scientific experimentation activities by triggering motivation and interest through engaging students in an innovative environment and exciting non-standard science topics. For example Cool Modes supports collaboration by allowing students to share workspaces and to construct and share artefacts using a Learning Object Repository [9]. The individual features of the learning scenarios supported by Cool Modes will be described below in detail.

3 The Learning Environment

All 3 scenarios have been carried out using the CoolModes environment [10]. CoolModes is a CBLE that supports scientific activities by engaging students in modelling tasks and scientific inquiry. Every scenario is represented through a specific palette in the software.

The maze scenario

The maze scenario is an approach to rule based programming using a very limited visual programming language. The scenario can be used by students from the age of 13 without any knowledge pre-requisites. The main challenge is to provide a robot with a strategy of how to escape out of an arbitrary maze. Virtual and physical mazes can be built and used for strategy testing. While working with the maze scenario the students can learn about

- algorithmic thinking,
- the basics of rule based programming,
- how to formulate and analyse rule based algorithms,
- how to develop classifications for complex objects (mazes and rule sets)
- redundancy within algorithmic specifications
- sophisticated strategies solving the specific challenge (Pledge algorithm)

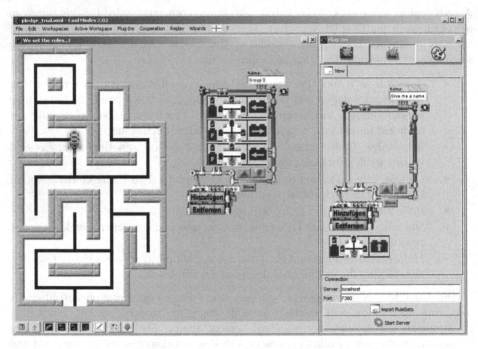

Fig. 1. Finding a way out of the maze: Maze scenario

The idea to develop formalized strategies to escape out of a maze is not new [11]. A robot with a sense of its direct environment and absolute heading can be instructed which way to take in a specific situation by formulating a set of rules like "when there is no wall to the right, turn to the right and move forward". Within the CoolModes environment, the students can construct different mazes and provide robots with rule sets describing how to behave within a maze. To lower the students' difficulties at the beginning a specific programming-by-example-mode can be used that helps the students to develop first rule sets. When being familiar with the learning environment, the students have to rethink their strategies and formulate them in a systematic way to achieve best results. The learning scenario normally is used to perform a competition between different groups of maze creators and rule set developers who try to overcome the results of the other groups. Simple strategies like wall following can be developed and programmed by the students quite easily, more sophisticated strategies normally need additional information input by the teacher. Another interesting group contest is to formulate the smallest possible rule set e.g. for wall following.

The moon scenario

The moon scenario enables students to calculate lunar heights based on digital measurements out of moon images. A detailed description can be found in Hoeksema et al. [12]. Only a few knowledge pre-requisites (mainly sentence of three and the similarity of triangles) are needed to enable the students aged about 14 years to work self-determined in groups. While working with the moon scenario the students can learn:

-   how cartographic measurements can be estimated by measuring visible shadow lengths,
-   how to model the geometrical relation between sun, earth and moon within our solar system,
-   the consequences for light and shadow on the moon,
-   how to abstract an algebraic formula out of a geometric model and
-   how to express an algebraic formula within a visual calculation language.

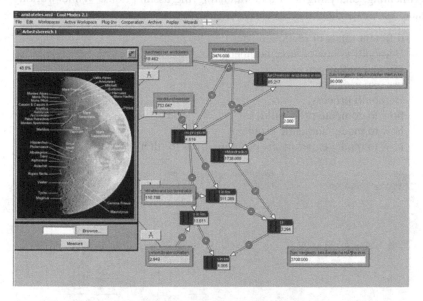

Fig. 2. Calculating lunar heights with the Cool Modes Moon palette

First, the students have to produce or retrieve applicable images of the moon. Within the CoolModes environment digital measurements can be taken out of these images. The measurements taken can be transferred to calculation trees to calculate a specific height. To solve this task the students first have to develop an understanding about the solar system, namely the rotation of the earth around the sun, the rotation of the moon around the earth, and the consequences for light and shadow that can be observed while watching the moon. Therefore, a dynamic geometric 2D model is provided to the students. The gained geometrical understanding has to be transferred to an algebraic formula. This formula has to be modelled using an operational visual language to express calculations. When successful, the built model can be reused easily to calculate arbitrary heights like lunar walls or craters. Later, a "moon lexicon" can be created collaboratively. Several group contests are possible (best estimation of a specific crater, location of the highest crater etc.). The comparison of the different operational models and their calculation precision is the basis for collaborative and competitive discussions and group exchange.

The stochastic experimenting scenario

The stochastic experimenting scenario [13] enables students to get practical experiences with probabilities setting up own, virtual experiments for simulation, analysing and validating their results. The scenario can be used by students from the age of 12. It was employed in introductory sequences with the "law of large numbers" as a central theme, for the exploration of betting e.g. lottery games or the birthday paradox and motivating inferential statistics through the study of Bernoulli processes. The main challenge is to facilitate discovery learning in the field of stochastics following an inquiry cycle comprising stating hypotheses, modelling and experimenting, analysing data and validating the assumptions. While working with the stochastic experimenting scenario the students can learn about

- different kinds of random devices
- Bernoulli's 'law of large numbers'
- fair and unfair games
- urn experiments
- Bernoulli processes
- how to compute probabilities
- how to model authentic problems
- how to model experiments using methods to filter and analyse data

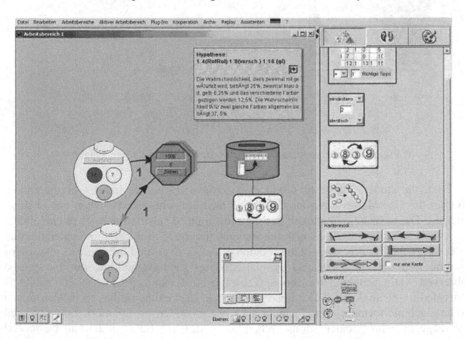

Fig. 3. Model of a stochastic experiment with hypothesis note

Stochastics is a prominent and challenging domain in math learning. Fischbein [14] exposed its importance for science learning: "Practical experience with probabilities provides an ideal way of familiarizing children with the fundamental concepts of science, such as prediction, experiment and verification". Pupils often start motivated to find out more about "chance", being confronted with complex challenges. Hands-on experiments e.g. throwing dice or coins are often used to help the students understand basic concepts. Normally the experimental work is limited to introductory lessons because it requires a lot of repetitive work and great patience and preciseness by the students.

Within the Cool Modes Stochastic environment students are supported in modelling and simulating multiple experiments with random generators like dice, coins and various urns. It contains other elements to build up a micro-world for exploring probabilistic problems through experimenting like control elements to repeat an experiment, data collectors to store the results, filters for automatic sorting or analysis e.g. in lotto experiments. Tables, bar charts for absolute or relative frequency visualize the outcomes and facilitate the examination and interpretation of data. Further elements support collaborative activities.

4 Focus

The focus of this study is the effect of the learning scenarios on motivation. Additionally general attitudes were assessed as background variables. The learning sequence for every scenario tested is not longer than several hours. Therefore we did not employ a pre-post assessment since changes in attitudes can only be measured over a longer time span [15]. Still we were interested in how general attitudes such as attitudes towards science and attitudes towards computers differ from perceived enjoyment and other motivational factors towards the activities that students carried out when participating in the scenarios.

One goal of the COLDEX project is to support scientific topics and activities with a non-standard science character. Even though the scenarios were developed for being integrated in school curricula, they promote non-standard science topics and approaches. Thus we aim at introducing authentic as well as exciting scientific activities to combine with traditional topics in the field of math and computer science. One question that seemed to be especially interesting was: "How did participating in the learning scenarios affect the students motivation"? In addition we were interested in the students general attitudes towards science and computers. Therefore attitudes were assessed as contextual variables. For this study we chose three different scenarios from the scenarios used in the COLDEX project. Therefore a second question was to look at differences in motivation between the three scenarios. An overall purpose of the study was to refine instruments for further assessment of attitudes and motivation in German schools.

5 Method

Participants and Learning Setting

101 participants were students in the age of 15 and 16 from school classes in North-Rhine Westphalia in Germany. Four classes participated in COLDEX scenarios with the topics Maze, Moon and Stochastics respectively.

Since this study was employed in classroom settings we must assume various influences affecting the results due to high heterogeneity. First the scenarios themselves vary in different aspects. One aspect is that the scenarios are to different degrees related to the curriculum (see Table 1, No.1). Thus the scenarios were more or less embedded in the lesson plan. Another aspect was whether prior knowledge was needed to be able to participate successfully (see Table 1, No.2).

Table 1. Scenario Charachteristics

No.	Scenario Characteristics	Stochastics	Maze	Moon
1	Curriculum related	+	-	-
2	Prior knowledge	-	-	+

All three scenarios took place in lab rooms, two at school and one at university. Students worked together in dyads in an open reciprocal environment. That means dyads working together were free to exchange with other groups or with the teacher. All groups had a teacher-centred introduction, a discovery session, Practice Sessions and a LOR session. In all scenarios the goal was to encourage students to solve problems using the modelling environment CoolModes.

Instruments:

For assessing motivation we used one modified scale to collect information about perceived motivation towards the learning activity. Motivation was assessed as post-assessment directly after the learning activity.

Two modified scales were used to test Computer and Science Attitudes in general. Both attitude questionnaires were administered beforehand to collect background information.

Translation Procedure:

The questionnaires were translated from the original (English) language into German in accordance to the translation guidelines for translating tests suggested by Van de Vijver & Hambleton [16]. Two independent translators with pedagogical background translated the questionnaire from English to Swedish. These three translations were discussed together with the translators and one external reviewer. After resolving inconsistencies one translation was developed. Two bilingual pedagogues translated back the Swedish version into the original language. The back-translations were then compared to the original questionnaire; the German version was again revised. Face-validity of the German questionnaire was afterwards tested in a pilot test with six students. Reliability was tested for each subscale separately during the study.

Motivation Scale

We adopted the "Intrinsic Motivation Inventory" developed by Deci and Ryan [17] to target the learning activity directly to find out how students perceived the learning activity. The inventory uses a seven point Likert scale where "1" represents "not at all true", "4" represents "somewhat true" and "7" represents "very true". The questionnaire consists of several subscales, wherefrom we chose three subscales: "Interest/Enjoyment" (7 items), "Perceived Competence" (6 items) and "Effort" (5 items).

Table 2. Reliability Analysis of IMI (Intrinsic Motivation Inventory)

Subscales	Number of Items	Cronbach's Alpha
Enjoyment	7	0.93
Competence	6	0.90
Effort	5	0.84

Attitude Scales

Science-related attitudes were measured with TOSRA. The TOSRA is based on the classification of students' attitudinal aims according to Klopfer's [18] six categories: Attitude to science and scientists, attitude to inquiry, adoption of scientific attitudes, enjoyment of science learning experiences, interest in science, interest in a career in science. The Questionnaire was developed by Fraser and uses a seven-point Likert scale. It was tested in several areas, especially for evaluation learning software [19], [20]. For this study we adopted the original design by Fraser, only choosing two of the seven subcategories [21]: Attitudes toward scientific inquiry, Enjoyment of science lessons. Reliability was acceptable for the Inquiry scale. We removed one item from the further analysis to gain higher reliability. Reliability of the Enjoyment scale was excellent.

Table 3. Reliability Analysis of TOSRA (Test of Science Related Attitudes)

Subscales	Number of Items	Cronbach's Alpha
Scientific Inquiry	10	0.80
Enjoyment of science lessons	10	0.93

For Computer Attitudes we adapted the CAQ questionnaire from the work by Knezek [22]. The original questionnaire contains 95, five-point Likert-type items including 9 subscales. We modified the scale from five-point to seven- point to have equal scale for all questions (TOSRA, IMI and CAQ). Due to the short learning activity we needed to stick to a reasonable amount of subscales, so we chose three subscales that seemed to be especially interesting for the evaluation: "Computer Enjoyment", "Computer anxiety" and "Computer Importance". Reliability was tested for all 3 subscales. To further investigate reliability, a factor analysis was conducted for the Computer Attitude Questionnaire. The factor analysis suggested two factors, merging enjoyment and anxiety, differentiating between "Computer Anxiety/Enjoyment" and "Computer Importance".

Table 4. Reliability Analysis of CAQ (Computer Attitude Questionnaire)

Subscales	Number of Items	Cronbach's Alpha
Anxiety/Enjoyment	9	0.83
Importance	7	0.75

6 Results

Motivation Toward COLDEX Learning Scenarios Using "Cool Modes". The three motivation subscales were analysed using ANOVA. A difference for enjoyment between the scenarios has been found (F (2, 92)= 19.873, p= .000). An analysis (Post hoc with Bonferroni correction) of the enjoyment subscale showed significant differences between Maze and Moon scenario (p= .000) and between Moon and Stochastics scenario. No significant differences towards enjoyment were revealed between Maze and Stochastics scenario. The perceived enjoyment towards the activity was significant lower for the Moon scenario than for both other scenarios. The Post hoc comparison with Bonferroni correction showed the same for the motivation subscale "competence". While students participating in the Stochastics and Maze scenario perceived themselves as competent during the activity, students participating in the Moon scenario (p= .000) felt significant less competent. There were no significant differences between the scenarios regarding effort invested. A Pearson correlation for all scenarios revealed high correlation between all motivation factors. Hence, we could find a linear relationship between all subscales of motivation.

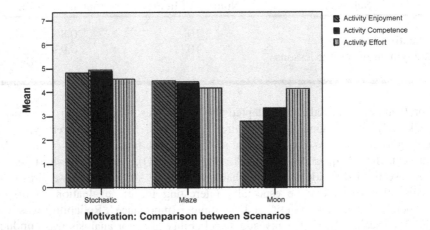

Motivation: Comparison between Scenarios

Fig. 4. Results Motivation for all scenarios

Table 5. Means for motivation

Descriptive Statistics

Scenario		Mean	Std. Deviation	N
Stochastic	Enjoyment	4.74	1.576	46
	Competence	4.89	1.256	46
	Effort	4.47	1.513	46
Maze	Enjoyment	4.38	1.133	29
	Competence	4.34	1.257	29
	Effort	4.02	1.196	29
Moon	Enjoyment	2.80	.913	28
	Competence	3.26	.958	28
	Effort	4.11	.921	28

General Attitudes. The results of the ANOVA showed no significant differences between the scenarios regarding general attitudes. Hence comparing attitudes between scenarios showed similar results for all scenarios. A correlation between the attitude scales for all scenarios using Pearson's correlation coefficient showed that both computer scales were related (Stochastics: r= .806; Maze: r= .853; Moon: r= .879). This was different for the both science subscales. There was no correlation between the subscales scientific inquiry and science lesson enjoyment. While scientific inquiry showed high results for all scenarios, science lesson enjoyment was significant lower in comparison to the other attitude scales.

Table 6. Attitudes for all scenarios

Descriptive Statistics

Scenario		Mean	Std. Deviation	N
Stochastic	Computer Enjoyment/Anxiety	6.04	.779	43
	Computer Importance	5.92	.790	46
	Science Enjoyment	4.78	1.326	46
	Scientific Inquiry	5.60	.932	46
Maze	Computer Enjoyment/Anxiety	6.06	.925	27
	Computer Importance	6.00	.970	29
	Science Enjoyment	4.73	1.588	29
	Scientific Inquiry	5.89	1.060	29
Moon	Computer Enjoyment/Anxiety	6.03	.978	28
	Computer Importance	5.84	.994	29
	Science Enjoyment	4.63	.909	29
	Scientific Inquiry	5.76	.566	29

7 Discussion

The means for motivation indicate that students of the Stochastics and the Maze scenario found the activities to be enjoyable and somewhat enjoyable. Accordingly students in both scenarios felt competent and somewhat competent. Since the Moon scenario showed significant lower results than the other two scenarios we will focus on it in more detail:

The results have shown that the motivation subscales in the scenarios did not differ significantly from each other except within the Moon scenario: Students perceived that they put significant more effort (M= 4.11; SD=0.91) in the Moon activity as they found it enjoyable. One possible explanation could be that the Moon scenario requires prior knowledge on the one hand but this knowledge was not available because of the scenario's extra curricular character. Students might have put extra effort into solving tasks in the Moon scenario but this effort was not sufficient so the students became discouraged. This led to low results on the enjoyment subscale (M=2.80, SD=0.91). If we see developing motivation within students as a dimension between amotivation, challenge and discouragement, then overchallenging would cause low motivation.

We found it interesting that attitudes towards computer and scientific inquiry all correlated highly. However that for all scenarios we found significant lower attitude results for enjoyment towards science lessons. This could indicate that attitudes related to school activities in general would be lower than to non-school related attitudes.

8 Outlook

In this study, we compared the motivation results between the scenarios and assessed general attitudes towards science and computers as background variables. In addition we assessed the learning outcome in each school class. Future efforts will include analysing the knowledge results in comparison to the motivation results. Also we plan to compare outcomes of this study with results from observational data published elsewhere [23] to co-validate both results and to enrich our findings.

Our approach gave us hints about the differences on motivation between scenarios, however a standard experimental design would have given us more clues about how the motivation differed between students who participated in COLDEX scenarios vs. students who participated in traditional classroom activities.

References

1. Liu, M. (2004). Examining the Performance and Attitudes of Sixth Graders During Their Use of A Problem-Based Hypermedia Learning Environment. Computers in Human Behavior, 20 (3), 357-379.
2. Kivinen, K. (2003). Assessing Motivation and the Use of Learning [online]. Available: http://acta.uta.fi/pdf/951-44-5556-8.pdf [15 March 2005]. Academic dissertation
3. Chinn, C.A., Malhotra, B.A. (2002). Epistemologically authentic inquiry in schools: a theoretical framework for evaluating inquiry tasks. Science Education 86, 175 – 218
4. Jonassen, D.H. (2000). Computers as Mindtools for Schools: Engaging Critical Thinking. Columbus, OH: Prentice-Hall.
5. Jonassen, D.H. (2005). Modeling with technology: Mindtools for conceptual change. Columbus, OH: Merrill/Prentice-Hall.

6. Hoppe, H.U. (2004). Collaborative mind tools. In Tokoro, M. & Steels, L. (Eds.): The Future of Learning. Amsterdam: IOS Press.
7. Project COLDEX (Collaborative Learning and Distributed Experimentation). Download from http://www.coldex.info
8. Baloian, N., Breuer, H., Hoeksema, K., Hoppe,U., Milrad, M. (2004). Implementing the Challenge Based Learning in Classroom Scenarios. In: Sofoklis Sotiriou (ed.). Proceedings of the symposium on Advanced Technologies in Education. July 2004. Argostoli, Greece
9. Pinkwart, N., Malzahn, N., Westheide, D., & Hoppe, H. U. (2005). Community Support Based on Thematic Objects and Similarity Search. In L. Aroyo & D. Dicheva (Eds.), Workshop proceedings of the 12th International Conference on Adaptive Hypermedia (p. 57-60). Amsterdam, University of Amsterdam
10. Pinkwart, N. (2003). A Plug-In Architecture for Graph Based Collaborative Modeling Systems. In U. Hoppe, F. Verdejo & J. Kay (eds.): Shaping the Future of Learning through Intelligent Technologies. Proceedings of the 11th Conference on Artificial Intelligence in Education, pp. 535-536. Amsterdam, IOS Press.
11. Abelson, H., di Sessa, A. (1981). Turtle Geometry: The Computer as a Medium for Exploring Mathematics. M.I.T Press, Cambridge, Massachusetts
12. Hoeksema, K., Jansen, M., Hoppe H. U (2004). Interactive Processing of Astronomical Observations in a Cooperative Modelling Environment. In: Kinshuk, Chee-Kit Looi, Erkki Sutinen e.a. (eds). Proceedings of the 4th EEEE International Conference on Advanced Learning Technologies, ICALT 2004, Joensuu, Finland, pp 888-889
13. Kuhn, M., Hoppe H. U., Lingnau A., Wichmann (2005): Computational Modelling and Simulation Fostering New Approaches in Learning Probability. Innovations in Education and Training International Journal (IETI)
14. Fischbein, E. (1975). The intuitive sources of probabilistic thinking in children. London: Reidel.
15. .Knezek, G., Christensen, R., Miyashita, K., & Ropp, M. (2000). Instruments for assessing educator progress in technology integration. Denton, TX: Institute for the Integration of Technology into Teaching and Learning (IITTL).
16. Van de Vijver, F. & Hambleton, R.K. (1996). Translating tests: Some practical guidelines. European Psychologist, 1(2), 89-99.
17. Deci, E. L., & Ryan, R. M. (1985). Intrinsic motivation and self-determination in human behaviour. New York: Plenum.
18. Klopfer, L. E. 1971. Evaluation of learning in science. In B. S. Bloom, J.T. Hastings, and G. F. Madaus (Eds.), Handbook of summative and formative evaluation of student learning. New York: McGraw-Hill.
19. Lott, K. (2003). Evaluation of a Statewide Science Inservice and Outreach Program: Teacher and Student Outcomes. Journal of Science Education and Technology, Vol. 12, No.1
20. Wood, M. S. (1998). Science-related attitudes and effort in the use of educational software by high school students. Unpublished senior thesis, Center for Educational Technologies, Wheeling Jesuit University, Wheeling, WV.
21. Fraser, B. J. (1978). Development of a test of science-related attitudes. Science Education, 62, 509-515.
22. Knezek, G. and Miyashita, K (1994). A preliminary study of the Computer Attitude Questionnaire. In Knezek, G. (Ed.) Studies on children and computers: The 1993-94 23. Fulbright Series. Denton, TX: Texas Center for Educational Technology.
23. Wichmann, A., Kuhn, M., Hoppe, U. (2006): Communication through the Artifact by Means of Synchronous Co-construction. ICLS Proceedings 2006, Bloomington, Indiana

Appendix

1. Post Hoc with Bonferroni Correction for all scenarios

Multiple Comparisons

Bonferroni

Dependent Variable	(I) Scenario	(J) Scenario	Mean Difference (I-J)	Std. Error	Sig.
Enjoyment	STO	MAZ	.374	.325	.757
		MOO	2.057*	.333	.000
	MAZ	STO	-.374	.325	.757
		MOO	1.682*	.368	.000
	MOO	STO	-2.057*	.333	.000
		MAZ	-1.682*	.368	.000
Competence	STO	MAZ	.510	.294	.256
		MOO	1.604*	.301	.000
	MAZ	STO	-.510	.294	.256
		MOO	1.093*	.332	.004
	MOO	STO	-1.604*	.301	.000
		MAZ	-1.093*	.332	.004
Effort	STO	MAZ	.377	.314	.701
		MOO	.435	.322	.541
	MAZ	STO	-.377	.314	.701
		MOO	.058	.355	1.000
	MOO	STO	-.435	.322	.541
		MAZ	-.058	.355	1.000
Computer Enjoyment/ Anxiety	STO	MAZ	-.019	.217	1.000
		MOO	.091	.222	1.000
	MAZ	STO	.019	.217	1.000
		MOO	.110	.245	1.000
	MOO	STO	-.091	.222	1.000
		MAZ	-.110	.245	1.000
Computer Importance	STO	MAZ	-.069	.227	1.000
		MOO	.159	.233	1.000
	MAZ	STO	.069	.227	1.000
		MOO	.228	.257	1.000
	MOO	STO	-.159	.233	1.000
		MAZ	-.228	.257	1.000
Science Enjoyment	STO	MAZ	-.112	.319	1.000
		MOO	.100	.326	1.000
	MAZ	STO	.112	.319	1.000
		MOO	.213	.360	1.000
	MOO	STO	-.100	.326	1.000
		MAZ	-.213	.360	1.000
Science Inquiry	STO	MAZ	-.289	.222	.586
		MOO	-.221	.227	1.000
	MAZ	STO	.289	.222	.586
		MOO	.069	.251	1.000
	MOO	STO	.221	.227	1.000
		MAZ	-.069	.251	1.000

*. The mean difference is significant at the .05 level.

Getting to Know Your Student in Distance Learning Contexts

Claus Zinn and Oliver Scheuer

DFKI — German Research Centre for Artificial Intelligence
Stuhlsatzenhausweg 3, 66123 Saarbrücken, Germany
Phone: +49 681 3025064
claus.zinn@dfki.de

Abstract. Good teachers know their students, and exploit this knowledge to adapt or optimise their instruction. Teachers know their students because they interact with them face-to-face in classroom or one-to-one tutoring sessions. They can build student models, for instance, by exploiting the multi-faceted nature of human-human communication. In distance-learning environments, teacher and student have to cope with the lack of such direct interaction, and this must have detrimental effects for both teacher and student. In this paper, we investigate the need of teachers for tracking student actions in computer-mediated settings. We report on a teacher's questionnaire that we devised to identify the needs of teachers to make distance learning a less detached experience. Our analysis of the teachers' responses shows that there is a preference for information that relates to student performance (*e.g.*, success rate in exercises, mastery level for a concept, skill, or method) and analysis of frequent errors or misconceptions. Our teachers judged information with regard to social nets, navigational pattern, and historical usage data less interesting. It shows that current e-learning environments have to improve to satisfy teachers' needs for tracking students in distance learning contexts.

1 Motivation

There is an increasing number of e-learning systems that aim at adding computer-mediated instruction to traditional classroom teaching, one-to-one tutoring, and individual learning. The use of such systems can be beneficial for teacher and learner, but it can also lead to frustration for both of them. Learners may not profit from e-learning tools because of incorrect or sub-optimal use, lack of guidance or discipline, the complexity of the software *etc*. Teachers may have problems to judge whether learners make proper use of the software, or achieve learning gains because of, or despite of, e-learning software.

In traditional settings, good teachers know their students, in terms of their mastery levels, motivation, learning progress, learning styles, and misconceptions. Good teachers can then exploit this information to adapt or optimize their instruction and to timely intervene in the learning process when problems occur. The importance of student monitoring is essential. Cotton, for instance,

W. Nejdl and K. Tochtermann (Eds.): EC-TEL 2006, LNCS 4227, pp. 437–451, 2006.

surveyed the literature in educational research and found that this discipline "identified the practice of monitoring student learning as an essential component of high-quality education" [1].

In face-to-face teaching instructors can build their student model by direct questioning, observations (*e.g.*, overall behaviour, visual cues as facial expression and gesture), and communications (*e.g.*, linguistic clues, intonational pattern). This is hard, if not impossible, in computer-mediated learning systems, which are far less perceptive to affective and motivational aspects of student behaviour and the subtleties of human-human communication. It seems that the often proclaimed advantage of e-learning, "learning any time, any place", turns to a major handicap when it comes to student tracking.

One-to-one human-human tutoring is costly, however, and one-to-many classroom instruction leaves little time to teachers to care for individual student needs. There is thus a justification for e-learning systems to complement human-human instruction with (one-to-one) computer-mediated learning. In fact, where human resources are scarce, intelligent e-learning systems can open new possibilities. They could monitor student activity by keeping track of all system-user interactions. A sophisticated analysis and use of such data can then provide valuable information to teachers, say, to better understand their (distant) students, and to point them to their students at risk.[1] The analysis process as well as the presentation of the results can be mechanised by software tools.

Our goal is to develop a student tracking tool for teachers in the context of ActiveMath, a web-based, user-adaptive learning environment for mathematics [http://www.activemath.org], and iClass, an intelligent cognitive-based open learning system [http://www.iclass.info]. The requirements analysis unfolds into two aspects. First, from the vast amounts of raw system-learner interaction data, we need to identify and extract information that is valuable for teachers. Second, from the various possible presentations for extracted information, we need to identify intelligible visualisation methods that allow teachers to interpret student actions effectively and efficiently. To investigate the first aspect, we have devised a teacher's questionnaire.[2] In this paper, we present the questionnaire, an analysis of the results, and derived requirements for a student tracking tool.

2   Related Work

2.1   Computer-Based Learning

There is a plethora of e-learning systems, ranging from general content management systems to domain-dependent intelligent tutoring system, using different

---

[1] Results from data analysis can also be presented to course designers to improve the content of instruction, to learners for self-reflection, and to system developers, say, to increase the usability of an e-learning system's graphical user interface.

[2] The questionnaire is still available on-line and accessible via the URL http://www.activemath.org/questionnaire/questionnaire.html as we continue to welcome teacher's contributions to student tracking tool requirements.

architectures, having various purposes, and offering different services and tools. There are standalone systems that run on your local machine; others follow a network-based client/server architecture; some use web-browsers, others have proprietary graphical user interfaces. Learning systems may support self-study, collaborative (peer-to-peer) learning, organized learning in supervised groups, web-based homework, or combinations thereof. Some systems emphasise services for students, others target teachers and course designers.

The features and limitations of student tracking software depend on the characteristics of the underlying e-learning systems. The overall architectural setting (local/network, browser/proprietary GUI *etc.*) has a major impact on logging mechanisms and the exploitation of log data. A local installation, for instance, excludes a centralized log data collection; and a standard web-browser requires sophisticated (client-side) scripting to get hold of tracking data.

In this paper, we ignore technical constraints of existing e-learning systems, and take a user-centered approach to requirements analysis. Given a set of common learning activities in e-learning contexts such as *reading* content material (provided as text, (graphical) illustrations, movies, animations, sound *etc.*), *communicating* with others (using email, discussion forums, chat *etc.*), *practicing and assessing* (say, answering fill-in-the-blanks questions, multiple-choice questions, puzzles, teacher-evaluated assignments *etc*), we need to identify those which analyses yield potentially valuable learner information for teachers.

2.2   Student Tracking Approaches

There is a wide range of student tracking approaches and implementations. Commercial course management systems like WebCT, for instance, track: the date of the first and most recent sign-on for each student in the course; the usage of the conference tool (number of articles read, number of postings and follow-ups to measure of involvement and contribution to the course); the use of various other tools (*e.g.*, notes, calendar, e-mail); and visits to the content material (page visits, view times) to monitor course usage, usefulness, and quality. Gathered data is then visualised in tabular form or with bar charts [2,14].

In [7], Mazza *et al.* critisise visualisations in tabular format as "often incomprehensible, with a poor logical organisation", and as "difficult to follow". As a result, they say, "tracking data is very rarely used by distance learning instructors". The information visualization approach followed by CourseVis [7] and its successor, the graphical interactive student monitoring system GISMO [8], uses graphical encodings of data (generated by course management systems) that are adapted to human cognition and that allow teachers to capture important relations and facts easily. The graphical representations provided are usually interactive and can be modified by the user (*e.g.*, rotatable 3D graphs).

In [4], Hardy *et al.* present a toolbox to "track, analyse and display learners interactions within a virtual learning environment". Student tracking data include, for instance, amount of time a user spends in different parts of system, number of accesses to the course material by date, or the navigational route taken through the contents. Whereas Mazza *et al.* have the main motivation to help instructors to build a mental model of their students, Hardy *et al.* emphasise that the provided information can be used as a "valuable input when evaluating the effectiveness of the e-learning materials and framework".

Merceron and Yacef pursue a data mining approach to student activity tracking [10]. Their tool for advanced data analysis in education (TADA-Ed) offers, for instance, an association rule algorithm that can be used to identify sets of mistakes that often occur together, or a decision tree algorithm to predict final exam marks given students' prior usage behaviour. Usage of the tool requires basic knowledge in data mining (and machine learning as its technological basis), and therefore, TADA-Ed is a tool that is primarily directed at educational researchers rather than professional teachers.

Some tutoring systems have a proprietary student tracking tool that depends on the domain of instruction. The LISTEN Reading Tutor, for instance, helps children learning to read [11]. The system displays stories, sentence by sentence, which children then have to read aloud. LISTEN's logging mechanism stores the children's utterances as well as other student-system interaction events into a relational database. The LISTEN student tracking tool processes interaction events by means of SQL queries and presents the results to the educational researcher [12]. The results are hierarchically structured: if the time interval of one interaction is contained in the time interval of another interaction of the same student, then there is a parent-child relation between the two interactions. A browser then shows the resulting tree; browsing is facilitated by expanding and collapsing tree nodes, or by defining interaction types filters. The tool is intended for qualitative case analysis.

A related strand of research deals with the visualization of learner models. Student modelling is a discipline in artificial intelligence which analyses the computer-tracked student behaviour and information provided by the student himself to build an internal representation (the system's beliefs about the student). This representation can then be used to adapt courses to the needs, goals, and preferences of individual students and to generate personalized feedback and help. The resulting model can also be visualised. The VisNet system visualises learner models that are based on Bayesian Belief Networks (BBN) [3]. VisNet is intended for "engineering and tuning BBNs and for engineering and maintaining BBN representations of learner models". In [15], Zapata-Rivera and Greer describe the VisMod system, another system for visualizing Bayesian learner models. The "inspectible learner models" provided by this system should also benefit instructors and learners: "Using ViSMod it is possible to inspect the model of a single learner, and compare several learners by comparing their models, navigate throughout the model changing focus according to learners and teachers interests, and use several sources of evidence to animate the evolution of a new model".

Given the large variety of student tracking systems and their rich sets of features, it is time to keep stock and ask teachers (in part, experienced with the use of such systems) to state their interests and requirements for the tracking and analysis of student activity in e-learning systems.

3   Teacher's Questionnaire

The questionnaire resulted from a multi-step process. First, candidate information units for student tracking was gathered. Then, to evaluate the candidates' usefulness as well as their description in terms of understandability and completeness, feedback was requested from a few teachers via email. Their answers were exploited to make questionnaire formulations less technical, and to add or elaborate explanations were necessary. The revised questionnaire was then encoded into hypertext and published on-line (in both English and German), together with a PHP script that stored submitted forms into a MySQL database.

Distant instructors were pointed to the questionnaire by personal contacts, hyperlinks from various web-sites[3], and postings with a call for participation in two highly frequented discussion forums for e-learning: the Distance Education Online Symposium (DEOS-L)[4] and the Edtech Discussion list[5].

3.1   Questionnaire Description

The questionnaire consisted of three parts. The introductory part motivated and explained its purpose. The second part, organised thematically, proposed actual candidates for student tracking information. Teachers were asked to evaluate those candidates with regard to interestingness on a scale with the values "not at all interesting", "not very interesting", "fairly interesting", and "very interesting". The value "I am not sure" was available to cover cases where participants could not assess the interestingness of a given proposal. Teachers were also asked to give qualitative feedback with regard to their preferences or to the appropriateness of our proposals. In other text input fields, they could contribute their ideas to improve or complement our candidate proposals for student tracking. The third part aimed at profiling those who participated in filling-out the questionnaire; this last part was adopted, with some slight modifications from [5]. The profile included, for instance, participants' role, instructional setting, and e-learning experience.

Fig. 1 display a shortened version of the questionnaire's second part.

3.2   Questionnaire Results

At the time of writing, 49 teachers participated in the study. Their votes on our proposals for tracking student activity were computed with the following weights:[6] "very interesting" (weight 5), "interesting" (4), "not very interesting" (2), and "not at all interesting" (1). The score value for a given proposal resulted

---

[3] http://www.activemath.org, ccel.dfki.de, and www.saarlernnetz.de.

[4] http://www.ed.psu.edu/acsde/deos/deos.asp.

[5] http://www.h-net.org/ edweb/list.html.

[6] Question category 11 (presentational issues) and 12 (free text input field for preferences, comments *etc.*) were not scored. They were also omitted in Fig. 1.

(1) Usage & Activity times
   (1.1) Amount of time the learner spends with the system (per session)
   (1.2) Number of learner actions with the system (per session)
   (1.3) Number of sessions
   (1.4) History of past usage
(2) Course coverage
   (2.1) Percentage of available material read
   (2.2) Percentage of available exercises tackled
   (2.3) History of past percentages
(3) Learning Content
   (3.1) Amount of time spent per concept/skill/method/competency
   (3.2) Number of learner activities per concept/skill/method/competency
   (3.3) History of past learning contents
(4) Activity types
   (4.1) Amount of time per activity type
   (4.2) Activity type distributions
   (4.3) History of past activity patterns
(5) Student assessment/aptitude
   (5.1) Overall success rate
   (5.2) Overall cancellation rate
   (5.3) Number of steps done (for multi-step exercises)
   (5.4) Ratio of correct to incorrect steps (for multi-step exercises)
   (5.5) Number of learner help requests
   (5.6) Replay of exercises (in discrete steps)
   (5.7) List of n most frequent diagnosed mistakes and misconceptions
(6) Learning gains
   (6.1) Mastery level for each concept/skill/method/competency
   (6.2) History of past mastery levels (for each concept/skill/method/competency)
(7) Learning interests
   (7.1) List of accessed (and potentially) read course material
   (7.2) List of teaching material's underlying concepts/skills/methods/competencies
   (7.3) List of most frequently looked-up terms (when a dictionary is available)
   (7.4) List of most frequently trained concepts/skills/methods/competencies
(8) Learner's navigational style
   (8.1) Learner classification
   (8.2) History of past learner classification
(9) Groups
   (9.1) Allow manual definition of groups and computation of group results
   (9.2) Allow automatic group clustering
(10) Communication tools
   (10.1) Number of communication actions (per tool)
   (10.2) Ratio of social activities to all activities
   (10.3) Number of thread initiations
   (10.4) Number of follow-up postings
   (10.5) Social Nets

Fig. 1. Questionnaire (simplified form without explanations). The full version is available at http://www.activemath.org/questionnaire/questionnaire.html.

Table 1. Highest scored proposals: 0 – "I am not sure" (or no vote), 1 – "not at all interesting", 2 – "not very interesting", 3 – "fairly interesting", 4 – "very interesting"

Nr	Proposal	Votes					Score
		0	1	2	3	4	
5.1	Overall success rate (for exercises)	3	0	0	12	34	93
6.1	Mastery level for each concept, skill, method, competency	8	0	0	13	28	92
2.2	Percentage of available exercises tackled	2	0	0	15	32	92
5.7	List of n most frequent diagnosed mistakes and misconceptions	5	1	1	11	31	90
2.1	Percentage of available material read	2	0	3	16	28	87
7.1	List of accessed (and potentially) read course material	5	1	3	12	28	86
3.1	Amount of time spent per concept, skill, method, competency	4	1	1	20	23	85
5.2	Overall cancellation rate	7	0	4	14	24	85
3.2	Number of learner activities per concept, skill, method, competency	4	1	5	11	28	83
4.2	Activity type distributions	6	2	4	11	26	82

from the addition of all votes with their corresponding weights, and a subsequent linear transformation that yielded a scale from 0 to 100. Note that "votes" of the form "I am not sure" did not enter the score.

We have summarised our results in two tables and figures: Tab. 1 shows the top-ten proposals with the highest scores, and Tab. 2 shows the ten proposals with the lowest scores. Fig. 2 and Fig. 3 show the distributions for the ten best and ten worst proposals, respectively. We will discuss the results in Sect. 4.

3.3 Questionnaire Participants' Profiles

In total, 49 teachers, representing 10 countries, participated in the study (USA: 63%, United Kingdom: 12%, Germany: 8%, and others).[7] The most frequently taken roles were instructor (91%), instructional designer (67%), and course co-ordinator (37%). Most of the participants were involved in 2-5 online courses (63%), with maximum course sizes of 20-50 students (50%). Most participants supervised learners in higher education: 76% worked with undergraduates, and 43 % worked with postgraduate students. Two thirds (65%) of the participants are engaged in pure distance courses, the remaining third (35%) work in blended learning scenarios. The main proportion of participants were rather experienced with an involvement of 5 years or longer in online courses (62%). A wide range of learning systems was used: 22 different systems were explicitely stated, headed by the commercial ones from WebCT (47%) and Blackboard (42%).

Participants used the following e-learning services or tools: content material (98%), email (93%), discussion forums (87%), chat tools (59%), and glossary

[7] The nationality was derived from IP addresses and email addresses (where supplied).

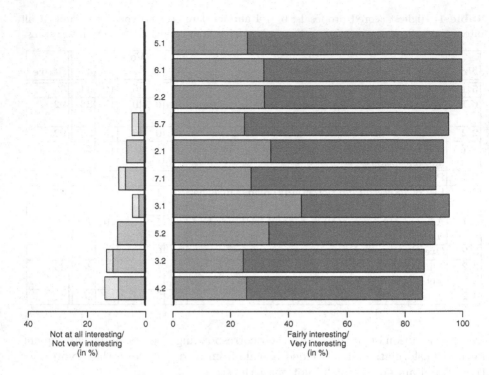

Fig. 2. Distributions of high-score proposals

(28%). Other tools (given in free text input) included video-conferencing, portfolios, field investigations, wikis and blogs.

Participants used the following assessment techniques: teacher-evaluated assignments (96%), quizzes, *e.g.*, multiple-choice and fill-in-the-blanks questions (76%), analysis of discussion forum contributions (61%), group work (59%), simple usage statistics (33%), and analysis of log files (28%). Other assessment techniques (given in free text) included portfolio, student self-evaluation, automatic essay scoring, peer assessment and self assessment, end of course paper, and student homepages graded by required criteria.

4   Discussion

Approval rates for individual proposals (measured as the proportion of participants stating "fairly interesting" or "very interesting") ranged from 63% to 100%, with an average value of 85%. Thus, all proposals were met with considerable approval. This also corresponds to some qualitative feedback: "I believe you have covered a great range of features.", "I think all those data should be available to the teacher", "In principle all proposals are well thought-out and justifiable ..." (translated from German) and "From the point of view of someone

Table 2. Lowest scored proposals: 0 – "I am not sure" (or no vote), 1 – "not at all interesting", 2 – "not very interesting", 3 – "fairly interesting", 4 – "very interesting"

Nr	Proposal	Votes					Score
		0	1	2	3	4	
1.2	Number of learner actions with the system (per session)	4	1	7	18	19	76
8.1	Learner classification (navigational style)	5	1	7	18	18	76
5.6	Replay of exercises (in discrete steps)	10	0	9	12	18	75
4.3	History of past activity patterns	6	2	5	20	16	75
9.2	Allow automatic group clustering	8	2	7	15	17	73
2.3	History of past percentages (course coverage)	7	0	10	18	14	71
3.3	History of past learning contents	7	2	8	18	14	70
10.5	Social Nets	5	4	7	16	17	70
10.2	Ratio of social activities to all activities	6	3	11	10	19	68
8.2	History of past learner classification (navigational style)	8	1	14	16	10	62

who likes investigating data to find patterns my answer to the majority of the questions is 'very interesting' ".

Although all proposals were assessed as at least "fairly interesting" by a large majority of participants, the computed scores reveal clear trends and favorites.

4.1 Proposal Ratings

Our teachers considered performance-related student tracking information particularly interesting. All of the top four entries in Tab. 1 address this issue. This high interest is not surprising as student assessment is a major teacher task. When teachers correct homework assignments or student exams, then notions like "overall success rate" and "percentage of available exercises tackled" are crucial to obtain a mark; the way students solve an exercise, or fail to solve it, gives teachers valuable information about students' level of mastery for exercise-related concepts, skills, and methods.

It is worth to note that teachers voted "list of n most frequent diagnosed mistakes and misconceptions" as particularly interesting (rank 4). The identification of typical student errors helps assess mastery levels, and also informs teachers' remedial feedback. Some anecdotal email-based feedback said:

> "For me, it would be more interesting to get feedback on the type of error; or in abort situations, feedback describing where pupils failed."[8]

On fifth and sixth position of the interestingness scale, we have student tracking information with regard to reading. Proposal 2.1 focuses on the percentage

---

[8] Translated from German: "Es waere fuer mich interessanter, Rueckmeldung ueber die Art der Fehler zu erhalten bzw. bei Abbruechen, an welchen Stellen die Schueler (innen) scheitern."

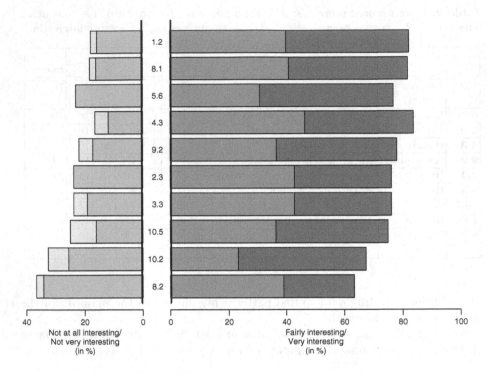

Fig. 3. Distributions of low-score proposals

of available material read, whereas proposal 7.1 offers an insight into a student's learning interest by listing all of the course material that the student has (potentially) read. It could be that teachers with frequent reading assignments gave high rating for these proposals; those teachers may welcome tools to check whether students carried-out their reading assignments in time, or even explored material of their own choosing.

On positions 7-10, we find information that only e-learning systems could provide. The amount of time (rank 7) and the number of activities (rank 9) can be used to estimate how much effort a student invests. The overall cancellation rate (rank 8) may indicate a student's perseverance in tackling problems. Together with other top-ranked proposals, this information can be used to derive a student's pace through the course material.[9] The activity type distribution (rank 10) shows how students divide their time; it may indicate whether students systematically evade certain activities, or whether they spend too much time on other, potentially distracting, tools.

Some teachers assign less importance to these lower-ranked pieces of information. One teacher considers teaching as "an amalgam of different activities". For

---

[9] Using this data in isolation is problematic; for instance, students may not read texts that were given to them, or they may start a large number of activities without being properly involved or motivated.

this teacher, "the way the student divides his/her time over these activities is of less concern...". Another teacher wrote the following comment:

> "As teacher, I am interested in what 'stuck' [with the students]. The way [towards understanding] is only of interest if there are problems in achieving a learning goal, and to analyse the causes for this"[10].

Another teacher agrees: "[...] often problems, misconceptions, negative emotions, and the like are more important to a facilitator than controlling the actual pathways (which are hidden inside the learners and partially take place outside the learning environment)".

This view is reflected by our ranking; navigational pathways and replay of learner actions received low scores. Also, historical information of student-system interaction in terms of past activity pattern, past percentages of course coverage, and past learner classification obtained a lower rating.

From the questionnaire's profiling section, we know that the assessment techniques "usage statistics" and "log data analysis" were only marginally used. The rather low rate for this kind of data indicates that current student tracking tools do not address instructors' needs.

4.2 Preferences, Appropriateness, and Completeness

In question 12, we asked teacher to rank given student tracking proposals as well as to comment on their appropriateness and completeness.

Preferences. Only 9 teachers from a total of 49 teachers stated their preferences. Two participants gave very general statements ("I believe you have covered a great range of features", "I think all of those data should be available...]"). The ranking of the remaining seven teachers is quite diverse, ranging from proposals that appear in the top-ten list to medium-scored proposals (*e.g.*, analysis of online time, amount of social activity) and low-scored ones. The small sample of 9 teachers, thus, only partially represents the 49 votes on our candidate proposals, which may be explained by the diverse teacher backgrounds:

> "The level of the learner has much to do with the answers given. We teach only graduate students pursuing masters or doctoral degrees. Our interests would be far different from those dealing with K-12 or undergraduates."

Appropriateness. We received controversial feedback with respect to the appropriateness of our candidate proposals for student tracking. Whereas one teacher sees online time as a valuable piece of information ("This gives me information on the time spent on different subjects, so this is a valuable addition"), another

---

[10] Translated from German: "Als Lehrer interessiert mich, was 'haengengeblieben' ist. Der Weg dahin ist nur dann von Interesse, wenn es Probleme bei der Lernzielerreichung gibt, um Ursachen zu analysieren".

one questions its usefulness ("On-line time barely tells me whether a student really worked through the content of the e-learning system")[11]. We obtained similar controversial remarks with regard to activity times. One teacher believes that the use of activity times "indicates which activities are time-consuming or not."; another teacher considers "teaching as an amalgam of different activities." For this teacher, "[T]he way the student divides his/her time over these activities is of less concern [...]."

There is no perfect profiler, since learning, as one teacher put it, "takes place within and outside virtual learning environments". There is thus a danger that student tracking tools may mislead teachers "to interpret the share of all activities performed in the learning environment for the whole picture." According to this teacher, some of our questions and proposals sound like implying the existence of perfect learner classification, when student models can only be based on imperfect beliefs.

Completeness. Less than a quarter of the participants stated an opinion on the completeness of our proposals for student tracking. One teachers found that "the number of metrics is sufficient". Another teacher is more sceptical:

> "I'm not sure any question can capture the essence of learning cognition and application- I think you might get some sense of it through a small group of questions."

In the completeness text field, teacher proposed to track: the number of times and duration of students viewing help materials, student inactivity, and meta-cognitive indicators (*e.g.*, confidence and prudence values derived from learner answers). One teacher would like to detect potential cheaters, and proposes to check whether students go online and take their tests at the same time.

4.3   Related Studies

The designers of the CourseVis system also devised a teacher's questionnaire to inform the formulation of system requirements for the tracking of distant students [6]. Their empirical study covered three aspects: social aspects (student-student, student-tutor, student-system, and vicarious interactions), cognitive aspects (*e.g.*, student performance), and behavioural aspects (*e.g.*, course attendance, student's pace).

In total, 98 distance learning instructors participated in the CourseVis study, most of them involved in university courses. The findings are as follows (in parentheses: the share of participants who voted for a feature as "extremely interesting" or "very interesting"): participation in discussions (66%), participation in group work (67%), overall performance (82%), and performance for certain domain concepts (63%). From the behavioural aspects, course attendance, access

---

[11] Translated from German: 'Die Onlinezeit sagt kaum etwas darueber aus, ob tatsaechlich im bzw. mit dem System inhaltlich gearbeitet wurde."

of and time spent for course material, performance for evaluation proofs, and participation in discussions earned the highest assessment.

There is high agreement between both studies as all teachers favoured performance-related student tracking data. In the CourseVis study, 82% of all teachers rated the feature "overall performance" as "extremely interesting" or "very interesting". In our study, "overall success rate" came out first. There is also agreement on the importance of mastery levels. The CourseVis category "performance for certain domain concepts" got a high approval rate of 63%, where our feature "mastery-level for concepts/skills..." took second place in our top-ten table. The relation between mastery levels and diagosed mistakes/misconceptions (our rank 4) was also drawn in the CourseVis study:

> "The importance of this information was also stressed by participants in the discussions we had. Almost all instructors wanted to use this information in order to identify and remedy learners' common misconceptions in their courses"

The CourseVis proposal to track students' progressing within the course' schedule yielded high ratings as well. This is in line with the rating of our teachers regarding percentages of exercises tackled (rank 3), and percentages of available material read (rank 5).

5 Conclusion

Good teachers know their students. In the words of Cotton [1]:

> "Research comparing effective and ineffective teachers cites the existence and use of a systematic procedure for keeping and interpreting data on student performance as a notable difference between these groups."

Student monitoring is thus a crucial ingredient to optimize instruction and to make learning a success. Teachers (and students) will only profit from the increasing market for e-learning products and services, when profiling tools help them getting to know their students in distance-learning contexts.

The participants of our study know this, of course. When we asked them how they would you use student tracking information (Question 13.9), their top-three choices were: "to respond to specific individuals in an appropriate way" (83%); "to adapt teaching to individuals or groups of learners" (73%); and "to identify and remedy common misconceptions" (73%).

It is therefore not surprising that teachers have a preference for pedagogically-oriented measures (overall success rate, mastery levels, typical misconceptions, percentage of exercises tackled and material read), which are, naturally, easy to interpret. On the other hand, teachers find fine-grained statistics of log data (replay of exercises, histories of past course coverages and activities, navigational style) too cumbersome to inspect or too time-intensive to interpret, and social data (social nets, ratio of social activities to all activities) of less interest.

Our ranking of student tracking proposals, however, shows no clear winner as the distance between any adjacent entry in Tab. 1 and Tab. 2 is at most three points. The separation of ranked proposals into two tables (top-scores, low-scores) is therefore artificial; a student tracking tool that will only contain our top-ten proposals will disappoint teachers with other preferences. Teachers, with their many different backgrounds, roles, instructional settings, and visualisation preferences should therefore be given an easy-to-use configuration mechanism to personalise their student tracking workbench. Also, given the rich e-learning experience of many of our participants, it would be an enormous advantage if a student tracking tool could interface to many e-learning systems, thus providing a uniform student profiling application across multiple e-learning platforms. A common, standardised format for log data would facilitate the construction of a multi-platform student tracking tool.

The adequate logging, filtering, and analysis of student log data is obviously constrained by the underlying e-learning system, which may or may not have the capabilities to properly log semantically rich student actions. Unfortunately, current state-of-the-art e-learning system only provide quite shallow data. They track accesses to teaching material (say, to compute course coverage), time-related information (say, to compute the number and duration of tutorial sessions), and they have simple student assessment methods where students are asked to answer closed questions (e.g., multiple-choice questions and fill-in-the-blank questions). This information makes it hard, if not impossible, to identify a student's conceptual understanding of the course, say, in terms of mastery levels or student misconceptions. As one teacher said: "Presumably, the pure number of successful steps will not tell me much, apart for closely-guided exercise solutions, which, however, tell me very little about [learners'] conceptual understanding." [12]

Teachers found tracking information on the student's mastery level for each concept, skill, method, or competency as well as the amount of time spent and the number of learner activities invested to acquire such level particularly interesting. The provision of this information, however, is only possible if content material, exercises, tool use *etc* is semantically annotated with adequate meta-data. The requirements of our teachers are partially met by intelligent tutoring systems [13]. The ActiveMath system [9], for instance, has a semantic annotation of learning content, interactive exercises that allow students to solve non-trivial, multi-step problems, and domain reasoners that support the system to perform deep analyses of student answers in terms of correctness and misconceptions. Such systems are expensive to build, but will help students to better learn, and — with appropriate student activity tracking tools — teachers to better getting to know their distant students.

Acknowledgements. We are grateful to Erica Melis for initial work on the questionnaire, and for publicizing its availability.The work presented in this paper is

---

[12] Translated from German: "Da sagt mir die Anzahl der erledigten Schritte vermutlich wenig aus, wenn es nicht streng gefuehrte Aufgabenloesungen sind, die dann aber wieder weniger ueber das entwickelte Begriffsverstaendnis aussagen."

supported by the European Community under the Information Society Technologies programme of the 6th FP for RTD — project iClass contract IST 507922.

References

1. K. Cotton. Monitoring student learning in the classroom. Northwest Regional Educational Laboratory, U.S. Department of Education, 1988. School Improvement Research Series (SIRS), http://www.nwrel.org/scpd/sirs/2/cu4.html.
2. M. W. Goldberg. Student participation and progress tracking for web-based courses using webct. In *Proc. 2nd N.A.WEB Conf.*, Fredericton, NB, Canada, 1996.
3. J. Greer, J. D. Zapata-Rivera, C. Ong-Scutchings, and J. E. Cooke. Visualization of bayesian learner models. In *Proceedings of the workshop Open, Interactive, and other Overt Approaches to Learner Modelling AIED 1999*, 1999.
4. J. Hardy, M. Antonioletti, and S. Bates. e-learner tracking: Tools for discovering learner behavior. In *The IASTED International Conference on Web-base Education*, Innsbruck, Austria, 2004.
5. R. Mazza. *Using Information Visualisation to Facilitate Instructors in Web-based Distance Learning*. PhD thesis, University of Lugano, 2004.
6. R. Mazza and V. Dimitrova. Informing the design of a course data visualisator: an empirical study. In *5th International Conference on New Educational Environments (ICNEE 2003)*, pages 215 – 220, Lucerne, 2003.
7. R. Mazza and V. Dimitrova. Generation of graphical representations of student tracking data in course management systems. In *IV '05: Proceedings of the Ninth International Conference on Information Visualisation (IV'05)*, pages 253–258, Washington, DC, USA, 2005.
8. R. Mazza and C. Milani. Gismo: a graphical interactive student monitoring tool for course management systems. In *T.E.L. Technology Enhanced Learning 04 International Conference*, Milan, 2004.
9. E. Melis, G. Goguadze, M. Homik, P. Libbrecht, C. Ullrich, and S. Winterstein. Semantic-aware components and services of activemath. *British Journal of Educational Technology*, 37(3), 2006.
10. A. Merceron and K. Yacef. Tada-ed for educational data mining. *Interactive Multimedia Electronic Journal of Computer-Enhanced learning*, 7(1), 2005.
11. J. Mostow, G. Aist, P. Burkhead, A. Corbett, A. Cuneo, S. Eitelman, C. Huang, B. Junker, M. B Sklar, and B. Tobin. Evaluation of an automated reading tutor that listens: Comparison to human tutoring and classroom instruction. *Journal of Educational Computing Research*, 29(1):61–117, 2003.
12. J. Mostow, J. Beck, H. Cen, A. Cuneo, E. Gouvea, and C. Heiner. An educational data mining tool to browse tutor-student interactions: Time will tell! In *AAAI 2005 Workshop on Educational Data Mining*, 2005.
13. D. Sleeman and S. J. Brown, editors. *Intelligent Tutoring Systems*. Computers and People Series. Academic Press, 1982.
14. WebCT. *WebCT Vista^{TM} 3.0 Designer and Instructor Reference Manual*, April 2004. Technical Communications, http://www.webct.com.
15. J. D. Zapata-Rivera and J. Greer. Externalising learner modelling representations. In *Workshop on External Representations of AIED: Multiple Forms and Multiple Roles. International Conference on Artificial Intelligence in Education AIED 2001*, pages 71–76, 2001.

The L2C Project: Learning to Collaborate Through Advanced SmallWorld Simulations

Albert A. Angehrn and Thierry Nabeth

INSEAD Centre for Advanced Learning Technologies (CALT),
Bvd de Constance, 77305 Fontainebleau Cedex, France
{albert.angehrn, thierry.nabeth}@insead.edu

Abstract. L2C - Learning to Collaborate - is an ongoing research project addressing the design of effective immersive simulation-based learning experiences supporting the development of collaboration competencies both at the individual and
organisational level. The key characteristic of such advanced learning tools consists in the integration of psychological, motivational, cognitive, organizational,
cultural and technological factors affecting the success of collaboration into the
modeling of a set of virtual characters with whom learners can interact dynamically within a challenging and realistic collaboration scenario (SmallWorld Simulations). This paper provides an overview of the project, the conceptual basis,
key design principles and expected pedagogical impact of this new type of immersive simulation-based learning experiences.

1 Introduction

Effective collaboration dynamics are fundamental to learning, knowledge exchange
and development/innovation processes in a wide variety of educational, economical or
societal contexts. In spite of the attention that the subject of collaboration has attracted over the last years in fields like organisational dynamics [1, 2] management
[3], and education [4], no traditional or computer-enhanced approaches and learning
solutions have emerged to-date to address efficiently and effectively the development
of collaboration competencies from an inter-disciplinary perspective, including:

1. Individual psychological and motivational factors determining knowledge seek-
    ing and sharing behavior of people involved in collaborating
2. Group, organizational and inter-organisational factors conducive or detrimental to
    collaborative behavior
3. Cognitive and behavioral mechanisms to support effective knowledge exchange
    processes to seek for and integrate knowledge from diverse sources taking into
    consideration their contextual embeddedness
4. Opportunities and pitfalls of technologies aimed at supporting distributed col-
    laboration
5. pragmatic aspects resulting from best/worst cases of collaboration patterns in
    different contexts (mergers, alliances, as well as other initiatives by global teams
    of business, educational or social entrepreneurs and distributed communities of
    professionals).

W. Nejdl and K. Tochtermann (Eds.): EC-TEL 2006, LNCS 4227, pp. 452 – 457, 2006.
© Springer Verlag Berlin Heidelberg 2006

In fact, in today's global environment, a very large number of collaboration initiatives fail to deliver the value expected [5, 6], as collaboration complexity is significantly increased by the diversity and the distributed nature of the people, groups, and knowledge sources, by the ICT technologies and e-Collaboration platforms involved to support such distributed processes, as well as by the complexity of the knowledge integration processes involved.

2   Addressing the Collaboration Challenge

If, under the best conditions, collaboration can be successful in "traditional" settings in which people and organizations are either co-located (such as in centralized R&D centers) or distributed but involved in "simple/highly structured" collaboration processes (such as software developers operating within open source communities [7]), we are reaching today a "Collaboration Frontier" (see Figure 1).

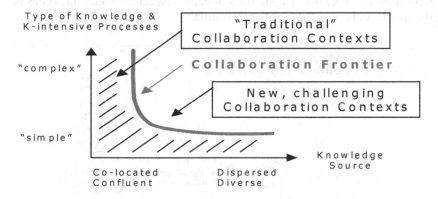

Fig. 1. Collaboration and Knowledge Integration Frontier

Our ultimate objective, however, is to acquire the competencies to move beyond the current "Collaboration Frontier" into contexts in which highly distributed and diverse groups are able to successfully collaborate on complex types of knowledge exchange and knowledge creation processes. This emerging need is calling for innovative approaches to design and deploy effective learning experiences aimed at stimulating and facilitating the acquisition and continuous development of collaboration and collaboration management competencies.

It is with this objective in mind that the project "**L2C: Learning to Collaborate**" was launched as an EC co-sponsored collaboration among European academic institutions and industry partners.

3   The "L2C: Learning to Collaborate" Perspective

The ongoing work on the L2C Project is progressively aiming at the design of immersive simulation-based learning experiences supporting the development of collaboration competencies at the individual and organizational level. The key characteristic of the project consists in the adoption of validated design principles (*SmallWorld Simulations* or SWS [8]) underlying the development of simulations which are currently extensively used in top business schools (such as MIT, Stanford, etc.) in managing change and innovation in different types of organizational contexts [see e.g. 9 and 10].

A concrete example of a learning experience which can be classified as a *SmallWorld Simulation* is the so-called 'EIS Simulation" [11, 12, 13, 14] which has been widely adopted over the last few years to substitute or complement traditional ways of teaching change management competencies. In this type of simulations, learners (operating in small teams) are projected into a realistic scenario in which they have to play the role of "change agents" sent into a company with the mission of introducing a major innovation (a new Information and Reporting System). Over a period of six simulated months their task is to get to know and convince more than 20 simulated characters (representing the top management of the simulated organization) to adopt the innovation by using different communication and intervention tactics and address different forms of resistance to change, by understanding and leveraging the formal and informal/social networks among the simulated characters, taking into consideration the specific culture of the target organization.

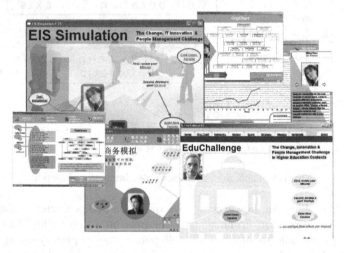

Fig. 2. Screens from different versions of the EIS Simulation

The EIS Simulation (see Figure 2) provides a concrete example of how the know-how of a specific complex domain (in this case: change and innovation management in organizations) can be embedded in a dynamic, computer-based simulation to provide a rich, intensive, and realistic game-like learning experience considered superior to more traditional ways of teaching such a complex subject [12].

4   Designing SmallWorld Simulations for Collaboration Competencies Development

The design challenge of SmallWorld Simulations addressing collaboration competencies development follows the structured process illustrated in Figure 3. The first step consists in identifying and selecting a set of models, dynamics and insights reflecting state-of-the-art academic literature (the "Knowing" dimension), current pedagogical approaches and learning objectives (the "Learning" dimension), and insights from collaboration practice (the "Doing" dimension) to be gradually embedded in simulation-based Learning Experiences.

As mentioned in the first part of this paper, the specificity of the targeted simulations is to integrate models of: (i) **individual behavior** (to allow learners to come into touch with different types of individuals displaying different types of attitudes), (ii) **group interactions** and **relationship network dynamics** (e.g. influence networks affecting the diffusion of attitudes in a group), (iii) **organizational contexts** and **dynamics** (e.g. specific cultures reflecting a given industry, a family business or an SME context), and (iv) **intervention dynamics** (e.g. what happens when the learners try to intervene in the simulated context using different approaches and tactics).

Key design guidelines also include a realistic scenario, a challenging management mission, a set of believable characters, a range of managerial actions and a realistic role for the players (operating typically in teams to strengthen the collaborative learning dimension of the simulation-based learning experience, [12])

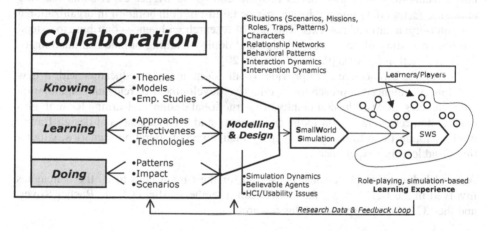

Fig. 3. L2C Simulations Design Process (adapted from [8])

In addition to **design guidelines**, the L2C Project is producing **pedagogical guidelines** describing the ideal educational settings and processes in which L2C Simulations can be deployed in universities or organizations. This is particularly important, as (1) L2C Simulations have the primary objective to stimulate and facilitate learning, and (2) the "learning-by-playing" approach employed [10] is not the currently dominant model for adult learning. The key role of games in triggering learning, knowledge structuring and cognitive change in children has been extensively analyzed in the work of Piaget and Vygotsky [15, 16]. In adult education, and particularly management development, computer games have been employed successfully over several decades. However, the successful deployment of "games" in organizational learning contexts remains a challenge in most cultures and organizations.

The key hypothesis we aim to test through the resulting L2C simulations is the extent to which ICT-based systems can be used to: (1) model cognitive and behavioral processes related to collaboration dynamics, (2) embed such processes in interactive game-like learning experiences, and (3) help individuals and organizations to diagnose and learn how to address cognitive and behavioral barriers (at both the individual and organizational level) to effective collaboration and knowledge sharing.

5 Conclusions

In the modern hyper-competitive business and social environment, effective collaboration competencies are emerging as a key condition for productive and sustainable value creation at the individual, team, organizational and inter-organizational level.

L2C Simulations, the design of which has been discussed in this paper, address the area of collaboration from a multi-disciplinary perspective, integrating insights and models from social sciences, knowledge management, collaboration-oriented ICT, and experiential, computer-enhanced learning.

Research-wise, our objective is to demonstrate how individual cognitive and behavioral processes and relevant organizational dynamics can be modeled using simulation technology in a way that is realistic enough to trigger experiential learning about the factors determining the success or failure of collaboration in organizational and inter-organizational contexts. This line of research will hence contribute to extend our understanding of how to best design and deploy learning-oriented simulations of social interaction contexts [9, 10, 17, 18, 19, 20].

The ultimate objective is to provide: (i) the community of educators with a new technology-enhanced approach to the effective development of relevant collaboration competencies, and (ii) the community of instructional designers, learning technologies experts and researchers with tools, components and a conceptual and design framework enabling them to design and deploy their own collaboration scenarios, simulations, and learning experiences.

Acknowledgements. A personal thank-you for their input goes to all the colleagues involved in the L2C Project, the CALT team members, Alicia Cheak, Rachel Royer, and the EC, which co-sponsored this research.

References

1. Mayer, R. C., Davis, J. H., and Schoorman, F. D. (1995). An integrative model of organizational trust. Academy of Management Review, 20, 3, 709-734..
2. Orlikowski, W.J. (1992). Learning From Notes: Organisational Issues in Groupware Implementation, Proceedings of the Conference on CSCW, Toronto, 362-369.
3. Hansen, M.T. and Nohria, N. (2004) How to Build Collaborative Advantage. MIT Sloan Management Review, 461 pp 22-30.
4. Pea, R.D. (1994). Seeing What We Build Together: Distributed Multimedia Learning Environments for Transformative Communications. J. of the Learning Sciences, 3, 3, 285-299.
5. Miles, R.E. and Snow, C.C. (1992). Causes of failure in network organizations. California Management Review, 34, 4, 53-72.

6. Labianca, G., Brass, D., and Gray, B. (1998). Social networks and the perception of inter-group conflict: the role of negative relationships and third parties. Academy of Management Journal, 41, 55-67.
7. Loebbecke C. and A.A. Angehrn (2004). Open Source Communities Reflecting Co-opetitive Learning and Knowledge Exchange Networks; Proceedings of the 2004 IFIP International Conference on Decision Support Systems (DSS 2004), 490-500.
8. Angehrn, A.A. (2006). SmallWorld Simulations: Experiences and Developments; The 6th IEEE Int. Conference on Advanced Learning Technologies (ICALT 2006), 413-414.
9. Angehrn, A.A. (2005). Learning to Manage Innovation and Change through Organizational and People Dynamics Simulations; Proceedings of the International Simulation & Gaming Association Conference (ISAGA 05), Atlanta, USA.
10. Angehrn, A.A. (2004a). Learning by Playing: Bridging the Knowing-Doing Gap in Urban Communities; In A. Bounfour and L. Edvinsson (Eds.), Intellectual Capital for Communities: Nations, Regions, Districts, Cities, Butterworth-Heinemann, 299-316.
11. Angehrn, A.A. (2004b). Behind the EIS Simulation: An Overview of Models Underlying the Simulation Dynamics; CALT Working Paper 10-2004.
12. Manzoni, J.F. and A.A. Angehrn (1997), Understanding Organizational Dynamics of IT-Enabled Change: A Multimedia Simulation Approach, J. of Mgmt Info. Sys., 14, 3, 109-140.
13. Angehrn, A.A. (2004/5). The EIS Simulation User Manual. (http:// www.calt.insead.edu/ eis)
14. Angehrn, A.A., Schönwald, I., Euler, D. and S. Seufert (2005). Behind EduChallenge: An Overview of Models Underlying the Dynamics of a Simulation on Change Management in Higher Education; SCIL-Universität St Gallen, SCIL Report 7, December 2005.
15. Wadsworth, B.J. (1979). Piaget's Theory of Cognitive Development. Longman.
16. Moll, L.C. (1990), Vygotsky and Education– Instructional Implications and Applications of Sociohistorical Psychology. Cambridge University Press, 1990.
17. Aldrich C. (2005). Learning by Doing: A Comprehensive Guide to Simulations, Computer Games, and Pedagogy in E-Learning and Other Educational Experiences, Jossey-Bass.
18. Gilbert N. (1993). Computer simulation of social processes, Social Res. Update, 6.
19. Gilbert, N. and Chattoe, E. (2001). Hunting the unicorn: an exploration of the simulation of small group leadership. In N. J. Saam & B. Schmidt (Eds.), Cooperative Agents: applications in the social sciences, Dordrecht: Kluwer, 109 – 124.
20. Salen, K. and Zimmerman, E. (2003). Rules of Play: Game Design Fundamentals, MIT Press.

Integrating Instructional Material and Teaching Experience into a Teachers' Collaborative Learning Environment[*]

Mírian C.A. Brito[1], Germana M. da Nóbrega[2], and Káthia M. de Oliveira

[1] Mestrado em Gestão do Conhecimento e da Tecnologia da Informação
Universidade Católica de Brasília, Brasília, Brazil
[2] Núcleo de Administração - Faculdades Alves Faria, Goiânia, Brazil
mcab@click21.com.br, {gmnobrega, kathia}@ucb.br

Abstract. Current trends from the Knowledge Management community, and particularly, toward learning organizations have been privileging collaborative work. When the considered organization is an academic institution, one might look at teachers as knowledge workers. In such a context, we see Technology Enhanced Workplace Learning as a process accounting for continuous development of teams' skills. In this paper, we propose a learning environment for Teachers, relying on progressive improvement of Instructional Material, as feedback from classes are collaboratively taken into account. We focus on the environments' design, founded on basis such as Experience Factory and Learning Objects Metadata.

1 Introduction

Graduating and under-graduating institutions (GIs) often work in accordance with a number of directives formulated by educational regulating organisms. Such organisms usually implement a number of policies for the educational area they govern, organizing information for the existing educational levels, under the light of statistic data and assessment they accomplish.

Constrained thus by a major regulating level, GIs draw their own goals and internal regulating directives. These are established, by their turn, as competent people consider a macro view of teaching-learning processes within the variety of programs the GI provides, inspecting whether those processes are responding to the institution's goals and social commitments, and yet to the external regulating directives.

While academic work may be discussed through the above upside-down whole perspective, we choose to address at first the teaching-learning process up to the point teachers have governability. From teachers' perspective, pedagogical practices and related daily activities within a GI may be thought-of as including planning a course, lecturing classes, managing temporary/definitive substitutions

---

[*] Work supported by CNPq (Brazil) under the grant MCT/CNPq/CT-INFO/506911/ 2004-7.

W. Nejdl and K. Tochtermann (Eds.): EC-TEL 2006, LNCS 4227, pp. 458–463, 2006.

Table 1. A synthesis of related work

Features	Buseti et al	QSabe	Cic	Debyte	Couses as seeds	EQO
Educational material sharing	Y		Y	Y	Y	Y
Learning Objects usage	Y					
Free discussion			Y	Y	Y	
Structured discussion						
Experiences sharing		Y		Y	Y	
Best practices sharing (consensus)				Y		

with colleagues, and so on. Within this context, the following questions might arise: (*i*) how to welcome a novice teacher, by creating a double-sense channel for exchanging experiences? (*ii*) How to consider teaching experience and to facilitate daily activities, such as to progressively improve teaching-learning process? (*iii*) How to reduce the impact of temporary or definitive absence of a teacher from the GI, being thus concerned with quality of teaching-learning process?

The state-of-the-art and of the practice in Education reveals that answers to the above questions would suggest the establishment of teachers networks, which can take place both formal and informally within a GI. As stated by Santaella in [15], collaboration between teachers reduces the lack of confidence, fear on making mistakes, motivates engagement and the progressive development of the group. While interacting, teachers reflect on problems and successful situations they daily go through, learning from experience [8]. Often, they create new situations for their own professional development, aiming to share ideas about lived circumstances, and finding new ways to solve common problems, thus establishing informal and spontaneous networks for exchanging teaching experiences.

The community concerned with Computer Science and Education has been investing in teachers formal nets supported by computational systems, let us highlight [6,2,4,11,13]. In Table 1, we present a synthesis of these environments, according to some features that we find relevant to our own work.

Considering open issues from there, in §2, we briefly describe a system - called doceNet - for supporting continuous improvement of skills (of teachers and of students as an expected consequence), within a process triggered by the experience teachers bring back from classes. In §3, we present our concluding remarks.

2   DoceNet: A Learning Environment for Teachers

We propose to look at doceNet as a learning environment for teachers on the basis that its main goal is to provide collaborative both analysis and synthesis of experiences teachers daily go through, as a means to continuously improve their skills.

2.1   On the Environment's Design

Fig. 1 depicts doceNet. we mainly instantiate the classical infrastructure of the Experience Factory from [5] and include the Models from AC-Hybrid [12]. The term Model here is referring to Learning Objects (LOs), including course Plans, which are considered here as LOs for teachers. In what follows we present firstly our application profile, containing the resulting metadata set. Then, the resulting instantiation of the Experience Factory steps are introduced within two main sub-phases: (i) Course Organization, including steps 1 to 4, and the (ii) Experience Factory itself, including steps 5 and 6. Sub-phase (i) is accounting for planning and administrating a course, while (ii) is supporting (i).

DoceNet application profile. From current standards (e.g. LOM [17] and Dublin Core [10]) and application profile specifications over them, for building LO repositories (e.g. Cancore [7], SCORM [1], ARIADNE [3]), we choose ARIADNE due to its closer proximity to our needs. In order to explore ARIADNE's profile within DoceNet, we inspect each of its metadata, such as to decide on suitability to our context.

An important feature within doceNet is registering recommendation (from experience) on *how, when* and *why* to use a certain LO in classes, i.e., information that might help teachers to learn, either from his/her or others' experiences, such as to allow one to repeat or to improve positive experiences and to avoid negative ones. In addition to that information, other aspects could be relevant for understanding stored information. We add, then, a new metadata category, called *Experience*, as described in Table 2.

In order to achieve our profile, we need to accomplish additional changes on ARIADNE metadata, such as: (i) wider account for information about relations between the objects in the environment, adding thus the generic category from

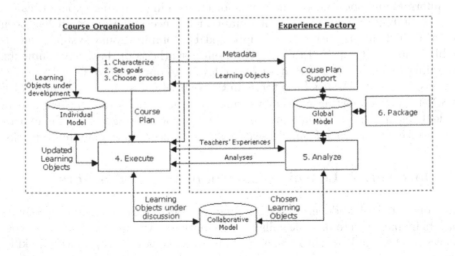

Fig. 1. DoceNet: a teachers' learning environment

Table 2. Experience metadata for doceNet application profile

Category	Metadata	Description
Experience	Experience-type	Stores if the teacher experience is positive or negative.
	Maturity	Stores validity level of the experience and may assume the following values:
		o *Initial*, needs more practice;
		o *Confirmed*, practiced several times;
		o *Consolidated*, practiced, discussed and refined.
	Statement	Stores the experience description itself (pedagogical situation, implications, problems, etc.)
	Recommendation	According to the 3 above metadata, what guidelines have been validated and accepted in order to solve or to improve the concerned material (why, how, and where to use it to a better extent).

LOM standard, called "Relations", in which two elements about relations from ARIADNE are included to foresee possible kinds of relations between LOs; (*ii*) identifying the contents of an object in a more detailed manner, adding thus the "Keyword" metadata to the "General" category; (*iii*) information on the situation of the object in the environment: under discussion or voting, etc., adding the "Status" metadata to the "General" category; (*iv*) identifying the thematic area (e.g., Artificial Intelligence and Theory of Computation, in a Computer Science program) to which the object is attached, adding thus the "Sub-area" metadata to the "Semantic" category; (*v*) registering the author of the last change carried out on the LO, adding thus the "Last update author" metadata to the "Indexation" category.

Course organization. Within doceNet, Course Organization supports a number of activities that usually take place in GIs, even without the existence of any computer system. These activities include planning a course and then lecturing classes. The result of organizing a course within the system is a document called *Course Plan*, according to the Plan structure established in the organizational level. Course organization includes then the Characterize, Set goals, Choose process, and Execute steps from the Experience Factory, as described below.

Characterize. Competent instances from the GI define a number of features identifying a course. Those features compose the header-part of a course Plan. Also, those features appear as metadata allowing the Teacher to search for LOs while preparing a Plan.

Set goals. Overall contents are also defined by competent people from the GI, along with course goals. For instance, "to be capable of building a Finite Automaton to accept a given Regular Language", within a course on Formal Languages. The Teacher, by his/her turn defines assessment criteria such as to measure whether those goals are reached by students.

Choose process. The Teacher defines the units needed to cover the contents. Also, he/she draws up a teaching methodology, and considers the bibliography previously established by competent people from the organizational level. In order to close the course Plan, the Teacher builds up a detailed activities schedule.

Execute. While lecturing classes, the Teacher executes the course Plan. He/she may carry out subtle changes on future activities (and corresponding LOs), according to how students are responding to the course. Yet, due to unexpected situations in classes, he/she may intend to modify LOs for further courses. The teacher may accomplish that within his/her Individual Model. When changes are done, he/she may transfer the LOs to the Collaborative Model, in order to trigger an asynchronous discussion with colleagues.

(Teachers') Experience Factory. The steps Analyze and Package correspond to the Experience Factory itself, allowing teachers to discuss and to search for a consensus on daily issues.

Analyze. The goal here is to analyze and to refine the suggestions/questions placed in the Collaborative Environment. In order to organize the discussions, we borrow the IBIS model [9,14]. Considering duration, we suggest discussions to have a fixed time, for instance, a semester-long. Results from discussions within the Collaborative Environment correspond to the dust knowledge from the Experience Factory.

Package. This step accounts for synthesis on discussions, for what we borrow vIbis model [16]). After all decisions are made, the group Coordinator transfers those validated LOs (and corresponding metadata) from the Collaborative Model to the Global Model.

3   Conclusion

In this paper we report part of the work developed within the context of a research project, which is concerned with computer-supported formal networks involving teachers. Considering the experience from the research group members themselves as teachers, as well as the lacks identified from inspecting the literature, we propose an environment for supporting the continuous improvement of instructional material. The environment relies on the collaboration between teachers within a thematic area in a (under)Graduating Institution, motivated by individual experiences from lecturing classes with that material.

Our current research agenda includes achieving the Web environment both modeling and implementation. Then, we intend to exhaustively submit the environment to real use situations, aiming to obtain empirical evidence that could support our initial assumptions, in terms of possible answers to the questions raised in §1. Further work include establishing metrics allowing to assess learning under the perspective of the organization itself as an entity.

References

1. ADL. Scorm metadata set. http://www.adlnet.org, 2001.
2. J. C. Andrade, J. C. Naidl, J. M. Pessoa, and C. S. de Menezes. Qsabe - um ambiente inteligente para endereçamento de perguntas em uma comunidade virtual de esclarecimento. In *Proceedings of the First Latin American Web Congress - LA-WEB 2003*. IEEE, 2003.
3. ARIADNE. Ariadne foundation. http://www.ariadne-eu.org/, 2001.
4. N. A. Baloian, J. A. Pino, and O. Motelet. Collaborative authoring, use, and reuse of learning material in a computer-integrated classroom. In *CRIWG 2003*, volume 2806 of *LNCS*, pages 199–207. Springer, 2003.
5. V. R. Basili, G. Caldiera, and D. H. Rombach. The experience factory. In *Encyclopedia of Software Engineering*, pages 469–476. 1994.
6. E. Busetti, P. Forcheri, M. G. Ierardi, , and M. Molfino. Repositories of learning objects as learning environments for teachers. In *International Conference on Advanced Learning Technologies - ICALT 2004*, Joensuu, Finland, 2004.
7. CanCore. Cancore application profile. http://www.cancore.ca, 2002.
8. M. H. Cavaco. Ofício do professor: o tempo e as mudanças. In A. Nóvoa, editor, *Profissão professor*. Pontes Editores LTDA, Porto, 1995.
9. J. Conklin and M. L. Begeman. gibis: A hypertext tool for exploratory policy discussion. *ACM Transactions on Office Information Systems*, 6(4):303–331, 1988.
10. DCMES. Dublin core metadata element set v1. http://dublincore.org/documents/1999/07/02/dces/, 1999.
11. J. F. S. de Araújo and M. da F. Elia. A capacitação em serviço de professores, via internet, através da discussão de questões. In *XIV Simpósio Brasileiro em Informática na Educação - SBIE 2003*, Rio de Janeiro, Brazil, 2003.
12. E. J. R. de Castro, G. M. da Nóbrega, E. Ferneda, S. A. Cerri, and F. Lima. Towards interaction modelling of asynchronous collaborative model-based learning. In J. Mostow and P. Tedesco, editors, *ITS 2004 Workshop on Designing Computational Models of Collaborative Learning Interaction*, pages 71–76. Maceió (Brazil), August 2004.
13. R. Depaula, G. Fischer, and J. Ostwald. Courses as seeds: expectations and realities. In *Proceedings of the Second European Conference on Computer-Supported Collaborative Learning - Euro-CSCL 2001*, pages 494–501, 2001.
14. A. Diaz and G. Canals. Divergence occurrences in knowledge sharing communities. In *10th International Workshop on Groupware - CRIWG 2004*, San Carlos, Costa Rica, September 2004.
15. C. M. Santaella. *Formación para la profesión docente*. Grupo FORCE y Grupo Editorial Universitario, Madrid, 1998.
16. J. Wainer and F. C. Lenz. vibis: a discussion and voting system. *LNCS*, 1(2):36–43, 1994.
17. IEEE Learning Technology Standards Committee WG12. Draft standard for learning object metadata. http://ltsc.ieee.org/wg12/files/LOM-1484-12-1-v1-Final-Draft.pdf, 15 July 2002.

A Neural Approach for Modeling the Inference of Awareness in Computer-Supported Collaboration

Thanasis Daradoumis[1] and Luis A. Casillas[2]

[1] Open University of Catalonia, Department of Information Sciences,
Av. Tibidabo, 39-43, 08035 Barcelona, Spain
adaradoumis@uoc.edu
[2] University of Guadalajara, Department of Computer Sciences,
Av. Revolucion, 1500, 44840 Guadalajara, Mexico
lcasilla@mail.fic.udg.mx, lcasillas@uoc.edu

Abstract. Individuals interacting in a computer supported collaborative learning (CSCL) environment produce a variety of information elements during their participation; these information elements usually have a complex structure and semantics, which make it rather difficult to find out the behavioral attitudes and profiles of the users involved. This work provides a model that can be used to discover awareness information lying underneath multi-user interaction. This information is initially captured in log files and then is represented in a specific form in events-databases. By using data mining techniques, it is possible to infer both the users' behavioral profiles and the relationships that occur in a CSCL environment. In this work we combine different data mining strategies and a neural-based approach in order to construct a multi-layer model that provides a mechanism for inferring different types of awareness information from group activity and presenting it to the interested parties.

1 Introduction

Online collaborative learning constitutes a complex task both as regards its utility and its capability to reach an effective and useful learning. Various research aspects such as group and individual evaluation, interaction modeling and analysis, and supporting several types of awareness (workspace, social, task, and concept) are in the way to get a satisfactory response [2]. However, as regards awareness support, many debatable matters are still waiting for a complete and formal response and solution [9]. These aspects justify the grown interest and development of technology for knowledge management, mobility and conceptual awareness in the area of distributed collaborative work and learning [6, 7, 8].

The automation of awareness support to both collaborative teams and their coordinator/evaluator in online learning environments is by no means solved by the current state of the art in awareness technology [1, 7]. Groups of dispersed people are enabled to work and learn together through enriched web-based environments which are capable of capturing important information from group interaction, but so far they fail to provide useful and easily handled representation of this information which may have a complex structure. However, the more complex the representation is, the richer

W. Nejdl and K. Tochtermann (Eds.): EC-TEL 2006, LNCS 4227, pp. 464 – 469, 2006.

is the knowledge that can be extracted and be used for evaluating and supporting individuals and groups [11]. Enriched knowledge representations imply new requirements and functionalities of Computer-Supported Cooperative Work (CSCW) and CSCL systems [5, 10].

In CSCL environments, in particular, the assessment plays a significant role and it is oriented to distinguish the different behaviors and attitudes adopted by the participants, which shows and represents specific user profiles [4]. These profiles are the key elements that provide assessment information. Taking into account that every user may produce a significant volume of actions, our approach considers it as a basic source to build the user profile. Though this is just one dimension of the user profile construction, the large amount of data generated by the users' actions in real online collaborative learning situations causes a complex problem, that of information and knowledge discovering, which we are going to deal in this work.

For this reason, we applied an approach that combines different data mining strategies and a neural-based method in order to construct a multi-layer model that provides a mechanism for inferring awareness information from group activity and presenting it to the interested parties at different levels of detail. This constitutes an important means for both evaluating and supporting the individual and group learning process in a principled manner. Here the paper focuses only on the evaluating issue.

The paper is structured as follows. First, we present a detailed analysis of the problem and then we proceed to describe the design of our model (Section 3). Finally, Section 4 discusses how our model was developed and used to infer awareness in a real collaborative learning practice.

2 Problem Analysis

Our generic approach aims at discovering the awareness regarding the behavior of students and groups, so that to assess four facets of group activity: *performance, group functioning, interaction* and *support*. To that end, in collaboration with the tutors of a real collaborative learning practice we set to test and validate our model, we identified twenty-nine potential variables that can provide the evaluation criteria for assessing group and individual behavior and performance. Our first decision was to filter them according to their influence and importance to group activity so that to avoid the complexity that derives from a possible combination explosion. This process ended up with a more structured, reduced list of indicators which were organized in two layers taking into account two criteria: first, their capacity to explain the overall group and individual behavior at different levels if description; second, the dependences that hold among them.

The middle level indicators detected are: individual presence, group presence, individual audience, group audience, individual persistence, group persistence, individual precision, group precision, individual seizing, group seizing, volume of active individual, interaction, volume of active group interaction, volume of passive (perceptive) individual interaction, volume of passive (perceptive) group interaction. The higher level indicators are: performance, group functioning, interaction, collaboration support.

3 Model Design

Based on the above set of indicators and variables, a list of direct dependences was developed. Every dependence was represented by an ordered pair. Then, some rules were constructed to build the critical paths from the input events to the higher level indicators. The resulting critical paths helped to build a network, which was the very first construction for the model to infer awareness from the stored events. Yet, this initial model resulted to be too heavy because of its size and redundancy.

As a consequence we simplified the model structure and dimensions by constructing a couple of models based on the performed analysis; one for student and another for group awareness. Finally, we proceeded to combine the two models in one integrated model. At that point the variable and indicator names were adjusted to represent a closer perspective to reality. Figure 1 sketches this model, including the connections and possible sources for the necessary input data.

The model processes the input data through a structure that uses weights during the propagation, employing the propagation algorithm (**1**), adapted from [3]. Every input data is multiplied by the connection's weight and is summed up to produce $f(X)$, then $f(X)$ is used to obtain the unit's threshold $t(f(X))$ which is sigmoid shaped. The thresholds are the inputs for the units of the following layer, and the process is repeated until the final output is generated [3].

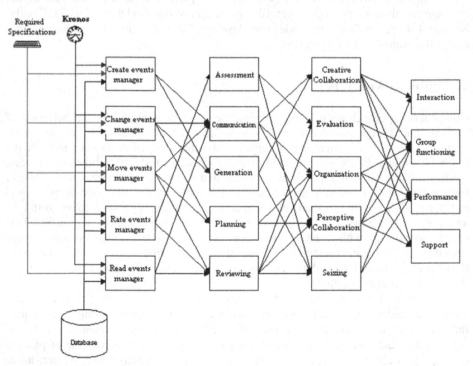

Fig. 1. A Model to discover awareness about student or group performance and functioning in a CSCL environment

Besides the main model, a complementary model was considered to measure and gather the awareness regarding the reactions (i.e., the perceptive behavior) of the members in a group with respect to the members' creative actions. To be able to collect the actions and reactions occurred inside a group, the complementary model was based on the information related to creative and perceptive collaborations along the different distinguishable moments in the whole model. This allowed the complementary model to collect a set of changes in the thresholds for member and connection values. Figure 2 sketches this social network.

$$f(X) = \sum_{i=1}^{n} (x_i * w_i)$$

$$t(f(X)) = \frac{1}{1 + e^{-f(X)}}$$

(1)

These interactions have an associated connection value (*VCxn*), which is initially assigned an extreme negative value; every time an interaction occurs between two members this value increases. An interaction could be creative (e.g., expressed by a create action) or perceptive (e.g., expressed by a read action). Similarly, each member has an associated participation value (*VPtn*) which is also initially assigned an extreme negative value; then, every time a creative or perceptive interaction takes place, it receives a quantity of points, being this quantity higher in case of creative actions. Finally, the *Kronos* element enables to reconstruct and evaluate specific periods of collaborative interactions. Doing so, we are able to verify the reaction and impact that a specific member action produces to the rest of group members.

In short, this rather simple model lets the teacher assess a member's performance, collaboration at pair and group level, and action-reaction for specific events and periods of time by employing principles based on unsupervised machine learning.

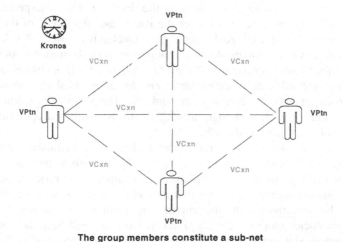

Fig. 2. A complementary model that gathers the awareness regarding the inner actions and reactions in a group

4 Model Implementation

Five event-families, *create*, *change*, *move*, *rate* and *read*, have been considered during the first stages as the main activity indicators. As shown in Fig. 1, the very possible events would produce a specific value in each of these five entry points to the model. Hence, when an event is processed a value is assigned to each of the five entry points in the model. In addition, it is possible to verify that every processing unit is reached only through some of the connections coming from the units in the previous layer. The connections in-between the layers are not complete, due to the dependences we want to model. Moreover it differs from the regular structure of a traditional multi-layer neural network, since the traditional training algorithms are not useful to train this model. Following the neural networks technology, the approach we are using is that of assigning weights to the connections and propagating the inputs to gather the results. Since there are different useful values within the model, a different training mechanism was required. Traditional training algorithms focus on the production of specific outputs, and internal thresholds are just part of the calculus to generate certain outputs. We discovered that no useful results were produced for internal thresholds when useful outputs were calculated. This inconvenience of the traditional neural approach led us to design a new training mechanism.

The new training model splits the main model in many small networks, one for every variable and indicators. Every small network is fed with the information coming from the processing units preceding it in the dependence hierarchy. Hence, every small neural network is trained using the classic back-propagation algorithm. After training all the small neural networks separately, the weights resulted from the distributed training were stored and used to build a network of networks. The new complex structure can produce specific outputs, whereby it also retains useful information for the internal slots representing variables and middle level indicators.

Nevertheless, the complex model did not show significant differences when processing different real data cases stored in the database. This unexpected behavior justified an additional research work over the nature and frequency of the events. In order to achieve this special goal, some new mechanisms were developed. This helped us to discover an interesting phenomenon as regards students' behavior and tendencies in their event generation. The event *read_event(all)* is always around 80% of the events generated, meanwhile *create_event(document)* is always around 7% and the event *create_event(note)* is always around 5%. The rest of the event categories have low significance values though, among them, the clipboard operations are the most popular with levels around 1.5%.

These tendencies can be discovered in the analysis of individuals, groups and the whole package of events. The interesting part in the analysis is that individuals and groups follow different plans, or their plans are not supposed to produce the observed tendencies. This phenomenon justifies that an additional study, e.g., an ethnographic one, should be integrated with the current approach for modeling the learners' behavioral tendencies more effectively. Finally, we combined both the main and the complementary model, embedding the weights, which were assigned and used in the main model, into the complementary model structure. The effect of this combination was a significant production of different types of awareness regarding behavioral attitudes in a group, as well as some interesting points about group functioning.

5 Conclusions and Future Work

This work focused on the design, construction and test of a data mining model to discover the hidden awareness by means of neural networks techniques and explain the individual and group's behavior. A couple of initial neural models gave rise to a complex model capable of analyzing interactions through a system that pondered different event-categories, whereas a neural model filled a set of variables and indicators. Members, group-leaders, tutors and course coordinators can gather awareness regarding group activity and correct those aspects that pertain to everyone's responsibility. The ultimate goal is to construct an abstract model containing general approaches for the analysis of collaborative interactions, which can be instantiated or inherited for developing analysis tools or specific groupware facilities. Moreover new frameworks can be built up based on a better understanding of the collaborative activity. Our future work aims to address and provide different types of awareness to different types of users, at different levels of detail, taking into account that the different users may specify their particular variables or indicators they want to study and monitor. The goal is to provide an information system to allow CSCL participants to gather the type of awareness that best conforms to their needs and interests.

Acknowledgments. This work has been partially supported by the Spanish MCYT project TSI2005-08225-C07-05.

References

1. Bentley, R., Appelt, W., Busbach. U., Hinrichs, E., Kerr, D., Sikkel, S., Trevor, J. & Woetzel, G.: Basic Support for Cooperative Work on the World Wide Web. Int. J. of Human-Computer Studies 46(6) (1997), 827-846.
2. Gutwin C., Stark G., Greenberg S. Support for workspace awareness in educational groupware. CSCL'95. Bloomington, Indiana, USA: ACM Press (1995) 147–156.
3. Haykin, S. Neural Networks, A comprehensive foundation. Prentice Hall, NJ (1999).
4. Herrmann, T., Hoffmann, M., Jahnke, I., Kienle, A., Kunau, G., Loser, K., Menold, N. Concepts for usable patterns of groupware applications. Conference on Supporting Group Work; ACM (2003) 349-358.
5. Horn, D., Finholt, T., Birnholtz, J., Motwani, D., Jayaraman, S. Six degrees of jonathan grudin: a social network analysis of the evolution and impact of CSCW research. ACM conference on Computer supported cooperative work. Chicago, USA (2004) 582-591.s
6. Jang, C., Steinfield, C., Pfaff, B. Supporting Awareness among Virtual Teams in a Web-Based Collaborative System: The TeamSCOPE System. Siggroup Bulletin 21(3) (2000).
7. Morch A., Jondahl S., Dolonen J. Supporting Conceptual Awareness with Pedagogical Agents. Information Systems Frontiers, Vol. 7, No. 1. (2005) 39-53.
8. Perry, M., O'hara, K., Sellen, A., Brown, B., Harper, R. Dealing with mobility: understanding access anytime, anywhere. Computer-Human Interaction. 8(4) (2001) 323-347.
9. Schmidt, K. The problem with 'awareness'. Computer Supported Cooperative Work vol. 11, (2002) 285–298.
10. Soller, A., Martínez-Monés, A., Jermann, P., & Muehlenbrock, M. From Mirroring to Guiding: A Review of State of the Art Technology for Supporting Collaborative Learning. International Journal of Artificial Intelligence in Education, 15 (4) (2005) 261-290.
11. Zumbach, J., Schönemann, J., Reimann, P. Analyzing and Supporting Collaboration in Cooperative Computer-Mediated Communication. T. Koschmann, D. Suthers, T. W. Chan (Eds.), CSCL 2005: The Next 10 Years! Mahwah, NJ: Lawrence Erlbaum. (758-767).

An Exploratory Study of the Relationship Between Learning Styles and Cognitive Traits[*]

Sabine Graf[1], Taiyu Lin[2], Lynn Jeffrey[3], and Kinshuk[2]

[1] Women's Postgraduate College for Internet Technologies,
Vienna University of Technology, Vienna, Austria
graf@wit.tuwien.ac.at
[2] Department of Information Systems, Massey University
Palmerston North, New Zealand
t.lin@massey.ac.nz, kinshuk@ieee.org
[3] Department of Management & International Business, Massey University
Auckland, New Zealand
l.m.jeffrey@massey.ac.nz

Abstract. To provide personalization and adaptivity in technology enhanced learning systems, the needs of learners have to be known by the system first. Detecting these needs is a challenging task and therefore, mechanisms that support this task are beneficial. This paper discusses the relationship between learning styles, in particular the Felder-Silverman learning style model, and working memory capacity, a cognitive trait. Due to this relationship, additional information about the learner is available and can be used to improve the student model. An exploratory study is presented to verify the identified relationship based on the literature. The results of the study show that the identified relationship between working memory capacity and two of the four dimensions of the learning style model is significantly supported. For the two remaining dimensions further research is required.

1 Introduction

Modelling the characteristics of learners is important for all systems that incorporate personalization issues and especially for systems that aim to provide adaptivity. Student models (for example, see [2]) are crucial components of technology enhanced educational systems dealing with personalized learning. They store information about learners such as personal data, domain competence, learning styles, and cognitive traits. To adapt to the learners' needs automatically, this information needs to be known by the system first. One challenge of student modelling is to identify the needs of the learners. The simplest approach to inform a student model is to ask the student for the required data. However, this approach is not suitable for getting accurate information for several components of a student model, such as cognitive traits,

---

[*] This research has been partly funded by the Austrian Federal Ministry for Education, Science, and Culture, and the European Social Fund (ESF) under grant 31.963/46-VII/9/2002 and partly by Online Learning Systems Ltd in conjunction with the New Zealand Foundation for Research, Science & Technology.

W. Nejdl and K. Tochtermann (Eds.): EC-TEL 2006, LNCS 4227, pp. 470–475, 2006.
© Springer-Verlag Berlin Heidelberg 2006

domain competence, and learning styles. For example, the estimation of domain competence is subjective and for identifying the cognitive traits and learning styles, comprehensive tests or questionnaire-based surveys have to be performed. An alternative approach is to track the students' behaviour and infer the required information from this behaviour. The challenge of this approach is to identify enough information from the learners' behaviour.

To support the information detection process, it is beneficial to find mechanisms that use whatever information about the learner is already available to get as much reliable information to build a more robust student model. In this paper we investigate the relationship between learning styles, in particular the Felder-Silverman learning style model (FSLSM) [5], and working memory capacity, which is one of the cognitive traits included in the Cognitive Trait Model (CTM) [8]. This relationship provides additional information which can be used to improve the identification process of both, the learning style and the cognitive traits, in an adaptive virtual learning environment.

In the next section background information about FSLSM and CTM is provided. Based on the identified relationship from the literature, we present in Section 3 an exploratory study to verify this relationship. Section 4 concludes the paper.

2 Background

In this section Felder-Silverman learning style model and Cognitive Trait Model are explained to provide the theoretical underpinning of the current investigation.

2.1 Felder-Silverman Learning Style Model

While there are several learning style theories, Felder-Silverman Learning Style Model (FSLSM) [5] was chosen for this study for the following reason: most other learning style models classify learners into a few broad groups, whereas Felder and Silverman describe the learning style of learners in more detail. It distinguishes between preferences on four bi-polar dimensions: *active* learners learn by trying things out and working with others whereas *reflective* learners learn by thinking things through and working alone. *Sensing* learners like to learn concrete material and tend to be practical whereas *intuitive* learners prefer to learn abstract material such as theories and their meanings and tend to be more innovative than sensing learners. *Visual* learners remember best what they have seen whereas *verbal* learners get more out of words, regardless whether they are spoken or written. *Sequential* learners learn in linear steps and prefer to follow linear stepwise paths whereas *global* learners learn in large leaps and are characterized as holistic.

Each learner has a preference for each of these four dimensions. The preferences are considered to be tendencies indicating that it is possible that learners with a high preference for certain behaviour may sometimes act differently.

2.2 Cognitive Trait Model

The Cognitive Trait Model (CTM) [8] is a student model that profiles learners according to their cognitive traits. The CTM changes the traditional idea of the student model as just a database sitting on the server which is full of numbers for only a particular task. The CTM provides the role of 'learning companion', which can be consulted by different learning environments about a particular learner. The CTM can still be valid after a long period of time due to the more or less persistent nature of cognitive traits of human beings [3]. When a student encounters a new learning environment, the learning environment can directly use the CTM of the particular student, and does not need to "re-learn the student".

Three cognitive traits, working memory capacity, inductive reasoning ability and associative learning skills, have been included in CTM so far. In the current investigation between CTM and learning style model, only working memory capacity is covered, and it is discussed briefly.

In earlier times, working memory was also referred as short-term memory. Richards-Ward [10] named it the Short-Term Store (STS) to emphasise its role of temporal storage of recently perceived information. STS allows us to keep active a limited amount of information (roughly 7+-2 items) for a brief period of time [9]. While Baddeley [1] defined working memory structurally, others defined it as a process [11]. Even though these two different points of views differ on the structure of the working memory, they both agree that the working memory consists of both storage and operational sub-systems [10].

3 Exploratory Study

In [7] investigations about the relationship between FSLSM and working memory capacity (WMC) are presented. Based on the literature, a relationship between high WMC and a reflective, intuitive, and sequential learning style can be identified. In contrast, learners with low WMC tend to prefer an active, sensing, and global learning style. Regarding the visual-verbal dimension, only a relationship in one direction could be identified. Hence, learners with low WMC tend to prefer a visual learning style but learners with a visual learning style do not necessarily have low WMC. On the other hand, learners with verbal learning style tend to have a high WMC but not all learners with high WMC tend to prefer a verbal learning style.

To verify the relationship identified from the literature, an exploratory study with 39 students was conducted. 19 of them are students at Massey University (New Zealand) and 20 are from Vienna University of Technology (Austria). To measure their learning styles, students completed a questionnaire developed by Felder and Soloman [6]. Their WMC was measured by a web-based version of an operation word span task [4, 12] developed for the study. Both instruments are described in the following section and results are presented after that.

3.1 Instruments

For identifying the learning styles according to FSLSM, the Index of Learning Styles (ILS) [6], a 44-item questionnaire developed by Felder and Soloman, was used. As mentioned earlier, each learner has a personal preference for each dimension. These preferences are expressed with values between +11 (e.g. strong active preference) to -11 (e.g. strong reflective preference) per dimension.

Regarding WMC, we developed a web-based version of the operation word span task (OSPAN) [12], Web-OSPAN. Procedures of GOSPAN [4], a computerized and group-administratable operation word span task, were adopted into Web-OSPAN. In the task, subjects are required to perform simple arithmetical operations such as (2 * 3) + 4 = 10. After each operation, a word is presented. The subjects are asked to answer true or false to a group of arithmetic operations and at the end asked to recall the words presented after each operation.

As proposed by Turner & Engels [12], the total number of correct calculations, the total number of correct recalled words, and the maximum set size the subject had the words recalled correctly are recorded and the total number of correctly recalled words is used as a measure of WMC. Both GOSPAN and Web-OSPAN follows OSPAN [12] in recording these measures.

3.2 Results

The data collected from the Web-OSPAN task and the ILS questionnaire were analysed and the results of this analysis are presented in the following.

Visual/Verbal Dimension. From the described relationship between the visual/verbal dimension and WMC, two conclusions can be drawn: (1) learners with a low WMC tend to prefer a visual learning style (but learners with a high WMC prefer either a visual or a verbal learning style) and (2) highly verbal learners tend to have a high WMC (but visual learners can have either high or low WMC).

Because our dataset includes only 2 students with highly verbal learning style, at this stage of analysis it is not possible to draw any reliable conclusions from these two students.

To answer the first statement, only the visual part of the dimension was analysed. The hypothesis to be tested was whether the learners with a low WMC have a highly visual learning style. The significance level is set to 5 %.

The variance for the LWMC group is 10.07 and that of the HWMC group is 12.54. A 1-tailed t-test with unequal variance was used. The T-Stat value 1.77 is greater than that of the critical value 1.69, with significance level at 0.04, indicating that the difference in visual preference is statistically significant. With the positive T-Stat value, the mean of the LWMC group is larger than that of the HMWC group, and it further confirms that learners with low WMC have a highly visual learning style.

Sensing/Intuitive Dimension. Before testing the relationship, an internal consistency reliability test for the questions of ILS was performed. In the sensing/intuitive dimension, three questions were stated as unreliable and therefore were removed them from further analysis. Hence, the instrument became more reliable and accurate.

As discussed earlier, the literature refers to a correlation between a sensing/ intuitive learning style and WMC, indicating that sensing learners tend to have a low WMC and intuitive learners are more likely to have a high WMC. According to the regression analysis, this trend can be seen but according to the conducted Pearson correlation at the 0.05 level, there is only a significant correlation between a sensing/intuitive preference and the time students needed to perform the task ($r=-0.35$).

Looking at the data and the subjects' characteristics in more detail, it can be seen that there are differences in language skills. Especially for the Web-OSPAN task, where students have to remember words, good language skills are crucial. The task was conducted in German for Austrian students and in English for New Zealand students. While all Austrian students have very good German skills, the English skills of New Zealand students varied quite markedly. Only a few students were native speaker and at least half of them had only moderate English skills.

Therefore, the results of the 20 students from Austria were analysed separately. The conducted Pearson correlation results in a significant negative correlation at the 0.05 level to the WMC groups ($r=-0.51$), the total number of correct recalled words ($r=-0.5$), and the maximum set size the subject had the words recalled correctly ($r=-0.56$). Therefore, we can conclude that for the students with good language skills, the expected relationship suggested in the literature is supported.

Active/Reflective and Sequential/Global Dimension. Regarding these two dimensions, no significant evidence supporting the identified relationship to WMC was found. The results of the Pearson correlation test showed no significant correlation. Therefore, further analysis aiming at identifying hidden variables is necessary and a study with a larger sample size is planned.

4 Conclusion and Future Work

In this paper we investigated the relationship between the Felder-Silverman learning style model and working memory capacity, one of the traits in the Cognitive Trait Model. This relationship can be used, on the one hand, to get additional information about learners in systems which are able to detect either learning styles or cognitive traits. For systems that already consider both, learning styles and cognitive traits, the relationship can be used to build a more robust student model by including the information about learning styles in the detection process of cognitive traits and vice versa.

According to current investigations, learners with a high WMC tend to favour reflective, intuitive, and sequential learning styles, and vice versa. On the other hand, learners with a low WMC tend to prefer active, sensing, visual, and global learning styles. To verify this relationship an exploratory study was performed. The relationship between the sensing/intuitive dimension as well as the visual/verbal dimension is supported by the results of the study. For the two other dimensions, no significant correlations were found. This might be because of the small sample size of the study (39 students) or because of the existence of hidden variables.

Future work deals with enlarging the study to get more significant results and also to be able to analyse the results in more detail. Furthermore, we plan to use the benefits of the verified relationships in a web-based educational system which is able to detect learning styles and cognitive traits. The additional information from the relationship will be used to improve the detection process of cognitive traits and learning styles.

References

1. Baddeley, A.D.: Working Memory. Oxford University Press, Oxford (1986).
2. Brusilovsky, P.: The Construction and Application of Student Models in Intelligent Tutoring Systems. Journal of computer and systems sciences international, Vol. 32, No. 1 (1994) 70-89.
3. Deary, I.J., Whiteman, M.C., Starr, J.M., Whalley, L.J., Fox, H.C.: The Impact of Childhood Intelligence on Later Life: Following Up the Scottish Mental Surveys of 1932 and 1947. Journal of Personality and Social Psychology, Vol. 86, No. 1 (2004) 130-147.
4. De Neys, W., d'Ydewalle, G., Schaeken, W., Vos, G.: A Dutch, computerized, and group administrable adaptation of the operation span test. Psychologica Belgica, Vol. 42 (2002) 177-190.
5. Felder, R.M., Silverman, L.K.: Learning and Teaching Styles in Engineering Education. Engineering Education, Vol. 78, No. 7 (1988) 674–681.
6. Felder, R.M., Soloman, B.A.: Index of Learning Styles Questionnaire, Online version (1997).Retrieved 6 May, 2006, from http://www.engr.ncsu.edu/learningstyles/ ilsweb.html
7. Graf, S., Lin, T., Kinshuk: Improving Student Modeling: The Relationship between Learning Styles and Cognitive Traits. Proceedings of the International Conference on Cognition and Exploratory Learning in Digital Age, Portugal (2005) 37-44.
8. Lin T., Kinshuk, Patel A.: Cognitive Trait Model - A Supplement to Performance Based Student Models. Proceedings of International Conference on Computers in Education, Hong Kong (2003) 629-632.
9. Miller, G.: The magic number seven, plus or minus two: Some limit of our capacity for processing information. Psychology Review, Vol. 63, No. 2 (1956) 81-96.
10. Richards-Ward, L. A.: Investigating the relationship between two approaches to verbal information processing in working memory: An examination of the construct of working memory coupled with an investigation of meta-working memory, Massey University, Palmerston North, New Zealand (1996).
11. Salthouse, T.A., Mitcheel, D.R.D., Skovronek, E., Babcock, R.L.: Effects of adult age and working memory on reasoning abilities. Journal of Experiemental Psychology: Learning, Memory, and Cognition, Vol. 15 (1989) 507-516.
12. Turner, M.L., Engle R.W.: Is working memory capacity task dependent? Journal of Memory and Language, Vol. 28 (1989) 127-154.

Automatic Semantic Activity Monitoring of Distance Learners Guided by Pedagogical Scenarios

Viviane Guéraud and Jean-Michel Cagnat

ARCADE Team
CLIPS – IMAG Laboratory,
BP 53, 38041 Grenoble Cedex 9, France
Viviane.Gueraud@imag.fr
Jean-Michel.Cagnat@imag.fr

Abstract. This paper describes how we propose to assist trainers in their tasks of monitoring a distant group, in the context of learning situations exploiting interactive learning objects (simulations, micro-worlds...). We describe the conceptual model on which we base the monitoring of such learning situations. A scenario, created by the trainer, describes the goal proposed and the various controls to be made during the learner's progression toward this goal. Our tools automatically use the scenario to control the learning object, to monitor the learners' activities and to provide tutors with semantic and synthetic representations of these activities. We also provide automatic assistance to learners. The context of this work is the FORMID project, which has resulted in a computer platform implementing our proposals.

1 Introduction

The use of Learning Management Systems for the development and exploitation of distance training via Internet is nowadays very common. However, we agree with [11] that "although these systems support many tasks related to teaching at distance, the instructors still face a number of problems with managing distance courses effectively; most of which are brought by the difficulty to gain sufficient understanding of [...] distant students." *Active learning situations* in which the learner interacts strongly with an educational tool (micro-worlds, simulations or interactive learning environments) require a specific monitoring approach.

Current Learning Management Systems usually offer the possibility to monitor the succession of activities, but do not provide enough information on the internal progression of each activity (Eifel[1], EduTools[2], LAMS[3]). Consider for instance an activity in which the learner must use a simulation tool. It is usually feasible to include such an activity [1]; if the simulation supports the SCORM standard, the LMS may obtain further information, for instance whether the learner has started or completed the activity. However, since the LMS does not provide detailed

---

[1] Eifel, http://www.eife-l.org
[2] EduTools 2006, Course Management Systems, retrieved from http://www.edutools.info
[3] Learning Management System LAMS, http://www.lamsinternational.com

W. Nejdl and K. Tochtermann (Eds.): EC-TEL 2006, LNCS 4227, pp. 476–481, 2006.

information, the tutor is not able to monitor and to assist the learners. In this paper, we propose a generic solution to this problem.

One of the ARCADE team objectives is to assist the trainer when he acts as an author during the creation phase and when he acts as a tutor in the exploitation phase with a virtual class. The *pedagogical scenario* concept is for us a key element: scenarios are created by trainers (instructors...) to propose a set of activities and goals on *Interactive Learning Objects*, such as simulations, micro-worlds...; scenarios are further used to assist trainers in their task of monitoring the class activity.

The complete exploitation phase concerns both learners and trainers; however, in this presentation we privilege the point of view of the trainer. The task of monitoring learners involved in active learning situations requires more functionalities than commonly offered by current open and distant training platforms.

2 Functions for Monitoring Distant Learning

We focus on what happens during an activity, rather than on the sequencing of activities in a learning unit or on the pedagogical structuring of the global curriculum. We consider situations in which the learner must accomplish a task or solve a problem, while interacting with a learning object. Furthermore, the results presented here concern mainly individual learning situations, and not collaborative activities.

The MDLA (Monitoring Distance Learning Activities) model [5] describes functionalities to assist the distant synchronous monitoring of learners involved in active learning situations. In our opinion, these functionalities provide a global answer to the monitoring requirements and this model, while designed for synchronous monitoring, is also applicable for asynchronous monitoring of the same kind of activities.

Our contribution is to propose monitoring tools that will automatically inform the tutor on the learners' activity (by offering a semantic perception of the activities and a synthetic view of the class activity) and provide assistance to learners.

What is the proper level of detail to monitor effectively the activity of a learner working on an exercise? A trace of elementary actions on the interface (e.g. mouse clicks at such and such locations...) would be useless because such events are too far removed from the task semantic and do not really inform on the learner's difficulties. The system must deliver indicators of a higher level of abstraction that help to appreciate especially the qualitative aspect of the work. There are a large number of possible levels of detail: operations on the learning objects (e.g., a switch has been closed), internal states (e.g., the object has been placed in state S), etc. We have to select the optimal level that will give the tutor the most efficient perception of the learner's activity. We propose the notion of "*semantic perception of the activity*", based on indicators produced by pedagogical scenarios all along the session.

In the MDLA model, the global perception of the class activity is supposed to result from the successive perception of the activities of the individual learners. In order to reduce the cognitive overload that this approach induces on the tutor, the FORMID project offers a *synthetic perception of the class* (or sub-group) activity, in supplement of the perception of the individual activity of each learner.

Another originality of the FORMID project is to provide an *automatic assistance* to the learner. The tutor is able to define by herself the specific assistance to provide to the learners in function of their progression.

3 FORMID Concepts, Mechanisms and Associated Tools

We describe now several FORMID concepts and their roles in the distance monitoring process [9].

The FORMID platform is a software implementation of our concepts. It is designed to host various *active learning situations*, composed of both an *interactive learning object* and a *scenario*. We have used various kinds of *Interactive Learning Objects* (ILOs): simulations (in various scientific domains [4]) and micro-worlds.

The learner must use these ILOs to execute specific tasks and reach specific goals described in *pedagogical scenarios* (*scenarios* in short) which have three roles: define precise activities/goals (*exercise*) proposed to the learners on an ILO.; specify controls to be made on the learner's progression during this activity; define the pedagogical support that will be provided automatically to the learner according to his/her progression [8], [9].

FORMID can integrate ILOs that satisfy at least the following general properties: *inspectability* (one must be able to consult from the outside some variables of the ILO); *scriptability* (one must be able to change from the outside the values of some variables). Our supervisor architecture includes an extensible set of "adapters" for ILOs of different origins. As an example, we have integrated Java simulations generated by *Easy Java Simulations* software [http://fem.um.es/Ejs] without any modifications of these simulations. We also have adapters for Java applets and Flash applications, satisfying varying constraints of inspectability and scriptability.

An *execution supervisor* (or *monitor*) is active on each learner workstation. This component takes advantage of the ILO inspectability and scriptability properties: it verifies the learner's progression with respect to the scenario steps; it transmits monitoring information towards the tutor workstation.

The learner communicates with this monitor through a simple interface (not shown in this paper) in order to select and start the exercise, read assignments and feedback, and request end-of-step validations.

A large part of the learner support is described in the scenario and delegated to the execution supervisor that will automatically assist the learner during the exercise resolution process. This automatic mechanism relieves the tutor of "routine" monitoring tasks, thus allowing him to spend a maximum of time on more difficult aspects requiring his full expertise.

4 Global and Detailed Perception of the Class Activity

The tutor must be able to compare the respective progression of learners among the complete sequence of exercises, as well as in the context of each exercise.

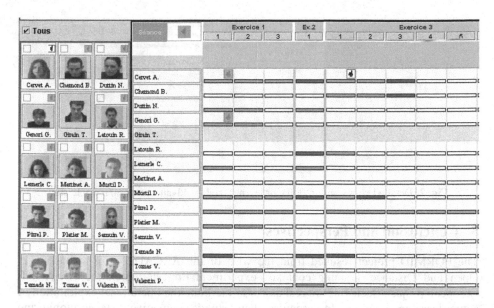

Fig. 1. Global view of the group progression

In the main FORMID interface (shown in Figure 1), the photo panel on the left represents the "virtual class" and identifies the learners. Grayed boxes correspond to non connected learners. In the upper part of the central "progression monitoring" zone, we have a set of exercises, and the various steps composing each exercise. This structure gives meaning to the content of the lines in the lower main part.

We have one line per learner. Different colors show the progression for each step: red (or dark) indicates a validation request issued by the learner, but refused by the monitor; green (or medium gray) indicates an accepted validation request.

This synthetic information is sufficient to make a diagnostic on the activity of the class, identify learners that progress either very slowly or very fast, locate quickly the main difficulties of the whole class. The tutor is thus able to react more efficiently to the class difficulties.

The automatic support mechanism delivers information to the learners without any intervention from the tutor, but two more detailed views are available to the tutor.

On the left (in Figure 2), we monitor the class activity for a chosen step (step 1 of exercise 1): detected controls and requested validation. Colors are again used to distinguish "bad" such as errors, "good", or "neutral" (no judgment value) situations.

We can also monitor the chronological activity of a single learner in a given step (on the right, in Figure 2). The central part gives a detailed chronology of the activity of this learner. Each line corresponds to the time flow (from top to bottom). The tutor may evaluate more precisely the approach used by the learner when facing problems.

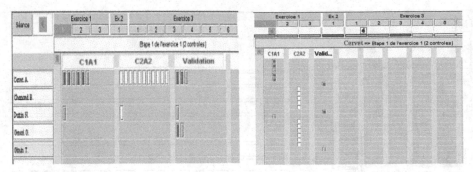

Fig. 2. Detailed views: group (left), or learner (right), advancement on a single step

5   Conclusion and Perspectives

The FORMID project resulted from the wish of the ARCADE team to pursue, in Open and Distance Training contexts, experimentation started in the ARIADNE European project. Scenarios are real assets to facilitate the operational exploitation of active learning situations. In particular, they provide innovative distance monitoring functionalities, as demonstrated by the FORMID platform. We are now validating their usefulness and their usability by experimentation in real instructional contexts, in the context of the European Network of Excellence Kaleidoscope[4].

The integration (in progress) of our tools in open and distance learning platforms will extend the usability of our tools and provide more experimentation opportunities. We will thus bring our contribution to the various researches on the definition of a tutor workstation for distant monitoring. In addition to the various functionalities discussed above, an ideal workstation should also let the tutor perceive various factors that influence learning. These factors can be related to emotional states [2], [3]; social behavior of learners [6]; group cohesion, group interactions [12]; information from collaborative dialog analysis [7], [14]. In parallel with research on each of these aspects, specific works consider how to better use the trails (or tracks) databases to give the tutor pertinent visual representations [11] or new information extracted by data mining techniques [13].

We facilitate the tutor's tasks by providing directly to the learners an appropriate assistance. Researchers should also be able to use our tools for the supervision of experimentation with virtual classes.

References

1. Burgos D., Tattersall C., Koper R., Re-purposing existing generic games and simulations for e-learning, Open University of the Netherlands, Nov. 2005, OUNL Dspace Service, http://hdl.handle.net/1820/508.
2. Chaffar S., Frasson C., Inducing Optimal Emotional State for Learning in Intelligent Tutoring Systems, International Conference Intelligent Tutoring Systems (ITS'04), Lecture Notes in Computer Science LNCS 3220, Brazil, Aug.-Sept. 2004, pp 45-54.

---

[4] http://www.noe-kaleidoscope.org

3. Conati C., Maclare H., Evaluating a Probabilistic Model of Student Affect, International Conference Intelligent Tutoring Systems (ITS'04), Lecture Notes in Computer Science LNCS 3220, Brazil, Aug.-Sept. 2004, pp 55-66.
4. Cortés G., Guéraud V., Experimentation of an authoring tool for pedagogical simulations, International Conference CALISCE'98, Göteborg, Sweden, 1998.
5. Després C., Synchronous Tutoring in Distance Learning: A model for the synchronous pedagogical monitoring of distance learning activities, Artificial Intelligence in Education (AIED 2003), IOS Press 2003, p271-278.
6. George S., Leroux P., An Approach to Automatic Analysis of Learners' Social Behavior During Computer-Mediated Synchronous Conversations, International Conference Intelligent Tutoring Systems (ITS'02), Lecture Notes in Computer Science LNCS 1363, Biarritz, France and San Sebastian, Spain, June 2002, pp 630-640.
7. Gerosa M.A., Pimentel M.G., Fuks H., Lucena C., Analysing Discourse Structure to Coordinate Educational Forums, International Conference ITS'04, Lecture Notes in Computer Science LNCS 3220, Brazil, Aug.-Sept.2004, pp 262-272.
8. Guéraud V., Pernin J.-P., Cagnat J.-M., Cortés G., Environnements d'apprentissage basés sur la simulation: outils-auteur et expérimentations, Revue Sciences et Techniques Educatives, Vol.6 n°1, p. 95-141, Hermès, 1999.
9. Guéraud V., Adam J-M., Pernin J-P., Calvary G., David J-P. L'exploitation d'Objets Pédagogiques Interactifs à distance: le projet FORMID. Revue STICEF, vol.11, 2004, ISSN: 1764-7223, pp 109-164 (www.sticef.org).
10. Mabbott A., Bull S., Alternative Views on knowledge : Presentation of Open Learner Models, International Conference Intelligent Tutoring Systems (ITS'04), Lecture Notes in Computer Science LNCS 3220, Brazil, Aug.-Sept. 2004, pp 55-66.
11. Mazza R., Dimitrova V., CourseVis : Externalising Student Information to facilitate Instructors in Distant Learning, Artificial Intelligence in Education, AIED 03, Eds U. Hoppe, F. Verdejo, J. Kay., IOS Press, July 2003, pp279-286.
12. Mbala A., Reffay C., Chanier T., Integration of Automatic Tools for Displaying Interaction Data in Computer Environments for Distance Learning, International Conference Intelligent Tutoring Systems (ITS'02), Lecture Notes in Computer Science LNCS 1363, Biarritz, France and San Sebastian, Spain, June 2002, pp 841-850.
13. Merceron A., Yacef K., A Web-Based Tutoring Tool with Mining Facilities to Improve Learning ant Teaching, Artificial Intelligence in Education, AIED 03, Eds U. Hoppe, F. Verdejo, J. Kay., IOS Press, July 2003, pp279-286.
14. Vieira A.C., Teixeira L., Timoteo A., Tedesco P., Barros F., Analysing Online Collaborative Dialogues, International Conference Intelligent Tutoring Systems (ITS'04), Lecture Notes in Computer Science LNCS 3220, Brazil, Aug.-Sept. 2004, pp 315-324.

Electronic Portfolios as a Means for Initializing Learner Models for Adaptive Tutorials

Zinan Guo and Jim Greer

ARIES Laboratory, Department of Computer Science, University of Saskatchewan
Saskatoon, Saskatchewan, S7N 5C9, Canada
zig094@mail.usask.ca, jim.greer@usask.ca

Abstract. Using electronic portfolios (e-portfolios) to assist learning is an important component of future educational models. We show how to use the information contained in e-portfolios to initialize learner models for adaptive tutorials. E-portfolios become sources of evidence for claims about prior conceptual knowledge or skills. An experiment is designed for testing how accurate a model can be built and how beneficial this approach can be for reflective and personalized learning. Monitoring this process can also help tutorial developers and experts identify how initial learner models may automatically arise from e-portfolios.

Keywords: electronic portfolio, learner model initialization, adaptive tutorial, adaptive learning environment.

1 Introduction

Electronic portfolios are defined as an organized collection of digital and/or analog artifacts and reflective statements that demonstrate a learner's intellectual development over time [1]. The rapidly growing use of e-portfolios in higher education, especially in online learning, provides students a user-centered file management option. Many schools and universities have developed e-portfolio systems where students are encouraged to store and organize artifacts during their formal schooling and to further carry on with augmenting that e-portfolio during lifelong learning. E-portfolios can offer advantages in demonstration of skills, learner reflection, collaboration, and assessment. The portfolio offers the possibility to show how the learner "conquers" the subject domain during the work or learning process. In this lies also the possibility to discover connections across subject areas and to develop a meta-perspective on the student's own learning and knowledge [7].

Research about adaptive tutorials [9] has identified why an adaptive tutorial is helpful for the learner and how maximum benefits can be gained. A suitable learner model for adaptive tutorial courseware includes four main categories: aptitude, prior learning experience, cognitive learning style, and personal characteristics. Adaptive tutorial systems hold much in common with the more mature research area of Intelligent Tutoring Systems (ITS), but ITS research focuses more on detailed problem-solving processes than on tutorial interactions. The common goal of both ITS and adaptive tutorials is to provide adaptive and individualized instruction.

W. Nejdl and K. Tochtermann (Eds.): EC-TEL 2006, LNCS 4227, pp. 482–487, 2006.

Learner models are specialized mechanisms for representing information and knowledge of learners inside adaptive/ personalized learning environments. In general, learner models are in the form of detailed cognitive models of the learner, and are maintained along with learning interactions in order to recommend suitable learning resources or to provide individualized help during problem solving. Learner models frequently contain information about the knowledge levels of learners on various domain concepts of interest.

In this paper, we investigate how a learner model can be bootstrapped using e-portfolios when a learner begins to interact with an adaptive tutorial. A standardized information model of e-portfolios is first discussed. A method of student model initialization with a system design is presented. An experiment, now underway, is also discussed where domain experts are invited to evaluate the method of bootstrapping and evidencing initial learner models from student e-portfolios.

2 E-Portfolio Information Model and Specifications

A standardized e-portfolio information model explains what information is generally contained in e-portfolios, while a set of specifications are defined to describe the organization of the e-portfolio. The IMS ePortfolio information model specifications have been proposed and deemed a plausible set. With these specifications, standardized meta-data can be bound to artifacts in an e-portfolio making them easier to interpret and maintain across different institutions and platforms/systems [5]. The content in an e-portfolio may be widely varied, but the associated meta-data should conform to more standard and predictable formats. An e-portfolio is defined as a collection of multiple portfolio parts that are collated in an IMS Content Package. All of the contextual information for a portfolio, e.g., presentation aids, relationships, etc., are also defined within the IMS Content Package. In essence the manifest file for the IMS Content Package is the XML representation of the Portfolio with each of the portfolio parts being supplied as resources in the content package. The set of resources contains any source materials that are described as part of the portfolio, e.g., examples of work, copies of certificates, etc. For the case of nested portfolios, each portfolio is defined in its own content package, i.e. with a single manifest file. Sets of portfolios are clustered by creating a top-level content package in which each portfolio package is a resource. This standard structure makes it easy for learners to query and track portfolio parts at different granularity levels and reference them in other applications by making reference simply to a universal resource identifier.

These features of e-portfolios proposed by IMS were defined and extended from the IMS Learner Information Package specification [6]. Types of portfolio parts are described in up to 18 catalogues that describe not only essential learner and learning information, e.g. identification, goal, competency etc. but also some contextual information for an e-portfolio, e.g. relationship, access and security control, etc. Some of these elements can be attached to learner models as a form of evidence for certain cognitive skills or learning acquisitions. The decision as to which elements should be used for which aspects of a particular learner model is made along with the process of bootstrapping the learner model.

3 Initializing a Learner Model

Many issues could arise in initializing learner models in different adaptive learning systems. However, these can be categorized into four general phases based on: who is being modelled, what is being modelled, how the model is acquired and maintained, and how the model might be used [4]. Traditionally, these questions are addressed by developers and answered through natural language interaction with students. The accuracy is strongly affected by domain/subject matter, and tends to be hard to verify. Extracting information as learning evidence from e-portfolios to initialize student models will enrich the content of learner models and make the model more likely to be browsed and edited by the students themselves.

Three main methods of bootstrapping a learner models are: 1. users outlining their own learning goals; 2. users providing a self-description (general personal information); 3. users being given a pre-test on the subject area [3]. Both 1 and 2 are easy to adapt to e-portfolio information extraction with partial automation and assistance, but achieving 3 requires fairly detailed e-portfolio instances that need to be mapped and interpreted from a standardized information model. For this reason, we are focusing on an approach where a customized interface is provided for permitting students (or teachers) to link evidence from an e-portfolio with answers to questions about their knowledge-state. Previous research has shown reflective comments (from human tutor and peers) about problem-solving activities to be effective in helping students reason about their own learning behaviours [8]. Since some students may have a hard time remembering details about their prior learning activities, this evidencing process is believed to be helpful as it "forces" students to browse their own learning records. The process of "evidencing" their claims is an important reflection activity, which we expect can be shown to support learning.

Table 1 presents some identified relationships between learner models and e-portfolio components at an abstract class level. It shows the potential that components of a standardized e-portfolio could be mapped to values in a learner model or linked as evidence. As shown in the table, artifacts in a standardized e-portfolio and their annotations may contribute to nearly all aspects of learner model information. For example, identification and participation can be mapped to general and personal learner information, while activity, assertion and reflection can be used to evidence and support (meta) knowledge and skill level. It seems also that attaching machine-generated meta-data to students' e-portfolios would be beneficial for further use by some other adaptive learning system. Thus, learner model information generated by an adaptive learning environment could itself be an important artifact in an e-portfolio and could potentially be transferable to other learning systems via the learner's e-portfolio.

3.1 System Design

An overview of our system with its high-level data flow is presented in Figure 1. The content and associated meta-data in an e-portfolio serve as the input. Although e-portfolios do not represent explicit models of cognitive capabilities, they contain evidence that may justify claims about the learner's knowledge or skills. The extension to the learner model is essentially a set of rules and an interface to e-portfolios. The process for populating the learner model must fit with the specific requirements of the adaptive tutorial system (ATS), and hence needs to be engineered by the learning environment developer. Students could/should be involved in the process of initializing learner models by using dialogue and message confirmation in three steps: 1. establish a set of essential questions about cognitive state based on the requirements of the ATS; 2. present these questions to the student with a suitable e-portfolio meta-data browsing tool; 3. monitor the student to locate evidence in the portfolio to confirm claims made in answer to these questions. The quality of the interpretation from e-portfolios to learner models is determined by a set of initialization rules and specialized interfaces, which in our system are to be pre-defined according to the expected format of the associated learner model. Interfaces to extract information and import it into the learner model will be affected by specific goals and design aspects of the adaptive tutorial system as well as domain ontologies. Currently, the learner needs to manually select a set of artifacts and annotations from all the e-portfolio data as evidence to build their learner models through pre-defined questions, in which the learner gains an opportunity for reflective learning. Domain ontologies will be used for searching required semantic terms that are related to key words in a pretest question in the e-portfolio repository.

The evidencing process has been applied in a web-based application where the learner uses a slider to justify the claim on their skill levels, and attaches evidence using browse and search functions in a pop-up portfolio browser. The portfolio browser has two highlight features to assist browsing: "search relationship" that finds a pair of artifacts according to <relationship> meta-data, and "ontological assistance" that help the learner identify all available related artifacts to a concept or a topic. For

Table 1. How an e-portfolio part could be linked to learner model as evidence

Main category	Details and Comments	IMS ePortfolio Spec
Who is being modelled	Degree of specialization Individuals/classes of learners	<identification> <participation>
	Temporal extent, Learner history	<activity>, <affiliation>, <qcl>, <transcript>
What is being modelled	knowledge and meta knowledge	<activity>, <assertion>, <product>, <reflexion>
	Learner goal/intentions	<goal>
	Capabilities	<competency>, <qcl>
	Preferences	<accessForAll>, <interest>
	Motivations	<interest>,<goal>,<reflexion>
How is the model to be acquired	users outlining own goals	*Packaging + Binding*
	users providing a self-description	*Packaging + Binding*
	users given a pre-test on subject	<competency>
How is the model to be maintained	Compare learning path and tutorial system planned strategy	<activity>, <assertion>
Why is the model there	Elicit info from learner	<assertion>, <competency>
	Provide advice/help	<assertion>
	Provide feedback	<assertion>
	Interpret learner's activity	<assertion>, <activity>

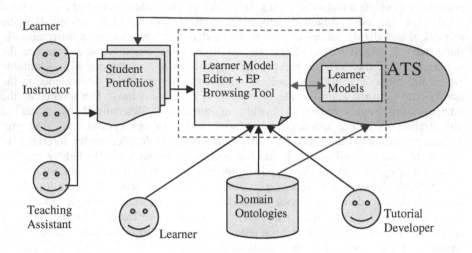

Fig. 1. An overview of the system

instance, when a product is found matched with a certain topic, associated meta-data such as assertion, goal and reflection are identified and made ready to link to a learner model.

An experiment using the system is being conducted to identify the feasibility of initializing an accurate learner model from an e-portfolio. We are utilizing domain experts to take actual student e-portfolios and proceed through the "evidencing" process for an adaptive tutorial on the topic of "Abstract Data Types (ADT) in Java". (The tutorial has not been fully implemented; however the ontology of the tutorial and expected learner models are.) The experts also will be invited to an interview where together they can share and discuss their judgments and comments on the proposed approach. The e-portfolio were built from real student learning materials and experiences collected from an entry-level Java programming, including assignments, quizzes, exams, Q&A, instructor's feedback and self-reflective comments. The topics covered in this course have overlaps with both the prerequisite and regular content of the ADT tutorial. The questions for evidencing student's knowledge mainly focus on concepts that fall in the overlap.

4   Conclusion

The artifacts in an e-portfolio should be browseable in human-readable form and this leads to the requirement that learner models, in order to be useful e-portfolio artifacts, be inspectable by users. Research in open learner modelling has shown that inspectable learner models can bring benefits to students and teachers. After completing a session with a learning environment, the learner model could be transferred as a new artifact to the learner's e-portfolio. Attaching inspectable learner models to e-portfolios may provide another means for learner reflection.

This research activity is also connected with the larger issue of e-portfolio assessment as well as prior learning assessment. E-portfolio assessment involves evaluating learner achievement relative to pre-defined rubrics and utilizing the e-portfolio elements as evidence sources for achievement of prescribed learning outcomes. This has some striking similarity to the method described in this paper for initializing learner models. It also bears some similarity to inspectable learner modelling. The use of e-portfolio allows qualifications to be changed to focus more on the actual core of what needs to be assessed, rather than peripheral efforts to record and administer students work [2]. The same could be said of learner models! Student self-assessment and portfolio assessment included in the e-portfolios can be beneficial for learner information management in personalized and adaptive learning environment.

This short paper provides a preliminary discussion about how standardized e-portfolios and learner models can be connected. It also presents a system with both a learner model editor and an e-portfolio visualization tool that may assist learners in initializing student models with portfolio evidence. It describes an experiment aimed at testing whether learners can gain any benefit in reflective and personalized learning from this approach. Monitoring this process can also help developers and designers of adaptive learning environment identify how an initial learner model can further automatically arise from an e-portfolio. It shows how learner reflection can be supported through the inspection of e-portfolios and demonstrates yet another way in which inspectable learner models can be used to enhance learning.

References

1. Barrett,H.C. (2001), "Electronic Portfolios—A chapter in Educational Technology; An Encyclopedia to be published by ABC-CLIO", [online].
   <http:www.electronicportfolios.com/portfolios/encyclopediaentry.htm>.
2. Grant, P. (2005) Enriching Assessment with ePortfolios, in proceedings of ePortfolio 2005, Cambridge UK.
3. Greer, J., & McCalla, G., (1994) Student Models: The Key to Individualized Knowledge-Based Instruction, NATO ASI Series F: Computer and Systems Sciences, vol. 125, Springer Verlag, Berlin Heidelberg.
4. Holt, P., Dubs, S., Jones, M., and Greer, J., (1994) The State of Student Modelling, "Student Models: The Key to Individualized Knowledge-Based Instruction", NATO ASI Series F: Computer and Systems Sciences, vol. 125, Springer Verlag, Berlin.5-20.
5. IMS ePortfolio Specification (2005), IMS Global Learning Consortium, Inc. http://www. imsproject.org/ep/index.html, accessed 6/15/2006
6. IMS Learner Information Package Specification (2005), IMS Global Learning Consortium, Inc. http://www.imsproject.org/profiles/index.html, accessed 6/15/2006
7. Nordeng, T.W., Dicheva,D., Garshol, L.M., etc. (2005), Using Topic Maps for Integrating ePortfolio with eCurriculum, in proceedings of ePortfolio 2005, Cambridge UK.
8. Pon-Barry, H., Clark, B., Schultz, K., Bratt, E O., Peters, S., & Haley, D. (2005) Contextualizing Reflective Dialogue in a Spoken Conversational Tutor .Educational Technology & Society, 8 (4), 42-51.
9. Toshiyuki Urata, Developing Adaptive Tutorial Courseware to Support Students in Distance Education, Presented at Poster Session, EDUCAUSE Annual Conferences, November 2003.

New Media for Teaching Applied Cryptography and Network Security

Ji Hu, Dirk Cordel, and Christoph Meinel

The Hasso-Plattner-Institute (HPI), University of Potsdam, Postfach 900460,
D-14440 Potsdam, Germany
{ji.hu, cordel, meinel}@hpi.uni-potsdam.de

Abstract. Considering that security education needs to train students to deal with security problems in real environments, we developed new media for teaching applied cryptography and network security. They permit students to gain real-life security experience from virtual laboratories on CD, DVD, or online. The application of those media is helpful to reduce investment and administration costs as well as effectively support security experiments which previously had to be done in conventional security laboratories.

1   Introduction

Teaching only theoretical facts has proved to be insufficient for today's IT security education because security teaching is focusing more on preparing the skillful workforce in response to increasing security challenges [1]. In this context, we must meet the need of training students to apply security technologies for real environments. So far, computer helps practical security instruction in four ways:

Multimedia courseware is digitized lectures [12]. It provides no user interaction or real experiences; Demonstration software, e.g. [3], [13] allows learners to play with cryptographic algorithms, but in very few cases, real tools or everyday environments are involved; Simulation systems let students accomplish security tasks in a very abstract and limited environment. This means that students have no chances to apply production tools [8], [11]; Dedicated computer laboratories [9] and [14] are practical for security training because security exercises are performed with production software on real systems. However, they require expensive hardware/software investment and intensive efforts to create, configure, and maintain laboratory environments. Moreover most security exercises require privileged access to the OS, which introduces the risk of misuse and inconvenience of administration [14]. For security reason, dedicated networks are isolated from production networks and not able to benefit the learners outside the campus.

The Tele-Lab IT-Security project of the Hasso-Plattner-Institute has developed new media to support learning/teaching applied cryptography and network security. In order to integrate hands-on experiences, Tele-Lab created virtual and

W. Nejdl and K. Tochtermann (Eds.): EC-TEL 2006, LNCS 4227, pp. 488–493, 2006.

lightweight laboratories on the CD, DVD, or online instead of constructing expensive traditional security laboratories. Students thus can gain real-life security experiences with CD/DVD or Internet connections without the limitation of time and place.

The following parts of the paper are organized as follows: Section 2 briefly introduces the Tele-Lab concept and architecture. Section 3 and Section 4 presents Tele-Lab CD/DVD and Tele-Lab server respectively. Then Section 5 describes application of Tele-Lab and shows how they can support daily teaching and learning. Finally, Section 6 concludes the paper.

2   The Tele-Lab Concept

Tele-Lab is intended to produce computer-aided tutoring systems that allow students to learn about IT security and also gain practical skills. Its contents cover many aspects of applied cryptography and network security such as encryption, authentication, email security, firewalls, intrusion detection, wireless security, etc. The originality of Tele-Lab is that it integrates real-life exercises and laboratory environments in e-learning/tutoring systems to help students understand how technologies are applied in reality. E.g. Tele-Lab not only explains and demonstrates encryption algorithms, but also offers students chances to apply cryptographic tools like PGP or OpenSSL to encrypt or digitally sign messages.

The concept of Tele-Lab is illustrated in Figure 1. Basically it consists of a Linux system and a tutoring system. The Linux system is equipped with various open-source security tools such as scanners and password crackers, and can be used as a virtual laboratory. The tutor is a local web server that presents teaching contents stored in a knowledge repository and manages exercises scripts. A user reads theoretical part by a web browser and finishes exercises by applying tools in Linux. User's results can be either text or data sent to the tutor or some changes on the operating system such as modifying configurations or opening/closing services. The tutor then evaluates the results by scripts. Hence, interactive and real-life exercises are realized.

Tele-Lab replaces most administration work by managing configurations and exercises with scripts. But security exercises introduce risk of misuses because

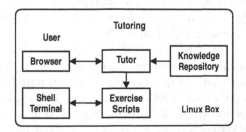

Fig. 1. The concept of Tele-Lab IT-Security

students are allowed to be a super user in many exercises, e.g. starting or closing services. Thus students might corrupt Tele-Lab by misusing their privileges, which results in administrative inconvenience and interruption of the learning process.

3   Tele-Lab CD: A Reliable and Portable Virtual Laboratory

In order to improve the reliability of the Tele-Lab and ease its administration, we developed Tele-Lab CD/DVD [5]. It integrates the entire Tele-Lab on a Knoppix live-CD. This kind of CD has a special feature to detect a rich set of hardware and run a complete Linux on itself instead of installing it on a hard disk.

By implementing Tele-Lab on live CDs, we have a portable and reliable virtual laboratory. It can be distributed to students for the training at home or in the workplaces on general PCs. Tele-Lab CD will not affect hardware and software installations and runtime failures can be simply handled by re-booting.

4   Tele-Lab Server: Virtual Laboratories on the Internet

Tele-Lab CD/DVD has its limitation of usability: it only runs on those machines which the Live CD supports and can not provide network security exercises because of its performance and space limits. From the point of view of e-learning, it is desirable that students can work with Tele-Lab over the Internet. Therefore, we came up with the idea to develop an online learning and exercising platform, Tele-Lab IT-Security Server [5]. Tele-Lab server differs from Tele-Lab CD by building virtual laboratories with virtual machines instead of Live CDs. Virtual machines (VMs) [4] are software copies of physical machines and can be connected to networks. This provides the possibilities to simulate real laboratory environments cheaply and for students to access them online easily.

The architecture of Tele-Lab server is shown in Figure 2. The user work environments are built with the User-Mode Linux virtual machines [2]. They behave normal applications running on a host computer and accessible from outside the host as any regular computer. Each VM is carefully installed and configured with security tools and user settings. Careful performance optimizations such as system resource allocations and separation among VMs are done for making VMs smaller and faster. A host can run multiple VM copies and their destruction would not result in any negative effects on the host. Therefore, it is possible to grant students super-user rights on a VM.

The user interface to VMs is realized by a remote desktop access service, VNC [10]. VNC implements a remote frame buffer (RFB) protocol which can collect inputs from a remote client, encodes the desktop updates of the VM, and sends them back to the client. VNC also supports java-applet clients, and then the VNC clients can run inside a browser. Such a thin user interface permits students to access VMs via a standard browser without installing special client software.

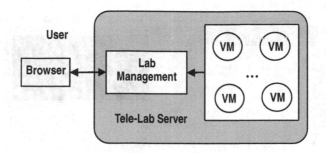

Fig. 2. Tele-Lab Server: a virtual machine based training system

Big concerns for running Tele-Lab online are its reliability and security. Firstly, VMs can be corrupted by users who have super-user rights. Second, it is also possible that VMs are converted to an attack station by their users for compromising production networks. Therefore, we developed VM management and security solutions to make Tele-Lab reliable and safe.

The status of VMs and user operations are monitored in real-time and defective VMs will be restored to default settings automatically. Security of Tele-Lab focuses on system and network level isolations which jail users inside the VM and prevent them from accessing production networks. The host OS is protected against intrusions from VM processes by separation between VMs and the host. We have a firewall between a VM and the production networks against network attacks from the VM. Further details about VM management and security can be found in [7].

5   Application

Tele-Lab mainly supports learning/teaching cryptography and network security. It can also be adapted for other subjects and user groups. E.g. Tele-Lab can provide exercises for lectures, can be a complete e-learning program, or can be customized for industrial training. The feedback from the students who tried using Tele-Lab shows it was easy to follow theoretical parts and complete most exercises without help of a human instructor. If students are unfamiliar with Linux, some exercises about Linux security (e.g. the iptables firewall) would be a little bit difficult for them. However, other more general exercises can be handled without special Linux skills. E.g secure email exercises only require the skills to use browsers and email clients in a graphical environment. This indicates that the use of Linux as a laboratory platform might bring some difficulties but it is still an effective solution for IT students.

5.1   Example Chapter: Password-Based Authentication

This chapter is about how users are authenticated by passwords and how passwords are protected in Linux. In its exercise, privileged operations are involved.

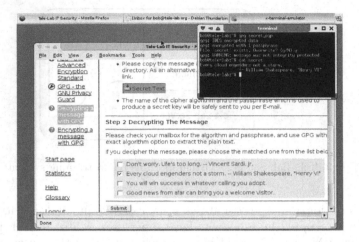

Fig. 3. Tele-Lab user interface

A user needs to crack a Linux passwd file with an open-source cracker, John-the-Ripper. The typical learning process includes following steps:

1. Concepts like password hashing (DES and MD5), "passwd/shadow" file, and advice on strong passwords are introduced.
2. Relevant password tools are presented. They include the "passwd" command, PAM (the Linux "Pluggable Authentication Modules"), and the John-the-Ripper password cracker.
3. In the exercise of password cracking, the work environment is prepared first. The system's password hashing mode is initialized to use DES algorithm.
4. A group of random passwords is generated and saved as a "passwd" file.
5. The user needs to download the "passwd" file and apply a root account for running the system level program, John-the-Ripper.
6. The user switches to the root user mode and runs John-the-Ripper to decode passwords. The user interfaces are shown in Figure 3.
7. After the plain passwords are found, the tutor examines the submission and saves completion records.

6   Conclusions

Tele-Lab IT-Security provides new media for teaching practical IT security. They allow students not only to learn security concepts and principles, but also to experiment security and gain hands-on experiences in a lightweight and safe laboratory environment. Tele-Lab is not to completely substitute the role of conventional security laboratories, e.g. it is hard to include those exercises which need complicated network environments; Security on Windows platforms has also not yet been addressed. Instead Tele-Lab is to provide more practical features and alternatives to traditional ways. In summary, Tele-Lab is a research attempt to fill the gap between e-learning and practical security training. This work has demonstrated the possibility to implement hands-on security laboratories on the Internet reliably, securely, and economically.

References

1. Bishop, M. (2000). Education in information security. IEEE Concurrency, 8(4):4–8.
2. Dike, J. (2001). User-mode Linux. In Proceedings of the 5th Annual Linux Show-case & Conference, Oakland, California, USA.
3. Esslinger, B. (2002). Cryptool - spielerischer einstieg in klassische und moderne kryptographie: Neue version - fundierte awareness in deutsch und englisch. Daten-schutz und Datensicherheit, 26(10).
4. Goldberg, R. P. (1974). Survey of virtual machine research. IEEE Computer, pages 34–45.
5. Hu, J. and Meinel, C. (2004). Tele-Lab IT-Security on CD: Portable, reliable and safe IT Security training. Computers & Security, Elsevier, 23(4):282–289.
6. Hu, J., Meinel, Ch., and Schmitt, M. (2004). Tele-Lab IT Security: An Architecture for Interactive Lessons for Security Education. In Proceedings of ACM SIGCSE Norfolk, Virginia, USA 2004.
7. Hu, J., Cordel, D., and Meinel, C. (2005). Virtual machine management for Tele-Lab IT-Security server. In Proceedings of IEEE ISCC 2005, pages 448–453.
8. Irvine, C. E. and Thompson, M. F. (2004). Expressing an information security policy within a security simulation game. In Proceedings of the Sixth Workshop on Education in Computer Security (WECS6), pages 43–49, Monterey, USA.
9. Ragsdale, D., Lathrop, S., and Dodge, R. (2003). Enhancing information warfare education through the use of virtual and isolated networks. Journal of Information Warfare, 2(3):53–65.
10. Richardson, T., Stafford-Fraser, Q., Wood, K. R., and Hopper, A. (1998). Virtual network computing. IEEE Internet Computing, 2(1): 33–38.
11. Rowe, N. C. and Schiavo, S. (1998). An intelligent tutor for intrusion detection on computer systems. Computers and Education, 31:395–404.
12. Schillings, V. and Meinel, C. (2002). Tele-TASK - tele-teaching anywhere solution kit. In Proceedings of ACM SIGUCCS 2002, Providence, USA.
13. Spillman, R. (2002). CAP: A software tool for teaching classical cryptology. In Proceedings of the 6th National Colloquium on Information System Security Ed-ucation, Redmond, Washington, USA.
14. Vigna, G. (2003). Teaching hands-on network security: Testbeds and live exercises. Journal of Information Warfare, 2(3):8–24.

Initiating Technology-Enhanced Learning at a Public-Sector Institution in a Developing Country

Muhammad F. Kaleem

COMSATS Institute of Information Technology, Lahore, Pakistan
farhat@gmail.com

Abstract. This paper describes the experience of the author in setting up a project for lecture delivery using electronic academic content with the aim of initiating technology-enhanced learning activities in a public-sector institution of higher learning in Pakistan. The project was aimed at undergraduate engineering students, and the author was the instructor of an engineering course. The paper will explain the background which influenced the scope of the project, and list out the objectives set for the project. The setup used for lecture delivery will be described, and the advantages and limitations of the approach will be highlighted. The paper will also present and categorize different problems faced during the project and highlight their impact on the project. Finally, the plans and work-in-progress to continue and enhance the scope of the project in the future will be presented.

1 Introduction

This paper will describe a project to initiate technology-enhanced learning undertaken at the electrical engineering department of a public-sector institute in Pakistan. The institute is relatively new, established in 2002, and offers a four-years (8-semsters) bachelor's degree in electrical engineering (the institute also offers degrees in other disciplines). The project was carried out by the author as an instructor to an introductory Electronics course taught to students in the third semester.

Since the institution is new, it lacks a general infrastructure which could facilitate initiation of technology-enhanced learning. Resources (e.g. financial resources) which could be utilized for technology-enhanced learning are also lacking. Therefore, any effort at technology-enhanced learning, while aiming at improving the efficiency of learning, should have the ability to improvise innovative methods and approaches which are cost-effective, as well as remain non-intrusive to the existing learning methodology.

In this context, the rest of the paper will be used to briefly describe details of the project. The background in which the project was initiated will be explained, and the main objectives of the project will be listed. The setup used for technology-enhanced learning will be described, and our observations with respect to the effort for technology-enhanced learning will be explained. Finally, some problems faced by us in the process will be mentioned, and some future plans will be highlighted.

W. Nejdl and K. Tochtermann (Eds.): EC-TEL 2006, LNCS 4227, pp. 494–499, 2006.
© Springer-Verlag Berlin Heidelberg 2006

2 Background

Almost all of the teaching at the electrical engineering department is done using the classical approach [11]. Some instructors occasionally use computer-based, or electronic slides, which are projected in the classroom using a data projector. However, any writing during the lecture is done on the whiteboard, and electronic slides are mostly used for demonstrative purposes. At present no course is conducted by lectures which are delivered entirely using computer-based slides. One other aspect of teaching engineering courses, though not limited to them, is that these are very writing intensive. This means that preparing electronic slides for lecture delivery, containing equations and diagrams, requires much effort. This also means that during lecture delivery, the instructor may need to write equations, or draw diagrams [9].

Though there is in general awareness of technology-enhanced learning, mainly among those instructors who have in the recent past studied in Europe or the USA, there is no effort at any technology-enhanced learning initiative at the institute. The campus is networked through a LAN, and broadband internet access is available to all teachers, and also to students through computer pools, however none of the courses being offered at the electrical engineering department has its webpage.

2.1 Objectives of the Project

Given the background as presented previously, the objectives of the project could be listed as the following individual points:

1. promote an efficient learning environment based on innovative use of inexpensive technology
2. enhance the teaching and classroom experience, providing flexibility in lecture delivery, as well as an effective interaction protocol between the instructor and students
3. allow active student involvement and interaction
4. supplement the classroom learning experience with the possibility of distance learning
5. allow adoption and gradual enhancement of e-learning activities on a sustainable basis

2.2 Lecture Delivery Setup Description

We used a setup that allowed us to use inexpensive technology innovatively, conformant to objective 1 as listed in section 2.1. The lectures were delivered using electronic slides projected in the classroom using a data projector. To prepare the slides, digital ink was used to draw figures, circuit diagrams, and also to write text. For using digital ink, a cheap USB based tablet pen device was used. The author used his own laptop for lecture preparation and delivery. The data projector was placed on a moveable trolley during the lecture. Figure 1 shows the lecture delivery setup. The instructor's position behind the trolley is depicted, which enables him to write on the tablet pen device while facing the students.

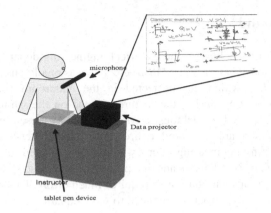

Fig. 1. Diagram showing the lecture delivery setup

The tablet pen device was also used during lecture delivery to write on the slides. For this purpose the tablet pen device was placed on the trolley along with the data projector. The height of the trolley was such that placing the tablet pen device allowed the author to write comfortably on the device at a natural angle. The laptop computer containing the slides was placed at a chair placed adjacent to the trolley, so that its screen was visible to the author.

The lectures were also recorded using a cordless microphone. Important here is that not only the voice of the instructor was recorded, but the screen of the laptop was captured simultaneously as well. Therefore it was possible to record the slides, the writing on the slides with digital ink during the lecture, as well as the voice of the instructor synchronised with the slides, and a freely downloadable software was used for this purpose. The recorded lectures were made available to the students after the lecture. For this purpose the lecture files were placed on a shared network folder.

3 Observations

In this section we will describe some of our observations about important aspects of our project for technology-enhanced learning. We will focus on the classroom impact of the project, as well as its advantages and limitations. We will also refer back to the objectives of the project as appropriate.

3.1 Classroom Impact

In the context of classroom impact we are interested in evaluating whether the methodology used for lecture delivery contributed to teaching, as well as to student learning.

– It was possible to eschew the use of the whiteboard (see section 3.2 for some exceptions to this). This made the use of electronic slides feasible, since the problems due to switching between slides and whiteboard could be avoided. Prepared electronic slides helped the instructor save time not having to write the lecture contents on the whiteboard during the lecture. In this context, 86 percent of the students found that the lecture delivery setup helped save time, whereas 74 percent of the students found using electronic slides and writing on them using digital ink during lecture more easy to view as compared to the whiteboard.

– The use of digital ink helped the instructor to spontaneously adapt to the students. Concepts could be explained, and students' questions answered by writing on the slides spontaneously, without causing any distraction to the students. 88 percent of the students felt that the lecture delivery setup enabled more interaction between the students and the instructor. Also, 83 percent of the students felt the lectures delivered using this setup to be better than those delivered using traditional techniques.

– By following the best practices in the use of digital ink [3], it was possible for the instructor to adopt a simple interaction protocol with the students, as well as to increase student engagement.

– Related to the previous point, the lecture delivery setup allowed the instructor to face the students at all times (91 percent of the students found this to be true). There was no disruption caused by the instructor having to turn towards the whiteboard to write. According to students' feedback, this allowed them to better engage with the instructor. 88 percent of the students found that the setup allowed the instructor to deliver better lectures.

– The methodology of lecture delivery also helped enhance the classroom experience. 89 percent of the students found that lectures delivered using this setup allowed them to take more interest in the lecture, whereas 83 percent of the students found the methodology to make the classroom experience more interesting.

All of the points mentioned in this section can be related to objectives 1, 2 and 3 as listed in section 2.1.

3.2 Advantages and Limitations

A big advantage of the project setup described in section 2.2 was its ease of use, and the fact that it allowed us to incorporate an effective method of lecture delivery using available and cheap resources. The whole setup did not take more than 10 minutes at the beginning of the lecture.

The setup was meant to supplement the classroom experience, not replace it, hence avoiding the problems that can accrue due to lack of personal contact between the instructor and the student [4]. The recorded lectures were, however, available to the students for use outside the classroom, thus allowing a very basic form of distance learning [6]. Based on students' feedback, it was ascertained that roughly 50 percent of the students were using the recorded lectures outside of the campus. We can relate this aspect to objective 4 of the list of the project's objectives listed in section 2.1.

The lecture setup also had some limitations which are worth mentioning. Among these is that the use of the whiteboard could not be completely eschewed. The setup using the USB-based tablet pen device, and the laptop connected to the data projector through a cable meant a tethered setup. Therefore, the setup, though offering a simple interaction protocol between the instructor and students, allowed for only one-way slide annotation.

Another limitation of the setup was related to only the instructor's voice being recorded. Since the cordless microphone was attached to the instructor's collar, any answers by the students to the questions posed by the instructor were not recorded. In this case the author adopted the practice of repeating the student's question before answering, so that the instructor's speech in the lecture recording could be put in context.

3.3 Issues with Lecture Preparation and Delivery

For lecture preparation and delivery with digital ink we used the guidelines as provided in [3]. However, at times we did face the problem of slide clutter (see Fig. 2) and sometimes the electronic slide proved to be small to write. For the latter, one easy remedy was to keep a blank slide in the slide deck after a slide where much writing was anticipated, thus avoiding clutter and the need to erase digital ink. The author also felt a tendency to use too much attentional ink [10], which also required occasional erasure of digital ink from the slide. However, on analysis of the recorded lectures, the effect of erasing digital ink was not found to be significant, since the context of the inking, as well as erasure, was available in the recording.

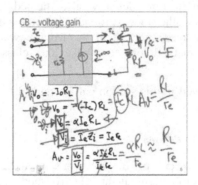

Fig. 2. A cluttered slide

4 Future Work

We have now run the project during a whole semester, and are using it again during the following semester. Presently work is underway to evaluate and deploy an open-source learning management system. As part of this step, a web-based learning management system has been installed at the electrical engineering department, and is being used initially by the author for the Electronics course. The recorded lectures of the new semester are being made available on this web-based platform, in contrast to the network drive-based approach used previously. We have also used the learning management system for student assignments, and have had very good response. We also plan to administer classroom quizzes online, which for the time being are paper-based. These efforts and plans are in accordance with objective number 5 listed in section 2.1.

The lectures recorded during the project have been shown to other instructors at the author's institute, and also at another engineering university in the same city. One other extension of the project we are planning goes in the direction of recording lectures at one institution, and making it available for students at the other, possibly using the institution's local learning management system. Though more elaborate programs (in scope and in use of technology) of distance learning are being used [5], we consider this to be a cost-effective method of knowledge dispersion, while also giving students more freedom by learning from courses without enrolling in them or being present at another institution.

Another application of the setup used in the project is to help improve the presentation and teaching skills of less experienced teachers, and plans are being made to effectively utilize the setup for this purpose.

References

[1] Richard Anderson, Ruth Anderson, Oliver Chung, K. M. Davis, et al. *Classroom Presenter - A Classroom Interaction System for Active and Collaborative Learning.* In Proc. First Workshop on the Impact of Pen-based Technology on Education. 2006.

[2] Valentin Razmov and Richard Anderson. *Pedagogical Techniques Supported by the Use of Student Devices in Teaching Software Engineering.* In Proc. SIGCSE'06. Houston, Texas, USA. 2006.

[3] Richard Anderson, Ruth Anderson, and Luke McDowell. *Best Practices for Lecturing with Digital Ink.* 2005. Accessed on *15.01.06* at: http://www.cs.washington.edu/education/dl/presenter/papers.html.

[4] Han-Zen Chang, Yi-Chan Deng, Mong-Chen Chiang, Hui-Chun Liao, et al. *Bringing Off-campus Students to the Digital Classroom Environment: The Design and Use of MSIE System.* In Proc. Fifth IEEE International Conference on Advanced Learning Technologies. 2005.

[5] Animesh Patcha and Glenda Scales. *Development of an Internet based Distance Learning Program at Virginia Tech.* In Proc. SIGITE'05. New Jersey, USA. pp: 379-80. 2005.

[6] Lester A. Gerhardt. *The Future of Distance Learning - The Process and the Product.* In Proc. ITHET 6th Annual International Conference. 2005.

[7] Sung-Bin Chang, Kuan-Jung Tung, and Tak-Wai Chan. *A Learning Strategy of Student Question Generation to Enhance Comprehension of Learning Materials in Digital Classroom Environment.* In Proc. Fifth IEEE International Conference on Advanced Learning Technologies (ICALT'05). 2005.

[8] M. Roldan. *Tablet PCs in the University: Ready for Prime Time.* In Proc. 6th International Conference on Information Technology Based Higher Education and Training. 2005.

[9] Richard Anderson, Ruth Anderson, Luke McDowell, and Beth Simon. *Use of Classroom Presenter in Engineering Courses.* In Proc. 35th ASEE/IEEE Frontiers in Education Conference. Indianapolis, IN, USA. 2005.

[10] R. J. Anderson, C. Hoyer, Wolfman S. A., and R. Anderson. *A study of digital ink in lecture presentation.* In Proc. CHI'04. pp: 576-574. 2004.

[11] Nenad Karlovcec, Tibor Skala, and Sabina Saina. *Computer Science Education: Differences Between Elearning and Classical Approach.* Accessed on *16.01.06* at: http://www.claroline.net/dlarea/Zagrebpaper1336.pdf.

Requirements and an Architecture for a Multimedia Content Re-purposing Framework

Marek Meyer[1], Tomas Hildebrandt[2], Christoph Rensing[2], and Ralf Steinmetz[2]

[1] SAP AG, SAP Research CEC Darmstadt, Bleichstr. 8, 64283, Germany
marek.meyer@sap.com
[2] KOM Multimedia Communications Lab, Darmstadt University of Technology,
Merckstr. 25, 64832 Darmstadt, Germany
{hildebrandt, rensing, steinmetz}@kom.tu-darmstadt.de

Abstract. Production of Learning Resources is very expensive. Hence re-use is a common way to lower these costs. In contrary to a re-use "as is" re-purposing means to transform a Learning Resource to suit a new learning or teaching context. We consider re-purposing to be a promising approach to improve the re-use of Learning Resources. As a basis for re-purposing tools, a re-purposing framework shall provide fundamental functionality in order to facilitate the development of re-purposing tools. This paper analyzes the requirements for such a framework, proposes an actual architecture and presents the current state of the implementation.

1 Introduction

E-Learning has gained a major role in eduction. Web Based Trainings (WBT) and other kinds of multimedia content are important especially for adult education. For these formats, powerful tools exist for creating Learning Resources. But once a Learning Resource is created and published, the work of these tools is considered to be finished. The challenge in re-using digital Learning Resources is the combination of content, multimedia and didactics.

From a didactical point of view, it would be best to design and produce learning materials completely from scratch, because this approach would lead to a maximum of quality. But the production of e-learning materials is very expensive. Therefore, new ways have to be found to reduce the costs of the authoring process. The common approach to lower production costs is to re-use existing content. The term Learning Object has been introduced to define reusable units of learning materials; re-use here means to use a learning object again without changing it.

A broader definition of re-use is based on the insight that re-use may include modifying the Learning Resource in order to use it (re-purposing) [1]. Re-purposing may consist of different steps, such as modularization and adaptation. A re-purposing tool is a tool that supports an author to transform a Learning Resource to suit a new learning or teaching context. It guides the author to reach that goal and should enable her to pursue the big picture instead of small editing steps.

W. Nejdl and K. Tochtermann (Eds.): EC-TEL 2006, LNCS 4227, pp. 500–505, 2006.

Developing such a re-purposing tool is a complex task. Therefore, this paper focuses on the development of a re-purposing framework, which facilitates the implementation of re-purposing tools.

This paper is organized as follows: In the second chapter, we analyze the requirements for a re-purposing framework. Related work is discussed in chapter three. Chapter four presents a brief solution approach which is then transformed into an actual architecture and implementation in chapters five and six. Finally, conclusions and an outlook are presented in the seventh chapter.

2   Requirements for a Re-purposing Framework

As shown in the introduction, there is need for a generic re-purposing framework. The requirements for such a framework are analyzed in this section. The re-purposing framework should not be one application with a fixed functionality and front-end, but a basis on which different applications can be built. The core requirements are:

Format Independence: The intended framework must be format-independent in a way that an application using the framework will be enabled to deal with resources in different formats. Ideally, applications should be format-independent.

Support for Structured Multi-Document Resources: Learning Resources may consist of multiple documents. Usually, there are links between these documents, which turn a set of single documents into a meaningful ensemble. Those links may be hyperlink-like references between content documents or references in a manifest document. Therefore it is necessary to regard several documents as one logical resource as well as to give the possibility to regard each single document.

Enhanced Support for Content Analysis: An intelligent re-purposing tool, which supports the user to reach her goals, has to know about the details of the Learning Resource contents. It would, for example, be helpful for restructuring tasks if the structure of a course could be shown to the user; possibly enriched with information about the relations between different text blocks (e.g. coherence of text blocks or which didactical roles they play).

Modification of Content Without Unintended Information Loss: Analysis of the content is only the first step of re-purposing. The data has also to be changed by the application. These changes should take place without losing relevant information (e.g. formatting). This is a challenge because the analysis works on an abstract data model.

Extensibility: The re-purposing framework should be designed as an open framework for various re-purposing applications. Hence, extensibility should be considered as one of the core requirements. Extensibility comprises especially new formats, new re-purposing processes and new content analysis methods.

3   Related Work

Authoring tools for Learning Resources mostly support creation and simple editing, but no re-purposing. Furthermore, many authoring tools bring along their own source format. A created Learning Resource is rendered into a target format for publishing. Those Learning Resources can only be edited by the authoring tool, and only if the original source is available. There are some tools that provide basic adaptation support. But the functionality is always restricted to a small set of document formats and adaptations types. Examples for such tools are SYSTRAN office plug-ins [2] and the slide master feature of Microsoft PowerPoint. However, the approach of using one separate tool for each adaptation type for each format leads to a confusing number of programs. And each of these programs behaves differently. We currently do not know of any editing tool that offers support for arbitrary adaptations for different document formats.

A wide-spread approach for covering several document formats by one tool is to use an abstract intermediate format. A popular approach is to use the XML File Format of OpenOffice as intermediate format and filters for importing and exporting various other document formats [3,4]. Another project that uses an intermediate format is ALOCoM [5]. ALOCoM uses a proprietary intermediate format in combination with a simple ontology for content elements.

Bayerl et al. have developed methods for semantic analysis of document markup (cf. [6]). They propose to use three levels of semantic document markup: a structural level, a thematic level and a rhetorical level. An implementation exists that uses XML as markup language and Prolog for semantic analysis. However, only one document format is supported: all contents have to be available as DocBook documents.

4   Application Examples

Two example applications may illustrate the use of a re-purposing framework. The first example is an adaptation tool that adapts a Learning Resource to a particular corporate design. The second example is a modularization tool, which decomposes a Learning Resource into several smaller Learning Resources.

A corporate design consists of several layout elements and styles, which form a unique appearance that is recognized by customers. Parts of a corporate design are e.g. logos, particular fonts, text colors and sizes, as well as rules for text alignment and image placement. The difficulty in changing the layout of a Learning Resource in order to fit a new corporate design is to identify layout elements with a particular meaning. For example, headlines have to be formatted different than plain text or image captures. If logos are to be replaced, we have to tell apart logos from all other images. An adaptation tool could benefit from a re-purposing framework by re-using existing functionality and focusing on the primary task.

As a second example we consider a tool that modularizes a Learning Resource into several smaller Learning Resources. Again detailed semantic information about the content elements would be required for performing the task. Consider that a modularization algorithm calculates module boundaries based on the similarity of text passages. Using the re-purposing framework, the modularization tool could first calculate the similarity of text passages and attach that information to the content elements. The boundaries would be technically realized by propagating the boundaries to the format-specific layer, where finally the Learning Resources are technically decomposed.

5   Re-purposing Framework

For realizing a re-purposing framework that fulfills the aforementioned requirements, we decided to create representations of the Learning Resource contents on multiple layers, each with an increasing abstraction level. The proposed layers are:

- A physical representation layer which represents the involved files as they exist on disk
- An object-oriented representation layer that represents the content structure as an object tree
- A semantic representation layer that represents the content structure as a semantic graph enriched by semantic information

On the object-oriented representation layer a so-called Object-Oriented Content Representation (OOCR) will represent the structural entities of the documents as a tree of objects. These objects are also the entities which provide methods for modifying the content.

The semantic representation layer will consist of an RDF model called Semantic Content Representation (SCR) that contains the structural information of the OOCR plus additional semantic markup and relations. The SCR also provides the required format abstraction by using a generic Content Ontology. The Content Ontology will provide the necessary concepts for interpretation of the SCR.

However, although an RDF model is very helpful for analysis, it is not suitable for changing the content. If changes were performed directly on the Semantic Content Representation, it would be necessary to transform this model back into

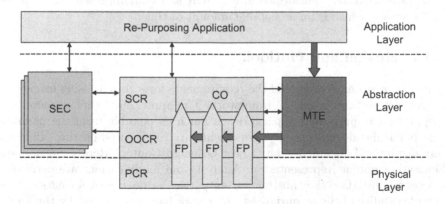

Fig. 1. Components of the Re-purposing Framework

the original format - which would lead to information loss. Therefore, all modifications are propagated by a Modification Transaction Engine (MTE) to the OOCR, where they can be performed format-specific. Content modifications are formulated by re-purposing applications as atomic, format-independent modification commands.

The complete architecture is illustrated in Fig. 1. Re-purposing tools mainly interact with the framework via the SCR.

The ability for handling particular document formats is added to the framework by format plug-ins. A format plug-in contributes format-specific extensions to the framework for handling this document format.

6 Implementation

We have implemented a first version of the presented re-purposing framework. Currently we provide support for two formats: HTML and the Sharable Content Object Reference Model (SCORM) [7]. The framework is combined with a simple SCORM editor that allows to edit and aggregate SCORM-compliant Learning Resources. Framework and SCORM editor together are planned as a basis for a sophisticated re-purposing tool.

The whole application is implemented in Java on top of the Eclipse Rich Client Platform (http://www.eclipse.org/rcp/). It is realized as multiple Eclipse plugins, which represent the different components of the architecture. There is one plug-in for the basis system and for each supported content format a separate plug-in. Re-purposing applications are integrated by adding a new Eclipse plug-in. For the Semantic Content Representation, we build an RDF model using the Jena semantic web framework.

Up to now, some simple adaptation processes have been implemented to prove the feasibility of the framework architecture. The results are quite promising, as the adaptation processes work satisfactory for the supported formats right now. We have used three different SCORM courses for testing (consisting of 27 to 95 HTML documents). The results of a performance measurement show that the tested courses can be transformed into OOCR and SCR representations in less that 7 seconds, which is an acceptable amount of time.

7 Conclusion and Outlook

In this paper, we have presented the requirements for a re-purposing framework and our architecture for such a framework. The approach of that framework is to separate a re-purposing application as much as possible from the handling of the particular documents. The documents are represented on three different layers as physical documents, an Object-Oriented Content Representation and a Semantic Content Representation. Analysis and modifications are performed via a generic interface that abstracts from particular document formats.

The feasibility of the re-purposing framework has been proven by the implementation of some basic adaptation processes. More sophisticated re-purposing applications, which use more of the framework's potential, are currently developed. One of the remaining tasks is to implement complex analysis methods in order to facilitate the development of those re-purposing applications. Also, additional format plug-ins for further document formats should be implemented to broaden the use of the framework.

Acknowledgments

This work is supported by the German Federal Ministry of Economics and Technology in the context of the project Content Sharing. We would like to thank Sonja Bergsträßer for developing the Content Ontology, Birgit Zimmermann for her implementation of an adaptation tool that runs as a first re-purposing application on top the framework and Heiko Schmitt, who implemented parts of a SCORM Format Plug-in.

References

1. Rensing, C., Bergsträßer, S., Hildebrandt, T., Meyer, M., Zimmermann, B., Faatz, A., Lehmann, L., Steinmetz, R.: Re-Use and Re-Authoring of Learning Resources - Definitions and Examples. Technical Report KOM-TR-2005-02, TU Darmstadt - Multimedia Communications Lab (2005)
2. SYSTRANS: SYSTRANS WebServer, (http://www.systransoft.com/products/client-server/webserver.html)
3. OpenOffice.org: OpenOffice filters using the XML based file format, (http://xml.openoffice.org/filters.html)
4. Rotard, M., Finsterle, L.: Creating and Publishing Courseware Independent of the Authoring System. In: Proceedings of the Technology Enhanced Learning Conference. (2003) 251–254
5. Verbert, K., Gasevic, D., Jovanovic, J., Duval, E.: Ontology-based learning content repurposing. In: WWW '05: Special interest tracks and posters of the 14th international conference on World Wide Web, New York, NY, USA, ACM Press (2005) 1140–1141
6. Bayerl, P.S., Lüngen, H., Goecke, D., Witt, A., Naber, D.: Methods for the semantic analysis of document markup. In Vanoirbeek, C., Roisin, C., Munson, E., eds.: Proceedings of the 2003 ACM Symposium on Document Engineering (DocEng-03), New York, ACM Press (2003) 161–170
7. Advanced Distributed Learning: Sharable content object reference model (SCORM) 2004, (http://www.adlnet.org)

Developing a Reference Model to Describe the Personal Learning Environment

Colin D. Milligan[1], Phillip Beauvoir[2], Mark W. Johnson[2], Paul Sharples[2], Scott Wilson[2], and Oleg Liber[2]

[1] Learning Services, University of Strathclyde, Alexander Turnbull Building,
155 George Street, Glasgow G1 1RD, United Kingdom
colin.milligan@strath.ac.uk
[2] Learning Support & Development, University of Bolton,
Deane Campus, Deane Street, Bolton, BL3 5AB, United Kingdom
{p.beauvoir, m.w.johnson, p.sharples. o.liber}@bolton.ac.uk,
s.wilson@bangor.ac.uk

Abstract. How can we ensure that our educational systems evolve to better serve the needs of learners? This paper reports on initial work to create a Reference Model for a Personal Learning Environment, where the emphasis is on facilitating learning, in contrast to traditional Virtual Learning Environments which exist primarily to manage the learning process. This paper describes the rationale underlying the Personal Learning Environment concept and the advantages gained by specifying a reference model to define the PLE domain, before presenting a summary of the reference model itself.

1 Introduction

There is an inherent conflict in formal education: the number of students, each with their own individual needs, always greatly exceeds the numbers of teachers available to teach them. In order that the system is efficient, the teacher is constrained in the pedagogical options open to them by organisational policy. This situation is exacerbated by technology: the institutional imperative is to manage the learning process and the technologies adopted are those which reinforce traditional modes of working and provide efficiency gains rather than new pedagogical opportunities.

This paper describes our work in exploring new models for learning environments which seek to facilitate the learning process. We first describe our rationale for a Personal Learning Environment and the emerging technologies which may facilitate it. We then describe how we have formally examined existing software tools and the ways in which they are used to define the elements of a Reference Model for Personal Learning Environments, including typical design patterns we would expect to see in a Personal Learning Toolkit and the services which such a toolkit might interact with.

The work was funded by the United Kingdom's Joint Information Systems Committee (JISC) as part of its contribution to an international e-Framework initiative [1]. The primary goal of the initiative is to produce an evolving and sustainable, open standards based service oriented technical framework to support the education and research communities.

W. Nejdl and K. Tochtermann (Eds.): EC-TEL 2006, LNCS 4227, pp. 506–511, 2006.

1.1   Current Online Learning Environments

Most higher and further education institutions in the United Kingdom now manage the delivery of online course content and provision of student communication facilities through some kind of Virtual Learning Environment (VLE) [2]. VLEs provide a number of benefits to students and staff within an institution. For the administrator, a VLE provides a set of tools which allows course content and student cohorts to be managed efficiently and provide a single point of integration with student record systems. For the tutor, a simple set of integrated tools allows the creation of learning content without specialist computer skills, whilst class administration tools facilitate communication between tutor and cohort (for class announcements) and individual learners (for feedback). For the learner, the VLE provides a single environment within which all online content can be accessed and communication can be managed.

VLEs first began to emerge around ten years ago, in the wake of the widespread availability of the World Wide Web. The technologies adopted by VLEs are largely standard, with most commercial (e.g. WebCT and BlackBoard) and Open Source tools (moodle, ATutor) exhibiting the same functionality, and overall pedagogical approach. But VLEs are fundamentally a conservative technology; they are a solution to a set of organisational problems: managing students, providing tools and delivering content, and whilst they serve the needs of the institution well, they are often ill suited to the needs of learners.

Can we re-examine the online learning experience and design a set of tools which more fully support the learning process and are more closely matched to the needs of individual learners. These tools would give the learner greater control over their learning experience (managing their resources, the work they have produced, the activities they participate in), reduce the range of tools they must interact with, and would constitute their own personal learning environment, which they could use to interact with institutional systems to access content, assessment, libraries and the like.

In a Personal Learning Environment (PLE), the learner would utilise a single set of tools, customised to their needs and preferences inside a single learning environment. The tools would allow the learner to:

- **Learn with other people:** managing their relationships with tutors, and peers, as well as form links between contacts who are not part of their formal learning network.
- **Control their learning resources:** enabling them to structure, share and annotate the resources they have been given along with those they have found or created themselves, or been given by their peers.
- **Manage the activities they participate in:** providing them with the opportunity to set up and join activities such as study groups, bringing together a specific group of people, together with the appropriate resources.
- **Integrate their learning:** allowing them the opportunity to combine learning from different institutions, re-using previously generated evidence of competency or making links between formal and informal learning.

Individual technologies which embody the spirit of the Personal Learning Environment have emerged over recent years. These include wikis and weblogs, along with newsreaders, communication tools, workflow, calendaring software, and so called 'Web 2.0' [3] tools such as del.icio.us, and flickr which facilitate sharing of resources through an individual's social network. To define a Personal Learning Environment, we must look at these tools, and the technologies underpinning them.

A key technological component of the Personal Learning Environment is the use of Web Services. Web Services underpin the Web 2.0 technologies described above, allowing different software tools to interact with each other to exchange data and information. This allows a separation of tools into those which people interact with (which will have a user interface) and those which interact with other tools (which have no need for a user interface, but store and make data available in a defined way such that other tools can access it).

A Service Oriented Approach (SOA) is at the centre of the e-Framework initiative described above [1] and of which this work forms part. Creating a framework for Web Services (where each service has been factored to ensure maximum flexibility) fundamentally provide a promise of interoperability.

Interoperability is vital because institutional Virtual Learning Environments are not suddenly going to disappear. Web Services provide the key to co-existence of VLEs and PLEs: as long as the VLE uses a web services approach, then content, discussions, class membership and the like can be exposed as services that the PLE can subscribe to. In this way, a student can sit at her laptop, and interact with a single environment, accessing content from all the institutions at which she is studying, allowing her to communicate with all her peers, wherever they may be registered.

2 Arriving at a Concept of a Personal Learning Environment

But what exactly is a Personal Learning Environment? The title embraces a variety of interpretations and has generated a certain degree of discourse [4]. For some, the PLE concept facilitates learner choice and control, allowing the selection and combination of informal and formal learning opportunities from a variety of sources. Others see the PLE as an extension of the portfolio, providing a learner centred environment in which learners can record achievement and plan and work toward new goals.

Our initial concept of a PLE came from a visual representation of a 'Future VLE' created by Scott Wilson [5]. In this early vision, the key element is that the Future VLE acts as a coordinator of a number of different services and agents. The learner may choose the tools to utilise within their learning environment, and aggregates learning content from formal education providers and informal sources. The future VLE also provides tools for managing resources and relationships. The architecture inherent is that of generic Web 2.0 web services such as RSS, FOAF and ATOM.

After the Future VLE vision was published and the initial work of the PLE Reference Model project presented and disseminated, a number of other authors responded with their own vision of what might constitute a Personal Learning Environment. Space does not permit a full survey of available models here, but two examples show the type of thinking which is ongoing.

The ELGG Personal Learning Landscape takes a similar approach to the Future VLE described above. The ELGG software developed by David Tosh and others [6] provides an environment for reflection (through weblog style posts) and peer communication (facilitated by FOAF). Together with a content repository and tools for managing resources, the Personal Learning Landscape strongly resembles the core PLE concept.

Jeremy Hiebert also draws heavily on ELGG and e-Portfolios in his Personal Learning Environment Model [7]. Hiebert shows how past, present and future learning can be managed through a set of self directed learning tools (for example: blogs, portfolios, feed aggregators) and a set of generic activities (collecting, reflecting, connecting, and publishing). This all occurs in the context of an individual's identity (contact information, interests, reputation, values) and their social network (contacts, collaborators, peers, mentors, tutors, friends, family ...).

Analysis of the PLE visions presented allowed us to identify some common features. These are:

- **Feeds for collecting resources and other data.** Each of the models uses a feed-based mechanism for collecting resources and other data; feeds are a useful generic mechanism for pulling together resources from a wide range of sources.
- **Conduits for sharing and publishing.** As much emphasis is placed on sharing (remixing) and publishing resources as on collecting and reading - the learner is expected to be an active contributor to their learning.
- **Services for interacting with organizations.** The boundary between individuals and institutions or organisations is mediated through services at the boundaries of organisations.
- **Personal information management.** The learner spends time organising and connecting together the resources they collect into meaningful collections and groups, for themselves and also to share with others. This is an important process for the learner, echoing the sentiments of 'Connectivism' [8].
- **Ambiguity of teacher - learner role.** All the models considered are heavily learner-centric, and omit to mention the role of teachers. Implicitly there seems to be a conception that the roles of teacher and learner may be interchangeable, and that tools for learners could, and perhaps should, be the same as that of teachers.

3   Creating a Reference Model for Personal Learning Environments

To develop the reference model for the PLE in general, and for the instruments provided by the Personal Learning Toolkit in particular, we used a pattern language approach. Alternatives such as UML process modelling were considered, however the diversity of possible solutions within the conceptual model of a PLE is too great for most UML-based approaches. Pattern languages enable the largest number of possible valid solutions while at the same time providing a coherent 'design vocabulary'.

What differentiates a Personal Learning Toolkit from any other type of tool is difficult to pin down in terms of features alone; the critical factors are primarily in how the system is used, by whom, and in the context of use. However, for the purposes of creating a useful reference model we took a pragmatic approach, identifying a wide range of tools and sites that exhibit what we felt were characteristics useful in a PLE context, and then identifying recurring patterns in this reference set. Tools surveyed included: *Email and personal information management tools, Chat and messaging tools, Groupware and community tools, Calendaring, Scheduling and time management tools, News aggregation tools, Weblogging and personal publishing tools, Social software, Authoring and collaboration tools,* and *Web Integration tools.* A selection of these tools used together, would in many cases constitute a Personal Learning Toolkit.

From this selection, we were able to identify a set of 77 relevant patterns. The language could be further refined, expanding to include new patterns, or subsuming patterns already identified. The pattern language created was aligned with other relevant work such as the Pattern Language for Groupware systems [9].

The patterns that emerge from the analysis of the tools above define a vocabulary that we could then use to plan the development of prototypes, and that others can use in the development of Personal Learning Toolkits.

The patterns that have been identified reflect the configuration of services that are likely to be required for the PLE to be an effective environment for learning. These patterns reflect current user behaviour and fall into 9 categories: *Context Patterns, Conversation Patterns, Network Patterns, Resource Patterns, Social Patterns, Team Patterns, Temporal Patterns, Workflow Patterns,* and *Activity Patterns.*

The patterns collected and described here represent current practice, and it is likely, that when a PLE is implemented, that new patterns of behaviour will emerge. These can be described and incorporated into the Reference Model at a later date. The reference model is not designed to be static.

As the general approach we wanted to use is service-oriented, using the e-Framework as its starting point, we described the patterns identified in the pattern language in terms of services as well as application functionality.

Some of the services that support these patterns already exist. For example, in supporting social patterns, FOAF is ideal. For both calendaring and workflow, a variety of technologies exist, and in the case of workflow, well-developed commercial products could be easily integrated. In addition to pre-existing technologies, we can also see where pre-existing protocols and standards may be integrated into the PLE: for example, the ATOM protocol is ideal for the implementation of conduits, and this compatibility opens up new possibilities for the incorporation of other ATOM-compliant tools and services.

We identified a number of key services that recur in the patterns: *Activity Management, Workflow, Syndication, Posting, Group, Rating, Annotating, and Recommending, Presence, Personal Profile,* and *Exploration and Trails.*

The PLE Reference Model is an aggregate of the Patterns described and Services identified. Some of the services already exist. For those new Services that we have identified, Service Definitions will be written.

In our model, the Personal Learning Toolkit, consisting of a set of tools as identified from the Design Patterns, is used by the learner to interact with a number of distributed and coordinated services. Service descriptions describe the interfaces and interconnection of services. In practice, different learners might utilise different tools: one student may prefer to read e-mail with Mozilla Thunderbird, whilst another reads e-mail through Microsoft Outlook In a similar way, the same learner might access the same type of service from more than on service provider, for instance utilising course content from two sources.

4 Discussion

This Reference Model attempts to provide a framework to enable us to understand the emerging concept of a PLE. Existing examples of Personal Learning Environments can be reviewed within the context of the model to ensure that it encompasses each approach.

In the short term, there will be continued use of Web 2. 0 technologies to support learning. New tools will arise, demonstrating new Design Patterns. These can be incorporated into the Reference Model at any stage.

We may also see an evolution of Virtual Learning Environments as vendors adopt a Service Oriented Approach. Once VLEs are opened up in this way, we may see more widespread adoption of the PLE concept within mainstram formal education.

We have used the Reference Model as a blueprint to create two prototype PLE toolsets (a standalone desktop application and a portal based solution). It will be interesting to see the production of other prototypes using different technologies (for instance by extending web browsers through plugins, or by developing within a desktop widget framework such as that provided by Yahoo), and the new opportunities ssthese afford.

References

1. The e-Framework initiative: http://www.e-framework.org/ (accessed 10 April 2006)
2. Managed Learning Environment Activity in Further and Higher Education in the UK, A study by JISC/UCISA. http://www.elearning.ac.uk/mle/MLElandscapestudy/mle-study-final-report.pdf (accessed 11 April 2006).
3. O'Reilly, T., (2005) What is Web 2.0?
   http://www.oreillynet.com/pub/a/oreilly/tim/news/2005/09/30/what-is-web-20.html (accessed 13 April 2006)
4. http://del.icio.us/tag/ple_workshop_2006/ (accessed 30 June 2006)
5. Wilson, S., (2005) Future VLE – The Visual Version
   http://www.cetis.ac.uk/members/scott/blogview?entry=20050125170206 (accessed 11 April 2006)
6. http://www.elgg.net/ (accessed 12 April 2006)
7. Hiebert, J., (2006) Personal Learning Environment Model
   http://headspacej.blogspot.com/2006/02/personal-learning-environment-model.html (accessed 13 April 2006)
8. Siemens, G., (2004) Connectivism: A learning theory for the digital age.
   http://www.elearnspace.org/Articles/connectivism.htm (accessed 12 April 2006)
9. Schümmer T., Groupware Patterns, http://www.groupware-patterns.org/ (accessed 12 April 2006)

Semantic Modelling of
Learning Objects and Instruction

Claus Pahl and Mark Melia

Dublin City University, School of Computing
Dublin 9, Ireland
{cpahl, mmelia}@computing.dcu.ie

Abstract. We introduce an ontology-based semantic modelling framework that addresses subject domain modelling, instruction modelling, and interoperability aspects in the development of complex reusable learning objects. Ontologies are knowledge representation frameworks, ideally suited to support knowledge-based modelling of these learning objects. We illustrate the benefits of semantic modelling for learning object assemblies within the context of standards such as SCORM Sequencing and Navigation and Learning Object Metadata.

1 Introduction

Cost-effective and educationally successful learning object development increasingly relies on reusable learning objects and their integration into a sound instructional design. Description and discovery mechanism are needed to allow learning objects to be published by providers and retrieved by potential users. Instruction needs to be designed separated from the learning objects themselves.

Two developments from software engineering and Web technologies, addressing composition and description, can provide solutions for the development of complex units of study from reusable learning objects. Firstly, model-driven development uses diagram-based models that are abstract, easy to comprehend and communicate. Modelling has been recognised as an important aspect in the development of software systems. Model-driven architecture (MDA) is a proposed standard that reflects this view [1]. MDA supports development through diagram-based modelling [2]. Secondly, semantic modelling is based on ontologies as sharable, extensible knowledge representation frameworks [4]. Ontologies and ontology-based modelling have been proposed to enhance classical UML-based modelling. The essential benefits of ontologies are, firstly, interoperability and sharing of descriptions and, secondly, advanced analysis and reasoning.

We present an ontology-based modelling framework that addresses the requirements of learning object and instruction development. The three different layers of the MDA framework – business modelling, abstract system design, and platform-specific modelling – shall be adapted to the learning technology context and shall be supported by combining different ontology-based modelling techniques that address the central concerns of these layers. These concerns are, firstly, subject domain modelling, secondly, instruction design, and, finally,

W. Nejdl and K. Tochtermann (Eds.): EC-TEL 2006, LNCS 4227, pp. 512–517, 2006.

platform-specific implementation. Instructional design through sequencing of reusable learning objects shall here be the central activity.

- Subject domain modelling is a concern that is independent of a concrete computational paradigm. Capturing the domain context of a unit of study is essential for learning content development.
- Instructional design on a platform-independent level is important since sound educational composition and sequencing are essential design issues.
- Explicit modelling of learning objects and instruction within the given platform technology supports the model-based discovery of learning objects and the deployment of sequenced instruction.

We also address the abstract description of learning objects through metadata in order to enable reusability. Our platform consists of SCORM Sequencing and Navigation [5] and the Learning Object Metadata standards [6].

2   Subject Domain Modelling

The focus of the first MDA modelling layer is to capture and conceptualise the objects and processes that form the central concepts of the subject domain. Ontologies consist of two basic entities – concepts of a domain and relationships between these concepts that express properties of one concept in terms of another concept. Classical ontologies relate concepts in a subclass hierarchy, which creates a taxonomy for a particular domain. Two kinds of concepts – objects representing static entities and information and processes representing activities and behaviour – can be distinguished. The set of relationships shall comprise a subclass relationship for concept hierarchies, a dependency relationship, and a composition relationship. The choice of relationship types here is critical to address the needs of activity-oriented domain modelling [7]. Dependency relationships express how information objects are processed by activities. Composition is important for both objects and processes. Our concern is domain modelling for course subjects. Domain activities and processes are important as they often form the starting point for detailed models including instructional aspects.

In Fig. 1, objects are elliptic entities such as learning objects. Processes are rectangular entities such as learning activities. These entities – concepts in an ontology – are represented from three viewpoints. This three-part ontology in Fig. 1 is a generic model template that can be refined for a particular subject:

- Classification: For a programming course, learning objects which address loops or specific data structures could be defined as refinements of the given learning object elements in the template.
- Behaviour: Subject-specific learning activities such as study units on different forms of iteration and loops in programming can be sequenced, i.e. instructionally designed, using diagrammatic process expressions.
- Structure: The hierarchy of composite learning objects can be presented.

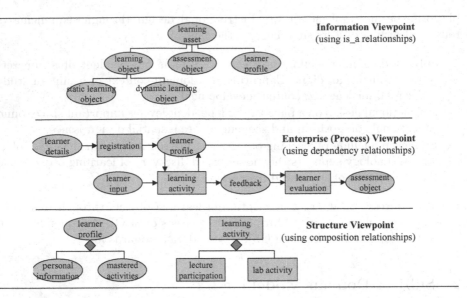

Fig. 1. Subject-level Excerpts from an E-Learning Domain Ontology

Sequencing constraints on activities and processes can also be expressed in ontological form in addition to concepts and relationships. Iteration, choice, concurrency, or sequence are process combinators that are often better expressed in a separate, textual sublanguage. Individual activity steps of a learning activity could be sequenced using additional constraints: *lecture; !(labExercise1 + labExercise2); selfAssessment*, which expresses that a lecture is followed by a repeated choice between two lab exercises followed by a test.

3   Instruction Modelling

This modelling layer introduces a learning design focus into the modelling process. Instructional design through sequencing is our focus. Instructional sequencing and interaction processes are part of the learning design, which determines how we assemble learning objects to sound educational units of study.

Looking into software technology can be beneficial due to similarities between instructional sequences and processes between software services. Various process-related ontologies exist [8] – in particular service ontologies appear suitable. WSPO – the Web Service Process Ontology – can be distinguished from other service ontologies such as OWL-S and WSMO through its process-orientation [9]. In WSPO, the focus is on the behaviour – i.e. processes and interaction – of software. WSPO ontologies are based on a common template (Fig. 2) that we utilise here to express the instructional design of learning object assemblies.

The central WSPO concepts are the states that separate individual activities – pre- and poststates of learning activities – and that characterise the state of the learning process in terms of objectives already achieved and prerequisites of further activities. Other concepts capture objects that might be processed in an

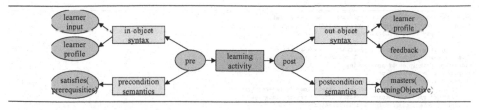

Fig. 2. Ontological Service Process Template (WSPO) – applied to E-Learning

activity (such as learner profile information) and conditions (such as prerequisites and effects in terms of learning objectives that are mastered after successfully working through a learning activity). Two forms of relationships characterise this ontology. The central relationship type is the instruction or learning process itself. This instructional relationship is enhanced by an instruction activity combinator sublanguage (*lecture*; !(*labExercise1* + *labExercise2*); *selfAssessment* is an instructional sequence of activities). These sequencing expressions describe a learning process in terms of state changes. Auxiliary relationship types are so-called descriptional relationships, which associate the auxiliary concepts such as learning objectives and prerequisites to states (see Fig. 2).

The instruction model focuses on activities and how they are sequenced to processes. The combinators that we use are ';' (sequential composition), '!' (iteration), '+' (choice), and '||' (parallel composition). The symbol ∘ says that the activity implementation might process these objects. The domain model process

$$lecture; \ !(\ labExercise1 + labExercise2 \ ); \ selfAssessment$$

can be mapped to a WSPO sequenced instruction expression

> *lecture* ∘ *profile*;
> ! (*labExercise1* ∘ (*profile*, *input1*); *labExercise2* ∘ (*profile*, *input2*));
> *selfAssessment* ∘ *profile*

4   Implementation Modelling

Implementation modelling relates the previous layers to the chosen platform. Our platform consists of SCORM SN as the instruction implementation language and LOM as the metadata notation for learning object reuse.

- LOM aims at the abstract description of learning objects by providing an interoperable form and vocabulary for semantic learning objects description and discovery in repositories. Some of the technical aspects in the domain and instruction model provide input for the transformation to LOM.
- Learning object-based instruction design is often called sequencing to indicate the process-like nature of learning object assemblies. SN is a sequencing language that supports the instructional design based on learning activities and associated learning objects. WSPO already captures the essentials of instruction and interaction processes and can easily be translated into SN.

```
xmlns:lom-general="http://ims.org/ims/schemas/lom-general"
xmlns:lom-tech="http://ims.org/ims/schemas/lom-technical"
xmlns:lom-edu="ims.org/ims/schemas/lom-educational"

<lom-gen:title>Introduction to Programming</lom-gen:title>
<lom-gen:description>A third-level course for computing students
addressing principles of programming
languages</lom-gen:description>
<lom-tech:format>text/html<lom-tech:format>
<lom-edu:interactivityType>active-simulation</lom-edu:interactivityType>
<lom-edu:description>learning objective: to master the language
concepts loop and choice</lom-edu:description>
```

Fig. 3. LOM Template – applied to an E-Learning Case Study

A learning activity could both be published (using LOM) and integrated in a learning object instructional sequence (using SN). LOM descriptions capture syntactic and semantic learning object descriptions, similar to WSPO with its prerequisites and learning objectives. It adds, however, various aspects that can also be included in discovery and matching. We have illustrated three categories of attributes - general, technical, and educational in Fig. 3. These descriptions are published by providers and can be searched by potential users in education-specific repositories. The benefit of ontologies is the improved support of semantic description and discovery compared to syntactical formats such as LOM.

SN is an XML notation, based on a WSPO-like operator calculus. Actions, which describe simple learning object applications, are assembled to define learning processes using combinators such as *sequence* or *iteration*. Instruction is an inter-learning object perspective on process assembly for these learning objects. An example showing a SN specification generated for a sequenced programming learning object is presented in Fig. 4. This excerpt is shortened and simplified. The complexity of this specification indicates the benefit of model-driven development and automatic code generation. Complex SN specifications can be

```
<item identifier="module">                                        <imsss:mapInfo targetObjectiveID="LAB_PREREQ"/>
 <imsss:sequencing>                                                  </imsss:primaryObjective>
  <imsss:controlMode choice="false" flow="true" forwardonly="true"/>  </imsss:objectives>
 </imsss:sequencing>                                               </imsss:sequencing>
 <item identifier="labex">                                        </item>
  <title>Lab Exercises</title>
  <item identifier="lab1" identifierref="ex1_res">                 <item identifier="asses" identifierref="asses_res">
   <title>Lab Exercise 1</title>                                   <title>Self-Assessment</title>
   <imsss:sequencing>                                               <imsss:sequencing>
    <imsss:controlMode choice="false" flow="true" />                 <imsss:controlMode choice="true" flow="false" />
   </imsss:sequencing>                                               <imsss:sequencingRules>
  </item>                                                             <imsss:preConditionRule>
  <item identifier="lab2" identifierref="ex2_res">                     <imsss:ruleConditions conditionCombination="any">
   <title>Lab Exercise 2</title>                                       <imsss:ruleCondition condition="satisfied" operator="not"/>
   <imsss:sequencing>                                                 </imsss:ruleConditions>
    <imsss:controlMode choice="false" flow="true" />                  <imsss:ruleAction action="hiddenFromChoice"/>
   </imsss:sequencing>                                               </imsss:preConditionRule>
  </item>                                                            </imsss:sequencingRules>
  <imsss:sequencing>                                                 <imsss:objectives>
   <imsss:controlMode choice="true"  flow="false"  />                 <imsss:primaryObjective objectiveID="ASSESS">
   <imsss:sequencingRules>                                             <imsss:mapInfo targetObjectiveID="LAB_PREREQ"/>
    <imsss:preConditionRule>                                          </imsss:primaryObjective>
     <imsss:ruleConditions conditionCombination="any">              </imsss:objectives>
      <imsss:ruleCondition condition="satisfied" operator="not"/>   </imsss:sequencing>
     </imsss:ruleConditions>                                       </item>
     <imsss:ruleAction action="hiddenFromChoice"/>                 <imsss:sequencing>
    </imsss:preConditionRule>                                       <imsss:controlMode choice="true" flow="false"/>
   </imsss:sequencingRules>                                         </imsss:sequencing>
   <imsss:objectives>                                              </item>
    <imsss:primaryObjective objectiveID=TEST">
```

Fig. 4. Generated SCORM SN Implementation (excerpt)

automatically generated if the user provides a simple abstract instruction specification, a chosen SN templates, and a few other default settings.

5   Conclusions

The benefits of ontologies match the requirements of a platform such as learning object development and deployment within SCORM, where often reuse of learning objects is the main style of development. This style relies on interoperable data formats and sound educational assemblies. In heterogeneous environments and cross-organisational development, information about a variety of aspects – represented in ontologies – is vital. Model-driven development defines a development process for this context. We have identified activity-oriented subject domain modelling, instructional design, and learning object implementation modelling as three central development concerns. Ontology technology provides an integrated, coherent solution for these concerns at all modelling layers. We have limited our investigation to inter-learning object aspects. Learning object development also comprises their generation from resources such as ontologies. Ontologies can be used to generate different learning object types [10].

While the aim in this paper was to outline a modelling approach and to demonstrate the feasibility and benefits, more needs to be done to implement and empirically evaluate the approach. We and others, like [3], have only made initial steps in this direction so far. Our aim is also to support our approach with a wider range of suitable, learning technology-specific tools and to use the proposed methodology for a wider range of subjects.

References

1. Object Management Group. *MDA Model-Driven Architecture Guide*. OMG, 2003.
2. H.-E. Eriksson, M. Penker, B. Lyons, and D. Fado. *UML 2 Toolkit*. John Wiley & Sons, 2004.
3. S.-C. Hu. Application of the UML in Modeling SCORM-Conformant Contents. Intl. Conf. on Advanced Learning Technologies ICALT'05. IEEE, 2005.
4. M.C. Daconta, L.J. Obrst, and K.T. Klein. *The Semantic Web*. Wiley, 2003.
5. ADLNet. Sharable Content Object Reference Model SCORM, 2004.
6. IEEE Learning Technology Standards Committee LTSC. *IEEE P1484.12/D4.0 Standard for Learning Object Metadata (LOM)*. IEEE Computer Society, 2002.
7. R. Wilson. *The Role of Ontologies in Teaching and Learning*. Technology and Standards Watch Report TSW0402. JISC Joint Information Systems Committee, 2004. http://www.jisc.ac.uk/uploaded_documents/tsw_04_02.pdf.
8. T. Payne and O. Lassila. Semantic Web Services. *IEEE Intelligent Systems*, 19(4), 2004.
9. C. Pahl. Ontology Transformation and Reasoning for Model-Driven Architecture. In *International Conference on Ontologies, Databases and Applications of Semantics ODBASE'05*. Springer LNCS Series, 2005.
10. C. Pahl and E. Holohan. Ontology Technology for the Development and Deployment of Learning Technology Systems. In *Intl. Conf. on Educational Hyper- and Multimedia Edmedia'04*. AACE, 2004.

Context-Aware Workplace Learning Support: Concept, Experiences, and Remaining Challenges

Andreas Schmidt and Simone Braun

FZI Research Center for Information Technologies
Information Process Engineering
Haid-und-Neu-Strae 10-14, 76131 Karlsruhe, Germany
{Andreas.Schmidt, Simone.Braun}@fzi.de

Abstract. Workplace learning offers the unique possibility of the immediacy of purpose and real-world context. In order to leverage on this, we have developed a context-aware method to support workplace learning. In this paper, we want to describe the concept of context-steered learning, both from a content-driven and communication-driven perspective, and present corresponding system functionality primitives.

1 Introduction

In the wake of constructivism dominating pedagogy research during the last years, the situatedness of learning has come to the center of attention, also a result of the insight that traditional learning methods in the form of large decontextualized courses lead to inert knowledge; i.e., knowledge that can be reproduced, but not applied to real-world problem solving [1]. In order to avoid the inertness, pedagogy tries to set up authentic learning settings, an approach increasingly shared in e-learning domain. If we consider professional training, it is the immediacy of purpose and context that makes it largely different to learning in schools or academic education. This immediacy has the benefit that we actually have an authentic context that we need to preserve. The majority of current e-learning approaches, however, ignores this context and provides decontextualized forms of learning as a multimedia copy of traditional presence seminars.

Technology-enhanced workplace learning tries to leverage on the work context by providing solutions to smoothly integrate learning processes into work processes and—in a more advanced stage—to consciously reflect the work situation e.g. in learning objects. In this paper, we want to present the conceptual foundation for technically realizing context-aware learning support systems in which *awareness* has the aspects both of *knowing about* and *taking into account*.

First, we introduce the notion of *context-steered learning* (section 2) before operationalizing it in a conceptual model and methodology for workplace learning support together with the associated system primitives (section 3 and 4). We conclude with a comparison to the state of the art (section 5) and a summary and outlook (section 6).

W. Nejdl and K. Tochtermann (Eds.): EC-TEL 2006, LNCS 4227, pp. 518–524, 2006.

2   Redefining Guidance: The Notion of Context-Steered Learning

With formal training support, the system role seems to be quite clear: (a) provide functionality to find or to assign and to access learning resources, (b) to assess and track learning progress and (c) to provide tutoring support. The system is mainly reactive in the sense that employees need to consciously access the system in order to learn. With an increased level of informality and the associated higher degree of integration into everyday work processes, this system paradigm does no longer fit. This has already been realized both in research and practice, but the answer to that challenge mostly is the salvation of self-steered or self-directed learning. If we translate this, it actually means that we completely give up the concept of pedagogical guidance; learners search on their own for suitable learning resources as soon as they know what they don't know. They pace their learning progress and look for additional support as soon as they get stuck. This view is definitely a bit too nave. Even research on information seeking and information behavior has shown in empirical studies that already initiating a search process is a cognitively challenging barrier (cp. [2]).

Furthermore, guidance is not only important for the individual learner, but also for the company and the alignment of individual learning with corporate strategies, e.g., in the context of competence management and other human resource development approaches. So the question is not whether guidance is important, but rather how and which form of guidance. To redefine guidance, we have analyzed two extremes of guidance (course-steered vs. self-steered) and developed a new form of guidance (context-steered learning) [3], which shall be briefly introduced in the following:

– **Course-steered learning** currently is in the focus of corporate learning strategies. Learning activity is controlled by the pre-defined course structure, where courses typically are relatively large learning units, which can be subscribed to or assigned to. It is important to note that this encompasses both e-learning courses and presence seminars (and, of course, blended learning arrangements).
– **Self-steered learning** implies that the learner initiates and controls the learning process herself. Typically, she actively searches for learning resources, which help to satisfy the current knowledge need. This includes purposefully contacting colleagues for help on a particular problem.

The main drawback of course-steered learning is that it only allows for a limited integration of working and learning activities due to the coarse-grained nature. Self-steered learning on the other hand allows for interweaving these processes, but it requires non-trivial cognitive abilities (e.g. becoming aware of knowledge gaps and formulating a corresponding query in whatever form). In order to overcome these problems, we have elaborated a third type of learning process: **context-steered learning**. Here, the system observes the (potential) learners work activities, while she interacts with her everyday applications. The system deduces from its domain knowledge and the learner's knowledge potential knowledge gaps. For these gaps, the system can compile small learning programs from available learning resources and recommend them to the learner, who can decide whether to learn now, to postpone it, or to discard the recommendation completely. In the following two sections, we want to present a conceptual model for context-steered learning and primitives in the system functionality to realize context-aware learning functionality. We divide context-steered learning basically into two cases: learning through content and learning through communicating with other humans.

3   Content-Based Context-Steered Learning

Context-steered learning seems to be a natural transition from e-learning and knowledge management approaches. It is based on the assumption that there are small learning units that can be used on demand. Context-steered learning can be visualized as a process cycle, which appears as an on-demand 'detour' of the working processes and can be broken down into the following system primitives (see fig. 1):

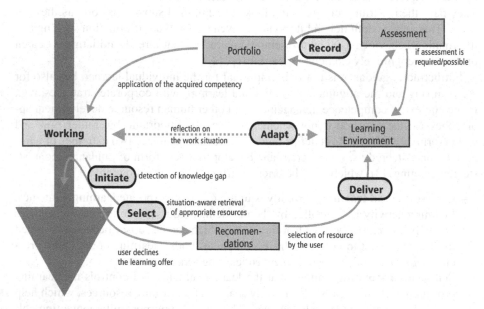

Fig. 1. Content-based context-steered learning

- **Initiate.** In the first phase, the system detects based on observations of the work context and background knowledge if there is a learning opportunity. This functionality refers to the timing *(when)* and modality *(how)* of interventions. These interventions can be interpreted as a sort of automated scaffolding activity of the system that tries to overcome learning barriers resulting from cognitive and affective factors typically associated with a knowledge gap. Timing and modality have to be carefully crafted (e.g., in the form of peripheral attention interfaces like balloon tooltips or tray icon animations) in order to avoid distracting and annoying the pontential learner.
- **Select.** Appropriate learning resources that help to satisfy the learner's knowledge need and that fit to the learner requirements are selected. Relevance criteria can range from current competencies or the current task or role via information about the technical equipment up to personal learning style and preferences. Some of

these criteria are hard criteria (mandatory for inclusion in the result set, e.g. objectives), others soft criteria (affecting ranking like interactivity level).

- **Deliver.** In contrast to traditional information retrieval & filtering (the paradigm of which is also prevalent in the domain of knowledge management), it is important to acknowledge that even for self-contained learning resources it might be not appropriate to deliver just a single learning object because the learner cannot understand it without learning other topics first. So the *what*-aspect of delivery cannot be restricted to simple filtering, but must also consider the aggregation of smaller parts into a delivery unit. Here, the context provides the constraints of this aggregation problem by specifying the prerequisites. This consideration of semantic constraints represent a form of pedagogical guidance [3], which avoids overstraining the individual with the unknown and thus helps to reduce (or at least not increase) the feeling of uncertainty typically associated with an information/knowledge need [4].

- **Adapt.** This is the domain of classical micro adaptivity in e-learning. This incorporates adaptive navigation support (to suggested further readings), the adaptation of presentation (e.g., in terms of verbosity or for mobile devices) and behavior of (active) learning content (*context-aware learning objects*) that directly responds to aspects of the situation (e.g., in simulations).

- **Record.** Moving from traditional formal training towards flexible on-demand learning implies that we can no longer rely on training certificates or impartial assessments. However, although often neglected, these certificates still play an important role in an employee's career. The most promising concept to overcome this problem are electronic portfolios [5]—in analogy to traditional portfolios documenting achievements in the area of creative arts. One often neglected aspect in the business context of classical formal training are certificates that can be obtained after successfully attending training activities. In the case of context-steered learning, electronic portfolios can form the basis for documenting the learning activity and its context in which it took place.

After completion of this micro learning process, the learner returns to his working process and has the possibility to apply the newly acquired competencies—and to return to the learning process if transfer to practice was not successful.

4 Communication-Based Context-Steered Learning

Although there is far more research on formal learning, learning objects and other explicit resources, the majority of learning activities informally takes place and within inter-human communication. Therefore, our research does not only comprise delivery of explicit learning resources, but also investigate how context can improve these informal processes. Apart from collaboration within teams or communities of practice, a very typical situation is what has recently been labeled as *informal teaching*: an employee asks her colleague about something, and the other side explains to her (cp. [6]). This situation is a generalization of the expert finder problem of knowledge management where the system knows about experts in certain subject areas and provides yellow pages to search for them.

In many practical cases, these expert finder applications are considered problematic because they lead to communication overload on the teacher's side. Also for learners, especially new and unexperienced employees who are almost always on the learner side, do not want to contact experts. They would feel more comfortable with *peers* with whom they can discuss their problem on a similar level. Obviously, establishing contact between an informal learner and an informal teacher cannot be reduced to the problem of identifying an expert for a subject area the learner wants to know about. Rather, this informal teaching must be supported in a context-aware way, which means negotiating between the teacher and the learner context. This can be broken down into the following functionality primitives (see fig. 2):

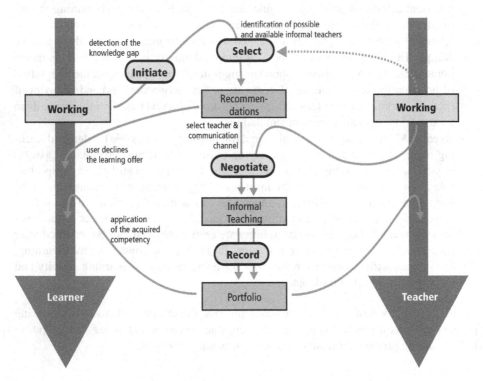

Fig. 2. Communication-based context-steered learning

- **Initiate.** This step is identical to the content-based approach.
- **Select.** In contrast to content (which is always available), informal learning through communication requires an informal teacher on the other side. Informal teaching is more complex than classical expert finding: learners often favour a person being on a par and at the same competence level; for instance, a person who has recently had the same problems and difficulties. Furthermore, before presenting recommended teachers, the system has to check their availability in a broader sense than pure presence. Availability signifies a person's receptiveness for communication and for the resulting interruption besides her physical presence and her reachability in terms of access to communication devices.

– **Negotiate.** To support the informal way of context-steered learning, it is insufficient only to recommend potential contact persons. Rather the system has to mediate the subsequent approach between the learner and the selected informal teacher. This reflects the problem that not only learning processes have to be integrated into the surrounding work processes, but also teaching processes. In this step, the system tries to find a compromise between the learner's need and the teacher's interest, taking into account contextual factors on both sides like current task, subject of the inquiry, urgency, and communication partner relationship. So the system has to balance the learner's need and the teacher's interest e.g. by delaying message delivery on the teacher's side, if the message is not urgent and the teacher is occupied, or by an explicit notification in the reverse case.

– **Record.** In addition to learning activities, also teaching activites are to be recorded.

5 Existing Approaches

Although context-aware learning support as a separate research field does not exist, there is prior work in many different fields:

Business-process-oriented knowledge management (BPOKM, e.g. [7]) has realized the importance of the process context for context-aware delivery and storage of knowledge assets. While it is true that business processes are an important element of the work context, they definitely are too narrow. Furthermore, BPOKM has so far completely ignored the concept of pedagogical guidance, viewing the problem mainly as a retrieval problem of the right content.

Macroadaptive e-learning approaches like [8] or [9] mainly adapt to the learner in terms of delivery. They filter the learning content based on the learner's competencies and the knowledge requirements of the current position or business process context. While this is an important step into the direction of context-aware learning support, they only consider rather static elements of the context, which does not allow for deeper integration of working and learning processes. **Microadaptive e-learning approaches** and adaptive hypermedia approaches are probably the area of research with the longest history and highest activity [10]. They focus primarily on the learning object behavior itself and how to adapt it to the learner and her characteristics. The main problem of current adaptive e-learning approaches is that they do not consider learning in a work context, but rather set up artificial contexts in learning labs.

6 Conclusions and Outlook

We presented a conceptual model that responds to the challenges of context-aware learning support: what is context, how to get it and how to make use of it. Context-steered learning provides a framework for on-demand learning support, both in the case of formal and informal learning. With an appropriate context infrastructure consisting of a sufficient amount of sensors and a management system that hides the complexity of dealing with contradictory, uncertain and aging information, this is also technically feasible. For the content-oriented part, this has been shown in the EU-funded project *Learning in Process* [3] and subsequent industry projects. The communication-based methods have been successfully demonstrated outside the learning domain [11] and are now developed further within the project *Im Wissensnetz*.

Currently, we are working on broadening the scope of awareness to making learning support *socially aware*, i.e. aware of the individual's perspective on social relationships, and on incorporating knowledge maturing processes [12] (with the learner as content generator) into the concept.

Acknowledgments. This work has been co-funded by the European Commission under contract IST-2001-32518 and the German Federal Ministry of Education and Research in the project *Im Wissensnetz*.

References

1. Bereiter, C., Scardamalia, M.: Cognitive Coping Strategies and the Problem of 'Inert Knowledge'. In Chipman, S., Seagal, J., Glaser, R., eds.: Thinking and Learning Skills. Volume 2. LEA, Hillside, NJ, USA (1985)
2. Niedzwiedzka, B.: A proposed general model of information behaviour. Information Research **9** (2003)
3. Schmidt, A.: Bridging the Gap Between Knowledge Management and E-Learning withContext-Aware Corporate Learning Solutions. In: 3rd Conference on Professional Knowledge Management (WM 2005). Volume 3782 of LNAI., Springer (2005) 203–213
4. Kuhlthau, C.C.: Seeking Meaning: A Process Approach to Library and Information Services. 2nd edition edn. Libraries Unlimited, Westport, CT (2004)
5. Tosh, D., Werdmuller, B.: The Learning Landscape: a conceptual framework for ePortfolios. interact **2004** (2004) 14–15
6. Grebow, D.: At the Water Cooler of Learning. Transforming Culture: An Executive Briefing on the Power of Learning (2002) 55–57
7. Abecker, A.: Business process oriented knowledge management: concepts, methods, and tools. PhD thesis, Fakultt fr Wirtschaftswissenschaften, Universitt Karlsruhe (2004)
8. Woelk, D., Agarwal, S.: Integration of e-Learning and Knowledge Management. In: World Conference on E-Learning in Corporate, Government, Health Institutions,and Higher Education. Volume 1. (2002) 1035–1042
9. Davis, J., Kay, J., Kummerfeld, B., Poon, J., Quigley, A., Saunders, G., Yacef, K.: Using Workflow, User Modeling and Tutoring Strategies for Just-in-time Document Delivery. Journal of Interactive Learning **4** (2005) 131–148
10. Park, O.C., Lee, J.: Adaptive Instructional Systems. In Jonassen, D.H., ed.: Handbook of research for educational communications and technology. 2nd edition edn. Lawrence Erlbaum, Mahwah, N.J. (2004) 651–684
11. Gross, T., Braun, S., Krause, S.: Matchbase: A development suite for efficient context-aware communication. In: Proceedings of PDP 2006, Los Alamitos, CA, IEEE Computer Society Press (2006) 308–315
12. Schmidt, A.: Knowledge Maturing and the Continuity of Context as a Unifying Conceptfor Knowledge Management and E-Learning. In: Proceedings of I-KNOW 05, Graz, Austria. (2005)

A Context-Model for Supporting Work-Integrated Learning

Armin Ulbrich[1], Peter Scheir[1], Stefanie N. Lindstaedt[1],
and Manuel Görtz[2]

[1] Know-Center, Graz, Inffeldgasse 21a
8010 Graz, Austria
{aulbrich, pscheir, slind}@know-center.at
http://www.know-center.at/
[2] SAP Research CEC Darmstadt, Bleichstraße 8
64283 Darmstadt, Germany
manuel.goertz@sap.com
http://www.sap.com/research/

Abstract. This contribution introduces the so-called Workplace Learning Context as essential conceptualisation supporting self-directed learning experiences directly at the workplace. The Workplace Learning Context is to be analysed and exploited for retrieving 'learning' material that best-possibly matches with a knowledge worker's current learning needs. In doing so, several different 'flavours' of work-integrated learning can be realised including task learning, competency-gap based support and domain-related support. The Workplace Learning Context Model, which is also outlined in this contribution, forms the technical representation of the Workplace Learning Context.

1 Introduction

Knowledge workers are workers whose critical work resource within their essential value creating tasks is knowledge [2]. In order to enhance the productivity of knowledge workers, their competency enhancement and learning has to take place directly at their workplaces. This work has been carried out as part of the APOSDLE project. APOSDLE[1] is a 48 months research and development (R&D) integrated project partially supported by the European Community under the Information Society Technologies (IST) priority of the 6th framework programme for R&D. Work-integrated learning aims at fostering the learning transfer (i.e. the application of what has been learnt to current job activities [4]). Work-integrated learning does not merely rely on pre-defined development plans and on learning resources, which are specifically designed and produced for dedicated learning situations.

Work-integrated learning instead mainly considers knowledge workers' actual tasks, personal competency disposition and work domain as relevant contextual information for deriving current learning needs. A knowledge worker's context provides the basic search criterion for retrieving 'learning' content from organizational

---

[1] http://www.aposdle.org

W. Nejdl and K. Tochtermann (Eds.): EC-TEL 2006, LNCS 4227, pp. 525–530, 2006.

memories during experiences of self-directed learning. By that several 'flavours' of workplace learning can be realised including the following:

- *Task learning*: At design-time, generic tasks are related to resources, which are considered relevant for executing the given task. The user-context-model allows for deriving these resources from the user's current task and presenting the user with them.
- *Competency-gap based support*: At design-time tasks are provided with competencies that are necessary for executing the task. At run-time the competencies a user possesses are compared to the competencies necessary for executing the task at hand. This comparison may result in a so-called competency gap. The user-context-model allows for deriving those competencies that are necessary to fill the competency gap.
- *Task execution support* and *domain-related support*: At run-time, tasks are related to domain concepts basing on the work domain, within which the task is going to be executed. The user-context-model allows for deriving these domain concepts.

In the next section the so-called 3spaces will be introduced. The 3spaces is a conceptual model providing an abstract view on those technical systems making up an IT-based workplace. Starting from the 3spaces the Workplace Learning Context Model will be presented. Its objective is to represent the knowledge worker's context in such a way that it provides a means to the end of exploiting the context for self-directed learning experiences.

2   3spaces and the Context of Knowledge Workers

A typical IT-based workplace of knowledge work does consist of at least three conceptual spaces ([7]), each of which can be composed of several technical systems.

- The *work space*: The work space represents work relevant devices, tools and resources and is typically structured according to the user's tasks and work processes.
- The *learning space:* The learning space represents the individuals' competencies that have been acquired during experiences of conscious learning as well as learning that unconsciously occurred during work execution.
- The *knowledge space*: The knowledge space represents the knowledge that is stored within organisational memories. Ideally, knowledge is structured according to relationships defined by the semantics inherent to a given knowledge domain.

For the rest of this contribution we refer to the three spaces introduced as the *3spaces* as depicted in Figure 1. It is important to note that all three spaces are typically structured differently (structural disconnection) and are implemented by heterogeneous systems (technical disconnection) (see [3]).

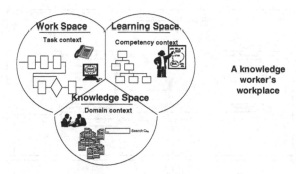

Fig. 1. A knowledge worker's workplace

From a user's point of view the 3spaces constitute what we will call the *Workplace Context* of a user. The Workplace Context is an abstract conception of the relevant conditions and factors influencing a user at her workplace resulting from the properties of the 3spaces. The technologies and concepts of the 3spaces provide the context in which a knowledge worker executes her value-creating tasks. It is our dedicated goal to exploit the knowledge worker's context in order to supporting her during experiences of self-directed learning and competency development.

We have provided a preliminary definition of what we consider the context to be made of. This definition proceeds on several different conceptualisations concerning context such as [1], [5], [9] and [10]: The context is the substrate in which events occur and allows a meaningful interpretation of data. A context is characterized by a relevant subset of all surrounding potentially dynamic (e.g. temporal, environmental) information and (external and internal) conditions. To assess the relevance a goal must be considered, which is bound to an entity.

3 Workplace Learning Context Model

The Workplace Learning Context Model is the technical representation of what we understand as being relevant information and conditions for the Workplace Context of a knowledge worker. The Workplace Learning Context Model is divided into three packages – competency, process, and domain – which are each directly related to one of the three diverse spaces of the 3spaces introduced above (see Figure 2 showing the diagram using the Unified Modelling Language (UML[2]) notation for class diagrams).

The integration of the three spaces is achieved by a loose coupling of the packages through connection of conceptually analogous elements from each of the 3spaces. The packages and their core elements are outlined hereinafter.

3.1 The Process Package

The *process package* (center in Figure 2) is directly related to the *work space* from the 3spaces. The link to the domain package (see Section 3.2) results from the presumption,

---

[2] http://www.uml.org/

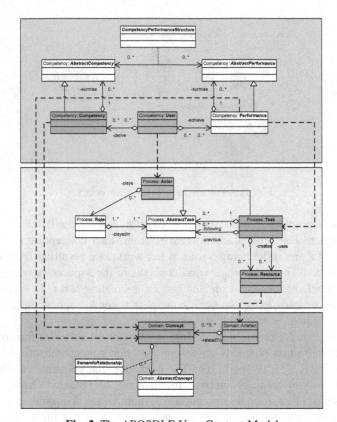

Fig. 2. The APOSDLE User-Context-Model

that information available for support of work-integrated learning is stored within the organisational memory. The relationship is modelled by the associations between the elements `Task` and `Resource` within the process package. A task is an activity a user performs. Resources are equivalent to elements of type `Artefact` from the domain package, which serves to model knowledge artefacts from the organizational memory. The link to the competency package (see below for a more detailed description) is provided by the relation between the elements `Task` and `Role`, where a role is incorporated by a number of actors. An `Actor` is equivalent to an element of the type `User`, which is modelled within the competency package.

3.2 The Competency Package

The *competency package* (top in Figure 2) addresses personal knowledge. Competencies represent the individual knowledge workers' competencies. The *competency package* is directly related to the *learning space* from the 3spaces. We will follow the understanding of competencies in [6]. Here a competency is perceived as non-observable, theoretical construct denoting a personal characteristic of a human person (e.g. knowledge or ability), which is applicable to differing contexts. A person shows evidence of possessing competencies in that she masters certain so-called performances (i.e. exercises and problems). The performances' outcomes are observable and measurable.

The links between the competency package and the other two packages are as follows: The modelling element `User` within the competency package is connected to the elements `Competency` (i.e. the competencies a user possesses) and `Performance` (i.e. the work-related activities a user has executed). A `User` is equivalent to an `Actor` in the process package (see above). The modelling element `Concept` from the domain package (see below) is used for labelling the elements `Competency` and `Performance`.

3.3 The Domain Package

The *domain package* is directly related to the *knowledge space* of the 3spaces. The domain package is linked to the other two packages in the following ways: The link to the process package is provided through the relationship between the model elements `Concept` and `Artefact`, where artefacts are equivalent to elements of the type `Resource` from the process package (see Figure 2 and above). The domain package and the competency package are related in such a way that the modelling elements `Concept` form the vocabulary for labelling the elements of type `Competency` and `Performance` in the competency package.

4 Conclusion and Future Work

With this contribution we have presented the Workplace Learning Context and the Workplace Learning Context Model. The basic objective of creating the Workplace Learning Context Model is to provide means to retrieve relevant resources from the underlying 3spaces. This is done to support workers during experiences of self-directed learning such as the following:

- Task learning
- Task execution support
- Competency-gap based support

For the future we are planning to investigate into how to model the actual user profile. We will aim at incorporating well-elaborated research results in that field (see for instance [8]). We will also have to integrate the Workplace Learning Context Model with the software architecture that is going to be developed for the APOSDLE platform. In that a retrieval infrastructure for retrieving and presenting work-relevant, context-dependent resources will be developed.

Acknowledgements

This work has been co-funded by the European Union through the IST program under FP6. The Know-Center is funded by the Austrian Competence Center program Kplus under the auspices of the Austrian Ministry of Transport, Innovation and Technology (www.ffg.at/index.php?cid=95) and by the State of Styria.

References

1. Dey, A.K., Abowd, G.D., Salber, D.: A Conceptual Framework and a Toolkit for Supporting the Rapid Prototyping of Context-Aware Applications. In: Human-Computer Interaction Journal, Vol. 16, Nr. 2-4 (2001) 97—166
2. Drucker, Peter F.: Post-Capitalist Society. HarperBusiness (1993)
3. Farmer, J., Lindstaedt, S.N., Droschl, G., Luttenberger, P.: AD-HOC – Work-integrated Technology-supported Teaching and Learning. Proceedings of the 5th Conference on Organisational Knowledge, Learning and Capabilities 2004, Austria (2004)
4. Haskell, R.E.: Transfer of Learning: Cognition and Instruction. Elsevier Academic Press (2001)
5. Kobsa, A., Koenemann, J., Pohl, W.: Personalised hypermedia presentation techniques for improving online customer relationships. In: The Knowledge Engineering Review, Vol. 16, Nr. 2 (2001) 111—155
6. Ley, T., Albert, D.: Identifying Employee Competencies in Dynamic Work Domains: Methodological Considerations and a Case Study. In: Journal of Universal Computer Science, Vol. 9, Nr. 12 (2003) 1500—1518
7. Lindstaedt, S.N., Farmer, J.: Kooperatives Lernen in Organsiationen. Haake, J., Schwabe, G., Wessner, M. (eds.): CSCL-Kompendium, Oldenbourg Wissenschaftsverlag (2004) 191-220
8. Montaner, M., López, B., De la Rosa, J.L.: A Taxonomy of Recommender Agents on the Internet. Artificial Intelligence Review, Vol. 19 (2003) 285—330
9. Oppermann, R.: From User-adaptive to Context-adaptive Information System. i-com Zeitschrift für interaktive und kooperative Medien, Vol. 4, Nr. 3 (2005) 4 – 14
10. Wessner, M.: Kontextuelle Kooperation - Unterstützung kooperativen Lernens auf Basis des Kontextes. In: J.M. Haake, U. Lucke, D. Tavangarian (eds.): Lecture Notes in Informatics, Vol. 66, GI-Edition LNI (2005) 57—68

Made-to-Measure Learning Materials

Magí Almirall, Muriel Garreta, and Josep Rivera

Universitat Oberta de Catalunya, Av. Tibidabo 39
08035 Barcelona, Spain
{malmirall, murielgd, jrivera}@uoc.edu

Abstract. This paper presents how we developed a solution to easily publish learning contents in the formats that best fulfill students' needs at each specific moment of their learning process. The basis is an XML standard file from which different format outputs are generated automatically. The output interface is designed using human-computer interaction (HCI) methodologies and following e-learning and accessibility standards. We describe here the creation process of three different formats: a paper format generated in two sizes (pocket and folio), a Web format based on standards of e-learning and an accessible Digital Talking Book (DTB) format. This adaptation of the output format to meet students' needs resulted in an increase of their satisfaction, not only regarding the interface but also the overall materials service. Therefore, by solely changing the output of the contents, students' perception - as shown by satisfaction surveys - was that the quality of the contents had increased.

Keywords: E-learning contents, e-learning standards, usability lab, human-computer interaction, accessibility.

1 Introduction

The UOC, in English, Open University of Catalonia, is a completely virtual university founded in 1995. It currently has more than 35,000 students and offers 19 official undergraduate degrees as well as several graduate programs. UOC's virtual campus is an integrated e-learning environment that allows students to pursue their studies completely online except for final exams when appropriate.

All UOC's learning materials were written specifically for e-learning purposes. As a result, a total of 1,000 course materials have been developed for our students. Since most of these materials were created some time ago, when it was required to update and improve them we encountered important inconveniences; for example, modifying their interface in order to increase accessibility and usability was extremely costly and by no means automatic.

The goal of the project described in the present paper was to explore the possibility of developing an automatic system for treating contents based on e-learning and accessibility standards and using human-computer interaction (HCI) methodologies to design the output, with the objective to increase students' satisfaction and therefore improve their learning experience. Consequently, the contents' edition would need to

W. Nejdl and K. Tochtermann (Eds.): EC-TEL 2006, LNCS 4227, pp. 531–536, 2006.

be independent of their output format. Empirical HCI methods were then used to evaluate and analyze the usability of those formats.

When we evaluated the possible initial formats to work with, we decided to focus on two main formats: paper and web, their accessibility and usability. The paper format best suits students when continuous reading is required; in this context, the student sometimes prefers a pocket book and other times, a folio size. The added value of the web format is the interactivity and the possibility to quickly search for a specific concept. Different formats are then needed to satisfy user's needs at different times, in different moments, and in different ways. Our study concluded that one same user may require all formats depending on their lifestyle and personal characteristics.

For example, a virtual university student that wishes to advance in her studies while commuting to work on the train will need a light weight and fit-in-the-bag format (i.e. chapter pocket book format). But she might also wish to work on an assignment during lunch hour at work for which she will need to quickly find the meaning of concepts, definitions, email the professor for questions, etc. (i.e. search-based course material), and will also want to work on her studies at night, when the children are asleep and the energy level is low and attention span barely gone. In this case, she will require a more passive yet stimulating format (i.e. a DVD format, so the user can sit down, relax and learn). In conclusion, user studies contributed to identify the above and other multiple formats that a virtual university would require to provide in order to facilitate users' learning experience.

Taking into account that user characteristics and abilities differ depending on their context and moment of use, accessibility and usability were then seen as intertwined and of utmost importance, as a user was able to access something at one time (web-based material during work hours) but was not able to access the same at a later time (during their train commute). In conclusion, if we needed to develop multiple formats from one same course material, we needed to find a way in which we could do so quickly and cost-efficiently.

Moreover, for web formats, we wanted to comply with the standard SCORM [1] to benefit from their functions of tracking and reuse. The accessibility format had two foci: to apply the section 508 norm [11] in the web format and to create a new format thought for the accessibility, a Digital Talking Book of DAISY type.

2 Developing Usable Interfaces

Several empirical and inspection methods exist for designing and evaluating interfaces. We decided to focus on empirical methodologies and more specifically we used the development of personas, interviews and iterative user testing.

Our initial task was to analyze UOC's statistical information to help us build user profiles. We decided to use this method because we consider user archetypes as a key factor in usability processes [12] as well as a powerful design and communication tool. However, and as opposed to Cooper's method [3], we believe that the persona creation process should involve both quantitative and qualitative information [5]. From our initial analysis consisting of 200 surveys, we defined different user profiles and then conducted user interviews for a qualitative validation of these personas.

Afterwards and in order to also validate these profiles from a quantitative point of view, we ran a second round of surveys to a higher number of students. With the obtained 1,108 responses we came out with four user profiles according to their usage of the learning materials including format, location, purpose, satisfaction and preference. Table 1 shows one of the variables used to define these profiles.

Table 1. Reading materials frequency depending on format and location by user profile

	Dedicated (11%)	Explorers (25%)	Standard (54%)	Noninvolved (9%)
Total 1108				
Support used				
Computer	86%	72%	73%	8%
Paper	96%	94%	98%	46%
Location of use				
Home	98%	98%	100%	49%
Work	51%	27%	35%	8%
Public place	9%	8%	7%	1%
Public transportation	15%	14%	13%	13%

The user profiles were the basis for the recruitment screening for the two rounds of user testing. In total, we run tests with thirty users. Although several authors proclaim that testing with fewer users is enough to find most usability problems [8], we also benefited of the possibility of observing more students using our materials given that the effort required to test more users is not much higher.

For the user tests, we decided to use a hi-fi prototype of the materials where students could reproduce the way they work with interactive materials. In order to select the tasks that would show us the way students use the course materials, we defined user scenarios based on the three personas developed. Each user profile had different goals when using materials and the accomplishment of these goals defined the tasks for the user test. The quantitative data from our web logs were also a source of information for the creation of the set of tasks and supported our conclusions.

For our portable usability laboratory we used Morae software [13]. With this software we captured a video image mixing the PC screen and the student's face. At the same time Morae can save all clicks and keyboard actions in a file. For the analysis of our tests, we took into account the number of clicks and the time needed to accomplish the task. Simultaneously, the users were observed and their expressions and comments noted to support the test results. These tests results were also shared with a multidisciplinary team of observers whose work was a key factor in this project. Specifically, the team was formed by two developers from the IT department, two persons from the content management group, one pedagogue, one psychologist and one graphical designer.

The observers' analysis of both the interactions and observations recorded was the basis for the interface improvements, and with their recommendations a new prototype was built, to run a second set of user tests. The results of the second iteration showed an improvement of more than 50% from the first set of tests.

3 Developing Accessible Interfaces

There are several actions on the Internet aiming to standardize accessibility. From these, two key norms have to be considered, the "section 508" [11] and the Web Accessibility Initiative (WAI) [15]. This last norm is divided in tree levels: A, AA, AAA. The level AA of WAI is similar to "section 508" as shown by the Thatcher analysis [14], which is the standard we aim to have for all our developments.

During our research process, we also found several proposals of specific formats for disabled people. One of these was the Digital Audio-Based Information System (DAISY) [4], a new technology to develop and distribute books and contents. With DAISY it is possible to use the Digital Talking Books (DTB) in order to meet the needs of visual impaired people. This format combines audio files with structure files in order to offer simple navigation for the user. Books in DAISY format grant greater speed of reading and greater easiness of access to different parts of the book. This format can be read by small portable devices and by a personal computer with special software like the system to play digital talking books on a PC analyzed by Morley [7].

Our work to design accessible interfaces undertook two parallel tasks. One focus was aimed to obtain interfaces designed by usability methods in WAI AA level, and the other, the development of an automatic generator of the DAISY format. The WAI AA level focus is straightforward and there is automatic software to analyze the results like Bobby [2]. However, to develop a digital talking book in DAISY format we needed to create a concrete file structure.

The file structure we developed has an initial file named discinfo.html, in which DAISY players can found all our books. From there, the DAISY players go to the first file of a book named ncc.html. The ncc.html file contains the book index to allow for easy navigation and the references to the *.smil files. With the smil files we synchronized the navigation and the audio files.

4 Advantages and Engines for Automatic Transformation

As we have seen, when learning materials are in XML format we can easily build many output formats. XML offers important advantages for big volumes of similar contents like our 1,000 different course materials:

- We can generate different output formats from one unique source with lower costs since the cost to generate XML is similar to the one to generate HTML.
- XML facilitates the introduction of a continuous improvement process of formats and interfaces, because by changing the XSL filter all contents are modified at the same time.
- It helps in the semantic markup, once the content has been atomized and identified as many superior markup layers (which relate elements) as needed can be created.
- The generation of SCORM-compliant materials from XML facilitates their later management in different e-learning platforms.

As mentioned earlier, for this specific project we automated the generation of four formats requiring the development of three different conversion engines. We fabricated two forms of book (pocket and folio), a Web format based in standards of e-learning and an accessible Digital Talking Book (DTB-DAISY). The engines for automatic transformation were developed in XSL technologies and Java when needed.

The engine for the web format works in two steps. First the engine creates the HTML pages and the manifest.xml SCORM file which contains the navigation data. Afterwards, using the SCORM information from the manifest.xml file, the engine creates the navigation menu and the search service.

The PDF format engine takes XML file and outputs the PDF format also with two steps like Leslie, D. M. [6]. This engine uses the specifications of the World Wide Web Consortium (W3C) about information presentation, Formatting Objects (FO) [9] and changes the XML to the FO language. Then the program uses the Formatting Object Processor (FOP) [16] to change from the FO to the PDF format.

For this project we developed two filters for the PDF format, the resulting output is of enough quality to directly produce books. These filters control columns, images, widows and orphan lines, etc. In these cases the XSL engine uses Java programs to count lines and control spaces. In order to obtain the best possible output, it was necessary to modify the FOP since it didn't cover the full FO standard, especially for orphans and widows lines. This gave us the opportunity to rewrite the code of this Open Source initiative.

Our engine to generate a material in the DAISY format has three parts. We have the XML content as we mentioned earlier and the first task is to clean the XML content to obtain a valid text for voice synthesizer. Second the engine sends the valid text to the synthesizer (we use Loquendo voice synthesizer [10]) and from this stage we obtain the audio files in wav format. The engine finishes its work by creating the smil, ncc and discinfo files.

5 Conclusion

The work described in this paper was the starting point to begin the transformation of our 1,000 learning materials. Now, using XML we can easily and iteratively work on the process of improvement based on usability and accessibility premises.

The students' feedback on the results of the project has been very positive as shown by the semiannual survey for the University students. The satisfaction regarding the learning materials went up ten points from 64% to 74 % in the courses where the new formats were used.

This project opens new possibilities such as the development of an editor engine to easily create XML files at editorial companies or the standardization of the XML in RDF to unify the e-learning content base. Regarding the output formats, we have now an easy way to develop many types of outputs: audio, DVD, contents for PDA, iPod, etc. The question is which formats are best for the students considering their goals, learning strategies and the context of study. Our plan is to keep using HCI methodologies in order to answer this and other questions.

Acknowledgements

This work is partially supported by the Spanish MCYT and the FEDER funds ref. FIT-350201-2004-6 (AMEDIDA) and FIT-350300-2005-20 (MAT 2).

References

1. ADL: Sharable Content Object Reference Model (SCORM) overview, http://www.adlnet.org.
2. Bobby, HTML analyser, Center for Applied Special Technology, http://www.cast.org/bobby.
3. Digital Audio-based Information System , http://www.daisy.org.
4. Dix, A., Finlay, J., Abowd, G., Beale R.: Human-Computer Interaction. Prentice Hall, Hillsdale, NJ (1998)
5. Kujala, S. and Kauppinen, M.: Identifying and selecting users for user-centered design. In Proc. of the Third Nordic Conference on HCI (2004)
6. Leslie, D. M.: Transforming documentation from the XML doctypes used for the apache website to DITA. Proc. of the 19th Annual international Conference on Computer Documentation. SIGDOC '01. ACM Press (2001)
7. Mor, E. Minguillón, J.: E-learning Personalization based on Itineraries and Long-term Navigational Behavior, In: Proc. of the Thirteenth World Wide Web Conference. (2004) 264-265
8. Morley, S.: Digital talking books on a PC: a usability evaluation of the prototype DAISY playback software, Proc. of the third international ACM conference on Assistive technologies (1998) 157-164
9. Nielsen, J.: Usability Engineering. Morgan Kaufmann, San Francisco, CA (1993)
10. Pawson, D.: XSL-FO. Making XML Look Good in Print , O'Reilly & Associates, Inc. Sebastopol, CA (2002)
11. Quazza, Silvia. Laura Donetti, Loreta Moisa, Pier Luigi Salza. Actor: a multilingual unit-selection speech synthesis system. Proc. of 4th ISCA (2001)
12. Section 508, http://www.section508.gov.
13. Sinha, R.: Persona development for information-rich domains. In CHI '03 Extended Abstracts on Human Factors in Computing Systems (2003) 830-831
14. Thatcher, J.: Compare WAI-section 508, http://jimthatcher.com/sidebyside.htm (2003)
15. Web Accessibility Initiative (WAI), http://www.w3.org/WAI
16. XML Graphic Project, http://xml.apache.org/fop

The Problem of LD Execution and the Need for an IMS LD Level B Ontology

Ricardo R. Amorim, Eduardo Sánchez, and Manuel Lama

Department of Electronics and Computer Science, University of Santiago de Compostela
Campus Univesitario Sur s/n, 15782 Santiago de Compostela, A Coruña, Spain
`rramorin@usc.es, eduardos@usc.es, lama@dec.usc.es`

Abstract. This paper presents an ontology describing the semantics of the level B of the IMS Learning Design specification. The ontology is aimed at supporting intelligent agents to automate the tasks involved during the execution of IMS LD documents. The work includes a taxonomy of concepts, a set of axioms formalized in first order logic, and a case study. The ontology was built with Protégé, represented in OWL, and finally translated in XML Schema for validation with the Reload tool.

1 Introduction

This paper focuses on the representational and runtime issues of the IMS Learning Design specification (IMS-LD) [1], a model of semantic notation describing content and process of unit of study[2]. In it information model, three levels of implementation and compliance are specified: *(1)* level A, containing the core concepts needed to support pedagogical diversity; *(2)* level B, extending level A with Properties and Conditions in order to support more sophisticated behaviours, personalization and learner interactions, and *(3)* level C, adding Notifications to the previous levels. With these elements, the IMS LD offers flexible expressiveness to represent any design as well as an XML Schema representation to execute IMS LD documents during runtime. However, this information model presents some important expressiveness limitations: *(a)* the meaning of concepts is usually expressed on *natural language* which difficult software implementation [3]; and *(b)* the XML-Schema provided [4] is not expressive enough to describe all semantics associated to the elements of IMS-LD (e.g., is-a relations, properties of relations and *axioms* cannot be represented) [5]. To solve this problem, a ontology [6] can be used to semantically describe both structure and meaning of the IMS-LD elements. In this way, an ontology of IMS-LD level A have been presented [3].

At this point, we address the problem of executing Learning Designs. For this task, IMS LD Level B is key to support a complete learning flow description of Units of Learning and ontologies are required to formally describe the semantics implicit in the information model. It enables software agents to perform complex tasks related to the authoring, production and delivery stages in a IMS-LD runtime system [7].

In the following section, a solution in terms of an ontology of the IMS LD Level B is presented; section 3 explores the possibilities of the ontology in a case study; and section 4 finally discusses the contribution of the presented work.

W. Nejdl and K. Tochtermann (Eds.): EC-TEL 2006, LNCS 4227, pp. 537–542, 2006.
© Springer-Verlag Berlin Heidelberg 2006

2 Ontology Description

The ontology was built on top of the IMS LD level A ontology presented in [4]. The Level B concepts were obtained from elements and relations explicitly represented in the IMS-LD information model document. A set of axioms was additionally included to guarantee the consistency of the definitions and to represent implicit knowledge.

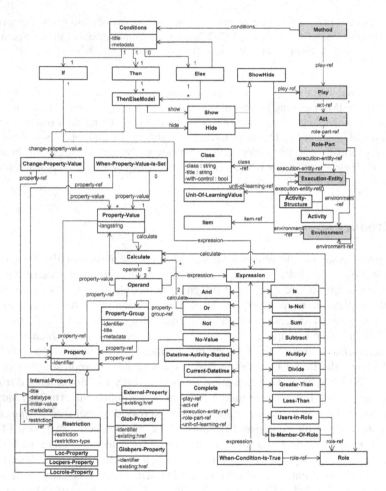

Fig. 1. The Level B concept taxonomy (concepts of level A in grey)

The IMS-LD level B adds the Property concept to the level A to extend the description of the elements of level A. Properties represent data that can be stored enabling to maintain information about Role, Learner and the execution state of some entities such as Play, Act, Activities. The properties constitute an essential part of monitoring, personalization, assessment, and user-interaction processes. Properties, for instance, can be used: (1) to represent personal preferences in a Learning Design such as the language preference required to adapt the Environment used during the execution of activities; and (2) to determine when an action is triggered (i.e. on the completion of an act). Considering the scope of a property and its relationship with the `Restriction` concept, we have classified the properties in *Internal Properties* (created by learning designer with their own names, types and values) that has a UoL scope and *External Properties* (defined according to an agreed vocabulary) with a runtime scope, which means that can be used by different UoLs. The `Restriction` concept allows the designer to constrain possible values (e.g. fractionDigits, Length, totalDigits) of an internal property. For example, a property related to a person's name could have a maximum number of characters (restriction=30; restriction-type=´maxLength´). The `Property-Group` concept allows the clustering of different properties.

The Conditions concept is aggregated into the Method concept and it is used along with properties to facilitate the learning design refinement. For example, in a Method, Conditions can be introduced either to show or hide entities such as Play, Activity and Environment in a personalized way. In this sense, the value of a Locpers-Property instance can be used to determine when the isvisible attribute of a specific Learning-Object (in an Environment) is true. The Conditions concept (figure 3) has a typical programming language structure: IF [expression] THEN/ELSE [show/hide something or change property-value]. In the `IF` concept, the `Expression` concept is related to a set of logical operators (i.e. `And`, `Or`, `Greater-Than`), a set of calculate operators (`Sum`, `Subtract`, `Multiply`) and some specifics LD expression operators (e.g. `Users-In-Role`, `Datetime-Activity-Started`). The `Then` concept is related to the statements which are executed when the evaluated expression in a `If` instance is *true* and the `Else` concept is related to the statements executed when the evaluated expression in the `If` instance is *false*. The `Show` and the `Hide` concepts specify the value of the `is-visible` attribute of an entity (`Item`, `Play`, `Environment`, `Execution-Entity`, `Class`) when an instance of the expression in a `If` instance is evaluated in runtime. For example, in a test, if the value of a property instance "Answer 2" corresponds to the correct answer, a message ("Congratulations") as instance of a `Class` concept is showed.

Following the same steps in [3], for the IMS-LD level B ontology, 20 axioms were found: firstly, the constraints in the text of the IMS-LD Information Model and the IMS-LD Best Practice Guide was identified, then the text was rewritten, and finally described in first order logic (*Formal Description*).

3 Case Study

To demonstrate the application of the IMS-LD ontology, the Jigsaw methodology has been chosen (Figure 2). Besides its popularity, this technique is suitable to understand how cooperation-based learning activities are carried out in activities that can easily be broken down into their constituent parts. In short, the Jigsaw consists on the following steps: (1) Jigsaw presentation, in which the directions are explained and the students are organized in groups of 4 or 5 individuals; (2) Jigsaw First Part, in which different learning material is assigned to each member of the group, so that each student receives a fragment of the information of any given topic that is the matter of the study, and then prepares the topic joining up with the members of the other groups who have the same topic; (3) Jigsaw Second Part, in which the students return to their initial groups in order to explain and discuss the topic along with the other members; and (4) a final evaluation.

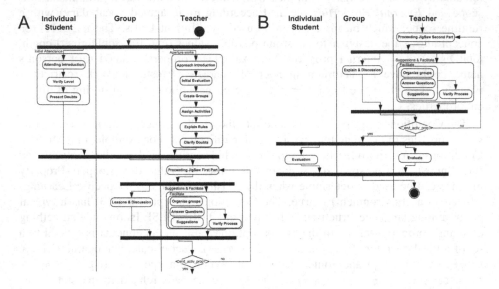

Fig. 2. (A) Jigsaw presentation and First Part; (B) Second Part and final evaluation

As it can be seen in Figure 3, the `Method` representing the Jigsaw approach has a `Play` made up of a set of `Acts`, which are executed in sequence. Each `Act` comprises a set of concurrent `Role Parts` that relates roles (professor, student, etc.) with activities. The `Complete Act` concept is used to control the end of an `Act`, either stating the maximum time for the realization of the `Act`, or the associated `Role Parts` that must be completed. For instance, the *Jigsaw presentation (JS-Pres)* `Act` refers to the activities to be performed during the initial stage of the Jigsaw and is made up of two `Role Parts`: *Aperture Works (Ap_Work)* and *Initial Attendance (In_Att)*. A relation *jsfm-wrpc:when-role-part-completed* between the instances *jsfm-cp* of `Complete Act` and *In_Att* of `Role Part` is used to indicate when this `Act` is completed. In this `Act`, the professor carries out the following activities with the groups: objectives presentation, in which he explains the topic of the subject; student assessment, in which an assessment in order to verify the students' prospects and needs is carried out; group creation, in which the activities to be realized and the rules and criteria of the evaluation are explained. These activities are represented by a series of `Support` or `Learning Activities` that are grouped into `Activity Structures`. Each `Role Part` associates a single `Support Activity`, `Learning Activity` or `Activity Structure` to a certain `Role`.

An `activity Structure` is completed when the value of the `number-to-select` attribute is equal to the number of the activities in the set that have been completed. The two `Acts` following the *Jigsaw Presentation* `Act` are the key moments in the Jigsaw technique. The *Jigsaw Part 1* comes when the groups are formed with students with the same study topic. Each topic is a part of the whole subject to be studied, around which the students carry out the activities according to the information that has been supplied by the professor. In the *Jigsaw Part 2* each group comprises students that, collectively, possess all the study material. In this Act, each student explains the topic that he has previously studied to the rest of the group. In parallel, the professor monitors and guides the activities carried out by each group.

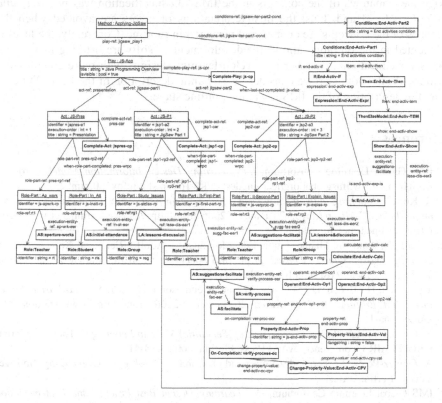

Fig. 3. Instantiation of the IMS LD Level B Ontology for the Jigsaw example

With IMS-LD Level B, more complex behaviours can be described. Using the Conditions concept and the Property concept, a sophisticated learning flow could be described. For example, in order to repeat the activities of the First Part and Second Part of the JigSaw, two Conditions were defined using an instance of the Property concept: *end-activ-prop*. The expression defined as an instance of the If concept (Is *end-activ-prop*, false) decides the value of the Show action, which determines the *isVisible* attribute of the activities suggestions-facilitate and lessons-discussion. When the activity verify-process is finished, an instance of On-Completion (*verify- process-oc*) change the value of *end-activ-prop*, setting it to true, what means the end of this part of the process.

4 Discussion and Future Work

The description of IMS-LD based on natural language imposes serious limitations for automated processing. Different implementers can include IMS LD misinterpretations during the development of applications Although the XML Schema used as a default IMS LD representation provides a formal model, it cannot represent all the knowledge contained in the IMS-LD information model. With the proposed learning design ontology the semantics of the concepts in the IMS-LD specification was *precisely and explicitly* defined and, thus, the misinterpretations or errors are avoided when the instances of the concepts are created and managed in runtime. Concretely, the level B represented in the ontology allows the development of software offering new possibilities for educational designer to develop learning designs with more complex behaviours. As the next step we consider the semantic description of the IMS LD Level C and,the description of the IMS LD at the runtime stage.

References

1. IMS Global Learning Consortium. *IMS Learning Design Information Model.*, retrieved from http://www.imsglobal.org/learningdesign/ldv1p0/imsld_infov1p0.html.
2. R. Koper. *Modelling units of study from a pedagogical perspective the pedagogical meta-model behind EML*, retrieved 26 January, 2006 from http://dspace.learningnet works.org/retrieve/33/ped-metamodel.pdf
3. Ricardo R. Amorim, Manuel Lama, Eduardo Sánchez, Adolfo Riera, and Xosé A. Vila. *A Learning Design Ontology based on the IMS Specification*. IEEE Journal of Educational Technology Society (Special Issue) , January, 2006.
4. Thompson, H., Beech, D., Maloney, M., and Mendelsohn, N. *XML-Schema Part 1: Structures 2nd Edition*, 2004, retrieved 26 January, 2006 from http://www.w3.org/ TR/ xmlschema-1.
5. Y. Gil and V. Ratnakar. *A Comparison of (Semantic) Markup Languages.* The 15th International FLAIRS Conference, AAAI Press, Florida, 2002, 413-418.
6. A. Gómez-Pérez, M. Fernández-López and O. Corcho. *Ontological Engineering*, Springer Verlag: Berlin, 2004.
7. IMS Global Learning Consortium, *IMS Learning Design Best Practice and Implementation Guide*. retrieved from http://www.imsglobal.org/learningdesign/ ldv1p0 /imsld_bestv1p0.html
8. N. Noy, R. Fergerson and M. Musen. *The knowledge model of Protege-2000: Combining interoperability and flexibility*. The 12th International Conference in Knowledge Engineering and Knowledge Management, France, 2000.
9. M. Dean and G. Schreiber. (editors). *OWL – Web Ontology Language Reference*, 2004, retrieved 26 January, 2006 from http://www.w3.org/TR/owl-ref.
10. Joint Information Services Committee(2004). RELOAD Editor. Introductory manual, retrieved May, 20, 2005 from http://www.reload.ac.uk/ex/editor_v1_3_manual.pdf

Taking Teaching Context into Account for Semantic Annotation Patterns

Faiçal Azouaou and Cyrille Desmoulins

CLIPS- IMAG, Université Joseph Fourier, Grenoble
BP 53 38041 Grenoble cedex 9 France
{faical.azouaou, Cyrille.desmoulins}@imag.fr

Abstract. In this article, starting from MemoNote pattern functionalities enabling teacher to memorize semantic and personal annotations, our objective is
to extend them with context-aware capabilities. MemoNote uses annotation patterns to deduce annotation semantics from the form chosen by the teacher. We
specify the annotation context, its capture from elements of the teaching situation and we model it with ontologies. Annotation context model is then directly
integrated into the previous pattern formalism in MemoNote, in order to obtain
context-aware pattern. Therefore, MemoNote can deduce annotation semantics
from the annotation form depending on the current context.

1 Introduction

The semantic annotation tool, MemoNote [1], dedicated to teachers, enables them to
annotate digital documents with their own comments as on paper, where each annotation has an explicit semantics for both the teacher and the machine. This is made
possible thanks to the use of ontologies, which are particular to teacher's activity. In
addition to be semantic, each annotation is subjective, reflecting teacher's personal
point of view in specific circumstances. Therefore, for each new annotation,
MemoNote stores three facets: a graphical, a semantic and a personal one.

To assist the teacher in creating these semantic annotations rapidly, the tool provides him/her with annotation patterns facility. Annotation pattern represents an annotation form (highlighting, circle…), which is linked to its semantics in a given context. MemoNote uses these patterns to deduce automatically annotation semantics
using its form.

However, the teacher during his/her activity can switch between different contexts,
where he/she annotates using different patterns and consequently uses a specific
group of patterns for each specific context. For example, whereas red highlighting
means an error indicator during his/her chemistry labs, it can mean an important pas-
sage to be used for discussing with other teachers during the same lab preparation.
Then the semantics deduced from a specific form use depends on annotation context,
and the application of a specific pattern is deterministic (annotation semantics can be
known) only if the context has been previously set. Consequently, MemoNote has to
be context-aware to adapt its behavior to each teacher's context state.

W. Nejdl and K. Tochtermann (Eds.): EC-TEL 2006, LNCS 4227, pp. 543 – 548, 2006.

The objective of this article is then to study and model the annotation activity context of the teacher, in order to take it into account into annotation patterns.

The article is organized as follows. In the first section, we propose a definition for the teaching annotation activity. In section 2, we identify the teacher's annotation context and in section 3 we specify how to capture it. Then, in order to implement this context, we propose to use ontological models to it (section 4). Using this model, we present in section 5 context-aware patterns, which enable MemoNote to deduce the annotation semantics from its form depending on the annotation context.

2 What Is the Context and Context-Awareness?

According to the Free on-line dictionary of computing [2] the context is *"that which surrounds, and gives meaning to, something else"*. The basis of this definition is that the context cannot be defined solely, without considering the object it concerns, the context of *something*. This definition states that from the various objects, events, person that surrounds something, the context is restricted to the meaningful elements as regards to this *something*.

Starting from this definition, we propose to define the teacher's annotation activity as the *meaningful properties about that which surrounds, and gives meaning to, teacher's annotation activity*. More formally it can be defined as follows:

The properties P of any element Y such as:
- Y is around the teacher's annotation activity
- Y gives meaning to the teacher's annotation activity
- P is meaningful to the teacher's annotation activity.

Generally speaking context awareness can be distinguished in [3]:

- Active context awareness. An application automatically adapts to discovered context by changing the application's behaviors (the aim is execution);
- Passive context awareness. An application presents the new or updated context to an interested user (the aim is information) or makes the context persistent for the user to retrieve later (the aim is memorize).

MemoNote is already a passive context-aware application, even implicitly. Indeed, for each created annotation, MemoNote memorizes its context of creation in the annotation personal facet [1]. But MemoNote lacks explicit and active context-awareness as it does not adapt its behavior to context changes. The objective of this article is to go beyond passive context-awareness by defining context-aware patterns as a kind of active context-awareness.

3 Teacher's Annotation Context

Starting from Schilit and Adams' categorization of important context elements[4], Chen & Kotz [3] claim that the important aspects of the context of a given user are :

1. *Computing environment.* Available processors, devices accessible for user input and display, network capacity, connectivity, and costs of computing.
2. *User environment.* Location, collection of nearby people, social situation...
3. *Physical environment.* Lighting and noise level.
4. *Time Context.* Time of a day, week, month, season of the year."

To identify the teacher's annotation context, we use educational models about teacher's activity [5] to adapt generic context models (as [6]) into Chen and Kotz's categories. Finally, we obtain the following elements of the teacher's annotation context (see Table 1).

Table 1. Annotation context elements

• Teaching elements – Name – Position – Place – Teaching situation • Computing elements – Material – Software (annotation tool) • Time elements – Date – Hour	The teaching situation is itself composed of • Teaching phase • Teaching domain • Teaching degree • Teaching activity

4 Context Capture

The annotation context has to be captured before being memorized into annotation objects. This capture depends on several criteria: availability, possibility to measure this context using sensors and so on. Three sources for information about context can be identified:

- **Machine software.** Operating system and other software running on the machine.
- **Device.** The tool uses external devices having sensors to check several data.
- **User.** He provides the data that cannot be obtained otherwise.

In the ideal case, context information must be available from surrounding software, primarily the operating system but more generally the software environment in which the teacher can open teaching documents. A Learning Management Content System (LMCS) is then the better source for the extraction of teaching elements context.

The following table presents for each element of teacher's annotation context the corresponding source (in decreasing order of interest).

Table 2. Capture of context information

Context category		Information	Sample values	Context source
Teaching elements		Name	Peter ELAPA	LMCS or LMS
		Position	Professor	LMCS or LMS
		Place	University + room 112	GPS device, LMCS, LMS or Calendar
	Teaching situation	Teaching activity	Design Labs…	LMCS, LMS, Calendar
		Learning Domain	Chemistry, physics	LMCS, LMS
		Learning Degree	Bachelor, Master	LMCS, LMS
		Learner Activity	Labs, Simulation, Exercise, Lecture	LMCS, LMS, Calendar
Computing elements		Software	MemoNoteWeb, MemoNote PC	Annotation tool itself
		Material	Tablet-PC, PDA, PC.	Annotation tool itself
Time		Date	01/01/2005	Operating system
		Hour	11h45	Operating system

5 Context Modeling

The nature of the processing which is applied to the context data differs according to the model we choose to represent them. For example, if we choose to represent the context using object-oriented model, it is interesting to use the object-oriented programming languages to process context data. On the other hand, if this data is modeled using relational model, a relational query language such as SQL is more suited.

From the various possible models to represent the context, a solution is to choose an ontological representation as it respects Buccholz assertion [7] "*A representation of the context information should be applicable throughout the whole process of gathering, transferring, storing, and interpreting of context information*".

Based on the context elements specified in section 2, we developed the following ontology of teacher's annotation context (See table 3).

Table 3. Context ontology

• Annotation context
   ○   Teaching elements
   – Name
   – Position
   – Place
   – Teaching situation
   ○   Computing elements
   – Material
   – Software (annotation tool)
	○ Time elements
	   – Date
	   – Hour

6 Context-Aware Pattern

Based on the annotation context model provided in the previous section, we are now able to define context-aware patterns.

The pattern context was first proposed by Alexander [8] to express the environment in which a pattern solves a particular problem. The first MemoNote pattern formalism [9] is based on Alexander's approach but the context is not formalized. At this stage, the context is only a textual description. In this formalism a pattern is described with the following elements:

- Name. The name should express the semantics produced by the annotation related to this pattern. This name should be significant.
- **Context.** A sentence to describe the context in which the pattern solves a particular problem.
- Problem to be solved. It is about the annotation objective which is carried out by the annotation act.
- Solution. A set of values for the annotation attributes, corresponding to the annotation semantics.
- Forces. It is about a description of the arguments justifying the use of this particular pattern to solve the current problem.
- Related patterns. It is about a list (if there are some) of patterns that have relations with the current pattern

Integrating context into patterns comes down to simply replace the textual description of context with an instance of the context ontology. Context is then composed of teaching elements, computing elements and time (see section 4). With this new model, each pattern becomes context-aware, extending the MemoNote capabilities.

7 MemoNote Context-Aware Functionalities

The current implantation of MemoNote's context-aware component provides three functionalities: pattern selection, context-aware annotating and pattern management.

Pattern selection. Currently, the context capture in MemoNote requires the teacher to provide values to all its attributes (except for the annotation time). MemoNote uses the current context values to select the relevant patterns and to activate them on the patterns palette. The other patterns are hidden.

Context-aware annotating. To annotate using a specific annotation form, the teacher chooses a pattern from the pattern palette and applies it to a specific anchor. MemoNote uses this pattern to deduce the annotation semantics and records in the annotation database the new annotation with its semantics and the context values.

Pattern management. MemoNote enables teacher to manage his/her patterns by creating, modifying, and deleting them. For example, to create a new pattern, teacher opens the new pattern form and specifies its properties. MemoNote assists the teacher in this creation process by predefining the context values.

8 Conclusion

Starting from the semantic and personal annotation patterns dedicated to teacher of the MemoNote tool, this article aimed at extending them with active context-aware capabilities that is the ability to adapt to the context of the current annotation situation.

Apart from computational and time element, what makes annotation context specific to teacher is its teaching situation elements, composed of teaching phase, domain, degree and activity. Its capture can be based on information taken from an LMS (Learning Management System) through which the teacher accesses to the annotated document, or from teacher's personal diary. The use of these two sources enables an easy and simple way to recover rich information about teaching situation.

This annotation context is represented with ontologies. We developed an ontology of the teacher's annotation context which is directly integrated into the initial pattern formalism, leading to context-aware patterns.

The potential ways to improve context-awareness in MemoNote are twofold. Firstly, there is a need to deeply model what are the relevant changes of the annotation context. How to define context change granularity and how to provide simple ways of expressing their relevance? Secondly, to avoid to the teacher the tasks of pattern management (like pattern creation), MemoNote should deduce teacher's patterns automatically and we could then develop machine learning algorithms.

References

1. Azouaou, F., Desmoulins, C Teachers' Document Annotating: Models for a Digital Memory Tool, *IJCEELL*, 16, pp. 18-34.2006
2. Howe, D. Free On-Line Dictionary Of Computing (London, UK, Imperial College Department of Computing).2006
3. Chen, G. & Kotz, D. A Survey of Context-Aware Mobile Computing Research *Technical Report: TR2000-381 Dartmouth College*, pp. 16 (Hanover, NH, USA).2000
4. Schilit, B., Adams, N. & Want, R. Context-aware computing applications, *WMCSA 1994*, Santa Cruz, California, December.1994
5. Grandbastien, M. Ontologies pour l'Utilisation de Ressources de Formation et d'Annotations sémantiques en Ligne, études et propositions à partir de cas d'utilisation., pp. 23 (OURAL report, French government grant. Paris, France).2005
6. Korpip, P., Mntyjrvi, J., Kela, J., Kernen, H. & Malm, E.-J. Managing Context Information in Mobile Devices, *IEEE Pervasive Computing*, 21.2003
7. Buchholz, S., Hamann, T. & Hübsch, G. Comprehensive Structured Context Profiles (CSCP): Design and Experiences, Paper presented at the *IEEE Workshop on Context Modeling and Reasoning (CoMoRea)*, Orlando, FL, USA, Mar 14.2004
8. Alexander, C., Ishikawa, S. & Silverstein, M. *A Pattern Language: Towns, Buildings, Construction* (Oxford, Oxford University Press).1977
9. Azouaou, F., Desmoulins, C., Mille, D Formalisms for an Annotation-based Training Memory: Connecting Implicit and Explicit Semantics, *AIED 2003*, Sydney, Australia, July.2003

Designing a Constructionistic Framework for T-Learning

Francesco Bellotti[2], Jaroslava Mikulecka[1], Linda Napoletano[3], and Hana Rohrova[1]

[1] Faculty of Informatics and Management, University of Hradec Kralove
Rokitanskeho 62, Hradec Kralove 50003, Czech Republic
{jaroslava.mikulecka, hana.rohrova}@uhk.cz
[2] Department of Electronics and Biophysical Engineering, the University of Genoa
Via Opera Pia, 11/a, 16145 Genoa, Italy
franz@elios.unige.it
[3] ORT France 10 Villa d'Eylau 75116 Paris, France
linda.napoletano@ort.asso.fr

Abstract. iDTV is a promising platform for education, since it can reach a large number of people and provide computing and communication interactivity. However, a number of key issues have yet to be faced, in a variety of fields, such as pedagogy, digital signal processing, and Human-Computer Interaction. Starting from pedagogical principles rooted in the constructionism theory, the ELU IST project presents a t-learning framework where learners are involved in compelling educational games through iDTV and engaged in their actual construction as well.

Keywords: iDTV, constructionism, t-learning, MHP, gaming.

1 T-Learning: Potential and Challenges

Analogical TV is a communication medium able to reach daily a huge part of the people. However, specific use of TV for educational purposes has not been very effective yet. We can explain this, from a pedagogical point of view, by considering two major drawbacks. First: the typical educational approach for assume a world of independent individuals who "acquire" knowledge according to universal principles, tempered only by general categorizations based on age and cultural interests. Second: the co-construction of knowledge in the learning process is relegated to pre-established paths that follow an abstraction-instantiation loop. Most of teaching is done through abstraction. The students are completely excluded from the possibility to produce institutionalised educational assets, even when the theory goes that proper understanding is achieved only by co-construction of knowledge [1].

In the recent years, digital TV has introduced significant novelties in the TV world. It provides bandwidth for much more channels than analogue TV and supports end-user interactivity with computer based applications that are broadcast together with the audio-visual stream. These applications allow the viewer to select content, access a variety of services (ranging from interactive advertising to healthcare, from e-Government to e-Banking, from games to weather forecasts) and send feedback through an Internet-based return channel.

W. Nejdl and K. Tochtermann (Eds.): EC-TEL 2006, LNCS 4227, pp. 549–554, 2006.

In the field of education and training, interactive Digital TV (iDTV) has spurred the t-learning concept, which is emerging as an important medium to create opportunities for learning, in particular at home. A recent study [2] supported by the European Union reports a number of reasons why it is important to consider the role that interactive digital TV has within a broader e-learning strategy:

- Most people have access to a TV set in their home. The television is a familiar, easy to use and reliable consumer device with around 95-99% penetration in European households.
- In the emerging era of lifelong learning, learning will take place in wide variety of context and locations. Informal learning will increasingly become as important as the more traditional forms of formalized learning.
- The TV has the potential to overcome the digital divide by reaching a much wider audience in particular people who is typically not familiar with information and communication technologies (ICTs).

Fundamental key issues need to be addressed in order to exploit the iDTV potential for education:

- How can the learning support systems (human as well as technological) be integrated within a TV-based learning environment?
- What types of interactivity are needed to enhance the learning through iDTV?
- What aspects of interactivity are requested for different learning contexts and how can they motivate learners?
- What conditions and requirements are demanded in order to create a compelling learning environment, and to turn a passive viewer into an active learner?

Internet and television are coming closer in many ways in iDTV, therefore the t-learning methodology can benefit from experience, gained within web-based learning. There has been deep discussion amongst educational theorists about the extent to which media affects learning. Research made by Salomon [3] confirmed that the choice of media does lead to differential learning outcomes both in terms of pace of acquisition and depth of understanding. However, the extent to which learning actually occurs greatly depends on learner's volitional mindfulness, itself partly determined by the nature of the materials encountered and partly by attitudinal factors.

We have been investigating these issues in the Enhanced Learning Unlimited (ELU) project funded by the European Union under the 6th Framework Programme [4]. ELU aims at increasing learning opportunities, mainly at home, through iDTV. Major ELU objectives are:

- the development of new t-learning formats
- the development of software modules able to enhance to the Multimedia Home Platform (MHP) iDTV standard in order to meet specific t-learning needs.

The ELU Consortium consists of 14 partners from 10 countries, with a significant presence of new accession Eastern Europe countries. Given the wide variety of themes to be addressed (from computing to broadcasting, from pedagogy to specific learning items, such as mathematics, history and computer science), the ELU design involves a multidisciplinary team representing the point of view of the actors involved in the t-learning process.

2   iDTV as a Learning Environment

iDTV, as specified through most widespread broadcast standards, in particular the MHP, provides a number of characteristics that are key to develop effective learning environments for a large number of people. We identify some features of the iDTV that have to be taken into account when designing t-learning processes:

a. Interactivity
iDTV technology allows information to travel both to and from the learner, using a combination of telephone, cable or satellite systems. This opens to the wide audience of TV viewers the potential for two-way communication, which is a fundamental prerequisite of an interactive adaptive learning system.

b. Video Learning experience
The video format allows characters, actions, and settings to be depicted in a rich, vivid, and realistic manner that is hard to achieve in text-only presentations. A second advantage of the video format is that it provides the ability to weave in related background information which might motivate the study of related problems in mathematics and other domains.

c. Adaptivity
Adaptive electronic programme guides (EPGs) filter the enormous number of programmes available every day, to recommend programmes to a viewer. Recommendations rely on predictions about the viewer's preferences, which itself is based on the viewer's behaviour in the past (content-based filtering) and the opinions of like-wise minded users (collaborative/social filtering) [5].

d. Narrative
The tradition of broadcast TV is strongly rooted in narrative and its potential to create stories that engage the audience. Bruner [6] celebrate narrative as "a mode of thought and an expression of a culture's world view", he claims that through the active generation of narrative we make sense of our own and other's experiences.

e. Informal learning/edutainment
The context (home) and the opportunities (edutainment applications) for t-learning impact the lifelong learning process that allows individual to construct knowledge, skills, values from the daily experiences [7]. The experiences of t-learning are characterised by a focus towards informal learning activities and a strong connection with the game world until now.

f. Social activity
Watching TV is often a social activity. This poses interesting issues from a personalisation point of view. Instead of user modelling we may need group modelling. The members of a group can, however, be quite diverse. It is an interesting question whether it would be possible to produce TV programs that allow all family members to simultaneously learn something, each one at her/his own level, and each one being kept motivated [8].

3 Pedagogical Principles for iDTV

The above discussed features make iDTV a very interesting tool for education, in particular from the point of view of the constructivist pedagogical theory. According to Constructivism, knowledge is constructed through a process stimulated by a problem, a question, a doubt, a dissonance by situating cognitive experiences in real-world performing authentic activities [6]. In fact, according to constructivism knowledge will be as increasingly significant as its context is increasingly rich and authentic [9].

Constructivism overturns the traditional instructional perspective that focuses on strategies and materials to help teachers instruct through an effective and easy to memorize organisation of contents. To design following a constructionist approach means to define the strategies, the tools and the materials to sustain the learner to construct her/his personal knowledge.

In this constructionist perspective, we aim at designing learning environment that supports Meaningful Learning (i.e. able to trigger active, constructive, intentional, authentic and cooperative learning processes).

4 The ELU T-Learning Framework

Relying on these principles, ELU has designed a t-learning framework based on game templates, particularly aimed at secondary school students. The idea is to define simple game models (templates) that can be instantiated with different contents and interfaces in different education contexts. The game templates idea has been proposed for the exploration of a urban artistic territory in mobile gaming [10] and for educational virtual tourism on the web [11].

Fig. 1. Game templates sample instances: Pairs, VisualQuiz, TextQuiz and SlidingMemory

We have defined a number of game templates for iDTV, including MemoryGame, Couples, VisualQuestions, Catch it!, etc. (see Fig. 1). We group the templates in 3 main categories, according to the type of skills they aim to stimulate in the player.

The categories are: observation games (manipulation of images), reflection games (quizzes, riddles) and action videogames (culturally-contextualized arcade games).

The games can be broadcast and played also in remote player interaction through the receiver Set Top Box' return channel. Interaction involves competition, as a global hall-of-fame is maintained to keep track of the highest scores. Interaction also involves collaboration, in some games the score is shared among cooperating players.

Games are not isolated but are broadcast as thematic libraries. Thus, a player can build her own knowledge acquisition path by selecting in the library the most suited game instances to achieve a specific educational goal (intentional learning). For instance, the "Charles Magne" theme may involve a library of a number of puzzles, memory games, historically-contextualized arcade games, etc. By playing with such games, the player should collect information to solve the final quiz on the item. Within a thematic library, games may be accessed through simple menus, or may be proposed to the end-user in predefined sequences.

The ELU framework also supports active involvement of the learners (players) in building the educational objects (i.e. the game instances). To this end, we are designing a web-based, visual content visual authoring tool through which young players can create their own instances of the game templates, by inserting contents (e.g. characters, images, sounds). Once finished, the author may submit the created games to the broadcaster, which will review and select the most suited games for actual broadcasting. Figure below depicts the overall schema that we have conceived to support the ELU t-learning framework.

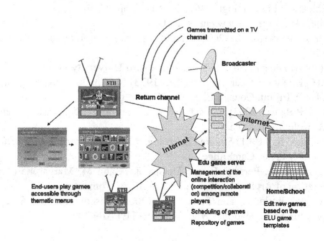

Fig. 2. Overall schema of the ELU t-learning framework, involving creation, scheduling, broadcasting and use of an educational iDTV packet based on the game templates

5   Conclusions

iDTV is a promising platform for education, since it can combine a huge user penetration with interactivity. However, a number of key issues have yet to be faced, in a variety of fields, such as pedagogy, digital signal processing, Human-Computer Interaction, multimedia production. ELU intends to explore new pedagogic theories, mostly based on constructivism that could be effective for iDTV. In particular, we are designing an education environment which stimulates the learner by engaging her in thematic virtual challenges (e.g. about a historical period, a scientific item, a statistic concept) that require a player to solve quizzes and other games on related arguments. The next phases of the project involve the implementation and test of the proposed framework in a number of courses in 4 countries of Eastern Europe.

Acknowledgements

This ELU project is partly supported by the 6th FP of the European Union. The authors would like to thank the coordinator and all the members of the consortium.

References

1. Rizzo, A. Brunk, J. Molari, G. Napoletano, L Toccafondi, G. Designing a knowledge building community. in Gherardi, S., Nicolini, D. (eds) (2005) *The Passion for Learning and Knowing. Proc. 6th Int. Conf. Organizational Learning and Knowledge* Univ. of Trento e-books, Trento, pag.208-226 vol. 2
2. Bates, P., J. (2003) t-learning Study - A study into TV- based interactive learning to the home. Final Report. pjb Associates, UK.
3. Salomon, G. (1983). The differential investment of mental effort in learning from different sources. Educational Psychologist, Vol. 18, No. 1, pp. 42-50
4. ELU website. URL: http://www.elu-project.com/
5. Masthoff, J. & Pemberton, L. (2003) Adaptive learning via Interactive Television. University of Brighton.
6. Bruner, J. (1996) *The culture of education.* Harvard University Press
7. Coombs P.H., Prosser R.C. and Ahmed, M. (1973) New paths to learning for rural children and youth. UNICEF Int. Council Educational Development
8. Atwere, D. & P.Bates. (2003) Interactive TV: a learning platform with potential. Learning and Skills Development Agency.
9. Lave, J., Wenger, E., (1991) *Situated Learning: Legitimate Peripheral Participation* Cambridge University Press, Cambridge
10. Bellotti, F., Berta, R., Ferretti, E. and DeGloria, A and M. Margarone (2003) VeGame: Field Exploration of Art and History in Venice, IEEE Computer.
11. Bellotti, F., De Gloria, A. and Ferretti, E. (2005) Discovering the European Heritage Through the ChiKho Educational Web Game, INTETAIN 2005.

Advanced Personalized Learning and Training Applications Through Mobile Technologies and Services

Giancarlo Bo

GIUNTI Interactive Labs S.r.l. – Via Portobello, Abbazia dell'Annunziata
16039 Sestri Levante, Italy
g.bo@giuntilabs.it

Abstract. This paper offers an overview on the concept of "personalization" applied to learning processes in a context of mobility, through an analysis of both the related open issues and the expected benefits that would come from the introduction of mobile technologies as a support to individual learning experiences. Relevant technical aspects are discussed too and a framework for creating pedagogically sound mobile services suitable to support ubiquitous enriched learning experiences is presented. This work mainly refers to the major outcomes from three very relevant EU projects – MOBIlearn, WearIT@Work and Natacha - where real users have been involved since the beginning in the research activities, thus helping in defining relevant generic mobile knowledge management use cases and pedagogical models. Some examples of potential learning/training applications and real-life use scenarios are provided to show how in practice mobile technologies can be fruitfully exploited to promote innovative, user-dependent, learning, training and edutainment strategies.

1 Introduction

Expert teachers and trainers know very well how much a personalized attention to learners during the learning process can make a huge difference with respect to its success, particularly when the peculiarities of individuals and their need to learn differently are recognized, exploited and supported. In traditional classroom-based teaching approaches, instructors intuitively manage key human factors (skills, passion, interest, will, frustration, satisfaction, fear, personal preferences, etc.) to promote learning. When the learning process goes online these factors run the risk of being underestimated and disregarded. On the other hand the recent availability of innovative mobile technology and the increasing popularity of handheld devices are offering new opportunities and paradigms for personalized education. In other words, the true potential of e-learning as "anytime", "anywhere" and "adapted to the user" could be realised through a proper application of the "mobile learning (m-learning)" concept.

Personalization in terms of m-learning suggests that a potential mobile learner could easily tailor a selection of available learning contents and services according to his/her interests and/or current pedagogical objectives. For instance, the ability to tailor the service in terms of topics and language, as well as selecting incoming newsletters and updates can help the viewer filtering knowledge, and making its acquisition more targeted and effective. The final goal of personalized learning is to provide a learning path that is matched to the learner's needs and abilities, resulting in

W. Nejdl and K. Tochtermann (Eds.): EC-TEL 2006, LNCS 4227, pp. 555 – 560, 2006.

a more efficient and high quality learning process. In order to match learner's profile and objectives, current learning context and available pedagogical resources, a well-defined description of each component involved in the process is needed, with a specific focus on the user model. An additional interesting aspect of the personalization process is that, once the user model has been identified, the accuracy of the personalization can be iteratively improved with time, as more dynamic data are collected and stored regarding the ongoing interactions of the user with the system and the continuous monitoring and re-assessment of the user's satisfaction. This also allows for a classification and "clustering" of learners.

From the conceptual and technological perspective, supporting the learning process personalization implies the design and development of suitable "services" to be integrated in a mobile learning application and able to provide content and learning process personalization features. In the following section a complex technological framework suitable to integrate, amongst others, personalization services for mobile knowledge management and learning/training applications is presented.

2 The *Open Mobile Abstract Framework*

A key objective of the EU MOBIlearn project, one of the most important worldwide initiatives related to the use of mobile technologies for learning, had been to improve the knowledge level of individuals by developing learning processes on-the-move. To this end, besides new pedagogical models, a robust, extensible, flexible and interoperable infrastructure was needed. The answer given by the MOBIlearn project to this need is the "Open Mobile Access Abstract Framework" (OMAF), a layered abstract model that has been designed and implemented as a service-oriented architecture [1], [2].

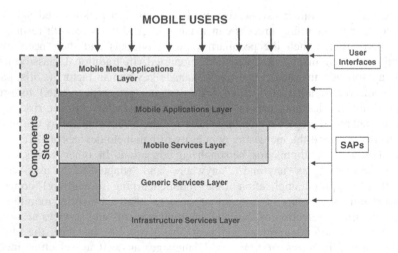

Fig. 1. The OMAF layered model

With reference to Fig.1, the following layers are included in the OMAF model:

- *Mobile Meta-Applications Layer (MmAL)*: the set of systems, tools and applications obtained as a combination/integration of two or more mobile applications, to provide extended and more complex functionalities to users.
- *Mobile Applications Layer (MAL)*: the set of systems, tools and applications specifically designed and implemented to provide a particular mobile functionality. They are built starting from the suite of mobile services and common services.
- *Mobile Services Layer (MSL)*: the set of components able to provide mobile specific services, which are used by the mobile applications.
- *Generic Services Layer (GSL)*: the set of components that provide generic services to be used by the application services.
- *Infrastructure Services Layer (ISL)*: the underlying services that enable to exchange data in terms of communications, messaging and transactions.
- *Service Access Points (SAP)*: interface to the corresponding service. Each SAP provides access to one service capability. SAPs will be implemented through APIs (Application Programming Interfaces)
- *Components Store (CS)*: a set of components and data models that has to be specified to support the Generic and Mobile services.

Developed by applying a user-centred design approach, based on the ISO13407 standard, the OMAF model addresses the conceptual layout of services needed to access knowledge, information, training and daily support in a mobile environment, for example via collaborative spaces, context awareness, personalized and location-based information delivery. At present, the top-level abstract components in the framework and their associated services have been identified: mobile client, portal management, content management, collaboration, communication, context awareness and user modelling, location and navigation, infrastructure. In practice, relying on these services, a mobile application developed as an instantiation of the OMAF model is able to support several relevant features like, amongst the others, contextualized multimedia information delivery and presentation, user positioning and guiding, multimodal interaction, collaborative working and group communication.

Currently, being the OMAF concept accepted and developed to a reasonable degree of maturity, the main goal is to design and instantiate a wide set of mobile end-user applications starting from the services already available in the framework and extending them when needed, according to new use scenarios and requirements. This has been achieved in other EU projects, where the OMAF has been proposed and is used as the reference for supplying innovative mobile solutions to different categories of users.

3 A New Way for Visiting a Museum

The Museum Mobile Application, conceived and developed in MOBIlearn as an instantiation of the OMAF model, represents a cutting edge support during a museum tour. According to his current position, a visitor receives on a PDA the most relevant

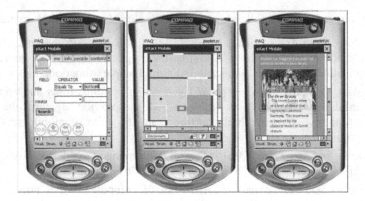

Fig. 2. Some screenshots of the museum application. Search for relevant contents (left), museum navigation (middle) and learning contents visualization (right).

information while he is freely wandering through the rooms. This application supports the location-based access to relevant multimedia and personalized information about work of art, both in push and pull modalities (see Fig.2).

The application offers also some interesting functionalities for supporting the work of museum managers in terms of an easy access to the spatial structure of the museum and the possibility of binding to physical locations the pedagogical objects created by means of a user-friendly content authoring tool.

4   Training and Daily Activities in Industrial Maintenance

One of the key application scenarios considered in the WearIT@Work project focuses on the support of maintenance activities and empowerment of professionals in the aeronautic industry through the adoption of wearable mobile technologies [3], [4] and [5].

The aeronautic industry takes maintenance aspects into account from the very beginning of the aircraft design in order to make maintenance tasks easier and faster. Through some scenarios based on a real case studies (removal and installation of equipment on the aircraft, inspection and trouble shooting), Giunti Interactive Labs is aiming at demonstrating how wearable technologies and a suitable application instantiated from the OMAF model can improve operators job and maintenance competitiveness by supporting continuous maintenance operators training, increasing mobility of workers, improving availability of task-dependent information, speeding up localization and detection of areas to be repaired or maintained, improving intra- and extra-team communication and knowledge sharing.

In the future working scenario fostered by the end users, the maintenance operators will be equipped with a Maintenance Jacket, with integrated wearable technologies in it, both early in the training phase and during daily activities. The wearable computer will be equipped with suitable input devices, which register measurements taken during the maintenance procedures, allows the user interacting with the system and displays task-relevant information according to the user profile (Fig.3).

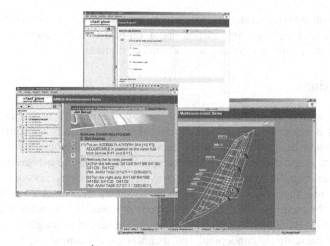

Fig. 3. Screenshots of the maintenance application

5 In-Flight Edutainment for Passengers

The Intranet Content Management and Delivery System (ICMDS), developed within the NATACHA framework is a complete OMAF-based platform devoted to the creation of informative and edutainment contents and their delivery to end users (passengers and/or crew members) through the NATACHA aircraft-ground network and/or a traditional IP infrastructure (wired/wireless Intranet or Internet). After registration to the main Portal, users are be able to retrieve information objects according to a specific need/interest and to enjoy the comfort of a personalized, on-demand, live information service.

Through a ground based mobile network (WiFi, GPRS) users would be able to ubiquitously access the service (on board and before/after the flight).On-demand edutainment and general purpose delivery services that have been identified as commercially relevant and can be provided on new generation aircrafts and/or in the airport using the

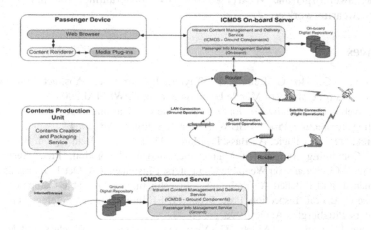

Fig. 4. The ICMDS architecture

ICMDS platform are contextualized tourist information and news, personalized edutainment, ad-hoc professional contents, information about on-board facilities/services, information about security procedures, advertising and commercial promotion.

6 Conclusions

User satisfaction is the ultimate aim of personalization. It is motivated by the recognition that a user has needs, and meeting them successfully is likely to lead to a satisfying relationship and re-use of the services offered. Beyond the common goal, however, there is great diversity in how personalization can be achieved. Information about the user can be obtained from a history of previous sessions, or through interaction in real time. "Needs" may be those stated by the customer as well as those perceived by the business. Once the user's needs are established, rules and techniques are used to decide what information content or service behaviour might be appropriate.

The paper presented a conceptual and technological framework, the OMAF, that can be extended and adapted in order to deliver personalized services, including those needed for supporting training and learning processes. Some real application, which have been tested and assessed with the involvement of real users, have been presented and discussed as well for showing the potentialities offered by the OMAF model. The research activities in this field are currently ongoing at Giunti Interactive Labs, aiming at defining further extensions of the model according to new use scenarios (e.g. moving from the mobile environments to the interactive digital TV). Results of this advanced research will be presented and discussed in future publications.

Acknowledgments

The research described in this paper has been carried out in three different international projects co-funded by the European Commission in the FP5 and FP 6: MOBIlearn (IST Programme, contract N° IST-2001-37187, http:// www. mobilearn. org), NATACHA (GROWTH Programme, contract N° GRD1-2001-40196, http:// www.natachaweb.org/) and WearIT@Work (IST Programme, contract N° 004216, http://www.wearitatwork.com/).

References

1. Da Bormida, G., Bo, G, Lefrere, P., Taylor, J: "An Open Abstract Framework for Modelling Interoperability of Mobile Learning Services". WSMAI 2003: 9-16
2. Bo, G.: Web services and XML for supporting new m-learning experiences. Design of an innovative architecture, Proc. LeGE Workshop 4, Stuttgart, Apr 2004.
3. Siewiorek, D.P., Smailagic, A., Bass, L., Martin, D., Siegel, J., Bennington, B.: Adtranz: A Mobile Computing System for Maintenance and Collaboration, Proc. Second IEEE International Conference on Wearable Computers, Pittsburgh, PA, Oct 1998, pp. 25-32.
4. Ockerman, J. and Pritchett A.: Preliminary Investigation of Wearable Computers for Task Guidance in Aircraft Inspection, Proc. Second IEEE International Conference on Wearable Computers, Pittsburgh, PA, Oct 1998, pp. 33-40.
5. Tummolini L., Lorenzon, A., Bo, G., Vaccaro, R.: iTutor: A Wireless and Multimodal Support to Industrial Maintenance Activities, Proc. Mobile HCI 2002, pp. 302-305

COOPER: Towards a Collaborative Open Environment of Project-Centred Learning*

Aldo Bongio[4], Jan van Bruggen[3], Stefano Ceri[2], Valentin Cristea[8],
Peter Dolog[1], Andreas Hoffmann[6], Maristella Matera[2], Marzia Mura[5],
Antonio Taddeo[7], Xuan Zhou[1], and Larissa Zoni[2]

[1]L3S Research Center, University of Hanover, Germany
[2]Politecnico di Milano, Italy
[3]Open University Netherland, Netherlands
[4]Web Models s.r.l., Italy
[5]Abbeynet S.p.A., Italy
[6]LT Design Software GmbH, Germany
[7]University of Lugano – ALaRI, Switzerland
[8]University Politehnica of Bucharest, Romania
cooper@l3s.de

Abstract. Nowadays, engineering studies are characterized by high mobility of students, lecturers and workforce and by the dynamics of multinational companies where "classes" or "students' teams" composed of persons with different competencies and backgrounds, working together in projects to solve complex problems. Such an environment will become increasingly relevant in multinational universities and companies, and it has brought a number of challenges to existing e-learning technologies. COOPER is an ongoing project that focuses on developing and testing such a collaborative and project-centred leaning environment. This paper proposes a COOPER framework and shows its approaches to address the various research challenges.

1 Introduction

More and more, in an environment characterized by high mobility of students, lecturers and workforce and by the dynamics of multinational companies, "classes" or "students' teams" are composed of persons with different competencies and backgrounds. Such working environments will become increasingly relevant in industry, with distribution of multinational companies all over the world and with extensive adoption of partnerships and outsourcing. Increasingly, project-centred teaching approaches, often in the context of workplace learning, are adopted in the case of scientific and technical studies, where teams rather than individual students will work on a given project and where teachers' support will often be substituted by interaction with a small group of advisors and tutors, possibly coming from different (remote) institutions and providing different competencies and approaches.

---

* This work is partially supported by EU/IST FP6 STREP project COOPER (contract number IST-2005-027073).

W. Nejdl and K. Tochtermann (Eds.): EC-TEL 2006, LNCS 4227, pp. 561–566, 2006.

Our project COOPER is focused upon the problem of creating and managing virtual teams of persons with heterogeneous backgrounds and competencies, of assessing their entry-level competencies and their "scientific growth", of coordinating their collaboration as well as facilitating their personalized growth, and even following them up after the end of their formal participation in the learning activities, when they constitute an alumni community. This approach is built upon project-centred learning and social network learning situation, which is seen as an important mechanism for breaking distance barriers and making effective use of e-learning technology.

The objective of COOPER is to create techniques and tools that support team-based, project-centred learning in the following circumstances:

- Graduate (or post-graduate) university studies involving students and lecturers participating in focused projects (e.g., masters or specialization courses) coming from different institutions and backgrounds;
- Company universities and company training, involving multi-national participants coming from company's sites or customers which are world-wide dispersed, participating in the launching of new product or technology, or in product- and project-centred training.

To accomplish this objective, we need to exploit several technologies, including collaborative learning, knowledge sharing, recommendation, social network, process modeling, (a)synchronous communication and so on.

Currently, COOPER is still an ongoing research project, and many research and development tasks are in progress. This paper is intended to give an overview of the project and present a high-level approach to tackle the challenges in project-centred learning in open environments.

The rest of this paper is organized as follows. Section 2 presents the COOPER scenario. Section 3 introduces the COOPER framework organized into 4 dimensions: processes, pedagogical scenarios and assessment, knowledge sharing and recommendation, and technical infrastructure. Section 4 concludes this paper with a project roadmap.

2   The COOPER Scenario

Basically, the COOPER scenario can be decomposed into three phases: *pre-project* phase, *project development* phase and *post-project* phase.

- In the *pre-project* phase, individuals and problems are described. Individuals are "applicants" described in terms of their background, objectives, and constraints. Problems, in turn, are described in terms of the identity and roles of stakeholders, their objectives, the technologies involved, their tutors, the expected results and expected duration. Then, the user makes candidate assignments and build a project team consisting from the applicants based on individual's portfolios assessments and the need of a project. The team is provided with the required infrastructure in terms of mentors (e.g., faculty and company representatives).

– The *project development* phase covers all the standard phases of project management. Events such as project's kick-off, evaluation workshops, milestones, and conclusion are scheduled, project deliverables are defined and then produced, and the classical project management artifacts are included or integrated. The distinguishing aspects of the delivered processes are: a tight integration between synchronous and asynchronous components. In addition, project team is provided with features like recommendation of active experts for advice, past experiences from similar projects, knowledge and context sharing between peers and groups, and so on.

– The *post-project* phase can be seen as a knowledge management opportunity for the purposes of further projects which includes the delivery of project results, its dissemination, and the persistent storage into a repository describing the full history of the project, available at the user organization premises and perhaps exported to the stakeholder premises. Project result becomes an asset of the alumni as his personal portfolio; an asset of the project's stakeholder, as an artifact of knowledge which can be further developed; and an asset for the "user" organization, who can indeed evolve it into a profile for follow-up projects.

3   The Approaches of COOPER

We have conducted extensive case studies in a number of organizations. They include the Advanced Learning and Research Institute (ALaRI)[1][2][3] and the Alta Scuola Politecnica (ASP)[2] representing the case in university studies, and the LT Design Software[3] representing the cases in company training. From these case studies, generalize the following most important technical requirements in the COOPER scenario.

– Defining a set of team management processes that are most suitable for supporting project-centered learning in the COOPER scenario.
– Creating knowledge sharing and recommendation services to facilitate collaborative teamwork processes.
– Proposing pedagogical tools to support competency building and competency assessment in heterogeneous virtual teams.
– Constructing an infrastructure with a set of telecommunication tools to support the distant cooperation in a distributed virtual team.

The approaches to address these requirements are elaborated Section 3.1, 3.2, 3.3 and 3.4 respectively .

3.1   Cooperative Teamwork Processes

In order to support the design of project-centered learning processes, we are working on the definition of a reference framework encompassing and generalizing the

---

[1] www.alari.ch
[2] www.asp-poli.it
[3] www.coware.com

needs of the three COOPER case studies. The starting point of our work is an existing model for Web application design, WebML [2], its recent extensions for process modelling [1], and the associated Web design product, WebRatio[4].

The framework will offer complete specifications of the process instances supporting team-based learning within the COOPER platform. In particular, it will cover both *structured* and *unstructured* processes. In structured processes, the different activities and the activity flow can be envisioned and specified at design time. For example, the pre-project phase in the COOPER scenario, which is especially focused on the team set-up, generally encompasses structured processes, whose activities adhere to well-established procedures deriving from the institution rules, and do not vary across teams. Unstructured processes still consist of a set of predictable activities. The behavior of the single activities is well-know, but it is difficult to predict their composition within processes, since their assignment to enrolled actors and their synchronization with other activities may depend on users' choices at enactment-time. We in particular observe that team cooperation processes during the project development phase are typical examples of unstructured processes: in order to reach a common goal (e.g., producing deliverables required by a project milestone), team participants execute some cooperation activities, mainly synchronous communication acts (e.g., virtual meetings, chats, audio/video conferences, etc), selecting them from a fixed set of existing "activity types". However, the flow of such activities, as well as the actors triggering their execution do not follow standard procedures, since they depend on the specific team cooperation policy.

For the specification of structured processes, we are developing visual editors for process modelling based on popular standard notations, such as the Business Process Modeling Notation (BPMN) [3], as well as the translation of process notations into WebML specifications. In order to support unstructured processes, we are defining *activity patterns*, namely "hypertext templates" supporting the execution of conventional cooperation activities, to be incorporated within the reference framework. Such templates will also allow users to dynamically "compose" their team cooperation processes, based on the configuration and personalization at enactment time of the different activities, of the enrolled actors, and of the activity flow.

3.2   Knowledge Sharing Services for Team Work Processes

We provide three functional components to support knowledge sharing.

The first component is a knowledge repository. There exit a variety of knowledge and learning resources in the COOPER scenario, including training courses given by tutors, internal documents produced by team members and external resources on the web. All the resources will be managed by a common knowledge repository, which will integrate Database and IR techniques to take full advantage of the richness of meta-data and semantics in the knowledge resources to enable easy browsing and search. The knowledge repository covers multiple projects, so that resources produced in one project can be reused by others.

---

[4] www.webratio.com

The second component is a set of the search and recommendation services. The former enables learners to actively search for knowledge resources or experts for advice. The latter discovers learners' knowledge vacancy and requirements, and recommends relevant learning resources and experts to them. Existing techniques in search engines and recommender systems will be adapted to this component. In addition, new solutions will be proposed for assessing learner's competence and preference (latent semantic analysis will be used in this context).

The third component is a platform for knowledge exchanging. Tools like forums and blogs will be used for exchanging learner experiences. Wiki will be used for collaborative knowledge construction. The knowledge and experiences produced on the platform will be imported to the knowledge repository so as to be shared with other projects. User profiles can also be extracted from the contents on these tools to reinforce the search and recommendation services.

3.3 Pedagogical Scenarios and Assessment for Virtual Teams

Knowledge sharing and co-construction in virtual teams will not emerge by itself, but requires that tasks, as well as social and technical environment are created that stimulate or even require these processes. To create such an environment new didactical approaches are needed that combine project-centered work with learning and knowledge sharing. Furthermore these approaches need to be accompanied by assessment strategies that support competency building as well as competency assessment in heterogeneous virtual teams in a variety of settings. Examples of the latter are portfolio assessment, self-assessment and peer assessments. Typically, these assessment forms are used not only to evaluate student development, but also to engage learners in critically analyzing what they are learning, to identify appropriate standards of performance and to apply these to their own work.

Cooper will model a number of pedagogical scenarios for collaborative learning in virtual teams and appropriate assessment strategies. One such scenario is that of the Virtual Company that was developed and implemented by the Open University of the Netherlands. The VC scenario engages virtual teams in authentic projects. The scenario covers the whole lifecycle of the Cooper model and it includes various assessment strategies, including assessments dealing with performance in a team.

IMS Learning Design, QTI and the OUNL-Citogroup assessment model are important specifications to guide the modeling needed for Cooper. They all also have clear shortcomings that Coopers underlying modeling may help to overcome. In Cooper we will test implementation of didactical scenarios and assessment by integrating them at the model level by means of operation and interaction units.

3.4 Infrastructure for Cooperative TeamWork Processes

The infrastructure and tools for cooperative teamWork processes will be produced by means of a framework which integrates the up-to-date technologies for Web development in a collaborative setting, with provisions for asynchronous and synchronous components such as integrated Voice Over Internet (VOI) softwares.

The framework will be totally Web-based and developed using the Web applications provided by the WebML design notation [2] and by the WebRatio tool both expanded with process modeling concepts and with standard application distribution primitives (based on Web Services).

The COOPER infrastructure will also provide a tight integration of the asynchronous Web application with synchronous tools, made up of state-of-the art VOI technology. In order for the communication platform to address the collaborative learning paradigms defined in Section 2, it will include a set of interactive tools for the synchronous communications, such as audio/video conference, application sharing, co-browsing, presence services and chat, based on IETF SIP standards (RFC f3261, RFC 3856, RFC 3903). Finally the integration of the synchronous activities within the asynchronous part of the platform will be supported by several asynchronous tools, such as audio/video session recording, discussion forum and logs storing.

4   Conclusions and Further Work

While there exist a number of research works that have partially addressed the issues described in this paper, they are not intended to support the project-centred learning scenario described in Section 2. On the one hand, significant work is required to adapt and integrate the existing techniques into the COOPER scenario. On the other hand, new solutions should be proposed and applied to overcome the unique challenges emerging in the scenario.

In COOPER, we will achieve it in 3 stages. The first stage is requirement analysis. The results of the requirements analysis have been documented in this paper. In the second stage, a number of novel tools and techniques will be developed within a work framework proposed in this paper. Finally, the tools and the techniques will be evaluated from technical (showing improved technical properties of the proposed methods) and user perspectives (showing effectivness of learning supported with the tools and techniques).

References

1. M. Brambilla, S. Ceri, S. Comai, P. Fraternali, and I. Manolescu. Specification and Design of Workflow-Driven Hypertexts. *Journal of Web Engineering 1,* 2 (April 2003), 1–100.
2. S. Ceri, P. Fraternali, A. Bongio, M. Brambilla, S. Comai, and M. Matera. *Designing Data-Intensive Web Applications.* Morgan Kauffmann, 2002.
3. S.A. White, et al. Business Processing Modeling Notation (BPMN), Version 1.0. May 3, 2004, available at www.bpmn.org.

Design of Web-Based Financial Learning Environment

An-Pen Chen[1] and Hsiao-Ya Chiu[2]

[1] Institute of Information Management, University of National Chiao Tung,
1001 Ta Hsueh Road, Hsinchu, Taiwan 300, ROC
apc@iim.nctu.edu.tw
[2] The Department of Management Information, Yu Da College of Business
No.168, Hsueh-fu Rd, Chaochiao Township, Miaoli County, 361 Taiwan, ROC
kates.chiu@msa.hinet.net

Abstract. This study proposes the designing concepts of developing a comprehensive financial learning environment which is valuable for business schools as a reference to construct their learning platforms. Modern education stresses both theory and field experience. However, students are unlikely to obtain sufficient investment field experience in the present educational environment because of the enormous capital needs of financial operations. Thus, a key limitation of financial education is the removal of investment risks associated with money flow during investment practice. In order to remove these educational limitations, this paper proposes an investment simulations environment to exercise real market practices in financial and investment courses and proposes a referential application of scenario-based learning for investment learning. The investigation results indicate that IFILE learning is more effective, interesting and realistic than learning in the traditional classrooms.

Keywords: Financial simulation games, web-based learning, scenario-based e-learning, technology enhanced learning, laboratories design.

1 Introduction

Information technologies (IT) such as computer-assisted instructions (CAI), virtual instrument technology and interactive learning environment have long been discussed in relation to education. Approaches have been widely adapted for integrating various teaching information systems, such as computer-based training (CBT), web-based instruction, and on-line simulation game, into a unified instruction environment. Accordingly, numerous studies on instruction reveal that appropriate use of IT can significantly enhance teaching and learning effectiveness.

In line with the growing popularity of Internet-based instruction applications, the integration speed of IT and education methodologies is increasing more rapidly than ever [4][10][11]. Although educational institutes have widely applied IT to learning, business schools have yet to fully exploit IT capabilities to enhance learning efficiency. Consequently, more and more business schools are attempting to upgrade their

W. Nejdl and K. Tochtermann (Eds.): EC-TEL 2006, LNCS 4227, pp. 567–572, 2006.
© Springer-Verlag Berlin Heidelberg 2006

instruction environments to meet industrial requirements [1][9][3] Although there are several investment simulation web sites running for virtual stock trading exercise, seldom literatures discuss the application example for academic environment.

This study introduces design concepts of Integrated Financial Investment Learning Environment (IFILE) including a basic web-based environment, laboratories, virtual trading center, and scenario generator. This study also presents preliminary evidence of the teaching/learning efficiency via questionnaires gathered from both students and teachers that have experienced IFILE learning.

2   System Framework

The IFILE focuses mainly on serving as a financial and investment learning environment for business schools through the learning path of investment skills. This study establishes an educational platform that provides an interactive learning environment with five investment labs for satisfying different curricula needs.

2.1   Web-Based Learning Environment

The bottom level of IFILE is a "web-based financial education platform" that provides an interface facilitating fundamental learning and research, combined with a virtual trading center that processes trading exercises without requiring real money. The entry portal of the education platform functions as a virtual learning environment on web site that consists of Virtual classroom, Virtual Financial building, E-Library, Teachers e-office, and Students Forum. Students can login to this web site and learn via online programs and materials. The web site comprises the following web pages:

(1) Virtual classroom: including functions of curriculum planning and online chat room that may be separate from real class schedules. (2) Virtual Financial building: integrated real-time quoting system to respond to student online inquiries regarding stocks, funds, derivative products, bonds, international markets and financial news. (3) Virtual Trading center: was originally designed for performing virtual trading based on the real-time data produced by actual financial markets while the transaction records of each student are reserved in the student historical database. (4) E-Library: provides a rich online data source, database and other learning resource. (5) Teachers e-office: facilitates teachers in releasing homework and publicizing tutorial materials.

(6) Students Forum: a web-based forum system where students can freely discuss their opinions.

As shown in Fig.1, the financial education platform provides the fundamental framework of the IFILE system, while all financial investment laboratories conduct their simulated trading through the virtual trading center.

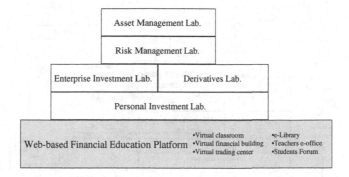

Fig. 1. The framework of IFILE includes a web-based financial education platform and five laboratories based on the learning path of Fundamentals of Investments

2.2 Laboratory Design

In order to design a learning environment that can best support the teaching needs, the IFILE designing group first investigated several popular textbooks [14] [2] [15] and built five financial laboratories based on the learning path of financial investment field, including: (1) *Personal Investment Lab* to familiarize students with securities trading operations. (2) *Enterprises Investment Lab* to simulate a professional investment institute. (3) *Derivatives Lab* enables students to learn how to control risks using derivatives. (4) *Risk Management Lab* aims to help students improve their skills in risk control and profiting, and draws on numerous financial skills and quantitative models. (5) *Asset Management Lab* helps students build up their capabilities in dynamic asset allocation, investment efficiency evaluation and asset portfolio optimization. The software systems used in IFILE labs are enhanced from popular financial industry packages by software vendors to adapt them for more specialized learning purposes.

2.3 The Virtual Trading Center

The learning software used in IFILE is connected to real-time market data sources and scenario generator, while practice orders are transmitted to a virtual trading center via a web interface to serve as real world exchanges linking buyers and sellers. The virtual trading center is designed to meet educational requirements by reproducing trading centers in real financial markets, effectively permitting students to learn how to make investment moves. Fig. 2 illustrates the software component and operating flows of IFILE virtual trading center.

2.4 Financial Market Scenario Generator

One of the educational goals of IFILE is to allow students practicing trading exercises under various market situations and thus the IFILE applied scenario-based technology to support these learning needs. Scenario-based learning [12] can be defined as learning that occurs in a context, situation, or social framework, which is based on the concept of

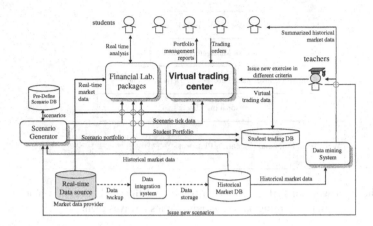

Fig. 2. System components and operating flows of the virtual trading center in IFILE

situated cognition [6][7] and constructivist learning[5][8][13]. The authors are now focused on design a financial market scenario generator (FMSG) system to support scenario-based learning needs.

Investment in real world moves correlate to timeline and market behavior that are never repeated as the moment passes. Moreover, financial models are applied differently as market situations change. To increase the effectiveness of instruction, an ideal financial investment learning system should accommodate repetition of practice exercises, thereby allowing students to compose various investment strategies to applied different financial models in specified scenarios.

3 Preliminary Survey

At the end of Fundamentals of Investments course held in June 2005 at NCTU, this study issued an anonymous questionnaire to 45 attending graduate students who have also experienced traditional classroom investment courses to examine the effectiveness of IFILE and classifying 33 semantic differential type questions into five major topics. Most students confer that IFILE can increase their learning interest, improve communication with other students, improve their trading experience, and improve self-learning achievements. Almost all students consider online learning can be efficient for this course.

Additionally, since the IFILE framework have introduced to business schools, some 31 schools have implemented IFILE classrooms. This study successfully conducted telephone or mail questionnaires in May 2005, sampling 27 teachers who have applied IFILE from those schools with conventional classroom teaching experience in financial investment courses. 41% of teachers used IFILE classrooms over ten times during the same course, where 72% of teachers used IFILE over five times. Thus, most of the comments came from teachers who had clearly understood the environment and had actually applied IFILE in their lectures. The result shows that 67% teachers believe that

IFILE can better fits their teaching needs, and 93% prefer IFILE to traditional classrooms if they can choose.

The investigation results from both teachers and students indicate that IFILE learning is more effective, interesting and realistic than learning in the traditional classrooms, especially when the course should applied conventional learning material and IT to practical exercise.

4 Conclusions

This study demonstrated the framework of IFILE, which provide an integrated learning environment comprising various topics such as laboratories design, virtual trading center, and financial scenario generator which never been discussed before. This study also applied questionnaires to both students and instructors, and results summarized that such an integrated learning environment like IFILE can help students increase their learning interest and improve their trading skills.

However, several topics remain to be resolved in the future. First, web-based simulation classrooms such as IFILE need further discuss from a psychological perspective to measure the concentration of students in the virtual environment. Second, a financial scenario generator as proposed in this article requires further enhancement. Finally, some problems should be further addressed when academic attention expand virtual learning environment from local to international market.

References

1. Albrecht W David. 1995. A financial accounting and investment simulation game, Issue in Accounting Education 10, 12-141.
2. Alexander, Gordon J. & Sharpe, William F. & Bailey, Jeffery V., 1993, Fundamentals of investments(2nd ed.), Prentice-Hall.
3. An-Pin Chen, Hsiao-Ya Chiu, Shinn-Wen Wang, and Chieh-Yow ChiangLin. 2003. Innovations in Financial Investment Information Education• Practical Financial Investment Simulation Programs. The 11th annual conference on pacific basin finance, economics, and accounting.
4. Brooks, D. W. 1997. Web-teaching• A guide to designing interactive teaching for the World Wide Web. Cambridge University Press.
5. Brooks, Jacqueline Grennon and Brooks, Martin G.,1993, The case for constructivist classrooms. Alexandria, VA: ASCD.
6. Brown, J.S., Collins, A., & Duguid, P.,1989, Situated cognition and the culture of learning. Education Researcher, 18(1), 32-41.
7. Collins, A., Brown, J. S., & Newman, S. E., 1990, Cognitive apprenticeship: Teaching the crafts of reading, writing, and mathematics. In L. B. Resnick (Ed.), Knowing, learning, and instruction: Essays in honor of Robert Glaser (pp. 453-494). Hillsdale, NJ: Lawrence Erlbaum.
8. Fosnot, Catherine., 1996, Constructivism: Theory, perspectives, and practice. New York: Teachers College Press.
9. Joseph Santos. 2002. Developing and Implementing an Internet-Based Financial System Simulation Game. Journal of Economic Education 33 , 31-40.

10. Khan, B.H. 1997. Web-based instruction. Englewood Cliffs, NJ: Educational Technology.
11. Myung-Geun Lee. 2001. Profiling students' adaptation styles in Web-based learning. Computer & Education 36, 121-132.
12. Randall W. Kindley, 2002, Scenario-Based E-Learning: A Step Beyond Traditional E-Learning, Learning circuits published on web site: http://www.learningcircuits.org/2002/may2002/kindley.html.
13. Steffe Leslie P. & Gale J. (Eds.), 1995, Constructivism in education. Hillsdale, NJ: Lawrence Erlbaum.
14. Ye Rih-Wu. 2000. Modern investment theory skills and application. FCMC press, Taiwan.
15. Zvi Bodie, Alex Kane, Alan J. Marcus, 1999, Investments (4th ed), McGraw-Hill.

Towards an Effective Instructional Engineering Analysis Method

David Díez Cebollero, Camino Fernández Llamas, and Juan Manuel Dodero

DEI Laboratory - Computer Science Department
Universidad Carlos III de Madrid, Spain
{david.diez, camino.fernandez, juanmanuel.dodero}@uc3m.es

Abstract. The analysis phase constitutes an essential step in the development of information systems. This fact is perhaps even more important in the development of learning software: the process of creating learning materials must take into account the range of abilities, needs, and interests of different stakeholders, adapting itself to a variety of contexts and pedagogical paradigms. It is therefore a complex process that must consider diverse perspectives and levels of abstraction.

Currently, there are two trends among others in Software Engineering engaged in optimizing the process of information systems development: Aspect-Oriented Software Development and Model-Driven Architecture. The combination of both mechanisms can facilitate the development of complex information systems like computer-supported learning systems. The intention of this paper is to propose an analysis method in learning material development process based on Aspect-Oriented Analysis and Model-Driven Architecture.

Keywords: Instructional design, instructional engineering, computer-aided education, analysis method, Aspect-Oriented, Model-Driven Architecture.

1 Introduction

Instructional Design and Technology (IDT) encloses the analysis of learning problems, as well as design, development, assessment and management of processes and resources intended to improve learning [1]. It is a complex and multidisciplinary discipline that involves several areas of knowledge, some of which present very diffuse boundaries. Given the difficulties and the complexity of this task, different authors have defined a series of methods [2,3] that, considering software engineering as a reference, try to optimise the learning material development process. The methods of information systems engineering suggest a methodological division of a system into modules, phases or stages in order to improve the learning systems development [4].

One of the essential phases of the development of information systems is the analysis phase. The analysis phase in software development processes aims to study and inform of the requirements and conditions of the system in order to determine the

W. Nejdl and K. Tochtermann (Eds.): EC-TEL 2006, LNCS 4227, pp. 573–578, 2006.

most appropriate solution to develop [5]. At the analysis phase, the learning systems share three fundamental characteristics:

- Different levels of abstraction. The problem is tackled by defining different stages, so that both the problem domain and the functionality provided by the system can be determined independently.
- Different perspectives. The definition of the problem is based on diverse points of view. The result is a series of models that represent the learning problem from different standpoints.
- Crosscutting concerns. There are dependencies and overlapping between such diverse perspectives, which makes it difficult to analyse each of them independently.

IDT known-methods only take into consideration the two first characteristics; unfortunately, the earlier instructional engineering methods do not resolve the overlapping and scattering problems at the analysis phase. In order to improve the learning systems analysis stage, we propose to turn to two increasingly used Software Engineering techniques:

- Model-Driven Architecture (MDA). MDA is an approach to using models in software development [6]. It is a specification that provides the tools for software development based on the definition of models with different level of abstraction.
- Aspect-Oriented Software Development (AOSD). AOSD is a paradigm of software development that leads to reducing the software system complexity through the separation of concerns [7]. The purpose is to facilitate the development of systems that take into account different overlapping perspectives or issues.

In this paper, we propose an analysis method for learning software using aspect-oriented and model-driven approaches aimed at improving the identification of the system requirements.

The rest of the paper is organized as follows. Section 2.1 and 2.2 motivate the need for an instructional engineering analysis method that supports multiple dimensions of decomposition. In section 2.3, our analysis method is described and shows how our approach has been realized, to end with some conclusions and future work.

2   An Instructional Engineering Analysis Method

Instructional Engineering is defined as a method that supports the analysis, the creation, the production and the delivery planning of learning systems, integrating the concepts, processes and principles of instructional design, software engineering and cognitive engineering [4]. To help perform these tasks thoughtfully and effectively, an instructional engineering method is needed.

The life-cycle of the earlier instructional engineering methods resembles the phases of the traditional software engineering process: analysis, design, development and evaluation. Taking as a starting point the opinion of diverse authors [8] that grant to the analysis a preponderant role, we will be focussed on the revision of the analysis phase. The aim is to know the features of the learning material analysis process in order to define a correct and useful instructional engineering analysis method.

2.1 Problem Description

In order to understand the complexity of the problem, we will consider a specific case study: the treatment of the user's profile from the point of view of instructional design.

The definition and treatment of the profiles of end users is a usual characteristic of information systems, being particularly relevant in learning systems. The profile can determine whether the end user is an instructor, who is in charge of monitoring the learning process, or a student. In this latter case, the competencies of the students must be taken into account to define the most appropriate course for their skill set. What is more, these skills might vary as the course progresses, creating the need for a constant readjustment of the contents and the way in which they are presented.

In brief, the analysis of the profile of the user is an essential aspect in the design of the system that must be carried out from diverse perspectives: from the point of view of the navigation model, the instructional model and the knowledge model. In turn, preliminary knowledge on the problem (for instance, the most suitable type of learning process depending on the abilities of the student or the aims of the instructor) can simplify both the analysis and comprehension processes of any scenarios.

2.2 Problem Evaluation

The complexity of learning systems, characterized by the great amount of information used, their high volatility and their multidimensional nature, determines the methodological approach for a correct analysis of the problem:

- Levels of abstraction. The analysis of the problem must be performed step by step, starting up with a global overview of the learning process and finishing off with a precise definition of the learning scenario to solve. The advantage of this approach is that the analysis of relevant aspects to the solution of the problem can be carried out at any moment, without paying attention to very general or excessively precise characteristics.
- Multiple perspectives. The problem must be analysed from diverse points of view [9]. These perspectives reflect the characteristics of the problem, the aspects of interest, for each of the models intervening in the solution: the pedagogical model, the instructional model, the navigation model, etc. This distinction of perspectives must be respected in each of the levels of abstraction defined for the problem.
- Overlapping of aspects. The analysis of the problem from different perspectives constitutes a widely-used and very advisable technique for highly-complex information systems [10]. Nevertheless, as the system grows, the number of elements and the relationships between them get increased, which impairs dealing with all aspects of the system separately, or circumscribed in a specific perspective. This problem is known as "Crosscutting concerns" [9,11]

The difficulty in the analysis of learning systems is depicted in figure 1. The problem must be observed from different perspectives and levels of abstraction (as proposed by the instructional design methods defined so far) but being aware of the existence of common relevant aspects in various models of the problem.

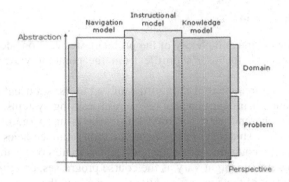

Fig. 1. The analysis phase decomposes the system into a multidimensional space of overlapping models. There are any relevant aspects that must be considered from diverse viewpoints.

2.3 Proposed Solutions

Once the problem is analysed, the next step is the establishment of mechanisms for solving it in order to define a correct and complete method of instructional design analysis. The most complex of the factors presented relates to the "Crosscuting concerns" problem. The problem occurs when there are aspects in the system (such as the profile of the user) that cannot be shaped independently; thus, the functionality of those aspects becomes scattered and tangled by the different models of the problem.

Currently, there are many approaches to deal with crosscutting concerns in early stages in software development. Probably, the most interesting is AOSD: a paradigm to reduce software system complexity through the decomposition of crosscutting concerns [7]. Separation of concerns is the ability to identify, summarize and utilize in an isolated way only properties that are relevant to a condition or objective. Based upon this idea, the objectives of the analysis phase are to:

- Identify the system properties.
- Define dependencies between these properties in order to determine which properties are interrelated.
- Choose the most suitable properties to be used as well-decomposed ones.

In turn, the development of complex learning systems poses a problem due to the large amount of information that must be processed. In these cases, a model-driven software development approach based on the definition of independent models for different abstraction levels might be substantially advantageous. The MDA approach defines a set of standards oriented towards an effective system development using model-driven development [6]. MDA proposes to make a distinction between system specification and its development for a specific platform [12]. For this reason, system development is driven by three different abstraction levels: Computation Independent Model (CIM), Platform Independent Model (PIM) and Platform Specific Model (PSM). Specifically, the analysis phase within the software development life cycle extends from the CIM level up to the first stages of the PIM level.

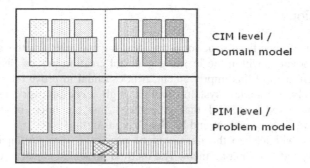

CIM level /
Domain model

PIM level /
Problem model

Fig. 2. Learning analysis. An instructional engineering analysis method based on AOSD and MDA. In each model we can identify two kinds of concerns: independent properties (vertical stripes) and crosscutting properties (horizontal stripes).

Having reached this point, it would be reasonable to propose an instructional engineering analysis method based on the use of AOSD within the MDA framework. Taking figure 2 as representative of the workspace in a learning system, our analysis method proposes the following guidelines:

- The analysis of the learning problem will be tackled at the CIM level. This involves mapping the problem description to properties in the system.
- The learning system functionality specification will be carried out at the PIM level. In this level two tasks are made: 1) The properties are designed independently. 2) The models will be recombined by composition rules.
- Each of these levels will be in turn divided into several perspectives, based on the viewpoints involved in the system.

Based on these guidelines, the design problem exposed in section 2.1 will be solved of the following way:

- The first step is to describe the learning problem using narrative scenarios for each perspective: pedagogical, instructional, delivery, etc.
- The different narrative scenarios may be translated into specific requirements. For instance, requirements describe behaviour associated with the user profile.
- Using aspect-oriented analysis techniques, like Theme/Doc [13], the system properties and the dependencies between perspectives are identified. In our case, the "user profile" property will be recognized in all perspective.
- The CIM level result will be an analysis model that identifies the system properties, grouping them and establishing relations between them. In our example, we define a user profile view that shows relationships between perspectives, as well as the relations with other properties of the system.
- At the first stages of the PIM, the "user profile" property will be designed independently, defining the composition rules between perspectives.

In our approach, Learning Analysis becomes a first-class activity of learning material development process. The dependencies model supposes a source of semantic information which promotes system evolution and maintainability.

3 Conclusions

The definition of specific instructional engineering methods for the analysis phase represents an advance within the learning material creation process. Nevertheless, to ensure the usefulness of this improvement, it is essential to prove the capacity of the method to analyze complex systems with a high level of overlapping. Learning analysis is an analysis method that guarantees this condition based on Aspect-Oriented Software Development and Model-Driven Architecture.

Future work will lead to the definition of properties that participate in learning process and dependences among them. The method presented is just a starting point. It must be refined, stretched, and modified, and it must be applied in real cases of study.

Acknowledgements

This work is partly funded by the MD2 project (TIC2003-03654) from the Spanish Ministry of Science and Technology.

References

1. Reiser, R A. Trends and Issues in Instructional Design and Technology. Merrill/Prentice Hall, Upper Saddle River, N.J. (2001)
2. Paquette, G, Aubin, C., Crevier, F. MISA: A knowledge-based method for the engineering of learning systems. Journal of Courseware Engineering. (1999) No 2, 63-78.
3. Uden, L. An engineering approach for online learning. Journal of Distance Engineering Education. (2003) Vol. 1, No. 1, 63-77.
4. Paquette, G. Instructional Engineering in Networked Environments. Pfeiffer, San Francisco. (2004)
5. Jacobson, I., Booch, G., Rumbaugh, J. The Unified Software Development Process. Addison-Wesley Professional, Reading. (1999)
6. Bichler, L. A flexible code generator for MOF-based modelling languages. 2nd OOPSLA Workshop on Generative Techniques in the context of Model Driven Architecture. Anaheim. (2003)
7. Filman. R. Aspect-Oriented Software Development. Addison Wesley, Boston. (2004)
8. Wiegers, K. E. Software Requirements: practical techniques for gathering and managing requirements throughout the product development cycle. Microsoft Press, Redmond. (2003)
9. Tarr, P, Ossher, H., Harrison, W, Sutton, S. N Degrees of Separation: Multi-Dimensional Separation of Concerns. ICSE 1999 Conference Proceedings. (1999) 107-119
10. IEEE Computer Society. IEEE Recommended Practice for Architectural Descriptions of Software-Intensive System. IEEE Std-1471-2000 (2000) 29p.
11. G. Kiczales, J. Lamping, A. Mendhekar, C. Maeda, C. Lopes, J.M. Loingtier, J. Irwin. Aspect-oriented programming. ECOOP'97—Object-Oriented Programming, 11th European Conference. (1997) 220-242
12. Czarnecki, K. Simon H. Classification of model transformation approaches. 2nd OOPSLA Workshop on Generative Techniques in the Context of the Model Driven Architecture Anaheim (2003)
13. Baniassad, E, Clarke, S. Finding Aspects In Requirements with Theme/Doc. In Proceedings of Early Aspects2004: Aspect-Oriented Requirements Engineering and Architecture Design, Lancaster. (2004)

The LEAD Project*: Computer Support for Face-to-Face Collaborative Learning

Wouter van Diggelen and Maarten Overdijk

Utrecht University, Research Centre Learning in Interaction,
Heidelberglaan1, 3584 CS Utrecht, The Netherlands
{w.vandiggelen, m.overdijk}@fss.uu.nl

Abstract. The LEAD project[1] stresses that one of the important challenges with regard to technology-enhanced learning is to develop effective networked-computing support for face-to-face collaborative learning. To achieve this one has to gain a deeper understanding of face-to-face collaborative learning *and* the technology that supports the communicative processes that are involved. The LEAD project will enhance state-of-the-art research by studying this complex interplay within a collaborative classroom setting, an arrangement that has hardly been addressed in educational research and practice.

Keywords: Collaborative learning, Problem solving support, face-to-face discussions.

1 Introduction

Most views of computer-supported collaborative learning emphasize that new ways of learning will occur outside the classroom, connecting learners who are dispersed in time and space. These views assume a situation of online collaboration, distance learning and virtual teaching. Although overcoming time and space has a direct added value, it also leads to a partial focus. There are characteristics of face-to-face interactions, particularly the space-time contexts in which such interactions take place, that the emerging technologies are either pragmatically or logically incapable of replicating [5].

The LEAD project stresses that tomorrow's learning will still take place in schools where learners *meet face-to-face to collaborate, discuss and solve problems*. Recent studies indicate that most of tomorrow's learning will take place on-campus and face-to-face. The use of ICT has become commonplace, but in a way that only gradually is

---

* Project team: Utrecht University, Research Centre Learning in Interaction; Centre Nationale de la Recherche Scientifique, Paris; Ecole Nationale Supérieure des Mines, St-Etienne; University of Salerno, Dipartimento di Scienze dell'Educazione; University of Salerno, Dipartimento di Informatica e Applicazioni; University of Nottingham, Learning Sciences Research Institute; ICATT Interactive Media, Amsterdam; Tilburg University, Faculty of Arts; University of Lyon, Interactions, Corpus, Apprentissages, Représentations.

[1] The LEAD project (IST-2005-028027) is partially funded by the European Commission under the IST Programme of Framework VI.

W. Nejdl and K. Tochtermann (Eds.): EC-TEL 2006, LNCS 4227, pp. 579–584, 2006.
© Springer-Verlag Berlin Heidelberg 2006

stretching traditional on-campus practice [e.g. 1]. These face-to-face learning situations are largely ignored by much of current research into computer-supported collaborative learning.

The LEAD project focuses on co-located collaboration. It calls into question the typical classroom situation where a group of learners sit together to discuss a topic. The LEAD project assumes that these collaborative situations can be improved with the appropriate collaborative technology. The goal of the LEAD project is to develop, implement and evaluate conceptual models, practical learning methods and associated networked-computing technologies for effective face-to-face collaborative learning.

2   Collaborative Problem Solving

The LEAD project focuses on one specific type of "higher-level cognitive" learning activity, i.e. collaborative problem solving.

Collaborative problem solving is an essential aspect of our day-to-day performance in society. In addition, when the conditions are right, people who solve a problem together may learn [3, 8]. Learning is viewed as a matter of participation in social activity and as the negotiation of shared meanings [7]. Part of the knowledge *emerges* during the problem-solving process. When learners share and discuss their experiences, perspectives and information, significant features of the problem space emerge or become apparent. Roschelle and Teasley [7] consider this *joint problem space* as an essential property of collaborative problem solving. The concept 'problem space' has its origin in cognitive analysis of human problem solving where it is defined as a person's internal representation of the task environment. The internal representation captures essential aspects of the problem and the desired end state. It also includes general knowledge associated with the problem and strategies, and plans and rules for solving the problem.

2.1   Problem-Solving Discussions

Collaborative problem solving normally takes its shape as a *problem solving discussion* that is directed towards the exploration of a particular subject or resolution of a problem.

Learners who solve a problem collectively have to manage different kinds of group tasks. On a general level two group tasks can be identified: learners have to *solve the problem* and they must *collaborate*.

2.2   Solving the Problem

With respect to first task of solving the problem, a first complicated factor is that the problems learners address are usually *ill-defined*. At the beginning it isn't clear what the problem exactly is *and* which actions may lead to solution of the problem. Learners have to identify and analyse the problem, they have to generate and evaluate ideas and choose a solution. Learners might disagree about every aspect of the problem-solving process. They may think differently about the nature of the problem, its causes and consequences or about potential solutions.

The interactions that constitute this aspect of a problem-solving discussion can be typified as *task-related interactions*. The task-related interactions are used to explicate task processes in groups, in that information made available to members and how they use it are directly related to task performance [6].

2.3   Maintaining an Acceptable Level of Collaboration

A second complicated factor has to do maintaining an acceptable level of collaboration within the group. When learners have to solve problems collectively they have to maintain durable relations and acceptable levels of participation. We will typify these interactions as *non-task related*. Non-task related interactions affect group members' perception of one another and the relationships they form [6]. Non-task related interactions can be typified as *social-emotional interactions*. These interactions are primarily directed toward the relationship between group members.

2.3   Computer Support for Problem-Solving Discussions

The LEAD project is about supporting problem-solving discussions in the classroom. With the addendum 'in the classroom' we want to emphasize that we deal with discussions where learners are located near each other. It means that learners communicate face-to-face *and* simultaneously use LEAD 's collaborative software system to solve the problem at hand. The computer support will focus on both aspects of the task-related interaction, i.e. the communicative processes and their outcomes.

3   Theory-Driven Design

The LEAD project adopts a *design research* approach that combines *theory-driven design* with empirical *educational research*. The design research approach entails both 'engineering' particular forms of learning *and* systematically studying those forms of learning within the context defined by the means of supporting them [3]. It explicitly exploits the design process as an opportunity to advance researchers' understanding of learning processes [4].

The research and development (R&D) approach consists of three successive phases of activities (**Fig. 1**):

1. problem analysis and theory development,
2. design of the technology and learning methods, and
3. the implementation and evaluation of the design in practice.

3.1   Problem Analysis and Theory Development

The R&D approach starts with a sense that an existing learning situation can be improved. In our case, it is the notion that small-group, face-to-face problem-solving discussions within the classroom may benefit from networked-computing support. This statement gives rise to a research and design process that aims to improve

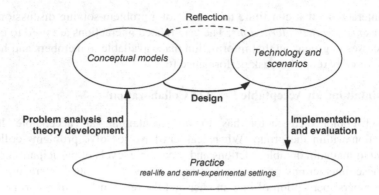

Fig. 1. LEAD's Research and Technical Development strategy

face-to-face discussions in the classroom. This educational improvement is guided by theories and models that apply to the specific learning situation where LEAD zeroes in on.

The development of theories and models is triggered by an *analysis* of the learning situation. This analysis starts with the identification of the *key issues* that pertain to the phenomenon of face-to-face discussions in the classroom. A deeper understanding of these key issues is crucial for the design of a learning environment for face-to-face problem-solving discussions. It leads to a phase of theory development that ends in several tentative conceptual models.

3.2 Design

The design activities are a natural continuation of theory development activities. The design aims at the development of a methods and tools for effective face-to-face problem-solving discussions. The educational part of the design leads to methods and guidelines for the arrangement of the learning environment. The technical counterpart produces a collaborative software system that forms an integral part of the learning environment.

3.3 Implementation and Evaluation

The principles and hypothesis developed during the theory development phase are made applicable for evaluation in practice through the design. Evaluation must account for when, how and why the design functions in practice. The practice may range from semi-experimental studies towards field study in real-life classroom settings.

Through research in practice we can draw conclusions about the theoretical foundation of the design. If necessary, we can adapt the conceptual models, and subsequently improve the design. The reflective aspects of the approach results in an *iterative design* cycle that gradually knits together a coherent set of conceptual models that reflects progress in understanding.

4 Expected Results

The expected results of the project are:

1. Conceptual models about collaborative problem solving in the classroom;
2. A collaborative software system for face-to-face problem-solving discussions;
3. Learning methods for technology-enhanced collaborative problem solving;
4. A tool for transcribing and analyzing learners' actions and interactions.

There are yet no self-contained theories and models that could apply to the specific learning situation that is the focus of LEAD, i.e. networked-computer support for face-to-face problem-solving discussions in the classroom. We lack detailed theories and models on which we can base the design.

For example, the insights gained from on-line learning environments don't provide us with the appropriate directions. Computer-mediated communication in co-located settings differs basically from on-line settings [5]. In on-line distance learning environments *all* communication takes place electronically and must be supported likewise. There is a fundamental shift in orientation when we move our attention towards face-to-face settings.

Because there aren't any theories and models available on which we can base the design, we have to invest time in theory development.

Theory and design are interwoven within the LEAD project. Theory development becomes a 'design' activity in itself and its outcomes will be part of the design. The development of conceptual models and the design of the collaborative system go hand in hand.

LEAD's collaborative system consists of two tools that aim to support specific problem-solving activities that are performed during a group discussion. The system provides learners with the appropriate structures to match the characteristics of effective task-related communication.

The two tools are:

1. A *text-based conferencing tool* that offers its users a variety of 'textures' for text-based computer-mediated interaction. The tool is based on a stratified structure that encompasses several layers, where each layer may reflect different aspects of the interaction. Furthermore, the 'textures' provided by the conferencing tool exceed the temporal order that is characteristic for a chat or face-to-face discussion.
2. A *graphical shared-workspace tool* that consists of a graphical, shared workspace with a pre-defined notation system. Within the shared workspace users create a graphical representation of the topic at hand and/or the process of discussion. The tool will provide its users with various structures that will guide their spatial behaviour within the graphical workspace.

The LEAD project will develop learning methods for effective networked-computing supported problem-solving discussions in semi-experimental or actual classroom settings. The learning methods involve concepts that can be traced back to the conceptual models. They also contain operational strategies in the form of practical guidelines for arranging the learning environment. These guidelines refer to e.g. the task, instructions, information, role of the teacher, technology to be used and the configuration of the technology.

The learning methods with associated collaborative technology have to be implemented and evaluated in practice. The LEAD project will also develop techniques for data collection, transcription and analysis of face-to-face and computer-mediated actions and interactions

References

1. CHEPS: CHEPS Scenarios. The European Higher Education and Research Landscape 2020. University of Twente. Center for Higher Educational Policy Studies (2004)
2. Cohen, E.G.: Restructuring the Classroom: Conditions for Productive Small Groups. Review of Educational Research 64 (1994) 1-35
3. Cobb, P., Confrey, J., diSessa, A., Lehrer, R. and Schauble, L.: Design Experiments in Educational Research. Educational Researcher 32 (2003) 9-13.
4. Edelson, D.C.: Design Research: What we Learn when we Engage in Design. The Journal of the Learning Sciences 11(2002) 105-121.
5. Olson, G.M. and Olson, J.S.: Distance Matters. Human-Computer Interaction 15 (2000) 139-178
6. Propp, K.M. Collective Information Processing in Groups. In Frey, L.R. Gouran, D.S. and Poole M.S. (Eds.): The Handbook of Group Communication Theory and Research. Sage Publications, Thousand Oaks (1999).
7. Roschelle, J. and Teasley, S.D.: Construction of Shared Knowledge in Collaborative Problem Solving. In O'Malley, C. (ed.): Computer-supported Collaborative Learning. Springer-Verlag, New York (1995)
8. Webb, N.M. and Palincsar, A.S.: Group Processes in the Classroom. In Berliner, D.C. and Calfee, R.C. (Eds.): Handbook of Educational Psychology. Simon & Schuster Macmillan, New York (1996)

On-Campus Blended Learning: Using Discussion Forums for Peer Collaboration on Tutorial Assignments

J.A. Gilles Doiron

Center for Teaching and Learning,
Zayed University, Abu Dhabi, U.A.E.
gilles.doiron@zu.ac.ae

Abstract. In this study, 165 undergraduate students were assigned to online tutorial discussion groups of 8 or 9 students per group, and during 9 weeks of the semester, these groups used discussion forums to discuss assigned readings, present opinions, debate issues and summarise papers or information they had researched for their weekly tutorial assignment. Student's postings were peer rated for their contribution to the discussion. Statistically significant ($p<0.01$) high correlations were found between performance, posting frequency and peer rating. During the semester, two attitude survey questionnaires were conducted, and within-survey correlations showed moderate correlations in Survey I, and high correlations in Survey II. Although this blended learning approach was successful in encouraging individual participation, resistance to change was still evident.

1 Introduction

The use of information and communication technology (ICT) for teaching and learning is providing new opportunities for the development of student-centred learning and collaborative learning approaches, and many researchers are investigating the advantages and drawbacks of online learning. The discussion forum, a computer-mediated communication (CMC) application, is one aspect of ICT that has generated much interest.

According to Karayan and Crowe [1], and Smith and Hardaker [2], the advantage of a discussion forum, as opposed to the traditional face-to-face class discussion session, lies in it's asynchronous nature which allows for a wider student participation and offers them more time to process their thoughts. While some researchers highlight the fact that shy students are more likely to participate in an online discussion because it is less intimidating than speaking up in class [3], Haythornthwaite et al [4] point to the growing concern that discussion forums are impersonal and may contribute to students feeling isolated.

Whereas discussion forums have been widely used in distance education, the rationale for their use in on-campus courses is substantively different [5]. More and more on-campus courses are supported with ICT learning management systems, and the "blending" of face-to-face and online activities is creating new approaches to learning [6], [7]. In an effort to identify sound teaching and learning strategies within this contemporary context, the design and evaluation of these novel on-campus

W. Nejdl and K. Tochtermann (Eds.): EC-TEL 2006, LNCS 4227, pp. 585–590, 2006.

blended learning approaches is vital. Hence, this case study examines how undergraduate health psychology students worked collaboratively in small work groups on weekly tutorial assignments over a period of nine weeks.

2 Background

Health psychology is an applied area of psychology and thus lends itself well to discussions of how psychological principles and findings can be applied to real world problems. Bishop and Doiron [8] believed that because of the availability and convenience of ubiquitous CMC, students in the health psychology course could benefit greatly from the use of online discussion forums to communicate ideas and comment on readings that relate theories in health psychology to specific health issues. In addition, since the launch in the late 1990s of its own online learning management system, known as the integrated virtual learning environment (IVLE), the university had made the use of IVLE mandatory in all courses. Consequently, the students in this study, being third year undergraduates, were already familiar with the use of the university's ICT tools.

At the outset of the semester, 165 students were randomly assigned to groups of 9 or 8, and during the subsequent 9 weeks, they used the discussion forums to address the weeks' tutorial question. Each group accessed its own discussion forum and students posted messages and replied to postings at their convenience from wherever they had access to the Internet. The course instructor did not take part in any of the forums.

Group leadership was rotated weekly and leaders were tasked to get the discussions started and keep the group on track for seven days. At the end of each week, the discussion forums were closed and each group leader wrote a paper on the assignment question. To familiarise everyone with what was expected on an assignment paper, an exemplar paper was made available on the module web site for students to consult, and as the group leadership was rotated weekly, each group member became the group leader for one assignment.

While tutorial papers counted for 25% of the overall course grade, each group member's contributions to the online discussions also counted for marks. Based on an individual's contributions towards helping the leader to address the tutorial question, the leader anonymously assigned a grade from 0 to 7 to each group member. At the end of the semester, these grades were tallied and used to calculate a 10% of the course grade that reflected the quality of participation from each student throughout the semester. To complete the declared 50% continuous grading for the course, 15% was allocated for a critique of another group's paper.

3 Methods

The subjects, 165 students in the Faculty of Arts and Social Sciences of a major university in South East Asia, were third year undergraduates. During the semester, two questionnaires were administered; the first was given after the third tutorial assignment and the second was given after the last assignment.

These surveys were designed to examine how the students felt about a) using online discussion forums; b) the quality of the online discussions; c) online vs. face-to-face discussions; d) relationships in online discussion forums; and e) online peer collaboration as a learning strategy. The question types included five point and three point Likert scale responses, dichotomous true/false responses, nominal selections, and open answer qualitative input.

4 Findings

Throughout the 9 weeks of the tutorial assignments the 165 students posted a total of 3,560 messages. Although total weekly postings dropped from 566 in the first week to 377 in week 4, postings maintained a weekly level above 300 thereafter. However, while most students posted in all of the 9 weeks, 37 students missed one week, 15 students missed two weeks and 13 students dropped out of the discussion forum activity in the first 6 weeks. The average number of postings per student was 21.58 (SD=11.45, Range: 2 – 70).

Usage statistics indicated a sustained involvement from most of the class, and as noted by the instructor, students expressed themselves at a level far beyond the interactions experienced in traditional face-to-face tutorial discussions. However, while the usage statistics alone do not reflect the quality of peer collaboration, the peer assessment ratings provide an indication of the level of satisfaction with the posting contents. The average rating was 4.13 (SD=1.05, Range: 0 – 6).

Continuous assessment (CA) marks (N=165) were made available for the study, correlations between the marks received for the tutorial assignment paper, the critique of another student's paper, the discussion forum peer ratings and the frequency of postings were investigated. As table 1 shows, correlation results using data from the entire class (N=165) showed statistically significant correlations (p>0.01) among most of the performance categories.

Table 1. Performance Correlations (N=165)

		Paper	Critique	Peer Rating	Postings
Paper	Pearson Correlation	1	.777	.352	.264
	Sig. (2-tailed)		.000	.000	.001
Critique	Pearson Correlation	.777	1	.277	.130
	Sig. (2-tailed)	.000		.000	.097
Peer Rating	Pearson Correlation	.352	.277	1	.589
	Sig. (2-tailed)	.000	.000		.000
Postings	Pearson Correlation	.264	.130	.589	1
	Sig. (2-tailed)	.001	.097	.000	
	N	165	165	165	165

Notably, there is a large correlation between total postings and peer ratings. This seems to indicate that group leaders based their group member ratings on the number of postings submitted.

One hundred and fifty-seven (157) students completed Survey I and results indicated that 87.3% of the students were comfortable working with the discussion forums, 70.1% felt confident about expressing their opinions in the discussion forums, while 15.6% of students said they felt insecure and 14.7% said that they had difficulty understanding discussion forum postings. Moreover, 20% of students said that they found it difficult expressing themselves in the discussion forum format.

When asked if they had contributed more opinions in discussion forums, as compared to face-to-face tutorial discussions, 56.4% of the students said that they had, while 21.8% disagreed. When asked if they had spent more time gathering information to prepare for the online discussion, 58.5% said that they had, while 8.4% indicated they had not. On the issue of trusting their group members to offer meaningful contributions in their postings, 40.2% of students said that they trusted their discussion forum group members, while 20.1% said they did not.

Interestingly, only 24.6% of the students thought they had learned more about the tutorial topics because of their participation in the discussion forum format, while 29.9% said they had not. Similarly, only 24.2% thought they had remembered more about the tutorial topics because they had participated in the discussion forum format, while 35.9% disagreed.

One hundred thirty-two (132) students completed Survey II, and most of the results did not differ substantially from Survey I. However, three areas that seemed to indicate a shift in attitude from Survey I were perceptions about a) the impersonal nature of the discussion forums, b) learning, and c) recall.

Students who felt their relationships were personal decreased from 15.7% in Survey I (n=155) to 10% in Survey II (n=131), and students whose opinions were neutral also decreased from 24.2% to 18.5%. In Survey II (n=131), 43.5% of respondents, up from 24.6% in Survey I (n=154), said they believed they had learned more from participating in the traditional face-to-face tutorial discussions. Similarly, 62.1% of the students in Survey II (n=132), up from 30.5% in Survey I (n=153), said they remembered more facts about the topics from participating in the traditional face-to-face tutorial discussions.

An analysis of bivariate correlations using a 2-tailed Pearson correlation coefficient test was run on the data and most questions within both surveys correlated well. Correlation coefficient descriptors from Cohen's [9] scale of correlations were used, and statistically significant correlations, ranging from moderate to small in Survey I and high to small in Survey II were found.

Notable correlations indicated that students who said they expressed themselves clearly in discussion forums, also said they clearly understood what others had written in the postings, were confident about expressing their opinions in discussion forums, had contributed more opinions in discussion forums, felt trust towards other discussion forum group members and believed they remembered more about the tutorial topics as compared to the face-to-face tutorial discussions. Students who said they had difficulty expressing themselves clearly in discussion forums, also said they felt insecure about expressing their opinions in discussion forums, had contributed fewer opinions in discussion forums, felt that they could not trust their group members, had spent less time gathering information for online discussions, preferred working alone rather than collaboratively and believed they had not remembered more about tutorial topics as compared to the face-to-face tutorial discussions.

Paired samples correlations showed a significant (p<0.01) correlation in all question pairs, and, as table 2 shows, paired samples t-tests revealed that 3 pairs of questions showed a significant difference between the means.

Table 2. Paired Samples T-tests and Effect Size

Question Pairs	Mean	SD	Std. Error	t	df	Sig. (2-tailed)	Effect Size
Survey I Q. 15 & Survey II Q. 14	-.224	.93	.08	-2.69	124	.008	.24
Survey I Q. 17 & Survey II Q. 17	-.384	1.42	.13	-3.03	124	.003	.27
Survey I Q. 19 & Survey II Q. 18	-.810	1.46	.13	-6.24	125	.000	.56

In order to establish whether any of these pairs actually had a practical or meaningful difference, a calculation of effect size was conducted. Cohen's d effect size calculation was used and d values of .2, .5 and .8 were rated as a small, medium and large effect size. The means and standard deviations in the data indicated a trend; namely that after a semester of using discussion forums for collaborating on tutorial assignments, students more readily agreed that their relationship with the other discussion group members was very "business like" and impersonal" (Pair 1), preferred the traditional face-to-face tutorial discussion as the format for "learning more" (Pair 2), and, more emphatically, preferred the traditional face-to-face tutorial discussion as the format for "remembering more" (Pair 3).

6 Discussions and Conclusions

In this case study, with approximately one in three students stating that they would rather not stray from the traditional face-to-face activity, resistance to change is evident. Further research will help identify more variables that affect and perpetuate the negative attitudes towards using discussion forums as a tutorial assignment workspace. The data gathered in this study is the basis for a post hoc discriminant function analysis (DFA) that will look at cognitive learning style groups as dependent variables.

In conclusion, while university lecturers are encouraged to devise teaching strategies that foster student independence and collaborative interdependence, we know that one size does not fit all. Hence, although small collaborative discussion forum workgroups are a viable alternative to the traditional face-to-face tutorial discussion format, we need a deeper understanding of the processes that lead to their adoption or rejection. The "blended learning" approach might be better served with a side order of structures designed to respond to individual preferences and tastes, making collaborative peer learning a more palatable dish for all.

References

1. Karayan, S. & Crowe, J.: Student perspectives of electronic discussion groups. THE Journal: Technological Horizons in Education, Vol. 24, No. 9, (1997) 69–71
2. Smith, D. & Hardaker, G.: e-Learning innovation through the implementation of an Internet supported learning environment. Educational Technology and Society, Vol. 3, (2000) 1–16

3. Citera, M.: Distributed teamwork: the impact of communication media on influence and decision quality. Journal of the American Society for Information Science, Vol. 49, No.9, (1988) 792–800
4. Haythornthwaite, C., Kazmer, M. M., Robbins, J. & Shoemaker, S.: Community development among distance learners: temporal and technological dimensions. Journal of Computer Mediated Communication, Vol. 6, No.1, (2000) 1–24
5. Davies, J. & Graff, M.: Performance in e-learning: online participation and student grades. British Journal of Educational Technology, Vol. 36, No.4, (2005) 657–663
6. Jaffee, D.: Institutionalized Resistance To Asynchronous Learning Networks. Journal of Asynchronous Learning Networks, Vol. 2, No. 2, (1998) 21–32
7. Spector, J.M.: An Overview of Progress and Problems in Educational Technology. Interactive Educational Multimedia, Vol. 3, (2001) 27–37
8. Bishop, G. D. & Doiron, J. A. G.: Using Online Forums as a Replacement for Face-To-Face Discussion Groups. In Proc. of FASS-CDTL Symposium, Singapore, (2003) 36–43
9. Cohen, J.: Statistical power analysis for the behavioral sciences (2nd ed.). New Jersey: Lawrence Erlbaum (1988)

Semantic Positioning as a Means for Visual Knowledge Structuring

Patrick Erren and Reinhard Keil

Heinz-Nixdorf Institute, University of Paderborn
Fuerstenallee 11, 33102 Paderborn, Germany
erren@zitmail.uni-paderborn.de
rks@uni-paderborn.de,
http://wwwhni.uni-paderborn.de

Abstract. This contribution introduces a new concept for the cooperative visual structuring of knowledge. We distinguish this from traditional
methods of knowledge organisation. We will show through an example of
use, based on virtual knowledge spaces, how our procedure can be used
productively in teaching. First experiences support the potential of this
concept, and raise associated new challenges. In the age of cooperative
distributed knowledge organisation we estimate a growing importance for
this type of structuring knowledge as a part of media supported learning
processes.

1 Introduction

We connect two basic qualities with the concept of hypertext, which after Ted
Nelson[7] can only be realized with help of computers. One the one hand this is
non-sequential writing, first enabling technically supported cooperative writing.
On the other hand it is semi-structured data management, allowing to incorporate semantic correlations without the need for fully structured and referenced
data material. The quality of semi-structured data management has long been
understood to equal the organisation of cognitive structures [9]. Thus hypertext
was regarded as a means for authors to enable alternative learning paths for the
reader.

The added value for the reader is quite limited, because even a printed script
or textbook can contain multiple references and is mostly read non-sequentially.
Today these concepts are still dominant especially in the area of web-based
learning. However, hypertext was originally conceived to provide readers with
the ability to create explicit internal and external links in and to documents,
encompassing their own semantic interests apart from those of the author(s).

We regard the development of new forms of cooperative structuring and presentation of knowledge structures to be of great importance. These use traditional visualisation and structuring methods and enrich them with the concept
of semantical positioning. An example depicts the current development in a
practical work context. Finally we will give a short outlook on future research
questions.

W. Nejdl and K. Tochtermann (Eds.): EC-TEL 2006, LNCS 4227, pp. 591–596, 2006.

2   Added Media Value

Classical learning management platforms like Moodle[1] or WebCT[2] put their
focus on documents, which are embedded in a context of use via certain management functions. Cooperation platforms like CommSy[6] or Cure[2] focus on
communication functions, without meeting the requirements of supporting the
persistency of objects and the ability for cooperative manipulation of their attributes. In both contexts of use it is often impossible to arrange or position
objects and documents spatially. Generally users only have access to a hierarchical list sorted after filename, creation date or other standard attributes.

The concept of virtual knowledge spaces[3] in contrast does not only offer basic
functions for virtual learning communities (awareness, role and rights management, event functions like automatic notices, etc.). It also offers basic possibilities for the cooperative semantical structuring of knowledge. With help of a
new Eclipse-based client named 'medi@rena', objects can be positioned freely,
arranged graphically with others and overlaid in spatial areas.

For us this marks the transition of current knowledge representation towards
cooperative visual knowledge structuring as a continuous, distributed and cooperative process. Here objects, documents and graphical elements are connected
in such a way, that the spatial arrangement of knowledge elements and their
visualisation allow for the deduction of the underlying knowledge structure. For
a practical implementation in e-learning further deliberations on the concept of
semantic positioning are necessary.

3   Structuring Knowledge Through Semantic Positioning

In addition to approaches of textual knowledge organisation via chapters, lists,
tables or even ontologies, mainly graphical structures have emerged since the
60s. These structures are employed to give a quick overview of a specific topic
area[8]. Such methods gain notable importance against the background of knowledge that needs to be accessible digitally over long periods of time. Consequently
knowledge structuring deals with semantics over multiple documents or structured views on document collections. Therefore time and place spanning cooperative accessibility is a requirement as well as non-sequentiallity and semi-
structuredness mentioned in the introduction. This also distinguishes knowledge
structuring from mere knowledge organisation which allows only for ordering
and categorization but cannot be based on semantics on a content level. The
structure needs to be expandable in the light of its long term usage capacity.
Compositions as much as learning are social processes in which knowledge that is
not fully compiled is gathered, edited, complemented and polished. Christopher
Alexander developed the concept of 'constructive diagrams' to support these
processes[1]. His census is that representations need to be developed in which
the problem structure is expressed in an adequate symbolic representation such

---

[1] Refer to: http://moodle.org
[2] Refer to: http://www.webct.com

as a map. Explorability as a requirement thus also means that graphical statements can be questioned critically just like textual ones.

In a first approach we have created a canonical framework of expressive means for knowledge visualisation structures. This framework allows to incorporate our concept of *semantic positioning* that will be explained subsequently.

- *PicMents (Picture Elements)*
  Basic elements of simple or complex atomic visual compositions used to create visual knowledge structures. These include lines, dots, surfaces, arrows, images (icons), etc.
- *MarkUps*
  Element attributes that allow for a specification of PicMents aside from spatial dimensions or type (Color, Shape, Caption, etc.).
- *Arrangements*
  Different basic methods of arranging PicMents. We distinguish relational, combinatorical, topographical and topological arrangements.

The mentioned basic arrangements use different methods for the visual semantic structuring of knowledge elements. These are explained in the following:

- *Relational*: graph structures where elements depicted as nodes are explicitly connected via (semantic) edges (e.g. Organigrams, Flow Charts, Mind Maps).
- *Combinatorical*: table structures where semantic meaning is derived from the respective combination of row and column.
- *Topographical*: diagrams encompassing sets and/or quantities depicted through linear or filled surface structures expressing semantic meaning through containedness or intersection (e.g Pie Charts, Venn Diagrams).
- *Topological*: Semantic closeness is expressed via spatial proximity of elements in n-dimensions. Each dimension carries its respective meaning (e.g. time axes, topology maps, alphanumerical orderings).

	Relational		Combinatorial	Topographical	Topological
	Semantic Nets		Matrices	Rooms/Spaces	Axes
	Relations		Combinations		Surface Areas
Flows	*Hierarchy*	*Graphs*		Venn Diagrams	
	Organigram				
	Mind Map				

Fig. 1. Categorised Arrangement Techniques for Knowledge Structuring

The combination of at at least two of said arrangements with PicMents (and MarkUps) in such a manner that a semantical relation is specified by the unique position of knowledge objects is what we call *overlays*. The notion of overlays however only refers to the structure of arrangement. For the applied technique, namely the utilization of the spatial dimension within the corresponding overlay of documents and graphical structures, we coined the term *semantic positioning*.

Its main advantage are the expanded information dimensions available through the possible layering of multiple arrangements, PictureElements and MarkUps. A knowledge document thus already gains recognizable meaning through its position within an overlay. The richness of expression and constructive power of this technique becomes apparent with the manifold relations expressible via graphical spatial arrangement (e.g. closeness of elements, similarity or bond strength). This is even deepened by the possible complexity of elementary shapes[5] through combination (e.g. with arrows). The versatile combinability has strengths but also weaknesses: On the one hand it allows to express yet unnoticed contexts, on the other hand formal verification is impossible, as is the extraction of meaning from a complex diagram with means of its elementary components. It however also becomes clear that, in contrast to the concept of semantic positioning, techniques simply based on PicMents such as mind maps only allow for rough categorizations but not for content based complex semantic statements.

4   Complex Statements Due to Semantic Positioning

Due to the complexity of information dimensions that can be arranged graphically in overlay structures, we propose the hypothesis that only semantic positioning allows for the formulation of *complex statements* (e.g. hypotheses, evaluations). These knowledge structures can then be explored, edited and expanded constructively on a visualisation level. This is in contrast to mere singular arrangements which can only cover factual knowledge or structures and are not open for interpretation. The following example was constructed by students as a graded presentation, utilizing our Java client the so-called medi@rena to create overlay structures. In the medi@rena objects are not only statically displayed (either positioned through the author or generated by algorithms) but are subject to continuous cooperative modifications especially regarding their arrangement. We will show how a complex statement can be constructed by the pragmatic visualisation concept of semantic positioning.

Time Tunnel
The time tunnel is an overlay of a time line (toplogy) and set structure (topography). It can narrow down and widen up along its course. Elements can be placed either around or inside the tunnel. Bottlenecks are used to show critical phases in which an accidental nuclear war was more likely to happen. Influence factors are depicted as diagram lines within the tunnel. A quantitative assertion about the weighed influence of factors in a certain situation would be possible if documents in the figure had not been placed on both sides of the tunnel, but for example on only one side with the height of a line depicting the influence of the corresponding factor in the respective situation. The result in both cases however is a complex statement that can be interpreted and argued against. In the figure above its creators asserted that there was always a mixture of influence factors responsible in every situation and that no grade of responsibility could be attributed to the three factors of humans, politics or technology. In the

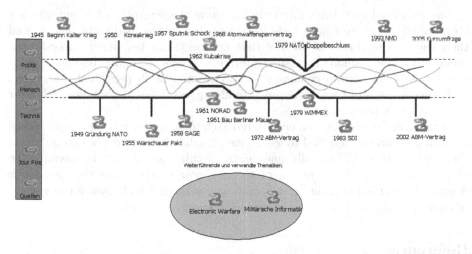

Fig. 2. Time-Tunnel Overlay Structure on the Topic of 'Accidental Nuclear War'

later discussion in class however other students noted that in contrast to the depicted statement humans had often ultimately been responsible for resolving critical situations that happened due to faulty technology. In this kind of discussion only based on a visual composition, it becomes evident how semantical positioning allows for complex statements through visual knowledge structuring.

5 Conclusion and Outlook

Semantic positioning for structuring knowledge has been utilized in several courses of the department of computers and society of the University of Paderborn. It was used by students within the framework of the Jour-Fixe concept[4] to build presentations in the form of virtual knowledge spaces, centering on a chosen topic. While many original design ideas for incisive structures were created, many students still intuitively resorted to building non-overlayed arrangements that would be hard to expand upon and which carried no complex statements. These students albeit agreed in the final evaluation that overlayed structures of other students had proven a better basis for discussion and interpretation. Overall we deem that our approach has potential based on these first experiences.

The new concept of semantic positioning provokes a lot of (heavy) discussions within student groups. This may be due to the complexity of statements expressable with visual overlay structures or the fact that they are questioned critically by other students and the teachers during consecutive presentation phases. We are under the impression that groups with a good deliberation culture (*Streitkultur*) produced the best results. In first aspects semantic positioning as currently implementable can already support life long, expandable learning processes, via visual knowledge structuring.

The produced structures often vividly show the interplay of a mutual view on a knowledge space (made technically possible by the medi@rena client) and their cooperative creation. We feel that an additional key benefit may be the possibility of individually accessible alternative views (equaling different overlay structures) for a certain content in a specific area with persistent documents and objects. Each of these structures could express different contexts with their respective semantics.

In the near future there is a need to research if basic overlays like the presented time tunnel can be identified to systemize visualisation approaches according to their pragmatics. Additionally one needs to think about how to advance the current medi@rena client in regard to offer new functions for the interactive work to further support and ease semantic positioning and allow for new ways of creating, editing, navigating or exploring overlay structures.

References

1. Alexander, C.: Notes on the Synthesis of Form. Cambridge (Mass.): Harvard University Press, 1964
2. Haake, J.M. et. al.: CURE - Eine Umgebung fuer selbstorganisiertes Gruppenlernen. i-com, 3. Jahrg., Heft 2 2004, S. 20-26
3. Hampel, T., Keil-Slawik, R.: sTeam: Structuring Information in a Team Distributed Knowledge Management in Cooperative Learning Environments. In: ACM Journal of Educational Resources in Computing 1(2) 2001, 1-27
4. Hampel, T.; Keil-Slawik, R.; Emann, B.: Jour Fixe We Are Structuring Knowledge Collaborative Structuring of Semantic Spaces as a Didactic Concept and New Form of Cooperative Knowledge Organization. In: Proceedings of E-Learn 2003, Phoenix, Arizona USA, AACE, S. 225-232
5. Hansen, Y. M.: Graphic Tools for Thinking, Planning, and Problem Solving. In Jacobson, R. (Hrsg.): *Information Design.* Cambridge: MIT Press, 2000
6. Jackewitz, I., Jenneck, M., Strauss, M.: CommSy: Softwareunterstuetzung fuer Wissensprojekte. In: Pape, B., Krause, D., Oberquelle, H. (Hrsg.): *Wissensprojekte - Gemeinschaftliches Lernen aus didaktischer, softwaretechnischer und organisatorischer Sicht.* Muenster: Waxmann, 2004, S.186-202
7. Nelson, Th. H.: Computer Lib/Dream Machines. South Bend, In: no publisher, First Edition, 9th printing, 1983, S. DM 29
8. Rewey, K. L., Dansereau, D. F., & Peel, J. L.: Knowledge maps and information processing strategies. Contemporary Educational Psychology, 16, 1991, 203-214.
9. Winkler, H.: Docuverse - Zur Medientheorie der Computer. Munich: Boer, 1997

Time2Competence: The PROLIX Project

Fabrizio Giorgini[1], Volker Zimmermann[2], Nils Faltin[2], and Luk Vervenne[3]

[1] Giunti Interactive Labs S.r.l., Via Portobello Abbazia dell'Annunziata,
16039 Sestri Levante, Italy
f.giorgini@giuntilabs.com
http://www.giuntilabas.com/research.html
[2] im-c, Altenkesseler Str. 17 D3
66115 Saarbruecken, Germany
{Volker.Zimmermann, nils.Faltin}@im-c.de
[3] Synergetics, Terlinckstaart 75
2600 Antwerp, Belgium
luk@synergetics.be

Abstract. The poster introduces PROLIX, an integrated project funded by the European Commission. PROLIX overall objective is to align learning with business processes in order to enable organisations to faster improve the competencies of their employees according to continuous changes of business requirements. To reach this goal, PROLIX is developing an open, integrated reference architecture for process-oriented learning and information exchange. The key innovation in PROLIX consists of a process- and competency driven framework for interlinking business process intelligence tools on the one hand with knowledge management and learning environments on the other.

1 Introduction

PROLIX (PRocess-Oriented Learning and Information eXchange) is a 48 months research and development integrated project funded by the European Commission under the Sixth Framework Programme, Priority 2 "Information Society Technologies" started the 1st December 2005.

The objective of PROLIX is to align learning with business processes in order to enable organisations to faster improve the competencies of their employees according to continuous changes of business requirements. PROLIX is developing a process- and competency driven framework for interlinking business process intelligence tools on the one hand with knowledge management and learning environments on the other.

2 Project Objectives

PROLIX is developing a process-oriented learning approach and a flexible and adaptive service-oriented architecture system which is capable of aligning training and knowledge product ion of people faced with so-called "complex situations" such as work and business process changes, or other complex multivariable learning

W. Nejdl and K. Tochtermann (Eds.): EC-TEL 2006, LNCS 4227, pp. 597–602, 2006.

environments, which cannot be solved with traditional eLearning or knowledge management approaches. In order to face these challenges, PROLIX will:

- *enable an organisation to close the learner's life cycle* by providing support for the implementation of the international acknowledged P(lan)-D(o)-C(heck)-A(ct) Philosophy within Organisations.
- *make it easier to define Learning Goals based on business needs and business processes* by providing methodologies, tools and services within business process management that link to learning design methodologies.
- *deliver a methodology for matching of needed competencies with "as-hoc" profiles* resulting in an accurate didactical learning scenario definition and configuration.
- *provide competence oriented process decision support through simulation* for the benefit of organisational and individual team learning with a quantitative feedback for business processes and required/ changed competencies by providing a concept for the PROLIX competency oriented process simulator, developing scenarios for competency oriented process simulations according to company needs and providing a service to simulate real work situations for the benefit of individual and team-oriented competence development in different branches, under different conditions and requirements.
- *integrate Learning Technology Solutions with Business Information Systems* by providing a Learning Process Execution Platform to enable the measurement of the individual qualification needs based on valid tests ("diagnosis") and instantiate configured learning processes based on the competency analysis and matching according to the learner, providing Learning Process Workflow Services (LPWS) to manage the learning processes. These Services have the "knowledge" of the configured learning processes and execute the various learning application services within SMS Skill Management, LMS Learning Management Systems, LCMS Learning Content Management Systems and KMS Knowledge Management Systems.
- *monitor Learner's Performance according to Business Needs* by providing services to measure the resulting learner performance both in terms of competencies acquired and in terms of effectiveness in solving the original problem, performing the 'job' or coping with the (business) process change and providing models for corporate learning success and react ion pat terns to training results.

3 Time2Competency

The delay between the identification of learning needs and actual learning effects the competitiveness of any Company. PROLIX will make people and organisations more competitive by reducing the time it takes to fill competency gaps and build proficiency according to the business needs and daily work processes. PROLIX couples business processes with learning processes in corporate environments, enabling business process driven learning at the workplace, taking into account the single learner and his needs as well as corporate requirements. PROLIX solutions support and enhance the speed and effectiveness of both formal and informal learning processes, integrating learning management platform technology (such as learn eXact [1] and CLIX [2]) and support services. The PROLIX project is aiming to reduce the time needed from identifying a business need to meeting the competency requirement through learning (Time-to-Competency) by an average of 20%.

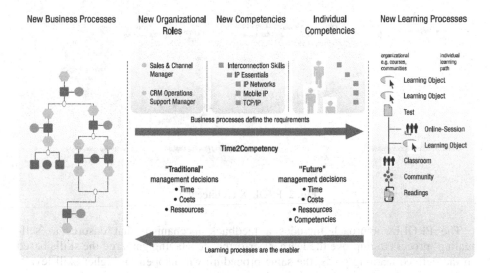

Fig. 1. Learning as „key enabler" for business process management

Overall and seen from an organizational point of view, PROLIX will significantly contribute to the change management within companies that needs to develop into a holistic learning organization enabling the integration of learning into the daily working tasks. Corporate culture requires the provision of strategies, methods and concepts to satisfy heterogeneous learning needs. Mechanisms and concepts for the organizational introduction of technology enhanced learning in corporations have to be coordinated with its philosophy and company vision.

4 Approach

PROLIX supports a complete learning process life cycle comprising (Fig. 2) 1) the analysis of complex business situations; 2) the identification of individual and organisational learning goals; 3) the analysis of competencies describe according to the IEEE standard RCD [3] and their matching with individual skills; 4) the definition of appropriate learning strategies according to the IMS Learning Design specification [4] and the simulation of competency-oriented processes; 5) the execution of improved learning processes; 6) the monitoring of learners' performance according to the goals defined.

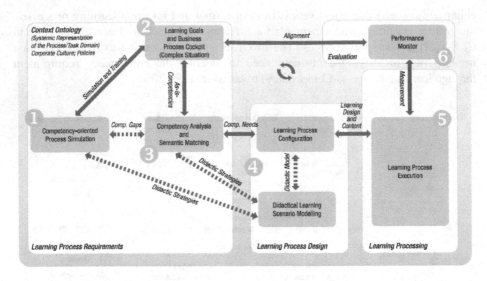

Fig. 2. PROLIX architecture

The PROLIX approach includes a feedback mechanism that ensures a ´self-healing´ process to improve the learner performance. Having gathered the skills based on the defined learning goals, the same procedure will happen on higher skill levels, so that a continuous procedure is a result.

PROLIX will deliver an open learning platform integrating the needed systems to close the learning life cycle by providing interfaces from learning management systems

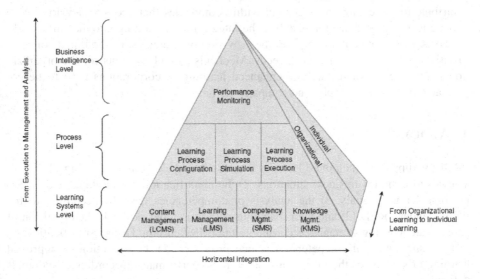

Fig. 3. Innovation dimensions of PROLIX

to business process management systems, competency management systems, learning content management systems as well as performance measurement systems (Fig. 3).

5 Test Bads

In order to demonstrate its concept, PROLIX set up three test beds in different fields of application. PROLIX will specify, design, implement and start to demonstrate its tools and services in more mature eLearning-aware and, therefore, lower risk environments, i.e. the "Government test bed" with UK Government Care Programme (Social Care Institute for Excellence), the "Telecom test bed" with British Telecom (BT) learning, and the "Educational Publishing test bed" with publishing houses Klett and EDITIS.

6 Open Business Enterprise Learning and Information Systems Exchange Reference Architecture (OBELIX)

PROLIX will deliver services (or alternatively called "modules") of process-oriented learning technologies that are integrated on the basis of a service-oriented architecture likely based on Web Services described in WSDL.

Based on the flexible PROLIX architecture, each module will be self-sustainable, thus reducing the risk of a single point of failure within the system. Furthermore, based on the company requirements PROLIX foresees the possibility that there might be several implementations of one module, each tailored to the needs of the various test beds.

PROLIX will open its results to the learning industry by developing an open reference architecture for process-oriented learning (OBELIX). This architecture will ensure that third party vendors can integrate specific solutions into the overall approach and by this replacing other components.

PROLIX will link learning with business; process-oriented learning will avoid outsourcing of personnel training and ensure learner's employability since they efficiently learn according to needs. Management will have a technology to see learning as the business enabler of competitive enterprises.

Acknowledgments

The PROLIX project is funded by the European Commission in the Information Society Technologies (IST) Programme - Project No. 027905. The partners in PROLIX include im-c, Synergetics, IDS, Giunti Interactive Labs, QPR, Imaginary, University of Hannover, Institut f. Arbeitswissenschaft u.Technologiemgmt, Wirtschaftsuniv. Wien, University Vienna, NCSR Demokritos NCSR,VUB/Starlab, DFKI, DANUBE, Klett, EDITIS, EEA, British Telecom, SCIE. Full details of the PROLIX project can be found at http://www.prolixproject.it

602   F. Giorgini et al.

References

1. learn eXact LCMS, http://www.learnexact.com
2. CLIX, http://www.clix.de/
3. IEEE RCD, Reusable Competency Definition,
   http://ieeeltsc.org/wg20Comp/ wg20rcdfolder/
4. IMS Learning Design, http://www.imsproject.org/learningdesign/index.html

Knowledge Fusion: A New Method to Share and Integrate Distributed Knowledge Sources

Jin Gou, Yangyang Wu, and Wei Luo

College of Information Science and Engineering, Huaqiao University
362021 Quanzhou, China
goujin@gmail.com, wuyy@hqu.edu.cn, weiluo@sogou.com

Abstract. This paper presents a new method to integrate and share distributed knowledge objects using fusion process. Knowledge objects are mapped to an ontology base and transformed to meta-knowledge set. A detailed knowledge fusion algorithm based on GA and semantic rules is proposed. Feedback mechanism is also discussed to optimize both the fusion process and knowledge space. Experimental results of a case study show the feasibility of design rationale in a knowledge-based service environment.

1 Introduction

Knowledge fusion is one of the most important components of knowledge management and knowledge engineering, which can transform, integrate and fuse distributed information resources such as DB, KB and data warehouse to obtain new useful knowledge elements, and diversiform knowledge objects can be shared and cooperative through it.

Presently most researches in this field focus on how to set up and improve the infrastructure of knowledge fusion. Two representative research projects are KRAFT [1] and EUREKA [2], which used multi-agent and middleware technology to implement the transforming and mapping process of knowledge objects.

Knowledge fusion algorithm is the core function module in knowledge fusion systems, which should be a programmable procedure and whose aim is to generate and formally represent new knowledge objects through some fusion operations such as comparing, combining and cooperating on existing knowledge elements according to restrictions. However, there are still less fusion algorithms now and most of them can only operate on given knowledge objects directly [3]. Such process increases the probability of illogical results.

On the other hand, knowledge objects have the character of fuzzy and knowledge fusion is a dynamic process. Therefore, the result of knowledge fusion could be evaluated only by application, while parameters of the fusion process should be adjusted according to the feedback.

The purpose of this paper is to describe a new knowledge fusion algorithm KFGS (Knowledge Fusion algorithm based on Genetic algorithm and Semantic rules) and a feedback mechanism to adapt to application requirements.

W. Nejdl and K. Tochtermann (Eds.): EC-TEL 2006, LNCS 4227, pp. 609–614, 2006.

2 Architecture

An overall architecture of the knowledge fusion is shown in Fig. 1.

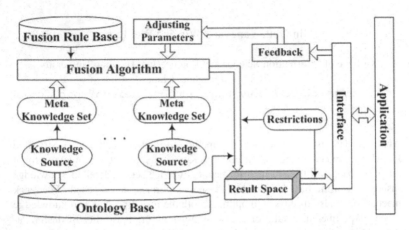

Fig. 1. The knowledge fusion process

From the framework above we can see that ontology base and meta-knowledge sets should be created before the knowledge fusion process as a connotational formalized representation of distributed knowledge sources. Fusion result is structured and stored in a knowledge space. Fusion algorithms based on semantic rules should be adjusted by the feedback from applications.

2.1 Ontology Base

Knowledge objects in a fusion system can be represented with ontology and meta-knowledge set. Let O and O_i denote the ontology base and the ith object instance in it. Let S_k denotes meta-knowledge sets of the kth knowledge base node.

$$O_i = \{(P_j^i, T_j^i, D_j^i)\}$$

$$S_k = \{((C_1^k, E_1^k), (C_2^k, E_2^k), \cdots, (C_n^k, E_n^k))\} \tag{1}$$

Where P_j^i denotes the jth attribute of the object O_i, T_j^i denotes the type of P_j^i, D_j^i denotes its value, expression or behavior, while C_i^k denotes the ith character object of S_k, E_i^k denotes the description content of C_i^k. Detailed description of O_i and S_k were given in another research paper of ours [4].

Some contents of a new ontology instance such as attributes name need manual work to create, while set of relationship can be semi-automatically generated according to semantic relationships between it and existing ontology objects. One of representative semantic relationships is similarity. Suppose existing ontology base is $\{O_1, O_2, ..., O_k\}$, then the similarity relationship must meet restriction rule as followed:

$$(O_{k+1} \cong O_i) \quad iff \quad (\{P_j^i\} \Leftrightarrow \{P_j^{k+1}\}) \,\&\,\&\neg(\{D_j^i\} \Leftrightarrow \{D_j^{k+1}\}) \tag{2}$$

Similarity denotes that those pairs have the same type of characters while at least one difference exists between their values. So they can be transformed partially when initializing ontology object as followed:

$$\{T_j^i = (T_j^i \cup (O_{k+1} \cong O_i));\ T_j^{k+1} = T_j^i\} \tag{3}$$

2.2 Meta-knowledge Set

Let the first element in S_k stand for its corresponding object in O instead of any material characters. Then the meta-knowledge set's creating process of a certain knowledge object should be described as followed:

Firstly, initialize ontology object corresponding to the knowledge object, transform it into standard form according to elements in the ontology relationship description.

Then generate the next $(n-1)$ elements in the meta-knowledge set in term of the content of ontology attributes in the result of the step above.

Based on the result of the procedures above, set value of the first element (C_1^k, E_1^k) in that meta-knowledge set based on the mapping relationship between the knowledge object and ontology conception. Create a new ontology object and description manually if there is not such an attribute value, then jump to the first step and go on.

3 Knowledge Fusion Algorithm

Knowledge fusion algorithm KFGS is based on both *GA* and semantic rules. The former provides mainly fusing operators, while the latter is used to reduce the dimension of result space and filter out illogic or mismatched pairs.

3.1 Fusion Rules

Let a pair of knowledge objects KO_1 and KO_2 are both represented as conjunctive normal form. $(A_1, A_2, ..., A_{n1}, RC_1)$ and $(B_1, B_2, ..., B_{n1}, RC_2)$ symbolize their atomic propositions. Then two basic semantic relations are described as followed:

***Definition*1:** Semantic Include relation between sets of atomic propositions. $\{A_i\}$ are semantic included by $\{B_j\}$ if and only if the former's semantically description is a subset of the latter's which can be symbolized as $\{A_i\} \subseteq^Y \{B_j\}$.

***Definition*2:** Semantic Intersect relation between sets of atomic propositions. $\{A_i\}$ and $\{B_j\}$ are semantic intersecting if and only if their semantically descriptions are not entirely same while repeating partially which can be symbolized as $\{A_i\} \cap^Y \{B_j\}$.

KO_1 and KO_2 can be fused if and only if the precondition of at least one followed rules is satisfied.

***Rule*1:** If semantically include relation is satisfied between their condition attributes but neither of these semantically relations is done between decision attributes, which also means $\{A_i\} \subseteq^Y \{B_j\}$ and $(RC_1 \not\subset^Y RC_2) \& \& (RC_1 \not\subseteq^Y RC_2)$, KO_2's condition attributes should be semantically partitioned based on KO_1's ontology content to keep only different parts, while extend and unite KO_1's decision attributes semantically to generate new values.

Rule2: If semantically include relation is satisfied between both their condition and decision attributes, formally as $(\{A_i\} \subseteq^Y \{B_j\}) \& \&(RC_1 \subseteq^Y RC_2)$, KO_1's corresponding knowledge object should be destroyed. On the other hand, if semantically relation between decision attributes is contrary to the one above, which is just as $(\{A_i\} \subseteq^Y \{B_j\}) \& \&(RC_2 \subseteq^Y RC_1)$, then elements' range of KO_2's meta-knowledge set should be partitioned and eliminate any values ever appeared in KO_1's.

Rule3: If semantically intersect relation is satisfied between both their condition attributes and neither of these semantically relations is done between decision attributes, equivalent to $\{A_i\} \cap^Y \{B_j\}$ and $(RC_1 \not\subset^Y RC_2) \& \&(RC_1 \not\subseteq^Y RC_2)$, divide their condition attributes semantically. Then each one keeps its own idiographic part and extracts the intersection to create a new knowledge object.

3.2 Fusion Procedure

The coding method and genetic operators introduced in [5] are referenced in KFGS. The detailed procedure of KFGS is summarized as followed:

Step1: Initialize. Compute initial fitness values of knowledge objects according to comparability of code bits.

Step2: If the fitness values of current knowledge set and the times of loop are both less than the respective arranged threshold, repeat the iterative sub steps:

Step2.1: Execute selection operator. For each pair of knowledge individuals, use rule1-3 above to decide whether they should be operated on with intercross and aberrance. If preconditions of all the four rules are not satisfied, do selection again.

Step2.2: Execute reversion operator if the pair meets requirement.

Step2.3: Transform result individual and output it into the knowledge space.

Step2.4: Update the set of knowledge objects and compute the new fitness values.

The definition and description of those four operators, selection, intercrossing, aberrance and reversion can be found in [5].

4 Feedback Mechanism

The quality of the knowledge service is evaluated by corresponding function in applications or manually. The result of that evaluation should be transmitted to the feedback module of knowledge fusion with the format of message as: $M = (KO_{id}, D_s, Le, Me)$. Where KO_{id} denotes the identity of knowledge object corresponding to M. D_s is the structural description of KO_{id} from application. Le denotes the level of service quality, which can be defined as a fuzzy value between 0 and 1. Me is the memo to explain reasons if Le is too low.

All the parameters of knowledge objects and knowledge fusion process should be adjusted with the feedback as followed formula:

$$P_s^{(T+1)} = g(Le) \cdot P_s^{(T)} + [1 - g(Le)] \cdot \Delta P \tag{4}$$

Where ΔP is a correctional constant for P_s. $g(Le)$ is a monotonously increasing function of Le.

A representative parameter of knowledge object KO_{id} for evaluation is logic dependability (α, β, γ), where α denotes the frequency of being used, β denotes the percentage of being correctly matched with application, γ denotes the average fuzzy degree of its avail. They are usually initialized as (1, 100%, 1.0). Their evolving equations with feedback are shown as formula 5.

$$(\alpha^{T+1}, \beta^{T+1}) = \begin{cases} (\alpha^T + 1, \dfrac{\alpha^T \cdot \beta^T}{\alpha^T + 1}), & Le < Le_{thre} \\ (\alpha^T, \beta^T), & Not \quad Used \ ; \\ (\alpha^T + 1, \dfrac{\alpha^T \cdot \beta^T + 1}{\alpha^T + 1}), & Le \geq Le_{thre} \end{cases}$$

$$\gamma^{T+1} = \frac{Le + \alpha^T \cdot \gamma^T}{\alpha^T + 1} \tag{5}$$

5 Case Study

To compare with two other knowledge fusion algorithms (marked as KFA-G and KFA-A whose detailed description can be seen in [4]), the same experimental environments as mentioned in [4] are chosen.

The result of qualitative comparison between KFGS and two other existing knowledge fusion algorithms is given in Table 1.

Table 1. The result of qualitative comparison

	New object	Semantic relation	Knowledge reuse	Amount tendency	Independence of object	Strategy for efficiency	Filter
KFA-A	No	No	Only current form	Decreasing	Without regard	None	No
KFA-G	Yes	Yes	No restriction	Increasing	Without regard	Controls parameter	No
KFGS	Yes	Yes	No restriction	Little change	Independent	Fusion rules	Yes

To analyze the relationship between parameters and Le, suppose Le to be distributed randomly. We collected evolving results of parameter γ at the first 50 cycles and drew the relationship scatter graph in Fig. 2.

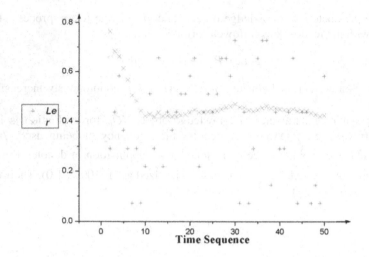

Fig. 2. Relationship scatter graph of *Le* and γ

From the figure above we can see that the feedback-adapting mechanism is convergent and effective.

6 Summary and Acknowledge

We present a knowledge fusion framework based on ontology and meta-knowledge set which filters out illogic knowledge object pairs with semantic rules and implement fusion process with GA. A feedback mechanism is also proposed to adjust parameters and optimize the fusion operations.

This work is partially supported by High Level Startup Research Project of Huaqiao University 06BS102 granted to Dr. Jin Gou and Fujian Province NSF Project A0510020 granted to Prof. Yangyang Wu.

References

1. Preece A D, Hui K Y, Gray W A, et al.: KRAFT: An Agent Architecture for Knowledge Fusion. Int. Journal of Cooperative Information Systems, 1-2(2001) 171-195.
2. Homepage of UMBC Agent Web. http://www.cs. umbc.edu/kqml/.
3. Brian J G, Dickson L.: Knowledge Fusion. In: Proc. of the 7th Annual Workshop on Conceptual Structures: Theory and Implementation. Springer-Verlag, Berlin Heidelberg New York, (1992) 158-167.
4. Jin Gou, Jiangang Yang, Qian Chen: Evolution and Evaluation in Knowledge Fusion System. In: Interplay Between Natural and Artificial Computation.Lecture Notes in Computer Science, Vol. 3562. Springer-Verlag, Berlin Heidelberg New York (2005) 192–201.
5. Ruqian Lu: Artificial Intelligence. Science Publishing Company, Beijing (1996)

Ontologies to Support Learning Design Context

Jelena Jovanović[1], Dragan Gašević[2], Christopher Brooks[3], Colin Knight[2],
Griff Richards[2], and Gordon McCalla[3]

[1] FON, School of Business Administration, University of Belgrade, Serbia and Montenegro
`jeljov@gmail.com`
[2] School of Interactive arts and Technology, Simon Fraser University Surrey, Canada
`{dgasevic, cjk2, griff}@sfu.ca`
[3] ARIES Laboratory, Department of Computer Science, University of Saskatchewan, Canada
`cab938@mail.usask.ca, mccalla@cs.usask.ca`

Abstract. This paper presents an ontology-based framework aimed at explicitly representing the context of use of a learning object inside of a learning design. The core of the proposed framework is a learning object context ontology that leverages a range of other kinds of learning ontologies (e.g. domain, user modeling, learning design etc.) to capture the context-specific metadata. On top of that framework, we develop the architecture of an adaptive educational system, in order to illustrate the benefits of our proposal for personalization of learning design. Finally, we reflect how two present educational tools (iHelp Courses and TANGRAM) correspond to the proposed architecture.

1 Introduction

The combined use of IMS Learning Design specification (IMS LD) [3] and IEEE Learning Object Metadata standard (LOM) [2] enables one to specify learning designs and learning objects (LOs) targeted for different learning situations, based on different pedagogical theories, comprising different learning activities where students and teachers can play many roles, and carried out in diverse learning environments. However, they cannot enable more advanced learning processes, such as dynamic adaptation of content in accordance with the students' objectives, preferences, learning styles, and knowledge levels. Further, if adaptation is to happen automatically information must be codified in an unambiguous manner. Ontologies help increase the consistency and interoperability of metadata. The Semantic Web community has already developed a number of different kinds of ontologies that can be integrated in an ontological framework in order to enable adaptive use of LOs inside a learning design. Our proposal for such a framework is the main subject of this paper.

2 Learning Object Workflows

The complexity of the process of using LOs is described in this section in order to identify the main actors in that process, as well as the types of metadata that can be employed to facilitate the process. The principle actors are subject matter experts

W. Nejdl and K. Tochtermann (Eds.): EC-TEL 2006, LNCS 4227, pp. 615–620, 2006.

(who create the learning content and provide initial metadata for it), instructors (who search for, obtain, modify, then wrap a LO in a learning design), and learners (who end up consuming the LO). These actors use different tools to complete their tasks. A subject matter expert generally uses an authoring tool (e.g. a HTML editor) to create content. In the best case, this content is published to a LO repository and annotated with metadata. An instructor creates an instruction plan for the students she anticipates will take the course. Initially, the instructor sets out the learning objectives the students must reach, and subsequently searches LO repositories for topics related to the specified learning objectives. In addition, she considers materials from previously given lectures and courses, lecture materials provided by colleagues, and other traditional sources (e.g. libraries, the web, etc.). Searching is typically limited to keywords, however LOM-aware repositories may also allow the instructor more advanced search options, such as typical amount of time to complete material or age range of the intended recipients. Using her domain knowledge and a general idea of the kinds of students that will take the course (e.g. their knowledge level), the instructor chooses the appropriate LOs and integrates them into the course. How successfully a designer can do this depends on a number of factors including: if the course has an open or closed (restricted) set of students, if the instructor has some experiences with the course, as well as the diversity of the student set (the problem gets more difficult with each new learner trait the instructor wants to take into account).

There are a number of issues with this kind of workflow. First, the need to access multiple repositories increases the amount of time an instructor must spend building a list of candidate LOs for a particular purpose. Once this list is built, it still takes a fair amount of time for the instructor to evaluate the suitability of each resource for the given objective. Even if these resources are annotated with metadata, the designer needs to absorb this information, consider the value of the metadata given the context of the publisher of the metadata, and finally make a decision as to which object fits the circumstances best. Our anecdotal observations suggest that instructors spend a minimal amount of time looking at metadata records, and then begin to browse the learning content directly. After a short review of the content, the instructor typically begins to modify the content (and thus create a derived LO) instead of reviewing other pieces of retrieved content. Third, if the desire is for highly personalized systems, the instructor must repeat this process for each student, or at the very least for cliques of students. Even when the instructor tackles all these challenges, the objectives of the class might change and the process of creating content must begin anew.

Finally, all of the information in the system flows in one direction – towards the learner. Once a LO is found, evaluated, and used in a course its lifecycle typically ends. While the instructor may keep the object, along with any modifications they have made, it is rare to see metadata in repositories updated with the results of how effective the object was in teaching a particular topic. While some LO repositories, (e.g. MERLOT), do provide a forum for community feedback, none provides facilities for directly modifying LO metadata or even supplying an alternative record.

We instead argue that a more dynamic workflow can be achieved by increasing the communication between tools and actors in a learning environment. Key to realizing a more dynamic workflow is being able to represent the context of use of a LO. By associating a LO with a user model, the learning objectives it was used for, and the observed interactions a user had with the LO, the process of inspecting metadata can be changed from a database lookup into a process of reasoning. This changes both the target and the scope of metadata – instead of being aimed directly at end users, metadata is now aimed at computational agents who can make sense of this data for end users. The remainder of this paper explores the notion of context, and describes how we see this notion fitting into our current e-learning systems.

3 Learning Object Context

When learning content is assembled into a learning design, many assumptions are made about the learners and the learning situation, e.g. assumptions about the learner's competencies, preferences, learning style, goals, and motivation. These assumptions are what we refer to as the *context* – the unique set of characteristics of the learning situation that govern how content should be structured into a flow of interaction for a particular learner. Learning specifications such as IEEE LOM, and IMS LD provide metadata elements aimed at representing some of these assumptions (e.g. 'learning objective' in IMS LD). However, these elements are usually not broad enough to capture all necessary information for effective learning, and not formalized enough to provide for automatic adaptation. In our previous work we addressed these concerns by developed an ontology-based framework enabling formal representation of:

- *Learning object content structure* – ALOCoM Content Structure Ontology formally defines the structure of a LO with the goal of making each component of the LO directly accessible and thus reusable [4].
- *Learning design* – LOCO ontology, based on the IMS LD Information Model, formally defines the concepts and the relationships of IMS LD specification [6].
- *Learning object context* – LOCO-Cite ontology formalizes the concept of learning object context and was originally developed to promote the integration and reuse of LOs and learning designs [6].

Our subsequent efforts to utilize the elements of context for personalization of learning designs revealed that the LOCO-Cite ontology needs to be further extended. Hence, we extended it to integrate connections to user models, competencies, user evaluation information and other relevant data. Specifically, these connections are established via an additional set of properties introduced in the LOCO-Cite ontology. The *LearningObjectContext* class, representing a specific context of use of a LO, is maintained as the central item of the ontology. A number of properties were introduced to enable formal description of the LO's context-related metadata:

- The *isContextOf* property refers to the actual learning content (i.e. LO) that the context is about. The range of this property is the *loco:LearningObject* class, defined in the LOCO to formally represent a LO.
- The *usedInActivity* property is actually a reference to the learning activity (*loco:Activity*) the LO was/is supposed to be used within.
- The *userRef* property refers to the user model of either the teacher/instructional designer who assigned the LO to the specific learning context during the design process or the learner who actually used the LO in that context. The range of the property is the concept of user as defined in the user model ontology developed for the TANGRAM project (explained in more detail in [4]).

- The *dateTimeStart* and *dateTimeEnd* properties store data about the date and the time when the learner started and finished working with the LO. Hence, the time period the learner spent dwelling on the LO can be deduced.
- The *evaluatedWRT* property reports on the user's evaluation of the LO in the given context. Specifically, we defined five different dimensions of users' evaluations: character, clearness, usefulness, stimulation level and pro-collaborative nature. Values for these characteristics are codified using a five item Likert scale. Additionally, users are encouraged to tag the LO with any term that reflect their view of the LO in that specific learning context..

4 Architecture for Learning Design Adaptation

We developed the architecture of an adaptive educational system leveraging the capabilities of the presented ontologies for discovery, reuse and adaptation of LOs and learning designs. The architecture comprises a repository of learning objects (LOR) and its accompanying repository of learning object context data (LOCoR). The LOCoR stores learning objects' context-related data in accordance with the LOCO-Cite ontology. The idea is that each object from the LOR has its corresponding learning object contexts in the LOCoR. A LO gets its first context instance in the LOCoR when an instructor integrates it in the course during the design process. As the time passes and the LO is used in different courses, its learning object context instances become available in the LOCoR.

Besides a LOR and a LOCoR, the architecture also comprises a repository of learning designs represented in accordance with the LOCO. A learning design stored in the repository does not directly reference concrete LOs. Instead, a learning design and a LO are only implicitly related via the learning object context. During both course design and run time, the LOCoR is searched for learning object context instances that 'match' the key features of the learning situation (prerequisites, learning objectives, etc.). In that way the context related data help both teachers and students to identify relevant LOs. The system does the search by submitting a query to the LOCoR. The query uses the concepts/instances from relevant ontologies and/or taxonomies whenever it is possible, since their usage provides for an advanced matching process. For example, if no learning object context instance can be found that 'has' the required learning objective (represented as the targeted competency), an instance with a 'similar' objective can be used instead (this similarity is inferred from the ontological representation of competencies). Accordingly, a course/lesson delivery system working on top of the aforementioned repositories is able to provide a learner with the best suited LOs for every learning activity specified in the learning design of the course/lesson plan she is following. To put it differently, we suggest providing the learner with a custom 'view' (analogous to those found in relational databases) of the LOR which is generated in accordance with the requirements of her current learning situation. The learner is free to search and browse through the customized view of the LOR. This way the learners are given a substantial level of control over their learning process (we believe in the active learning approach), whereas, at the same time, the usage of custom views over the LOR protects them from cognitive overload. The learner's browsing behavior can be tracked, and data from this tracking can be mined to infer the learner's preferences, as well as some dimensions of her learning style. Based on the insights acquired into the learner's preferences, the view of the LOR for every subsequent activity the learner performs is further customized. One should also note that each time a learner selects a LO from the LOR, a learning object context instance of that LO is created in the LOCoR and all relevant context-related data for that usage are stored in it.

5 Tools

The section describes two educational systems closely related to the proposed solution for adaptive use of LOs.

The first one is iHelp, a web-based suite of tools[1] that includes *iHelp Courses*, a standards-based learning content management system, an asynchronous discussion forum, and a synchronous chat system. iHelp Courses is deployed within the Department of Computer Science at the University of Saskatchewan and is used to deliver the introductory course in computing concepts for non-majors in both pure online and blended environments. The system enables instructors to deploy LOs and sequence them in different ways for different cohorts of students [1]. Content can also be associated directly with collaborative tools (e.g. discussion forums), hence allowing for context-specific collaboration between learners.

iHelp Courses keeps fine grained knowledge about learner interactions with LOs. Specifically, for every LO a learner has viewed the system knows how long she was viewing that LO, what interactions (via synchronous/asynchronous discussions) were undertaken, and the results of any quizzes associated with that LO. We are currently transforming the content of this large database of end use data to be compliant with the LOCO-Cite ontology. Our intention is to apply various machine learning and data mining algorithms on this end-use data in order to find interesting patterns of actual usage of LOs. For example, what kind of learners they are suitable for, which kinds of learning activities they suit the best, etc. Likewise, valuable information can be inferred about learners and their characteristics, preferences and interests.

The second system is TANGRAM, an ontology-founded adaptive learning environment for the domain of Intelligent Systems [5]. TANGRAM illustrates how Semantic Web technologies, particularly ontologies and ontology-based reasoning, enable on-the-fly assembly of personalized learning content out of existing content units[2]. Its principle functionality is to enable reuse of existing content units to dynamically generate new learning content adapted to a learner's knowledge, preferences, and learning styles. Additionally, the use of ontologies enable advanced searching of repositories using of Semantic Web reasoners. For example, one can search for a content unit of a certain type (as defined in the ontology of pedagogical roles, e.g. "definition"), dealing with a certain topic (from the domain ontology) and being at a certain level of granularity (as defined in the structure ontology, e.g. "slide"). Accordingly, TANGRAM provides students with quick access to a particular type of content about a topic of interest, e.g. access to *examples* of RDF documents or

---

[1] See http://ihelp.usask.ca for more information.
[2] Content unit is an abstract concept aimed at representing content of any level of granularity.

*definition*s of the Semantic Web. We intend to improve TANGRAM's personalization capabilities through the use of and reasoning over context related data.

6 Conclusions

Researching the potentials of personalized use of prominent learning technology efforts, we have developed a novel ontology (LOCO-Cite) for bridging them. This ontology makes use of several other kinds of learning-related ontologies in order to capture information about the context of use of a LO inside of a learning design. Information of this kind is useful for personalization of learning designs – for example, during learning design playback a query specifying the main features of the current learning situation can be sent to the repository of learning object contexts in order to identify learning object contexts representing similar learning situations and from them infer the most suitable LOs for the present.

Our future research will be focused around the implementation of this architecture with the hopes of leveraging the presented ontologies to enable personalization and reuse of LOs and learning designs within the iHelp Courses and TANGRAM environments.

Acknowledgment

The work of the University of Saskatchewan and Simon Fraser University is funded in part by Canada's LORNET NSERC Research Network.

References

1. Brooks, C., Kettel, L., Hansen, C., Greer, J.., "Building a Learning Object Content Management System," *In Proc. of E-Learn 2005 Conference*, October. 24–28, 2005. Vancouver, Canada.
2. Duval, E. (Ed.), 1484.12.1: IEEE Standard for Learning Object Metadata, IEEE LTSC, 2002
3. IMS Learning Design Information Model. Version 1.0 Final Specification, rev.20, 2003, http://www.imsglobal.org/learningdesign/ldv1p0/ imsld_infov1p0.html.
4. Jovanović, J., Gašević, D., & Devedžić, "Dynamic Assembly of Personalized Learning Content on the Semantic Web," *In Proc. of the 3th European Semantic Web Conf.*, Budva, Montenegro, 2006.
5. Jovanović, J., Gašević, D., & Devedžić, V., "TANGRAM: An Ontology-based Learning Environment for Intelligent Information Systems," *In Proceedings Proc. of the 10th E-Learn Conference*, Vancouver, Canada, 2005, pp. 2966-2971.
6. Knight, C., Gašević, D., & Richards, G., "An Ontology-Based Framework for Bridging Learning Design and Learning Content," *Educational Tech. & Society*, Vol. 9, No. 1, 2006.

TENCompetence:
Lifelong Learning and Competence Development

Christopher Kew

CETIS, University of Bolton,
Deane Road, Bolton BL3 AB
UK
c.kew@bolton.ac.uk

Abstract. TENCompetence is an integrated project which will support individuals, groups and organisations in Europe in lifelong competence development by establishing the most appropriate technical and organizational infrastructure, using open-source, standards-based, sustainable and innovative technology. To achieve this, the project will conduct RTD activities to further develop and integrate models and tools in the respective fields of knowledge resources, learning activities and units of learning, competence development programmes and network data for lifelong competence development. The result will be the creation of new pedagogical approaches, new innovative software, and the integration of isolated models and tools into a common framework for competence development.

1 Introduction

According to a recent report from the World Bank, 21st century economies can only remain competitive if their workforces are able to adapt to the ever-changing demands of the labour market on the knowledge economy [1]. Such demands, coupled with advances in technology, have highlighted the need for a more flexible and knowledgeable workforce. With lifelong learning increasingly being accepted as a prerequisite to a career path that will typically span in excess of forty years, the EU is supporting the TENCompetence[1] project (The European Network for Lifelong Competence Development). The project aims to establish a technical and organisational infrastructure that uses open-source, standards-based, sustainable and innovative technology to support the lifelong development of competence which will, in turn, support the European Union goal of transforming the EU into "the most dynamic and competitive knowledge-based economy in the world"[2].

In order to better understand the work undertaken by the consortium, it helps to place it in the context of the project framework, and, to this end, this document outlines the rationale and the objectives of the overall project.

---

[1] http://www.tencompetence.org

W. Nejdl and K. Tochtermann (Eds.): EC-TEL 2006, LNCS 4227, pp. 621–627, 2006.

2 Learning for Life

The concept of Lifelong Learning has emerged in response to the need to provide EU citizens with the opportunity to continue learning regardless of age, social status or situation, through a range of formal and informal channels. The basic aim is to help people to update their skills set, and /or to help them to retrain for work in a new field of activity. Moreover, there is now a consensus amongst economists, educators and politicians that this concept of lifelong learning is integral to the economic vitality of European society [2].

In keeping with the recommendations of the 1999 Bologna Agreement [3], which set out to construct a European Higher Education Area (EHEA), changes to learning infrastructures will include the creation of a system of equivalent qualification ratings in higher education institutions throughout Europe. This initiative is intended to afford students the freedom to study in a country of their choice without the problems associated with weighing one set of qualifications against the equivalent in the host country. Moreover, it is anticipated that such a system will help to further secure the position of lifelong learning in higher education.

A further recommendation is that the use of information and communications technologies should be central to the realisation of this vision. This has led to the conception and launch of TENCompetence, a four year IST^2 project funded by the EU. In many countries the use of information and communications technology (ICT) is now considered as key to involving more people in adult learning due to its ability to widen access to education, to increase participation and to reduce delivery costs [4].

3 Project Aims and Solutions

Put simply, the project remit is to provide a means by which individuals, groups and organisations in Europe are able to gauge their operational knowledge in a given domain. Users will subsequently receive advice and facilitated access to a network of resources that are designed to help them fulfil the competence requirements of, for example, a potential or current employer, or a place of learning (College, University etc).

The mechanics of the proposed learning network will include a framework capable of assessing competence in different lines of work and fields of knowledge. This will be combined with a range of both informal and formal learning facilities such as dedicated personal learning environments, accessed through rich clients, that will allow individual and group clients to perform various roles in the TENCompetence infrastructure, and to share knowledge, activities and learning programmes at any level (from primary through to tertiary) via a system of ICT facilitated social exchanges.

The benefits of this network are potentially invaluable to the concept of Lifelong Learning which has been struggling to meet the needs of today's users. These needs have been identified by the project as:

The need for new pedagogical and organisational models of learning that fulfil the potential of the latest technologies

---

^{2} http://www.cordis.lu/ist/

Throughout the history of e-learning, the use of educational technologies has been largely bereft of any meaningful pedagogical underpinning mainly due to the primacy of the learning object. This object-centric approach to learning has fostered a generation of "hollow" pedagogical models which have systematically failed to actively engage the learner in anything beyond electronic page-turning and the passive consumption of knowledge. Moreover, a tendency to simply employ traditional face-to-face pedagogies in an e-learning context fails to take account of the new paradigms that learning technologies can support.

The TENCompetence project will develop new pedagogical models that integrate individual learning, collaborative learning, organisational learning and knowledge management. The TENCompetence infrastructure will be designed for informal, self-directed learning within companies or at home. Furthermore, these approaches will allow for the use of ambient technologies in the support of humans in their tasks.

The need for individuals and organisation in Europe to have access to information detailing all formal and informal learning opportunities

TENCompetence will provide tools that will work with existing repositories to locate suitable learning opportunities, knowledge resources, units of learning, programmes and learning networks based on the prior knowledge, preferences and circumstances of the user.

The need to encourage and facilitate sharing of knowledge and learning

Given the difficulties implicit in sharing learning resources [5], TENCompetence will devise and disseminate policies, business models and software agents that adhere to the principles of social exchange theory in order to promote the pro-active sharing of knowledge and learning resources.

The need for a system to help European organisations to effectively assess the competences and skill sets of job

The ability to assess the competencies of potential employees and learners who have studied and worked in a variety of settings is a complex task. To facilitate this process, TENCompetence will provide assessment models and software tools in the form of person and group portfolios, personal development plans, and interoperable competence definitions.

The need for improvements in supporting the use of e-learning and knowledge management environments to support effective task performance

TENCompetence will provide software to facilitate and support the creation, storage, and use of knowledge resources, learning activities, units of learning, competence development programmes and networks for lifelong competence development.

The need for a decentralised management model

Given the heterogeneous nature and the extent of the competition in European markets, no one centralised network could effectively accommodate the various users of a learning network. Moreover, individuals and organisations who collaborate in lifelong learning want to maintain their autonomy and maintain control over their learning. To this end, TENCompetence will apply principles of self-organisation and social exchange theory to the production of a decentralized, self-organized and empowered management model for use within the TENCompetence infrastructure.

The need to consolidate the best of the tools currently available to provide a stable and consistent environment in which to work

TENCompetence will locate and integrate isolated tools that are available in the fields of Knowledge Management, Human Resource Management and e-Learning. Furthermore, the integrated tools will be adaptable and will support a variety of teaching methodologies while incorporating the more innovative aspects of the web; and such tools will also be open standards compliant, and plug-and-play.

3.1 Specific Objectives

In order to fulfil the above needs, the TENCompetence project comprises three main activities including Aspect Research and Technological Development (RTD), Integration RTD and Valorisation. Taken together, Aspect RTD, Integration RTD and Valorisation envelope the ten objectives (listed below) that underpin the project rationale. This section provides an outline of the various activities and the objectives that they fulfil.

Aspect RTD. The Aspect RTD activities are concerned with the research and development of new software tools, materials and models in four specific areas:

Knowledge resources and knowledge management

This area encompasses the fields of knowledge management, digital repositories, learning management systems that work on learning objects, etc.
Objective: To research and develop innovative methods and technologies for the creation, storage, use and exchange of knowledge resources related to lifelong competence development.

Learning activities and units of learning

This area includes work on the semantic modeling of teaching-learning systems, pedagogies for formal and informal learning, assessment models and tools, computer supported collaborative learning or work (CSCL/CSCW).
Objective: To research and develop innovative, standards-based methods and tools for the creation, storage, use and exchange of formal and informal learning activities and units of learning. This includes tools for the assessment of the learning process and learning outcomes.

Competence development programmes and informal programmes for competence development

This area covers such issues as the identification and accreditation of competences, personal development programmes, supporting users in the navigation of a collection of learning activities and interoperable portfolios.
Objective: To research and develop innovative methods and technologies for the creation, storage, use and exchange of formal and informal competence development programmes (including the assessment of previously required competence levels, navigation support, and the sharing of successful formal and informal learning tracks).

Networks and communities for lifelong competence development

This area includes initiatives designed to encourage and promote the use of self-directed learning, interoperable formal programmes, (e.g.,Bologna Bachelors/Masters) communities of practice, learning communities and reusable competency definitions. *Objective:* To research and develop models, methods and technologies for the creation, storage, use and exchange of networks of competence development programmes from different sources around Europe in order to support lifelong competence development.

Integration RTD is concerned with orchestrating Aspect developments from a usability perspective. To this end the project includes three integrated project objectives which are defined as follows:

To research and develop a sustainable European infrastructure for lifelong competence development

Developed in line with user requirements and relevant RTD results, the TENCompetence infrastructure will commit to providing solutions to the seven needs stated above.

To ensure the validity and viability of the approach during the project by performing real-life pilot implementations in different organisational and international settings

The consortium will conduct three cycles of pilots in competence development in the areas of digital cinema, health work, water management and city-wide contexts. The first cycle aims to provide "proofs of concept" while the second is intended to test the usability of the infrastructure. The third and final cycle of pilots takes the form of "business model demonstrators" which will help define the different ways in which the project's outcome can connect with the market. As well as helping to raise user awareness and comprehension of the infrastructure, the demonstrators will serve to encourage associated technology partners and the wider community to adopt and/or build upon the tools and methods established and the services used.

To ensure the sustainability of the infrastructure

In order to sustain both the infrastructure and the services delivered by TENCompetence, the project will be supported by awareness raising activities, dissemination / exploitation activities, training activities, usability support, community development around the software products, and support to incubation activities. Sustainability is closely linked to the valorisation activities (See Valorisation).

To advance the state-of-the-art in the underlying research fields

Further research will be conducted and a number of support tools will be created to support collaborative knowledge, embedded learning, knowledge engineering, learning communities & communities of practice, e-learning, lifelong learning, learning technology specifications and standards, intelligent software agents, semantic modeling and ontologies for learning, social exchange theory and self-organized learning. It is also anticipated that the project will deliver innovation in existing and newly created applications that will function as services in an interoperable service-oriented approach.

To provide input to international, national and professional standardisation bodies

The consortium is composed of partner institutions known for their activities in standards-based work, including the majority of the European members of IMS Global Learning Inc. Together, their expertise will be used to help identify those specifications and standards best able to help achieve the aims of the project. Further input to standardization bodies will include the extension of IMS QTI, the integration of new assessment methods for lifelong competence development and the development of a learning path specification to describe the structure of programmes (curricula, training programmes, personal development programmes, etc.) in an interoperable way.

Further details pertaining to the ways in which the tools, UoLs and models will be integrated are expected to emerge as a result of ongoing research and pilot testing.

3.2 Valorisation

"Valorisation" is used here to refer to the promotion and dissemination of project results beyond the inner circle of the project partners. This final set of activities is intended to facilitate the training of researchers and key staff including the associate partners that join the TENCompetence community.

As part of the valorisation strategy, the project will undertake to provide training in the deployment of the project tools, methods and services to both professionals and general stakeholders. This will involve the development of activities and materials for use in face to face and blended competence development situations using social and collaborative scenarios which will be facilitated by the TENCompetence systems as they become available. To test, then use, and finally sustain the infrastructure, associate partners will be actively recruited from the outset. With their help, the business models that enable the infrastructure to be sustained will be realistic, practical and tested.

The exchange of research and research results also constitutes a major goal in relation to the valorisation strategy. To this end the project will support a community of PhD students in line with the research activities carried out in the Aspect RTD activities and exchanges between academic and other project partners will be encouraged.

4 Conclusion

It will be understood from the above that the TENCompetence project recognises the need to prepare employers and employees for the ever-evolving demands in skills and knowledge requirements which underpin a successful economy. The project will seek to help individuals and organisations alike to meet such demands by developing an organisational and technical infrastructure based on a service-oriented approach. To achieve its aims the project has enlisted the help of thirteen "core" partners known for their activities in either learning technology or standards-based work and drawn from nine different European countries (Belgium, Bulgaria, France, Germany, Greece, Italy, the Netherlands, Spain, and the UK), to produce a consortium of diverse but complementary organizations that include research groups, universities, software companies and SMEs. More information on the various partners and their involvement in the project can be found on the TENCompetence website[3].

---

[3] http://193.63.48.115/tenc/node/13

References

[1] The World Bank (2003) Lifelong Learning and the Knowledge Economy – Summary of the Global Conference on Lifelong Learning. Stuttgart, Germany, October 9-10, 2002 Available: [http://siteresources.worldbank.org/EDUCATION/Resources/ 8200-1099079877269/547664-1099079984605/lifelong_KE.pdf]

[2] European Commission (2001). Making a European Area of Lifelong Learning a Reality [online] Available: [http://europa.eu.int/comm/education/life]

[3] European Commission (2005). The Bologna Declaration on the European Space for higher education: an explanation [online] Available: [http://europa.eu.int/ comm/ education/ policies/educ/bologna/bologna.pdf]

[4] Selwyn, N. (2003) ICT in Adult Education: Defining the Territory [online] Available [http://www.literacy.org/ICTconf/OECD_Selwyn_final.pdf]

[5] Littlejohn, A. and Buckingham Shum, S. (2003). (Eds.) Reusing Online Resources (Special Issue) Journal of Interactive Media in Education, 2003 (1). ISSN: 1365-893X Available: [www-jime.open.ac.uk/2003/1/]

A Storyboard of the APOSDLE Vision

Stefanie Lindstaedt[1] and Harald Mayer[2]

[1] Know-Center, Inffeldgasse 21a,
8010 Graz, Austria
slind@know-center.at
www.know-center.at
[2] Joanneum Research, Steyrergasse,
8010 Graz, Austria
harald.mayer@joanneum.at
www.joanneum.at

Abstract. The goal of the APOSDLE (Advanced Process-Oriented Self-Directed Learning environment) project is to enhance knowledge worker productivity by supporting informal learning activities in the context of knowledge workers' everyday work processes and within their work environments. This contribution seeks to communicate the ideas behind this abstract vision to the reader by using a storyboard, scenarios and mock-ups. The project just started in March 2006 and is funded within the European Commission's 6th Framework Program under the IST work program. APOSDLE is an Integrated Project jointly coordinated by the Know-Center, Austria's Competence Centre for Knowledge Management, and Joanneum Research. APOSDLE brings together 12 partners from 7 European Countries.

1 Motivation

In current business practice and eLearning research projects, most spending is applied to enhancing *knowledge transfer* of formal training interventions. Haskell [4] informs us that in 1998 US$ 70 billion were spent on formal training and Back [1] states that in 2000 US$ 78 billion were spent on corporate training and continuing education. Studies on the other hand have revealed that in today's economy only a small amount of knowledge that is actually applied to job activities comes from formal training. On average people only transfer less than 30% of what is being learned in formal training to the professional workplace in a way that enhances performance. This is independent of the kind and quality of the courses taught but mainly depends on too little consideration of work environment needs during and after formal training efforts [8]. 80 – 90% of what employees know of their job, they know from *informal learning* [7]. Initiatives aiming at enhancing knowledge transfer of formal training try to answer the question: "How much does the learner know after engaging in the formal training?" Instead, as suggested by the above numbers, the question which should be asked is: "To which extent can the learner apply the newly acquired skills to her work tasks?"

W. Nejdl and K. Tochtermann (Eds.): EC-TEL 2006, LNCS 4227, pp. 628–633, 2006.

In order to answer this second question one has to look at the theories of *learning transfer* [5] and design computational learning support based on them. A simple taxonomy of six levels has been proposed which reach from nonspecific transfer over application and context transfer to near, far and creative transfer. Transfer on all these levels involves the application of what has been learned to situations which are more or less similar to the one in which the knowledge was acquired. Within this contribution we focus on application situations stemming from the work tasks and processes.

Work-integrated learning happens to a tremendous degree during social interaction, while knowledge workers collaborate on digital artifacts or communicate aspects of these artifacts. The role a knowledge worker embodies in social interaction is subject to continuous change: At one point in time, a knowledge worker acts as a learner, at another point in time, the same knowledge worker acts as an expert (teacher) depending on her expertise with regard to the subject matter at hand [6]. Hence, when we learn there is always explicitly or implicitly some teaching involved. In the case of formal trainings we usually encounter one teacher or trainer who conveys the content to be learned. But in other situations – such as reviewing code – this teaching role is not so obvious to the expert herself. In the following we will refer to such episodes as *work-integrated teaching*.

2 APOSDLE Goals and Challenges

Triggered by the identified, unsatisfactory situation above the APOSDLE (Advanced Process-Oriented Self-Directed Learning Environment) project addresses underlying research challenges such as:

- Understanding and defining work-integrated learning and teaching
- Supporting learning transfer instead of knowledge transfer
- Integrating this support within real world application cases
- Measuring learning transfer within real world environments

Thus, the APOSDLE goal is to enhance knowledge worker[1] productivity by supporting informal learning and teaching activities in the *context* of knowledge workers' everyday work processes and *within* their work environments. APOSDLE leads the way towards the seamless integration of learning, teaching, and working at the future professional workplace.

The key distinction of the APOSDLE approach as compared to more traditional (e)Learning approaches is that APOSDLE will provide integrated support for the three roles a knowledge worker fills at the professional workplace: the role of learner, the role of expert, and the role of worker.

Learner Support. APOSDLE provides learners with support for self-directed exploration and application of knowledge. This is done within their work environment such that learning takes place within the learner's current work context. APOSDLE provides learners with guidance through the available knowledge by applying novel

---

[1] Knowledge workers (here often simply referred to as workers) are members of organizations whose essential operational and value creating tasks rely on knowledge as their critical work resource [3].

learning strategies. Content from knowledge sources are presented to learners even if the content provided has originally not been intended for learning. The main learning strategies that we use in APOSDLE will be based on the principles of *Cognitive Apprenticeship* [2]. This principle is widely recognized as a fruitful approach to learning in realistic situations and it combines aspect of problem-based learning and self-directed learning. Within cognitive apprenticeship scaffolding is a central technique for supporting learning. Cognitive scaffolds are tools that enable learners to perform processes they would not be able to perform proficiently without the support of the tool. Scaffolds help learners to go just beyond the level of proficiency they have on their own.

Expert Support. APOSDLE acknowledges that most effective learning transfer happens during communication, collaboration and social interaction. APOSDLE lowers the hurdles for knowledge workers to informally convey knowledge via their computational environment in that it captures the context of the creation, evolution and usage of artifacts. APOSDLE enriches artifacts with context information and therefore allows artifacts to be turned into true learning artifacts (contextualized collaboration). Based on existing approaches to capture knowledge, APOSDLE will develop new methods and tools which support the capturing of knowledge as it shows up in processes of collaboration. Especially, it will support communication and collaboration between people about an artifact (e.g. a document, a graph, or a piece of code). By doing so APOSDLE taps into collaborative learning episodes and makes the results available to other people in their own informal learning processes. This emphasizes the importance of group learning and communication support within the APOSDLE framework.

Worker Support. APOSDLE tightly incorporates learning and teaching episodes into the work processes in that it takes care of several aspects of workers' work contexts such as worker's competencies, work situation, and application domain. Workers are provided with context sensitive knowledge, thus raising their own awareness of learning situations, content, and people that may be useful for learning. APOSDLE enables workers to access content from several diverse knowledge sources without having to change the environment. Within APOSDLE we are concerned with the modeling and acquisition of context. Here, we define context as a set of relevant information and constraints that an individual (learner, tutor) needs in order to reach an individual or shared (learning) goal [9]. The relevance of information depends on the individual perspective and the goal that has to be achieved. We focus on the context of a task as the set of information and constraints which are relevant to a certain worker in a certain situation when trying to accomplish this task. In this narrow meaning, context is worker and situation-specific.

To work, learn and teach efficiently and effectively, a knowledge worker must be provided with optimal guidance to manage the large variety of knowledge artefacts available in the corporate infrastructure. Therefore the seamless integration of the underlying information spaces into an integrated semantic knowledge structure is of paramount importance. APOSDLE will therefore create such an infrastructure (referred to as APOSDLE platform) to support the integration of the three roles.

The outcome of APOSDLE will be a methodology, software framework and reference architecture for work-integrated learning enhancing the learning and teaching processes for the individual and the organization. In order to ensure the general applicability of this outcome an application-driven approach is used to cover the needs of three fundamentally different organizations: a network of SMEs, a public organization, and a large corporation.

3   APOSDLE Usage Scenario

This usage scenario shows how the different roles of a knowledge worker – Learner, Expert and Worker – will be supported within *one integrated* APOSDLE Environment.

Background. Sandra is a technical expert at HighTech. She has recently been promoted to project manager. In this new role she has now also the responsibility of directly working with the customer to elicit the user requirements of the software application to be developed. In addition, she is responsible for ensuring that the requirements are updated, linked to the design documents, and finally used for testing. In the past she was involved with requirements management (RM) but never in the elicitation process (RE). Also, she feels a little uncomfortable since she is not sure that her team handles requirements according to the company standard.

Worker Support. A new project is about to start and so Sandra instantiates a new project folder in the common file system, sets up a common e-mail repository, etc. By analyzing these actions (which Sandra is executing within her work environment) an APOSDLE Work Tool automatically identifies that Sandra currently is in the project management phase "ProjectStart". Another APOSDLE Work Tool unobtrusively offers all information relevant to the ProjectStart phase. This helps Sandra to remember all the steps which need to be done. In addition, the APOSDLE Platform keeps a user profile of Sandra. In this profile Sandra's expertise in RE has been recorded as low. One of the important first tasks associated with the ProjectStart phase is that the user requirements for the system to be developed need to be elicited. Due to Sandra's profile the APOSDLE Work Tool makes Sandra aware that more detailed and more introductory information about RE is available. Since Sandra is happy about all the help she can get she selects the offered APOSDLE Self-Directed Learning (SDL) Tool.

Learner Support. By glancing at the window offered by the APOSDLE SDL Tool Sandra notices a number of very different available resources associated with RE, structured neatly into categories: *templates* to document user scenarios, a *frequently asked questions* list, *questionnaires* for structured interviews, *example* documents from other projects, a *tutorial* about scenario-based RE, a *link* to a community of practice (COP) platform within HighTech related to the topic, and even an announcement for a RE *class* to be held in a few weeks. The APOSDLE SDL Tool

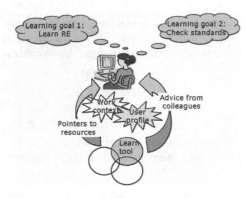

explains which resources can be used for which purpose and how it all fits into the RE process. In addition, the tool provides Sandra with guidance about how best to approach to learn RE.

Right now Sandra is in a bit of a hurry since the first customer meeting will be held tomorrow. So the first thing she does is look at the COP platform. This platform is an APOSDLE Teaching Tool which knows about Sandra's work and competency context and helps her identify people with the right know-how to help her learn. She immediately asks some urgent questions and is pointed to a little pre-recorded tour through the available methods. Based on this information and the advice given Sandra decides that she will use the scenario-based RE approach. She switches back to her APOSDLE SDL Tool and selects this approach. She accesses the user scenario templates, skims through the tutorial, and looks at some examples from projects she was involved in. But since Sandra is not only interested short-term in RE but also wants to establish a better RE practice in her team she also signs up for the course offered.

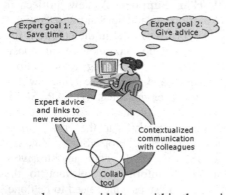

Expert Support. Some weeks later Sandra reviews the use case descriptions of one of her newer team members. By now she has learned quite a bit about RE and especially is knowledgeable about the RE standards employed within HichTech. She immediately notices that her colleague started to document design options instead of focusing on the user requirements. Since this is a typical mistake most beginners make and which she has made herself, she already has compiled a number of reference materials, examples, and guidelines within the review environment (an APOSDLE Collaboration Tool). She now marks the suboptimal parts in the use case, links the relevant material to it and writes a short explanation in the chat window about how the material applies here. She also points him to other such use case examples done before. In addition, by using another APOSDLE Collaboration Tool she records a short tour of the available use case modeling resources in the APOSDLE environment and makes this guided tour (including her voice annotations) available to all her team members by associating it to the project management phase ProjectStart. From now on inexperienced use case designers will be offered this tour automatically by the APOSDLE system.

Acknowledgements

APOSDLE is partially funded under the FP6 of the European Commission within the IST work program 2004 (FP6-IST-2004-027023). The Know-Center is funded by the

Austrian Competence Center program K plus under the auspices of the Austrian Ministry of Transport, Innovation and Technology (www.ffg.at/index.php?cid=95) and by the State of Styria.

References

1. Back, A., Bendel, O., & Stoller-Schai, D. (2001). E-Learning in Unternehmen. Grundlagen - Strategien - Methoden - Technologien. Orell Flüssli Verlag.
2. Brown, J. S., Collins, A., & Duguid, P. (1989). Situated cognition and the culture of learning. Educational Researcher, 18.
3. Drucker, P.F. (1993). Post-Capitalist Society. HarperBusiness.
4. Haskell, R.E. (1998). Reengineering Corporate Training. Intellectual Capital and Transfer of Learning, Quorum Books.
5. Haskell, R.E. (2001). Transfer of Learning: Cognition and Instruction. Elsevier Academic Press.
6. Lave, J., & Wenger, E. (1991). Situated Learning – Legitimate Peripheral Participation, Cambridge University Press.
7. Raybould, B. (2002). Performance Support Engineering Part One: Key Concepts. Ariel PSE Technology, 2000. Cited in Dickover, N.T.: The Job is the Learning Environment: Performance-Centered Learning to Support Knowledge Worker Performance, JIID, Vol.14, No. 3.
8. Robinson, D.G. (2003). Skill and Performance: They are not equal. Apartment Professional Magazine.
9. Wessner, M. (2005). Kontextuelle Kooperation in virtuellen Lernumgebungen. Lohmar: Eul-Verlag.

Blended Learning Technologies in Lifelong Education: Lessons Learned from a Case Study

Konstantinos Liotsios, Stavros Demetriadis, and Andreas Pombortsis

Informatics Dept., Aristotle University of Thessaloniki, P.O. Box 888, Thessaloniki, Greece
{liotsios, sdemetri, apombo}@csd.auth.gr

Abstract. The combination of the traditional form of education and e-learning activities (blended learning) constitutes an important possibility for the higher education, so that they reach the flexibility which is considered to be necessary for their adaptation to the trainees' needs within the frame of socio-cognitive needs created by the information society. We present the principles of the application of blended lesson designs in graduate level and of its evaluation by the students. Based on our experience we support the opinion that the blended design may constitute the most important example of the organization of education in the information society. Could cope also with the needs and characteristics of lifelong learning, as it seems to provide both the necessary flexibility and the support for the development of the skills for the management of technology and time which are not confirmed by the traditional designs.

Keywords: lifelong learning, e-learning, blended learning, action research.

1 Introduction

The socio-cognitive transformations caused within the frame of the information society make it necessary for the educational institutions of all levels (especially Universities) to "provide for a larger and more diverse cross-section of the population, to cater for emerging patterns of educational involvement which facilitate lifelong learning and to include technology-based practices in the curriculum"(Renner, 1995, as quotation in Hicks, Reid and George, 2001). Within this frame the e- and lifelong learning services plainly emerge as important mechanisms to the newly formed needs.

By "e-learning" we refer to the use of Information and Communication Technologies (ICT) to provide educational services from a distance. The asynchronous ICT can facilitate simultaneous both independent and cooperative learning experiences (Garrison & Cleveland-Innes, 2003; Swan, 2001). We believe that these services, besides the natural distance between the trainers and the trainees, can and must bridge other kinds of distances as well, such as "transactional distance" (Moore, 1993). It refers to the differentiation between the trainee's actual learning goal and the one s/he finally achieves through the specific arrangements which are effective in the educational environment (arrangements such as the analysis of the educational unit available, the possibilities of dialogue and interaction between the trainees and the trainer, etc).

W. Nejdl and K. Tochtermann (Eds.): EC-TEL 2006, LNCS 4227, pp. 634–639, 2006.
© Springer-Verlag Berlin Heidelberg 2006

Respectively the idea of "lifelong" learning may be simply described as every learning activity during a person's life which extends beyond the education offered by the typical educational environments (school, University). We also believe that a more essential understanding is offered by the description of lifelong learning as "The process of change of perceptions and practices in educational issues aiming at the confrontation of continuous needs emerging within the frame of the information society. This change of our comprehension removes from the significance of learning as preparation for the professional life and brings to us nearest in the significance of learning as basic element of life and professional career of each one" (Birmingham University, 2005).

2 Blended Learning and Lifelong Learning

By the term "blended" or "hybrid" learning we refer to forms of education which combine activities taking place in traditional places (i.e. classroom, laboratory) with the use of synchronous of asynchronous educational activities offered from a distance with the support of synchronous technology (e-learning activities). (Hamburg, Cernian & Thij, 2002). It appears that the blended education emerges as an interesting learning model which could allow educational organizations to help their students adjust from the traditional educational experience, to the e-learning in small, gradual steps so that this change is more easily manageable and comprehensible by them, and the trainees are supported to develop the skills required (i.e. management of available time) (Aycock, Garnham & Kalet, 2002).

The up to the present day available research provides proof that blended learning can be equally or more effective and efficient compared with the model of entire e-learning and with the model of entirely traditional education. The students participating in programs of blended learning achieve the same of better learning results besides being more contented with the combining process. (Garrison and Kanuka, 2004).

Within the frame of the present project by the term "lifelong" learning we mainly refer to the possibility offered to people older than 25 years of age, to be trained according to specific learning needs related to their educational training. This category of trainees is usually characterized by:

- Restriction of free time available especially in the mornings (working professionals)
- Prohibited possibilities of movement (working, family people)
- Moreover their educational needs may be characterized as :
- Immediate (updating information/specialization to agree/correspond with their current needs)
- Timely (learning offered at the moment it is needed)
- Focused (usually in connection with the profession they already practice)
- Short-dated (short duration of rapid education/training)
- Flexible (adapted to individual needs and learning pace)

Thus, lifelong learning within the frame of the information society appears to be inevitably related to the need for a flexible and just in time offer of education on issues which may be of highly focused interest.

On the other hand, blended education may respond to the flexibility demands set by lifelong learning (due to the component of e-learning), may offer focused and self-regulated learning (also due to the component of e-learning) and may even create and maintain much more effectively the sense of the learning community (due to the component of traditional education). It may also constitute form a perfect environment of introduction to the regulations and the cultivation of skills which are required for the attendance of lifelong e-learning programs, such as the familiarization with technology and the skill of time management (due to the component of e-learning).

3 Educational Activities

In this unit we present the educational activities which we organized within the frame of blended education in graduate level. For the creation of e-learning activities the Blackboard^{TM} environment was used (https://blackboard.lib.auth.gr).

For the investigative study of the activities we followed the model of Action Research (Leh, 2002). According to the model the researcher participates actively in the materialization of the learning activity interacting with the trainees, recording their opinions, attitudes and suggestions and readjusting its plan taking into account the recorded data.

The design of the activities was based on the simple model of "Backward Design" (Wiggins and McTighe, 2000) which starts from the learning goals to be achieved (final element) and leads to the assignment of the necessary activities in components of traditional education and e-learning as well as the restoration of relations between them (initial element).

We organized the subject "Constructing learning environments with the use of Information and Communication Technologies (ICT)" in a thoroughly blended form (graduate Computer Science Department Program specializing in "ICT in Education", 11 participating students, 2nd semester of studies). Following the backward model the design was as follows :

- *Learning Goal 1*: Students should be able to explain, understand and comment on the basic concepts and methods of the constructive approach.
  - *Educational Activity*: The students study representative texts of the theoretical principles of the constructive approach and discuss them so that they reach clear conclusions. This activity is supported with 5 sessions: one initial session of traditional form as introduction to the goals and the contents of the subject, followed by 3 online asynchronous sessions, where the participants study texts based on the lecturer's instructions and discuss the texts in asynchronous discussion groups and in the end a traditional session where they discuss the issues on which the 3 online sessions focus as a whole.
- *Learning Goal 2*: Students should be able to compose theory and practice analyzing materializations of constructive educational designs.
  - *Educational Activity*: The students are asked to study in co-operation from a distance (3 online sessions) representative cases of innovative educational designs with the use of technology within teaching places of traditional school and present their project in a traditional session.

- *Learning Goal 3*: Students should get familiar with specific subjects which may offer design specifications of thorough constructive environments on the Internet.
  - – *Educational Activity*: As in activity 2 the students co-operate from a distance (3 sessions) for the study of particular subjects which they present in a traditional session.
- *Learning Goal 4*: Students should design their own constructive environment on the Internet.
  - – *Educational Activity* : Based on their experience on phases 1-3 the students are asked to suggest and design environments of constructive training (3 online sessions) and present and evaluate them in a final presentation (traditional session).

All in all of the thirteen sessions anticipated by the schedule of the subject the 4 are conducted in traditional form and the remaining are offered from a distance. The 4 traditional sessions function as review sessions of a unit (of one educational goal) which was completed and at the same time introduce the students to the next unit.

4   Results

In order to reach to conclusions concerning for the evaluation of the educational process, for the final outcome of the implementation of the blended model and the improved re-design of the blended approach, a final research based on interviews was conducted. The teaching assistant of the class assigned to the 11 students the guidelines of the discussion for the interviews which were recorded thus making easy their processing and at the same time ensuring the accuracy and validity of the answers. The first results we recorded are summed up as follows:

- *There is an initial satisfaction* of the part of the participants about the form of the lesson. The satisfaction has to do as much with the authentic "constructive" experience which the lesson offers (according to a student's statement "we learn about constructivism in a constructive way") as with the flexibility characterizing it (two of the students attending the class are appointed teachers in a long distance from University and otherwise they would not be in a position to attend).
- *However*, the students pointed out certain points in the lesson which they did not like due to the implementation of the blended model and which they would characterize as deficiencies such as :
  - – about the *learning community* it was not cultivated among the students the acquaintance, the strengthening of relations, the sense that they belong to the same learning community with negative results in the co-operation, interaction, asking of questions/question wording and mutual assistance.
  - – Likewise *there was no sufficient help* – support on the part of the lecturer for the preparation of the projects.
  - – *The lecturer's demands* on the self-regulation of the study time and the self-determination of the learning pace (composition of long projects, in very short periods of time, demanding in both length and time) were also *recorded as highly increased*.

- *The Discussion Board* in its offered structure and organization did not create the necessary conditions for co-operative learning, but was ended up in a simple service of project presentation, something which was also tiring because of the constant repetition of the same comments – remarks (of the projects) due to the way of the students' participation in the asynchronous online discussions (where the ones who simply agree with the "previous speakers" must still "upload" their own messages as a an indication of their participation in the process of the material).

- Finally *the participants' suggestions* are recorded for the improvement of the design on the following points:
  - *the increased time of preparation* which is required for every online session (at least on the first sessions),
  - *the participation in the asynchronous online discussions* (where the ones who simply agree with the "previous speakers" must still "upload" their own messages as a sign of their participation in the process of the material) and
  - *the necessity for the development* of time management skills (to this direction the design helps as specific short-length projects are determined for each online session – every week – so that the phenomenon of the accumulation of the project before the deadline of the project handing in is avoid.

5 Conclusion

In this article we supported the opinion that the blended organization of education may constitute the proper adaptation process (and an example of realization of lifelong learning programs as well) in relation to the needs it generates and the skills required for lifelong learning. To this objective we presented the basic characteristics of the blended organization of education in connection with the lifelong learning needs, while we proceeded to indicate the application elements and the evaluation of blended designs of education in graduate level of higher education.

Based on our up to the present day experience, from our above case study, we support the opinion that the blended design can form the ruling example of the learning organizing in the information society as it deals with increased flexibility with the problems of the trainees' movement and the resources management on the part of the trainer. Moreover it offers the ideal environment for the gradual initiation of the trainees in the organizing and the skills the e-learning activities require. We believe that these characteristics make – in principle – the blended design an interesting and efficient model of organizing education in relation to the needs and characteristics of lifelong learning.

References

1. Aycock, Garnham, Kalet.: Lessons Learned from the Blended Course Project, Teaching with Technology Today, Vol.8, No. 6, (2002) 9-21.
2. Garrison, D.R., Cleveland-Iness, M.: Critical factors in student satisfaction and success: Facilitating student role adjustment in online communities of inquiry. Invited paper presented to the Sloan Consortium asynchronous Learning Network Invitational Workshop, Boston (2003).

3. Garrison, D.R., Kanuka, H.: Blended learning: Uncovering its transformative potential in higher education, Internet and Higher Education 7, (2004) 95-105.
4. Hamburg I., Cernian O., Thij H.: Blended Learning and Distributed learning Environments, in ViReC e-Initiative project (2002). Online, retrieved from http://cs.ucv.ro/ViReC on March, 15/ 2005.
5. Hicks, M., Reid, I., George, R.: Enhancing on-line teaching: Designing responsive learning environments, The International Journal for Academic Development, 6(2) (2001) 143-151.
6. Leh. A.: Action Research on Blended Courses and their Online Communities, Educational Media International, 39:1 (2002) 31-38.
7. Moore, M. G.: Theory of transactional distance, In: Desmond Keegan (Ed.): Theoretical principles of distance education, London, New York: Routledge, (1993) 22-38.
8. Swan, K.: Virtual Interaction: Design factors affecting student satisfaction and perceived learning in asynchronous online course, Distance education, 22(2) (2001) 306-331.
9. Wiggins G., Mc Tighe J.: What is Backward Design ? ASCD Books for Educators NEWS (2000).
10. University of Birmingham. Online retrieved from www.ao.bham.ac.uk/aps/glossary.htm, on March, 23/2005.

iCamp – The Educational Web for Higher Education

Barbara Kieslinger[1], Fridolin Wild[2], and Onur Ihsan Arsun[3]

[1] Centre for Social Innovation,
[2] Vienna University of Economics,
[3] Austria, Isik University, Turkey
kieslinger@zsi.at, fridolin.wild@wu-wien.ac.at,
arsun@isikun.edu.tr

Abstract. iCamp is an EC-funded research project in the area of Technology Enhanced Learning (TEL) that aims to support collaboration and social networking across systems, countries and disciplines in higher education. The concept of an iCamp Space will build on existing interfaces and integrate shared community features. Interoperability amongst different open source learning systems and tools is the key to successful sustainability of iCamp. The content for this collaboration within social communities is provided via distributed networked repositories including, for example, content brokerage platforms, online libraries, and learning object databases. The innovative pedagogical model of iCamp is based on social constructivist learning theories. iCamp creates an environment for a new way of social networking in higher education that puts more emphasis on self-organised, self-directed learning, social networking and cross-cultural collaboration.

1 Introduction

iCamp has the vision to become the higher educational web in an Enlarged Europe of 25+ (Fig. 1.) [1]. We pursue the idea of gathering people (learners, facilitators, peers, etc.) into one common virtual learning environment. This virtual environment does not consist of a single software system, but is composed of various interoperable tools and platforms. Each element of this patchwork of open-source solutions and the entire space are compliant with an innovative pedagogical model built upon a social constructivist approach. This pedagogical model encompasses social networking, scaffolding for self-directed, self-organised learning, incentives, and cross-cultural collaboration aspects.

iCamp validates its pedagogical model in combination with its interoperable system & tools portfolio – the iCamp building blocks. The efforts will result in guidelines on pedagogical and technical issues as well as in an open-source software package of constructivist learning tools.

In the future the users shall have seamless access through their own learning platforms and tools to services and artifacts offered by remote systems. The pan-European higher education network created by iCamp will comprise institutions, departments, units, and institutes, enabling their students and staff members to collaborate on a group or individual level.

W. Nejdl and K. Tochtermann (Eds.): EC-TEL 2006, LNCS 4227, pp. 640–645, 2006.

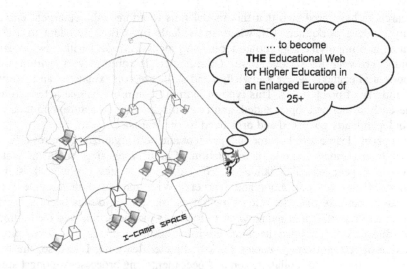

... to become
THE Educational Web
for Higher Education in
an Enlarged Europe of
25+

Fig. 1. iCamp Vision

2 Project Objectives

The main research objectives in iCamp are driven by pedagogical, technical and social challenges that aim to [2]:

- Investigate, develop and validate innovative pedagogical models for social instruction that support learners in achieving their learning goals in a self-directed manner and to establish social networks
- Provide a validated portfolio of constructivist learning tools that support these innovative learning models
- Provide an open virtual learning environment consisting of a network of learning tools, platforms and repositories
- Develop and describe open source code for connecting to the iCamp network and to provide interoperability amongst different systems
- Document and describe best practices to be derived from the validation trials for universities that may benefit from iCamp in the future
- Assess the actual and potential impacts of the iCamp network on Higher Education Institutions at different levels and from different perspectives

In the following sections we will describe the objectives in more detail.

2.1 Pedagogical Objectives

The pedagogical approach in iCamp starts from the constructivist learning theory with a focus on the learner and his or her way of constructing knowledge. The challenge that we still face with many learning environments today is that they have been developed following the transmission model of teaching and learning, where information is transferred from experts to novices. For quite some time educational researchers have predicted that this model fails to address the emergent demands of many modern workplaces [3], where individuals must flexibly adapt to a changing context and improvise appropriate tools and processes to deal with new domains or a rapidly growing knowledge base. Often, such learning occurs within informal, experiential contexts where knowledge and skills are contextualized and defined by a community of practice [4]. This type of learning can often be characterized as being inherently ill-defined, open-ended, and cross-disciplinary in nature, and thus needs to be independently governed and organized by the learner.

Preparing learners to become independent and self-organized requires a facilitative rather than a didactic mode of instruction. iCamp emphasizes social networking to meet this pedagogical challenge. This implies a new role and shifting in responsibilities for educators and learners. With the rapid development of ICT, educators can take over the role of mediators, mentors, and thus become facilitators. iCamp will provide tools and services to facilitate the mentoring and mediating role of the educators in an open learning environment as well as the development and practice of relevant competencies for self-directed learning. Likewise, the tools and services will allow for collaboration and peer mentoring processes amongst students.

The iCamp pedagogical model will be drafted out of four models that are all guided by the overall principle of self-directed learning. Scaffolding self-directed learning will support the learners in identifying their needs and in planning and carrying out learning projects in non-formal and informal settings. An incentives

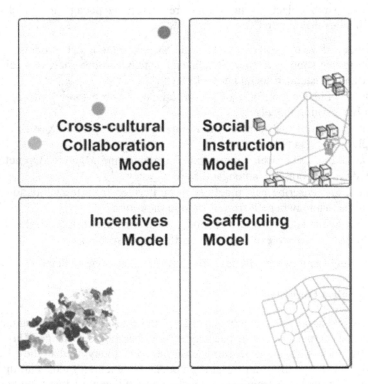

Fig. 2. iCamp Pedagogical Models

model shall provide new approaches to learning contracts combined with an easy access to distributed and networked resources, and personal and collaborative Web publishing tools. Weblog authoring has not only been identified as being instrumental for the formation of informal learning networks that are highly decentralized and self-organizing, it has also been documented that technologies, tools, and practices related to personal and collaborative Web publishing create a fruitful context for developing open, unstructured, and supportive learning environments.

The collaboration amongst students across countries also implies cultural differences in learning and these have to be respected and supported by the learning environment. In this context, iCamp will perform an analysis of emerging personal and collaborative web publishing practices such as Weblog authoring in order to provide insights into the codification and standardization of cross-cultural and cross-disciplinary social networking and information sharing [5] in open, networked environments.

2.2 Technical Objectives

In terms of collaboration and communication iCamp will focus on the potential of new tools that support the creation of social networks amongst the students and other peers. These new tools shall support the personal preferences of the students.

iCamp will offer students as well as any academic staff access to large content repositories that go beyond the currently existing learning object repositories. Thus iCamp will bridge the currently existing gap between different repositories. The community members of iCamp will have access to a network of content repositories, from digital libraries to online bookstores. The challenge for iCamp is to further explore ways to retrieve important information from the deep web by extending the Simple Query Interface (SQI) [6] and thus provide interoperability amongst the various systems.

iCamp will also develop strong interoperability amongst different open source learning platforms. With the developments of the last few years, the eLearning market has been (over-)populated with tools and platforms to support different types of learning communities with learning management, content management and communication tools. Currently, open source tools in that area are gaining more and more reputation and have had a high uptake especially in the NMS and AC. However, there is still a lack of interoperability between the various systems. Standardisation work is trying to overcome these interoperability problems, but has only done so to a minor extent. Here again, the SQI has started to tackle the problem by connecting different systems. So far, the SQI has been concentrated on querying for learning resources. The challenge for iCamp is to allow cross-collaboration of users amongst various eLearning systems and to facilitate the joint use of community features. In iCamp we are dealing with system, syntactic and semantic interoperability of heterogeneous information resources (digital repositories, learning service providers, learning resource brokers, iBlogs, etc.) to create the iCamp Space, an enlarged European educational network.

2.3 Social Objectives

In order to assess the potential of iCamp in supporting and fostering the creation of social networks the project will apply a social network analysis approach. The research questions tackled are related to the theory of relational/social capital. Social capital refers to the value derived from social ties or social networks [7]. Social capital has the potential to explain many phenomena in expertise sharing networks. However, the concept still lacks good theoretical grounding. Based on such a theoretical foundation social research in the iCamp educational environments will be carried out to examine the explanatory power of a social capital theory in a cross-cultural setting.

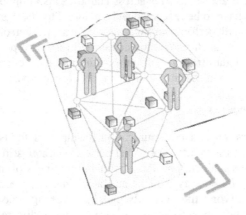

Fig. 3. iCamp Social Networks

The cooperation and collaboration of students from different countries in an enlarged Europe also implies social challenges related to cross-cultural aspects and diversity. Whereas the exchange of students and study visits across Europe are already a very common means for students to get in contact with other cultures, a virtual collaboration such as the one proposed by iCamp is still a challenge for diversity management. Social networks generally create social capital value through face-to-face contact among a limited number of people who share social norms and gestures. Broadening social networks online requires the development or invention of conventions and codes that support interaction. Social software generally codifies and structures interaction and limits the expression of the culturally specific. While this is often perceived as a disadvantage of mediated communication in comparison to face-to-face interaction, it might prove useful in the cross-cultural context of iCamp. It is the objective of iCamp to provide a careful exploration and evaluation of these aspects.

3 Conclusion

In conclusion, iCamp will strengthen the educational landscape in Europe and drive it towards a sustainable infrastructure. Since iCamp is not creating an additional eLearning system, but facilitates interoperability, a main advantage is that universities and students can continue to use and further develop their tools and services, while at the same time connect to other systems. In addition, learners and facilitators can practice and challenge a constructivist approach to learning in a mediated and networked environment. The wide collaboration space envisioned by iCamp will facilitate up-take and deployment. iCamp will provide pedagogical guidelines as well as a software toolkit to ease integration into the iCamp Space.

References

[1] iCamp Consortium, iCamp Technical Annex, 2005.

[2] Kieslinger, B., *Deliverable 6.1 – Project Presentation*, 2006.

[3] Brown, S. J. and Duguid, P. (1992). Stolen knowledge. Educational Technology, 33 (3), 10-15.

[4] Brown, S. J. and Duguid, P. (1998). Organising knowledge. California Management Review, 40(3).

[5] Davies, W. (2003). You Don't Know Me, but... Social Capital & Social Software. London: The Work Foundation.

[6] Simon B., Massart, D., Duval, E. (2004). Simple Query Interface Specification, Whitepaper. http://nm.wu-wien.ac.at/e-learning/inter/sqi/sqi.pdf (last access: April 5th, 2006).

[7] Field J., (2005). Social Capital and Lifelong Learning. Bristol: The Policy Press.

The Study on Effective Programming Learning Using Wiki Community Systems

Soo-Hwan Kim, Hee-Seop Han, and SunGwan Han

Dept. of Computer Education, Gyeong-in National University of Education,
Gyeyang-gu, Incheon, 407-753, Korea
love0jx@hotmail.com, anemon@korea.com, han@gin.ac.kr

Abstract. This study suggests the effective learning programming method using the Wiki Community Systems. In an e-Learning setting, it is hard to expect the growing learners' ability of thinking and collaboration when programming learning focuses on learning content. The Wiki Community systems we suggested, which are community-centered, however, can foster learners' ability of algorithm thinking through processing of sharing ideas and collaborating on a work with learners. We applied learning programming method using the Wiki Community systems to the fourth-grade elementary students. As a result, learners could share their ideas about solving problems and collaborate on the entire processes of learning. Furthermore, this system makes learners' knowledge for algorism to be more elaborate during learners are finding out the optimum algorithm and improve learners' thinking power.

Keywords: programming learning, Wiki system, Knowledge management.

1 Introduction

The main object of learning programming in computer science is to promote learners' logical thinking and problem-solving skills. Explanation and manuals-oriented methods are mainly instructional methods for learning programming language. These instructional methods, however, can not offer a learner an opportunity that a learner learns programming with his or her interest and ability to learn. There are various ways to solve problems in terms of programming algorithm. Accordingly, it is useful for learners to share the ideas or strategies for solving a problem and collaborate through the entire process of programming. We designed the Wiki Community system and examined how to elaborate learners' knowledge and the rate of formation of knowledge. Further, we analyzed the effectiveness of collaborative learning when learners learned programming using the Wiki Community system.

2 Background

Smith et al. said that the difficulty of programming is represented by Grand Can-yon [8]. Howell proposed five essential elements in teaching the first programming language course [2]. Papert wrote the history of LOGO and introduce

W. Nejdl and K. Tochtermann (Eds.): EC-TEL 2006, LNCS 4227, pp. 646–651, 2006.

of LOGO [6]. Saper suggested that the LOGO is clearly better choice of a language in preparation for computer science [7]. McNemey provided a historical overview of educational computing research at MIT from the mid-1960s to the present day [5]. Bo Leuf and Ward Cunningham described that Wiki is unusual among group communication mechanisms. in that it allows the organization of contributions to be edited in addition to the content itself [3]. David Mattison said that at its narrowest point, we will continue to find Wikis filling the humble role of helping shape people's attitudes and knowledge about Web-based, collaborative content creation and editing [4]. Takeda T. and Daniel Suthers provided the proposal of online workspace for annotation and discussion of documents [9]. Maria de Los Angeles Constantino-Gonzalez and Daniel D. Suthers analyzed automated coaching of collaboration based on workspace [1]. However, there are few examples that apply the Wiki system to programming learning.

3   Design and Implementation of the Wiki Community System

The Wiki Community system consists of five modules; editing module, navigation module, searching module, user module and interface module (See Fig 1). Editing module is designed that learners can add, modify and delete program sources at will. Knowledge expressed by editing module is saved into Wiki History DB. Navigation module offers the knowledge and information accumulated in Wiki system in the shape of schematization. Searching module helps learner to find knowledge created by editing module in a breeze. User module saves users' preference and basic information on User DB. Interface module helps learners to access the Wiki system.

We developed this system using Linux and Apache web Server and programming language Python, MySQL as DB. The first page of the developed project site is like the left of Fig. 2. The project task and LOGO code are as the right

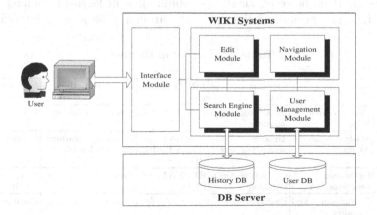

Fig. 1. Architecture of Wiki community system

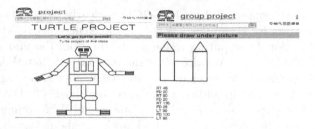

Fig. 2. Project page and LOGO code example

of Fig. 2. Project page is composed of Insert window, Explanation window for the program, Task presentation window, and Help window for glossary and programming commands.

4   Programming Learning with Wiki Community Systems

This study was conducted in learning programming for the fourth-grade elementary students as beginners. We selected LOGO. By learning LOGO, beginners can learn the basic of programming and promote their thinking power [1,6]. Table 1 shows the learning programming content that learners performed. The course for programming includes from basic command language to advanced language for command and to project learning for problem solving. However, the target learner of this study is beginner, so learners do not learn advanced algorithm. As you can see Table 1, learners learn the concepts of functions and variables. And then learners revise others' errors and perform project for the ideal programming.

Learning programming we conducted proceeds by three stages like Fig.3. First, Preparatory lesson stage is that a learner learns how to use LOGO program and acquires abilities for performing project by a teacher. When a teacher gave examples for that, however, there were differences in learners' understanding. Second, Learners performed their project through Wiki site by interchanging

Table 1. The plan of learning

Step	Contents	Capacity of learning	LOGO example	Learning method	Leaning media
1	Programming basic	Basic command language	FD, RT, LT, BK, CS	Direct-instruction	Contents
2	Master command language	Advance command language	REPEAT, HT, ST, PU, PD	Discovery learning, research learning	Community
3	Optimized programming	Correcting, optimization	REPEAT, TO END	Project based learning	Wiki community
4	Evaluation and Advance	Feedback		Discussion learning	Community

information. At this time, the formation of knowledge and the process of optimization occurred. Learners showed their own problem solutions and compared their solutions with others. Through this process, learners can acquire good ideas and solutions can be getting more and more optimized. Third, By trial and error, learners accomplished the project. In reality, learners overcame themselves through sharing their ideas and exchanging information. For learners with low levels, they could learn as seeing others' correction to their errors and the process of optimization.

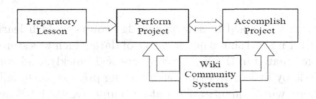

Fig. 3. The process of programming learning

5   Experimental Results and Discuss

Regarding correction of programming errors, we found many errors which beginners were likely to mistake from using basic commands to using variables and functions. Correction of programming errors usually was conducted by learners with high levels (see. Table2). As a result of that, we suggested that Wiki system is very useful to encourage collaborative learning among learners who have various learning capabilities and to foster sharing of learners' programming abilities.

For optimization of algorithm, we presented the project task which necessitated loop and function. Although participants were beginners, we could find some phases of optimization using loop and function. In addition to that, participants could understand the necessity and fundamental principle of commands.

Table 2. Pattern of correct errors

Pattern	Before correct errors	After correct errors
Command language	REPEAT 3 [FD100 RT90]	REPEAT 3 [FD 100 RT 90] // spacing after FD and RT
function	TO TRIANGLE REPEAT 3 [FD 100 RT 120]	TO TRIANGLE REPEAT 3 [FD 100 RT 120] END // add END
Move command language	PU FD 100 RT 90 FD 50 RT 90	PU FD 100 RT 90 FD 50 RT 90 PD //add PD
Using loop	FD 100 RT 90 FD 100 RT 90 FD 100 RT 90	REPEAT 3 [FD 100 RT 90] // use REPEAT
Using function	RT 90 FD 45 RT 90 FD 10 RT 90 FD 45 RT 90 FD 10	TO REC RT 90 FD 45 RT 90 FD 10 END REC();// use function

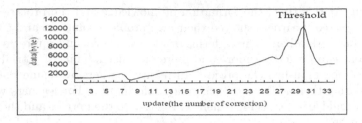

Fig. 4. Knowledge creation graph

This system was designed to save knowledge sources which learners created into History DB. Figure 4 shows quantitative of data which was stored in History DB. Knowledge created in the first stage increased quickly, and times went by, it decreased little by little. After that, as following process, we found the process of sophistication, which quantitative data became regularly. When threshold appeared, we allowed learners to access for revising of others' programming.

6   Conclusions and Future Works

The result we found in this study is that learning programming is more effective in the community setting than content-centered setting. Further, to harmonize community with plentiful content can be a better model for learning programming. Collaborative learning via Wiki system could be used not only learning programming but also learning in other areas of computer science. Especially, it is more valuable when learning necessitates diverse problem-solving skills or process of elaborating knowledge. Although this study was examined effectiveness of learning programming, especially, LOGO, using Wiki system, we expect that Wiki system can be developed for learning other computer programming language, such as C and JAVA. For the future research, we suggest that the study on developing navigation and interface for effective using of Wiki system is in need.

References

1. M. de los Angeles Constantino-Gonzalez and D. D. Suthers. Automated coachin of collaboration based on workspace analysis. In *Proceedings of the 36th Hawaii international Conference on System Sciences*, 2003.
2. K. Howell. *First computer languages*. PhD thesis, Colorado state University, 2003.
3. B. Leuf and W. Cunningham. *Wiki Way: Quick collaboration on the Web*. Addison-Wesley Longmann, April 2001.
4. D. Mattison. Quickwiki, swiki, twiki, zwiki and plone wars as pim and collaborative content tool. Technical report, British Columbia Archives, Canada, 2003.
5. T. S. McNeme. *From turtles to Tangible Programming Bricks : explorations in physical language design*, volume 8, pages 326–337. Pres Ubiquitous Computing, 2004.

6. S. Papert, D. Watt, A. Sessa, and S. Weir. Final report of the brookline logo project part : Project summary and data analysis. Technical report, Massachusetts Institute of Technology., 1979.
7. D. Shaffer. The use of logo in an introductory computer science course. *SIGCSE bulletin*, 18(4), Dec 1986.
8. D. C. Smith, A. Cypher, and K. Chucker. Making programming easier for children. *Interaction*, pages 60–67, 1996.
9. T. Takeda. and D. D. Suthers. Online workspaces for annotation and discussion of documents. In *Proceedings of the international Conference on Computers in Education*, 2002.

Analysing Graphic-Based Electronic Discussions: Evaluation of Students' Activity on *Digalo*

Einat Lotan Kochan

School of Education, Hebrew University of Jerusalem, Mount Scopus, Jerusalem, Israel
einat.lotan@gmail.com

Abstract. *Digalo* is a graphic based electronic discussion tool developed for educational purposes. These purposes are varied: learning to argue and discuss, learning through argumentation and discussion, and creating shared knowledge, are only some of them. This diversity, together with the unique graphic activity that *Digalo* requires, makes the analysis of *Digalo* e-discussions more complex compared to the analysis of other types of e-discussions (e.g. discussion forums). Models developed by educational researchers for analyzing electronic discussions, turn out to be insufficient for the analysis of *Digalo* activities, as they neglect some of the distinctive learning aspects *Digalo* activities contain. We therefore decided to develop a new method of analysis. This paper describes our considerations at the beginning of the development process, while focusing on the problems and challenges identified so far.

1 Introduction

Group discussion has long been recognized as an essential learning activity [5], [12], [17]. In the field of education it holds the potential not only for bringing on a cognitive conflict, or introducing the learner to new ideas, but also for the construction of shared knowledge [15], [16].

Many computerized tools have been developed during the last few decades to serve as platforms for communication between people who are remote in place and/or in time. Such tools use one or more communication channels (e.g. text, audio, video) and enable either synchronous or asynchronous communication. Another important differentiation is between tools that use verbal (or discursive) representations to support the discussion (ontologies, sentence openers, speech acts) and tools that use structural and graphical representations (discussion forums, discussion trees, argumentative maps). *Digalo* - a graphic-based discussion tool that is the focus of this paper - combines both kinds of representations. The rationale of this combination is that we see discussion as a valuable springboard to learning – both as process and as a goal.

The adoption of such tools in the educational context has generated the need to assess whether and how they promote learning, and to identify what kinds of activities they offer for teachers and learners. Some methods for the analysis of electronic discussions have been developed (e.g. [6], [8], [10]). However, most of these methods focus on analysing interactions in discussion forums and chats and were found inadequate to account for the special character of synchronous graphic-based discussions in which argumentative moves and structures are represented, as in *Digalo*-based discussions.

W. Nejdl and K. Tochtermann (Eds.): EC-TEL 2006, LNCS 4227, pp. 652–659, 2006.

2 From Technology to Methodology

The lack of adequate tools for analyzing *Digalo* e-discussions presented a major challenge throughout the DUNES project (IST-2001-34153, http://www.dunes.gr), which focused on developing and implementing *Digalo* – a graphic-based electronic tool for synchronous group discussions. The need for a sound and specially tailored model for the analysis and assessment of students' activities on *Digalo* - increased with the implementation of the tool in real educational contexts. We were committed not only to developing a reliable research tool that would account for the unique features of *Digalo* as a discussion tool, but also for supplying teachers with the appropriate instruments for the assessment of their students' learning through *Digalo*.

2.1 The Technology: Digalo, a Graphic-Based Tool for Electronic Discussions

Digalo is a software tool for knowledge sharing through visually supported discussions. Originally it was developed to support argumentative discussions, but it is not limited to any specific type/genre of discourse, and has been used for different goals.

Using *Digalo* consists of synchronously co-creating maps (see Fig.1) built of written notes inside different cards (represented by several geometrical shapes), as well as using different arrows to represent various types of connections between the cards or contributions (see also [7]).

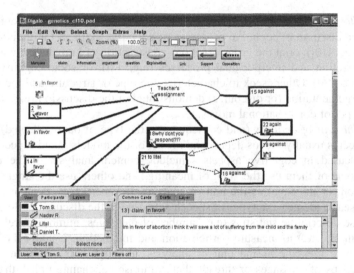

Fig. 1. A Digalo discussion map

These 'cards' and 'arrows' represent the ontology or the "grammar" of the discussion, which is usually predefined by teachers. The ontology constrains but also facilitates the discourse [4], [7] by guiding the learners to use specific speech acts (or argumentative moves). These speech acts, or moves correspond to the preferred type of discussion on each activity.

2.1.1 What Type of Discussion Does *Digalo* Intend to Promote?

Digalo was originally designed to promote argumentation. In the educational context argumentation is embodied in three activities:

(1) Logical-deductive reasoning [14].
(2) A form of rhetorical speech [18].
(3) A special form of dialogue – a reasoned debate or an argumentative discourse [1].

Digalo can serve for promoting all three types, but is mainly aimed to be used as a platform for argumentative discourse or interaction. In other words, *Digalo* is particularly designed to support and promote dialogical argumentative activities or systematic social reasoning [4]. The main goal of such activities in *Digalo* is to encourage critical dialogue, which is believed to foster understanding and accommodation of divergent viewpoints [11]. Although this aspect was recognized as a fundamental element in the development of *Digalo*, it was unclear in what ways we could demonstrate that such discussions actually take place. In other words, we lacked a method for analyzing *Digalo* discussions.

2.2 The Methodology: Analysis of Electronic Discussions

Models and methods for the analysis of electronic discussions differ in two main ways:

A) *The focus of analysis*: each model or method emphasizes a different aspect of the discussion: cognitive processes or cognitive skills at the individual level (e.g., [10]), or at the group level (co-construction of knowledge, e.g., [8]); interaction and interpersonal processes (e.g., [2]), or socio-cognitive aspects (e.g., [6]). Others seek to characterize the type or structure and the quality of argumentation (or discourse) demonstrated in the discussion (e.g., [1], [7]) or types of conversational moves.

B) *The unit of analysis* (and consequently, the type of data collected). This aspect is usually "focus dependent". Most of the models – and especially those focused in cognitive aspects - include content analysis of the messages. Some of them use the "unit of meaning" and others use the single contribution (or message) as the unit of analysis. In other cases, content analysis is used to identify the types of speech acts used in the discussion. Some models use descriptive statistics (e.g. number of messages, number of references to others, etc.) to measure participation and interaction. Usually they take the single message as the unit of analysis, although some of them recognize groups of messages or threads that comprise "exchange units" that become their unit of analysis.

Although models such as [10] and [6] incorporate several aspects of the electronic discussion, they are still deficient in coping with the complexity of such discussions [2] and especially of graphic-based discussions. In other words, they fail to reveal the quality of collaborative processes and the ways in which collaborators shape each other's reasoning [9].

De Laat and Lally [2] argue that due to their complexity, no single theoretical model is sufficient for analysing electronic interactions. To solve this problem they suggest using a multi-method empirical approach (based on triangulation of data). Further, Häkkinen et al. [9] discuss the need for *complementary* analysis methods to overcome the methodological complexity in the context of studying CSCL processes.

2.3 The Challenges: Why not Apply Existing Methods?

Digalo offers a complex activity, which consists of several different aspects that need to be taken in account when analyzed: the cognitive (content and discourse related) aspect [7]; the meta-cognitive aspect (awareness and reflection); the social and inter-personal aspect; the organization of the shared workspace [3]; the visual aspect or the

Table 1. Some essential aspects for the analysis of *Digalo* discussion maps as dealt with by 3 key-models

Aspect/ Indicator	Henri (1992)	Gunawardena et al. (1998)	Garrison et al. (2001)
Visual & practices with the tool: Discourse (emergent) structure.	None	None	None
Meta/cognitive & practices with the tool: Argumentative moves.	None	None	None
Meta/cognitive: Argumentative moves (discursive expressions)	Partially ("what was said").	Partially/ implied	Implied in cognitive presence & social presence
Management of the shared workspace (group and individual practices).	None	None	Partially (social presence)
Social: means of interaction (graphical and verbal)	Partially ("how it was said")	Partially/ implied	Partially (Social presence)
Social: type(s) of interaction and degree of interaction	Social and interactive dimension	None	Social presence
Social/cognitive: participation measurements and characteristics/ roles	Participative dimension	None	Social presence & cognitive presence
Cognitive (individual): ideas and concepts (quality, novelty, diverse sources).	Cognitive dimension	Partially / implied	Cognitive presence
Metacognitive: awareness and reflection (self, group, workspace, task), critical thinking	Partially (meta-cognitive dimension)	Implied	Partially (cognitive presence, social presence)
Socio Cognitive: knowledge sharing/ co-construction	Partially (social dimension)	Core of the model	Cognitive presence & social presence
Visual, social and cognitive: Breadth and depth of discussion	None	None	None
Moderation: types of moderation moves and their impact	None (teacher centered perspective)	None (student-student interaction)	Teaching presence
Moderation: students vs. teachers moderation	None	None	Teaching presence (teacher) implied in cognitive presence (students).

emergent structure of the discussion; the group (and individual) practices in using the tool and issues of facilitation and moderation of the group activity. The complexity is realized not only in the variety of different aspects, but also in the possible connections between them. Such connections imply that analysing from a narrow perspective (focusing on one or two aspects) might lead to a partial understanding of the *Digalo* discussions. Beyond these, the mode of communication possible through *Digalo* is unlike any familiar form of discussion (electronic or other), a fact that further complicates the analysis of *Digalo*-based discussions. In light of the above mentioned problem of complexity, these factors suggest that existing models and methods are insufficient or even inappropriate for analysing *Digalo*-based discussions. *Table 1* roughly demonstrates how some aspects, identified as essential to analysing *Digalo* activities, are "dealt with" by 3 key models: [6], [8] and [10].

While a proper empirical approach – like the multi-method investigation suggested by [2] and [9] - may assist in grasping the complexity of graphic-based electronic discussions, some challenges are still presented when known methods and models are applied for analysing discussions on *Digalo*. To mention just a few of them: (1) All known models are based on linear sequencing of the discussion – while in *Digalo* the discussion is not necessarily linear. As [3] showed learners tend to contribute both in parallel (independently) to each other or in response to each other. Different sub-discussions or separate threads of argumentation can develop independently of each other during the same activity, but unlike in discussion forums, it will not necessarily be visually evident. Furthermore, we found that sometimes students return to previously created contributions (cards) and change their contents (text). This forces us to use special tools and procedures to restore the linear sequence (timeline) of the discussion. (2) Most of the models we know measure processes at the individual level, while *Digalo* offers inevitable inter-subjective or group processes as well (implied by the shared workspace). Such processes are difficult to identify and measure. (3) Most models use a single unit of analysis, be it the single message, a whole segment of exchanges or any other form. Although some experiments in DUNES took this approach (e.g., [3], [7]), the complexity - resulting from the various processes taking place during the *Digalo* activity - entails a more flexible approach that incorporates a few different units of analysis or grain sizes [13]. Such an approach is difficult to develop and it turns the analysis work into a complex and time consuming process.

2.4   Towards a New Methodology for the Analysis of *Digalo*-Based Discussions

The challenges in developing a proper method for evaluating *Digalo*-based discussions result not only from the inability of existing methods and models to cope with the discussed complexity, but also from drawbacks in the implementation and use of the tool itself and the pedagogical method it accompanies. The main problem is that both teachers and students have difficulties in appropriating the tool as a mean of expression, or in accommodating the new language or type(s) of dialogue [11] integral to the use of the software.

Currently, most of the *Digalo* users are new to the pedagogical method of argumentative learning and to the software in particular, hence are still learning the language and are gradually acquiring essential skills; Consequently, any effort taken so far at evaluating the discussions has been affected by three interrelated factors: (a) the inappropriate use of the tool; (b) teachers' difficulty in fostering and delivering argumentative skills and practices, and consequently their students' difficulty in articulating their ideas in an argumentative manner; and (c) students' difficulty in using *Digalo* to collaboratively discuss issues. We believe engaging in a long-term research process will help us overcome this problem, mainly by training students and teachers and facilitating their learning of the tool. Our group is presently involved in a few EU-funded projects[1] that will hopefully guarantee such a process should actually occur.

Great efforts are still being invested in the process of developing a new method that will account for the several obstacles mentioned above. So far we have worked out a few principles that such a method should include: (1) using complementary research methods (e.g. quantitative and qualitative, direct measures and indirect interpretations, etc.); (2) using a few different units of analysis (a single contribution, a group or cluster of contributions, a whole map, and even a group of maps dealing with the same topic); (3) analyzing both at the individual level and the group level, trying to recognize processes of knowledge constructions at both levels; (4) referring to both content and structure (i.e. visual-spatial aspect) of the discussion; (5) accounting for both the process of discussion and the end-product (discussion map).

These principles, of course, require further processing in order to implement them synchronously, in a way that won't be too expensive in terms of cognitive load and time required. However, we believe these principles will serve as foundations for a future model of analyzing complex interactions such as those in *Digalo*. One weakness of these principles is that they do not guarantee a proper way to deal with the possible connections between different aspects of the *Digalo* discussions.

Up until now we have focused on theoretical and methodological aspects of developing an analysis and evaluation framework. One of the main challenges we will need to face is that of testing the validity and reliability of the model we are developing. Generally, validity will be addressed by the triangulation of data collected using different methods, as well as by comparisons of different objects (such as face to face lessons, students' individual products, etc.) we might find relevant for the evaluation of the different aspects. This in itself requires a thorough process of investigation that might take long. Reliability will be addressed by having teachers and researchers from different institutions participating in the development of the model and coding of data. Nonetheless, it is important to keep in mind that our main goal – regarding the implementation of *Digalo* - is primarily not to reach statistically valid conclusions but rather to develop an evaluation tool for teachers who use *Digalo* in their classrooms. We believe that different teachers have different goals when using *Digalo* in their classrooms, hence, the evaluation model must be flexible and comprised of different indicators that each teacher can choose from, in accordance with his/her specific goals. Only when we reach this phase, the model is rooted in pedagogical practices, will it be possible to consider this evaluation model through other "lenses" and test its validity and reliability.

3 Summary

Analysing *Digalo*-based discussion requires the development of an innovative methodology. This process of development might include the appropriation of existing

---

[1] ARGUNAUT (IST 027728), ESCALATE [020790 (SAS6)] and KP-LAB (IST 027490).

methods for analysis of electronic discussions, but also an investigation of the unique aspects of *Digalo* as a graphic-based argumentative-discussion tool, that existing models do not apprehend. Moreover, we are currently working to identify problems characterizing the specific application of *Digalo* in educational contexts. By doing so, we will progress towards a more comprehensive empirical method of analysis suitable for evaluating *Digalo* activities while dealing with their complexity. This will also contribute to our pedagogical understanding of the various educational activities which *Digalo* enables.

So far we have reached some insights about the factors needed to be taken into account in developing an appropriate analysis and evaluation model. These insights were formulated as the essential aspects of the (*Digalo*) graphic-based discussions and as the principles for the investigation of such discussions. These will serve in future developments of the envisioned analysis and evaluation framework. Such processes are essential elements that are taken up in the ARGUANUT project (http://argunaut.org).

Acknowledgement. I would like to thank Baruch Schwarz and Reuma De Groot for their support and faith in my work. I am also grateful to Amnon Glassner and Sarah Schrire for their insightful comments and to Raul Drachman and Rakheli Hever for their helpful contributions. This paper is a result of our group's (lead by Prof. Schwarz and Mrs. De Groot) participation in two EU-funded projects: the DUNES project (IST 2001-341653, 2001-2004, http://www.dunes.gr/) and the ARGUNAUT project (IST-027728, 2005-2008, http://argunaut.org/).

References

1. Baker, M. J. (1998). The Function of Argumentation Dialogue in Cooperative Problem Solving. In F.H. van Eemeren, R. Grootendorst, J. A. Blair and C. A. Willard (Eds.), *Proceedings of the 4th International Conference on Argumentation* (ISSA'98) (pp.27-33). Amsterdam: SIC SAT Publications.
2. De Laat, M. F., & Lally, V. (2003). Complexity, Theory and Praxis: Researching Collaborative Learning and Tutoring Processes in a Networked Learning Community. *Instructional Science*, 31, 7-39.
3. Diggelen, van, W., Overdijk, M. & Andriessen, J (2004). Constructing an Argumentative Map Together: Organizing Principles and Their Application. Paper presented at the ORD 2004 symposium, June 9-11 2004, Utrecht University, the Netherlands.
4. Diggelen, van, W., Overdijk, M., & De Groot, R. (2005). 'Say it Out Loud in Writing': A Dialectical Inquiry into the Potentials and Pitfalls of Computer Supported Argumentative Discussion, paper presented at CSCL2005, May 30 - June 4, 2005, Taipei, Taiwan.
5. Dillenbourg, P. (1999). Introduction: What Do You Mean by "Collaborative Learning", in P. Dillenbourg (Ed.), Collaborative Learning: Cognitive and Computational Approaches (pp. 1 –19). Oxford: Pergamon.
6. Garrison, D.R., Anderson, T., & Archer, W.(2001).Critical Thinking, Cognitive Presence, and Computer Conferencing in Distance Education. *American Journal of Distance Education*,15(1),7-23.
7. Glassner, A, & Schwarz, B., B. (2005). The Role of Floor Control and of Ontology in Argumentative Activities with Discussion-Based Tools. Paper presented at CSCL2005, May 30 - June 4, 2005, Taipei, Taiwan.

8. Gunawardena, C. N., Lowe, C. A., & Anderson, T.(1998).Transcript Analysis of a Com-
    puter-Mediated Conferences as a Tool for Testing Constructivist and Social-Constructivist
    Learning Theories. In: *Proceedings of the Annual Conference on Distance Teaching
    &Learning*. August 5-7 ,1998,Madison, Wisconsin.
9. Häkkinen, P., Järvelä, S. & Mäkitalo, K. (2003).Sharing Perspectives in Virtual Interac-
    tion: Review of Methods of Analysis. In: B. Wasson, S. Ludvigsen and U. Hoppe (Eds.),
    Designing for Change in Networked Learning Environments, Proceedings of the Interna-
    tional Conference on Computer-Support for Collaborative Learning 2003 (pp.395-404).
    Dordrecht: Kluwer Academic Publisher.
10. Henri, F.(1992).Computer Conferencing and Content Analysis. In: A. Kaye (Ed.), Col-
    laborative Learning Through Computer Conferencing: The Najaden Papers (pp.117-136).
    London: Springer-Verlag.
11. Keefer, M. W., Zeitz, C, M., & Resnick, L. B. (2000). Judging the Quality of Peer-Led
    Student Dialogue. *Cognition & Instruction*, 18 (1), 53-81.
12. Kuhn,D.(1991).The Skills of Argument. Cambridge: Cambridge University Press.
13. Lotan-Kochan, E. (2005). The Effect of Teacher Intervention on the Quality of Students'
    Discussion using Digalo: Developing and Testing an Evaluation Tool. Unpublished Mas-
    ters Dissertation, The Hebrew University of Jerusalem.
14. Means, M. L., & Voss, J. F. (1996).Who Reasons Well? Two Studies of Informal Reason-
    ing among Children of Different Grade, Ability and Knowledge Levels. *Cognition and In-
    struction*,14(2),139-179.
15. Scardamalia, M., & Bereiter, C.(in press).Knowledge Building: Theory, Pedagogy, and
    Technology. In K. Sawyer (Ed.),Cambridge Handbook of the Learning Sciences, New
    York: Cambridge University Press. [http://ikit.org/fulltext/KBTheory.pdf].
16. Scardamalia, M., Bereiter, C., & Lamon, M. (1994).The CSILE Project: Trying to Bring
    the Classroom into World 3.In: K.McGilly (Ed.),Classroom Lessons: Integrating Cognitive
    Theory and Classroom Practice, (pp.201-228), Cambridge: MIT Press.
17. Veerman, A. L.,Andriessen, J. E. B., & Kanselaar, G. (2000).Learning through Synchro-
    nous Electronic Discussion. *Computers &Education*,34 (2-3),1-22.
18. Voss, J.F., & Van Dyke, J.A. (2001).Argumentation in Psychology: Background Com-
    ments. *Discourse Processes*, 32 (2&3),89-111.

LeActiveMath

Erica Melis, Jeff Haywood, and Tim J. Smith[*]

German Research Institute for Artificial Intelligence (DFKI)
66123 Saarbrücken, Germany
University of Edinburgh
Tel.: +49 681 302 4629
melis@dfki.de

Abstract. LeActiveMath (Language-Enhanced, User-Adaptive, Interactive eLearning for Mathematics) is an interdisciplinary European effort that develops an internationalized Web-based intelligent e-Learning system for mathematics that can be used in high school and university as well as for self study. The many technological innovations serve a moderate constructivist and competency-based pedagogical approach. LeActiveMath integrates a number of services and tools and advances the state-of-the-art in semantic search and other usages of semantic representations, presentation of maths on the Web, course generation, coherence of material, exercise selection, modeling of motivation, modeling of competencies, annotation and structure of exercises, feedback and tutorial dialogues in exercises, First evaluations are completed and large ones ahead.

1 Introduction

LeActiveMath (*Language-Enhanced, User-Adaptive, Interactive eLearning for Mathematics*) is a European research project (STReP) funded by the 6th Framework Programme-Priority "Information Society Technologies", key action *Technology-Enhanced eLearning* in call FP6/2002/IST/1. This project is coordinated by the German Research Center for Artificial Intelligence.

The goal of LeActiveMath is to develop an innovative Web-based intelligent e-Learning system for mathematics that can be used in high school and university as well as for self study. The content and some input evaluation tools are specific for mathematics, but the main technology is not restricted to mathematics. The benefits of the new technologies are demonstrated with mathematics for which currently moderate constructivist approaches to education are even less common than for other domains. On the one hand, mathematics has the advantage of being clearly structured and to address concepts with a relatively clear semantics. Mathematics, on the other hand, poses additional challenges, e.g., in the delivery of formulas on the Web.

Since Web-technologies alone are insufficient LeActiveMath is a multidisciplinary effort which includes disciplines such as artificial intelligence, pedagogy,

---

[*] This publication was funded by the 6th Framework Program of the European Union (Contract IST-2003-507826). The author is solely responsible for its content.

W. Nejdl and K. Tochtermann (Eds.): EC-TEL 2006, LNCS 4227, pp. 660–666, 2006.

techniques and experiences from Intelligent Tutoring Systems (ITS) and representations developed for eLearning and the semantic Web. LEACTIVEMATH provides a synthesis of both worlds – ITS and eLearning – and it is one of the few mature and ready-to-use, multi-lingual, intelligent Web-based learning environments (not to be confused with Learning Management Systems). LEACTIVEMATH features generic technologies and services that are interoperable and can be reused.

LEACTIVEMATH effectively supports learning and stimulates the learner's initiative by providing interaction tools, (multi-modal) feedback and tutorial dialogues. It can suggest different levels of guidance, can follow a chosen pedagogical strategy, and reacts to the learner's motivational state. It puts the student in a more responsible position for her learning, grants students' self-guidance and supports meta-cognition where possible.

2   Pedagogical Fundament of LEACTIVEMATH

The purely instructivist approach seems to fail in many learning situations. Learning mathematics should not only aim at *solving* the problem but also at *thinking mathematically* and *arguing* about the correctness or incorrectness of the problem solving steps and involved methods, to perform simple and complex *computations*, etc. This is the idea behind **competency-based** pedagogy which provides dimensions on what to train and to evaluate, e.g., in the PISA studies.

The constructivist view of learning is based on the theory that knowledge cannot be directly taught to a student but has to be constructed by every single student with respect to her prior knowledge and experience [5]. Recent research suggests that the instructivist point of view is less efficient than a **moderate constructivist** view on learning and instruction. The term *moderate constructivism* defines a teaching and learning approach that mixes many of the fundamental features of (pure) constructivism with more instructional elements. For an eLearning environment this definition translates to a mixture of constructivist and instructivist elements in a problem-oriented learning environment. Learning is conceived as an individual, mostly active and self-regulated, situational and social process that is strongly influenced by the student's motivation and zone of proximal development.

Moreover, moderate constructivism addresses authentic problems, multiple contexts and perspectives, and learning with instructional support. It reconciles the strict constructivist with cognitive and instructional principles. This model suits the practical requirements of schools and its effectiveness has been shown in numerous empirical investigations.

3   How to Work with LEACTIVEMATH

With LEACTIVEMATH a student can choose one or several learning goals, a context and a pedagogically granted learning scenario. After such 'planning' activities she receives personalized learning material including dynamically produced narrative bridges such as summaries and introductions, as well as personalized suggestions. This helps in classroom differentiation as well as in focused self-learning. Even more actively, the learner can assemble her course manually from elements of existing courses.

An adaptive pretest with the integrated Siette system initializes the student model. The student can inspect her student model and this can help to motivate and guide meta-cognitive activities. The student's motivation and affects, e.g., being bored, unfocused, or overwhelmed, is monitored and reacted to, e.g., by providing more animated or less difficult examples and exercises, by changing the tutorial dialogue strategy, or by providing more or less interaction facilities in menus.

In the learning process, the student works on various kinds of interactive examples and exercises with the additional possibility to access dynamically linked factual knowledge and explanations. During the problem solving process she will receive feedback or be involved in a multi-modal tutorial dialogue in which the student or the system asks questions, points to problems, and gives hints. When the student makes a mistake while exercising, feedback and hints support her in discovering and correcting a misconception. Overall, LeActiveMath aims at combating shallow learning through engaging students more explicitly in the knowledge construction process.

Apart from exercises that come with tool support (concept map, search, function plotter, computer algebra systems (CAS)), other tools are available through a tool menu. For instance, she can assemble the material in her own way, she may consult the semantic lexicon, she can acquire printed material, she can enageg in an exploration and negotiation process with her student model, or she can use a CAS or another back-engine to solve problems she states herself. An input editor eases the input of mathematical expressions in exercises and the dictionary. Its simple usage helps the student to focus on the problem solving rather than on the handling of the system.

How are the Pedagogic Ideas Realized? In LeActiveMath, the following features contribute to the moderate constructivism:

- truly interactive problem solving with back-engine support;
- open, inspectable learner model (OLM) and negotiation that can be initiated by the learner. This fits a Piagetian line and involves the learner continually managing the process of comprehending new information and assimilating/accomodating it.
- inclusion of situational, emotional, and motivational features into the learner model;
- the indication of related concepts and learning objetcs as one of the results of the semantic search;
- Socratic tutorial dialogue with active turn-taking by student which allows the learner to take the initiative in discussions;
- suggestions that can be actively followed by the student;
- the possibility for the student to actively choose problems and topics to learn and to request more material or information;
- the design of the content.

4   Reusable Learning Tools and Components

Quite a number of isolated tools for learning have been developed world-wide: search tools, highlighting tools, exercise back-engines, simulation tools, mind map tools, modeling tools, assessment tools, CASs. Now, LeActiveMath integrates a number of components and tools, and has developed an open architecture and event framework (for asynchronous communication) shown in Figure 1. It eases the integration of components and tools and a collective use and updating of one and the same student model.

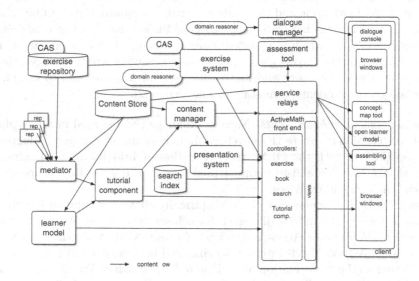

Fig. 1. LeActiveMath' coarse architecture

Technically, some of the components directly interact via procedure calls: e.g.. the Tutorial Component and the tutorial dialogue component; the input editor with the knowledge base and exercise back-engines; the interactive concept map with the knowledge base and the student model; the dictionary with the knowledge base and the learner model. All components report events which can be processed by other components. Web services communicate via events and XML-RPC.

Similar to its predecessor system ActiveMath [4], LeActiveMath relies on the semantic XML representation standard for mathematics, OpenMath, which is augmented with pedagogical metadata. The various tools and components build on that foundation and provide/use the semantics and/or the metadata information: the presentation engine adapts the content presentation according to metadata and customizes mathematical notation (e.g., to the country's common notation); the input editor produces OpenMath; the semantic lexicon can search for (a combination of) mathematical expressions, metadata, and text; semanitcs can be dragged into applications; the interactive concept map evaluates the user's input against metadata and semantics; the course generator utilizes metadata for its decisions; a mediator translates metadata of external repositories to make the course generation service available externally; the exercise repository is one particular open repository that is used.

Student modeling. Student modeling has been a research topic in artificial intelligence since the mid 1970's. Various techniques have been used to recognize and adapt to the student's behavior and knowledge. LeActiveMath takes up some of the most recent research challenges in student modeling:

It investigates the use of a range of factors for student modeling relating to affect, attitude, motivation and the student's goals It employs Bayesian belief networks for modeling the motivation and affect of the learner. A competency model has been developed which is updated using a variant of Dempster-Shafer. LEACTIVEMATH further investigates open learner modeling which has been shown to improve the involvement and motivation of students, and also to encourage reflection on the student's own state of knowledge [2].

Natural language enhancements. Natural language (NL) is used in many places in LEACTIVEMATH, where the novelties include natural language dialogue for the negotiations with the OLM, the generation of bridging and introductory texts that help to establish mental transitions in the generated courses, and tutorial dialogues in exercises.

Since tutorial dialogues have been empirically shown to improve learning in human tutoring [1], tutorial dialogues have been used in the American tutoring systems AutoTutor Atlas-Andes, and Circsim/APE. Now, the tutorial dialogue in LEACTIVEMATH integrates principled and flexible dialogue management based on the "Information State Update" approach of Trindi and planning of multi-turn tutorial dialogue strategies, in the domain of symbolic differentiation. It employs a dedicated domain reasoner as well as NL-understanding and NL-generation and copes with the student's initiative and student input that mixes informal language and mathematical formulae.

5   Formative Evaluation

As LEACTIVEMATH brings together a large number of innovative tools and components the successful implementation of these components and their integration is crucial to the success of the system. User-testing, expert evaluation, and usability testing of LEACTIVEMATH have been performed throughout the systems development to ensure that the goals of the system are met. Evaluations have taken place in Germany, Great Britain, and Spain. We include summary results from an initial formative evaluation conducted at the University of Edinburgh, UK. The results of this study has been used to improve the implementation.

Design. The formative evaluation focused on the user interface and its associated tools. This evaluation was lab-based with users working collaboratively with the evaluator to critique and assess the system (see [3] for details of this methodology). The users worked through a series of unguided tasks and were asked to describe their thought processes i.e. "Think Aloud", critique the system, and discuss improvements whilst they used the system. Users were also required to fill in pre- and post-use questionnaires about their experience of using LeActiveMath.

Results. Eleven students (6 male; mean age 19.45 years) from University of Edinburgh first year Mathematics courses took part in the first evaluation. All users were experienced in learning calculus, using computers and the Web, and most had previous experience of maths software although the tasks they had performed were mostly limited to generating graphs and inputting mathematical formulae. These students were considered representative of the university-level target users of LeActiveMath.

Overall the ratings of LeActiveMath were very positive. On average, their experience of using LeActiveMath was rated as "enjoyable". All but one of the participants said they would use LeActiveMath again and, on average their experience of using LeActiveMath was rated as "better" than that of existing maths software. All participants would recommend LeActiveMath to their peers irrespective of whether they had previous experience of maths software or not.

LeActiveMath was rated as more practical than existing software for performing a variety of tasks: learning a maths concept, solitary tutorials performed in a classroom, solitary tutorials at home, supplementing bookwork, and revision. LeActiveMath was rated as being as practical as existing software for group tutorials at home, entering mathematical formulae, and generating graphs. The only tasks for which LeActiveMath was rated less practical were group tutorials in a classroom and performing mathematical computations although this could be because the participants were not introduced to the CAS.

Ratings were also collected for the ease and usefulness of specific components within LeActiveMath. As mentioned previously (section 3 paragraph 3), LeActiveMath implements a *moderate constructivist* approach to teaching by providing contextualised feedback and hints in response to exercise answers and syntactical errors made when constructing formulae using the input editor. The hints provided during exercises were rated as "quite" useful and the input editor was rated as "very" useful. Users commented found the feedback useful for identifying their conceptual errors and essential for identifying syntactic errors.

LeActiveMath's semantic dictionary can be used to find definitions of mathematical concepts either via a search interface or by following hyperlinked concepts direct from content pages. The dictionary was rated as "quite" useful and easy to use by users. Several usability issues were identified during the evaluation that made it difficult for users to realise the full potential of the dictionary. However, even with these limitations users quickly developed a strategy of constantly referencing the dictionary for definitions and examples. The design flaws are currently being fixed and the resulting version of the semantic dictionary should function as an integral component of LeActiveMath.

6 Conclusion

LEACTIVEMATH brings together a number of "cutting edge" components in an attempt to maximise their benefit to the student. This benefit has been iteratively evaluated during development of LEACTIVEMATH to ensure that each component is optimized in its implementation and remains user-centred. A large-scale trans-national summative evaluation of the system will take place after those optimisations.

Details of the system, its components and tools are described in a number of articles which are not cited because of space limitations. Please visit our web site www.leactivemath.org or www.activemath.org for more specific publications.

References

1. M.T.H. Chi, S.A. Siler, Jeong H, T. Yamauchi, and R.G. Hausmann. Learning from human tutoring. *Cognitive Science*, 25:471–533, 2001.
2. V. Dimitrova, J. Self, and P. Brna. Applying interactive open learner models to learning technical terminology. In *8th Conference on User Modelling*, 2001. Springer-Verlag.
3. A.J. Dix, J.E. Finlay, G.D. Abowd, and R. Beale. *Human-Computer Interaction*. Prentice Hall, 1998.
4. E. Melis, E. Andrès, J. Büdenbender, A. Frischauf, G. Goguadze, P. Libbrecht, M. Pollet and C. Ullrich. ACTIVEMATH: A Generic and Adaptive Web-Based Learning Environment. *International Journal of Artificial Intelligence in Education*, 12(4):385–407, 2001.
5. J. Piaget. *Equilibration of Cognitive Structures*. Viking, New York, 1977.

Language Technology for eLearning

Paola Monachesi[1], Lothar Lemnitzer[2], and Kiril Simov[3]

[1] Utrecht University, Uil-OTS
Trans 10, 3512 JK Utrecht, The Netherlands
{Paola.Monachesi}@let.uu.nl
[2] University of Tübingen
Wilhelmstr. 19, 72074 Tübingen, Germany
{lothar}@sfs.uni-tuebingen.de
[3] LML, IPP, Bulgarian Academy of Sciences
Acad. G. Bonchev 25A, 1113 Sofia, Bulgaria
{kivs}@bultreebank.org

Abstract. Given the huge amount of static and dynamic content created for eLearning tasks, the major challenge for extending their use is to improve the effectiveness of retrieval and accessibility by making use of Learning Management Systems. The aim of the European project *Language Technology for eLearning* is to tackle this problem by providing Language Technology based functionalities and by integrating semantic knowledge to facilitate the management, distribution and retrieval of the learning material.

1   Introduction

In the *Language Technology for eLearning project* (LT4eL), we address one of the major problems users of ever expanding LMSs will be confronted with: how to retrieve learning content from an LMS. We tackle this problem from two different but related angles: from the content end and from the retrieval end.

On the content side, the fast growing content cannot be easily identified in the absence of systematic metadata annotation. It should thus be common practice to supply metadata along with the content, however this is a tedious activity which is not widely accepted by authors, as part of their tasks. The solution we offer is to provide Language Technology based functionalities, such as a key word extractor and a glossary candidate detector. They allow for semi-automatic metadata annotation on the basis of a linguistic analysis of the learning material. We provide these functionalities for all the nine languages represented in our project, that is Bulgarian, Czech, Dutch, English, German, Maltese, Polish, Portuguese and Romanian.

On the retrieval side, the standard retrieval systems, based on keyword matching, only consider the queries. They do not really take into account the systematic relationships between the concepts denoted by the queries and other concepts that might be relevant for the user. In the *LT4eL* project, we use ontologies as an instrument to express and exploit such relationships, which should result in

W. Nejdl and K. Tochtermann (Eds.): EC-TEL 2006, LNCS 4227, pp. 667–672, 2006.
© Springer-Verlag Berlin Heidelberg 2006

better search results and more sophisticated ways to navigate through the learning objects. An ontology of at least 1000 concepts for the domain of *ICT and eLearning* is being developed as well as an English vocabulary and English annotated learning objects. Language specific vocabularies for the other languages of the project are created which will be linked to the ontology as well as to the metadata of the learning objects. The ontology should facilitate the multilingual retrieval of learning objects.

The functionalities developed within the *LT4eL* project could be integrated in any open source LMS, however, for validation purposes the ILIAS Learning Management System (www.ilias.de) has been adopted.

The contribution of the project consists thus in the introduction of new functionalities which will enhance the adaptability and the personalization of the learning process through the software which mediates it. In particular, the system enables the construction of user-specific courses, by semantic querying for topics of interest through the ontology. Furthermore, the metadata and the ontology are the link between user needs and characteristics of the learning material: content can thus be personalized. In addition, the functionalities allow for retrieval of both static (introduced by the educator) and dynamic (learner contribution) content within the LMS and across different LMSs allowing for decentralization and for an effective co-operative content management.

The project is in its intial phase since it started in December 2005 and it will last for 30 months.

2   Semi-automatic Metadata Generation Based on Language Technology

In eLearning, we deal with learning objects of varying granularity. A learning object should be accompanied by metadata which describes it: the "Learning Object Metadata" (LOM) [1] has become the most widespread and well-known standard for the encoding of the metadata. The aim of the *LT4eL* project is to improve the retrieval and accessibility of content through the identification of the learning material by means of descriptive metadata. To this end, we employ available Language Technology resources to develop functionalities which facilitate the semi-automatic generation of metadata from content. The result will be two modules: (1) semi-automatic selection of keywords; (2) selection of definitory contexts, to be used for glossary entries, which can be used stand-alone, as web services, or integrated into Learning Management Systems.

2.1   Key Word Detection and Extraction

Keywords which describe the topics and contents of a document are essential for the retrieval and accessibility of this document and are therefore a key feature of the metadata. A software assistant will support authors and content managers in selecting appropriate keywords.

The keyword selector can draw on quantitative and qualitative characteristics of keyword candidates. Keywords are supposed to characterize the topic(s) of a learning object. They therefore tend to appear more often in a document than can be expected if all words would be distributed randomly. Keywords tend to cluster in certain documents and will not appear at all in other documents. A statistics which is frequently used to model the distribution of words in texts is Poisson or, alternatively, a mixture of Poissons (cf. [2]). While the distribution of function words is close to the expected distribution under these models, good keyword candidates deviate significantly from it. The score of this deviation can be used as a statistics by which the lexical units are ranked (cf. [3]).

A second distributional characteristics of keywords is their *burstiness*. Good keywords tend to appear, within documents, in clusters. Once a keyword appeared in a text, it tends to appear in shorter intervals. After a while, the word might disappear and appear – and burst – again, if the topic is resumed. Reference to a certain topic is a local phenomenon. The concept of term burstiness can be formalized by measuring the gaps between the individual occurrences of each term in the text. Sarkar et al. use a combination of two exponential functions the distribution within burts and outside bursts. Through an iterative process the variables values in these functions are modified to optimize the fit between observed and expected distribution values.Optimal values for these three variables are derived once the fitting reaches a stable maximum. These values turn out to be a good indicator for the "keywordiness of words in texts ([4]).

In the project, we employ linguistically annotated texts since it has been shown that the results of the keyword selection, measured against the performance of human readers, improves significantly if the text is annotated linguistically (cf. [5]).

We will experiment with different statistics. These statistics are:

- tf.idf, a standard term weighting measure in Implementation Retrieval
- Residual Inverse Document Frequency (cf. [3]).
- Term burstiness (cf. [4])

Our experiments are based on the assumption that the distributional characteristics of good keywords are similar to that of good terms, in the sense used in Information Retrieval.

The output of the various statistics will be compared to manual keyword annotation, performed by experienced annotators. A comparison of high ranking keyword candidates with keywords selected by humans will approximate recall and precision values. The (mix of) statistics which we will use in the final system will be selected on the basis of these evaluation results.

2.2   Detection of Candidates for Glossary Entries

Research on the detection and identification of definitory contexts has been pursued mainly in the context of question answering systems, where finding answers to definitory questions is a particularly difficult problem (cf. [6], [7]). In the field of eLearning, this work is relevant for the construction and maintenance of glossaries.

Glossaries are an important kind of secondary index to a text. They can be seen as small lexical resources which support the reader in decoding the text and understanding the central concepts which are conveyed. A glossary can be built on the definitory contexts which are presented in the learning objects themselves.

A glossary supports the non-linear reading of learning materials. The reader will not necessarily start at the place where the author defined the central terms and therefore be in need of a definition when he first encounters the term. An exploratory and self-guided learning style is supported (cf.[8]).

Glossaries should be derived from the learning objects in order to capture the exact definition which the author of these documents uses. This definition in many cases overrides a more general definition of the term.

The linguistic structure of definitory contexts is language specific. But within each language, there is not so much variation in the patterns of these contexts. In the project, definitory contexts are identified and learned in a bottom-up manner. First, a substantial amount of definitions are identified and annotated manually in the learning objects which are the asset of this project. From these examples, local grammars with the complexity of regular languages are abstracted. These language-specific local grammars are applied to a test set from the same language in order to estimate their coverage (cf. also [10]). A major issue will be the precision of these methods: it has been shown that too simple local grammars also capture text snippets which are not definitions (cf. [9]). This has to be taken into account when drafting and refining the local grammars for the involved languages.

3 Enhancing eLearning with Semantic Knowledge

An additional aim of the project is to enhance LMSs with semantic knowledge in order to improve the retrieval of the learning objects. We employ ontologies, which are a key element in the architecture of the Semantic Web, to structure the learning material. The ontology layer presents the appropriate level of abstraction over the meaning in general (upper ontologies) and in concrete domains (domain ontologies). We integrate the use of ontologies to structure, query and navigate through the learning objects which are part of the LMS. We take two groups of users into account: (1) Educators who want to compile a course for a specific target group and who want to draw on existing texts, media etc.; (2) Learners who are looking for contents which suit their current needs, e.g for self-guided learning.

The primary key for the access of contents are their metadata. In many cases, learners additionally want to consult the full text of a learning object. However, the search with a standard search engine too often leads to results which are undesirable. The set of documents might be too large and too unspecific (low recall, low precision of the retrieved documents). We improve the retrieval of the learning objects with the use of ontologies which will be integrated within the

LMS to structure the learning material. Each learning object will be indexed by an ontology 'chunk' that will allow for more detailed search. An ontology chunk is a part of the classes and relations encoded in the ontology which are consider relevant to the topic of the learning object — see [12].

In our work, the ontology is closer to a taxonomy, that is a set of concepts arranged in Is-a hierarchy. The ontology allows for the classification of learning objects since they will be connected to a set of concepts in the ontology. This classification will allow ontological search, i.e. search based on concepts and their interrelations within the ontology. Furthermore, multilingual search for learning objects will be possible. In this case the ontology plays the role of Interlingua between the different languages. Thus the user might specify the query in one language and get learning objects in other language(s).

Within the *LT4eL* project, we are developing a domain ontology in the area of our sample learning materials, that is *ICT and eLearning*. Furthermore, vocabularies related to the languages in the project will be aligned to this ontology. The development of the domain ontology will be done as a specialization of a upper-level ontology — DOLCE (see [11]). As criteria for the selection of this upper-level ontology, we can point to the following: (1) the ontology should be constructed on rigorous basis; (2) it should be easy to represent it in an ontological language such as RDF or OWL; (3) there are domain ontologies constructed with respect to it; (4) it can be related to lexicons - either by definition, or by already existing mapping to lexical resource. All of the above points apply to DOLCE.

The alignment of vocabularies with the ontology will ensure an appropriate way of searching over the same learning materials in different languages. Inference mechanisms can be assumed for searching the appropriate learning objects. We expect that the integration of ontologies within an LMS will facilitate the construction of user specific courses, by semantic querying for topics of interests; will allow direct access of knowledge; will improve the creation of personalized content and will allow for decentralization and co-operation of content management.

4 Conclusions

With *LT4eL*, we want to use Natural Language Processing techniques and resources to enhance the effectiveness of eLearning systems and processes.

On the one hand, we want to support authors of learning materials in the tedious task of metadata generation. This part of the task should neither be avoided by the author, nor should it detract too much from the original task, the generation of high-quality learning material. On the other hand, we want to employ language resources, in particular ontologies, to help users find the best learning material they can get to satisfy their current information needs.

We consider the diversity of languages in the European context not as an obstacle to an international eLearning infrastructure, but as a challenge. By tackling multilingual issues we want the broaden the horizon of the learner beyond what is available in his native language and in English.

For the sake of validation, we will integrate the tools and resources into the ILIAS Learning Management System, but we will make them available for other LMS as well. In the validation process, we will take four dimensions into account in order to evaluate the success of the project: (1) the usability of the platform itself, and in what way it is affected by the integration of the new functionalities; (2) the pedagogical impact of integrating the functionalities; (3) the consequences of incorporating multilinguality; (4) the social impact on virtual learner communities - and crucially, how this is affected by multilinguality.

References

1. *Final Draft, Standard for Learning Object Metadata*, IEEE, 2002 – P1484.12.1
2. K. Church and W. Gale. 1995. *Poisson mixtures*. In: Natural Language Engineering. Vol. 1, No 2, pp 163–190.
3. K. Church, W. Kenneth and W. Gale. 1995. *Inverse Document Frequency (IDF): A Measure of Deviations from Poisson*. In: Proc. of Third Workshop on Very Large Corpora.
4. Avik Sarkar, Paul H. Garthwaite, and Anne De Roeck. 2005. *A Bayesian Mixture Model for Term Re-occurrence and Burstiness*. In: Proc. of the Ninth Conference on Computational Natural Language Learning (CoNLL-2005). Ann Arbor, Michigan. ACL. pp 48–55.
5. Anette Hulth. 2003. *Improved Automatic Keyword Extraction Given More Linguistic Knowledge*. In: Proc. of the 2003 Conference on Empirical Methods in Natural Language Processing. pp 216–223.
6. S. Miliaraki and I. Androutsopoulos. 2004 *Learning to identify single-snippet answers to definition questions*. In: 20th International Conference on Computational Linguistics (COLING 2004). pp. 1360–1366
7. S. Blair-Goldensohn, K. McKeown and A.H. Schlaikjer. 2004. *Answering definitional questions: a hybrid approach*. In: New directions in question answering. pp. 47–58
8. B. Liu, C.W.Chin and H.T. Ng. 2003. *Mining topic-specific concepts and definitions on the web*. In: WWW 03. Proc. 12th Internat. Conf. on World Wide Web. pp 251–260
9. Ismail Fahmi and GosseBouma. 2006. *Learning to Identify Definitions using Syntactic Features*. In: Proceedings of the EACL 2006 workshop on Learning Structured Information in Natural Language Applications.
10. Judith Klavans and Smaranda Muresan. 2001. *Evaluation of the DEFINDER System for Fully Automatic Glossary Construction*. In: Proc. of AMIA Symposium 2001.
11. Claudio Masolo, Stefano Borgo, Aldo Gangemi, Nicola Guarino, Alessandro Oltramari, Luc Schneider. 2002. *WonderWeb Deliverable D17. The WonderWeb Library of Foundational Ontologies and the DOLCE ontology*. Preliminary Report (ver. 2.0, 15-08-2002).
12. Atanas Kiryakov and Kiril Simov. 1999. *Ontologically Supported Semantic Matching*. in the Proceedings of NoDaLiDa'99 (Nordic Conference on Computational Linguistics). Trondheim, Norway.

An Approach for Online Assessment in the Multinational EU Project: POOL Project Organization OnLine

Anke Mündler[1], Frank McCurry[2], Peter Haber[1], and Enrique Benimeli-Bofarull[1]

[1] Salzburg University of Applied Sciences
Urstein Süd 1, 5412 Puch / Salzburg, Austria
{amuendler.tks2002, peter.haber,
enrique.benimeli}@fh-salzburg.ac.at
[2] Galway Mayo Institute of Technology
Dublin Road, Galway, Ireland
frank.mccrurry@gmit.ie

Abstract. This paper deals with the different kinds of assessment possibilities in a virtual environment, assessing engineering students' project management knowledge, skills and competencies developed during online project management training. The first part will provide information about the EU Leonardo da Vinci II project: POOL, Project Organisation OnLine and the second part will focus on the assessment model, developed for the POOL project as well as the used methods.

In industrial projects it is widely common to have distributed teams, which have to communicate and work effectively. Therefore it is necessary to prepare engineering students to cope with real live project situations. As a matter of fact engineering students are not always aware of the possible cultural and virtual communication problems particularly in an international setting. They have to develop other skills for online communication and processing as in face to face meetings.

Keywords: Project Management, Intercultural Communication, Virtual Collaboration.

1 Introduction

The POOL project is a Leonardo Da Vinci EU project which intends to achieve two major outcomes:

First, innovative curriculum design aimed eventually at the main beneficiaries, the students. The work packages centered around and prototypically implemented in the student-industry project result in independent modules each addressing specific aspects of online project management such as quality assurance, intercultural communication, presentation skills, virtual group collaboration, and standardization of project documentation as shown in figure one.

Second, the experiences gained in the course of this project feed directly into the online handbook. This serves as a guideline and reference source for curriculum designers at higher educational institutions as well as in companies and will support the implementation of transnational online project management (training) [1].

W. Nejdl and K. Tochtermann (Eds.): EC-TEL 2006, LNCS 4227, pp. 673–678, 2006.

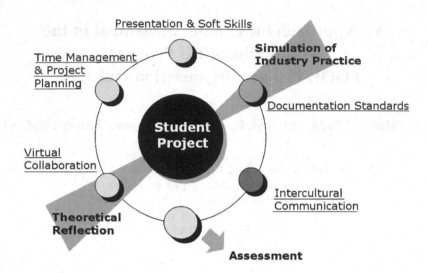

Fig. 1. The workpackages which are centered around the student project, with special focus on the assessment workpackage [1]

Owing to the modular structure, the resulting curriculum for online project management training allows enough flexibility for its concrete implementation in a wide range of higher educational institutions.

The centerpiece of the POOL project as mentioned above was the student project. Three student teams from three countries (Austria, Finland and Romania) were developing an Open Distributed Sensor Environment (ODSE). During their 3rd academic year students had to attend online project management courses. Each workpackage as mentioned above had a distinct area of project management, and provided an online course to the students during the year.

During the whole course students gained knowledge in Virtual Project Management (VPM) areas like project planning and time management, virtual collaboration, presentation and soft skills, documentation standards and intercultural communication. In addition to the technical knowledge students gained through the project, they were equipped with soft skills required for a virtual environment and non face-to-face / online communication. As it is increasingly common to use online tools for communication and meetings in industry projects, it is especially necessary to prepare engineering students for the future and equip them with soft skills, needed in a virtual environment and intercultural communications.

The success and the efficacy of the work packages and the overall module had to be assessed, reviewed and improved. The purpose of the assessment work package was to develop techniques, select suits of software and platforms, applying them in the integrated course structure of the POOL project. Furthermore the work package developed assessment strategies for each course, the final assessment and the evaluation of the overall module.

2   Assessment in the POOL Project

Because of the nature of project management, it provides challenges in providing on-line assessment of a number of skills and knowledge developed in each course. The courses provided by the different work packages have been taught in different ways depending on the content. Diversification of learning and assessing students is one advantage of online assessment and furthermore the independent delivery of content and the instant feedback increases the learning curve of a student [2].

An assessment should not be seen as a tool of pressure, to keep students silent and attentive but it should be used and seen to support students learning through formative and summative assessment and feedback [3]. There is always the need to measure, grade and evaluate students' achievements during and after a course. Assessment has great significance in education, since it is an ongoing process throughout the whole course [4, 5].

Especially in the POOL project where students are taught project management, continuous online assessment and feedback are very important both, to reflect the student's development and the achievement of each course and to guarantee quality and success of the overall model.

In general terms an assessment should be [6]:

- Valid, should review how well the assessment measures the intended student learning outcome in terms of choice of techniques, marking scheme and criteria, duration and coverage.
- Reliable, which implies that same results occur no matter when the assessment is processed and no matter if a different assessor, accomplishes the assessment.
- Fair: "allow for students of both genders and all backgrounds to do equally well. All students should have equal opportunity to demonstrate the skills and knowledge being assessed." Other aspects concerning fairness are the assessed content, given time, student effort and the transparency to students. Teachers should not abuse their role and power to take somehow "revenge" of the students. The assessment should be clear stated and there should not be any hidden questions. Students should not have to guess what is in the teachers mind.
- Secure in the case of online assessment

To establish a valid, reliable and fair assessment it is absolutely necessary to define clear learning outcomes of each course and assessment criteria [7]. Assessment criteria are necessary to compare and evaluate the assessment of prove of validity and reliability, as well as fairness [8]. As this is common in the traditional classroom it is the same procedure in a virtual environment.

After matching the assessment criteria to the learning outcomes it is necessary to establish the assessment for the course, using different methods and question types. Question types matching the thinking levels of Bloom's Taxonomy [9, 10] were used to assess the students knowledge, competencies and skills developed after each course.

Evaluating the higher level thinking like synthesis and evaluation skills can were realized through explanation questions, like a description of a scenario or essays. Assessment methods like formative and summative, criterion and non criterion referenced and self/group/peer assessment, are nearly used the same way as in the traditional classroom [11, 12].

Figure two shows the formative assessment after each module, depicted as light grey boxes. The final summative assessment, which covers all the different modules before, is processed together with the final student project presentation and demonstration.

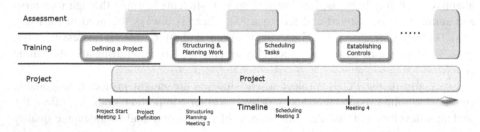

Fig. 2. Assessment, Training and the Project are done parallel to optimize learning by doing

The complete assessment model of the POOL student project comprises formative and summative assessment of each course including the platform usability with clearly defined criteria and finally the Minutes Sheet, which could be formative as well as summative.

For instance in the summative assessment part there was a combination of skills which had to be assessed, technical knowledge and presentation skills.

An important feedback for tracking is the minutes' sheet, which was used to get information from the students after a meeting, to ascertain their understanding of the progress and decisions which were made in the meeting. Through the use of this kind of online form, misunderstanding and duplication could be avoided, and problems were discussed again.

In the first stage of evaluating the assessment model of the POOL project two online assessments were done using the course *Project Planning and Time Management – WP4*. Doing the first assessment, the VLE platform was used to create the assessment supporting the QTI standard, where just basic question styles could be used (MCQs, short answer,…). To validate the questions/assessment concerning validity, reliability and fairness, a second assessment was established by using external software and integrated in the VLE as a SCORM package. More interactive questions (Hot Spot, Drag & Drop,…) were possible and therefore the feedback from the students was very positive.

The POOL project will end in October where all the results including the curriculum and the developed handbook as well as the courses and assessment results will be published on the POOL website [1] for further information. At this stage the curriculum and handbook are compiled and reviewed.

Table 1. The POOL Assessment Model

1. Summative assessment	2. Formative assessment	3. Platform usability	4. Meetings
Final project presentation Presentation and Soft Skills WP 5	*WP 3 – Virtual Collaboration Knowledge* Assessment VC Rubric	Time, spent on the platform Hours per week: Hours per month: Compared to others, and to the project schedule	Minutes sheet: Group/Self/Peer assessment, for project progress and collaboration review
Final demonstration System is working Student technical competency Knowledge	*WP 4 – Project Planning and Time Management* Knowledge assessment Student project plan, report	Uploaded documents VC Rubric Posts, emails, Sticks Usage as well in the VC Rubric	
Project report Documentation Standards WP 7	*WP 5 – Presentation & Soft Skills* Final presentation Knowledge assessment		
Poster (optional) Synthesis and Evaluation skills Full understanding Abstraction	*WP 6 – Documentation Standards* Knowledge assessment Project plan & additional documents		
	WP 7 – Intercultural Communication Knowledge assessment Minutes sheet, communication tools		

3 Conclusion

Assessment is a very important part in online teaching and online learning. The assessment methods listed in the student project of POOL are now undergoing test. Feedback from the students about the methods and strategies used will be evaluated and, if necessary, used to modify the techniques that are used for assessing higher level skills in a VLE. The overall evaluation of the POOL project will show how such an online project management course can contribute to successfully complete a distributed, international student project.

The assessment area of e-learning needs to further evolve, so that teachers can more fully exploit the advantages that are inherent in current technology where distance and diversity is no barrier. Generally, in the recent past, more effort has been expended on the development of course content and course delivery in VLE's than in developing suitable and effective online assessments. This area of e-learning is now attracting more attention and is increasingly becoming more and more importance.

References

1. POOL Project Organisation OnLine, http://www.pool.fh-sbg.ac.at, Salzburg University of Applied Sciences (2004)
2. CSHE: Why consider on-line assessment?. Australian Universities Teaching Committee. Retrieved May, 2006, from http://www.cshe.unimelb.edu.au/ assessinglearning/docs/Online.pdf
3. Race P. and Brown S. 500 Tipps on Assessment. RoutledgeFalmer (2004)
4. Howell, S.L, Hricko, M.: Online Assessment and Measurement, Foundations and Challenges. Information Science Publishing (2005)
5. Howell, S.L, Hricko, M.: Online Assessment and Measurement, Case studies from higher education K-12 and corporate. Information Science Publishing (2005)
6. NCERL: Reliability, validity, and fairness of classroom assessments. North Central Regional Educational Laboratory, Illinois. Retrieved March, 2006, from http://www.ncrel.org/ sdrs/areas/issues/methods/assment/as5relia.htm
7. Moon, J.: Linking Levels, Learning Outcomes and Assessment Criteria. Exeter University, Bologna Seminar (2004)
8. Assessment Criteria. University of Technology Sydney. Retrieved March, 2006, from http://www.iml.uts.edu.au/assessment/criteria/.
9. Bloom B.S.: Taxonomy of Educational Objectives, Handbook I: The Cognitive Domain. (1956)
10. Anderson, L.W., Krathwhol, R.D.: Taxonomy for Learning, Teaching, and Assessing, A: A Revision of Bloom's Taxonomy of Educational Objectives. Allyn & Bacon (2000)
11. Bull, J., McKenna, C.: Blueprint for Computer-Assisted Assessment. 1st edt. RoutledgeFalmer (2003)
12. Bull, J.: Computer assisted assessment: Impact on higher education institutions. Educational Technology & Society, 2(3) (1999).

Extending SCORM to Create Adaptive Courses*

Marta Rey-López[1], Ana Fernández-Vilas[1], Rebeca P. Díaz-Redondo[1],
José J. Pazos-Arias[1], and Jesús Bermejo-Muñoz[2]

[1] Department of Telematic Engineering, University of Vigo, 36310, Spain
{mrey, avilas, rebeca, jose}@det.uvigo.es
[2] TELVENT Interactiva S.A., Sevilla, Spain
jesus.bermejo@telvent.abengoa.com

Abstract. Current e-learning standards have been designed to provide reusability of educational contents and interoperability between systems. Besides these features, content personalization is also necessary, although current standards do not fully support it. In this paper, the ADL SCORM (Sharable Content Object Reference Model) adaptation possibilities are studied and an extension to this standard is presented in an effort to create adaptive courses that should be personalized before shown to the student.

1 Introduction

Due to the rapid progress of e-learning, diverse standardization efforts have emerged to allow reusability of educational objects and interoperability between systems. Among them, the ADL SCORM (Sharable Content Object Reference Model) [1] standard has reached great acceptance, since it brings together several standards of diverse institutes in different fields of e-learning. However, reusability and interoperability are not enough and adaptation of learning elements to suit user's characteristics is also necessary.

Concerning content adaptation, SCORM repeatedly mentions the importance of personalization in education. However, its current adaptation abilities are restricted and focused on two main aspects. On the one hand, SCORM allows to define several content organizations for the same course. The LMS (Learning Management System)[1] is responsible for deciding which one suits the user profile better, before he/she begins the learning experience. On the other hand, sequencing information allows to establish a set of rules —mainly based on the completion of the objectives of the activities— used by the LMS to decide which one is the next activity to be shown. However, sequencing information cannot be considered adaptivity [2] since it is centred in the instructor rather than in the learner.

As these abilities are not enough to offer personalized courses to the student, in this paper, a solution is exposed to extend SCORM with the purpose of providing it with adaptation ability. So as the course creator can be able to offer a series of options instead of a fixed one in some points of the course, indicating, for each of them, the characteristics of the target user. As a result, adaptive courses are created to be adapted

---

* Partly supported by the R+D project TSI 2004-03677 (Spanish Ministry of Education and Science) and by the EUREKA ITEA Project PASSEPARTOUT.

[1] In e-learning terminology, the term LMS is used to refer to the system designed to deliver, track, report on and manage learning content, learner progress and learner interactions.

W. Nejdl and K. Tochtermann (Eds.): EC-TEL 2006, LNCS 4227, pp. 679–684, 2006.

according to the user's characteristics before he/she studies it, although they can show its default behaviour when adaptation is not possible.

In this paper, the basis of this proposal and its scenario are firstly presented (Sec. 2). Next, the adaptation parameters, consisting in some user's characteristics, and the mechanism to obtain the values for these parameters from the user profile are introduced in Sec. 3. In order to provide SCORM with adaptivity, two extensions are proposed, and the one which permits to adapt the structure of the course is exposed in Sec. 4. Finally, Sec. 5 discusses some approaches related to this proposal and exposes the conclusions and further work .

2   Scenario

For the objective of this paper, the most relevant SCORM component is the SCORM Content Aggregation Model (CAM) which defines three main elements used to build a learning experience from learning resources (Fig. 1). An **asset** is an electronic representation of media, more than one asset can be collected together to build other assets. If this collection represents a single launchable learning object that utilizes SCORM RTE to communicate with a LMS, it is referred to as a **SCO**. The third component is called a **Content Organization**, a map that represents the intended use of the content through structured units of instruction (Activities). To deliver these elements to the LMS, SCORM defines the Content Package, compressed file containing the physical resources and a structured inventory of the content of the package, called manifest.

As SCORM adaptation abilities are very limited, in this paper a solution is suggested. Its aim is providing SCORM courses with adaptivity, based on a set of adaptation parameters obtained from the user profile (Sec. 3) at two levels (Fig. 1). Adaptivity at **SCO level** is achieved defining a new type of SCO: the self-adaptive SCO, which self-configures based on certain adaptation parameters [3]. Adaptation at **activity level** consists in offering a set of options for some of the activities, i.e. the objective of an activity can be achieved in different ways, depending on the user's preferences and background. The best option for the user should be chosen based on a set of adaptation rules for this activity, which relate the concrete subactivities to adaptation parameters (Sec. 4).

Fig. 1 shows the scenario for this proposal, where three different roles can be identified: the vocabulary creator, the content creator and the user. The two systems needed to make the educational process possible are also shown: the ITS and the LMS. It is worth mentioning that this proposal takes place into a broader work whose objective is developing t-MAESTRO (**M**ultimedia **A**daptive **E**ducational **Sys**Tem based on **R**eassembling TV **O**bjects), an Intelligent Tutoring System (ITS) for t-learning — education over Interactive Digital TV [4]. This ITS will be alluded all through the explanation, but the extension proposed equally works using any other one.

First, the **vocabulary creator** extends the SCORM Data Model with new vocabularies of adaptation parameters and provides t-MAESTRO with inference rules. These rules permit to obtain the actual values of these parameters from the user's characteristics stored in his/her profile. They also make possible that the proposed extensions work independently of how the user profile is stored in the ITS. Next, the **content creator** composes SCORM-conformant courses. He/she is responsible for searching, organiz-

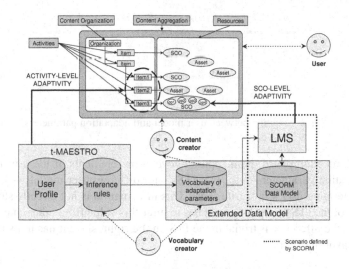

Fig. 1. Target scenario

ing and labelling learning content. Concerning the extension proposed, he/she should know the available adaptation parameters and generate the appropriate adaptation rules for the activities and SCOs based on these parameters.

t-MAESTRO maintains the user profile, which stores the user's preferences, knowledge and history. The existence of this profile is basic in order for the ITS to keep up to date the actual values of the adaptation parameters using the inference rules for these parameters provided by the vocabulary creator. These values allow t-MAESTRO to apply adaptation rules in order to adapt the course to user needs at activity level. Finally, the **LMS** has the responsibility of storing the actual values of the adaptation parameters and showing the course to the **user**. This system has to provide the values of adaptation parameters to self-adaptive SCOs when requested, so as they can resolve the adaptation rules and show the appropriate behaviour to the student [3].

3   Adaptation Parameters

Every user characteristic stored in the user profile could be used as an adaptation parameter. However, apart from constituting an unmanageable amount of information for a human course creator, these characteristics are different depending on the ITS used and, as aforementioned, a major concern of this proposal is that it should work in different ITSs. Bearing this in mind, the vocabulary of adaptation parameters will be common to all the ITSs and each one should deduce the values for these parameters from its user profile information. In order to carry out this task, a set of inference rules are needed. These rules are provided by the vocabulary creator and establish relationships between the concrete elements of the ITS user model and the adaptation parameters. A set of adaptation parameters considered relevant in the field of t-learning are presented in [3].

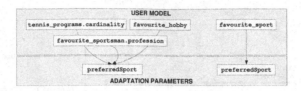

Fig. 2. Mapping between user model and adaptation parameters

In Fig. 2 an example of the mapping between the elements of the user model and some adaptation parameters —for two ITSs with different user models— is shown in order to determine user's favourite sport. This information is not directly stored in the user model of the ITS on the left, so, it has to infer this value from other characteristics. Conversely, the inference is trivial in the ITS on the right, since it has in its user model the user's favourite sport.

4   Extension at Activity Level

In this section, one of the extensions proposed is described, to obtain adaptivity at activity level. This serves to allow the course creator to establish a group of activities that all achieve the same learning objective. The learner does not need to study all of them but only those that match his knowledge state or are best adapted to his/her preferences. To make this selection possible, the course creator should provide a group of adaptation rules. Each rule consists of some conditions that are fulfilled by the student if this option is appropriate for him, and the action to be performed when it happens.

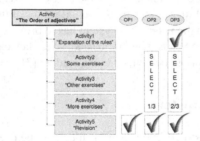

Fig. 3. Example of adaptation at activity level

In Fig. 3 an example is depicted to understand what has been explained. The learner is following a Spanish course and the lesson he/she has to study next is about the order of adjectives. This lesson consists of 5 activities: the first one exposes the theory, from second to fourth several exercises are proposed and the last one deals with revision. The course creator has established three adaptation rules: if the user has a Romance language as a mother tongue or has a high writing level in any of these languages, he/she should already know how to place the adjectives, that is why the the only activity needed is the revision one (OP1 in Fig. 3). If this is not the case, but the user have at least a medium level reading Spanish, he/she will have some basics about the order of adjectives, so, only one of three exercises activities and the revision one should be studied (OP2). If none of these conditions evaluates to true, the student has to study two of three exercises activities and the revision one (OP3). These rules are shown next in pseudocode.

```
if ((motherTongue IN (french, italian, portuguese)) OR (french.writing_level >= 7)
    OR (italian.writing_level >= 7) OR (portuguese.writing_level >= 7))
then
    show(activity5);
if (spanish.reading_level >= 5)
then
    show(1/3(activity2, activity3, activity4) AND activity5);
else //Default option
    show(activity1 AND 2/3(activity2, activity3, activity4) AND activity5);
```

As shown in this example, the actions to carry out if one of the conditions evaluates to true do not need to be fixed ones, on the contrary, they are expressed as a set of activities related through a logical expression to be decided by t-MAESTRO using the metadata describing those activities.

In order to express this set of adaptation rules, this proposal adds a new category to the SCORM manifest, named <adaptation>. It can be placed under several tags in the manifest: as a child of <organizations> —with the information needed for selecting the most appropriate organization—, as a child of <organization> —containing all the adaptation information for a single organization— or as a child of <item>— embodying the adaptivity information related to this activity.

5   Discussion, Conclusions and Future Work

One of the most promising fields to offer personalization on the field of e-learning is Adaptive Hypermedia, which tries to overcome the problem of having users with different goals and knowledge by using information represented in the user model to adapt the contents and links being presented to the user [5]. Several proposals try to introduce adaptivity in current e-learning standards. For example, the KOD (Knowledge on Demand) project [6] builds on an extension of the content packaging specification, for the description, in a common format collections of learning objects and rules to determine how they should be selected for different learner profiles.

On the other hand, some research works suggest expressing learning strategies at the competence level rather than at the level of the specific resources, as instead done by the SCORM manifests. The idea of [7] is to introduce at the level of the learning objects some metadata that describe both their pre-requisites and effects. Alternatively, a new element (*adaptivity*) within the educational block of metadata schemas is defined in [8] to express some aspects such as competencies of the learner before or after studying this educational element, learning styles and special needs.

In this paper, an extension to the ADL SCORM standard has been described, in order to permit the creation of adaptive courses, which present a set of options to decide the most appropriate one for the student. Its difference with respect to the aforementioned proposals is that it permits offering the student concrete alternative learning elements when those presented by default are not appropriate for him/her. This proposal presents some advantages related to the structure of the suggested scenario and the encapsulation of adaptation information. On the one hand, it is modular both for individuals and systems. Each individual implied in the process has its own function. Moreover, it works for every ITS on reception as long as the vocabulary creator had previously provided it with inference rules according to its user model. Concerning the systems developed up to now, it allows running adaptable courses in systems which do not understand the proposed extensions.

As a future line of work, a method to compare the user profile stored in t-MAESTRO with metadata describing learning contents is needed, with the purpose of selecting the most suitable activities when more than one is offered in a given option. In addition to that, t-MAESTRO should be able to update the user profile based on the information collected by the LMS in the Data Model, related to the objectives of the studied courses, and the metadata accompanying the elements the learner has studied. In order to make this process easier, an ontology based on SCORM CAM to allow t-MAESTRO reasoning over those elements has been already defined in [9].

References

1. ADL: Sharable Content Object Reference Model. http://www.adlnet.org (2004)
2. Abdullah, N.A., Davis, H.: Is Simple Sequencing Simple Adaptive Hypermedia? In: HYPERTEXT '03, ACM Press (2003) 172–173
3. Rey-López, M., Fernández-Vilas, A., Díaz-Redondo, R.P., Pazos-Arias, J.J., Jesús Bermejo-Muñoz: Adaptive Learning Objects for T-learning. In: ICWL 2006, Malaysia (2006)
4. Rey-López, M., Fernández-Vilas, A., Díaz-Redondo, R.P.: A Model for Personalized Learning through IDTV. In: AH2006, Ireland (2006)
5. Brusilovsky, P.: Methods and techniques of adaptive hypermedia. UMUAI (Special issue on adaptive hypertext and hypermedia) 6(2-3) (1996) 87–129
6. Sampson, D., Karagiannidis, C.: Re-using Adaptive Educational e-Content: the KOD VLP. In: ICCE'02, New Zealand (2002)
7. Baldoni, M., Baroglio, C., Patti, V., Torasso, L.: Reasoning about learning object metadata for adapting SCORM courseware. In: EAW'04, The Netherlands (2004)
8. Conlan, O.: The Multi-Model, Metadata Driven Approach to Personalised eLearning Services. PhD thesis, Trinity College, Dublin (2005)
9. Rey-López, M., Díaz-Redondo, R.P., Fernández-Vilas, A., Pazos-Arias, J.J.: *Entercation* Experiences: Engaging Viewers in Education through TV Programs. In: EuroITV 2006, Greece (2006)

The AtGentive Project:
Attentive Agents for Collaborative Learners

Claudia Roda[1,3] and Thierry Nabeth[2,3]

[1] American University of Paris, Computer Science Department,
112, rue du Bac, 75007 Paris, France
croda@aup.fr
[2] INSEAD Centre for Advanced Learning Technologies,
Bvd de Constance, 77305 Fontainebleau Cedex, France
thierry.nabeth@insead.edu
[3] AtGentive consortium
http://www.atgentive.com/

Abstract. Attention, which intervenes at many different levels such as the perception of the environment and the allocation of cognitive resources, appears to represent one of the key factors of learning and working performance. This poster presents AtGentive, a project which aims at investigating the use of agent-based ICT systems for supporting the management of the attention of young or adult learners in the context of learning and collaborative environments.

1 Introduction

Attention appears to represent one of the key factors of learning or working performance. The most effective learners and knowledge workers are often those people capable of filtering and selecting the most relevant information and at allocating their cognitive resources in the most appropriate manner.

This ability to manage efficiently attention can be considered as even more critical in the new learning and working contexts [see for example 1, 2, and 3]. For instance, in an online learning setting, the learners are more on their own; they have less guidance; and cannot situate themselves with others and adjust their behaviour. Even in presence of strong commitment, it is harder to evaluate optimal time allocation, and effectiveness of learning or collaborative processes. In this context, the learners have fewer points of reference to situate themselves, may not receive any direct pressure from a tutor or from their peers, and can more easily procrastinate, or engage into learning activities that are very ineffective. In the "knowledge economy", employees are engaged in a multitude of projects involving a variety of actors from different horizons with which they have to collaborate. They also have to process more information and solicitation than in the past, originating from a variety of sources, and available in different forms (news, email, instant messaging, etc.). Finally, they are more autonomous and more responsible for their lines of actions. As a consequence, the knowledge workers have more risk to be overwhelmed by too much information and too many interruptions, and also to manage inefficiently the execution of the

W. Nejdl and K. Tochtermann (Eds.): EC-TEL 2006, LNCS 4227, pp. 685–690, 2006.
© Springer-Verlag Berlin Heidelberg 2006

many tasks they have to accomplish for their work [1]. These new conditions typically results in a situation of information and cognitive overload for the learners and for the knowledge workers that represent a real challenge that need to be addressed so as to facilitate the setting up and the adoption of new methods of learning and work in the Information Society.

The AtGentive project is born from the idea that such a challenge can be addressed with the help of ICT systems that are aware of this attentional dimension, and that are able to support the individuals or the groups at filtering and selecting the most relevant information for them and helping them allocating their cognitive resources. Practically, the objective of this project is to investigate how to design such attention supporting systems, and in particular to explore how artificial agents, that may be embodied into artificial characters, can be used to provide more active and intelligent support to attention.

The first part of this poster will present the AtGentive project: what are the objectives of this project, what are the principles that will be used to design attention supporting systems for elearning and collaborative working context. The second part of this poster will present how these principles are going to be applied to design and to test "attention support" in two applications: (1) **AtGentSchool**: an elearning application for child education; (2) **AtGentNet**: an advanced virtual community platform supporting knowledge exchange of communities of distributed managers. The last part of this poster will conclude, and will indicate the future work.

2   A Project Aiming at Supporting Individual and Group Attention

2.1   An Overview of the AtGentive Project

The AtGentive project explores the links between learning and attention and it includes: (1) the definition of a model of attention for the learner (low-level & high level, individual & social); (2) different mechanisms to capture or infer information about the state of attention (both at a low and high level) of the user in agent-enhanced collaborative learning platforms; (3) Intervention mechanisms using attentive agents informed about users attentional state, providing guidance, helping users to better manage their attention to achieve their learning objective, reducing information overload, and therefore improving the effectiveness of the learning & working process.

More specifically, the important foci of the project include:

- A model of attention of the user, and the support of this attention by attention informed systems. A deep understanding of attention (importance, impact, processes to support it, etc.) will be elaborated
- The "sensing" of the environment and in particular the different means for collecting information that can be used to profile the user's attentional state.
- The design of a set of mechanisms for supporting the management of the attention of users and groups (for instance enhancing the user perception).
- The design of an artificial agent cognitive architecture able to proactively and intelligently support the user attention.

Practically, the technical infrastructures that will be designed in this project will consist in ICT platforms that are enhanced with different components (intelligent or not) providing different level of attentional support such as:

- Components and approaches helping to enhance the <u>perception</u> of the user by filtering or emphasizing the information presented or delivered to the user, and therefore contributing to the reduction of information and cognitive overload. Examples of such approaches include the information design of the spaces facilitating the user perception, the use of visual tags emphasizing the most important items, or the ordering of the information according to the importance of the item (relevance for the user, freshness of the item, popularity of the item).
- Components and agents facilitating the <u>organization</u> of learning and work processes. For instance, this support can be provided for the execution of activities in presence of multitasking, frequent interruptions, and large information sources. Examples of such mechanism include enhanced notification mechanisms and interruption management (e.g. delaying a notification, or delivering it in a way that does not break the concentration of the user), and the support of task resumption (saving and restoring a context for a task that has been interrupted).
- Intelligent agents and mechanisms able to <u>coach</u> the learners or the knowledge worker in reaching higher level of performance in managing their attention. These agents will in particular help the user to acquire attention management skills. Examples of these agents and mechanisms can include the provision of statistics displaying the different activities of the user and the time he/she has allocated to them, but also proactive agent interventions making suggestions to the user (for instance the agent may suggest a new focus, or may encourage the user to adopt a more effective learning or communication practice)

2.2 A First Sketch of the AtGentive Internal Architecture

The agents, which may appear embedded in a artificial characters, are able to profile the learners' attentional state (short or long term) by observing their actions. On the

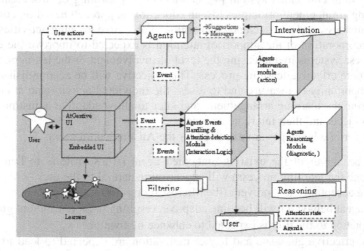

Fig. 1. A first sketch of the AtGentive internal architecture

basis of this profile, Atgentive agents can assess, analyze, and reason about user's attention, and provide assistance (for instance automating some tasks) and proactive coaching (assessment, guidance, stimulation, etc.).

Fig 1. represents a first sketch of the AtGentive architecture that will be further elaborated and then implemented during the project.

The main components of this architecture are:

- The attention detection module which monitors and profiles the learner's attentional state.
- The attention reasoning module. This module represents the main intelligent reasoning part. Its function is to (1) Assess the situation; (2) Identify and build a selection of possible assistance and coaching interventions.
- The Intervention module. The function of this component is to select and execute the interventions that are the more appropriate (having the maximum impact on the user, and do not unnecessary distract the user).
- The interface. The user interface will rely on well designed interaction portals and artificial characters (artificial agents may intervene as embodied agents) that are attention "friendly".

3   AtGentSchool and AtGentNet: Two Applications Applying the AtGentive Principles

Two different "attentive" applications are used to validate the principles elaborated in the AtGentive project: (1) **AtGentSchool**: an active elearning platform for child education; (2) **AtGentNet**: an advanced virtual community platform.

3.1   AtGentSchool: An "Attentive" Active Elearning Platform for Child Education

AtGentSchool is an e-learning application for child education that will be built upon on the existing Ontdeknet system [4]. Ontdeknet is a learning environment founded on learning arrangement principles [5], an educational approach based on constructivism, situatedness, and active engagement into collaborative learning activities.

The incorporation of the support of attention is expected to improve the effectiveness of these systems by increasing the level of involvement of the learners, and leading to a more effective learning process. This objective will be accomplished by having the opportunity to measure and to assess the individual activity and attention patterns, during the learning arrangement, and later to allow adaptive adjustments to the learning objects and their interconnections.

A number of advantages are expected for the AtGentSchool users:

- The behaviour of the existing embodied agent (whose role is to help children through the learning process) will appear more natural to the user, which will enhance acceptance and prevent (the Microsoft dog) irritation.
- The agent behaviour will become adaptive, resulting in more efficient guidance
- Adaptation to the user is expected to enhance motivation
- More effective guidance and higher motivation are expected to lead to more effective learning experiences

3.2 AtGentNet: An "Attentive" Advanced Virtual Community Platform for Supporting Knowledge Exchange

AtGentNet will consist in the design of an advanced virtual community platform supporting knowledge exchange of communities of distributed managers, relying on a model structuring of the communication using spaces currently implemented in the ICDT platform [6].

The incorporation of the support of attention in the ICDT platform will result in a set of mechanisms helping to enhance communication and knowledge exchange inside the platform.

Examples of mechanisms include:

- Advanced communication filtering and management mechanisms helping to reduce the knowledge and information overload associated with interaction with the other members of the community.
- Social awareness and translucence mechanisms displaying the activity happening in the community, helping to orient the attention of the users.
- Advanced monitoring capabilities (capturing the actions of the users, and basic filtering about these behaviours conducting to the generation of events that can be exploited by human or artificial agents)
- Artificial agents having some capacities to observe and to reason about the environment and about the users and to intervene proactively.
- "Attentional" expertise, allowing the agents to support managers in managing their own attentional state, both at the low level, and at the higher cognitive level.
- Artificial character interface, displaying agents as an anthropomorphic characters.

4 Conclusion and Future Work

The project has already started, with the involvement of the end users, to draft a series of scenarios. Such scenarios explore different ways to provide support for attention in an ICT platform. A few of the mechanisms have already been incorporated into first prototypes.

The AtGentive project is still at a too early stage to draw any definitive conclusions. However we have already observed that the concept of attention, by providing a new angle of analysis taking into account deeply human cognition, appears to be very useful to guide the design of mechanisms addressing the real issues that people are facing today (such as information overload, and the complexity of user-computer interaction). In some cases the concept of attention has provided us with a new angle of analysis of existing mechanisms that were not initially intended for supporting attention.

The second phase of this project, and its validation with the different pilots (one in schools, the second in a learning network), will help us to better understand which are the mechanisms supporting attention that are the most useful, and in particular will help us to assess the effectiveness of the new mechanisms (such as agent-based support) that will be elaborated for this projects.

Acknowledgments. The work described in this paper was partially sponsored by the EC under the FP6 framework project Atgentive IST-4-027529-STP. We would like to acknowledge the contribution of all project partners including: Laurent Ach, Albert A. Angehrn, Jaroslav Cech, Eugeni Gentchev, David Kingma, Pradeep Kumar Mittal, May Liem, Ivana Mala, Inge Molenaar, Koen Molenaar, Benoit Morel, Thierry Nabeth, Barbora Parrakova, Paul Rudman, Hari Siirtola, Toni Vanhala, Maurice Vereecken, Deng Ye, Mary Zajicek.

References

1. Davenport, Thomas and Beck John (2001); The Attention Economy; Harvard Business School Press, 2001
2. Roda, C., & Nabeth, T. (2005). The role of attention in the design of learning management systems. Proceedings IADIS International Conference CELDA (Cognition and Exploratory Learning in Digital Age), Lisbon, Portugal, 148 - 155.
3. Roda, C., & Thomas, J. (2006). Attention aware systems: Theories, applications, and research agenda. Computers in Human Behavior, 22(4), 557–587.
4. Ontdeknet: http://www.ontdeknet.nl/
5. Simons, P.R.J., Van der Linden, J.L., & Duffy, T. (Eds.) (2000). New learning. Dordrecht: Kluwer.
6. Albert A. Angehrn (2004); Designing Effective Virtual Communities Environments: The ICDT Platform; INSEAD CALT Report 10-2004

Meaningful Pedagogy Via Covering the Entire Life Cycle of Adaptive eLearning in Terms of a Pervasive Use of Educational Standards: The aLFanet Experience

Olga C. Santos and Jesus G. Boticario

aDeNu Research Group, Artificial Intelligence Dept., Computer Science School, UNED,
C/Juan del Rosal, 16. 28040 Madrid, Spain
{ocsantos, jgb}@dia.uned.es
http://adenu.ia.uned.es/

Abstract. Learners have different learning styles, background knowledge, interests and alternative evolution of their learning over time, which makes ineffective offering the same packaged course to each learner. Learning should be a user-centred process focused on learning activities adapted to learner's needs and preferences. However, authoring of adaptive courses traditionally requires massive customisations and complex design procedures. A methodological approach to support authors in designing reusable, platform independent, objective-based and adaptive courses has been defined at aLFanet project (IST-2001-33288). This proposal is only possible if educational standards (IMS-LD, IMS-MD, IMS-QTI, IMS-CP and IMS-LIP) are used. To test our approach, we have built a prototype which considers the full eLearning cycle (design, publication, use and auditing) based on pervasive use of the educational standards. In this paper, we describe the authors' experience in aLFanet as well as the main lessons learned from running a course at UNED.

Keywords: Metadata and Learning, Learning Objects, Learning Activities, Learning Design, Semantic Web, Pedagogy guidelines, Educational standards, Design templates, Adaptive eLearning.

1 Introduction

Learning should be a user-centred process focused on learning activities and objectives which can be adapted to learner's needs, preferences, and learning evolution over time. To support this adaptive approach based on educational standards design guidelines are needed. A practical experience has been addressed by the aDeNu research group at aLFanet project (IST-2001-33288) to provide adapted online course delivery based on pervasive use of standards (IEEE-LOM, IMS-LD, IMS-CP, IMS-QTI and IMS-LIP) and several user modelling techniques in a multi-agent architecture. The purpose here is not only to facilitate the implementation of courses based on explicit didactic methods (i.e. learning objects, learning activities and learning design) but also to face the entire life cycle (design, publication, use and auditing) of the learning process by offering adapted courses to each individual learner [1]. aLFanet allows the design of adaptive instructional design scenarios with

W. Nejdl and K. Tochtermann (Eds.): EC-TEL 2006, LNCS 4227, pp. 691–696, 2006.

advanced pedagogical models described in terms of standards. These adaptive scenarios designed by the course authors are combined with runtime adaptive tasks which take into account the actual use of the course by students. Furthermore, authors get sensible reports of the course based on learners' interactions by comparing the design and the expected results with the actual use and performance.

In this paper we describe the work done in aLFanet project to help authors translate the pedagogical and adaptation requirements to the learning process via the definition of design templates, learning scenarios and the use of educational standards.

2   Authors' Experience in aLFanet

The design phase is the starting point for the learner's driven process based on a strong pedagogical support and the combination of design and runtime adaptations. This process is performed thanks to the support given by the educational standards. It requires a four step process. First, to create the course materials as a set of learning objects. Second, to add metadata to those learning objects in order to be properly used in the course. IEEE-LOM/IMS-MD allows to specify what are the features of each of the learning objects used in the course. The third step is to define the instructional design (pedagogical support) to be applied in the course, which should be guided by learning objectives. To facilitate the specification of learning scenarios it is advisable to use learning design templates [4]. Finally, the fourth step is to build an adaptive scenario for the course, which allows delivering the course adapted to the individual learner needs from the combination of design and runtime adaptations.

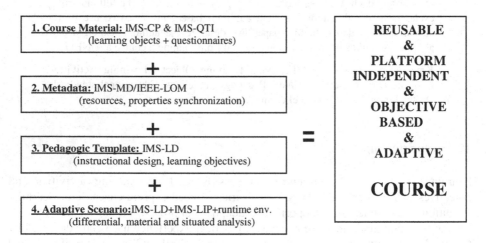

Fig. 1. Design phase process

Educational standards help to describe the learning process in a structured and organised way and makes possible to reuse the course in any compliant platform. To facilitate authors the description of the learning process, a template was designed at aLFanet. The purpose here is to use typical instructional arrangements for concept learning, assumed to be generic and applicable for any situation across problem domains. Concept learning approach [2] was selected because it is one the most used design setting and a considerable amount of experience based on research and practice has been accumulated so far.

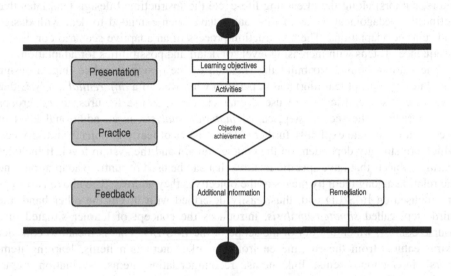

Fig. 2. Pedagogical guidelines for the concept learning template (high level activity diagram)

Figure 2 shows the three instructional design tactics (presentation, exercising/ practicing and feedback) valid for all types of concept learning (i.e. concept definition, concept classification and causal-effect understanding). The *Presentation* tactic implies to arrange explanation for each learning objective. The *Practice* tactic includes activities to ensure that learners are able to understand a particular concept. The template supports two scenarios in the practice tactic: pure **self-learning** and **explicit collaboration**. It's up to the designer to select and work out one or both scenarios for each practice. *Feedback* tactic aims to inform the learner about the level of performance, to determine remediation and/or to motivate.

Moreover, in aLFanet we have specific scenarios, explicitly described in terms of IMS-LD made up of learning activities and materials (packaged in IMS-CP), well known types of users with their corresponding roles (tutor, learners, moderators, etc.), relevant features to define users' profiles (learning style, knowledge, background, preferences, etc.) (managed with IMS-LIP), clear learning objectives to achieve and measurements (defined with IMS-MD) to evaluate (using IMS-QTIs) the effectiveness of the adaptive tasks. In more detail, the IMS-LD allows to describe the advanced pedagogical models dealt within aLFanet. In turn, IMS-LIP is used as a solid starting point for building the user model and exchanging it with different components. IEEE-LOM/IMS-MD describes the learning resources which facilitate providing the most appropriate learning resource to a certain learner in a certain situation. IMS-QTI is used to generate adaptive questionnaires by applying selection and ordering rules based on metadata integrated in the LD. IMS-CP defines a standardised set of structures to collect reusable content objects and packages the materials produced at the authoring tools. The intensive use of standards provides interoperability with different LMS.

To provide adaptive eLearning capabilities to various types of users (learners, tutors, authors) along the eLearning life-cycle the instructional design templates that define the pedagogical needs of the course have been extended to deal with design and runtime adaptations. The construction process of an adaptive scenario consists of a sequence of steps with increasing levels of detail and possibilities for adaptation.

The starting point is to build the skeleton of the design template (e.g. a design template for concept learning) and to perform what we call a *differential analysis* that guarantees the identification of users' characteristics, course features, users' groups characteristics. The second step, called *material analysis*, is an additional level of specification to state explicitly further characteristics of learning objects and services, which are strongly dependent on the course domain and the system level. It includes learning objects that have specific features that can be used in runtime adaptations and the relation among them by means of the objectives they address. The above two steps are focused on IMS-LD and, thus, easily described with it. On the other hand, the third step, called *situated analysis*, introduces the concept of learner situated in a course context, which are out of the scope of the IMS-LD. This is meant to consider extra features from the runtime environment like interaction items, learning item, users' interaction events, link items, recommendation items, evaluation items, sessions, and a navigation path.

3   A Course Experience in aLFanet

UNED pilot site (adapted from a course on *How to teach through the Internet[1]*) was designed following the steps identified in Fig. 1 and using the authoring tools developed as open source at aLFanet project: LD AT[2] and QTI AT[3]. The course flow is defined at design time based on the expected results of different questionnaires (learning styles, cognitive modality and pre-knowledge test) and the evaluation of the modules performed by the learner in the previous modules' objectives (from the assessments questionnaires). The usage of standards in the course was as follows:

- Learning objects characterised with IMS-MD (type, interactivity level, interactivity type, usage, difficulty level, format, duration).
- Activity structures with associated environments and resources (IMS-LD).
- Diversity in learning material and activities taking into account the properties defined in IMS-LD (inductive/deductive, beginner/advanced, visual/verbal learners) which are related to the learner profiles defined in IMS-LIP.
- Users characteristic considered are cognitive modality, learning styles, interest, knowledge level, level of activity and similarity between learners
- Learning objects and questionnaire items packaged in IMS-CP.

---

[1] http://www.ia.uned.es/~jgb/docencia/apr-for/introduccion.html
[2] http://sourceforge.net/projects/alfanetat/
[3] http://rtd.softwareag.es/alfanetqtitools/#QTIAuthor

- Banks of IMS-QTI items defined for learning styles and cognitive modality identification, pre-knowledge assessment, self-assessments, objective assessment, module assessment and final exam.
- Learning objectives, which establish the corresponding relationships among IMS-LD learning activities and environments, IMS-MD learning objects and IMS-QTI items.

The course was evaluated at UNED pilot site by 40 users. From the evaluation the following strengths were mentioned:

- Dynamic adaptation and recommendations supplied
- Flexibility of task order
- Variety of different exercises and assessments
- Good guidance and feedback by the use of tests (i.e. interactivity and direct self-assessment of the level of understanding of the course material)
- Course material is adapted to each personal learning profile.

The effectiveness of the learning process from the learners' experience in aLFanet was rated positively, in the sense that it is possible to reach the learning objectives (obviously depending on the quality of the course contents). Week points were detected on the design phase. Authors asked for improvements of the authoring tools and more documentation explaining how to implement different adaptive scenarios.

4 Lessons Learned

First, there is a big difference between aLFanet and other LMS in the sense that central in the authoring process is the design created in IMS-LD. This design contains the pedagogical guidelines and logic for pre-designed adaptations, and provides the hooks and the information upon which the runtime adaptation bases its reasoning. Since the author's design is to be applied in runtime, norms to be monitored during the execution of the course are needed to compare the real interaction with the author design, as well as metadata have to be added to activities, environment and learning objects to provide the appropriate material according to the design.

Secondly, the authors' feedback from the course experience gave special attention to the creation of assessments. Assessments pay an important role in the course design since a model focused on the student's performance in the learning process is commonly used. Authors suggested designing the course with a set of questions that will serve for the purpose of measuring the degree of understanding by the learner. Although aLFanet does not support the creation of question items (an external QTI compliant tool is used), it provides a QTI AT that allows the definition of dynamic questionnaires that can be adapted to each learner in terms of available metadata.

Thirdly, the LD AT supports the definition of the course components and method in IMS-LD, generating the complete course package (IMS-CP) that contains both the course definition and the course resources (contents). It allows also the definition of rules for adaptation in IMS-LD level B. Moreover, the learning design definition can benefit from information derived from QTI questionnaires.

To summarize, from the evaluation activities at aLFanet it was concluded that the design phase is experienced as a complex task. Although there are facilities addressed to the authors to define the instructional design and adaptations within a course (i.e.

the methodological approach provided in aLFanet and described in Fig. 1) there is still a need for a technical knowledge and skills in order to successfully orchestrate the pedagogical requirements in the course flow, experiencing adaptation requirements and open design that provides diversity in learning materials, open learning paths and user characteristics.

5 Discussion

The main conclusion after evaluating the prototypes in the different pilot sites is that although learners gave a high value to the adaptive features, authors were not very enthusiastic in developing adaptive learning scenarios based on educational standards due to the complexity of the process. For this reason, providing support to authors at design time is a critical issue. From the results of the evaluation it was shown that it is possible to create complex examples of adaptive instructional design by combining the expressiveness of IMS-LD together with other educational standards, and take advantage of existing services that make use of interaction data. However, despite the tools and documentation offered, only the university authors were capable of implementing the desired adaptation scenarios without support.

The challenge, not yet met in aLFanet, is to have the tasks to be accomplished not only clear at a general level but also to facilitate the technical authoring, providing technical integration between the tools. It has to be mentioned that IMS-LD standard was delivered some months after aLFanet project started and no LMS gave (and neither now gives) fully support to the learning cycle [3].

Acknowledgements

Authors would like to thank the EC for the financial support for the project and aLFanet consortium for their active participation.

References

1. Boticario, J.G., Santos,. Issues in developing adaptive learning management systems for higher education institutions. ADALE workshop. Fourth International Conference on Adaptive Hypermedia and Adaptive Web-Based Systems. (2006).
2. Leshin, C.B, Pollock, J., and Reigeluth, C.M. Instructional Design Strategies and Tactics. Englewood Cliffs, NJ. Educational Technology Publications. (1992).
3. Van Rosmalen, P.M., Vogten, H., Van Es, R., Passier, H., Poelmans, P., and Koper, R.. Authoring a full life cycle model in standards-based, adaptive e-learning. Educational Technology & Society. (2006).
4. Bailey, C., Fill, K., Zalfan, M., Davis, H.C., Conole, G. Panning for Gold: Designing Pedagogically-inspired Learning Nuggets. IEEE Journal of Educational Technology and Society - Special Issue, Theme: Learning Design 9(1) pp. 113-122. (2006).

A Context-Aware Service Oriented Framework for Finding, Recommending and Inserting Learning Objects

Xavier Ochoa[2], Stefaan Ternier[1], Gonzalo Parra[2], and Erik Duval[1]

[1] Dept. Computerwetenschappen, Katholieke Universiteit Leuven,
Celestijnenlaan 200A, B-3001, Heverlee, Belgium
{Stefaan.Ternier, Erik.Duval}@cs.kuleuven.be
[2] Information Technology Center,
Escuela Superior Politécnica del Litoral, Ecuador
{xavier, gparra}@cti.espol.edu.ec

Abstract. In this paper, we will propose a framework for finding, recommending and inserting learning objects in a digital repository, exploiting the user context that is captured from the Learning Management System (LMS). The framework we propose builds on top of the ARIADNE service oriented architecture for learning object repositories, abstracting from the technicalities of low level metadata and resource management. As a case study, the framework has been applied in a university learning management system (SIDWeb). The intent is to exploit contextual information from the learning management system in digital repositories.

Keywords: Service Oriented Architectures, Learning Management Systems, Recommender services.

1 Introduction

Learning Object Repositories are digital libraries with a special focus on storing resources that can serve in a learning scenario. As creating learning resources is expensive in time and hence in costs, it is vitally important that reuse of these materials is as easy as possible. Recently, a lot of effort has been put in standardizing both the metadata and services for describing and managing a learning object. Learning Object Metadata enables tools to attach properties on Learning Objects in a standardized way so that it does not matter where the metadata was produced, facilitating the reuse of the metadata. Standardization efforts like the Simple Query Interface [1] or the Open Archives Initiative for Metadata Harvesting [2] provide means to query or harvest repositories in a standardized manner so that searching materials over the boundaries of different repositories results in a critical mass of learning content that is now available.

While most of the technical barriers for the sharing of learning objects have been eliminated, the whole process of sharing, that is publishing the metadata in a repository and finding relevant objects, is outside the workflow of the intended users. LORs are stand-alone entities, usually separated from the normal environment (usually a Learning Management System) where the instructor uploads learning

W. Nejdl and K. Tochtermann (Eds.): EC-TEL 2006, LNCS 4227, pp. 697–702, 2006.
© Springer-Verlag Berlin Heidelberg 2006

materials for his/her students. In this paper we will present an architecture that enables eLearning users to share their content automatically each time that they add it to their environments and to find new materials while they are working, rather than have to search for them. With this approach, we hope to create a scenario of publishing and finding resources that fit better in the workflow of an LMS user as he/she might already find a reusable piece of content before realizing the need for it. As an example of this deep integration we will glue together an existing Learning Object Repository (ARIADNE[3]) with a run-of-the-mill Learning Management System (SIDWeb[4]).

2 Use Cases

To extend the capabilities of SIDWeb (and other LMSs), we envision different scenarios where the work of the instructor or learner could be improved by the use or more sophisticated (tailored) learning object services. Those scenarios are summarized in the following use cases:

- Instructor searching for new material
- Instructor is creating content
- Instructor is inserting a new object and gets recommended similar complementary objects.
- Student is reading content and wants to explore more material
- Teachers/students want to tag/annotate a learning object

A major ingredient to be able to provide this use cases is capturing the context. The paper doesn't aim to present a general way to deal with context, but will present an adhoc representation of the format of context as it is available in SIDWeb and most LMSs.

3 Core Services

In this chapter, we will present the core services necessary to provide implementations for the use cases presented above. Some of these services have already been standardized. The advantage of such a standardisation is that a repository that implements them can easily be plugged in a framework that consumes these services. These core services do not only make repositories more pluggable, they also intent to make them interoperable. Using these core services, repositories can be dealt with in a more generic way.

With core services we aim to describe indivisible units of interactions that provide some basic interaction. That means services that do not invoke other services in the background. The needs drawn from our use cases will require 2 kinds of services:

- Repository: User authentication and configuration management, insertion and searching for material
- Third Party Services: Metadata generation, keyword extraction, tracking services, etc.

In the following, we will go in more on detail on each of these services. For each service, a programming language-agnostic signature of the methods involved will be provided as well as a description of the context in which this service is to be used. Apart from that, we will outline in what specials cases exceptions can occur.

3.1 Repository

Session Management (SM) is the first core service and allows for making abstraction from access and security issues. A session will be identified by a token and can last either for a fixed period or forever. Session Management services provide means to request and terminate tokens that are used to invoke the other core services.

For the query service, we will take over the methods provided by the **Simple Query Interface** (SQI) [1]. Using this standard a source can transport a query to target either synchronously or asynchronously. For more information about this standard, we encourage the reader to consult [6].

The **insert service** (IS) is a service that allows for inserting and updating resources together with a description into a repository. It offers an insertResource method that enables shipping a resource together with the metadata to a repository.

Apart from the insert service that provides support for submitting the learning object and its metadata, there is also a need to submit user related information to the repository. The **annotate service** (AS) is meant to submit metadata about the usage of the object rather than the object itself. This information can be a comment written by a user, but it can also be a label that the user or the system wants to attach to the object.

3.2 Third Party Services

3.2.1 Translate Service (TS)
This service will translate a word or a sentence into another given language, indicated by the parameter toLanguage. This specification of this service is agnostic about the way it is implemented. It can work with a small fixed set of keywords or can use a full-fledged dictionary in the background. Context is an optional parameter that meant to can solve ambiguity.

3.2.2 Keyword Generator Service (KGS)
This service will extract the keywords from a piece of free text. The array that is returned has the length specified by the amountOfKeyword parameter.

3.2.3 Automatic Generation of Metadata (AMG)
This service performs automatic metadata extraction from the content and context of learning objects. More information about this service could be found at [5]. The most important function of this service is:

3.2.4 Tracking Service (TS)
With this service, applications can send data about the actions of users to a server. This information can help later with recommending materials to that user.

4 Tailored Services

With tailored services, we target services that consume other services and are hence not atomic. The tailored services that will be described in this section are tailored to needs outlined in the use cases. Using these tailored services offers 2 main advantages over using core service.

- Just like core service abstract from the way resources and metadata are managed by a repository, these services will hide the specific implementation of a service. In that respect the implementation of these services is not meant to be unaltered. The API that is offered by this service should be kept stable.
- These services are designed so that they fit the needs and specificities of a LMS and hide the implementation details. It is thus easier to integrating them into an LMS.

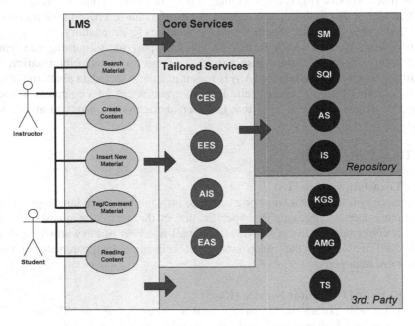

Fig. 1. An LMS can either directly access the core services or manipulate them through the tailored services layer

4.1 Example Enhanced Search (EES)

This service recommends new objects based on an already existing resource. An LMS invokes this service with a metadata instance and the context, describing e.g. the user of the course in which the object should be used. A valid metadata instance might be e.g. one that only contains the identifier (of an instance available in the digital library). This service will return a list of objects that are recommended.

4.2 Context Enhanced Search (CES)

With this service the context in which a query is executed can be taken into account. Context information can be used here to provide better results and as input for a ranking algorithm. This service will first feed the context as text to the Keyword Generator Service, which will return a list of keywords. These keywords will next serve to enhance the query that will be sent to SQI. In practice, as most of the SQI implementations provide a keyword based query format, the query that will be sent to SQI will be a list of search terms.

4.3 Automatic Insert Service (AIS)

As a learning management systems focuses on how learning objects are used, we need a service that fits this approach. With this service, an LMS can submit a learning object together with information describing the context in which the object is to be used. With such a service being invoked in the background, a learning management system no longer needs to provide the metadata describing a learning object manually.

4.4 Enhanced Annotation Service (EAS)

This service will help to enrich the annotations made by the user, including into the annotation contextual information that facilitate the understanding of it by other users.

5 Future Work

This paper presents an analysis of the requirements of an LMS and derives from these requirements context-aware services. Future work will focus on filling the gaps that this paper does not address:

- A query language for SQI. Keyword based query languages are easy to implement and to use by an end user. A context enhanced search service could however benefit from a richer query language. As an example, it could use such a query language to limit queries to a given age span or discipline, using the information available in the context
- Generalize Context. This paper uses as an example the contextual information that SIDWeb can deliver. In order for the framework to become useful in other learning environments, the schema that describes the contextual information the can be captured should be further enriched.

References

1. Simon, B., Massart, D., van Assche, F., Ternier, S., Duval, E., Brantner, S., Olmedilla, D., Miklós, Z.: A Simple Query Interface for Interoperable Learning Repositories. Workshop on Interoperability of Web-Based Educational Systems in conjunction with 14th International World Wide Web Conference (WWW'05). Chiba, Japan (2005)
2. OAI. The Open Archives Initiative. http://www.openarchives.org

3. Ariadne. http://www.ariadne-eu.org
4. SIDWeb, Information Technology Center, ESPOL. http://sidweb.espol.edu.ec
5. Ochoa, X., Cardinaels, K., Meire, M., Duval, E., Frameworks for the Automatic Indexation of Learning Management Systems Content into Learning Object Repositories, Proceedings of EDMedia 2005, Montreal, Canada, (2005) 1407-1414
6. LOR Interoperability. http://www.prolearn-project.org/lori

Trialogical E-Learning and Emergent Knowledge Artifacts

Yannis Tzitzikas[1,2], Vassilis Christophides[1,2], Giorgos Flouris[2],
Dimitris Kotzinos[1,2], Hannu Markkanen[3],
Dimitris Plexousakis[1,2], and Nicolas Spyratos[4]

[1] Computer Science Department, University of Crete, Greece
[2] Institute of Computer Science, FORTH-ICS, Greece
[3] EVTEK University of Applied Sciences, Finland
[4] Laboratoire de Recherche en Informatique, Universite de Paris-Sud, France
{tzitzik, christop, fgeo, kotzino, dp}@ics.forth.gr
hannu.markkanen@evtek.fi, spyratos@lri.fr

Abstract. According to the recently emerged, *trialogical learning* (TL) paradigm, learners are collaboratively developing shared objects of activity in a systematic fashion. In this paper we propose a basic learning scenario according to the TL paradigm. With this scenario as gnomon, we elaborate the technical issues that are raised for supporting it and we propose a flexible novel method for defining various aspects of the group knowledge.

1 Introduction

Classical learning theories are based either on the *knowledge acquisition* metaphor (i.e. a learner facing a body of knowledge), or on the *social participation* metaphor (i.e. a group of learners collaborate to assimilate a body of knowledge). Although widely accepted, these theories do not provide sufficient models for capturing innovative practices of both learning and working with knowledge ("knowledge practices"). To address this problem, a novel theory emerged recently, called *Trialogical Learning* (TL) [6], that emphasizes on the collaborative knowledge creation process. According to TL, learners are *collaboratively* developing *shared objects* of activity in a *systematic fashion*. We could therefore consider as cornerstone of trialogical learning the notion of shared objects, a notion that is quite general and can capture a plethora of application scenarios. For instance, a video that records how group members carry out their tasks, could be considered as a shared knowledge artifact which the group could annotate (with free text or with respect to an ontology), analyze and further discuss (e.g. for capturing tacit group knowledge). Moreover, and more interestingly, a knowledge artifact could take a more formal substance as in the case of documents (e.g. a survey paper), conceptualizations (e.g. a data/knowledge base), or even software code exchanged within a group. Hereafter we shall use *knowledge artifact* to refer to what is being created and/or shared by a group of learners (and could be a set of words, documents, concept maps, ontologies, annotations, etc).

W. Nejdl and K. Tochtermann (Eds.): EC-TEL 2006, LNCS 4227, pp. 703–708, 2006.

Models and techniques that allow diversification and flexible amalgamation of different world views are still in their infancy. In this paper, we investigate various ways to build emerging knowledge spaces within a "Trialogical Learning" scenario. In particular, we focus on the various methods to form the common knowledge of a group by combining the individual knowledge of its members. The provision of flexible methods for defining various aspects of the group knowledge is expected to foster TL knowledge creation processes and could lead to the development of tools that overcome the inelasticities of the current knowledge creation practices.

2 Motivating Scenario for *Trialogical* Learning

A set of N research papers, say $P = \{p_1, \ldots p_N\}$, is given to a set of K learners $A = \{a_1 \ldots a_K\}$ who could be students, researchers, or co-workers in a company. The goal of this group is to understand the topics discussed in these papers and to build an ontology, say O, that represents the main issues discussed in these papers. Moreover the group has to annotate these N papers according to the derived ontology, i.e. specify $d(p)$ for each $p \in P$ where $d(p)$ denotes the description of p with respect to O. We could also assume that there is an additional constraint saying that the ontology should not have more than C concepts. The learners, hereafter *actors*, have to collaborate (synchronously or asynchronously) in order to carry out this task.

Note that various combinations of (N, K, C) values describe different real-life scenarios. For instance, $(50, 1, 20)$ could describe what a MSc student should do in order to write the state-of-the-art of his MSc thesis. Of course, this scenario does not fall into trialogical learning, but is rather an instance of monological learning (acquisition metaphor). Values like $(150, 2, 50)$ might describe the collaboration between a professor and a graduate student for finding a topic for a PhD thesis. Values like $(100, 10, 10)$ may describe a group (comprising 10 members) of a research lab that is trying to join a research area by studying the 100 related papers that have been published the last 5 years and trying to identify the 10 main topics of the area (subsequently each member of the group would be responsible for one topic). Finally, big values for K, say 1000, could model the effort for developing an international standard.

A related rising question is whether the "quality" of the result of this collaboration (i.e. of O and $d(p)$'s) should be measured and if yes how. We can identify two broad cases. According to the first, there is an external (human or machine) observer who can grade the result, while according to the second there is not any external party. For instance, we may assume that there is a certain "solution" ontology (ideal or criterion), denoted $O^{(i)}$ that it is unknown for members of the group. For example, $O^{(i)}$ could have been provided by a tutor if there is one (or the tutor instead of one ontology he might have provided a set of admissible ontologies). Subsequently, appropriate metrics could be employed in order to measure the "distance" between $O^{(i)}$ and O_{s_i} and at every point in time (state s_i), so that the members of the group can judge if they progress or not.

Of course not only the group work but also the individual work could be graded. Recall that according to [7,2], for effective collaborative learning, there must be "group goals" and "individual accountability". Based on the successful results of experiments reported in [2]: fifty percent of each student's individual grade was based on the average score (of the group members) while the remaining fifty percent of each student's grade was individual.

In the case where there is not any external party we could probably only measure the degree of agreement between the members of the group. If O_A expresses the knowledge that all members of A accept to be correct, then the bigger O_A is, the better the group goes (assuming there is not any other constraint like C in the previous scenario).

3   General Principles and Issues

This section discusses issues that are important for supporting the previous scenario. In particular, Section 3.1 introduces personal and shared knowledge artifacts and clarifies their relation, while Section 3.2 shows how a set of learners can interact on the basis of the shared knowledge artifacts. Finally Section 3.3 synoptically discusses additional issues.

3.1   Personal Versus Shared Knowledge Artifacts

To abstract from representation details we shall hereafter use the term knowledge base (KB) to refer to an ontology or to an ontology-based information base (i.e. to a set of objects annotated with ontological descriptions).

Although trialogical learning focuses on shared artifacts, learners should be able to construct and evolve their own models. Let KB_a denote the knowledge base of an actor a. Now let KB_A denote the "shared" (or common) knowledge base of a set of actors A. The important issue here is the relation between KB_A and KB_a (for $a \in A$). Below we identify three broad cases:

- *UNION-case.* Here KB_A is obtained by taking the union of the KBs of all participants, i.e.: $KB_A = \cup\{ KB_a \mid a \in A\}$. Note that KB_A could be inconsistent if there is a notion of consistency. For example, if the task is to annotate a video with argumentative maps, then consistency is not a very strict issue. If on the other hand the task is to develop an ontology (for subsequently building a bibliographic database) or a software module, then consistency is a very important issue.
- *INTERSECTION-case.* Here KB_A is obtained by taking the intersection of the KBs of all participants, i.e.: $KB_A = \cap\{ KB_a \mid a \in A\}$, so it comprises statements "accepted" by every participant.
- *QUANTITATIVE-case.* Here KB_A is defined by a quantitative method, e.g. it may comprise all sentences that are accepted by at least a percentage of the actors. Obviously, UNION and INTERSECTION are special cases of this case.

3.2   Interaction Through Knowledge Artifacts

Suppose that we want to design and develop an application for supporting various forms of collaboration (e.g. asynchronous and synchronous) and supports private and shared knowledge artifacts. Figure 1 sketches a possible UI for that application that could serve as a proof of concept and as a gnomon for identifying and analyzing the associated technical requirements and challenges.

The UI is divided in two main areas: the left area allows managing the personal space, while the right area allows managing the group space. In the left area each learner is free to do whatever she wants, so everything is editable in that area. The right area shows the shared artifacts and this area is the key point for collaboration and for supporting trialogical e-learning. For instance, and assuming the scenario described earlier, each user may develop her own ontology at the left area, while the right window shows the group ontology O (according to the method that O is derived from the personal ontologies).

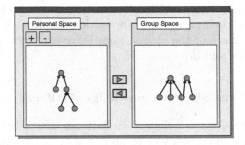

Fig. 1. An indicative UI for trialogical E-learning

The relationship between personal space and group space is very important. The button labeled by "→" allows a user to copy the desired parts from her ontology to the group space. The button labeled by "←" allows a user to copy the desired parts from the group ontology to her personal space.

An option that keeps the button "→" permanently pressed would allow synchronous collaboration in the sense that every change at a learner's ontology is immediately reflected (propagated) to the group ontology (e.g. blackboard-based collaboration). Symmetrically, an option that keeps the button "←" permanently pressed would propagate the changes on O to the personal space. This is not reasonable if O is defined by union, but it could be reasonable if O is defined by intersection or quantitatively. Deletions are handled analogously.

3.3   Auxiliary Functionalities

Above we have sketched the basics of a trialogical e-learning scenario. Of course, the scenario (and the UI) can be enriched with a plethora of auxiliary functionalities. Below we identify the most important ones according to our opinion:

- The *group space* view could be *customizable*, e.g. instead of showing the group ontology, one participant may want to see the ontology derived by considering the ontologies of only a *subset* of the participants. In general, the shared knowledge base could be defined with a set theoretic expression over subsets of A. For example, $K_{(\{a_1\}\cap\{a_2\})\cup(\{a_3\}\cap\{a_4\})}$ could capture the scenario where two groups (a_1, a_2) and (a_3, a_4) collaborate in the sense that the joint work of each group is integrated. Moreover, the group space could be *optionally managed* by a person whose role would be to accept or reject the changes that the participants forward to the group ontology.
- The *provenance* of every statement should be saved and be available at any time (e.g. this link was added by learner a_2). Moreover, the participants should be able to *annotate* every element of their personal or group space. The annotations could be textual or ontology-based.
- *Usability* is always a very important issue. For instance, by placing the mouse on top of an element of the group ontology, a balloon should open showing who provided this info (or what percent of the actors agree with this). Moreover the *visualization* of knowledge artifacts is a very important, challenging and open issue (some related issues are discussed in brief in [4,8]).
- The UI could be enriched with *teleconferencing* services allowing the participants to discuss in real-time while using the system.

4   Concluding Remarks

This paper described a specific scenario for collaborative knowledge creation in the spirit of the trialogical learning paradigm. According to this scenario the group knowledge base is formed by combining the KBs of the participants according to various methods. The provision of flexible methods for defining various aspects of the group knowledge is expected to enhance synergy in the knowledge creation process and could lead to the development of tools that overcome the inelasticities of the current knowledge creation practices. An indicative UI was sketched enabling us to scent the most important issues that are raised for its realization.

We plan to further investigate and experiment with these issues in the context of the Knowledge Practices Laboratory (KP-Lab) project (co-funded by the IST programme of the EU 6) and on the basis of the RDF Suite [1,3,5].

References

1. FORTH-ICS. The ics-forth rdfsuite: High-level scalable tools for the semantic web, 2005. http://139.91.183.30:9090/RDF/.
2. Anuradha A. Gokhale. "Collaborative Learning Enhances Critical Thinking". *Journal of Technology Education*, 7(1), 1995.
3. G. Karvounarakis, V. Christophides, and D. Plexousakis. "RQL: A Declarative Query Language for RDF. In *Eleventh International World Wide Web Conference (WWW)*, Hawaii, USA, May 2002.

4. Thorsten Liebig and Olaf Noppens. "OntoTrack: A Semantic Approach for Ontology Authoring". *Journal of Web Semantics*, 3(2-3):116–131, 2005.
5. M. Magiridou, S. Sahtouris, V. Christophides, and M. Koubarakis. "RUL: A Declarative Update Language for RDF". In *Procs. 4th Intern. Conf. on the Semantic Web (ISWC-2005)*, Galway, Ireland, November 2005.
6. S. Paavola, L. Lipponen, and K. Hakkarainen. "Models of Innovative Knowledge Communities and Three Metaphors of Learning". *Review of Educational Research*, 74(4):557–576, 2004.
7. R. E. Slavin. "Research on Cooperative Learning: An International Perspective". *Scandinavian Journal of Educational Research*, 33(4):231–243, 1989.
8. Yannis Tzitzikas and Jean-Luc Hainaut. "On the Visualization of Ontologies". In *Proceedings of the X Int. Conf. on Advanced Visual Interfaces, AVI'2006*, Venice, Italy, May 2006.

ARiSE - Augmented Reality in School Environments

Manfred Bogen, Jürgen Wind, and Angele Giuliano

Fraunhofer IMK, Schloss Birlinghoven, 53754 Sankt Augustin, Germany
manfred.bogen@imk.fraunhofer.de,
juergen.wind@imk.fraunhofer.de
AcrossLimits, Gateway Centre, Kappillan Mifsud Street, Hamrun HMR 10, Malta
angele@acrosslimits.com
http://www.arise-project.org/

Abstract. ARiSE is an exciting IST project funded under the 4th Call for proposals that will develop a new technology, the Augmented Reality Teaching Platform (ARTP) by adapting existing augmented reality (AR) technology for museums to the needs of students in primary and secondary school classes. Building on existing open platforms, the new technology will promote team work, collaboration between classes in the same school or even remote collaboration between schools in different countries in a learner-centered approach. Using 3D presentations and user-friendly interaction techniques will lead to better understanding of scientific and cultural content coupled with high student motivation.

Keywords: Augmented reality, e-learning, open platform, 3D, IST, FP6.

The project aims at integrating an AR teaching platform into the everyday environment of teachers and students, displaying audiovisual and multi-media content in line with the needs identified by education experts and researchers in the relevant areas. A major part of the project work is dedicated to the development of tools necessary for the easy production of content by non-AR-experts, to facilitate deployment in different countries of Europe at a moderate effort. Market analysis and suggested product development activities will be elaborated within the project.

At the same time, ARiSE benefits from an enlarged Europe, as the majority of the consortium members are chosen from relevant organizations in the new member states. The platform and example scenarios will be implemented independently of the countries involved. Two representative schools from two different countries in Europe (Lithuania and Germany) are partners in the consortium and will test the platform in realistic pedagogical scenarios. Research results will be validated using sound research methodologies from all addressed research areas.

Other schools from Romania and Malta will also participate in the testing but will not be formal partners in the project. Summer schools will provide intensive testing scenarios with students from schools not involved in the project. Furthermore, school classes will be invited to visit the participating research facilities and participate in single day events. The project therefore aims at integrating an AR teaching platform into the everyday environment of teachers and students, displaying audiovisual and multi-media content in line with the needs identified by education experts and researchers in the relevant areas.

W. Nejdl and K. Tochtermann (Eds.): EC-TEL 2006, LNCS 4227, pp. 709–714, 2006.
© Springer-Verlag Berlin Heidelberg 2006

1 Main Objectives

The main objective of the ARiSE project is to test the pedagogical effectiveness of introducing augmented reality (AR) into the classroom and creating collaboration between remote classes around AR display systems. ARiSE will develop an AR platform and associated pedagogical use cases, enabling teachers to develop, with a moderate effort, new teaching practices for teaching scientific and cultural content to their primary and secondary school classes. The aim is to give to a group of students a possibility to 'play' with the virtual objects and thereby perform learning by doing instead of learning by reading.

1.1 Detailed Objectives

The above main objective can therefore be split into the various areas that define also the work that is being done throughout the project.

Adapt existing AR platform and applications to school specific needs
ARiSE will develop a new type of teaching aid, namely an Augmented Reality Teaching Platform (ARTP). Based on the experience with existing augmented reality display systems and software toolkits for museums the ARTP will evolve through adaptation, integration and new developments in hard- and software. It will focus on the specific needs of students for interaction with three dimensional objects and using real objects together with superimposed information.

Develop associated use scenarios promoting team-work between students in a class and between classes in different countries
Realistic pedagogical scenarios will be developed for the use in European primary and secondary schools where students will work in groups collaboratively. The ARTP will thus support team-work in the same class as well as remote pan-European collaboration.

Develop tools for easy use of an AR platform by teachers (with very moderate effort to use existing or to create new content adaptable easily to local curriculum)
The project will develop tools for content creation and modelling of the teaching material, consisting of virtual objects and a description of their behavior. Such tools must enable didactics experts, authors of school books or movies, or even teachers, who might have no computer programming background, to model a dynamic virtual environment in a realistic way.

Demonstrate pedagogical effects of AR platform supported exercises (on the motivation of learner, on the quality of transfer of knowledge)
The ARTP will be designed and developed to deliver better understanding of scientific or cultural content, high student motivation through more comprehensible presentations and more intense social interaction in learning groups. Results will be measured in schools in 4 member states. The ARTP will therefore be developed together with a sound concept for didactics and pedagogy in these new teaching situations.

Enhance task modelling to deliver a fully user-centered new teaching aid
One objective of this project is to build a design framework able to support usability of interactive systems oriented on user tasks. The framework will be based

on a structured corpus of heuristics and design guidelines, with application-domain specific heuristics at the top and usability guidelines at the bottom. It will also be designed to serve in the evaluation process.

2 High-Level Architecture

An overview over the architecture of the project is shown in figure 1. On the left side of the picture the ARTP is presented, surrounded by students. The real teaching object is located in the center on a table with semi-transparent mirrors above it; so the real object is presented with overlaid 3-dimensional information.

The teacher 'stands' in the back, supports the students and answers questions. In the beginning when the new teaching platform has to be evaluated for its ideal application in class, the teacher and students will give feedback to a didactics and pedagogy expert and the teacher will get hints from this person.

Through the network connection one platform reaches another platform at a remote location and allows the concurrent teaching of two groups in different countries, whereas the teachers mediate between the different students. For homework and follow-up course work the students use their PCs, PDAs, or laptops at home to deepen the understanding of the learned content.

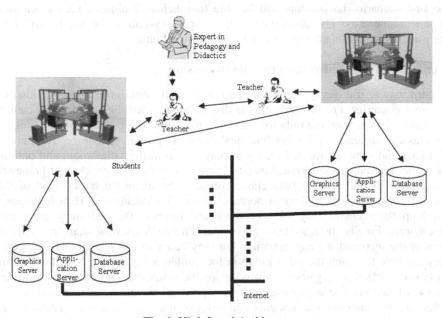

Fig. 1. High-Level Architecture

3 Content and Research Prototypes

Scenario 1: Process Visualization

A class of students in a school has to learn about a specific scientific content, for example a human digestive tract. The students will form a group around the augmented reality display system. A normal plastic model will sit in the middle while dynamic generated pictures illustrate the digestive process. The teacher can either explain or stand in the back to answer questions. Students can learn about the digestive process, the functionality of organs and their arrangements by watching the visualization, but also by intervention. They can watch different virtual food to be processed, inflict malfunction on certain organs, and they can virtually dissect the whole system. So the students influence the virtual demonstration and through this, the visual presentation of the model. Having understood the principles, they can download their generated protocol data and take the virtual models home for their homework. The assignment could be to answer questions about the digestive process, using the data and images from the virtual model generated in class.

Scenario 2: Construction with Guidance

In education it is mostly desired to have the students actually do something actively (for example build something) instead of just watching. One may think about a chemistry class where students should learn about the complex reaction of some isomer hydrocarbon with some halogen. These reactions are not only fundamental for plastics production, but also depend vitally on the participating molecules' structure in 3 dimensions. Once again the students will work in a team around a table. Unlike the first scenario the students will be able to touch real objects, i.e. the molecule toolkit components. The augmented reality display system in the middle will guide the students in building the molecules by visualizing hints.

Scenario 3: Tele-Presence and Remote Discussion

A third way to use the system would be remote collaboration in between classes of different countries. For this scenario the display system will be enhanced by cameras and microphones, used not only for augmentation but also for video conferencing. So, the classes can teach each other historical events important to Europe. Both classes will have the same augmented reality display set up in their classroom and both use the same 'real object': a physical map of Europe. In a preparative class or homework assignment the students of both classes prepare the historical background of their specific topic, like dates, lines of borders, reasons for events etc. Then both classes build up the scenario they want to show and develop the necessary augmenting projections. Finally, both systems go online. The students now share not only the view at the map and the augmentation, but they can also use speech and gestures, as they are able to watch the other group in the conferencing set-up. Now the teaching class summarizes their gained knowledge for the other one and explains events and course of action. The augmentation shows political developments or border lines. After the presentation the students can discuss the facts and ask questions. The teachers assist in answering questions, moderate the discussion and help with possible problems arising from language barriers.

4 Project Partners

- Fraunhofer Gesellschaft (FhG IMK), Germany
- Siauliaui University, Lithuania

Fig. 2. Design of the ARiSE poster for ECTEL poster session

- AcrossLimits, Malta
- Institutul National de Cercetare-Dezvoltare in Informatica (ICI), Romania
- Czech Technical University in Prague, Czech Republic
- Siauliai City Juventa Basic School, Lithuania
- Freundes-und Förderkreis des Rabanus-Maurus-Gymnasiums Mainz e.V., Germany

Professional Learning in Europe and Beyond Structures for Sustainable TEL-Research

Martin Wolpers[1], Margit Hofer[2], and Gunnar Martin[3]

[1] Katholieke Universiteit Leuven, Belgium
martin.wolpers@cs.kuleuven.be
[2] Centre for Social Innovations, Austria
hofer@zsi.at
[3] German Research Center for Artificial Intelligence (DFKI)
gunnar.martin@dfki.de

Abstract. This paper outlines how the Network of Excellence in professional learning (PROLEARN) influences European and world-wide research in the area of technology enhanced professional learning. Two new European projects, iCamp and Prolix serve as excellent examples of the impact of PROLEARN. The establishment of the professional learning cluster (PRO-LC) that bases on PROLEARN and its results further proves the urgency for a European wide organization in the area of research in technology enhanced professional learning.

1 Network of Excellence in Professional Learning – PROLEARN

While eLearning is increasingly influencing university and workplace education in Europe, several critical issues still have to be solved in order to achieve the full potential of technology enhanced learning in many of these learning scenarios. The EU/IST FP6 PROLEARN Network of Excellence in Technology Enhanced Learning (http://www.prolearn-project.org/) is focussing on these issues, and advancing the state of the art in this area, through a large concerted effort of more than 350 research institutions and companies working together in the PROLEARN Consortium and as PROLEARN Associated Partners. The PROLEARN key areas cover the use of software systems like brokerage platforms and services, appropriate business models and networks for specific markets, and advanced workplace arrangements integrating eLearning and knowledge work management with social software. Key issues also involve advanced production, deployment and exchange of professional learning resources and the use of these learning resources for professional training in small and medium-sized enterprises (SME) and larger companies.

It is the goal of the PROLEARN Network of Excellence to substantially increase the interlinking between these communities and to integrate the various research communities as well as eLearning providers and companies through joint research, grand challenge workshops, best practice forums and initiatives for enhancing the quality of eLearning in crucial application areas. In the context of the PROLEARN *Academy,* the PROLEARN summer schools specifically target young researchers and

W. Nejdl and K. Tochtermann (Eds.): EC-TEL 2006, LNCS 4227, pp. 715–718, 2006.

professionals to advance their knowledge on the state of the art in technology enhanced learning, as well as their networking in a joint research environment y. The PROLEARN Virtual Competence Centre embeds consulting services, dissemination and networking initiatives between research and company partners, and tightly couple advanced research and application scenarios for technology enhanced (workplace) learning in the PROLEARN context [5].

Two PROLEARN driven results clearly show the impact of its identified future developments inside and outside the participating partners. Inside the consortium, PROLEARN established a new working area on Social Software to address the emerging research issues. Based on the understanding that knowledge management and professional learning are tightly coupled, the PROLEARN partners will investigate the use of social software in the context of professional workplaces and how it supports the creation of social networks and communities.

While social software was not intended to be used in the context of Professional Learning a lot of challenges are raised by the enormous acceptance of these technologies by the people. The integration of social software within learning management systems and professional learning settings requires an intensive discourse between practitioners, professionals, and scientists from both. The established project iCamp (http://www.icamp-project.org/) addresses these needs in its research by creating an infrastructure for collaboration and networking across systems, countries, and disciplines. It is specifically targeting higher education, research bases on constructivist learning theories that put emphasis on self-organized learning, social networking and the changing roles of educators.

The area of competence modelling, development and the integration into professional learning is also one of the established focus areas in PROLEARN. It is becoming obvious that competency models can facilitate the combination and integration of work and learning scenarios. In this context, PROLEARNs partner were able to successfully propose the EU/IST funded integrated project PROLIX (http://www.prolixproject.org/) that aims to combine business with learning processes. The past has proven that effective business operations can only be reached by critically rethinking organizational structures and business processes focussing on an optimized relation to internal and external target groups [4]. Promising concepts for the acceleration, cost reduction and transparency of business processes result from the process-oriented approaches such as Business Process Reengineering [2] and Continuous Process Improvement [3; 7]. The implementation of enhanced or new (designed) processes – usually supported by adequate ICT infrastructure – shall lead to the targeted improvements of efficiency and effectiveness. While setting up such new processes, the impact of knowledge and competence is still frequently neglected or at least not well supported. As the knowledge at the workplace affects exceedingly the execution of business processes and its performance, it should be in the centre of contemplation: The employees act as a central resource that holds the companies "intellectual asset". Thus, their current qualification as well as the constant enhancement of their knowledge constitutes an important precondition for process optimization and its benefits. Therefore, the inherent mutual interdependencies between business processes and corporate training ask for accommodation by developing methods, technologies and tools to implement this linkage.

In order to leverage the true potential of technology enhanced learning within companies, PROLIX considers tight integration between corporate training efforts and the business processes carried out at the workplace of paramount importance.

Furthermore, the newly established professional learning cluster (PRO-LC) integrates the relevant European projects in the area of professional learning to achieve an even tighter integration of the European research area. PRO-LC facilitates activities of the participating projects in areas like dissemination and standardization, but also aims at identifying new research topics and striking up new research areas.

Naturally is PROLIX together with PROLEARN a founding member of the PRO-LC cluster. How these projects will work together within the PRO-L cluster will be described in the next chapter.

2 Professional Learning Cluster – PRO-LC

The Professional Learning Cluster (PRO-LC – http://www.professional-learning-cluster.org/) clusters the major European research projects in the area of Technology Enhanced Learning focusing on professional learning. It is driven by the recognition of the EC that the communication between research areas must be one of the priorities in Europe [6]. In establishing and organising the cluster, we put into practice the suggestions of communicating European research as developed by the European Commission and outlined in [1]. Beside PROLEARN, iCamp and PROLIX the cluster consist of the IP PROLIX, APOSDLE and TENCompetence, the Specific Targeted Research Project COOPER, BASE2 as well as the affiliated projects "Embedding ICT/Multimedia Standardisation Initiatives into European Vocational Training Development Strategies" (Leonardo-da-Vinci), EUCAM (Multilingual Communication in European Car Manufacturing). The close cooperation of these projects will increasingly strengthen European research and industry in the area of technology enhanced (professional) learning, e.g. through joint work in standardization bodies like CEN/ISSS and IEEE, e.g. the standardization of the Simple query Interface (SQI) for federated search.

Each project targets specific aspects of technology enhanced professional learning. For example, PROLIX will provide solutions for the modular combination of eLearning environments with business process modelling tools, TENCompentence (http://www.tencompetence.org) will support lifelong competence development of individuals, teams and organisations by developing a service-based and open source European infrastructure. APOSDLE (http://www.aposdle.org/) will enhance knowledge worker productivity by supporting informal learning activities in the context of knowledge workers' everyday work processes and within their computational work environments.

The main goals of the professional learning cluster are the provision of a forum for communication within the projects, joint forces in dissemination and best exploitation of results, standardization, and sharing research results with the focus on future developments in TEL. The participating projects are supported by the European Commission.

Joint activities include coordination and dissemination actions. Apart from the standard tool for cooperation like joint mailing lists, we envision joint project meetings and workshops to exchange and discuss the research findings and identify new challenges. Furthermore, we will jointly identify and define target groups and ways on how to promote our findings among them to bridge the gap between science and implementation in real learning environments. The target groups will enable the cluster to promote its findings tailored to the requirements of each group, thus improving the throughput of research findings from academia into industry. At the same time, this linkage of industry and academia will allow for the simplified intake of requirements from the industrial and economical world into research, so that the influence of industry on ongoing and emerging research fields improves significantly.

3   Conclusion

This paper outlines the evolution of PROLEARN inside the consortium and outside. With the establishment of the research area on social software PROLEARN tackles the most recent and emerging future research needs stemming from combining advanced knowledge management with professional learning. By focussing on competency modelling and knowledge workers PROLEARN establishes a tight coupling also into the third key are of professional learning, namely direct business and industry needs. The PRO-L cluster will provide the necessary sustainability for PROLEARN to carry its work on after the initial EU funding in an established excellent joint European research network.

References

1. European Commission (Eds.): European Research – A guide to successful communication. Office for Official Publications of the European Communities, Luxembourg, 2004.
2. Hammer, Michael; Champy, James: Reengineering the corporation: a manifesto for business revolution, 1. Ed., Brealey, London, 1993.
3. Imai, Masaaki: Kaizen (Ky'zen) : The key to Japan's competitive success. 1. Ed., McGraw-Hill, New York [et al.], 1986.
4. Martin, Gunnar; Leyking, Katrina; Wolpers, Martin: Business Process-driven Learning. In: European Commission (Eds.): Proceedings of the IST-Africa 2006 Conference and Exhibition, Pretoria, South Africa, 2006.
5. Nejdl, Wolfgang; Wolpers, Martin: European E-Learning: Important Research Issues and Application Scenarios. In: Cantoni, Lorenzo; McLoughlin, Catherine (Eds.): Proceedings of ED-MEDIA 2004 World Conference on educational multimedia, hypermedia & telecommunications, June 2004, pp. 2054-2068.
6. Potocnik, Janez: Let's make Science the next headline. Speech at the European Conference on Communicating European Research 2005, Brussels, 14.11.2005.
7. Scheer, August-Wilhelm: ARIS – Business Process Frameworks, 3 Ed., Springer, Berlin [et al.], 1999.

Author Index

Lecture Notes in Computer Science

For information about Vols. 1–4131

please contact your bookseller or Springer

Vol. 4180: M. Kohlhase, OMDoc – An Open Markup Format for Mathematical Documents [version 1.2]. XIX, 428 pages. 2006. (Sublibrary LNAI).

Vol. 4179: J. Blanc-Talon, W. Philips, D. Popescu, P. Scheunders (Eds.), Advanced Concepts for Intelligent Vision Systems. XXIV, 1224 pages. 2006.

Vol. 4178: A. Corradini, H. Ehrig, U. Montanari, L. Ribeiro, G. Rozenberg (Eds.), Graph Transformations. XII, 473 pages. 2006.

Vol. 4176: S.K. Katsikas, J. Lopez, M. Backes, S. Gritzalis, B. Preneel (Eds.), Information Security. XIV, 548 pages. 2006.

Vol. 4175: P. Bücher, B.M.E. Moret (Eds.), Algorithms in Bioinformatics. XII, 402 pages. 2006. (Sublibrary LNBI).

Vol. 4174: K. Franke, K.-R. Müller, B. Nickolay, R. Schäfer (Eds.), Pattern Recognition. XX, 773 pages. 2006.

Vol. 4173: S. El Yacoubi, B. Chopard, S. Bandini (Eds.), Cellular Automata. XV, 734 pages. 2006.

Vol. 4172: J. Gonzalo, C. Thanos, M. F. Verdejo, R.C. Carrasco (Eds.), Research and Advanced Technology for Digital Libraries. XVII, 569 pages. 2006.

Vol. 4169: H.L. Bodlaender, M.A. Langston (Eds.), Parameterized and Exact Computation. XI, 279 pages. 2006.

Vol. 4168: Y. Azar, T. Erlebach (Eds.), Algorithms – ESA 2006. XVIII, 843 pages. 2006.

Vol. 4167: S. Dolev (Ed.), Distributed Computing. XV, 576 pages. 2006.

Vol. 4166: J. Górski (Ed.), Computer Safety, Reliability, and Security. XIV, 440 pages. 2006.

Vol. 4165: W. Jonker, M. Petković (Eds.), Secure, Data Management. X, 185 pages. 2006.

Vol. 4163: H. Bersini, J. Carneiro (Eds.), Artificial Immune Systems. XII, 460 pages. 2006.

Vol. 4162: R. Královič, P. Urzyczyn (Eds.), Mathematical Foundations of Computer Science 2006. XV, 814 pages. 2006.

Vol. 4161: R. Harper, M. Rauterberg, M. Combetto (Eds.), Entertainment Computing - ICEC 2006. XXVII, 417 pages. 2006.

Vol. 4160: M. Fisher, W.v.d. Hoek, B. Konev, A. Lisitsa (Eds.), Logics in Artificial Intelligence. XII, 516 pages. 2006. (Sublibrary LNAI).

Vol. 4159: J. Ma, H. Jin, L.T. Yang, J.J.-P. Tsai (Eds.), Ubiquitous Intelligence and Computing. XXII, 1190 pages. 2006.

Vol. 4158: L.T. Yang, H. Jin, J. Ma, T. Ungerer (Eds.), Autonomic and Trusted Computing. XIV, 613 pages. 2006.

Vol. 4156: S. Amer-Yahia, Z. Bellahsène, E. Hunt, R. Unland, J.X. Yu (Eds.), Database and XML Technologies. IX, 123 pages. 2006.

Vol. 4155: O. Stock, M. Schaerf (Eds.), Reasoning, Action and Interaction in AI Theories and Systems. XVIII, 343 pages. 2006. (Sublibrary LNAI).

Vol. 4154: Y.A. Dimitriadis, I. Zigurs, E. Gómez-Sánchez (Eds.), Groupware: Design, Implementation, and Use. XIV, 438 pages. 2006.

Vol. 4153: N. Zheng, X. Jiang, X. Lan (Eds.), Advances in Machine Vision, Image Processing, and Pattern Analysis. XIII, 506 pages. 2006.

Vol. 4152: Y. Manolopoulos, J. Pokorný, T. Sellis (Eds.), Advances in Databases and Information Systems. XV, 448 pages. 2006.

Vol. 4151: A. Iglesias, N. Takayama (Eds.), Mathematical Software - ICMS 2006. XVII, 452 pages. 2006.

Vol. 4150: M. Dorigo, L.M. Gambardella, M. Birattari, A. Martinoli, R. Poli, T. Stützle (Eds.), Ant Colony Optimization and Swarm Intelligence. XVI, 526 pages. 2006.

Vol. 4149: M. Klusch, M. Rovatsos, T.R. Payne (Eds.), Cooperative Information Agents X. XII, 477 pages. 2006. (Sublibrary LNAI).

Vol. 4148: J. Vounckx, N. Azemard, P. Maurine (Eds.), Integrated Circuit and System Design. XVI, 677 pages. 2006.

Vol. 4147: M. Broy, I.H. Krüger, M. Meisinger (Eds.), Automotive Software – Connected Services in Mobile Networks. XIV, 155 pages. 2006.

Vol. 4146: J.C. Rajapakse, L. Wong, R. Acharya (Eds.), Pattern Recognition in Bioinformatics. XIV, 186 pages. 2006. (Sublibrary LNBI).

Vol. 4144: T. Ball, R.B. Jones (Eds.), Computer Aided Verification. XV, 564 pages. 2006.

Vol. 4143: R. Lämmel, J. Saraiva, J. Visser (Eds.), Generative and Transformational Techniques in Software Engineering. X, 471 pages. 2006.

Vol. 4142: A. Campilho, M. Kamel (Eds.), Image Analysis and Recognition, Part II. XXVII, 923 pages. 2006.

Vol. 4141: A. Campilho, M. Kamel (Eds.), Image Analysis and Recognition, Part I. XXVIII, 939 pages. 2006.

Vol. 4139: T. Salakoski, F. Ginter, S. Pyysalo, T. Pahikkala, Advances in Natural Language Processing. XVI, 771 pages. 2006. (Sublibrary LNAI).

Vol. 4138: X. Cheng, W. Li, T. Znati (Eds.), Wireless Algorithms, Systems, and Applications. XVI, 709 pages. 2006.

Vol. 4137: C. Baier, H. Hermanns (Eds.), CONCUR 2006 – Concurrency Theory. XIII, 525 pages. 2006.

Vol. 4136: R.A. Schmidt (Ed.), Relations and Kleene Algebra in Computer Science. XI, 433 pages. 2006.

Vol. 4135: C.S. Calude, M.J. Dinneen, G. Păun, G. Rozenberg, S. Stepney (Eds.), Unconventional Computation. X, 267 pages. 2006.

Vol. 4134: K. Yi (Ed.), Static Analysis. XIII, 443 pages. 2006.

Vol. 4133: J. Gratch, M. Young, R. Aylett, D. Ballin, P. Olivier (Eds.), Intelligent Virtual Agents. XIV, 472 pages. 2006. (Sublibrary LNAI).

Vol. 4132: S. Kollias, A. Stafylopatis, W. Duch, E. Oja (Eds.), Artificial Neural Networks – ICANN 2006, Part II. XXXIV, 1028 pages. 2006.